Migration, Migration History, History

Old Paradigms and New Perspectives

edited by
Jan Lucassen and Leo Lucassen

PETER LANG

Bern · Berlin · Bruxelles · Frankfurt am Main · New York · Oxford · Wien

Die Deutsche Bibliothek – CIP-Einheitsaufnahme

Bibliographic information published by Die Deutsche Bibliothek
Die Deutsche Bibliothek lists this publication in the Deutsche Nationalbibliografie;
detailed bibliographic data is available in the Internet at ‹http://dnb.ddb.de›.

British Library and Library of Congress Cataloguing-in-Publication Data:
A catalogue record for this book is available from *The British Library*,
Great Britain, and from *The Library of Congress*, USA

ISSN 1420-5297
ISBN 3-03910-864-6
US ISBN 0 8204 8045 2

Third revised edition

© Peter Lang AG, International Academic Publishers, Bern 1997, 1999, 2005
Hochfeldstrasse 32, Postfach 746, CH-3000 Bern 9, Switzerland
info@peterlang.com, www.peterlang.com, www.peterlang.net

Printed in Germany

Contents

Preface to the third edition

It is now eight years since the first edition of this volume appeared; it was followed by a second one in 1999. Because the book is still in demand we decided to publish a third edition, which has not been revised.

It is impossible to do justice to all the fine research that has enriched our insights and knowledge in the last decade, especially since the field lacks a coherent institutional framework. The only important recent initiative is the new list server H-Migration. Notwithstanding the poor organization of the field, it is possible to distinguish a number of new benchmark publications.

In Europe there is the second, revised edition of Leslie Moch's *Moving Europeans: Migration in Western Europe since 1650* (Bloomington, 2003), which remains one of the best overviews on migration history for this part of the world. A perfect complement is Klaus J. Bade's *Migration in European History* (Oxford, 2003), which pays more attention to the political dimension of migration and settlement processes. More focused on the integration process is Leo Lucassen's *The Immigrant Threat: The Integration of Old and New Migrants in Western Europe since 1850* (Champaign, 2005). Furthermore, there is the forthcoming *Migration – Integration – Minorities since the 17th Century: A European Encyclopaedia* (edited by Klaus J. Bade et al.).

Other scholars have concentrated on a more global view: Dirk Hoerder's *Cultures in Contact: World Migrations since the Second Millennium* (Durham, 2002) is the first serious attempt to avoid a Eurocentric perspective and to bring together the existing knowledge on migration and cultural exchanges since 1000 A.D. (cf. also the review symposium in the *International Review of Social History* (volume 49 (2004), pp. 475-515).

We should also like to call attention to three important recent contributions. First, the collection edited by David Eltis, *Coerced and Free Migration: Global Perspectives* (Stanford, 2002), which contains a number of excellent contributions about various parts of the world. Second, the article by Adam McKeown ("Global Migration 1846-1950") in the *Journal of World History*, which criticizes the Atlantic-centred bias in most historical migration studies. Third, the new book by Patrick Manning, *Migration in World History* (New York [etc.], 2005), which begins 40,000 years ago and uses the newest insights in "hard" science: human genetics, entomology, biology, and comparative linguistics, as well as world history. Finally, the field will also profit from the new series of books, *Global Migration History,* edited by Leslie Page Moch and Donna Gabaccia, and published by Illinois University Press.

Jan Lucassen and Leo Lucassen, July 2005

Migration, Migration History, History: Old Paradigms and New Perspectives

Jan Lucassen and Leo Lucassen

1. Introduction[1]

During the last decade it has become more than clear to historians working in the field of migration that this phenomenon has to be regarded as a normal and structural element of human societies throughout history.[2] Generally, migration is no longer viewed as a sign of crisis,[3] as a phenomenon exclusive to the industrial period, as an element of the "modernization" transition,[4] or as a typically Western occurrence. Nor do scholars stress only political factors in explaining large movements of people. Finally, the time when peasants in pre-industrial Europe were perceived as a stable, non-moving, and sedentary world, or when Handlin portrayed immigrants as rootless and desperate lies behind us.

The new paradigm, presented by Frank Thistlethwaite in an embryonic format 35 years ago, teaches us that migration is part of the general human pattern, essential for the functioning of families and crucial to the operation of the labour market. Most basic decisions by human beings – the choice of a profession or a partner – often entail leaving their place of birth or residence. While they may not go far, their moves nevertheless lead them to other social and sometimes geographical environments. As Charles Tilly aptly summarized: "The history of European migration is the history of social life."[5]

So far, we have said nothing new. The recent works of Moch and Canny, among many others, have argued this point convincingly.[6] Why then this book,

---

1. We are grateful for the thorough comments made by Leslie Page Moch and Dirk Hoerder on an earlier draft of this introduction.
2. See e.g. McNeill, *Human Migration*, although his speculative interpretation of the period from 1700 onwards becomes rather apocalyptical. He argues that the declining death rates in cities and the peopling of new continents have turned migrants into an ever-growing problem because they can not be taken in anymore.
3. The persistence of this interpretation becomes painfully clear in one of the few general reference works available, i.e. the study by Potts (*World Labour Market*), in which she depicts migration (be it slaves, indentured labourers, or guest workers) as a sign of crisis within the capitalist world.
4. Zelinsky, "Hypothesis of the Mobility". For a critique see Nugent, *Crossings*, pp. 7-8.
5. Tilly, "Migration in Modern European", p. 68.
6. Moch, *Moving Europeans*; Canny, *Europeans on the Move* and Hoerder and Moch, *European migrants*.

and why just now? What makes this book special? First, during the last decade more historical studies on migration and settlement have appeared than ever before. A state of the art as such therefore seems to be fruitful. Second, migration historians have substantially broadened their conceptual, temporal, and geographical scope. This development is even more cause for a reconsideration of current theoretical perspectives encompassing the gains in insights in divergent areas of specialization in the field of migration history, such as slavery studies, ethnic history, macro-economic migration studies, and gypsy studies.

This book shows such substantial progress that this work could hardly have been written even five years ago. At the same time, this introduction and the other chapters in this book clearly convey the monumental proportions of the current task and the need for a modicum of modesty. Little wonder, twenty-five strangers gathered in a room for two days cannot achieve a miracle. Collectively, however, these essays represent a pioneering effort in our field.[7] They are also an attempt to integrate migration and settlement processes in the general historical picture. This introduction addresses some key issues in this transition.

Migration historians face two major problems, which will be addressed in this introduction: 1) the widespread breakdown into myriad sub-specialties, both between and within disciplines; and 2) the difficulties of integrating the consequences of this new paradigm into general histories.

2. From Typology to Dichotomy

The migration landscape is full of canyons and fast running rivers. The deepest canyon separates social scientists from historians, and swift rivers divide scholars *within* disciplines. Intellectuals are often unaware (or only vaguely aware) of each other's progress. Focusing mainly on historical or historicizing studies manifests this flaw in the form of a great number of typologies intended to grasp the huge and intricate migration phenomenon. Intrinsically, these shortcomings are of course useful and even necessary. The problem, however, is that the rapid reduction of many of these typologies to fixed dichotomies often causes the dividing and isolating capacity of an analytical framework to overshadow its clarifying and explanatory potential. We will illustrate this danger by concentrating on three dominant modes of classification: a) the separation between coerced and voluntary forms of migration; b) the separation between studies on settlement and movement; and c) the restrictions of political, temporal, and geographical frameworks. Finally, this historiographical exercise will be combined with discussions about the major findings of the chapters in this book.

---

7. The names of the authors are italicized. For more information on the conference, see the acknowledgements at the end of this introduction.

2a. Different types of migration

Free versus unfree migration

As a rule, migration historians consider the very fundamental distinction between free and unfree migration only implicitly. Most exclude unfree or involuntary migrations from their definitions. Scholars who include these processes, however, sometimes adopt such an intense focus that they overlook free migration. Historians writing on European migrations rarely discuss the transportation of Jews, gypsies, and other victims to concentration camps or the forced movement of European labour into the wartime factories of the Nazis as forms of migration. Likewise, the Gulag is not commonly seen as a system of labour migration (albeit a forced one). Overall, migrations by prisoners of war, prisoners in general, and convict labourers are not regarded as part and parcel of migration history.[8] Yet the opposite seems to apply among historians writing on non-European migrations. In *The World Labour Market: A History of Migration*, Lydia Potts depicts migration in the Third World in terms of the forced recruitment of Indian labour in Spanish America, chattel slavery from Africa, coolie labour from Asia, forced labour for Japan's war industry, and the homeland system in South Africa. Although she skips over forced mass migrations in Mao's China, these examples suggest that free migration is virtually unknown in the "Third World" (with the possible exception of today's predominantly Asian "guest workers" in the Middle East). Potts's discussion of European migration, however, despite the mention of forced migrations in Nazi Germany (but not one word about Russia under Stalin), concentrates on the "guest worker" issue.[9]

Ulrich Herbert is one of the few historians who integrates forced labour migrations into the general migration history of a specific country. This approach is indicated by his subtitle "Seasonal Workers/Forced Laborers/Guest Workers". With respect to Germany, he correctly stresses that Germans and immigrants experienced both unfree and free migration situations. This finding presents migrations as a unity, although the motives among individual migrants may have differed substantially.[10]

The clarity in distinction between voluntary and forced migrations leaves something to be desired for other reasons. All kinds of non-economic coercion could induce people to accept work elsewhere under conditions that we would consider unfree without being the result of well-planned enslavement. Take the case of the seasonal migrants from the Apennines who descended annually to

---

8. Moch, *Moving Europeans*, p. 168 devotes some lines to coerced work in Nazi Germany.
9. Potts, *World Labour Market*.
10. Herbert, *History of Foreign Labor*. A similar approach is followed by Dohse, *Ausländische Arbeiter*; Lehmann, "Ausländerbeschäftigung und Fremdarbeiterpolitik"; Elsner, "Ausländerbeschäftigung und Zwangsarbeitspolitik".

the Campagna Romana to reap the harvest. This action initially appears to be one of the thousands of examples of movement by free migrant labourers. Closer examination reveals, however, that these workers, braving the dangers of imminent malaria in travelling to the coastal plains, were more or less forced to migrate because of their debts to the wealthy landowners in the lowlands. These landowners had agents who took advantage of shortages among the mountain dwellers at the end of the winter by advancing grain to those in need. They required that their debtors work the harvest in summer to repay part or all of their loans.[11]

Diana Kay and Robert Miles have identified other examples of unfree aspects of free labour migration in Western Europe in their book on the European Volunteer Workers in Britain between 1946 and 1951.[12] They show that these "volunteers" (who were recruited from refugee camps in Germany and Austria) "had freely volunteered to work in Britain, their consent to its terms had been obtained through each individual having signed [...]". The organizations of these workers, however, had good reason to define their status "with some exaggeration, as a form of 'serfdom'". *A fortiori*, the situation continues among today's illegal immigrants in the welfare states of the West.

Another example of more or less forced migration concerns women giving birth out of wedlock. As has been demonstrated for France, they were in no position to compel men to marry them. Many such women left their villages during their pregnancy and went to Paris or other major cities. There they delivered their children and tried to find work, mostly in the service sector. Although the urban labour market – especially positions for wet nurses – clearly played a role, this form of gendered migration also "illuminates a complex of non-economic motives".[13]

Recent studies on free and unfree labour in general have shown the virtual impossibility of clear-cut distinctions between free and unfree labour. Instead, they suggest a continuum from chattel slavery via serfdom and debt peonage[14] to free labour combined with the abandonment of a uni-linear or modernization perspective on the transition from unfree to free labour.[15] This assertion, together with the serious critiques by migration historians, leads to the conclusion that *a priori* distinctions between free and unfree migrations are difficult to substantiate. Our analytical framework should include all types of migrations.

11. J. Lucassen, *Migrant Labour in Europe*, p. 118.
12. Kay and Miles, *Refugees or Migrant Workers*, p. 145. Similar systems were tried in Belgium: Caestecker, *Vluchtelingenbeleid in de naoorlogse periode*, pp. 41-50.
13. Fuchs and Moch, "Pregnant", p. 1030. See also Fuchs, *Poor and Pregnant*.
14. See the fundamental remarks by Steinfeld, *Invention of Free Labour*. See also the contributions of David Eltis and Donna Gabaccia in this book.
15. Brass *et al.*, *Free and Unfree Labour*.

After justifying explicit assumptions, concentrating on some specific types according to degrees of freedom in labour relations may be useful.

Several contributions in this book successfully present structured comparisons between "free" and "unfree" migrations. *Pieter Emmer* bases his analysis of the different forms of migration on two major migration circuits. His economic focus renders a clear-cut distinction between free and unfree migration of minor importance, as his primary interest involves the economic costs and benefits from migration in general. *Ralph Shlomowitz* takes a similar approach in his examination of immigration to Australia from the standpoint of the state. This perspective furthers his fruitful comparison of state-financed migration (forced convicts and free assisted immigrants) and state regulated migration (indentured immigrants from India and the Pacific islands). *Eric Richards* also concentrates on Australia as a labour importing country and illustrates "the smooth passage from convictism to the civilian society and economy". When convict labour ceased to satisfy the demands of the Australian economy, assisted immigrant schemes emerged. Richards also submits a review of the work of Nicholas and others (who principally analyse convicts as migrants and oppose the notion of a "criminal class"[16]) by noting the socio-economic similarities between the convicts and the assisted migrants.

The common thread of these three contributions (which explains their opposition to the dichotomy free-unfree) is that they do not primarily view the majority of indentured and forced immigrants – except for slaves – as victims as opposed to free migrants. These chapters argue that the migrants had their own aspirations and actively sought to improve circumstances both for themselves and their families. This new paradigm ties in with more general insights on migration theory concerning networks and is also supported by *Arjan de Haan*. His careful analysis of intra-Indian labour migration demonstrates the importance of the subjective view of the migrants themselves. Most of the workers from the countryside migrated in networks and were not down-and-out elements of the community. Nor was the decision to migrate to the Jute mills in Calcutta the last option after proletarianization. According to their own perception, their choice was perfectly rational and indicative of upward social mobility because they could earn higher wages and support their relatives in the home villages. Forms of coercion and restrictions were apparently accepted as part of the bargain. The chapter by *Donna Gabaccia* reveals a similar situation among the so-called free Italian and unfree Chinese labour migrants, thereby illustrating the fluidity of the distinction between free and indentured workers.

David Eltis launches the most fundamental attack against the view that free and unfree labour are mutually exclusive. He shows that the two forms are

16. Nicholas, *Convict Workers.*

interdependent and in fact should be seen as part of a consistent unity rather than a dichotomy. Seeking an explanation for the emergence of the slave trade after the mid-seventeenth century, Eltis shows a narrow interaction between the "modernization of the English wage workers" (who increasingly refused to work for low wages and on unhealthy plantations) and the subsequent increase in the emigration of African slaves to the New World. He therefore concludes that "At some fundamental level the factors responsible for free migration from Europe also had a major shaping influence on the slave trade."

Labour migrants versus refugees

Another clear-cut distinction within migration studies, also derived from the difference between forced and voluntary moves, is that between labour migrants and refugees. The cause of mobility differs between the two groups. While economic motivations prevail among labour migrants,[17] persecution, war, indiscriminate violence, or massive natural disasters drive refugees from their homes.[18] Viewing them from the same perspective would only complicate a better understanding of the migration process. Various authors on migration theory have therefore dealt with refugees as a separate category, characterized by terms such as involuntary, pushed, and forced to leave because of distress.[19] Although the motivations of refugees and labour migrants undeniably differ in principle, the disparities are less obvious in practice than is commonly assumed.[20] The first problem with refugees is that they are defined by the governments of the receiving countries on the basis of ideological and economic considerations. Well-known examples are the indiscriminate welcome extended by the United States to people from behind the Iron Curtain in Europe and to Cubans.[21]

Closely related are the German *Aussiedler*, as certain descendants of German emigrants in Russia and other Eastern European countries are called. Immediately after World War II, it was clear that the *refugees* from the East had suffered far greater losses than the Germans in the West. The legislature passed a compensation scheme. Those who remained in the East had been resettled by Hitler to enlarge the contiguous German-settled areas in Central Europe and

17. See e.g. Moch, *Moving Europeans*, pp. 26-28. While she convincingly debunks the traditional crisis-interpretation of migration by focusing on labour migration, she tends to underestimate the economic motivation and importance of refugees.
18. Loescher and Scanlan, *Calculated Kindness*. For a classical overview of the history of refugees, see Marrus, *Unwanted*.
19. See Kuhlman, "Towards a Definition". He discusses among others the theories of Petersen ("General Typology") and Lee ("Theory of Migration").
20. See especially Richmond, "Sociological Theories", pp. 19-20.
21. Portes and Rumbaut (*Immigrant America*, pp. 241-242) cite the example of the heavy bias of the Reagan administration towards escapees from communist-controlled nations. In the years 1981-1987, 91.3 percent of all legal admissions of refugees and asylum seekers fell in this category.

were then moved a second time when the Allied troops came from the East. Others had been deported to Siberia immediately after the German invasion in 1941. It was argued that their double sufferings entitled them to compensation. Since nobody could help them in the East, the German government decided to admit them as citizens whenever they returned to Germany. Everybody assumed, however, that the *Aussiedler* would never come. At the moment, this migration basically results from economic motives rather than from persecution. Their arrival cannot be regarded as return migration either, since many have been away for several generations.[22]

To a certain extent the discrepancy between policy and motivation applies to Jewish emigrants from the USSR as well. After a turning point around 1974, the primary incentive among most Jews who left Russia was not ethnic discrimination but the possibility of upward social mobility and economic opportunities. As Zaslavsky and Brym noted, the bulk of the emigrants was only nominally Jewish; Israel "simply represented the West insofar as it was the only liberal-democratic country ready to take them in during the first years of the movement." Many Russian Jews in Israel did not feel comfortable there. They found Hebrew too difficult and were not at ease with the foreign culture.[23] In the period 1974-1979 the majority did not even go temporarily to Israel, but travelled through Vienna directly to Western Europe, the United States, and Canada.[24]

A striking contrast involves the *denial* of refugee status to most Jewish immigrants in Western European countries in the 1930s. The fear of offending the powerful and intimidating Nazi regime and concern about the high unemployment among the indigenous population led the Dutch government to instruct the border patrol to send back every asylum seeker (including Jewish ones) as late as 1938, unless he or she could prove "an immediate danger to life."[25] In this case historians have not been blinded by the contemporary opinion and have analysed Jewish emigrants from Nazi Germany as refugees. One may wonder, however, whether historians would have taken the same approach in the hypothetical event that the Nazis had refrained from their extermination policy.

Reviewing the more distant past further complicates labelling migrant streams. Immigrants from the southern parts of the Netherlands at the end of the sixteenth century, for example, may be considered refugees. As Protestants they were oppressed by the Catholic rulers from Spain. On the other hand, economic concerns also played a major role in their decision to leave. The textile industry

---

22. We thank Dirk Hoerder for this information. See also Lehmann, *Im Fremden ungewollt zuhaus*; Bade, "Fremde Deutsche", p. 409; and Muus, *Internationale migratie*, p. 61.

23. For personal accounts see Duwidowitsch and Dietzel, *Russisch-Jüdisches Roulette*, pp. 15-19.

24. Zaslavsky and Brym, *Soviet-Jewish Emigration*, p. 41. See also Salitan, *Politics and Nationality*, pp. 45-48. After 1989, direct emigration to Germany and the United States became much more difficult (*Ibid.*, pp. 106-107).

25. Moore, *Refugees from Nazi Germany*, p. 83; Marrus, *Unwanted*, p. 169.

in the South was crumbling, and many expected better opportunities in the newly independent Dutch Republic. In fact almost all refugees combine political with economic motives.[26]

This observation finally leads to some important general trends underlying the migration of refugees. Anyone who decides to leave his or her country of birth because of oppression has to choose whether to go and where to go. These two considerations become apparent in the *characteristics* of the people who eventually take flight. Most such individuals are young males who are fairly well educated or skilled.[27] Only in recent decades has this pattern changed in regions where civil wars have erupted. Here women and children are most likely to flee, whereas men stay behind to fight.[28] Since no one will deny that women and the elderly suffer from oppression as well, this selection process reveals that economic motivations clearly play a role. These situations also indicate the link with labour migration. In both cases migrants base their decision to move on expectations and information about work and opportunities from their respective networks.

Likewise, the host countries of refugees are imbued with economic considerations as well. People fleeing from behind the Iron Curtain (especially after the revolts in Hungary in 1956 and in Czechoslovakia in 1968) were ostensibly welcomed by Western countries for ideological and humanitarian reasons. In practice, however, each country tried to select the most able and best educated among the refugees. No one was interested in people who were elderly, sick, or disabled. Research has revealed that the labour market generally exerted a major influence on admission policies towards refugees.[29] Economic considerations of host countries play a more significant role in the countries of resettlement than in the countries of first reception. While Austria had little choice but to accept all Hungarian refugees who came, the countries that subsequently admitted a certain number of Hungarian refugees from Austrian camps were able to pick and choose. An illustrative example appears in the study by Kay and Miles mentioned earlier. Their analysis of the policy towards refugees in Great Britain after World War II (known as European Volunteers) clearly reveals the

---

26. Lucassen and Penninx, *Nieuwkomers*, p. 153, Lucassen and De Vries, "Leiden als middelpunt".
27. *Ibid.* A well-known example is the uneven sex ratio of Jewish refugees in the 1930s. In 1933, 52.3% of the Jews in Germany were women, compared with 57.5% in 1939. As a result far more women than men died in the concentration camps (Kaplan, "Jewish Women", p. 597).
28. We thank Dirk Hoerder for drawing our attention to this phenomenon. See also Zolberg *et al.*, *Escape from Violence*, pp. 114-115. Other examples include forms of female seasonal labour, such as servants and agricultural workers (J. Lucassen, *Migrant Labour in Europe*; Sogner, "Young in Europe"; Henkes, *Heimat in Holland*).
29. Marrus, *Unwanted*; Wolken, *Grundrecht auf Asyl*, pp. 344-347, for Germany; Loescher and Scanlan, *Calculated Kindness*, pp. 217-218, for the United States; Doesschate, *Asielbeleid en belangen*, for the Netherlands. For a more general overview of the relation refugees-labour migrants, see Hammar, *European Immigration Policy*, p. 242.

prevalence of economic motivations among the receiving governments. About 77,000 "volunteers" were obliged to work for twelve months at a designated workplace. Only if the authorities considered them "worthy members of the British community" were they allowed to stay permanently.[30]

General immigration policy in receiving countries reveals additional similarities between refugees and labour migrants. During periods of labour shortage (between 1955 and 1973 in Western Europe) entry and settlement was relatively easy. Some refugees in this era remained unnoticed because they came as "guest workers". When the oil crisis induced governments to discontinue the recruitment of foreign labour, however, this channel was closed, and, as a result, more people applied for asylum.[31]

Finally, most refugees do *not* come to countries in the Western world. They usually stay in camps close to or sometimes even inside their home countries, especially in Africa. As Aristide Zolberg has remarked, this indicates the absence of a direct link between the refugee problem and migration to the affluent West.[32] Only when refugees have contacts and prospects of earning a living in the West are they likely to migrate.

Notwithstanding the difference in motivations between refugees and labour migrants, the two groups have a lot in common with respect to migration. Both are looking for work and better opportunities. Both use information-gathering and support networks upon reaching their destination. Analyses of the migration process and its influences on receiving societies therefore have little reason to distinguish refugees from labour migrants. In this respect we fully agree with Anthony Richmond's conclusion concerning the similarities between refugees and other migrants:

> "[...]migratory decisions, even those taken under conditions of extreme stress, do not differ from other kinds of decisions governing social behaviour. The same sociological model of motivation is applicable. Second, the distinction between 'free' and 'forced' or 'voluntary' and 'involuntary', is a misleading one. All human behaviour is constrained."[33]

The good, the bad, and the ugly, compounded by the confusing vagrant concept[34]

Almost every important immigration flow incites officials in the receiving country to distinguish between good and bad immigrants. As the chapter by *Colin Holmes* makes clear, this principle applied to migration by Jews from Eastern

---

30. Kay and Miles, *Refugees or Migrant Workers*.
31. Lucassen and Penninx, *Nieuwkomers*, p. 47.
32. Zolberg *et al.*, *Escape from Violence*.
33. Richmond, "Sociological Theories", p. 17.
34. See also the contribution by Leo Lucassen in this book.

Europe to the West at the end of the nineteenth century (with a general emphasis on the "bad" category);[35] as well as to immigration by Europeans to the United States before World War I (with a distinction between Northwestern and Southeastern Europe); and to the 300,000 "repatriates" from the Dutch East Indies who moved to the Netherlands after 1945. In the case of the Dutch East Indies a combination of racial and cultural arguments served to prevent immigration by people with Oriental backgrounds.[36] Officials and politicians in many European countries continue their efforts to identify *true* refugees. In addition to separating the sheep from the goat *within* a certain immigrant group, an emerging selection trend tends to view the most recent immigrants as bad and their counterparts who arrived earlier as somewhat better. In fact, perceptions of immigrants seem to become rosier as the chronological spectrum is extended.[37]

Migration historians, who by definition deal with migrations further back in time, often express strong criticism of the negative views within receiving societies. Numerous studies have debunked much of the contemporary discourse. The old stereotype that Jewish immigrants from Russia or Italians who left their home country after 1890 were incapable of assimilation or tended to be parasites or vagrants has fallen into disfavour. Especially in the United States, these immigrant groups have joined the heroic ranks of national immigrant history.

A few categories remain, however, where negative contemporary opinions still dominate historical reflection, which is in turn imbued with negative contemporary opinions. These unpopular groups include vagrants, peddlers, and people travelling with their families and performing all kinds of itinerant occupations, often labelled as "gypsies" or "tinkers".[38] The dichotomy between vagrants and migrants is also linked to the more prevalent distinction between "subsistence" and "betterment" migration: people in the former group comprising people so poor they have to move to avoid dying from hunger and misery, whereas people in the latter group are motivated to improve their situation. This typology, which has been around for quite a while in a variety of formulations, has received a new impetus from social historians since the 1970s. Examples are the studies by Olwen Hufton on the poor in eighteenth-century France and by Carsten Küther on German vagrants in the same period.[39] Both scholars take a more critical view of their – often moralistic – sources than

35. Green, *Pletzl of Paris*; Holmes, *John Bull's Island*, pp. 65-68.
36. Cottaar and Willems, *Indische Nederlanders*.
37. A similar dichotomy was observed by Thistlethwaite in his famous programmatic article from 1960, "Migration from Europe", p. 18), in which he contrasts favourable writing about earlier immigrants in the United States (Germans, Scots, etc.) with descriptions of the more recent immigrants from Southern and Eastern Europe, who were problematized by sociological scholars at the time.
38. L. Lucassen, *Men noemde hen zigeuners*; Cottaar *et al.*, "Justice or Injustice".
39. Hufton, *Poor of Eighteenth-Century France*; and Küther, *Räuber und Gauner in Deutschland*.

their racist predecessors,[40] while nevertheless producing a general picture filled with beggars, con men, and thieves. Migration clearly signifies a crisis. The "bad" migrants ("vagrants", "vagabonds", "*herrenloses Volk*") are implicitly juxtaposed against the diligent, resourceful, and successful migrants. This dichotomy implicitly or explicitly excludes the "bad" migrants from the normal and accepted migration category. The result is that historical analyses actually reproduce the contemporary vision of migrants, which regarded vagrancy as a crime. This line of reasoning has been extended beyond early modern Europe to encompass other periods. An illustration of this trend involves the "subsistence-betterment" typology, used by the English historians Clark and Souden in the introduction to their collection on migration in early modern England.[41] Based mainly on the contribution by their colleague Slack (who analysed thousands of records of "vagrants" from the first half of the seventeenth century), Clark and Souden note a significant difference between the migration patterns of vagrants and all other migrants. While betterment migrants remained within a local or regional setting, vagrants travelled greater distances and tended to stay on the move. Moreover, the social characteristics of vagrants were quite distinct from other poor migrants because they were predominantly poor, young, male, able bodied, single, or involved in unstable relationships.[42]

Notwithstanding the stimulating quality of Clark and Souden's book, their differentiation between successful and unsuccessful migrants obstructs a more general view. The problem with this typology lies in the implications of the different migratory behaviour. *First,* linking a certain pattern of migration to the motivation of the people involved seems quite problematic. Why would poorer migrants *set their sights* on sheer survival and the somewhat more comfortable on upward mobility? Moreover, the distinction between these two categories was not as fundamental as is often assumed. "Vagrants" could break away from their seemingly hopeless predicament or at least give their children a better start in life, and "betterment migrants" could end up in the vagrant category. In an even more complicated scenario, one and the same person could be regarded quite differently depending on the stage in his or her yearly working cycle.[43] "Vagrancy" could thus be a temporary status in periods of unemployment or might reflect the inability of authorities to perceive the true migratory motive. French studies have revealed cases of such confusion in the accounts of seasonal migrants being arrested by the *maréchaussée* on their way to or from their work.[44]

---

40. For an analysis cf. L. Lucassen, "Blind Spot".
41. Clark and Souden, *Migration and Society*, pp. 11-48. In the area of subsistence migration, they rely mainly on Slack's contribution to their collection. See also Clark, "Migrant in Kentish Towns".
42. Slack, "Vagrants and Vagrancy", pp. 56-57.
43. For this concept see J. Lucassen, *Migrant Labour in Europe*, p. 97.
44. Gutton, *État et la mendicité*, pp. 180-181.

Second, indiscriminate use of the vagrancy concept easily opens a Pandora's box filled with stigmatizing ideas, thus virtually precluding any view of poor travellers or vagrants as normal migrants. The problem in other words is the moralistic associations inextricably linked with the term "vagrant". The same holds true for terms such as "gypsies" and "tramps". Distinguishing these groups from other migrants reinforces the contemporary idea that these people lived predominantly from begging and crime and formed a subculture dominated by other standards and values.

Admittedly this kind of critique is neither new nor original. Clark and Souden, as well as Slack, for example, are aware of such pitfalls. They even warn against overly simplistic use of the subsistence-betterment dichotomy by rightly arguing that many local migrants (such as apprentices and servants) had little prospect of betterment and noting that people with aspirations sometimes travelled greater distances.[45] They do not, however, draw the more radical conclusion that the typology as such is of very limited use and obscures more than it enlightens. The same holds true for the idea that subsistence migration by the poor posed a threat to society as a whole and could cause serious social problems. On this subject Clark and Souden point to the burden on poor relief and the downward pressure on wages. The root of the problem, however, was not migration but the general socio- economic and political developments that exacerbated poverty.[46] Finally, we should keep in mind that labour markets were highly segmented. An increase of poor immigrants did not automatically affect wages, at least not in general.[47]

In this book *Leo Lucassen* deals with the "vagrant theme", while *Georg Fertig* also offers valuable contributions on the subject. One of the main explanations for the very long history of stigmatization, which merits a separate study,[48] appears closely linked to the functioning of poor relief systems: because vagrants, gypsies, and the like lacked a fixed administrative abode, authorities (both local and central) feared they would become a financial burden and devoted major efforts to keeping them out of their territory.[49] The fact that most of them earned a living (albeit a modest one) did little to assuage this fear. An additional

---

45. Clark and Souden, *Migration and Society*, p. 31.
46. Lis and Soly, *Poverty and Capitalism*. In fact, poverty was widespread during the Ancien Regime. According to a recent study this situation resulted in a structural malnutrition that inhibited some 20 percent of the labour force from working more than a few hours a day and was responsible for huge numbers of beggars (Fogel, "Economic Growth", pp. 6-7).
47. A wealth of literature covers the dual economy or segmented labour-market, especially with respect to immigrants. We refer to Morawska, "Sociology and Historiography" (pp. 198 ff. and note 41 on p. 229).
48. For a thorough analysis of the ideas about gypsies in Western Europe, see Willems, *In Search of the True Gypsy*.
49. For a more systematic treatment of the poor-relief theme see also Cottaar, *Kooplui, kermisklanten*; and L. Lucassen, *Zigeuner*.

explanation for the stringent laws against vagrancy submitted by *David Eltis* notes the attempts by the English authorities in the seventeenth century to extract labour from "those unwilling to volunteer it for wages"; *Leo Lucassen's* contribution makes clear that this policy had emerged in the fourteenth century and has not disappeared since.

A final dichotomy, both today and in previous centuries, which combines elements from the "good-bad", "betterment-subsistence", and "voluntary-coerced", typologies, is the separation between high and low-income migrants. The first category (good and voluntary), including employees working for multinationals, for example, is rarely even regarded as a group of immigrants or aliens in everyday discourse, whereas the second category (bad and to a certain extent coerced) is seen as *the group of* immigrants whose very presence is deemed problematic. As a result of this mode of thought, their migration patterns, motives, and economic functions are rarely interpreted in one and the same framework. The fruitful nature of this combination appears in the work of Sassen, who uses Manhattan as an example to demonstrate that both categories are closely linked and form *one* segmented migration system, for example because the professionals create jobs for low-income "migrants", thus attracting new migration flows.[50]

2b. The isolation of settlement studies and the dearth of long term analyses

Another major gulf separating migration scholars internally is the distinction between the ones who are primarily interested in the movements of people and their counterparts who focus on the settlement process of migrants and on topics such as integration, assimilation, racism, and ethnicity. Historians who are interested in settlement issues (many of whom have published fundamental and important studies[51]) are greatly influenced by social and political scientists. As a result, many of these scholars tend to concentrate on the negative aspect of the settlement process. Immigration is not intrinsically considered problematic. In fact, settlement scholars love this process and earn a living from studying the subject. Often, however, they stress that immigration – regrettably – leads to problems. They attribute such problems to the monolithic wall of rejection that often confronts migrants, leading to expulsion, ghettoization, discrimination, and racism. In rare instances these scholars defend the opposite position and present immigration as a smooth and carefree process of assimilation.

---

50. Sassen, *Global City*, pp. 285-286.
51. Among others Bodnar, *Transplanted*; Morawska, *For Bread with Butter*; Gabaccia, *Militants and Migrants*; Noiriel, *Creuset français*; Bade, *Deutsche im Ausland*; and Engman, *Ethnic Identity*.

According to the long-term perspective, however, neither the problematic nor the happy description actually applies. The problematic aspects mostly pale into insignificance. Notwithstanding an often difficult start, most immigrants in Europe and America (with the notable exception of slaves) find their place, ascend the social ladder, and are absorbed by the native population.[52] Moreover, the insightful chapter by *Kenneth Lunn* disproves the concept of *a* receiving society by showing huge national differences as well as differences between central and local authorities in the treatment of aliens.[53] Furthermore, native populations comprise groups with conflicting interests and loyalties, which – with respect to the question of immigration – lead to coalitions of "strange bed fellows", as formulated by Zolberg.[54]

Another conspicuous trait of many settlement studies is the view of migration by specific ethnic groups (e.g. Italians, Poles, and Jews in various American cities) as a unique phenomenon and ethnic groups as primordially different, or at least tenacious. Much of the research – characterized by Morawska as the "ethnicity-forever approach"[55] – concentrates on the first or first few generations and ignores similar experiences by other immigrants. Even Robert Swierenga, an eminent migration scholar, revealed a partial weakness for this current in American ethnicity studies when he wrote:

> "Migration was a rational process and the outcome was homogeneous ethnic communities, held together by shared familial, religious, and social bonds. Cultural maintenance and distinctiveness, not assimilation, was the end result."[56]

Once again, the main problem with this approach is the short-term analysis and the fixation on unique characteristics among specific immigrant groups.[57]

---

52. Lucassen and Penninx, *Nieuwkomers*; Lieberson, *Piece of the Pie*. We therefore reject the recent interpretation by the French anthropologist Todd (*Destin des immigrés*), who argues that societies are characterized by immutable anthropological structures (especially traditions among the indigenous population of marrying inside or outside the ethnic group) determining whether immigrants have a chance to assimilate.
53. For a balance of capita selecta of the policies on the local level in Western Europe see also Soly and Thijs, *Minderheden in Westeuropese steden*.
54. Zolberg, "Reforming the Back Door".
55. Morawska, "Sociology and Historiography", p. 218.
56. R. Swierenga, "Ethnic History", *Ethnic Forum*, 4 (Spring 1984), p. 4, cited by Puskas, "Hungarian Overseas Migration", p. 229.
57. For a fundamental criticism on the "ethnic approach" see Morawska, "Sociology and Historiography"; and the contribution by Nancy Green. Note that many immigration studies use a restricted time frame (with a predilection for the period c. 1850-1940), thereby complicating an analysis of the long term process of assimilation (see e.g. Barton, *Peasants and Strangers*; Yans-McLaughlin, *Family and Community*; Bodnar, *Immigration and Industrialization*; Lovoll, *Century of Urban Life*; Emmons, *Butte Irish*). An exception is the interesting study by Halter (*Between Race and Ethnicity*) on the Cape Verdean immigrants, even though she focuses heavily on ethnic continuity and cultural links.

Instead, we propose avoiding an *a priori* focus on ethnicity and remaining open to other kinds of affiliations. Panikos Panayi wrote an interesting study on this subject about Germans in Great Britain during the nineteenth century, and concluded that:

> "[...] we cannot speak of a single German ethnicity. Germans maintained a consciousness with regard to their religious roots, while the organisations which they decided to join relied fundamentally on their occupations, political affiliations, and, above all, class."[58]

Second, scholars need to acknowledge the general long-term process of integration and assimilation. Rather than espousing the traditional and simplistic model of a rapid linear progression toward a common indigenous amalgamate of lifestyles, cultural values, and social patterns,[59] we define assimilation as the state in which immigrants or their descendants do not regard themselves primarily as different from the native-born population and are no longer perceived as such.[60]

In this respect we fully agree with Herbert Gans that the occasional and non-frequent "ethnic identity needs" that are especially apparent among third and fourth generation immigrants entail no fundamental conflict with the process of assimilation and acculturation.[61] More implicitly, Humbert Nelli reached the same conclusion. Notwithstanding the somewhat misleading title of his book (*From immigrants to ethnics*), he shows that most descendants of Italian immigrants have assimilated to a great extent after three generations. The invention of their Italian roots by the third and fourth generation immigrants, which results in a form of what Gans called "symbolic ethnicity", does not signify major changes.[62] A useful counterweight to the ethnicity trend appears in the work of the anthropologist Louise Lamphere, who stresses the importance of "mediating institutions" in the integration process, such as the state, schools, and corporations. According to this view, depriving immigrants of an opportunity to escape their initial social isolation will block assimilation.[63]

A new marker, suggested by anthropologists and political scientists alike, ties in closely with the "ethnicity forever" approach. This concept of transnationalism has become the vogue in the past decade or so.[64] According to this argu-

58. Panayi, *German Immigrants in Britain*, p. 225. See also Nadel, *Little Germany*.
59. Cf. Morawska, "Sociology and Historiography", pp. 212-213.
60. Lucassen and Penninx, *Nieuwkomers*, pp. 100-101.
61. Gans, "Symbolic Ethnicity", p. 1.
62. Nelli, *From Immigrants to Ethnics*, pp. 175-192.
63. Lamphere, *Structuring Diversity* and Hoerder, "From Migrants to Ethnics".
64. Cf. Heisler and Schmitter-Heisler, *Foreign Workers*; and Schiller *et al.*, *Towards a Transnational Perspective*. The essentialist cultural flaw that underlies this way of thinking (also inherent in the "ethnic history approach") has a broader influence. See for example the interpretation of the new immigration by Moch (*Moving Europeans*, p. 175) and the criticism by L. Lucassen ("Book Review of Leslie Page Moch"). Admittedly, though, other definitions of transnation-

ment, immigration to Western Europe and the United States after 1960 differs substantially in form, magnitude, and consequences from earlier mass movements.[65] On the one hand these immigrants were assumed to be very distinct in cultural respects and opposed to assimilation due to a strong return myth promoted by the sending state. On the other hand, the receiving state expected sojourners and therefore made no initial attempt to assimilate them. Modern communication and fast transport purportedly reinforced this situation by enabling immigrants to maintain strong links with their country of birth and create their own ethnically distinct networks. The new *problématique*, as formulated by Heisler & Schmitter-Heisler, is:

> "The open-ended, semi-settled position of large majorities of the migrant populations in most of the host societies."[66]

From a historical perspective, however, the issue arising from the transnational concept is that the settlement process of these new immigrants is still so fresh that such sweeping judgements are premature, to say the least. Moreover, many indications suggest that for example second – and sometimes third – generation immigrants from Morocco and Turkey in Western Europe are integrating and slowly are giving up their ambivalent position.[67] Finally, a short glance at the available historical literature reveals that various links with the country of birth are a very old and therefore probably a structural trait of the migration process,[68] and that the perception of immigrants as culturally different is far from a recent phenomenon. A well-known example is the contemporary attitude towards the new immigrants from Southern and Eastern Europe who entered the United States roughly between 1895 and 1921. Although collective memory has come

---

alism are also used, notably as an ideological movement that transcends nationalism (Bamyeh, "Transnationalism").

65. Apart from the "ethnic interpretation" of the immigration after World War II, there is a strong tendency to view the more recent immigration to Western Europe and the United States, implicitly or explicitly, as different and unprecedented. See Castles, *Here for Good*, p. 1; Cross, "Black Workers, Recession", p. 77; and King, *Mass Migrations in Europe*. The similarities between the policies towards labour immigration before and after World War II are especially easily forgotten. For example, Castles's statement that the period after 1945 is different because the state began to interfere actively only at this point by reducing immigrants to "unfree labour" ignores the developments during the Interbellum, when immigrants had even fewer rights and could be expelled far more easily (Castles, "Migrants and Minorities", p. 38; Cross, *Immigrant Workers in Industrial France*, pp. 218-219; Caestecker, "Vreemdelingenbeleid in de tussenoorlogse periode" and L. Lucassen, "Paspoort als edelste deel").

66. Heisler and Schmitter-Heisler, *From Foreign Workers*, p. 18.

67. Penninx *et al.*, *Impact of International Migration*. Cf. in this respect see also the interesting conclusion of Doomernik ("Institutionalisation of Turkish Islam") that the institutionalization of the Islam in the Netherlands is less a sign of ethnic cohesion than a bridge towards integration.

68. It is significant that Heisler and Schmitter-Heisler refer to Park's outdated work to support their thesis that the assimilation process has changed (*From Foreign Workers*, p. 14).

to consider them an integral part of the European immigration, commentators at the time proclaimed that they belonged to a "different civilization from that represented by the Anglo-Saxon race" and demanded curtailment of this immigration, which followed in 1924.[69]

This tendency of stressing the uniqueness of the group studied is not exclusively confined to settlement studies. Nor is the inability or unwillingness to establish comparisons restricted to ethnic historians. As the previous paragraph has revealed, many migration scholars lack any interest in comparisons with other forms of migration or in a unifying migration concept. Finally, this fragmented approach obstructs the diffusion of new insights in other parts of the migration field and occasionally confronts students with a cesspool of exploded theories. Morawska remarked with respect to the mutually exclusive American schools of ethnic historians and immigration sociologists:

> "Although they ran parallel for considerable stretches, these two intellectual movements are not sufficient aware of each other. Students in one discipline 'discover' what has been acknowledged and treated in the other's research for quite some time. Not infrequently [...] I hear comments like that of an ethnic historian reacting to the latest 'vogue' in immigration research [...], 'But we have known that for a decade!' And an immigration sociologist had a similar response to some new volume put out by ethnic historians: 'Well, don't they ever read what we write?'"[70]

The problem of comparisons (or the lack thereof) receives special attention in the fundamental contribution by *Nancy Green*. She suggests several desirable structures in such comparisons. To improve their insight into settlement processes, ethnic historians should not only compare ethnic or national groups as such, but first and foremost need to choose other units or levels of comparison (e.g. the position of immigrants in specific industries in various countries or patterns of social mobility over an extended period). This approach is necessary to detect common traits between immigrant groups and between immigrants and natives as a means of identifying specific traits among certain groups. *Dirk Hoerder's* chapter applies this strategy in practice by stressing the general function of networks built and used by migrants. He also shows how macro migration systems can be integrated in the everyday decisions of individual migrants. Finally, *Donna Gabaccia* illustrates these methodological considerations in her chapter, which contains the first structured account of the migration process of Chinese and Italians around the world. By concentrating on their function for the labour market and their indentured status, she shows that these groups have a lot more in common than is usually assumed.

---

69. Speech by Senator Simmons of North Carolina during the 1906 debates in Congress, cited by Goldin, *Political Economy of Immigration*, p. 25.
70. Morawska, "Sociology and Historiography", p. 188.

2c. Political, temporal, and geographical frameworks

While historians necessarily concentrate on certain cases and research some topics more thoroughly than others, some important trends in scholarship omit the general picture and obscure insight into migration and settlement processes. In this last historiographical paragraph we want to address three of the most influential frameworks in migration studies: 1) *state-centrism*, the tendency to study migration streams and settlement processes mainly from national perspectives; 2) *modernization-centrism*, the explicit or implicit idea that the Industrial Revolution is the most important temporal dividing line; and 3) *Euro- or Atlantocentrism*, the almost exclusive attention to transatlantic migration from Europe to the New World.

State-centrism

In keeping with the general dominance of political history, migration has long been studied almost exclusively from a state angle. Migration figures in standard histories only when it results from state policies, for example colonial settlement efforts, the expulsion of unwanted groups, or the prohibition of emigration.[71] Internal and labour migration fall by the wayside in this context. As the contributions by *Robin Cohen* and *Aristide Zolberg* illustrate, such a viewpoint is useful because it highlights the role of the state and places the phenomenon in a global perspective. Furthermore, it cannot be denied that the growing influence of the state in the twentieth century undeniably altered the settlement process fundamentally. The achievement of the modern nation-state coincided with increasing linkage of rights and obligations to citizenship. Being an "alien" – at least with respect to the central state – is now of far greater importance than it was during the Ancien Regime. Clear insight into the settlement process therefore requires a legal and social definition of immigrants.[72]

Assuming that migration is mainly triggered by state action or that settlement processes are determined only by the state, however, raises problems. In the first place, during the medieval and early modern periods, cities, rather than states, determined migration by actively attracting foreigners and assigning them a place in the local society. Likewise, local politics in the modern period did not merely mirror those at the national level, as the contributions by *Kenneth Lunn* and *Leo Lucassen* illustrate. In the second place, major discernible migration streams are

---

71. On this subject, see also Thistlethwaite's explanation for the lack of interest among European historians in transatlantic migration: "[...] European history has been the history of nations and, from this point of view, overseas migration is essentially negative." ("Migration from Europe", p. 21).
72. Brubaker, *Citizenship and Nationhood*. For a critique of his work see L. Lucassen, "Onontkoombare nationaliteitsbeginsel". See also Silverman, *Deconstructing the Nation*.

defined by labour markets rather than by state policies. Concerning the early modern period, the paper by Aristide Zolberg in the well-known collection by William McNeill & Ruth Adams (1978) is a good example. This study deals with migration mainly from the transatlantic perspective and views the process as primarily concerted by state policies motivated by imperialism and mercantilism. Zolberg's analysis of intra-European migration is restricted to state expulsions on political-religious grounds, as with the Huguenots and the Iberian Jews. According to this perspective, only the laissez-faire system in the nineteenth century led to a short period of free migration.[73]

Since the publication of Zolberg's paper almost twenty years ago, the subsequent dramatic expansion of knowledge has clearly shown the importance of remembering that however the state may attempt to control migration, worker movements are very much defined by the functioning of labour markets. The presence of illegal aliens in Europe and the United States, who are often essential for certain economic sectors (such as the garment industry and agricultural work), is tangible proof.[74] The manifestations of migration, characterized by networks and chains, have also remained very similar to preceding movements in earlier centuries. Even where the regulating character of the state seems abundantly clear at first glance, as in the case of the recruitment of guest workers in the 1950s and 1960s, traditional and informal contacts among labour migrants were at least as important.

Finally, the unintended paradoxical and contradictory effects of state policy are important with respect to settlement. The emergence of the welfare state in Western Europe yielded all sorts of unintended and unexpected benefits for migrants. Helping to build this welfare state provided many temporary immigrants (guest workers) with rights, thus enabling them to bring over their families and become permanent residents in the long run. Even the very restrictive German and Swiss nationality acts have been unable to prevent the settlement of considerable Turkish minorities within the borders of Germany and Switzerland. Most likely, these migrants are there to stay.[75]

---

73. Zolberg, "International Migration Policies", pp. 244-251.
74. Social and political scientists have yet to reach a consensus regarding the possibilities of the state for controlling immigration (see e.g. the conflicting opinions of Garry P. Freeman versus Rinus Penninx and Hans van Amersfoort in Miller, *Strategies for Immigration Control*). Convincing arguments against the power of state control are offered by Ogden, "Immigration to France"; Singer-Kérel, *Foreign Workers in France*; and Gemery, "Immigrants and Emigrants". For a more economic approach, see the work of Sassen (*Mobility of Labor*), who stresses the importance of "objective linkages", such as the military and economic interference of the United States in countries such as Haiti, the Dominican Republic, and Mexico, which "promoted the whole notion of migrating to the U.S." (p. 8).
75. In the last decade a wave of studies has gotten under way analysing the immigration policies of Western European countries since World War II. See among others: Hammar, *European Immigration Policy*; Hammar, *Democracy and the Nation State*; Hollifield, *Immigrants*; and Miller, *Strategies for Immigration Control*.

Modernization-centrism

Nine out of ten migration studies selected at random contain a tale about the industrial period.[76] Moreover, such books probably deal with intercontinental and transatlantic migration.[77] The choice for this approach often reflects the assumption that the Industrial Revolution triggered migration on a massive scale. Earlier occurrences of migration are dismissed as less interesting and to a certain extent of another nature. On the other hand, Herbert (who so elegantly avoids the free versus unfree labour migration dichotomy[78]), for example, uses the framework of "industrialized societies in which the dynamics of the economy, high mobility, and periods of boom and recession induce strong fluctuations in the labor market."[79] Moreover, the intercontinental mass migration in the nineteenth century is implicitly considered more fundamental than individual moves from one village to another or from one region to another.[80]

Criticism of the focus on the industrial period has been submitted by various scholars, including *Ida Altman, Leslie Page Moch, Dirk Hoerder*, and *Georg Fertig*. Their contributions in this book point to the fundamental and structural function of local and regional migration in the pre-industrial period and to the resemblances between these kinds of "moves" and migration on a larger scale. The study of small-scale forms of migration is essential for a good insight into international and intercontinental migrations. Daniel Courgeau has written:

> "Migration should no longer be seen as independent of the other stages of the familial and economic life cycle. It must be seen in the context of much wider processes of social change. The research [...] has involved us in the study of many different types of mobility: moving house, migration from one *département* to another, migration towards very urban and less urbanized areas, departure from the countryside, international migration and so forth. These varied forms of mobility must be related to the various stages of the life cycle, not in a fixed but in a dynamic framework."[81]

Ida Altman's chapter uses the case of Spain to demonstrate that patterns of local, regional, and transatlantic migrations were already interconnected in the sixteenth century, and that these links would become stronger in the centuries that followed. From the eighteenth century onwards Italian seasonal labourers gathered

---

76. See e.g. Ogden and White, *Migrants in Modern France*; Guerin-Gonzales and Strikwerda, *Politics of Immigrant Workers*; Castles and Miller, *Age of Migration*; and Hatton and Williamson, *Migration*.
77. See for example Vecoli and Sinke,*Century of European Migrations*; Emmer and Mörner, *European Expansion and Migration*; and Erickson, *Leaving England*.
78. See paragraph 2a, pp. 11ff, of this contribution.
79. Herbert, *History of Foreign Labor*, p. V. A comparable view in Wolf, *Europe and the People Without History*, pp. 362-363.
80. Notable exceptions are the works of Ogden and White, *Migrants in Modern France*; and Pooley and Whyte, *Migrants*.
81. Courgeau, "Recent Conceptual Advances", p. 73.

the harvest in France every year. At the end of the nineteenth century the Italians traded this work venue for the grain fields of Argentina. Every year they travelled there, together with many Galician farmhands, as *golondrinas* (Spanish for swallows),[82] only to return to Italy after a few months. The structural causes of migration remained largely the same. Only the scale and distances changed. For many migrants, crossing the ocean was a less permanent and fundamental move than is often assumed. Systems of chain and return migration kept the ties with the Old World intact.[83] Moreover, as stressed by *Dirk Hoerder* and others,[84] the decision to go work somewhere else continued to follow careful deliberation within the family, also when the labour market had assumed global proportions.

Nevertheless, comparisons between pre-industrial and industrial migration or between internal and international migration[85] are rare.[86] One exception is Stanley Lieberson's model study on internal black migration in the United states, which the author compares with the immigration from Southern and Eastern Europe after 1880. His perspective leads to surprising results that have enriched our insights into the social mobility of both categories, as well as the settlement process at large.[87]

In an even rarer work of scholarship, Moch links the pre-industrial and the industrial periods. Her excellent and path breaking study starts a full century earlier in 1650. Although she is aware of previous migrations in Europe,[88] she submits that migration before 1650 differed from migration during the following three and a half centuries. The major changes around the middle of the seventeenth century were both qualitative and quantitative according to Moch. Following Charles Tilly's seminal ideas about proletarianization, she notes qualitative changes in the European countryside that triggered important migration movements, such as the loss of small landholdings because of the increase of larger farms, growing employment demands as a result of the emerging protoindustry, and the demise of the European marriage pattern, thus curtailing fertility.[89] She also stresses a quantitative change in the location of capital holdings. These assets were still restricted to a few prosperous regions such as Amsterdam and London in the

---

82. Nugent, *Crossings*, pp. 104 and 119; Moch, *Moving Europeans*, p. 152.
83. See e.g. Morawska, "Return Migrations"; Wyman, *Round-trip to America*; and Baines, "European Labor Markets".
84. Baud, "Families and Migration"; Morawska, "Sociology and Historiography".
85. Tilly, "Transplanted Networks", pp. 79-95.
86. A notable exception is Baines (*Migration in a Mature Economy* and "European Labor Markets"), on the relation between internal English and transatlantic migration.
87. Lieberson, *Piece of the Pie*.
88. Moch, *Moving Europeans*, pp. 10-12, 23, 26-30 (Jewish and Huguenot refugees) and p. 6 (the growth of cities as an important "subplot").
89. *Ibid.*, pp. 7-8, 13 and 23.

seventeenth century, but spread to many more centres after that point.[90] Quite honestly, Moch is not concentrating on changes in the seventeenth century. Her focus lies on the eighteenth century, when proto-industrialization restricted migration that had been more intense during the preceding period.[91]

However valuable these observations may be, any increase in the intensity of migrations around 1650 remains to be ascertained. If international migrations may be seen as the tip of the iceberg, recent data concerning many European countries do not support this assumption and sometimes even indicate the contrary. Some examples may illustrate this point. Thomas Christopher Smout and others have produced estimates for Scottish emigration revealing that the first and the second half of the seventeenth century did not differ with respect to emigration, and that the eighteenth century even showed a decrease.[92] Wrigley and Schofield's reconstructions of English net migration losses in the sixteenth, seventeenth, and eighteenth centuries do not indicate major fluctuations that would signify clear sub-periods, which in fact means that international migration in relation to total population figures diminished in importance after the second half of the seventeenth century.[93] A rather complicated interpretation combines these figures with separate emigration and immigration streams, as submitted by Canny for England and Cullen for Ireland, in addition to the data on Scotland that was already mentioned. Canny explains that English emigration was far more important in the seventeenth than in the eighteenth century. Only Irish emigration increased during the eighteenth century.[94]

Not surprisingly, emigration from Spain was more important before 1650 than afterwards.[95] The fact that immigration into the Dutch Republic was more important during its earlier period than in its later years is equally understandable.[96] France is the final example here of a change in the importance of migration. Emigration from France in the late Middle Ages and sixteenth century was important, as revealed both by the initial colonization efforts in the Mediterranean and by the subsequent ones on Madeira. The renowned French migration to Spain in the sixteenth and early seventeenth centuries – also mentioned by Moch – seems to link up with these early colonization movements and contrasts sharply with the inability of the French to colonize America in the following century.[97]

90. *Ibid.*, p. 31.
91. *Ibid.*, p. 73.
92. Smout, "Scots and Emigrants in Europe" and Smout and Devine. "Scottish Emigration".
93. Wrigley and Schofield, *Population History of England*, p. 227.
94. Canny, *Europeans on the Move*; on London during the sixteenth and seventeenth centuries, see Archer, "Responses to Alien Immigrants".
95. Sánchez-Albornoz, "First Transatlantic Transfer".
96. J. Lucassen, "Netherlands".
97. S. Phillips, "Medieval Background"; Moogk, "Manon's Fellow Exiles"; Moch, *Moving Europeans*; and Cavaciocchi, *Migrazioni in Europa*.

Proletarianization and proto-industrialization have undoubtedly induced people in the European countryside to migrate. Whether any substantive change or increase in overall migration resulted from these phenomena, however, remains highly uncertain. We would like to suggest that such a change had already taken place at least one century earlier, and that the trend stabilized from around the middle of the seventeenth century until around the end of the Ancien Regime. It has become clear that European migration history does not start with the Industrial Revolution or even with proto-industry. Dating the beginning of such a history around the advent of the modern era with the great discoveries, the religious wars, and similar major events that triggered long-distance migrations is tempting. Such a clear-cut alternative is premature, however, and would simply elicit criticism from a specialist in medieval history.[98] We agree with Leslie Page Moch, who writes: "Migrations are not a signal of the modern age but rather [here she quotes Paul White and Robert Woods] 'continuous phenomena which are embedded in the social and economic framework of human organization'".[99]

Euro- or Atlantocentrism

Finally, some observations are in order regarding the dominance of migration studies on Europe and transatlantic migration. However understandable this predilection may be, it has led to a gross neglect of other migration systems. The contribution by *Georg Fertig* shows that hardly anybody noticed that migration from Germany to Eastern Europe considerably exceeded the westbound movement in the seventeenth and eighteenth centuries. Hoerder elaborates on this argument by noting the emergence of a Russo-Siberian system involving tens of millions of people in the nineteenth century. In both cases migrants formed a frontier society in their search for arable land and mineral sources.[100]

In a later publication Hoerder chooses a global perspective by taking into account colonial migration circuits in and from Asia and Africa and the Pacific rim migration (Chinese and Japanese) to North America and concluding with an exhortation to all migration historians to abandon their cosy and well-known niches for a "world systems" approach.[101] Various contributors have taken

---

98. S. Phillips, "Medieval Background"; W. Phillips, "Old World Background"; Matschinegg and Müller, *Migration – Wanderung* already contains 1,233 titles mainly on German-speaking countries between ca. 1350 and 1600. See also Jaritz and Müller, *Migration in der Feudalgesellschaft*.
99. Moch, *Moving Europeans*, p. 6.
100. Hoerder, *People on the Move*, pp. 18-21. See also Morawska, "Return Migrations", p. 279.
101. Hoerder, "Changing Paradigms".

Hoerder up on his recommendation, as indicated above.[102] *Pieter Emmer, Ralph Shlomowitz, Eric Richards,* and *Donna Gabaccia* have all succeeded in presenting their own global perspective and have thereby considerably enriched our understanding of migration and settlement.

To what extent have these new directions helped us construct a better analytical framework to study and understand migration? What kind of typology has a greater explanatory power and enriches our insights by linking migration phenomena that are normally confined within separate spheres? As always, criticism comes more easily than a constructive response. Nevertheless, the contributions in the present book contain more than enough fuel for starting a new engine. The main conclusions are:

1) Following *Leslie Page Moch*,[103] let us stick to the basic migration definition used by migration sociologists ("a permanent or semi permanent change of residence").[104] Let us avoid fundamental distinctions on the basis of distance, magnitude, or motive. The classifications suggested by migration sociologists such as Lee and Petersen can be useful, but should not obstruct our general view. We need to consider similarities between different forms of migration far more carefully and should therefore undertake more comparative studies. Although sub-specializations are unavoidable, this general conceptual model is important. In addition to facilitating the exchange of research results, this model offers a better guarantee for scientific progress.

2) We should also keep in mind the essential function of migration networks within human societies, especially with respect to the family and the labour market.

3) This structural socio-economic approach to migration does not diminish the importance of the emergence of the nation state. This development ushered in the end of the free migration, with World War I as the turning point. For the first time in history, state-run bureaucracies came about and controlled the entrance of aliens at the national borders.

These starting points yield two possible research strategies. One approach focuses on the reaction of family tactics to political processes. How did acts and regulations concerning migration and settlement, as well as local arrangements,[105] influence people's decisions as to whether and how to migrate? To what extent did individual decisions link up with family strategies? The other approach uses economic structures as a basis and focuses on the reaction of political structures. How did state and local authorities, as well as employers and unions, react to

---

102. Paragraph 2a, pp. 11ff of this contribution.
103. Cf. also Courgeau, "Recent Conceptual Advances".
104. Lee, "Theory of Migration", p. 49.
105. See Kenneth Lunn's chapter in this book.

the attraction of migrants to satisfy increased demand for labour? What kind of solutions were preferred by the state and which alternatives ignored?

3. Out of the Ghetto

Our plea for a more synthetic and unified approach should not be construed as an end in itself. Rather, this strategy is necessary for weaving the principal results and insights into the fabric of general social, economic, and cultural histories.[106] This observation leads to the second main theme of this introduction: the integration of migration studies into mainstream history. Such incorporation is especially important because outside the specialized domain of migration studies the phenomenon is still treated as a sign of crisis (uprooting) or as a modern occurrence (assuming a static pre-industrial society as in Peter Laslett's "The world we have lost"). We will illustrate this need on the basis of historiography in the Netherlands and other Western European countries.[107]

Most general Dutch history books largely neglect migration, despite the profound influence of immigration on the development of the Netherlands. For example, the sea provinces depended on foreign labour for 50 percent of their male workforce during the seventeenth and eighteenth centuries. Most textbooks, however, mention only the spectacular immigration flows, such as the Huguenots, the Jews, and the immigrants from the Southern part of the Netherlands (present-day Belgium and Northern France). Emigration to the Americas, repatriation from the Dutch East Indies, and the immigration of the guest workers receive only cursory mention: migration represents an incident. The Jews are the only group that receives more attention, although the focus lies on their religious position.

Books that specialize in socio-economic and demographic history may be expected to incorporate migration as a structural factor. Although such works address migration more extensively, they do not really integrate the phenomenon.[108] At first sight, this shortcoming seems unexpected. The dominant methods of demographic history, a specialization that one would expect to take a primary interest in movements of people, prescribe the opposite approach. Analyses of population growth between two available sets of data are based on

---

106. Jackson and Moch, "Migration and the Social History".
107. Based on Lucassen and Lucassen, "Van incident tot structurele factor".
108. An exception is the recent work by De Vries and Van der Woude (*Nederland 1500-1815*), who devote a paragraph to migration in the early modern period and acknowledge its structural importance (pp. 95-102). For the book as a whole, however, such migration remains a somewhat isolated topic. To date, only Van Zanden (*Rise and Decline*) has considered migration a structural factor in a general study with respect to the explanation for the economic growth of the Dutch Republic.

figures for births and deaths, after which a migration balance remains. Once this calculation is done, most historical-demographers lose interest in migration and concentrate on analysing natural growth (i.e. changes in birth and death rates). This migration balance reveals nothing about the size, the direction, or the backgrounds of the individual migration flows. The migration balance in the Netherlands since World War II (1945-1984) is a fine example of such an oversight. The very low migration balance of 370,000 people conceals a total emigration of 2,360,000 and a total immigration of 2,730,000. Figures from other European countries show similar orders of magnitude between net migration, immigration, and emigration.

Another method involves family reconstitution, which has become quite popular in the past few decades and can easily lead to a gross underestimation of migration. This technique groups all persons from a community – often a small village – into families on the basis of the registration of marriages. The analysis concentrates on complete families, that is to say the most stable and sedentary ones. Both the emigrants (whose destination are unknown as a rule) and the immigrants (whose backgrounds tend to be relatively unknown as well) are excluded for practical reasons. This once promising method thus leads to serious distortions. Moreover, it is often combined with a predilection for calculations reflecting the net migration. The separate immigration and emigration flows (and consequently the migrants as well) remain concealed. In several cases, both approaches have therefore reinforced the myth of an immobile Ancien Regime.[109]

The dismal circumstances regarding the role of immigration in historical studies on the Netherlands differ little from the situation in other Western European countries. Virtually everywhere, general histories tend to overlook migration nearly as much as accounts of demographic, social, and economic history. Migration history may thrive, but only within its own sphere.

Shifting the focus to Belgium, we see only a brief enumeration of migrations in general historical works. Ostensibly, hardly anybody seems to have left or entered this country after the nineteenth century. Only very recently has a different impression emerged from general overviews, such as the volumes edited by Anne Morelli and Els Deslé.[110]

The example of Roubaix is illustrative for France. At the beginning of the Third Republic the majority of the city's population consisted of Belgians. Nevertheless, J. Toulemonde does not mention them once in his typically thick French monograph about the growth of this city.[111] The French historian Gérard

---

109. A full elaboration of the net migration approach and family reconstitution method appears in Wrigley and Schofield, *Population History of England*. For a critical reappraisal see Houston, *Population History of Britain*, pp. 25, 58, 63-64; and Oeppen, "Back Projection".

110. Morelli, *Histoire des étrangers*; Deslé et al., *Denken over migranten*; and Caestecker *Ongewenste gasten*.

111. Noiriel, *Creuset français*, p. 19. For an interesting recent contribution on the Belgian migration

Noiriel (who provided us with this example) reflected extensively on the negligence of his French colleagues with respect to the history of immigration in their own country in his path-breaking work *Le creuset français* – a more than incidental reference to the American melting pot.[112] The term "negligence" is especially appropriate with respect to the recent past. Since 1935 the population growth of France has been entirely due to immigration, and the percentage of people born abroad even higher than the corresponding rate in the United States, the immigration country par excellence.

Somewhat unexpectedly, Noiriel places most of the blame on the world famous school of the *Annales* (especially on its foremost representative Fernand Braudel) for this state of affairs.[113] In a chapter with the rhetorical title "Questions to Fernand Braudel", Noiriel asks himself why so few pages from his last great work *L'identité de la France* (1986) are devoted to immigration. Only 35 address the subject out of a total of almost 1,000, and even these pages are filled with mere anecdotes. Noiriel primarily attributes this shortcoming to the inability of Braudel and his followers to analyse the post-revolutionary period. He also notes the impossibility of integrating the political history in Braudel's holistic approach. Instead, Braudel reveals a predilection for the *longue durée*, borrowed from *le temps long* of Vidal de la Blache, the founding father of geography. The population's regional and national ties – formulated by the French word *enracinement*, which means "being rooted in" – to the soil reflect this tradition. Regional developments are therefore addressed in detail in the long run.[114] This strategy easily leads to mechanistic approaches in which man and his geographic origin cease to be relevant. Noiriel overstretches the interesting quality of his argument by attacking Braudel too severely, at the same time forgetting that France – as we already indicated – did not experience much immigration or emigration compared to other countries from the late sixteenth and early seventeenth to the mid-nineteenth centuries. Braudel is very much aware of both this situation and the fact that a great deal of internal migration took place in France during the same period.[115] Thus, the demographic peculiarities of France may be an additional cause for the country's inattention to international migration before 1850. Compounded by the consequences of the family reconstitution method, which arises from the *Annales* school, the

to the North of France see Strikwerda, "France and the Belgian Immigration".

112. Noiriel, *Creuset français*, pp. 15ff.

113. *Ibid.*, pp. 50-67.

114. On this subject see also the interesting remarks by Burke ("French Historians and their Cultural Identities", pp. 159-160), who shows that many Annales historians (such as Febvre, Roupnel, Agulhon, and Croix) were downright patriotic and expressed a strong sense of identification with the *pays* which they originated from and which they chose as the subject of their doctoral thesis.

115. Braudel, *Identité de la France*, Vols. I, pp. 136-140, and II, pp. 185-200; see also footnote 97.

circumstances may adequately explain the failure of many French historians to integrate immigration in their work.

On the other hand, the few historians who study migration sometimes reach bizarre conclusions. Poitrineau, who wrote meritorious studies on the migration from the Massif Central to Spain (especially that which occurred during the eighteenth century),[116] believes there is an essential difference between the entrepreneurial mentality of "his" typically French migrants and the present day "good-for-nothings" from North Africa who pose a threat to French cities.[117]

Poitrineau's work is not the only example of the inclination of historians to contrast the supposedly negative characteristics of present-day immigrants with the qualities of their counterparts from the past. The English historian William Cunningham, who wrote an extensive monograph around 1900 on the history of immigration in Great Britain,[118] manifests a similar tendency. His entire book serves to prove a single thesis, namely that the activity and success of the British isles was made possible by a constant stream of immigrants. Cunningham's epilogue, however, indicates one exception: he is unable to identify any positive contributions on the part of the Jewish immigrants from Eastern Europe, the most speechmaking immigrants of his time.

The ubiquitous nature of this phenomenon[119] calls for a general explanation that transcends the failure of individual historians and schools. As Noiriel has shown, the problem is rooted in the genesis of history as an academic discipline in the nineteenth century. Almost all historians have always regarded the national state as their point of departure. In this perspective it is understandable that migration has been treated primarily as a sign of crisis or weakness.

4. Conclusion

This critical reappraisal of largely historical migration and settlement studies leads to the conclusion that notwithstanding inevitable specialization, a more fundamental accumulation of knowledge requires a comprehensive concept of migration, as offered at the end of the second section. Without arguing that all migrations are equal or identical, an awareness of similarities between the various types of movements is more useful in the final analysis. A general definition of

116. Poitrineau, *Remues d'hommes*.
117. Cf. Poitrineau's participation in the "Conseil scientifique" (founded in 1989) of the extreme-right French Front National (see: "Le conseil scientifique au 1er janvier 1990" in a leaflet of the Front National issued in 1990). We thank Nancy Green who brought this detail to our attention.
118. Cunningham, *Alien Immigrants to England*.
119. For Germany see the pioneering works of Dohse, Hoerder, Bade, Herbert, and Elsner.

migration is necessary to accomplish the integration of migration studies into mainstream social, economic, political, and cultural histories.

The first paragraph of this introduction asserted that the essays in this book collectively represent a pioneering effort in migration history, especially with respect to the two problems concerning the massive fragmentation into sub-specialties and the difficulty of integrating migration history into general history. We trust that the foregoing introduction has shown both the monumental task that awaits and the achievements in this book.

First, the conceptual gulf between free and unfree migrations has been narrowed and at the same time specified. Second, the same effect has been achieved regarding the antitheses between labour migrants and refugees and between the "good" and the "bad" migrants, which has resulted in a reha-bilitation of travelling groups. Third, new venues are available for reintegrating ethnic and migration studies, especially by focusing on long term developments. Fourth, the history of migration and settlement extends beyond modern periods and modern states in a small part of the world. Well-structured comparisons across time and space bring about fascinating insights and theoretical progress.

Finally, it may have become clear that the results have to be integrated in local, regional, and national histories. Historians as well as social scientists have to take an active stand, both to promote new insights in a wider circle and to prevent the specialization from turning into an end in itself. We therefore fully endorse and recommend the point of departure in Moch's *Moving Europeans*:

> "By writing this history of migration, I hope to bring the patterns of mobility into our thinking about preindustrial life, rural industry, the industrial revolution, and urbanization. Migration is present in every level of historical study. It should enliven the historical study of the family, the most intimate of social groups. On the village and regional levels, migration constitutes a part of the 'social glue' of subcultures and responds to economic and social change. State politics themselves both inspired and inhibited migration. Finally, European mobility responds not only to familial and local demands but also to those of the world economy."[120]

5. Acknowledgements

This book is the result of the conference "Migration and Settlement in a Historical Perspective: Old Answers and New Perspectives", held at the Netherlands Institute for Advanced Study (NIAS) on 23 and 24 September 1993. The workshop "The Importance of the Migration Factor in History Teaching at Secondary Schools in Europe", which took place at the International Institute

---

120. Moch, *Moving Europeans*, p. 21.

of Social History (IISH) in Amsterdam on 25 September 1993, was closely linked to the conference.

We wish to thank everyone who helped to make this project possible. First of all, Peter Klein (History Department of Leiden University) and Eric Fischer (IISH) who formed a joint organizing committee in which we cooperated with Piet Emmer, Herman Obdeijn, and Wim Willems of Leiden University and Marcel van der Linden and our indispensable secretary Annemarie Woudstra of the IISH.

We received financial support for the conference at NIAS from the Dutch Ministry of Education and Culture, the Humanities Faculty of Leiden University, the Royal Dutch Academy of Arts and Sciences, the Leids Universiteits Fonds, the Centre for Asian Studies Amsterdam (CASA) and the IISH. Euridice (European Commission, Brussels), an organization involved in the introduction of intercultural elements in national curricula, funded/contributed funds for the workshop at the IISH.

In addition to the authors in this volume, the scholars who presented papers at the conference included Jan Breman, Gérard Noiriel, and Herman Obdeijn. Marcel van der Linden and Peter Klein actively took part in the conference as chairpersons. At the workshop in Amsterdam the following persons delivered introductions and comments: Jan van Belle (Ghent), Colin Holmes (Sheffield), Gérard Noiriel (Paris), Diethelm Knauf (Bremen), Herman Obdeijn (Leiden), Marie Poinsot (Paris/New York), and Fritz Wittek (Euridice, Brussels).

Finally, we thank Lee Mitzman for the careful corrections to the texts by authors without a native command of English, Alice Mul for the desk-editing and the compilation of the collective bibliography, Mona Hilfman for the meticulous corrections in the final phase, and Aad Blok (Publications department IISH) for his coordinating role in preparing and producing this publication.

Amsterdam (IISH)/Leiden (Leiden University, Department of History), November 1996
Jan Lucassen/Leo Lucassen

PART I

THEORY AND METHODOLOGY

Dividing Time:
An Analytical Framework
for Migration History Periodization[*]

Leslie Page Moch

Historians of migration, contemporary social observers, and historians with more general interests seize upon the importance of the industrial revolution to human mobility. Indeed, the innovation of factory industry signaled a great age of migration to the city – and much of it to the new, brick factory cities that mushroomed during the nineteenth century where only villages or small trading towns had been before.[1] The visibility of factory towns such as Roubaix or Duisburg lay not only in their newness and enormous growth, but also in the problems of their newly-arrived workers. The deplorably unsanitary living conditions, crowded housing, alcoholism, and in some regions the high incidence of out-of-wedlock births served to rivet attention upon the migrants, caricatured by contemporaries like Emile Vandervelde, who in 1903 described urban migrants as "uprooted from the earth [...] conscripted by the barracks, store and factory, hypnotized by the city lights like the sea birds who, after sunset, fly bewildered under the beam of the lighthouse."[2] The factory and mining labor force of the late nineteenth century was all the more linked to migration because it was a multinational one: Dutch and Poles worked in the Ruhr valley; Belgians manned the looms in Roubaix; Italians stood at the embroidery machines in Switzerland; and Irish labored in the mills of Lancashire.[3] Finally, migration for the industrial age is more surely documented than for earlier periods with the advent of regular census returns, migration statistics for Prussian cities, and the widespread innovation of population registers.[4]

---

[*]   The author would like to thank Jan Lucassen and Leo Lucassen for their helpful comments on the earlier version of this essay.
1.   Vries, *European Urbanization*.
2.   Vandervelde, *Exode rural*, pp. 18-19. Engels's thoroughgoing description of Manchester set the tone for many others; Engels, *Condition of the Working Class*.
3.   Franchomme, "Évolution démographique"; Holmes, *Forgotten Migrants*, p. 93; Lowe, *Irish in Mid-Victorian Lancashire*; J. Lucassen, *Migrant Labour in Europe*, pp. 188-190.
4.   An entree for these sources includes Hochstadt and Jackson, "'New' Sources for the Study of Migration"; Gutmann and Van de Walle, "New Sources for Social and Demographic History"; Kälvemark, "Country That Kept Track". For the census, see Pinchemel, *Structures sociales et dépopulation rurale*, p. 21.

Yet migration has a long history apart from the industrial revolution; human movement was essential to the settlement of early medieval Europe and an integral part of early modern life in Western Europe. In the countrysides, regional migration routines were part of the agricultural cycle, family formation, and the supply of the rural labor force.[5] Harvest work took thousands of men out of their own regions and in many cases across national borders.[6] Migration to large and small cities provided an alternative to village life for young people and added newcomers to urban demographic systems which were chronically in deficit.[7] Migration from Europe was part of state mercantile and imperial agendas.[8]

Nonetheless, some scholars have maintained that a "sedentary model" characterizes early modern life. The French emphasize peasant attachment to the soil, arguing for an essentially sedentary society. At the same time, scholars of French migration recognize the "micromobility" associated with marriage, rural service, and sharecropping; they are experts in the importance of seasonal and temporary migration; and they have elucidated in great detail the migrations to – and through – early modern cities.[9] It is sensible to conclude that there was enough mobility in France so that a sedentary model may impede an understanding of its early modern migration patterns. Indeed, a sedentary model may be particularly inappropriate to France. In the north, its people were animated by the activities and attraction of Paris (the largest city on the continent north of Italy), which more than doubled in size in the seventeenth century; in the south, men moved to the rhythms of seasonal and temporary migration.[10] The virtue of the French model is that a fundamental shift in migration patterns is seen as dating from about 1750, rather than from the industrial revolution. Nonetheless, like a focus on the industrial era, this perspective enforces a dichotomous historical model of migration.

The fact that migration was embedded in rural life, family patterns, and agricultural routines long before the age of factory industry points to the inadequacy of a two-stage view of migration centering around the industrial revolution, or any other single historical period. Rather than jerry-build a dichotomous history, we are better served by an analytical framework with which to diagnose fluctuating migration itineraries. In this essay, I will sketch the elements of a framework for Western European historical migrations since 1650.

---

5. For a summary, see Moch, *Moving Europeans*, ch. 2.
6. J. Lucassen, *Migrant Labour in Europe*, ch. 6.
7. Vries, *European Urbanization*, pp. 175-214; Hohenberg and Lees, *Making of Urban Europe*, pp. 85-98.
8. Hoerder, "Migration in the Atlantic Economies"; Zolberg, "International Migration Policies".
9. For a summary of this argument, see Poussou, "Mobilité et migrations".
10. For the growth of Paris, see Vries, *European Urbanization*, Appendix I, pp. 269-278. For temporary migration in the south, see Poitrineau, *Remues d'hommes*.

This analysis of human mobility defines migration as a change in residence beyond a communal boundary, be it a village or town. Geographically, then, migration includes moves from one village to another as well as those across national borders and oceans. Temporally, migrations may be short-term or permanent; seasonal harvest movements and permanent departures from home are both migrations. The spatial and temporal breadth of this definition is designed to capture the full range of historical change. Perhaps more important, such an inclusive view of geographical mobility recognizes the interconnections among regional, national, international, and transoceanic migrations and the necessity of considering them as a whole in order to understand human mobility. If we consider international migration, ignoring the regional and national moves created by the same economic and social situation, for example, our understanding of migration will be impoverished.

An analytical framework for changing migration itineraries

I argue that the primary determinants of migration patterns consist of the fundamental structural elements of economic life: labor force demands in countryside and city, deployment of capital, population patterns (rates of birth, death, marriage), and landholding regimes. Shifts in these elements underlie changing migration itineraries. Incontestably, other forces shape migration patterns as well; among these is the political economy which, for example, gave such a different configuration to rural England (where enclosure and proletarianization released people from the land early on) than to France (where the peasantry survived into the twentieth century).[11]

A focus on the politics of migration reveal dramatic alterations in state policies that do not follow the rhythms of economic change. State politics and policies provided forceful incentives for migration under mercantilist regimes for such groups as Iberian Jews and French Huguenots in early modern Europe. European states generally adopted laissez-faire policies in the nineteenth century.[12] In the twentieth century, however, more proactive policy patterns have emerged with the aggressive policing of wartime labor, refugees, and foreign workers.[13] The states of Western Europe currently demonstrate great concern with migrants, especially those from outside European Union nations.

---

11. See, for example, Lis and Soly, *Poverty and Capitalism*, pp. 97-104.
12. The exception to general laissez-faire migration policies is Germany; see Herbert, *History of Foreign Labor in Germany*.
13. Herbert, *History of Foreign Labor in Germany*; Noiriel, *Creuset français*; Zolberg et al., *Escape from Violence*.

As compelling as it is to focus on the state and politics, such a perspective is not entirely useful for long-term historical periodization. State migration policies concern groups from beyond the borders of the national state, and particularly the issues of exclusion, expulsion, and citizenship.[14] These questions were not nearly so salient in the eighteenth and nineteenth centuries as they are today. More important for this essay, a focus on the state blinds us to the more mundane and numerous migrations internal to the national state and fails to explain trends in human mobility. This is partly a function of European history, where there were few large-scale state coerced migrations in the two centuries between those of the Huguenot refugees from the France of Louis XIV and the Jewish refugees from the Russian pogroms of Alexander III. Consequently, as important as the state – or at least attempted state control of international migration – has been to migration in this century, it is not the focus of an historical analysis over the long term.

On a more intimate level, European family systems played a direct role in migration, encouraging mobility precisely because the incest taboo forced many to travel at least to the next parish for a mate. Additionally, inheritance systems – both partible and impartible – encouraged the departure of some siblings.[15] Which family member left home and for what kind of work depended on individual demographic traits: gender, marital status, birth order, and age. Of these, gender is particularly important; it produced, for example, an aspect of what Pier Paolo Viazzo calls "the Alpine paradox," an apparently closed, endogamous society in which men and women formed two "sharply distinct sub-populations" – one conspicuously immobile, the other annually on the move to the lowlands. The women, reported one elderly villager to Viazzo, "would stay at home 'like moles'" while their husbands and brothers traveled widely.[16]

In addition social systems, operating at what Dirk Hoerder calls the "meso level" in this volume, mediated these familial and demographic distinctions; people traveled with kin or compatriots when possible, heading toward a destination where they knew someone who would help them. Most migrants were neither rootless nor friendless. Finally, local traditions that bred positive or negative ideology about departure distinguished one village from another.[17] Thus although macroeconomic structures molded migration in a general way, specific migration systems operated within meso-level social networks and local ideologies.

14. See, for example, Brubaker, *Citizenship and Nationhood in France and Germany*.
15. See, for example, Berkner and Mendels, "Inheritance Systems"; Viazzo, *Upland Communities*, pp. 258-261.
16. Viazzo, *Upland Communities*, p. 136.
17. Laurence Fontaine describes the peddling tradition that animated entire villages in "Solidarités familiales et logiques migratoires"; Abel Poitrineau indicates the proximity of Auvergnat villages that sent migrants to the lowlands to those who did not in "Aspects de l'émigration temporaire".

Here I will focus on the macroeconomic structures that shape general migration patterns: labor force demands, population growth rates, landholding regimes, and capital deployment. Changes in rural labor force demands have transformed the Western European countryside since the seventeenth century, first calling for an army of manufacturing labor in the eighteenth century, then for more specialized – and fewer – agricultural workers in the nineteenth and twentieth. Likewise, urban labor force demands have evolved from the need for a skilled artisanal force to the expanded demand for less skilled factory workers and increased numbers of tertiary sector employees and, in this century, a highly skilled white-collar labor force. With these transformations have come the shift from a low-growth population with high death and birth rates, to a fast-growing population with high birthrates and low death rates, to the present-day configuration of low population growth and low rates of fertility and mortality. Over the same period, peasant land ownership patterns have given way to a mass proletariat. Finally, the wealth of seventeenth-century western Europe lay primarily in the land, but since that time capital has come to be concentrated in urban production and trade.

Each of these shifts has worked to transform Western European life in ways, and at times, that have varied by region. The contingent and particularistic nature of history dictates that large-scale economic change has been uneven and varied. Nonetheless, patterns of migration have been affected in similar ways by macroeconomic change. Consequently, a periodization of European migration will not follow specific dates, as does a periodization of political history; rather it will divide on the most important shifts in economic and social life. I argue that migration followed a pattern in the preindustrial era (to ca. 1750 in many regions), altered by the proliferation of early industry into the countryside (beginning in the eighteenth century on the western edge of the continent). In the nineteenth century, the patterns of migration that supported early industry shifted with its collapse and expansion of factory production. The urbanizing, industrial Western Europe – its economy strong but its reproductive patterns weak by the mid-twentieth century – generated immigration from the outside, producing today's patterns of international migration.

The age of early industry (ca. 1750-1850)

The most significant development of labor demand in the age of early industry was the unprecedented development of rural industry – the manufacture of goods in village settings for distant markets.[18] Although rural production was

18. For the vast and fascinating literature on protoindustry, rural industry, and early industry,

hardly new, it employed greater numbers of villagers than ever before, and where manufacturing was intense, it employed a significant proportion of the population. Although no survey gathers the data on all rural production, it was particularly dense on the littoral of Northwestern Europe. A quarter of the population of county Ulster in Ireland (about 200,000 in 1800) produced linen. Westphalian villages produced linen, and in Minden-Ravensberg, 70 percent of the population worked in linen by 1800. On the Flemish plain, production tripled from 1746 to 1788, employing three out of four villagers. Just to the south, the number of workers producing a cotton-linen blend (*siamoise*) expanded from 57,000 to 188,000 in the middle years of the eighteenth century so that one-third of the population in upper Normandy worked in textiles by 1782. The greatest proportion of rural workers in any nation overall was found in Switzerland because mountain production was common; for example, 48.8 percent of the people in the Zurich highlands spun cotton for a living in 1878.[19]

Cities and the urban labor force played a particular role in the early industrial economy. In the previous century, large capital cities and ports had expanded; after 1700, small cities prospered and centers for rural manufacturing grew. Towns of 5,000 to 10,000 were the most likely to expand. These were the centers of administration, markets, and production that coordinated commercial information, decision making, and exchange. Towns and cities garnered the massive capital required for large-scale trade, and well as the petty amounts of capital doled out, penny by penny, to rural workers.[20] Around cities grew "para-urban agglomerations" that gathered artisans from the countryside.[21]

This period marks a watershed in the population history of Europe. After the crises of the 1690-1730 period, the population expanded quickly, from 81 million in 1700 to 123 million in 1800. Population growth was especially rapid between 1750 and 1800, when the French population expanded by 18 percent, the German by 33 percent, and the English by 50 percent.[22] Almost forty years of scholarly evidence attests to the fact that the most intense population increases of the period occurred where rural industry was most dense.[23] Intimate links bound rural economic and natural increase; expanded village manufacturing enabled rural people to marry and to provide employment for their children.

see Clarkson, *Proto-Industrialization*; Gutmann, *Toward the Modern Economy*; Kriedte et al., *Industrialization before Industrialization*.

19. Pfister, "Proto-industrialization and Demographic Change", p. 636; for a survey of rural industry, see Lis and Soly, *Poverty and Capitalism*; Gullickson, *Spinners and Weavers*, p. 69; Gutmann, *Toward the Modern Economy*, chs 5, 6, and 7.

20. Vries, *European Urbanization*, pp. 68-69; Gullickson, *Spinners and Weavers*, pp. 45-46, 65-67; Hohenberg and Lees, *Making of Urban Europe*, p. 130.

21. Deyon, "Fécondité et limites", pp. 870-871.

22. Anderson, *Population Change in North-Western Europe*, p. 23.

23. Chambers, "Vale of Trent", p. 20; Mendels, "Industrialization and Population Pressure".

In some areas, a greater proportion of women married, and married earlier, supported by the wages of cottage industry.[24]

Both in regions with intense rural industry and those without, a trend to proletarianization accompanied population increase. An expansion in the proportion of proletarians at the expense of the peasantry between 1650 and 1800 signaled a major change in the populations of western Europe. A marked decline from the high-water mark of the peasantry occurred from England east to Saxony and from Scandinavia to southern France. The eighteenth century saw an increase in peasants whose landholdings were too marginal to support families without supplemental wage work and an increase in *de facto* proletarians, cotters, and renters who did not own any land to speak of.[25] By the 1830s, the peasant economy had totally disappeared from England. In France, where peasant ownership was much stronger, Albert Soboul estimated that 40 percent of the rural population was semi-proletarian or proletarian by 1790. There was a visible minority of proletarians even in peasant strongholds like rural Brittany (20-25%) and the mountain parishes of the Pyrenees (30-40%).[26]

Changing migration patterns in the early industrial era

This period presents a conundrum to students of migration because changing rural conditions both contained and inflated migration. On one hand, rural industry enabled a great proportion of villagers in manufacturing areas to earn a living at home. Industrial villages and small towns were able to absorb much of the growing population of eighteenth-century Europe. In focussing on the mechanics of population increase via increased fertility, earlier marriage, and drops in mortality, the role of migration in rural manufacturing populations has been overlooked. Admittedly, this is in part because neither eighteenth-century population data nor family reconstitution techniques make it easy for researchers to appreciate rural migration. Yet mobility in the countryside was crucial to the growth of manufacturing villages and this is borne out by inspection of settlement laws. Cottage production was most successful where free settlement obtained, such as the English freeholding settlements where manors did not restrict settlement. Within the canton of Zurich, rural industry thrived most where a minimal *Einzugsgeld* fee was charged to newcomers and communal

24. Braun, "Early Industrialization and Demographic Change"; Vries, *European Urbanization*, p. 238; Levine, *Family Formation*, ch. 5; Medick, "Proto-Industrial Family Economy"; Wrigley, "Growth of Population in Eighteenth-Century England".

25. For example, see Kisch, *From Domestic Manufacture*, pp. 95-153, 221; Lis and Soly, *Poverty and Capitalism*; C. Tilly, "Demographic Origins of the European Proletariat"; Poussou, *Bordeaux et le sud-ouest*, pp. 292-301.

26. Soboul, *Civilisation et la révolution*, Vol. 1, pp. 125-126.

charters did little to block new settlement.[27] Comparisons between rural production in Silesia and the Rhineland, between the Austrian Waldviertel and the French pays de Caux, demonstrate that rural manufacturing grew most vigorously where legal space existed for a full-time cottager class originating with landless folk and poor cottagers. In the Caux, for example, the village of Auffay increased from 164 to 270 households in the boom weaving period of 1750-1789 – a 65 percent increase fueled not only by native-born villagers, but also by men and women from the region.[28] Additionally, manufacturing villages attracted and retained people more than other kinds of settlements. In comparing mobility among 16 English villages, David Souden found that industrial villages had relatively high levels of inward movement.[29]

Established rural manufacturing villages also retarded emigration, because more men and women were able to stay in their home arena to earn a living.[30] This is especially apparent in mountain villages from which emigration was necessary for many young people before rural industry expanded local employment, such as those in the Zurich highlands and the Swiss Canton of Glarus, where emigration dropped by half with rural manufacturing. In less mountainous England, the industrial villages studied by David Souden retained their populations better than pastoral and farming communities. Generally speaking, there was a smaller rate of emigration from villages of the industrial northwest than from those of the agricultural south (and by the 1780s, there was net immigration to the northwest). Peter Clark offers the general observation that growing industrial employment in villages helped to slow subsistence migration in the eighteenth century.[31] As Christiaan Vandenbroeke wrote of Flanders, "one should search for the underlying causes of demographic change above all in migration, or to be more precise, in the absence of cityward migration."[32] Vandenbroeke shows that the villages of the Flemish littoral lost population to the manufacturing villages of the interior in the eighteenth century.[33] Evidence from the early nineteenth century shows that the industrial villages of the Düsseldorf district of Prussia had lower migration rates than agricultural villages in the 1820s.[34]

By contrast, the migration scenario was quite different that emerged in regions where rural industry was less vigorous. For villages engaged in seasonal migra-

27. Pfister, "Proto-industrialization and Demographic Change", pp. 653-655.
28. Gullickson, *Spinners and Weavers*, pp. 16, 134, 136.
29. Clark, "Migration in England", pp. 81-83; Souden, "Movers and Stayers", pp. 20-21, 24.
30. See, for example, Vardi, *Land and the Loom*.
31. Clark, "Migration in England", pp. 81-83; Deane and Cole, *British Economic Growth*, pp. 118-127; Head, "Quelques remarques sur l'émigration"; Souden, "Movers and Stayers", pp. 20-21, 24; Viazzo, *Upland Communities*, p. 154.
32. Vandenbroeke, "Formes protoindustrielles", p. 934.
33. *Ibid.*, p. 918.
34. Hochstadt, "Migration and Industrialization in Germany", pp. 448-449.

tion, the growing population, combined with proletarianization, expanded established migration systems. More people joined the seasonal and temporary migration repertoires in place; for example, increasing numbers of men left the villages of the central French highlands to labor in the expanding cities of the plains and more men departed the villages of northwestern Germany for haying and digging peat in the Netherlands.[35] Impoverished country people stretched longstanding migration systems to the limit as they left home without the skills or itinerary of experienced migrants.

However, there was not enough work for the generations facing the crises of the 1780s, so that, increasingly, men – and women as well – sought work where ever they could find it. By 1790, economic and demographic factors produced a crisis that forced people onto the roads from industrial, agricultural and pastoral regions. Neither manufacturing villages, nor growing industrial *bourgs*, or even the busy outskirts of industrial cities could contain the growing population. Many migrants were what Peter Clark and Paul Slack call "subsistence migrants," but what the police called vagrants, whom they would confuse with the considerable numbers seasonal workers and with of men and women in travelling trades such as peddling and chimney sweeping.[36] The response to this subsistence migration was a fearful and punitive one that incarcerated growing numbers of underemployed men and women.[37] The increase in migrants and the focus on them at the close of the eighteenth century foreshadowed the urban industrial period to come.

Migration in the Age of urbanization and industrialization (ca. 1800-1970)

Although the booming factory town described at the opening of this essay provides an enduring symbol of the industrial age, one of its primary hallmarks is to be found in the countryside. Declines occurred in rural economies, as work in rural manufacturing, agriculture, or the combination of the two was endangered. Rural manufacturing waned as pay rates were reduced in region after region for village spinning, then weaving, as well as knitting and nailmaking.[38] The increase in commercial farming of potatoes, grains, and sugarbeets undermined existent patterns of farm labor like service in husbandry, producing intense short-lived work periods that demanded many seasonal workers, but less year-round labor. By the mid-nineteenth century, farm servants had virtually

---

35. J. Lucassen, *Migrant Labour in Europe*; Poitrineau, *Remues d'hommes*.
36. Clark and Slack, *English Towns in Transition*, pp. 92-93; Fontaine, "Solidarités familiales"; L. Lucassen, "Blind Spot".
37. See Lis and Soly, *Poverty and Capitalism*; Schwartz, *Policing the Poor*.
38. An exemplary description of this process is in Gullickson, *Spinners and Weavers*.

disappeared from southeastern England, where large farms and enclosures were most common.[39] At the core of these changes lay the demise of old agricultural and manufacturing systems, with their concomitant social supports and migration routines.

Ironically, populations grew as never before as rural earnings became less secure, fueled by improvements in the distribution and production of food (especially the potato) and the decline in demographic crises. The European population of 187 million in 1800 grew to 266 million in 1850, then to 468 million by 1913, an increase of 42 percent in the first half of the century and another 76 percent before World War I.[40] The increased population shared finite land resources, and as a consequence, the proportion of rural proletarians rose during the century. The landless were most willing to move. The magnitude of population growth and proletarianization varied; nonetheless, with or without economic crises, rural areas could not support the tripled population of Denmark, Britain, or Finland; the doubled populations of Belgium, Italy, the Netherlands, Austria-Hungary, or Germany; or even the 50 percent increase in France.

In the long run, the economic and demographic changes in rural Europe created a larger, relatively stable, urbanized labor force by about 1970.[41] But before this would be effected, changes in rural and urban economies produced unprecedented volumes of migration – climaxing in the opening years of the twentieth century.

First, cities themselves engendered seasonal migration for construction work. The great booms in city-building that provided housing, commercial spaces, public facilities, and urban infrastructures such as sewer systems were based on the summer work of men in the construction trades. Like the "swallows" from Spanish Galicia and northern Portugal who built Madrid, and construction workers from Poland and Italy who labored in the Rhine-Ruhr zone, masons from the Limousin built Paris and Lyon. The *département* of the Creuse in the central highlands of France alone exported over 10,000 masons annually in 1810; their numbers had increased to 30,000 by 1848. By 1907, over 30,000 Italians were at work in excavation and masonry in Germany, and over 57,000 in construction.[42]

Second, the labor for infrastructure work beyond the city – the construction of roads, railroad systems, and tunnels – was seasonal. Generally, teams of migrant workers built the railroads; only they were willing to live in makeshift barracks, located in rural areas that could be hostile and remote. Foreign labor

39. Kussmaul, *Servants in Husbandry*, pp. 121, 127, 131.
40. Armengaud, "Population in Europe", pp. 28-30.
41. Hochstadt, "Migration and Industrialization in Germany."
42. Brettell, *Men Who Migrate*, ch. 2; Chatelain, *Migrants temporaires en France*, Vol. 2, pp. 820-821; Rosoli, "Italian Migration", p. 109.

took much of the work: Irish in England, Belgians in Northern France, Poles in Germany, and Italians in Germany, Switzerland, and France.[43]

Urbanization and net city growth built on voluminous movement to and from urban areas. Research from Prussian records, for example, shows that as the city of Duisburg gained 97,836 residents in the 1848-1904 period, 719,903 men and women registered their arrivals to and departures from the city.[44] City growth and urbanization occurred in the context of a relatively high volume of human movement.[45] Of course, how much urban growth depended upon migrants varied by demographic regime. In England, where urban death rates were relatively low, migrants engendered only 16 percent of London's growth between 1852 and 1891. Where mortality remained very high, as in Italy, migration was more crucial to city growth, accounting for 80 to 89 percent of the growth of Rome, Turin, and Milan. French cities relied on immigration for urban growth because their birthrates were exceptionally low; migrants accounted for 64 percent of the increase in Paris.[46]

The combination of demand for labor and abundant supply of needy workers pushed international migration, that most visible kind of mobility, to new levels after the turn of the twentieth century. Foreign workers joined the agrarian, industrial, and commercial labor forces, recruited especially to the most successful regions. These included, first and foremost, the Ruhr Valley area, but also the commercial farming areas of Eastern Germany, Northern France, and South-western France, the industrial belt of Northern France, and Switzerland. By 1910, of the over one million foreign workers in Germany, 580,000 were Poles and 150,000 were Italians; foreigners were about 1.7 percent of the total population of the country. France, too, included over a million foreigners, of whom Italians numbered 419,000 and Belgians 287,000 in 1911, when foreigners were 2.9 percent of the population. Foreign populations played a much more important role in Switzerland, where there were over 552,000 foreign-born, including 219,000 Germans and 203,000 Italians; indeed, in 1910, 14.7 percent of the Swiss population was foreign and 16.7 percent of its labor force were foreigners. By contrast, England required little foreign labor by 1900.[47]

High volumes of transoceanic migrations coincided with intense movement on the continent. An estimated 52 million Europeans departed in the 1860-1914 period, of whom about 72 percent traveled to North America and 21 percent to Latin America. Mass migrations began in the 1840s, when the demand for

43. Chatelain, *Migrants temporaires en France*, Vol. 2, pp. 813-819; Rosoli, "Italian Migration", pp. 95-116.
44. Jackson, "Migration and Urbanization in the Ruhr Valley", pp. 247-279.
45. Hochstadt, "Migration and Industrialization in Germany"; Kertzer and Hogan, "On the Move".
46. Weber, *Growth of Cities*, pp. 233-241.
47. Cross, *Immigrant Workers in Industrial France*; Holmes, *Forgotten Migrants*, p. 14; J. Lucassen, *Migrant Labour in Europe*, pp. 189, 199-200.

labor increased in the farmlands and cities in North America and the sugar and coffee plantations of Latin America. They escalated as 13 million migrants departed between 1840 and 1880 and another 13 million in the last twenty years of the century.[48]

The prosperous regions of the global economy seemed insatiable in their need for labor in the thirty years before World War I, despite periodic downturns. Italians, for example, worked in their own growing cities, such as Turin, and were recruited to agricultural work, construction and textiles in France, Switzerland, Germany – and throughout the globe, as Donna Gabaccia's essay in this volume shows.

Transoceanic migrations were inspired by the same changes in home economies as shorter-distance movements and, like other migrations, they operated through personal networks of contact and labor recruiters. Like migrants within Europe, many of the men and women who went to the Americas did not stay at their destination, but returned home. After 1860, the reduced fares and travel time of the steamship made return more possible; while an estimated 25 percent of migrants to the U.S. returned to Europe in the 1870s, an estimated 45 percent did so in the 1890s.[49]

This pattern of laissez faire migration came to an end with the opening shots of World War I. Most foreign laborers quickly returned home, where armies and the war effort absorbed the young men who otherwise would have been out searching for work. During the war, governments of Western Europe defined, restricted, and used foreign labor; France, for example, required identity cards of foreigners beginning in 1917; both France and Germany imported foreign workers for wartime production.[50] After the war, the Johnson-Reed act imposed severe restrictions on European emigration to the U.S. in 1924. As the Great Depression cast a pall over the world economy, international migration remained muted, reinforced by state restrictions on entries.[51]

The increased regulation of international migration has averted attention away from continuing prewar migration patterns. Although demographic pressure in rural areas was less intense because the drop in birth rates slowed population growth, the shortage of rural resources and upgrading of urban opportunities continued after World War I. Low agricultural prices, mechanization, and a lack

---

48. Armengaud, "Population in Europe", pp. 62, 66-67; Mörner and Sims, *Adventurers and Proletarians*, p. 47.
49. Gould, "European Inter-Continental Emigration", p. 606.
50. Over 300,000 Russian Poles working in Germany when hostilities broke out were not allowed to return home; Herbert, *History of Foreign Labor in Germany*, pp. 87-119; Noiriel, *Creuset français*, pp. 89-90; Stovall, "Color-blind France?".
51. Herbert, *History of Foreign Labor in Germany*, pp. 126-127; Noiriel, *Creuset français*, pp. 24, 156-157; Singer-Kérel "Foreign Workers in France", pp. 287-289.

of jobs decimated rural areas; on the other hand, employment and capital lay in towns and cities.

People continued to move to cities, and to stay for urban work. For example, the industrial city of Turin doubled in size between 1881 and 1939. Maurizio Gribaudi has shown how the clear majority of the migrants to Turin from the Piedmont village of Valdoria (60 percent) remained in Turin, and increasingly traversed blue-collar positions for white-collar work as the generation of the 1870s gave way to the generations of the 1920s and 1930s. If the villagers of Valdoria are typical, they suggest that workers in urban areas experienced social mobility as they became a longstanding part of the urban labor force.[52]

After World War II, rural and agricultural employment declined precipitously as the "rural exodus" and urbanization continued. Between 1950 and 1972, the agricultural labor force in Italy and France decreased by more than half, and that of West Germany and Belgium by two-thirds. At the same time, urbanization was marked in France, West Germany, Sweden, Denmark, Finland, Norway, Ireland, Spain and Italy; it was less important in the United Kingdom and the Netherlands only because these countries were already so urbanized. By 1970, the vast majority of Europeans lived in urban areas: 91 percent of the British, 78 percent of the French, 85 percent of the West Germans, and 69 percent of the Italians.[53]

Despite the visibility of state intervention, migration continued on the same general pattern that had emerged gradually after the Napoleonic wars – a pattern of rural decline and urban expansion. The primary shift in fundamental patterns of European migration came not in 1914, but in the prosperous years after World War II, when the indigenous populations of northwestern Europe – highly educated and slow to reproduce – would be inadequate in numbers to supply labor to their own national economies. Northwestern European nations would recruit workers from southern Europe, as before, but also from the south and east Mediterranean basin and beyond, from as far away as their colonial regimes had stretched.

Migration in post-colonial Europe (from circa 1960 onward)

By the 1960s, migrants within European nations were relatively highly-paid and well-educated. French migrants in the 1980s, for example, were no longer poor montagnards who could not support themselves at home, but rather managers

52. Gribaudi, *Itinéraires ouvriers: Espaces et groupes*, pp. 15-16, 70-75; see also Kertzer and Hogan, "On the Move".
53. Ogden, *Migration and Geographical Change*, pp. 58-59; these figures are based on national definitions of urban areas.

and members of the liberal professions; mobility declined with social class to manual laborers. Property owners, especially farmers and shopkeepers, were the least likely to move. Historically, "internal migration was an activity of the poor," observed geographer Paul White, "today it is becoming more and more an activity of the rich."[54]

The indigenous labor force was not adequate to the demand for workers because population structures had changed. The falling birthrates of the interwar years had reduced the cohort of men and women going to work in the 1950s. In addition, these young men and women stayed in school longer than before, in training for white-collar and skilled jobs. Although rural migrants and women could fill some positions, the old pattern of hiring foreigners was vigorously renewed.

Foreign workers and their families arrived in unprecedented numbers in the 1960s. By the mid-1970s, over 8 million foreign men, women, and children resided in northwestern Europe. One in seven manual laborers in Germany and Britain was an immigrant; one in four industrial workers in France, Switzerland, and Belgium was a foreigner. Migrants came primarily from nine countries in southern Europe and North Africa: Portugal, Spain, Italy, Yugoslavia, Greece, Turkey, Tunisia, Morocco, and Algeria. Their destinations were France, Germany, Switzerland, the Netherlands, Belgium, Luxembourg, and Sweden. In addition, over a million more people from the worldwide British Commonwealth resided in Britain.[55]

In terms of their occupations and home conditions, these foreign laborers resembled historical migrants. Like nineteenth-century immigrants, they worked in agriculture, construction, and mining. The disagreeable and disruptive jobs were theirs. When the city of Geneva tunneled a comprehensive drainage system underneath the city, it hired men from Italy, Spain, and Yugoslavia to do the job. When northern French textile factories needed workers for a third shift, they looked to Algerians to take work that Belgians would not and that women could not legally accept under protective legislation. Since domestic service had become intolerable to the women of northwestern Europe, foreign women became servants.[56] These newcomers also resembled historical migrants because they came from areas of high natural increase, low incomes, and underemployment exacerbated by changes in landholding. This was true of Turks, for example, in whose homeland the population increased by 2.7 percent per year

54. White, "Internal Migration", pp. 25-27.
55. Berger and Mohr, *Seventh Man*, p. 12; Castles *et al.*, *Here for Good*, p. 43; Rogers, "Post-World War II", p. 21.
56. Berger and Mohr, *Seventh Man*, pp. 152-171; Berrier, "French Textile Industry"; Moch and Tilly, "Immigrant Women in the City".

and the annual per capita gross national product was $353, compared with $2,324 for France in the mid-1960s.[57]

These migrants contradicted earlier trends as well, reversing the historical movement of Europeans into Asia, Africa, and the Eastern Mediterranean. They traveled in the context of state regulation and control that had been relatively unusual before the twentieth century. Many arrived as part of bilateral labor agreements between the home and host nations. Others traveled to Europe after protracted and violent struggles of decolonization, in which they had been the political losers, like the 80,000 Algerian Harkis arriving in France after the Algerian struggle for independence.[58]

Postwar migrants were perceived as being more different from indigenous people than those of the previous centuries, because many originated in Muslim countries like Turkey, Algeria, or Pakistan, or were phenotypically distinct. Newcomers did make Europe more culturally heterogeneous in terms of gender relations, religion, reproductive patterns, and education; some faced high levels of hostility and racism. It is easy to conclude that these are new phenomena until one considers the fervent disregard in which, historically, Germans have held Poles, English have held Irish, and the Dutch have held Westphalians.[59]

The migration history of these diverse groups has, generally speaking, followed three stages. Initially, non-colonial groups began as labor migrants recruited to work in specific public works projects or factory jobs; they consisted of single men, for the most part, who were expected to return home. Between 1967 and 1973, the number of foreign workers expanded enormously and family reunification became more important. Wives, children, and other relatives who were not employed (or not reporting employment) expanded and changed the nature of migrant communities. As in the past, word of mouth and personal contacts worked in conjunction with labor recruitment to inflate migration streams. Since the oil crisis, inflation, and recession that began in 1973, hostility to foreigners and efforts to remove them have been endemic to the politics of western European nations. Immigrants have not increased as rapidly as before, yet they have not decreased; they are a permanent component of European society.[60]

Immigration into Europe is not at an end; as newcomers from East Germany and the Soviet bloc flooded into West Germany in the fall of 1989, it became clear that the long-standing migration to the west from central and eastern Europe had been staunched only temporarily by Soviet and cold war policies, and then only for a short period of some 28 years between the building of the

57. Castles and Kosak, *Immigrant Workers and Class Structure*, pp. 27-28.

58. Zolberg *et. al.*, *Escape from Violence*, pp. 227-234.

59. See, for example, Herbert, *History of Foreign Labor in Germany*, pp. 28-30; J. Lucassen, *Migrant Labour in Europe*, pp. 44-47.

60. Castles *et. al.*, *Here for Good*.

Berlin Wall in 1961 and its destruction in 1989. In 1990, an estimated 1.3 million people left the dissolving Soviet bloc.[61] Post-cold war migration patterns, then, resemble those of the post-colonial era. It remains to be seen how, and how well, the press of migrants will be managed by the countries of western Europe and by the collective body of the European Union. History has taught us that pressure from the east will subside only when social and economic conditions improve.

Conclusion

The very long-term view of European migration history shows only a few fundamental shifts in patterns of geographical mobility since the early modern era. Beginning in the eighteenth century, villages and small towns thrived, attracting newcomers and keeping the growing population at home; early industry promoted a more sedentary population. A long trend to urbanization, high migration rates, and rural-urban migration followed as urban economies grew while crises dislocated rural areas after the Napoleonic wars. By the time urbanization had peaked in 1970, the urbanized, educated, and relatively sedentary labor force native to northwestern Europe sought workers beyond its borders, and indeed, beyond the continent.

61. Tagliabue, "Europeans Fleeing West"; the figure of 1.3 million is from the United Nations High Commissioner for Refugees in Bonn.

The Comparative Method and Poststructural Structuralism: New Perspectives for Migration Studies*

Nancy L. Green

"I was constantly referring my new world to the old for comparison, and the old to the new for elucidation. I became a student and philosopher by force of circumstances."[1] Mary Antin, a young Russian Jewish girl who arrived in Boston at the turn of the century and became a successful writer, was acutely conscious of the comparative nature of the migration experience. The immigrant represents the Other in the nation-state, but the new land is the referential Other for the newly-arrived. The migrant embodies an implicit comparison between past and present, between one world and another, between two languages, and two sets of cultural norms. The immigrant's observations fall somewhere between the tourist's hasty generalizations and the social scientist's constructed comparisons.

Yet for migrants and social scientists alike, the comparative nature of observation is more often implicit than explicit. Historians, for example, usually ignore the temporal comparison implicit in most research. What I would like to examine here are the possibilities for explicit comparative research projects and their impact on migration studies.

I will first of all argue for the importance of comparison as a way of going beyond national categories. This necessarily implies a more general level of analysis in interpreting migration patterns. Yet while insisting on the importance of the comparative method, I will also emphasize the ways in which comparisons are constructed. Two examples will be studied. The first involves the use of national comparisons by looking at how French and American historiographies of migration have compared themselves to each other. The second concerns national group comparisons, and the different ways of comparing immigrant groups to each other. These examples illustrate the importance of recognizing the intellectual underpinnings of the "comparative imperative".[2] I then conclude

---

* This contribution was first published, in a slightly longer form, in the *Journal of American Ethnic History* (Summer 1994).
1. Antin, *Promised Land*, p. xxii.
2. I elaborated some of these ideas in an earlier form in two articles that have appeared in French: "L'histoire comparative et le champ des études migratoires", and "L'immigration en France et aux États-Unis".

with some considerations on the usefulness of a "poststructural structuralism". Comparisons can help us understand both the structural constraints and individual cultural choices framing the migration experience.

The Comparative Method

Historians, by our nature or by the nature of our archival research, have been more reticent than other social scientists to move from the particular to the general. The minutiae of archival research, the barriers of geographically (most often nationally) defined fields, and the monograph as principal product are perhaps some of the material causes for this reticence. Yet there have been several specific if sporadic calls to the comparative method in French, English, and American historiography since the turn of the century. These appeals to comparison have argued for its use on several grounds: to make history more of a social science; to rise above nationalism; to seek causes and origins of historical phenomena; and to clarify the specificity or similarity of historical processes.

In 1903, François Simiand issued one of the first calls for a comparative method in order to render the historical method more "scientific". In his desire to combat the orthodox, so-called objectivist historians of the nineteenth century who claimed to reproduce a simple representation of the past, Simiand argued that comparisons allow that classification which is the stuff of which social science is made. As Henri Sée later explained it, more "scientific" methods were necessary to move history from a descriptive practice to an explanatory one. William Sewell continued this line of argument in 1967: "The comparative method is an adaptation of experimental logic to inquiries where a true experiment is impossible."[3]

In addition to rendering the historical profession more "scientific", early calls for comparison stressed the importance of comparison in order to avoid the nationalism inherent in nation-based historical practices. Both World Wars concretely reinforced this line of reasoning. At the first International Historical Conference after World War I, in 1923, Henri Pirenne gave an impassioned plea for a comparative, scientific method in order to rid historians, and hopefully the world system, of the pitfalls of national prejudice inherited from nineteenth-century romanticism. Following World War II, Geoffrey Barraclough issued a similar call for comparison, pleading fervently for a less ethno-centric history in which comparisons, among other methods, would play an important role.

---

3. Simiand, "Méthode historique et science sociale"; Sée, "Remarques sur l'application"; Sewell, "Marc Bloch and the Logic". See also Grew, "The Case for Comparing Histories"; "Editorial", *Comparative Studies in Society and History*, 22 (April 1980), pp. 143-144; and more generally the October 1980, December 1980 and February 1982 issues of the *American Historical Review* and the March-April 1988 issue of the *Annales ESC*.

When the journal *Comparative Studies in Society and History* was founded in 1958, a telling phrase by Lord Acton served as epigraph and justification for the new approach: "The process of Civilisation depends on transcending Nationality."[4]

However, there are two other purposes for comparison, as Marc Bloch argued in his oft-cited article of 1928. Less defensive and more programmatic with regard to the use of comparison, Bloch pointed out that comparisons can help us understand the causes and origins of specific phenomena. And, more importantly for our purpose, he argued that comparisons permit an analysis of that which is specific and that which is general in all phenomena.[5]

This last issue is that which can be of particular interest to migration historians. What is specific and what is general in the migration phenomenon? I will argue that we cannot understand that which is individual and specific without understanding that which is structural and vice-versa. As one sociologist put it, "the comparative approach yields contradictory processes of unification and diversification."[6] Through a comparative method (or, as we will see, comparative methods), we can explore the universalism inherent in certain processes while understanding the diversity of both their representations and realities.

Yet to compare is not enough. While two cases are better than one, we also need to be aware of how comparisons are constructed. As Simiand himself wrote, "In any science, there is no statement which is not already a choice, there is no observation which does not presuppose some idea."[7] There is also no comparison, like any another research, which is completely neutral. By the level of generalization chosen, the variables chosen, the method of agreement or difference used, the accent is placed on diversity or unity. The way in which the question is asked implies part of the response.

Take "French Jews" for example. The subject may seem neutral, but much depends on the comparison. French Jews may be studied implicitly or explicitly in comparison with: French Catholics or Protestants; Italians or Poles in France; or with American Jews. In each case, the comparative perspective implies a different query, regarding religion, ethnicity, or nationality. The subject is almost but a pretext for very different questions: the place of religion in the nation-state; the importance of ethnicity for acculturation; the impact of the Diaspora on the Jews. In the first two cases, French Jews are compared to their compatriots in France; their "Frenchness" is essentially being scrutinized. However, in the third

4.   Pirenne, "De la methode comparative"; Barraclough, *History in a Changing World*; Thrupp, "Editorial", p. 1.
5.   Bloch, "Pour une histoire comparée". See also Sewell, "Marc Bloch and the Logic"; Hill and Hill, "AHR Forum"; and Atsma and Burguière, *Marc Bloch aujourd'hui* (Paris, 1990).
6.   Bouvier, "Différences et analogies", p. 14.
7.   Simiand, "Méthode historique et science sociale", p. 159.

case, the Diasporic perspective highlights the differences among Jews around the world; the French Jews' Frenchness becomes a given.

The comparative project thus implies a triple choice: that of subject, that of unit, and that of the pertinent level of analysis. While the choice of subject – migration and settlement, for example – is often explained, the unit and level rarely are. Yet the level of analysis is both subjective and crucial. As Adam Przeworski and Henry Teune have written, "Social phenomena do not have a property of 'being comparable' or 'not comparable'. 'Comparability' depends upon the level of generality of the language that is applied to express observations."[8] For Lévi-Strauss, the "significant distance" ("l'écart significatif") between units is constructed in "function of the type of research envisaged".[9] The logic of the comparison is thus constructed with the level of analysis chosen. Levels of comparability depend upon the perspective of the observer.[10]

Furthermore, the choice of unit is closely tied to the level of analysis. Since the advent of the nation-state, the most common unit of comparison has been that of a country. Although Marc Bloch, the medievalist, argued for more imaginative regional comparisons, and William Sewell, in his important gloss on Bloch, suggested that units do not even have to be geographic, the nation-state has remained the most visible unit of comparison for the last century.[11]

From the micro to the macro level, nation-states have also been the building blocks of migration studies. Political scientists, sociologists and economists (more than historians) have compared national policies on immigration and integration. Immigrant groups have also, for the most part, been defined by their national source, regardless of their regional origins. Community studies of the last twenty years have helped consecrate the terms and identities of "Jews", "Italians", "Poles", etc. However, while the nation-state has been an important legal and historiographic unit in constructing immigrant identities over the last two centuries, it is not the sole unit imaginable. The macro study of other forms of migration and settlement in other periods and other places may point to other pertinent units of analysis: the Atlantic slave trade, the Mediterranean, etc.

---

8. Przeworski and Teune, *Logic of Comparative Social Inquiry*, p. 10. The debate over the comparative method has been particularly engaged by those working at the boundary between history and sociology. See Skocpol and Somers, "Uses of Comparative History"; Skocpol, *Vision and Method in Historical Sociology*. See also Stuart Mill, "Two Methods of Comparison".
9. Lévi-Strauss, *Anthropologie structurale*, pp. 312-313.
10. Katznelson, *Black Men, White Cities*, pp. 29-30.
11. Bloch, "Pour une histoire comparée", p. 37; Sewell, "Marc Bloch and the Logic". Katznelson, *Black Men, White Cities*, has also suggested that we can compare "social time" – different periods in two different countries in which similar phenomena occurred. This is commonly the case in comparative studies of ancient and modern slavery. See also my study of the stock market crashes of 1929 and 1987, seen from American and French perspectives, "Leçons d'octobre – 1929, 1987".

What I would like to suggest here is that, even for the last two centuries, we can nuance our notion of the nation-state as a unit of analysis through the comparative method. In the rest of this contribution I would like to suggest two types of comparisons for migration studies, each of which go beyond the nation-state framework in a different way. First, I will compare two national historiographies of immigration and more particularly the ways in which comparisons have been used by them. By comparing the French and American historiographies' use of each other, we can understand some of the problems of the ways in which comparisons are constructed. Secondly, I will show how comparing different immigrants within the nation-state can provide a middle-level comparison of groups that may be more fruitful than nation-state comparisons. By changing the unit of analysis to compare immigrant groups to each other in their cities of settlement, for example, we can focus on an intermediary – "mezzo" – level of analysis which can be more pertinent to the understanding of the social construction of immigrant identities.[12]

In each case, comparison is salutary. It takes the perspective to a more general level of analysis and provides what social science is supposed to provide: wider categories of analysis for the understanding of human society. However, as will also become clear, the choice of the comparison implies certain presuppositions. Migration studies can in turn illustrate the possibilities and limits of the comparative method.

Comparative Historiography: The Migration Story in France and the U.S.

We can use the nation-state itself to transcend its meaning via comparison. By comparing nation-states with regard to migration patterns and policies, we can construct larger generalizations about migration processes.[13] But at the same time we must recognize two elements that necessarily structure such comparisons. The first may be tautological. Nation-state comparisons often only tell us what we already know: that the difference lies in the difference between the nation-states themselves. Second, we can ask how each nation compares itself to another. Thus, while arguing for the merits of comparison, I would also like to examine some of the limits of that comparison.

---

12. The term was suggested by Hervé Le Bras. On "middle level", "middle range" or "meso" comparisons, see Grew, "Case for Comparing", p. 773; Fredrickson, "Comparative History"; J. Lucassen, *Migrant Labour in Europe*.
13. For two particularly interesting wide-ranging approaches, see Zolberg, "International Migration Policies"; and C. Tilly, *Big Structures*. For two other particularly interesting comparisons, see Burawoy, "Functions and Reproduction of Migrant Labor"; and Freeman, *Immigrant Labor and Racial Conflict*.

Both France and the United States have been major countries of immigration over the last century. That they have dealt with that fact, that history, and that memory in very different ways is at the crux of the comparative problem. At a general level, French and American immigration histories in the nineteenth and twentieth centuries are similar. Their open immigration policies arose within the global context of industrialization. Both countries turned to immigrants for labor recruitment and population increase. Yet at the same time, both countries had to deal with contradictory rhetoric which distinguished "good" immigrants from "bad" and which led to notions of triage.

I would argue that the major historical differences in the immigrant histories of France and the United States are two: (i) timing; and (ii) the immigrant groups which came to their "shores". The United States cut off immigration in the early 1920s, whereas France maintained an open-door policy until the Depression. In both cases, growing xenophobia fuelled the fires of triage.[14]

The historiographic differences are perhaps even more interesting. Why is it that if both countries have been major countries of immigration, they have represented their immigration history so differently? Ironically, the United States, which cut off immigration earlier, has maintained a strong open door image, while France, more generous into the inter-war period, has subsequently largely ignored that portion of its history.

Furthermore, the way in which immigration history is perceived in both countries has had an implicit if not explicit comparative component to it. In comparing how they have compared themselves to each other, two facts stand out. American historiography has ignored French migration history while French historiography has often referred to the American model in order to understand its own immigration history.

The American reticence towards comparison is not the province of migration studies alone. One historian characterized the isolationist nature of American historical writing as the "Monroe Doctrine of American historiography".[15] Comparisons have been rejected all the more to underline the exceptional character of the American destiny. Indeed, the history of immigration has been used to reinforce if not found the notion of American exceptionalism (itself a comparative concept). Only occasionally have other models – Canadian, Argentine – been examined.[16] But by and large the history and memory of

14. General histories of immigration to the United States are by now numerous. Three recent overviews are: Archdeacon, *Becoming American*; Bodnar, *Transplanted*; and Daniels, *Coming to America*. For France, see Noiriel, *Creuset français*; Lequin, *Mosaïque france*; and Kaspi and Marès, *Paris des étrangers*.
15. Cited in Hartz, "Comment", pp. 281.
16. One of the rare attempts was the anthology edited by Vann Woodward at the behest of the Voice of America: *The Comparative Approach to American History*. See especially John Higham's article, "Immigration", where he shows how proportionately many more immigrants went

immigration have served to help define and construct American identity. The refusal of comparison reinforces specificity.

In France, on the other hand, the "discovery" of immigrants (via the "immigrant problem" coming to the fore in the 1970s) has taken place within an at times explicit reference to the American model.[17] One of the first articles in this regard was by Dominique Schnapper, comparing Italians in France and the United States.[18] Her title sets up the Tocquevillian dichotomy: "Centralisme et fédéralisme culturels" or American cultural pluralism versus French cultural jacobinism. In other words, the true melting pot occurred in France.

Yet French writings on the subject have gone through two periods, corresponding to shifts in the more general politics of immigration. A first period emphasized the pluriethnic nature of French society. Pro-immigrant and second generation groups, sociologists and historians firmly defended the "droit à la différence". The American example of cultural pluralism was often cited as a model for minority interaction with the nation-state. More recently, however, this "right to be different" has undergone retrenchment. And this has led to a re-evaluation of American cultural pluralism in a new, menacing, light.[19]

French historians in the last ten years have sought to reclaim the history of immigration to France. Gérard Noiriel made a deserved splash with his *Le Creuset français*, followed closely by Yves Lequin et al's *Le Mosaïque France*.[20] These works sought not only to re-balance the history of France but to implicitly if not explicitly combat the exclusionism of the far right through an appeal to a revised memory about immigration. However, the implicit and often explicit historiographic reference was that of American history.

But which American model? From the Chicago School of the 1920s to the fileo-pietistic histories of immigrant groups to Handlin's *The Uprooted* (1951) and Higham's *Strangers in the Land* (1955) to the new social history of the 1970s, the immigration story itself has evolved. As we know, after the years of consensus in the 1950s and the years of contestation in the 1960s, ethnic studies took

to Canada and Argentina than to the United States. He suggests that the true specificity of the U.S. was rather the diversity rather than the quantity of immigrants who arrived. See also Fredrickson, "Comparative History".

17. Pinto, "Immigration: L'ambiguïté". On the more general issue of the French love-hate relationship with the United States, see Lacorne *et al.*, *Rise and Fall of Anti-Americanism*; and Portes, *Fascination réticente*.

18. Schnapper, "Centralisme et fédéralisme culturels".

19. Vichniac, "French Socialists".

20. An early article on the subject by an Australian historian deserves note: Dignan, "Europe's Melting Pot".

off in the 1970s.[21] At the same time the research was reoriented. From the difficulties and xenophobia of the immigrant experience studied by Handlin and Higham, a new emphasis evolved stressing the immigrants' own agency, especially via their community and kinship structures. Pessimism gave way to (sometimes unbridled) optimism.

What is interesting is the choice of the socio-historical products imported by French historians and sociologists. The American model referred to in France has been, logically, the new social history, but with a twist. Having become interested in American immigration history during our own "roots revival", many French academics took this model as a symbol of all American immigration history and memory. Thus American periods of anglo-conformity and assimilation have been absent in the French representation of American immigration history.

Furthermore, this coincided with a growing French interest in the Chicago School of sociology. The Chicago School has become the obligatory reference for French sociologists and historians (to most Americans' surprise).[22] Louis Wirth has replaced Al Capone as the French academic's symbol of the Windy City, and a direct line of continuity from the 1920s to the 1970s has been drawn with regard to American historiography and memory of migration. The years of consensus, when immigrants were invisible, or the years of pessimism, when the portrayal of the American model was far from rosy, have been ignored along with the fact that immigration historians in the United States have been far from sanguine about the state of their specialty within American history as a whole.[23] Yet by taking American cultural pluralism for granted, there has been little understanding, as Olivier Zunz has pointed out, of how Horace Kallen's formulation of the term in the interwar period only became popular when it was rediscovered in the 1970s.[24]

21. The publication history of Higham's book is revealing: First published in 1955, it "took off" along with ethnic studies. From 1963 to 1978, the book was reprinted twenty times. Higham, "The Strange Career of *Strangers in the Land*". Higham adds that the "paperback revolution" also undoubtedly helped explain the book's success.

22. Grafmeyer and Joseph, *Ecole de Chicago*. On the impact of the Chicago School in Europe, see Oriol, *Bilan des études*, pp. 28-32.

23. Marcus Lee Hansen's seminal article of 1927 remained but an isolated call for immigration studies at the time it was written: "History of American Immigration as a Field of Research"; and the same author, *Atlantic Migration, 1607-1860* (1940). Nor did Frank Thistlethwaithe's now often-cited article have much impact at the time: "Migrations from Europe Overseas in the 19th and 20th Centuries" (1960).More recently, see, for example, Vecoli, "European Americans: From Immigrants to Ethnics"; Vecoli, "Return to the Melting Pot"; and Archdeacon's thoughtful, "Problems and Possibilities in the Study of American Immigration and Ethnic History", in which he calls for more comparative work in the field.

24. Kallen, *Culture and Democracy in the United States*; Zunz, "Genèse du pluralisme américain". See also Higham, *Send These to Me*, ch. 10.

During a second period, however, as calls for multiculturalism have receded in France (in part due to specific political factors such as the debate over a reform in the nationality law), the French view of American cultural pluralism has changed as well. French use of the term melting pot illustrates this shift.

Admittedly, the notion of the melting pot has had a complex history in the United States itself. As Philip Gleason has stressed, it contained a theoretical ambiguity from the beginning.[25] I would suggest that there have been at least five different meanings to the term. (1) In its most basic, popular usage, the term is often simply used to refer to the history of immigration to the United States. This, curiously enough, implies diversity. (2) The etymological root of the term, however, means the opposite – a process of homogenization. And there are both positive and negative assessments of that process. (3) In the initial, Zangwillian vision, the transformation of immigrants into Americans is seen as positive, both for the country and for the immigrants. (4) But the Kallenian critique (re-emphasized since the 1970s) challenges the value of melting on behalf of the immigrants;[26] whereas (5) the conservative critique (from Henry Ford to Henry Fairchild's *The Melting Pot Mistake*[27]) disputes the melting pot's virtue for the country.

But again what is interesting is to see which references are imported to France in the search for a new (comparative) history of immigration. At first, the most popular meaning of the term – that of a country of immigrants – was used. The "melting pot" became such a frequent reference in French that it lost its quotation marks (but added a hyphen, *le melting-pot*). Yet the use of the term has ultimately become as variable in French as its multiple meanings in English. During the (short) period of French interest in multiculturalism, it became the symbol of an immigrant society or shorthand for cultural pluralism.[28]

However, as the "right to be different" has given way to strong integrationist sentiment (on the part of immigrants and their defenders), the American melting pot has been redefined as a "juxtaposition of communities"; ethnic groups are "cultural ghettos" barricaded against each other in a "soft form of apartheid".[29] The terms ethnicity and community have similarly come under attack as reifications, like lobbies, which are foreign to the French nation's notion of individual rights.[30] American immigration history has thus been used first to

---

25. Gleason, "Melting Pot"; Sollors, *Beyond Ethnicity*, pp. 88-99.
26. Glazer and Moynihan, *Beyond the Melting Pot*.
27. Fairchild, *Melting Pot Mistake*.
28. It also designated a peaceful merging of peoples and was occasionally also decried as a homogenizing blend. See, for example, Etienne Balibar's article in *Le Monde*, 1 December 1984.
29. Robert Solé, "Un modèle français d'intégration", commenting on a talk by Michel Rocard, *Le Monde*, 7 December 1989.
30. Horowitz, "Europe and America".

prove that France is a country of immigration, and then to represent a frightening image of tribal ghettos in battle with each other. In its ultimate formulation, however, the etymological meaning of melting has been reclaimed as the truly French model of immigration.[31]

The migration of concepts merits a study of its own.[32] Concepts and words are imported, criticized, and rejected from one country to another, from one period to another. Popular terms and academic references can be introduced to one country totally out of synchronization with their use in their country of origin. I would suggest two explanations for the resulting discrepancies. First, the travelling across national boundaries of terms is usually accompanied by a selective use of the complex and changing definitions embedded in the original concepts. Second, the partial reading which occurs is clearly a function of the needs of the country of arrival.

To compare itself to the American case has had several functions in French historiography. First it served to insist on a (similar) tradition and history of immigration in France. Second, the comparison became a reproach in order to spur French historians on to narrow their historiographic lag with Americans in this field. But there has more recently been a significant distancing from the American model in order to emphasize a more specifically French immigration model. That the latter is celebrated as the true melting pot, in the assimilatory sense, is but a final ironic twist in the study of comparative historiographies.

Looking across the Atlantic thus becomes not simply a way of measuring one country's history against another, but of constructing national identity itself. In France, this dialogue (monologue) with the American model has taken place within a context of return to analyses of the nation itself.[33] For the United States, the discovery of French immigration could lead to a re-evaluation of American exceptionalism. If immigration is considered to be a fundamental differentiating factor from other countries, what happens when the same phenomenon is found elsewhere? Specificity must be reexamined.[34]

Nation-state comparisons may thus tell us more about the migration of concepts than the migration of peoples. Furthermore, they most often seem to postulate difference. Perhaps we have to look elsewhere, to another level and another unit of analysis to ask other questions about similarity (and difference) and immigrant agency in the migration process.

31. Schnapper, "Host Country of Immigrants". See also the editorial preface to the issue. The article originally appeared in *Le Genre humain* in 1989.
32. Or, as one screenwriter commented with regard to transatlantic cultural migrations: "There is a constant war between the United States and France. We sent them Jerry Lewis, so they retaliated by sending us deconstruction.", quoted in the *New York Times Magazine* 21 October 1990, section VI, p. 41.
33. Most notably with Pierre Nora's major editorial project: *Lieux de Mémoire*.
34. Higham, "Immigration".

National Group Comparisons

A more "mezzo" level of comparison may be more satisfying. For migration studies, this can mean the comparison of groups within one country. Here, too, the comparative method can take us beyond culturally-embedded explanations linked to national attributes. Indeed, the comparative method frontally asks the question of structure versus culture. What has been more important in shaping immigration patterns: the social, economic, and political factors in which the migration decision is made, or the individual, cultural traditions inherent in the decision? Three basic types of international comparisons are possible, which I call linear, divergent, and convergent. But each comparative project implies certain assumptions which also need to be addressed. Until recently, historical community studies, while questioning an assimilationist model, have importantly told the immigrants' story "from below" and have provided a necessary corrective to the homogenizing tendency of the nation-state. Nevertheless they have perhaps inherently prevented certain types of comparative questions. As Rudolph Vecoli stated at one point:

> "Single group studies have the merit of permitting the analysis of the migrant experience in depth, but they are open to the criticism that they neglect the common aspects of that experience which transcend ethnic differences."[35]

By underlining the importance of the values, customs and skills imported by the immigrants, we have emphasized culture over structure. But even in this poststructural world, I would argue that structure must be understood in conjunction with culture. What I would like to argue here is that a comparative study, at an intermediary level, can help us reexamine both differences and similarities in the migration experience. At least three types of fruitful comparisons are possible. However, it is important to understand how each implies different perspectives on the culture/structure issue.

Linear Model

To follow an immigrant from Vilna to New York or from Venice to Paris, from one point to another, is to compare past to present, a before to an after, and ultimately the experience in the country of arrival with that in the country of departure. The Neopolitan in Chicago is thus the subject through which life in Italy and life in the United States are compared. What can be called a linear form of comparison is in fact often used but rarely made explicit. Yet the debates

---

35. Vecoli, "European Americans", p. 418; Archdeacon, "Problems and Possibilities".

over continuity or change have fundamentally been comparisons of this sort. John Briggs, in a rare example of an explicit analysis of the linear comparison, has criticized the general terms that are often used to compare fertility in Italy with fertility in the United States. More generally, he insists that

"Researchers must choose a baseline from which to judge change, and they must locate evidence from different times, places, and groups that is similar in level and intensity of observation. [...] The question of change from Italian norms requires a comparison of similar forms of evidence from sources before and after migration."[36]

Not only does Briggs stress the importance of a nuanced understanding of the culture of origin, but he suggests that even a linear comparison is not neutral. It must be carefully constructed in order to properly evaluate continuity or change.

Convergent model

The convergent model is that which has been most frequently undertaken in American migration studies (although still absent in France). To compare Jews, Italians, and Poles in Chicago, or the Irish and Italian in Boston generally means comparing relative success or failure, or, in more discreet social science terminology, "social mobility". By taking a place, the city, as the constant, the comparison implies from the outset that difference will be found at the level of the immigrant groups themselves. Cultural origins thus explain the varying modes of adaptation to the city. Blacks and immigrants,[37] Jews and Italians[38] have been the groups most often compared. But at the same time, some more global convergent studies have compared multiple groups within one area: Olivier Zunz on Detroit, John Bodnar on Pittsburgh, Ron Bayor on New York.[39] These works have helped make the convergent model more complex, including

36. Briggs, "Fertility and Cultural Change", p. 1131. See also Briggs, *Italian Passage*; Gabaccia, *From Sicily to Elizabeth Street*; and Yans-McLaughlin, *Family and Community*.
37. E.g., Appell, "American Negro and Immigrant Experience"; Bodnar *et al.*, *Lives of their Own*; Gutman and Berlin, "Natives and Immigrants"; Lieberson, *Piece of the Pie*; Light, *Ethnic Enterprise in America*; Perlmann, *Ethnic Differences: Schooling and Social Structure*; Thernstrom, *Other Bostonians*.
38. Kessner, *Golden Door*; Schnapper, "Quelques réflexions sur l'assimilation"; Smith, *Family Connections*. For other convergent studies, see, e.g., Barton, *Peasants and Strangers*; Cole, *Immigrant City*; and Mormino and Pozzetta, *Immigrant World of Ybor City*.
39. Zunz, *Changing Face of Inequality*; Bodnar, *Immigration and Industrialization*; Bayor, *Neighbors in Conflict*. See also the debate between Zunz and Bodnar in Olivier Zunz, John Bodnar "Forum: American History"; and Steinberg, *Ethnic Myth*.

such factors as timing and economic opportunity at the time of arrival to explain varying "success stories".

However, if most convergent studies draw on national origins as the explanation of differentiation, the same type of study, at a more general level of analysis, can yield different results. Elizabeth Ewen's study of Italian and Jewish women in New York, for example, which is not presented as an explicitly comparative study, in fact compares two groups as immigrant women rather than as Italians or Jews.[40] The pertinent categories of analysis for Ewen are "immigrant". "women", or "family" rather than Italians or Jews. The evidence she presents from both groups, and the way in which it is presented – the structure of her chapters, the close use of Jewish and Italian examples from one paragraph to another and within one paragraph – emphasize above all the similarities in the immigrant women's experience on the Lower East Side. At this level of analysis, the differences between the two groups are almost invisible.

To a great extent, the comparative project as well as the level of analysis chosen thus structure the conclusions. There is no right or wrong way to construct a comparison, but it is necessary to be aware of the ways in which certain choices at the inception reflect options concerning the similarities or singularities of the immigrant experience. In one case difference may exclude resemblance. In another, semblance may hide uniqueness from sight.

Divergent Model

If most convergent studies take differentiated origins as their starting point, what I would call divergent studies locate the explanation of difference at the point of arrival, not at the point of departure. Following Poles throughout Polonia, Jews throughout the modern Diaspora, or Italians across the continents is another way of examining the questions of tradition and culture, continuity and change. Divergent studies are, however, rare.[41] Perhaps, as has been suggested for the Jews, it is because the premise of such comparison implies a differentiation which works against the notion of group unity.[42] The study of single national groups across space is however particularly interesting in order to

---

40. Ewen, *Immigrant Women*.
41. See, however, Samuel Baily's thoughtful analysis, "Cross-Cultural Comparison and the Writing of Migration History"; along with his: "Italians and the Development of Organized Labor"; and his, "Adjustment of Italian Immigrants in Buenos Aires and New York". Also, Briggs, *Italian Passage*; Gabaccia, *Militants and Migrants*; Klein, "Integration of Italian Immigrants"; Reutlinger, "Reflections on the Anglo-American Jewish Experience".
42. Schnapper, "Jewish Minorities and the State"; Green, "Diversité et unité".

evaluate the relative importance of cultural baggage or social-economic factors with regard to emigration and adaptation.

Two articles, admittedly by non-historians (anthropologists), illustrate particularly well how a divergent comparative approach can nuance linear or convergent comparisons in explaining immigrant behavior. Nancy Foner, in trying to understand the relative "success" of West Indians in New York, has questioned explanations based on the functioning of the ethnic network.[43] If a cultural explanation were sufficient, the same success should be found in other settings. However, West Indians in London are not nearly as successful as those who have emigrated to New York. Other explanatory factors must therefore be addressed: the immigrant cohort in each city, the nature of the neighborhoods in which they settle (the African-American clientele in New York). What is of interest here is how different comparative perspectives lead to different conclusions. Studying West Indians in New York (and implicitly comparing them to African-Americans) yields one result; comparing West Indians in New York to West Indians in London leads to another explanation.

Caroline Brettell has used a comparative approach to revise her own work on Portuguese immigrants in Toronto.[44] After subsequently studying Portuguese immigrants in Paris, she concluded that (linear) studies based on a single community are very often tautological: "One chooses a community to find or prove 'community'. The assumptions become the conclusion."[45] In Paris, unlike Toronto, Brettell found no "little Portugal" and few Portuguese voluntary associations, leading her to question her previous conclusions about the immigrants' behavior. The explanatory factor now became the difference between France and Canada and particularly the fact that France's proximity to Portugal sustains an active vision of return. Thus Brettell's article shows how different comparisons can create a chain reaction of questions, each relativizing previous conclusions, but therefore deepening our knowledge of the complexities of the migration process.

Different comparative studies thus provide different perspectives on migration. In asking who are more alike, an Italo-American and an Italo-Frenchman or an Italo-American and an American Jew, the answer already varies in function of the way in which the question is posed. The constant implied – country of origin or country of settlement – in many ways structures the comparative project from the outset.

Divergent and convergent histories can lead to different questions and different conclusions about immigrant itineraries. One way in which this can be done is by choosing neither a group (or two) nor a place, but a cross-study. By

43. Foner, "West Indians in New York City and London".
44. Brettell, "Is the Ethnic Community Inevitable?".
45. *Ibid.*, p. 1.

focusing on an economic sector as the "constant", for example, we can circumscribe the socio-economic context and then seek ways of more closely defining the variables pertinent to understanding immigrant work and lives. The garment industry is a particularly obvious example.[46] Jews, Italians, and Chinese, among others, have converged on the sewing machines in New York, while Polish Jews, Armenians, North African Jews, Turks, and other immigrants have moved into the garment district in Paris over the last century. Do they bring their skills with them in a linear trajectory? How do their (convergent) histories compare? And if we compare Polish Jews (or Chinese) in Paris and New York, what do their divergent stories tell us about immigrant adaptation?

Immigration essentially raises the question of the relationship of the particular to the general. As a result, not only have Mary Antin and others become comparativists by force of circumstance, but immigrants as groups have raised the question of difference within the nation-state and with regard to each other. Comparisons can help us understand both the structural constraints surrounding individual experience and understand the specificity of responses to that global experience.

Towards a Post-Structural Structuralism?

We have thus seen how comparisons have been used (or not) in nation-state historiographies and how comparisons may be used to go beyond the study of single nationality groups. The comparison makes us question generalizations based on single case studies while also questioning the conceptualizations behind the nation-state and nationality terms. In both cases comparison can offer a way around either the glorification of exceptionalism (American or French) or a structuralism that reifies "immigration". If comparisons generally take us to a higher level of generality (yes, apples and oranges can be compared), they also necessarily show variety within the structure and differentiated responses to it.

From heroic adventurers to downtrodden pawns, the image of migrants changed radically over the past half century. In the last two decades, community studies and micro-historical approaches have in turn rightfully restored the voices of the immigrants themselves and have been the crucial foundation stones of the field. However, perhaps the community paradigm has reached its limit, bound by national boundaries. Is it possible to re-integrate a structural approach which

---

46. For a mixed, convergent and divergent, approach, see Daniels, "On the Comparative Study of Immigrant and Ethnic Groups in the New World"; and his, "Chinese and Japanese in North America". Also Green, *Ready-to-Wear*. The industry of course is not an absolute constant either; Green, "Immigrant Labor in the Garment Industries". See also Waldinger and Ward, "Cities in Transition".

looks at individual decisions, cultural choices, *and* structural constraint? By examining individual and group choices within comparative, historical frameworks, we can perhaps move toward a "post-structural structuralism". For migration studies, this means examining and reinterpreting the structures surrounding the migration process in light of individual choice and vice versa. In this respect, comparisons bring us back to the question of generality and difference. But while regulating the macro- or micro-scope to stress one or the other, we cannot truly understand the one without the other. Similarity and specificity, structures and their variants can only be understood in relation to one another.

Segmented Macrosystems and Networking Individuals: The Balancing Functions of Migration Processes*

Dirk Hoerder

Until a decade ago, scholars dealt with migration as a process of disruption, even though Handlin's notion of uprootedness was discarded in the mid 1960s.[1] The pressures currently exerted by immigration on countries in the northern hemisphere (especially the ones within the Atlantic economies) have led politicians and a considerable part of eligible voters to fear disruption and to demand restrictionist or exclusionist policies.[2] Continuities of culture and migration flows, however, characterize migrations, as Leslie Page Moch has emphasized in her study on intra-European moves. Walter Nugent has noted the continuity in the process that used to be considered demographic transition.[3]

This paper begins with the assertion that migration balances rather than disrupts society by redistributing human resources according to the interests of all parties involved (whether migrants or persisters) and according to the interests of the sending and receiving societies. Since forced migrations (whether slave transports or streams of refugees) do not serve the interests of the migrants, the scope of the preceding assertion is questionable. It has been argued that "migration (even when forced) is a good thing" because some descendants of slaves will lead better lives. As first-generation slaves and forced labourers would disagree with this interpretation, it is one-sided ex-post accounting.[4] In a comparative analysis of voluntary and forced migrations based on Italian and Chinese worldwide migration, Donna Gabaccia supports the intermediate semi-voluntary and forced stages.[5] The concept of balancing processes that is advanced here applies to voluntary migrations and may be extended by taking

---

*   This essay is dedicated to Christiane Harzig, my partner in work and everyday life, who has shared many of her insights with me.
1. Vecoli, "Contadini in Chicago"; Bodnar, *Transplanted. A History.*
2. Hostility towards de jure foreigners and de facto immigrants has surged in Germany; in the March 1993 French election, LePen's rightist party garnered over 12 percent of the vote. Both the German and the Austrian governments refuse to consider their countries immigration countries.
3. Moch, *Moving Europeans*; Nugent, *Crossings.*
4. Cf. Pieter C. Emmer's contribution to this volume.
5. See the essay by Donna Gabaccia in this volume.

uneven power relationships into account. Slave labour or forced labour (e.g. in Nazi Germany) balance supply with demand to benefit the side in control. Similarly, present-day migrations from impoverished regions to the wealthy nations represent efforts to rectify the unequal distribution of goods and economic wealth, although they are obstructed by the entrance restrictions of the powerful states. Only by day-to-day resistance or by militancy under changed relationships of production or clandestine entry can such migrants hope to balance the various interests.[6]

Second, the relationship between the approach by the world systems and an analysis of behaviour among individual migrants from the bottom up can be extended beyond abstract push and pull forces by discussing the larger systems on a meso-level in terms of segmentation and by considering individual actions in terms of networks and family economies.

Third, I will emphasize the temporal and spatial overlaps between migration in the reproductive, commercial, and productive spheres. The emphasis on the productive spheres, for example (whether settlement migration to North America and Australia or labour migration within Europe and to the United States), has led to a dichotomy between pre-industrial and industrial migration that is at best only partially sustainable.

The "Extended Economist Approach" to Migration: The Material and the Emotional

Migration permits matching human resources with perceived opportunities. Such migration may be circular or directed outward.[7] In circular processes, individual migrants or persons with similar characteristics return to the place of departure. Seasonal migrants in agriculture and multi-annual labour migrants in industry temporarily venture into a different location and usually into a different economic stage of development (a wage economy) and, thirdly, into different concepts of time. They plan to return. Circular migration may also mean that the people returning are different from the ones who leave. In marriage migration, for example, some women leave, others arrive. In the exchange of commercial or intellectual elites between towns or areas, outward and inward migration take place simultaneously. Unbalanced circulation leads to a brain drain or mismatched sex ratios. Circular migration may also be career migration, as in the case of artisans or younger sons of merchants who leave or are sent away for training purposes. Circular migration increases the available

---

6. Nonini, "Popular Sources of Chinese Labor".
7. For a different usage of the terminology see Moch, *Moving Europeans*, pp. 16-17, based on
     C. Tilly, "Migration in Modern European History".

options, both in terms of marriage partners from outside the nearest circle of kin, friends, and fellow villagers and in terms of jobs from different crafts and skills and forms of income. It permits better information, acquisition of new skills, and establishment of regional and international trading networks.

Permanent out-migration connects areas with a demographic surplus to comparatively "understaffed" agricultural or industrial segments in distant regions. In some cases, areas of outward migration are replenished by inward migration from different sources: labour or land is in demand, but at prices that the part of the population migrating outward considers unsuitable. Outward migration may become inadvertently permanent, as when men or women leave temporarily but postpone return until death. Such migration may thus arise from circular migration.

In an approach that I call economist in the sense that costs and benefits are weighed both by societies and by individuals, outward migration – viewed from a top-down perspective – involves reallocation of human resources in regional, national, and international economies by administrative decree, via market forces, or via a combination of the two. The administrative regulations include government inducements, such as bonuses, tax rebates, homestead laws; coercion, such as deportation, involuntary contract labour, and forced labour; and prohibitions (e.g. of slavery).[8] Market forces include comparative levels of wages or total income, job opportunities, and travel costs. Such an emphasis on economic factors has been criticized for shortchanging human agency and individual interests in migration processes.

The concept of family economies[9] and the inclusion of non-measurable emotional and spiritual factors in the balancing process permit a reformulation of the economist approach to include the whole collection of factors that influence decisions. Family economies (whether in peasant, wage, or consumer societies) combine the income-generating capabilities of all family members with reproductive needs (e.g. care for dependent children or elderly relatives) and patterns of consumption to achieve the best possible results according to traditional norms for all members of the family and their standing in the community. Allocation of resources depends on the respective stage of the family cycle as well as on the stages in the lives of the individuals concerned. The allocation of time, labour power, and the skills of all parties concerned has to be negotiated in terms of the benefits for each: maximization of income or of leisure, child-care or work outside the home, education or wage work for children, traditional networking or individualist separation from the community.

---

8. Administratively induced migration will not be discussed separately, since arriving migrants come to terms with labour market conditions or agrarian practices, just as other newcomers.
9. The classic formulation of this approach is L. Tilly and Scott, *Women, Work and Family*, pp. 12 passim.

An inward-migrating new member of a family (a bride) is judged in terms of her labour capacity, family status, and, of course, child-bearing capability. Only after such assessment by the entire family, can the two prospective partners consider objecting because of emotional incompatibility.[10]

Viewed from the bottom up, the extended economist approach regards individuals as making deliberate choices with respect to perceived opportunities. Since individual decisions about life-courses, levels of subsistence, and interests in improvement consist of a conglomerate of traditional cultural norms and practices, of prevailing emotional and spiritual needs, and of economic rationales, the non-material sphere has to be included in scholarly analysis. Emotional and spiritual well-being and material security are, of course, linked. Immigrant women workers in the United States wanted "bread and roses, too".[11] This complex of factors poses a methodological problem for research. Loss of relationships, sadness, and homesickness (which I prefer to call network deprivation) or happiness and social contacts defy measurement by the single scale that applies to wages. Considered on a subjective basis in the individual decision-making process, they figure in the calculations of prospective migrants. In terms of traditional norms and practices, family economies and networks, and prospects, decisions about migration are made to satisfy the interests of the ones who remain behind as well as the ones who leave.

The economic gains of migration influence status in the culture of origin. They may be used to increase landholdings even in times of bountiful harvests because land provides status. They may facilitate ostentatious consumption, as with American houses or gold watches. Loss of status may arise from working conditions or societal demands and different cultural norms in the host society that induce migrants (both male and female) to change to an degree that is unacceptable to fellow villagers and non-migrating kin.

The intricate connection between economic and emotional factors is also manifested by the timing of decisions to leave. Both economic slumps in material status at home or in the receiving society with a resulting decrease in earning opportunities and emotional downturns in family relations influence the timing of departures. Again, the macro-economic aspect is well-known. The downturn of economies in receiving countries is followed (after an interval of a year, caused by the time lag of information flows) by a decline in inward migration. Similarly, the changes in intra-familial relationships at the time of the death of a parent (especially the mother) or the arrival of a new parent by remarriage

10. See for a case study and theoretical reflection Schiffauer, *Die Migranten aus Subay.*
11. Kornbluh, *Rebel Voices*, p. 195.

(especially a stepmother) increases outward migration.[12] At a time when all emotional relationships within the family unit require rearrangement, latent migratory potential is activated. When emotional ties are relaxed or changed, departure becomes easier and less costly.

The extended economist approach based on the inclusion of all socio-cultural aspects is conducive to understanding acculturation processes. Migrants, whether moving for commercial, agricultural, or wage-work purposes, have to come to terms with the receiving society sufficiently to achieve their goals. The quick insertion (assimilation) demanded by a number of receiving societies thus serves the interest of the newcomers – unless the pursuit of their economic goals becomes personally more costly than their return. In terms of loss of quality of life, goal-achievement by migration may appear overpriced to a degree that renders the benefits negligible. In such cases, decisions to leave are postponed, return migration occurs, and migration patterns may be changed.[13]

This insertion and matching of interests of migrants and of the receiving society occurs amid unequal bargaining power. Newcomers can rarely demand a high price for their labour. Only after establishing an economic foothold will migrant workers undertake mass strikes or other struggles for improved conditions. In fact, most of the early bargaining process concerns only the migrant, who has to decide how much of the old-culture customs, values, and habits to surrender in return for new job and income opportunities.[14]

Understood as a combination of measurable material benefits or losses with objectively non-quantifiable but subjectively considerable emotional and spiritual benefits or losses, the extended economist approach is no longer concerned merely with improving the balance between demographic and economic structures across geographic space. It now encompasses the family economy and its networks (i.e. the entire human side). A restricted "human-side" approach that merely juxtaposes loss of old-world everyday culture, social networks, and relationships against the pursuit of economic opportunities neglects the complex calculation or

12. This process is described in Kaztauskis, "From Lithuania to the Chicago Stockyards", especially pp. 104-105. Gabaccia, *Militants and Migrants*, p. 80. Diner argues that in Ireland the post-famine "rearrangement of family life" caused out-migration. See *Erin's Daughters in America*, pp. 31-32.

13. I have argued elsewhere that the minimal funds ($21.50 per person) that turn-of-the-century labour migrants brought with them when arriving in the United States necessitated immediate entry in the new labour markets and work places for sheer survival. Hoerder, "From Immigrants to Ethnics". Reports of the Immigration Commission, 41 vols (Washington, D.C., 1911), III, pp. 349-354. A cooperative research project on Swedish, Irish, German, and Polish immigrant women in Chicago, directed by Christiane Harzig (Universität Bremen), has shown an unexpected loss of rural traditions following arrival in urban society. Harzig, *Peasant Maids, City Women*.

14. Immigrant letters and autobiographies sometimes graphically depict the pros and cons, as my ongoing study of Canadian life-writings shows. See e.g. Bruser Maynard, *Raisins and Almonds* or Grönlund Schneider, *Finnish Baker's Daughters*.

evaluation of costs and benefits that are part of individual decision-making processes. This perspective shortchanges the material improvements in the same measure that a narrow economist approach disregards non-material factors.

Communities of Individuals and Segmented Structures: The Meso-Level

Migration, which was formerly considered in terms of isolated events (e.g. the flight of the Huguenots), is now regarded as a process (proletarian mass migration). The macro-level world systems approach is frequently applied irrespective of micro-level life course analysis of individuals. Neither the world economy nor the worldwide pool of cheap and obedient labour explain the complexities of economic sectors or offer insight into the diversity of labour migrations. I propose dealing with a meso-level comprising segments of larger systems and networks of individuals.[15] The worldwide systems approach requires adaptation to local circumstances or specific groups. Networks of families, larger kin groups, and neighbourhoods integrate individuals into local units that form societal segments. Migration offers spatial options in other parts of the world for specific family economies and village or neighbourhood groups, for members of specific crafts, and for families active in commerce.

The approach to segmented systems takes up research on economic sectors and labour markets.[16] Recently, James Barrett proposed replacing the notion of fragmented class consciousness in immigration societies with the notion of class segmented by ethnic culture.[17] The approach to networks considers research on the family economy and on neighbourhoods.[18]

The concept of economic segmentation postulates three levels, including primary or growing, secondary or stagnating, and tertiary or marginal sectors in national systems, which are sub-divided into different branches. International connections based on capital and skill exist within sectors. Thus, Manchester's cloth manufacture interacted and competed with corresponding centres of production in Bombay, New England, and (later on) in Lodz. The industry maintained connections with cotton-growing areas, whether in the American South, Egypt, or Uganda. Both entrepreneurs and their sons migrated between similar firms all over the world. Owners often brought skilled labour from the society of origin to their new factories for investment purposes. Thus, Saxony cloth manufacturers establishing a mill in Passaic, New Jersey also founded a

---

15. See the essay by Nancy Green in this volume for a plea to use the meso-level for comparative approaches.
16. Kerr, *Markets and Other Essays*; Gordon et al., *Segmented Work*.
17. Barrett, "Americanization from the Bottom Up".
18. L. Tilly and Scott, *Women, Work and Family*.

community of skilled German workers, who subsequently trained unskilled immigrants from elsewhere.[19] While segments exert a reciprocal influence, work and production require particular skills and expertise that cannot simply be passed on to other segments. Although capital was transferable between segments, investment depended on knowledge of production and marketing opportunities before the advent of finance capitalism.[20]

As for labour markets, migrating men and women do not move into one single reserve labour pool. Rather, they enter a specific labour market segment of the receiving society. Masons do not compete with tailors, and seamstresses do not vie with pastry cooks. Marginal farmers in search of wintertime employment move into lumbering but not into skilled cabinetmaking. Thus, competition between workers did not occur between each and every immigrant and between each and every native-born worker. Instead, it existed within individual segments only or arose when workers from one segment began to enter another. Such competition might result from a lack of jobs in one segment, from higher wages or better working conditions in another, or from deliberate employer hiring practices. Competition became particularly acrimonious whenever the entering group undercut the wages earned by the resident labour.[21]

Among immigrant workers of different cultural backgrounds, an "ethno-cultural or segmented class formation" process takes place. While this development occurs "simultaneously in various ethnic communities", the whole process has been characterized by "relations between the generations of immigrant workers and the various ethnic working-class communities" (i.e. by interaction across boundaries).[22]

Individuals depart from meso-level units, families, and communities because of prevailing interests or frictions. Families operationalize "objective" economic and social push and pull factors and "subjectively" chart the best course for survival or improvement. Balancing interests within a gendered division of labour established family economies that took into account (depending on societally determined gender-specific power distribution in families) the interests of all family members. The intra-familial negotiations combine material and emotional well-being. Migration out of a family often implied change for all members. A family economy based on joint labour on a subsistence plot lost part of its labour force and might be supported from afar by wages. This change brought such a family closer to the stage of a family wage economy.

19. Beckert, "Migration, Ethnicity and Working Class".
20. Hodson and Kaufmann, "Economic Dualism"; Licht, "Labor Economics".
21. Piore, *Birds of Passage*; Harrison, "Human Capital, Black Poverty", p. 285; Bonacich, "Theory of Ethnic Antagonism"; Christiansen, "Split Labor Market Theory"; see also Pierenkemper and R. Tilly, *Historische Arbeitsmarktforschung*; Valkenburg and Vissers, "Segmentation of the Labour Market".
22. Barrett, "Americanization from the Bottom Up", pp. 999-1000.

The choice of a destination by a prospective migrant depended on migration patterns comprising networks of friends and kin as well as fellow-villagers providing information and, sometimes, prepaid tickets. Just after 1900, 94 percent of the newcomers arriving in the United States was bound for relatives or friends.[23] Although the immigrants were moving across the world, they did not leave their networks. These ties channelled migrants into particular segments of the receiving society's labour market or into specific agrarian areas. This trend also kept migrants within communities of fellow countrymen or even fellow villagers. Communities are meso-level segments established from the bottom up, whereas segmented labour markets are units established from the top down. Both systems interact. Communities provide assistance in entering the job market and also create ethnic firms and new labour markets.

In their letters, immigrants directed their fellow villagers to follow their example according to earning capacity rather than personal affection, at least in the initial stage of community formation. Women in domestic service invited other women to come and offered to help them find jobs. Men brought over other strong and healthy men to work and earn money. Only later did immigrants send for their wives, husbands, or children. If, however, labour was needed that was considered to be women's work, women were brought over earlier by men.[24] One immigrant put matters squarely: "Those men in the iron mines in Missouri need women to do the cooking and washing. Three men have sent back for their wives, and two for some girls to marry."[25] Other strategies involved balancing interests within uneven power relationships. The emphasis on earning capacities included the non-economic aspect of building a secure foothold permitting residential and emotional stability and mutual support during crises.

Specific villages might be connected to different labour market segments in various parts of the world (depending on the gender and the stage of life of the migrants). For example, in a village near Milan, young girls were sent into silk mills not more than a day off (child labour within the context of family economies), young men went to southern France over the summer, usually for road or excavation work (medium-distance seasonal migration into an unskilled segment close to work patterns in agriculture), and others journeyed to the Missouri iron mines for several years or longer (long-distance multi-annual migration into an unskilled segment different from work patterns in agriculture). Several expert female silkworkers were invited to Japan to teach Japanese silkmakers Italian work procedures (long-distance migration of experts within

23. Reports of the Immigration Commission, III, pp. 358-359, 362-365.
24. See collections of immigrant letters, e.g. Thomas and Znaniecki, *Polish Peasant*; Barton, *Letters from the Promised Land*; Kamphoefner *et al.*, *News from the Land of Freedom*.
25. Hall, *Rosa*, p. 160.

one craft segment). Upon marrying, women moved within the village, to neighbouring villages, or to America (migration into unpaid service work).[26]

Continuities of Migration in Europe and the Atlantic Economies

Continuity and complexity of migration has been eclipsed by the sheer volume of transatlantic migration. The only pre-industrial movement within Europe that aroused any interest was the rural-urban migration in the centuries before the French Revolution. Evaluations of the movement were reduced to a cliche, "*Stadtluft macht frei*" (freedom in the European cities – to be followed in the nineteenth century by: freedom in America). The political interpretation of this image disregarded economic implications and changes of everyday living patterns. Both the pre-nineteenth century urban migration and the nineteenth-century transatlantic mass migration no longer seem extraordinary upon analysing the multidirectional character of migrations and expanding the narrow view of migrations in the productive sphere (whether agrarian or industrial) to include migrations in the reproductive sphere.[27]

Labour migration in the harvest season from naturally less productive regions to fertile valleys and easily tillable plains had been part of rural life for centuries. Demographic pressure might reverse this direction. People moved up increasingly steep hills, terracing them in the process. None of these migrations, which were part of traditional daily life, played a role in contemporary debates and consciousness. Only unusual events, such as moves of rural groups to distant lands (which involved smaller numbers of people), aroused the attention of observers (e.g. the *Schwabenzüge* into the Danubian hills or the South Russian Plains).

Parallel to the migration of agrarian labourers or smallholders, countless interurban migration streams existed. In commerce, merchants sent their sons to firms elsewhere to receive training and to establish commercial connections.[28] In intellectual circles, educated men left for universities or Latin schools. Again, only certain movements were registered as noteworthy events. The University of Prague drew men of learning from much of Europe, and St. Petersburg attracted artisans and merchants from a particularly large catchment basin. At this time, none of the points of destination was considered especially alluring. None became myths similar to the one surrounding "America" that emerged in the nineteenth century.

---

26. *Ibid.*, pp. 21, 24, 84, 120, 137.
27. See Moch, *Moving Europeans.*
28. Friedrichs, *Urban Society in an Age*; Moch, *Moving Europeans*, pp. 43-58. From Bremen, a circular migration of clerks in merchant firms and sons of merchant families proceeded back and forth to the United States.

One type of widely practised migration (involving journeymen artisans) did attract notice. The migrating men and their guilds developed a specific culture. They made themselves visible, by their bundles and their dresses (carpenters), by both their decorum and their occasional bouts of boisterous behaviour, and by their team spirit. Parallel to these male migrations, young women left home to work as farm help (*Gesinde*) or as domestic servants in urban households. Like the journeymen's migrations, the migrations by women were circular. Most returned to their town of origin at the time of their marriage. Women, however, did not and by law could not form guilds or develop rituals. This work, which was part of everyday culture in a stage of the life cycle and was performed in the privacy of households (the reproductive sector) was regarded as a natural and therefore not as a memorable occurrence.

Migration in the reproductive sphere was, as we might expect, gender specific.[29] Brides moved into the households of their husbands. Only widows with an established economic basis (whether a farm or an artisan's shop) could induce men to move to their residence. Thus all married women had moved, even though only moves that crossed parish boundaries at the very least may be considered proper migration.

Economic interests, which formed the basis for viable family economies, were also part of marriage arrangements. The need to earn a dowry and to achieve status in the marriage market at home motivated women to move into domestic service. Dowry patterns, the economic nexus, changed in the nineteenth century. Women emigrated to North America for reasons that included escaping degrading dowry negotiations and intra-family workloads assigned to women in Europe. In other cases, women consented to marriage in exchange for travel funds (the pre-paid ticket). Finally, in the age of mass out-migration of men, women had to follow if they wanted to marry. Viewed from the opposite perspective, men had to bring over women. All these aspects are neatly combined in a vignette from Italian migration. Men from one village had preceded women to a particular labour market in North America. One woman following her husband epitomized the combination of tradition-bound notions, marriage, and new expectations concerning America when she noted about her friend Emilia: "She was so happy she was going to America and going to get married that she didn't care who the man was."[30] The custom among men who were looking for wives of sending home for "helpmeets" or, quite explicitly, for

---

29. The question of visibility may not only be gender-specific, but may also refer to food production or agrarian lifestyles. At least since the increase of urbanization and, later on, industrialization, most attention has been directed toward cities and industries. In the modern period this interest is reflected in peasant incomes, which are as much below national averages as women's incomes. The topic exceeds the scope of this essay.

30. Hall, *Rosa*, p. 163.

women to clean their shirts and cook their food shows that labour power had become more important than cumbersome dowry traditions. This situation drives home the combination of emotional and economic considerations and makes explicit the economics of love and labour, which entailed unpaid reproductive labour in the case of marriage.

Given that migrations had been part of everyday life in most of Europe for centuries, did these patterns change during the period following the French Revolution and the Age of Enlightenment? Was anything different, other than the quantity of the transatlantic flow and the increase of out-migration over circular migration? The remark about Emilia offers a clue. She travelled not to the United States, but to "America", a conglomerate of often unjustified hopes, myths, concrete pieces of information, and real improvements. Thus, in conclusion, mentalities merit consideration.

People who moved across space lacked the minds of geographers or the instruments of land surveyors: they did not measure distance. Nor did they consciously move between nations. They did not travel from Italy to the United States, but from a town either to "America" or, more precisely, "to the iron mines of Missouri", a labour market segment with an ethnic community in the making. This particular community of male migrants was in the process of adding women to achieve permanency. In addition to Lombardos, it comprised Toscanos and Southern Italians. Thus, women had to start by changing their cooking. Food now had to be palatable to men from many regions of Italy. According to this homogenization of regional cultures in a foreign context, Lombardos and Toscanos became "Italians" shortly before turning into Italian-Americans.[31]

New information flows and improving means of transportation resulted in new mental maps of life-course development across space. They also resulted in deep misunderstandings. Changed notions about individuality and religion permitted more personal freedom in decision-making. New administrative and political structures brought about mental constructs of national culture that had a profound impact on the acculturation of migrants.

At the beginning of the nineteenth century, people in one craft knew about nearby markets for their skills and about production centres, although their horizon remained limited. When new tariffs cut Prussian weavers off from their traditional markets in Russia, they and their families crossed the Russian border to stop their descent into poverty and to ply their craft. They did not, however, consider other destinations. Persons with low incomes in Mecklenburg-Strelitz crossed into nearby Prussia where wages were somewhat higher.[32] All these moves concerned limited perspectives in limited regions. Among the many

---

31. Hoerder, "Labour Migrants' Views"; Hoerder and Rössler, *Distant Magnets*.
32. Lubinski, "Überseeische Auswanderung"; Reich, "Auswanderung aus dem Regierungsbezirk".

lower-class migrants, only journeymen artisans had established an information network and migration routes encompassing the continent. Long-distance moves were few and far between. They occurred, for example, in response to active recruitment (whether by the Russian Czarina or the Habsburg administration) and were often guided by recruiting agents.

By the end of the nineteenth century, however, long-distance moves had become commonplace. They connected specific villages and towns to specific areas of settlement or labour markets over large distances. World geography was segmented according to self-sustaining information flows and means of transportation. Measured in terms of travel cost and migratory experience, the Argentinean wheat growing areas were thus closer to the Italian reservoir of labour than the East Elbian plains.[33] With respect to cultural proximity, Buenos Aires was considerably less distant from Italy than New York was.[34] Selective mental maps registered only the segments of the world relevant to the particular user.

The system-based approach to migration, extending over time, using a conceptual framework linking individuals to world systems on a meso-level of mediating networks and interacting segments, and including mental maps of the world systems, offers a more comprehensive perspective on migration processes.[35]

33. Sartorius von Waltershausen, *Die Italienischen Wanderarbeiter*.
34. Baily, "Adjustment of Italian Immigrants".
35. Jackson and Moch, "Migration and the Social History".

PART II

BETWEEN FREE AND UNFREE LABOUR MIGRATION

Seventeenth Century Migration and the Slave Trade:
The English Case in Comparative Perspective[*]

David Eltis

By 1700, and possibly through to the twentieth century on a cumulative basis, the British were preeminent in the business of free as well as coerced long-distance migration. It is possible that more long-distance slaving voyages and migrant ships have set out from England, and later Britain, than from any other state in the history of the world.[1] Between 1600 and 1700 over 700,000 people left England, or about seventeen percent of the population in 1600. About 60 percent (or approximately 420,000) of these went to the Americas, with Ireland absorbing much of the rest. This outflow contributed to a thirty year decline in the population of England at the end of the seventeenth century. Over the same period, the English carried approximately 370,000 people from Africa.[2] Thus more British than African people went to the English Americas, with three quarters of the former arriving before 1675, and almost all the latter after 1625. In the second half of the century between 10,000 and 20,000 people a year were leaving for the English colonies – the most concentrated migration to any jurisdiction within the Americas up to that time. It was also among the largest on a cumulative basis. Spanish and Portuguese America each accounted for more

[*] The research for this paper was supported by the Canadian Social Science and Humanities Research Council and funds made available by the Queen's University Principal's Advisory Research Committee. I would like to thank Stanley Engerman and conference participants for comments on an earlier draft of this paper.

1. As a national group the Portuguese may have been responsible for a larger share of the Atlantic slave trade than the English, and in the eighteenth century may well have supplied more people per capita to their overseas possessions than did the British. On the slave trade, however, most Portuguese slave traders were based in Brazil, and a quarter of the Brazilian based traffic occurred after Brazilian independence when it becomes difficult to separate out Brazilians from Portuguese. The Portuguese trade, moreover, spanned more than four centuries.
2. Calculated from Wrigley and Schofield, *Population History of England*, pp. 528-529. Gemery, "Emigration from the British Isles"; Eltis, "British Transatlantic Slave Trade". This last essay has detailed estimates for arrivals of Africans only from 1662, and between this year and 1700 suggests 256,000 arrivals in English ships. For the period prior to 1662, I have allowed 2,000 per annum 1651-61, 1,500 per annum, 1640-50, and 1,000 prior to 1640. Shipboard mortality was in the order of 20 percent. In addition the English sold a few thousand of this total to the Spanish Americas.

than a million free and coerced migrants – but not much above a million – over two centuries, and the English, about 800,000.[3] The French and Dutch, even counting Brazil as Dutch in the second quarter of the century, brought a fifth or less of the English total. The English contribution was thus rather exceptional in its intensity, if not in its mix of peoples from Africa and Europe.

Free or indentured European labour predominated at first. In the mid-seventeenth century, there were probably just under 100,000 English settlers evenly split between mainland North America and the Caribbean. Between them they owned a very few thousand slaves. Coerced African labour was largely confined to Brazil and Spanish America. Fifty years later more than 150,000 African slaves laboured under English masters, most of them in the Caribbean. There were probably more African slaves under English control in 1700 than in the rest of the European Americas combined, with the possible exception of Spanish America.[4] The shift in the centre of gravity of plantation produce – for plantations colonies were the major target of both groups – was just as sharp. The English Caribbean had overtaken Brazil as the leading sugar produc-ing region in the world before the end of the seventeenth century and by 1700 the value of English plantation produce – sugar, rum, tobacco, ginger, indigo – probably rivalled that produced in the rest of the Americas.[5] But the growth of the white population from both migration and natural population increase was also rapid. By 1700 there were 260,000 of British descent in the Americas, in excess of those des cended from the Portuguese in Brazil, and while still

3. Peter Boyd-Bowman has estimated 437,000 migrants to the Spanish Americas down to 1650 and Magnus Mörner using the Chaunu's shipping data has estimated 750,000 down to 1700. Unlike the Wrigley and Schofield estimates for England neither of these allow for return migration. The number of people leaving Africa for the Spanish Americas before 1700 was probably less than 600,000 (Curtin, *The Atlantic Slave Trade*, 116, 119; Lovejoy, 1983, 479-482). For Brazil emigration from Portugal has been estimated at 600,000 before 1700, to which should be added 400,000 from Africa. This last figure assumes those arriving in Brazil during the Dutch period should be classed as arriving in the Dutch Americas, and that after 1650 estimates of the Portuguese slave trade should be reduced to at least half of what Curtin estimated. For my argument on this last point see Eltis "Relative Importance of Slaves".
4. Calculated from McCusker, *Rum Trade*, pp. 584, 692-708; Schnakenbourg, "Statistiques pour l'histoire", pp. 41, 44. Cf. Watts, *West Indies*, pp. 311-320, although Watts does not appear to have incorporated either the Schnakenbourg or McCusker archival data in his estimates. Population data for seventeenth century Brazil are limited. Simonsen, *Historia Economica do Brasil*, p. 271 suggests 110,000 slaves in Brazil in 1660. For my own assessment I have taken the relatively solid data for the Captaincy of Bahia in 1724 from Schwartz, *Sugar Plantations*, p. 88, and adjusted them downward in proportion to changes in sugar exports between 1698-1702 and 1721-25 (*ibid.*, pp. 502-503). I have further assumed that the slave population of Brazil was double that of the Captaincy of Bahia in 1700. This suggests a slave population of about 55,000 in that year. The great unknown is Spanish America. The low level of specie exports from and slaves imports into this region at the end of the 17th C. would suggest a small slave population.
5. Schwartz, "Colonial Brazil", pp. 430-431; McCusker, *Rum Trade*, p. 896.

below their Hispanic counterparts, they were increasing much more rapidly and would overtake them in the next century.[6]

From an even longer and wider perspective, the English experience is just as striking. The English who accounted for less than five percent of western Europe's population in 1550 made up nearly seven percent in 1680 and fifteen percent in 1900. If we include the neo-Europes then the English at home and abroad constituted 7.5 percent of Europeans at home and abroad in 1680. Thus, well before the eighteenth century began, the English had already become 50 percent more numerous than other Europeans in relative terms in a century or so, and, as argued below, with no obvious loss of material well-being.[7] In the slave traffic they were probably responsible for one out of every two Africans taken to the Americas between 1662 and 1807. Their dominant position from 1500 to 1862 is eroded only because they came on the slave trading scene relatively late and departed relatively early. In the process of shipping people from two continents to the Americas and eventually establishing the most sophisticated form of labour exploitation developed anywhere to that point, the English created a network of "communication and community" across the Atlantic unrivalled in its depth, complexity and reliability of contact, and quite unprecedented in the history of long-distance migration.[8]

I

These crude estimates and comparisons raise two major issues. First, what can explain the sudden and somewhat unprecedented English activity. Whatever the origins of this impulse, it seems clear that it affected African as much as English people. Second, how do these two streams compare to one another?

6. Gemery, "Emigration from the British Isles", p. 212, estimates 257,000 in English America in 1700. McCusker, *Rum Trade*, pp. 584, 586, 712, whom Gemery did not use indicates 262,000, but includes non-British residents. For Brazil, Oliver Onody has 300,000 non-indigenous residents at the end of the seventeenth century, with about one third slaves – consistent with the comments in note 3 above ("Quelques traits caractéristiques", pp. 335-337). For Spanish America there are estimates of 575,000 for 1650 in Rosenblat, *Poblacion Indigena*, Vol. 1, p. 59. Immigration into Spanish America was at very low levels in the second half of the seventeenth century and comparison with data for 1825 (*ibid.*, p. 36) indicates an average annual growth between 1650 and 1825 of about one percent, though this growth was probably less at the beginning and greater at the end of this period. On the basis of Rosenblat's figures we might hazard 8 to 900,000 people in 1700.
7. Wrigley, *People, Cities and Wealth*, p. 216 calculates English ratios for western Europe alone. For the English share of the neo-Europes, I have used population data for the English Americas from Gemery, "Emigration from the British Isles", pp. 211-212, and have assumed that the English living in Ireland in 1680, were as numerous as those living in the Americas (certainly an underestimate).
8. Steele, *English Atlantic*.

Comparisons that go beyond the volume, direction and degree of coercion of the two should provide fresh insights for both. Analyses of migrations have not only been overwhelmingly country-specific, they have also focussed exclusively on either free or coerced streams of migrants, at least insofar as transoceanic movements of people are concerned. Yet European migration across the Atlantic clearly interacted with the slave trade from Africa. Certainly in the seventeenth century, periods and places which saw the transatlantic migratory stream overwhelmingly African or overwhelmingly European were the exception from an overall perspective. It is unfortunate that the literature, except when addressing the switch from servant to slave labour (and vice-versa, later), has not integrated the two. At some fundamental level the factors responsible for free migration from Europe also had a major shaping influence on the slave trade.

English hegemony in transatlantic migration could hardly have been predicted. In 1630 English possessions in the Americas were trivial by comparison with those of the Portuguese, Spanish and Dutch. English domestic society and the economy must have appeared similarly disadvantaged. Per capita income lagged behind that of the Dutch, and total output was dwarfed by that of France and Spain. Yet it is within the domestic sphere that we must begin investigations of the free and coerced migration that the English organized. From an economic perspective, the major external stimuli – a land-abundant Americas and the desire for imports and a high export demand – affected all countries. Holland, Spain, Portugal and France stood to gain from rising Atlantic demand as well as England. Yet the benefits apparently accrued to the latter in particular, despite the fact that the first three in this list had a head-start. Apart from lacking diverse and well-established overseas links, the English could not even produce most of the goods they traded in overseas markets. As late as the 1680s – and long after for some items – the English obtained iron bars, spirits, a wide range of textiles and hardware that they traded in Africa and the Americas from foreign suppliers, not from their own manufacturers.[9] What was it that shaped the strong English response to generalised extra-European stimuli?

Part of the answer is to be found in the social and economic trends that England shared with the Netherlands. Changes in the English and Dutch domestic economies and societies – experienced to a lesser degree by other West Europeans – in effect allowed the merchant elite of these two countries to invade and greatly expand external markets including those in the Atlantic. The starting point of the argument is the recognition that free migration is no more associated with economic destitution – at either point of origin or point of arrival – than is its coerced counterpart. More specifically, free transatlantic emigration was not a sign of desparate economic circumstances in early modern Europe. The decline of the Spanish economy and the "seventeenth century crisis" did

9. K.G. Davies, *Royal African Company*, pp. 165-179.

not generate a mass movement to the Americas despite the abundance of land in Meso and South America. Indeed migration from Spain was much greater in the century before 1600 than the century after. Similarly German migration was far more important in the eighteenth century than during and after the Thirty Years War. Before the cheap passages of the nineteenth century, transoceanic population shifts were apparently associated with economic expansion, a measure of prosperity in the donor as well as the recipient region, and a rising potential for ocean-going trade, rather than with economic contraction.

This was not just a question of accumulating enough to pay for the transatlantic fare. Economic motives have usually provided the basic reason for migration, but given the absence of a durable "peace beyond the line" before the eighteenth century, individuals usually made the transatlantic move without stepping outside the political boundaries in which they were initially located – except for persecuted minorities such as the Jews and Huguenots. In broad terms the ability to establish and hold transatlantic territory, and provide a market for its exports implied both economic strength on the part of colonisers, and the flexibility to ship resources, particularly people, across the oceans. Thus prosperity at the end of the voyage – the point of attraction – was normally associated with a measure of material well-being and the availability of a pool of labour and capital at the beginning – the zone of provenance.

The English and Dutch cases demonstrate the point. Overseas expansion was both preceded and accompanied by profound changes within the domestic sphere which made the economy both stronger and more flexible. While the changes themselves are well known, their implications for transoceanic expansion and migration in particular have received much less attention. Indeed, despite the clear chronology, scholars have generally searched harder for the effects of overseas expansion on European economic performance than vice-versa. Three inter-related characteristics of English and Dutch agriculture and family life, each of which were less common elsewhere, are pertinent. One was the early emergence of the nuclear family. A second was the non-feudal nature of land ownership together with the early move to enclose common lands. A third was the related productivity advancements in food production that permitted a larger non-agricultural population.[10]

The first of these is not an indicator of economic well-being, so much as a prerequisite of enhanced responsiveness to economic opportunities, or at least an ability to absorb changes in the socio-economic system. Wrigley and Schofield have pointed out the key role of nuptiality and the nuclear family in the link between fertility and real income in pre-industrial England. In a regime

10. See the discussion in Braudel, *Identity of France*, Vol. 1, pp. 103-109; MacFarlane, *Origins of English Individualism*, pp. 135-140, 174-175; De Vries, *Dutch Rural Economy*, pp. 107-173; De Vries, *European Urbanization*, pp. 116-118, 210-212.

of nuclear families, marriage is a crucial economic decision, and the incentive to search for economic alternatives, one of which might be emigration, is altogether greater than in a system of extended families.[11] On the land tenure issue, heritable peasant tenure in parts of both England and The Netherlands was already lost by the end of the middle ages, and customary dues payable to the lord had evolved into variable rents. The replacement of copyhold by leasehold between the fifteenth and seventeenth centuries was more complicated than a simple landowner-initiated conversion at the death of a tenant posited by Brenner. Courts could interpret copyhold as carrying with it rights of inheritance. However, outright purchase of freeholds by either tenant or owner was at least as common as conversion to leasehold, and larger assemblies of land by even sub-tenants of copyholders not unknown.[12] The point for the present argument is that both the average size and the market orientation of English farming operations increased in the early modern period, a trend reinforced by gentry enclosure of common land. Attachment to the land was simply weaker and less widespread in England and the Low countries than elsewhere, and the dependence on wages greater. But the major link between agriculture and migration is not landholding tenure, but rather agricultural productivity. English and Dutch agriculture proved capable of supporting a steadily increasing non-agricultural population after 1600 with little dimunition in general living standards in the long run.[13] The non-agricultural pool of people were not bound to migrate, but were likely to prove responsive to opportunities that might include internal or overseas migration. From one perspective this was underemployment of the domestic labour force, from another, improved responsiveness to market forces.

Improved productivity was not confined to the agricultural sector. The advances in manufacturing and services, particularly transportation are well known in the case of the early modern Netherlands. For England, the vagrancy issue and subsistence crises between 1500 and 1660 have supported a large literature and have tended to obscure the fact that in the non-agricultural sphere too, the English position improved over this period relative to all Continental states except perhaps for the Dutch. Between the mid fourteenth and the early sixteenth centuries the basic English export, which throughout the middle ages had comprised raw wool, became woollen cloth.[14] In the first half of the

11. Wrigley, *Peoples, Cities and Wealth*, pp. 215-241; Rogers, *Family Building*, pp. 1-15.
12. Brenner, "Agrarian Class Structure"; Hoyle, "Tenure and the Land Market".
13. There is still considerable debate on when yields per acre began to increase, but probate studies and a new approach using labour inputs suggest 1600 as a likely starting point in England. See the essays by Robert Allen, Gregory Clark and especially Paul Glennie ("Measuring Crop Yields in Early Modern England") in Campbell and Overton, *Land, Labour, and Livestock*, pp. 255-283; and Clark, "Yields per Acre".
14. Carus Wilson, "Trends in the Export"; Bowden, *Wool Trade*, pp. 37-38. The same pattern

seventeenth century new woollen fabrics supplemented and eventually overtook the traditional English shortcloths among exports from London. Major developments in the substitution of coal for wood occurred, as well as new processes in metallurgy. The relative position of English technology in Europe improved markedly in two centuries before 1700.[15] Import substitution policies, aggressively pursued by the English, but not by the Dutch, may have been significant in the eighteenth century.[16] But neither this nor simple export demand, however rapid its expansion, can explain early English growth: all governments attempted to substitute domestic goods for imports. On the eve of the English Civil War per capita exports were £0.32 in official values – including reexports. By the 1660s this ratio had more than doubled to £0.72, and by 1700 amounted to about £1.27.[17]

Similar trends are apparent in the service sector. The shipping of general cargoes from England had been dominated by non-British shippers in the Middle Ages. The Hanse towns played a dominant role in the woollen trade with Flanders, for example. In the seventeenth century the Dutch dominated the bulk commodity trades of northern Europe, but in the "rich trades" of the Atlantic and the East Indies, requiring a ship quite different from the Dutch fluit, the English were able to hold their own with the Dutch.[18] Overall English mer-

of structural change as that presented here is traced in Inikori, "Slavery and the Development of Industrial Capitalism". For Inikori, however, the source of structural change in the English economy is shifts in demand, in particular export demand, and more especially demand from the Atlantic system. As suggested below, the absence of a generalised growth and industrialization process similar to the English pattern in those other western European economies that had large connections to the Atlantic system (France, Holland and Portugal) would seem to question this approach.

15. Nef, *Conquest of the Material World*, pp. 121-328; Fisher, "London's Export Trade".
16. O'Brien *et al.*, "Political Components of the Industrial Revolution". For the argument that such policies were critical before 1700 see Inikori, "Slavery and the Development of Industrial Capitalism".
17. The calculation of these ratios is as follows: for 1640 Fisher ("London's Export Trade", pp. 153-154) lists values of commodities other than shortcloths exported from London by English and foreign merchants at £694,856 of which £454,914 are woollens. Shortcloths "almost equalled in value the trade in [...] the newer fabrics" and the value of these is set at £400,000. To convert London trade into English trade a ratio of 0.67 is used as the divisor. For the 1660s – actually an average of 1663 and 1669 – and 1700, export data are from Davis, "English Foreign Trade", p. 166. For population data (for 1641, 1666 and 1701 respectively) see Wrigley and Schofield, *Population History of England*, pp. 528-529. Europe in the last phase of the Thirty Years War could not be expected to provide strong markets for English exports and the 1640 figure is likely below the long term trend. Nevertheless, this is strong growth indeed, and the growth rate in the generation before the 1660s was probably in excess of that in the last third of the century. We should also note that reexports were important in this process, but this drew on many regions outside the Americas, and the root of its growth lay in a highly competitive English merchant fleet and a bulking, credit and distribution system in London, the chief entrepot in this business, as well, of course as the Navigation Acts.
18. Barbour, "Dutch and English Merchant Shipping".

chant shipping tonnage increased fivefold in the century after 1582. The rate
of growth was somewhat faster after 1629 than before, but there was little
difference in this growth in the quarter centuries before and after 1660.[19] Large
increases in mercantile credit and insurance facilities occurred, much of it before
the massive growth of re-exports – the most important source of the general
expansion of English trade in the second half of the seventeenth century.[20] It
is also clear that London's ability to generate large pools of capital was established
early. The London of the 1640s and 1650s was well able to organise credit for
Cromwell's ventures as well as the multitude of private opportunities for
investment that those ventures provided – not least in Ireland.

The cumulative impact of these trends was that the relative position of the
small English economy in Europe improved substantially well before industrialization as conventionally defined or the establishment of significant colonies.[21]
Such trends made possible both a strong expansion of all English foreign trade
and the creation of overseas colonies. The most prosperous of these used capital,
skills, and initially labour from the metropolitan centre to produce commodities
which supplemented in a small way the dietary, recreational and fashion needs
of the English.

The discussion so far has stressed the common trends in English and Dutch
domestic developments. Two obvious questions arise from this. First why, with
this shared domestic experience, was Dutch overseas expansion so markedly
different from its English counterpart – especially in relation to settlement
colonies and migration? A second, and as we shall see, related question, is why
the streams of migration became geographically more separate toward the end
of the seventeenth century: the African going to the tropical and semi-tropical
Americas, the European increasingly to the temperate zones.

On the first of these, the missing term on the Dutch side of the Dutch-English
equation is emigration. In the two centuries before 1800, the Dutch experienced
net *im*migration of half a million people, almost all of them from other parts of
north-western Europe. The English over the same period, had a net *e*migration
of 1.25 million, almost all of whom settled around the Atlantic basins. Perhaps
a mere 30,000 people left The Netherlands for the Americas and Africa on a
net basis, and many of these were not Dutch. The East Indies were rather more
important, but even there, probably less than 1,000 different Dutch individuals

19. Davis, *Rise of the English Shipping Industry*, pp. 11, 15.
20. Barbour, "Marine Risks and Insurance"; Davis, "English Foreign Trade", pp. 150-166.
21. There is remarkable unanimity on the economic and social trends that preceded English –
    and indeed European – overseas expansion. Three major syntheses on European expansion
    in the early modern period – familiar to countless students in the English speaking world –
    are by Eric Jones, Eric Wolf and Immanuel Wallerstein. Each is written from a radically
    different world view (literally). Yet the uniqueness of late-Medieval and early modern Europe,
    and more specifically England is a theme common to all three.

a year left for the East Indies on a net basis – or less than 200,000 in total – most of them sailors and soldiers rather than labour for an export sector. Such departures from The Netherlands were always swamped by arrivals from all sources.[22]

The reasons for this discrepancy, so critical for explaining patterns of early modern overseas migration are to some extent the obvious ones. The English population was two and one half times the size of the Dutch. The structural changes undergone by the English economy in the early modern period may have led to improved living standards and international competitiveness, but the Dutch economy in the same period did much better again. Like the English, the Dutch may have had lacked the ties to the land and pre-modern social structures that inhibited migration, but more important, with relatively high incomes they also lacked the English incentive to emigrate. In addition, the location of the Netherlands and the internal waterways that linked it with the poorer areas of Europe, especially Germany, ensured a steady flow of migrants into the country. England was much more isolated by comparison. A dispropor-tionate share of immigrants into The Netherlands served in the army and merchant marine, and indeed became emigrants. For every Dutch there was at least one non-Dutch overseas migrant between 1600 and 1800, and the above estimates of Dutch emigration have to be doubled to take these into account. After making all allowances for these factors, however, the difference between the English and the Dutch experiences – the net emigration of the one and the net immigration of the other – still stands out, and there may be a case for less tangible factors.

Despite the progressive Dutch agricultural and manufacturing sectors, the elites of Zeeland and Holland who organised overseas endeavours appear to have placed rather more emphasis on exchange than the production activities stressed by their London counterparts. Perhaps because of the shaping influence of the war with Spain, investors in Amsterdam organised first around large companies and sent out expeditions aimed at plunder and creating and protecting trade routes. By contrast, and at considerable risk of over-simplification, the miriard of small overseas English ventures in the first half of the seventeenth century, most of which failed, were constantly searching for something to grow – in the aftermath, of course, of the search for precious metals which preoccupied everyone at first. The Royal African Company and official Plantations corre-spondence has abundant evidence of the search for new plants and methods, and the post-Columbian global exchange of flora acquired a modern, systematic and purposeful form in the seventeenth century. When the English found what they were looking for – varieties of cotton, tobacco and eventually sugar – often with

22. J. Lucassen, *Dutch Long Distance Migration*, pp. 20-23, 35-42; and Wrigley and Schofield, *Population History of England*, pp. 528-529.

Dutch help, it was usually the Dutch that carried it back to Europe. Indeed between 1600 and 1650 there was some specialisation of labour in Dutch and English activities in the Atlantic world. When Dutch plantations did take root as in Surinam, they had a large English component. The Dutch Americas, like the Dutch East Indies and the Dutch Gold Coast, comprised trading emporia: St. Eustatius and Curacao in the slave trade, Nieuw Amsterdam in the fur trade.

II

Yet the English drive for plantations, in the seventeenth century sense of that word, nevertheless changed form after 1650. Closer examination of this permits some fresh insights into not just English migration, but that of other European and African as well. At one level – the level in fact on which most of the literature on the switch from white to black labour in the Americas is to be found – the disengagement of English and African migrant streams appears driven by demographic and economic change. At another level, however, there were clearly some critical non-economic, socio-cultural forces at work that historians might profitably reexamine. We take up each of these major areas in turn.

A fresh perspective may still be possible on the economic- demographic front. The above discussion of the domestic English economy suggests that the lower cost of English services, the sophisticated London credit facilities, and the availability of English labour for migration made possible the establishment of the English plantation system using white indentured rather than slave labour initially.[23] Between one and two thousand Africans a year arrived in Barbados in the 1640s, rising to 2,000 a year in the 1650s. By 1660 the island's white and black populations were in rough balance, though whites were still more numerous elsewhere.[24] Throughout this period more whites than blacks arrived in the Caribbean, however, and far more white people went to the Caribbean than to the North American mainland before 1660. The fact that the African

23. Morgan, "Labor Problem at Jamestown"; Beckles, *White Servitude and Black Slavery*; Eltis, "Labour and Coercion in the English Atlantic World".
24. Population data form an important part of any assessment of arrivals prior to 1660. The best review of the evidence on the white population of Barbados is Gemery, "Emigration from the British Isles", pp. 219-220. John J. McCusker has also done the basic archival work on this and in addition presents the evidence on the black population in the Caribbean in McCusker and Menard, *Economy of British America*, pp. 153-154. Few Africans could have arrived in the English Americas outside Barbados before 1660. As late as 1672 there were less than 2,600 Africans in the whole of the English Leewards with nearly three-quarters in Nevis ("A particular of the Leeward Islands", British Library, Egerton mss. 2395, fol. 530). For direct evidence of slave arrivals before 1660 see Puckrein, *Little England*, pp. 67-72; and Eltis, "British Transatlantic Slave Trade".

population climbed more rapidly than its white counterpart in Barbados at least, is because white people could leave, particularly servants and prisoners at the end of their term – perhaps in search of land. Well over 100,000 people left England in each of the 1640s and 1650s decades – the largest decadal net migration of English up to that point. With Ireland in rebellion, Jamaica not acquired until 1655 and a new demand for labour triggered by sugar, it seems likely that many of them went to sugar growing areas.[25] Barbados exported 11,500 metric tons of sugar on average in 1665 and 1666.[26] Fifteen years earlier at mid-century, sugar output in the English Caribbean could not have been more than one or two thousand tons, but the major part of the labour force of both the Barbadian sugar and the Chesapeake tobacco sectors was likely of English origin until well into the 1650s.

After 1650 the continued expansion of the English economy, both domestic and colonial, was threatened by a diminishing population.[27] There were actually more people living in England in the mid-1650s than at any time thereafter down to the 1720s. For the three decades, 1651 to 1680, the mean rate of natural increase was actually negative. In the 1680s there were perhaps eight percent fewer people in England than a quarter of a century earlier. Estimated age and sex distributions suggest that the impact on the domestic labour force was not as immediate as for the population as a whole, but this was nevertheless the only time between the sixteenth and twentieth centuries that the English population declined.

The domestic response to this was rising real wages and decided swing in the pamphlet literature against emigration and in favour of coercing those who would not offer more work in response to rising wages. In Scotland there was first the reinstitution then the intensification of serfdom.[28] In England there were revisions of the Poor Laws in 1662, 1683 and 1697. These encouraged local authorities to establish permanent physical facilities for the poor and facilitated a shift from the concept of the poorhouse to that of the workhouse. Children and the old were to be set to work at as early and as late an age as possible, in the former case in the hope of encouraging "habits of industry" in later life.[29]

25. Gemery estimates 95,000 English emigrants heading for the Caribbean 1640-1660 ("Emigration from the British Isles", p. 215. Dunn, *Sugar and Slaves*, pp. 20, 55. Sugar production in Jamaica began slowly.

26. Eltis, "New Estimates". The mean of London imports for 1663 and 1669 taken from CO 388/2, fol. 7-11, 13-17 is 7,500 long tons.

27. This paragraph and part of the next are based on Wrigley and Schofield, *Population History of England*, pp. 207-209, 227, 441-449.

28. For the literature on this and a fuller presentation of these ideas see Eltis, "Labour and Coercion in the English Atlantic World".

29. Spinning flax was widely advocated for this group "who cannot see to wind Silk, nor yet stitch bodies, or work with a needle." Firmin, *Some Proposals for the Imploying of the Poor*, p. 8. One of the best discussions of the attempts to extract work from the poor after 1660 is still

Several pamphleteers advocated the use of machines in special workhouses to increase the pace of work in a striking parallel to the gang-labour system on Caribbean sugar plantations. Schools for the poor – and almost everyone who addressed the issue advocated these – were aimed at both increasing hours of work as well as work intensity during those hours.[30] Success from the employers standpoint is suggested by rising per capita export ratios and the growth of exports to continental Europe which suggest continued improvement in the productivity of the English relative to other Europeans.

For the colonies, rising real wages reinforced the impact of a declining English population. The labour crisis was more severe for plantation Americas, especially the sugar colonies, than for the domestic economy.[31] In the 1650s English emigration was nearly twenty percent larger than in the 1640s, but by now there was much stronger competition for migrants from elsewhere in the English Empire, noticeably Ireland. Here and, increasingly as the century wore on, in the Chesapeake too, mortality rates for migrants were less severe than in the West Indies and lower, too, than in the very earliest days of settlement. It is also likely that the availability of land in North America drew people away from Barbados. After 1655 English emigration in general declined slowly at first and then drastically, approaching the lowest levels estimated in the modern era at the end of the century. For the English Caribbean, the pressure on the supply of labour from England must have begun shortly after 1650, and in the Chesapeake, the same pressures began to be felt after 1660.

Table 1 shows the destinations and status, broken down by quinquennia, of 21,254 emigrants in the years 1651 to 1680 (though precise destinations in the Americas are available for only 17,557 of these). The data are the product of genealogical research, and comprise 11 percent of total departures for the Americas from England as estimated by Henry Gemery. The major single source is the registrations of indentured servants at Bristol, but other sources containing data on non-servant migrants contribute over half of the sample, so that investigation beyond previously published work on servants is possible.[32] To facilitate

Tawney, *Religion and the Rise of Capitalism*, ch. 4, sect. iv. See also Appleby, *Economic Thought and Ideology*, pp. 129-157; Furniss, *Position of the Laborer*.

30. The question of how much exploitation of the poor actually increased after 1650 has yet to be addressed systematically. There are relatively few known cases of the grandiose plans for extracting labour progressing beyond planning (e.g. the odd linen producing workhouse in London). In the end the high population densities and "the threat of starvation" meant that for domestic employers of labour such centres of coercion were unnecessary.

31. The importance of British demographic trends for immigration into Maryland is stressed in Green Carr and Menard, "Immigration and Opportunity".

32. For discussion of these data drawn from Coldham, *Complete Book of Emigrants, 1607-1660* and *ibid.*, *1661-1699* – particularly their representativeness in the light of various published estimates of transatlantic in the seventeenth century English Atlantic – see Stott, "Emigration from England". Migrants listed as "shippers" or merchants (5,000) have been excluded from

analysis the destinations are grouped into four major geographic and socio-economic categories: the export oriented Caribbean – Nevis, Jamaica, Barbados; the rest of the Caribbean; the export oriented mainland – the Chesapeake; and the rest of the mainland including Newfoundland. The first row of each of the panels of table 1 shows total departures for each region and five year period.

Inspection of the breakdowns in table 1 provides support for propositions that have become familiar from recent research on indentured servants and overall migrant flows. First, migrants were powerfully attracted to regions that had established export sectors. In effect, the Chesapeake and the Caribbean sugar islands were the destinations of 95 percent English migrants at this time. Second, the total number of migrants to all destinations declined steadily after 1660, though the decline here is somewhat sharper than scholars working with estimated data have found. Third, within the overall decline, the data here show the swing from the Caribbean to the North American mainland that has emerged from studies of both indentured servants and overall migrant flows. If we leave aside the large prisoner inflow to the Chesapeake in the early 1650s, discussed below, table 1 shows the Caribbean receiving more English emigrants down to mid 1660s, after which the Chesapeake and then the mainland broadly defined became the dominant destinations.

It is thus apparent that the broad trends of timing and direction that indentured servants exhibited are also valid for other European migrant streams. Yet the parallel is not exact, and the deviations are critical for the present analysis. Table 1 also presents data for prisoners sent from England to the Americas. This group are of particular interest because, like African slaves, they were forced to leave the Old World against their will and were the only group from Europe that as a matter of course had no choice over destination. The prisoner category actually combines the two rather distinct groups of prisoners of war and convicted felons. The former account almost entirely for the large exodus of prisoners in two batches to Virginia in 1651 and 1653, comprising Scots and Irish in the main. Convicts, the product of the English judicial system, account for almost all the rest. Virginia and Maryland received very few prisoners other than the Scots and Irish group at this time, and there must have been particular reasons, not yet apparent, for sending the latter to the Chesapeake. A comparison of the sugar islands with the Chesapeake shows that the former region received 88 percent of the prisoners in the sample leaving England after 1655. This is not far from the 95 percent of all slaves carried on English slave ships that Jamaica, Nevis and Barbados absorbed in the 1662-1680 period, and given the eighteenth century

the data because many of these individuals appear more than once either for the same voyage or different voyages. In addition Coldham's sources seem particularly thin for the 1642 to 1650 period for which there are records of only 491 migrants, with only single entries for some years. Analysis here is thus confined to the post 1650 period.

history of transportation to the Chesapeake, legislation in Virginia banning convict migrants in 1670 (and Maryland in 1676) is scarcely an adequate explanation of the pattern.[33] More important, table 1 also shows that prisoners made up a steadily rising share of all English emigrants leaving for the sugar islands after 1650. As emigration to the sugar islands declined, the share of those migrants comprising convicts grew from one or two percent in the 1650s to over half the total flow in the 1670s. Although the numbers never approached those from Africa and never compensated for the fall in servant and free migration, it is clear that the slave trade was not the only coerced migration that accelerated after 1650.[34]

English convicts notwithstanding, the dominant migrant stream to the sugar islands was the one from Africa by the early 1660s. English merchants who had first created the plantation complex with indentured labour, were able to fashion an unprecedented reponse to the colonial labour crisis. Indentured labour was replaced with slaves, and to a lesser extent convicts, and the English plantation complex assumed characteristics not seen before in the Americas. By no later than the 1660s, and probably from the 1640s the English were supplying almost all their own slaves and many too for the Spanish, a half-century prior to their formal accession to the asiento privilege in the Treaty of Utrecht. At a time when shipping costs absorbed half the price of an African slave in the Americas, the key to English domination of the slave trade was the productivity of the slave trading sector of its shipping industry. A crude comparison of total factor productivity in the English slave trade from the late 1670s with that of the French trade from the early eighteenth century suggests that the former group, mainly the monopoly Royal African Company, were significantly more efficient than their French counterparts.[35]

The Dutch were probably more of a competitive threat to the English slave trader than the French at this time. Postma's data do not allow direct comparisons because they contain no data on crew sizes, but it should be noted that between 1660 and 1713, for every slave shipped by the Dutch, the English shipped between three and four. It should also be noted that both nations were trying to sell to the Spanish, and the Dutch had as great an access to the English Caribbean islands as did the English interloper traders (those English who were separate from the Royal African Company).[36] Despite the Dutch role in selling

---

33. Convict labour and political prisoners are discussed in Beckles, *White Servitude and Black Slavery*, pp. 52-58. The slave ratio is calculated from Eltis, "British Transatlantic Slave Trade".
34. For early transportation see Beattie, *Crime and the Courts*, pp. 470-483; Coldham, *Emigrants in Chains*, pp. 3-43.
35. Eltis and Richardson, "Productivity in the Atlantic Slave Trade".
36. Postma, *Dutch in the Atlantic Slave Trade*, p. 110. For Dutch sales to English islands see Henry Carpenter and Thomas Belchamber, Nevis, June 3, 1686, in Public Record Office (henceforth PRO) series T70, Vol. 12, p. 128; and Edward Parsons, Sept. 7, 1688, Montserrat, *ibid.*, p. 101.

slaves to all-comers in the Caribbean, gold remained their chief concern in Africa throughout this period. Indeed the Dutch Atlantic trade by comparison with its focus on gold evokes more of a past Spanish than a future English preeminence. The English increased their market share in the slave trade as the Dutch share declined. This occurred, moreover, in a period when the price of African slaves in the Caribbean fell and quantities carried increased.[37] In short, the rise of English slave trading after 1650 was even more spectacular than the rise of the English slave system as a whole.

In summary, expansion at home and abroad coincided with a tightening supply of white labour in both England and the Americas. In the colonies the productivity of the English slave fleet allowed the expansion to proceed. Given an export market, ocean-going and plantation technologies, a sophisticated structure of financial intermediation, and a refusal of either English or Africans to work in plantation agriculture voluntarily, land abundance dictated slavery, an issue to which we will return in the next section. Labour costs (slave prices) fell from the 1650s to the 1680s, and then began to increase. At home there was a combination of higher wages and increasingly draconian social legislation, underpinned by relatively high population densities. But the end result was from one perspective remarkably similar. Exports from both England (woollen textiles) and the colonies (sugar and tobacco) increased strongly in the face of declining prices for all these commodities.[38] Thus the explosive rise to preeminence of the English slave system was stimulated and shaped by two major influences. One was the performance of the English economy relative to its continental counterparts. The English economy probably experienced productivity gains in excess of those of any other European economy in the century before the creation of the English slave colonies suggesting that in this case slave regimes existed because of European economic expansion, not the reverse. The other was the decrease of the English population in the second half of the seventeenth century, coupled with the appearence of attractive alternative destinations for those that did seek to leave England.

III

The preceding discussion is to some extent a gloss on the analysis of the switch from European to African labour that Galenson and Menard among others

37. Manning, *Slavery and African Life*, p. 178; Beckles, *White Servitude and Black Slavery*, p. 117.
38. Rogers, *History of Agriculture and Prices*, Vol. 5, pp. 462-463; Posthumus, *Inquiry into the History of Prices*, Vol. 1, pp. 503, 507, 515-516. The volume of English cloth exported to major markets in continental Europe for selected years is in Priestley, "Anglo-French Trade", pp. 46-47.

provided over a decade ago.[39] Yet to leave the discussion at this level is unsatisfactory because the switch was something much more than either an attempt
to increase or maintain profits, or an attempt to cope with the epidemiological
environment of the Americas. If it had been the former, planters would have
used Europeans as slaves, not Africans; it was obviously cheaper to bring people
from Europe, especially if they were already convicts, than to bring them from
Africa. If it had been the latter, in other words if European life expectancy on
Caribbean sugar plantations had been too short, then we should expect to find
some evidence on which planters based their decision. The reason there is none
is because planters never tried to use European slaves, and indeed could not even
conceive of this option. There are really two issues here which the literature
has conflated. First why was slavery reintroduced when it had already died out
at least in north-west Europe, and second why were the slaves non-European.
Economics and demographics certainly explain the former. They cannot account
for the latter.[40]

Africans went to the Americas as chattel slaves for life. Any progeny were also
slaves. In Coldham's sample of 21,254 emigrants between 1651 and 1680, the
mean length of term for 10,011 servants was 53.1 months (SD 14.2). Pregnancy
could result in a lengthening of this term, but of course the master had no claim
over the newborn child. Convicts in the same sample are much less well
represented, but the mean term for 76 of these was 114.2 months (SD 13.6),
with the difference between these means significant at the .01 percent level.[41]
It might be added that no sentence in an English court at this time required hard
labour from a convicted felon. It was the merchant and the owner of the
contract in the Americas that exacted the labour – in effect, to pay transport
costs. The fact that the term was longer than for indentured servants was
probably because convicts were less subject to careful selection and were more
likely to escape. The term thus incorporated a risk premium. Life sentences did
not exist, much less penal servitude for life, and as with servants, no planter had
any claim over the progeny of convicts. All Europeans exacted capital punishment, and some applied torture, but slavery apparently was something worse
than either (despite millenia in which it was accepted as an alternative to death),
and had come to be reserved for non-Europeans.

A closer examination of English and African migrant flows provides further
evidence of just how differently the English, and by implication other Europeans, viewed Africans from themselves. In the process it shows some of the

---

39. Galenson, *White Servitude in Colonial America*; Menard, "From Servants to Slaves".
40. For a full presentation of this argument see Eltis, "Europeans and the Rise and Fall of African
    Slavery".
41. Length of term for the Monmouth rebels in 1686 was ten years. See Hotten, *Original Lists
    of Persons*, pp. 315-345.

profound non-economic factors that shaped the shift of peoples from the Old World to the New. Table 2 shows male and child ratios of samples of major categories of migrants into the English Americas. Contrary to what much of the literature has led us to expect, the forced migrants from Africa were much more demographically representative of the societies they left behind than were any of the European groupings.[42] Thus men made up just under half of the flow of slaves from Africa at this time, but close to three-quarters of all servants, over eighty percent of convicts, and most surprising, almost all of a rather limited sample of free emigrants. Children comprised just over ten percent of the African flow, but contributed trivial numbers to any of the English streams. Family migration did not exist for either free or coerced groups, though for rather different reasons. A large female presence was likely only when the family unit was involved or when governments intervened directly, and neither of these were common. Indeed the domination of families and free migrants in the Great Migration to New England in the 1630s – like the latter's religious overtones – was probably quite exceptional before the redemptioner movement from Germany in the next century. Certainly women were lacking in the earlier movements to the Spanish Americas.[43]

The relative absence of women in the European flows and their strong presence in the African provides insight into one of the driving forces behind migration. European women were not regarded as suitable for field labour, African women were. There was no more strictly economic reason for women forming a minor component of European streams than for Europeans not being slaves. The division of labour that kept European women from acquiring skills outside the home and generally kept them from field labour was a purely cultural construct. And like slavery it applied to Europeans, but not, in European eyes to Africans.[44] Europeans were prepared to see African women work in the plantation fields (though not, curiously, to learn skilled tasks on the plantation), but had barriers against using European women for most tasks outside the home. At a more fundamental level the differences in gender roles assigned to Europeans and Africans in the Americas reflected the "insider" status of the former and the "outsider" status of the latter.

The same point is apparent in the legal status and treatment of English indentured servants and African slaves in the early plantation colonies. One of

---

42. For a fuller discussion of this see Eltis and Engerman, "Was the Slave Trade Really Dominated by Men?".

43. See most recently Anderson, *New England's Generation*, pp. 12-45, especially 21-23. For Spanish migration see Boyd-Bowman, "Patterns of Spanish Emigration", p. 584; Altman, *Emigrants and Society*, pp. 176-178.

44. For a similar argument made two decades ago see Morgan, "Slavery and Freedom", p. 21. For the domestic servant orientation of female indentures in a later period at least, see Salinger, "'Send No More Women'", and Grubb, "Servant Auction Records".

the more recent contributions to this very old debate draws strong parallels between the social and material conditions of white and black labour in the early sugar economy of Barbados.[45] Yet it is the differences rather than the similarities that stand out. Apart from the length of servitude and heritability of status, servants had first claim on skilled occupations and when they rebelled or ran away they were less likely to suffer death as punishment. But perhaps the most dramatic evidence of the different status of black and white workers arises in the voyage to the sugar islands. Between 40 and 50 ships a year arrived at Jamaica from England in the 1680s and at least as many again at Barbados and the Leewards. Given the nature of the colonial trade, these one hundred or so ships always had less merchandise cargo on the westbound journey than when returning. In the same period perhaps three thousand migrants per year left England for the Caribbean.[46] Even allowing for the seasonal nature of migration or the heavier migration in the 1650s, it is unlikely that any ship carrying indentured servants, convicts or troops had a density of people per ton on board that approached that of a slave ship leaving Africa.

Early in 1686 in the aftermath of Monmouth's rebellion and about the time that 300 of their fellow rebels were executed – many hung, drawn and quartered – three ships left Weymouth and one Bristol carrying 376 rebels to plantations in Barbados and Jamaica. These ships carried from 81 to 103 prisoners with a mean of 94. Tonnage averaged 130, so that the prisoner/ton ratio was only 0.72, less than one third of the 2.3 Africans per ton on 281 English slavers between 1676 and 1700. A total of 33 prisoners died on the voyage. Shipboard mortality in the North Atlantic could be high, and servants and convicts endured experiences they had never before encountered, but it is unlikely that transportation history can provide any parallel to the transatlantic slave ship, even though profits for shipper and planter alike could have been increased by imposing slave-traffic like conditions on servants.[47]

45. Beckles, *White Servitude and Black Slavery*. The thrust of this work is broadly consistent with the positions of Emerson Smith, *Colonists in Bondage*; and Williams, *Capitalism and Slavery*, pp. 3-29, though it is interesting that Beckles rightly rejects the Handlin's position that in mid seventeenth century the English were not prejudiced against blacks. Much of this paragraph is based on Beckles's work, though the interpretation here is rather different.

46. Derived by doubling the net figure of departures estimated at 1,000 to 1,500 in Gemery, "Emigration from the British Isles", and Galenson, *White Servitude in Colonial America*, pp. 212-218. For the number of ships sailing to Jamaica see Gary M. Walton, "Trade Routes, Ownership Proportions and American Colonial Shipping Characteristics", in *Las rutas del Atlantico: trabajos del Noveno Coloquio Internacional de Historia Maritima* (Seville, 1969), pp. 471-502, cited in: Minchinton, *Naval Office Shipping Lists*, p. 9.

47. Calculated from Hotten, *Original Lists of Persons*, pp. 317-342, and CO 33/14. Beckles describes one of these ships, the "Betty" as disembarking 49 out of 100 embarked. In fact Beckles's source, Hotten, lists by name 81 prisoners embarked, lists seven by name who died (in a complete, not an incomplete bill of mortality as Beckles describes it), and then lists the 72 prisoners who landed

Finally in this section we should note one further intangible in European and African migration which is difficult to reduce to the immediate economic (or more accurately pecuniary) interests, of the migrants themselves. It was not only those organizing and drawing on migration that were influenced by cultural or at least non-economic factors in the sense that a traffic in European slaves, or a traffic in servants conducted in slave ship like conditions – could have generated more profits. Non-pecuniary motives were also important for the migrants themselves, those at least who were permitted to exercise choice. Early English transatlantic migration was intimately connected with the modernization process, the focal point of which – the creation of a modern labour force – is increasingly viewed by labour and economic historians as cultural rather than economic. The creation of a pool of potential workers is a separate issue from the mix of incentives and coercion best suited to obtain labour from those workers.[48]

Seventeenth century England may not have had slavery, but it did have severe laws against vagrancy and idleness the aim of which was the extraction of labour from those unwilling to volunteer it for wages. Waged labour in Christopher Hill's view had a very low status among the non-elite, and migration – perhaps within England, but increasingly without – may be viewed as an attempt to avoid this status and achieve the pre-modern ideal of a piece of land and independence from the labour market. The fact that smallholdings might mean less income than reliance on the labour market did not matter. Freedom dues in the form of land disappeared early for servants moving to the Americas, especially for those sailing to Barbados. But the prospects of land were as enticing for migrants as for the Diggers that chose not to migrate, and some Chartists nearly two hundred years later who attempted to set up a land-bank scheme. From this perspective indentured servitude was something to be entered into voluntarily and endured temporarily by young people as an escape route from waged labour in much the same way as Eric Foner has posited for the Republican working class of the mid-nineteenth century urban United States.[49]

At some point in the centuries touched on here, however, worker aspirations shifted. Perhaps the essential meaning of modernization is worker acceptance

---

at Barbados and the planters to whom they were sold. One prisoner presumably died or escaped before sale. Beckles also cites a ship owned by Thomas Rous in 1638 that arrived with only 80 servants alive out of 350. In fact the 80 refers to the number that died at sea, not the survivors. Apart from these cases Beckles presents firm mortality data on only one ship carrying servants or convicts and the mortality rate on this was 7 percent. Support for his approving quote of a 19th century writer that "one fifth of those who were shipped were flung to the sharks" is thus lacking. He is much closer to historic reality when he writes that "[i]n comparison with the slave trade, the numbers (in the servant trade) were considerably smaller and the conditions less barbaric" (Beckles, *White Servitude and Black Slavery*, pp. 65, 67).

48.   Engerman, "Coerced and Free Labor".
49.   Hill, "Pottage for Freeborn Englishmen"; Foner, *Free Soil, Free Labor*, pp. 11-29.

of waged labour and a stress on consumption of goods and services – for which pecuniary income is necessary – over non-pecuniary rewards in the form of leisure or independence. In the English case there was certainly a clear change in the tone of the pamphlet literature circulating among the elite away from low wages and coercive social legislation, and toward the advantages of high wages in creating both enhanced worker productivity and a market for goods. It is hardly surprising to see these arguments appearing in the second half of the seventeenth century as transatlantic labour markets tightened.[50]

Less is known about the aspirations of seventeenth century Africans. The scarcity of voluntary migration from Africa to the Americas would suggest not only that Europeans saw Africans as slaves, but also that land was abundant in Africa as well as the Americas. This is consistent with the low population densities in Africa and the stress in many African cultures on acquiring people as opposed to land.[51] It is also of note that when Africans and those of African descent obtained an element of choice at emancipation, those that could, left the plantations in search of land – the goal of seventeenth century English workers and some in the nineteenth century too. Nevertheless it would be surprising, given the very different cultural backgrounds of seventeenth century Africans and Europeans, if the aspirations of the two groups were the same. But because those who became slaves were not given choice, it is the goals of European workers that concern us here.

The major point is simple, though not widely explored in the literature: it was not just the refusal or inability of European merchants to organize a European (or more probably in the English case, an Irish) trade in slaves that ensured Africans would become slaves in the Americas, it was also the aspirations of the European worker. The demand for cheap plantation produce was part of the gradual, but nevertheless secular rise in well-being that set in after 1650 in the English case at least. This was accentuated by changing values on the part of the worker as plantation produce formed a part (albeit small) of the goods that the "modernised" worker was now beginning to demand. But it was not just the higher wages available in England after 1660 that reduced emigration, but a willingness to respond to those higher wages on the part of more English workers. Modernisation of the English work force thus meant more slavery in the Americas for Africans. From the mid-seventeenth century the English increasingly refused voluntarily field labour on sugar estates, though in the absence of Africans (and after the attendant rise in wages) some would no doubt have chosen such conditions.

---

50. Coats, "Changing Attitudes to Labour"; Engerman, "Coerced and Free Labor".
51. See Thornton, *Africa and Africans in the Making of the Atlantic World*, especially pp. 72-97; Miers and Kopytoff, "African Slavery".

The main thrust of this argument is not without irony. For English merchants, the cultural values, shared across English society, that ensured the classification of English workers as "insiders" and therefore exempt from slavery, generated a transatlantic slave trade in Africans. A more pecuniary or profit-maximising or "capitalist" attitude would have meant less African slavery in the Americas. For English workers, the opposite holds. "Modernisation" meant a greater responsiveness to incentives and acceptance of a labour market. Until the free labour markets of the North Atlantic became more integrated, this ensured fewer English emigrants, particularly to plantation areas, and more pressure on Africa. Ultimately, perhaps the irony evaporates. Modernisation, twentieth century European history notwithstanding, meant not only a conception of insider that went beyond Europe, but the acceptance of this conception by much of non-European world.

We can now return to the issue of the seventeenth century spurt of migration from both Europe and Africa, largely dominated by the English. Economic and social change within England (and in this, England was a precursor and an analogue for Europe) created a pool of potential migrants, and the technological and material means to realise this potential. Cultural values were, however, just as important as economic and demographic factors in shaping the direction and composition of migration to the English (and by implication, non-English Americas). Specifically these values ensured the growth of the slave trade from Africa when English population levels declined after 1660. Attitudes to consumption and work within Europe and shifting European perceptions of insider and outsider are just as important as developments in ocean-going technology and the skills of merchants in explaining the nature of transatlantic migration – particularly in the switch from the mainly European to the mainly African stream that the English initiated.

Table 1: Destination of Migrants Leaving England for the Americas by Prisoner and Non-Prisoner Status and Quinquennia, 1651-1680

Destination	1651–55	1656–60	1661–65	1666–70	1671–75	1676–80
Virginia/Maryland						
Total migrants	2376	846	1383	994	1027	958
Prisoners	2110	0	11	28	87	145
Row 2/Row 1	0.89	0	0.01	0.03	0.08	0.15
Other North-American mainland						
Total migrants	5	3	68	24	33	343
Prisoners	1	0	1	0	0	0
Row 2/Row 1	0.20	0	0.01	0	0	0
Sugar islands★						
Total migrants	269	4254	2091	813	910	617
Prisoners	3	79	719	380	513	328
Row 2/Row 1	0.01	0.02	0.17	0.46	0.56	0.53
Other Caribbean						
Total migrants	41	333	67	2	24	76
Prisoners	0	0	0	0	0	0
Row 2/Row 1	0	0	0	0	0	0
All destinations★★						
Total migrants	5778	6153	3352	1936	2015	2020
Prisoners	2152	92	842	416	600	473
Row 2/Row 1	0.37	0.02	0.25	0.21	0.30	0.23

★ Sugar islands comprise Jamaica, Barbados and Nevis
★★ Includes some with no specified destinations other than "the Americas".

Total migrants include some with no status defined. The possibility of such migrants being convicts is not very high given the nature of the records.

Source: Calculated from data entered from Coldham, *The Complete Book of Emigrants, 1607-1660*; idem, *The Complete Book of Emigrants, 1661-1699.*

Table 2: The Sex and Age Structure of Free and Coerced Migration to the English Americas, 1651-80: Major Regions of Disembarkation by Decade (Sample size in parentheses)

A Male ratio						
Destination	1651-60		1661-70		1671-80	
Virginia/Maryland						
Slaves	–	–	–	–	0.543	(541)
Convicts	1.0	(500)	0.837	(43)	0.922	(232)
Servants	0.718	(1004)	0.751	(2498)	0.768	(1533)
Free migrants	1.0	(1000)	–	–	–	–
Sugar islands★						
Slaves	–	–	0.536	(7067)	0.595	(21188)
Convicts	1.0	(82)	0.783	(1017)	0.705	(837)
Servants	0.710	(5012)	0.795	(1565)	0.805	(624)
Free migrants	0.999	(1209)	–	–	0.750	(4)
B Child ratio						
Destination	1651-60		1661-70		1671-80	
Virginia/Maryland						
Slaves	–	–	–	–	0.044	(541)
Convicts	0.0	(500)	0.0	(43)	0.0	(232)
Servants	0.0	(1004)	0.0	(2504)	0.003	(1543)
Free migrants	0.0	(1000)	–	–	0.041	(117)
Sugar islands★						
Slaves	–	–	0.121	(7067)	0.091	(20763)
Convicts	0.0	(82)	0.003	(1144)	0.0	(841)
Servants	–	–	0.001	(1569)	0.016	(628)
Free migrants	0.0	(1209)	–	–	0.0	(4)

★ Jamaica, Barbados and Nevis

Source: For Europeans see table 1. For Africans, a new slave ship data set; for a description of this see Eltis and Engerman, "Fluctuations in Sex and Age Ratios".

Was Migration Beneficial?*

Pieter C. Emmer

Introduction

Is migration economically beneficial? The theory holds that without migration the geographical differences in personal and national incomes would be even greater than they already are. Migration is economically beneficial for the sending region. Exporting people should provide sending regions with a more favourable combination of the factors of production. Migration is economically beneficial for migrants in that the value of their marginal product is higher in the receiving economy than in the sending economy. Migration yields the same economic benefit for the receiving areas in that they will – like the sending region – be able to obtain a more favourable composition of labour, nature, and capital.[1]

This theoretical framework will no doubt present problems when applied to historical material. In the past several waves of migrants either had no say in their migration or did not profit directly from the increased value of their labour after their move. A free market for migrants seems to have developed relatively recently in Africa, where much of the past internal migration and virtually all the migration movements to other continents consisted of slave traffic. Similarly, a small percentage of Asian migrants were unable to maximize their earning potential immediately after moving, since they had signed long-term contracts of indenture that severely restricted their position on the labour market in the new host countries.[2]

Second, migrants usually paid a price for moving. Such payment included both the actual defrayal of the transportation costs and the social and emotional costs of leaving behind family, relations, and their home environment. Adapting to a new environment and creating new social structures can also be included among the costs of migration.

*   I would like to express my sincere gratitude to David Eltis, Stanley Engerman, Farley Grubb, and Ralph Shlomowitz, who read an earlier version of this contribution and offered very valuable comments. None of these readers, however, is to blame for any shortcomings in this overview.
1.   Simon, "Economic Effects of Immigration", pp. 109-116.
2.   Miles, *Capital and Unfree Labour*.

Third, part of the intra and intercontinental migration was caused not by the quest for better economic opportunities, but also by ideological and political pressures. From the Jews and Huguenots of the seventeenth century to the population of the former Yugoslavia, refugee migrants did not move to improve their socio-economic position. In fact, the majority of political and religious refugees moved because they anticipated that their economic status would decline more at home than abroad.[3]

As for the sending regions, some of the negative aspects of migration are of great significance. Emigration entails a financial loss for the sending region in that the emigrants consumed food, labour, and medical and educational services before their departure. In the case of free migration the remittances sent home by the migrants did not necessarily repay these costs in full. In the African slave trade, however, these costs could have been recovered by charging a price for the slaves before departure. While this practice prevailed, the recipients of the price were not always the individuals who had invested in rearing the slaves. Moreover, the selling price of slaves may have reflected their market value, rather than their actual "production" costs (which could be considerably higher). The impact of emigration might also extend beyond a random reduction of the population. Some migration movements consisted mainly of highly skilled and wealthy people able to take along their expertise and money. In these migration movements, the usual beneficial effect of reducing the pressure of overpopulation might be offset by a disproportionate loss of educational, commercial, and financial expertise. Page Moch has argued that such a situation occurred when the Huguenots left France and the Sephardi Jews the Iberian peninsula.[4]

In addition, the beneficial effects of large-scale emigration may be counteracted in areas with low population densities by a disproportionate reduction in the infrastructure of roads, villages, and cities. Some Africanists have observed that tropical Africa was a relatively sparsely populated region, and that the external slave trades to the Atlantic and the Indian Ocean caused the growth of the population to stagnate. In turn, this stagnation prevented the construction of large cities and long-distance transportation networks, which were both crucial factors in the economic development of other continents.[5]

Last but not least, the various negative aspects of migration for the receiving societies merit consideration. The European successes overseas are in part attributable to their pathogens, which created large empty areas for settlement in the New World and Australasia by killing many millions of Amerindians, Aborigines, and Maori.

---

3. Durckhardt, "Glaubensflüchtlinge und Entwicklungshelfer", pp. 278-287.
4. Moch, *Moving Europeans*, p. 29.
5. Manning, *Slavery and African Life*, pp. 133, 134; Thornton, *Africa and Africans*, pp. 72-74; and Inikori (ed.), *Forced Migration*, pp. 51-58.

Despite the drawbacks of emigration, this practice usually increased the rate of economic growth in both the sending and receiving areas, as well as in the personal incomes of the migrants. Europe, North America, and Australasia, which were the continents most affected by internal and international migration, are now the wealthiest areas in the world. During the period 1781-1932, the United Kingdom and Portugal experienced a mass exodus of more than 40 and 30 percent of their respective populations, which surpassed emigration from any other country, region, or continent.[6] This finding raises the question as to whether the United Kingdom would have been the first industrial nation if emigration had not achieved a reduction in the size of its population during the seventeenth century and slowed the rapid growth of its population during the nineteenth century. In Portugal, however, the reduction in the size of the population and the lower growth rate alone were apparently not sufficient to initiate a process of industrialization. Asking the same question with respect to Asia hardly seems useful, given the relatively small volume of both internal and external migration. Last but not least, the demographic impact of the slave trade on the demography of Africa should be mentioned, especially since this issue is a subject of debate. It would be difficult to argue that forced emigration had a dramatic demographic impact on Africa as a whole. Without the slave trade, the West African population would have been only several million more than it actually was, as David Eltis has noted. While the slave trade must have caused depopulation in specific regions and during certain periods, it seems unlikely that the – counterfactual – demographic growth in Africa in the absence of the slave trade would have generated more economic growth. In fact, it is doubtful whether African agriculture could have supported many more people than it actually did. Recent research on nutrition and disease in Africa provides no grounds for reversing the argument that emigration rarely diminished and usually increased the incomes of both the people who stayed behind and the people who moved or were forced to move.[7]

6. Eltis, *Economic Growth*, p. 67.
7. Jones, *The European Miracle*, pp. 70-85; Eltis, *Economic Growth*, pp. 64-73. Manning, *Slavery and African Life*, p. 85 argues that without the slave trade, the population of sub-Saharan Africa would have been 40 percent larger. The author does not indicate that Africa could have fed a much larger population. Also see Inikori and Engerman, "Introduction: Gainers and Losers", p. 6. The impact of emigration on the population of England is discussed in: Wrigley and Schofield, *Population History of England*.

The Development of Two Migration Circuits Between 1500 and 1800 and the Atlantic

Much of the literature on early migration across the Atlantic provides a false sense of magnitudes. Usually, historians stress the large volume of two groups of migrants: those who voluntarily left Europe and those who involuntarily left Africa. The actual numbers were quite modest between 1500 and 1800: about 3 million Europeans and about 9 million Africans. On the average, therefore, 6,500 Europeans (or 0.03 percent of the contemporary population) left Europe per year. While the number of slaves transported annually from Africa to the New World was triple the average figure for European migration, it amounted to only 0.12 percent of the estimated population of West Africa at the time.[8]

In fact, the volume of trans-Atlantic migration is less impressive than the demographic development of these migrants once they reached the moderate zones of the New World. Four figures prove this assertion. The influx of about 3 million Europeans during the years 1500 to 1800 resulted in an estimated 13.5 million inhabitants of European descent in the New World around 1800. The corresponding figures for Africans differed dramatically: 9 million emigrated as slaves, and about 6 million individuals of African descent lived in the New World in 1800.[9]

These figures clearly demonstrate the existence of both a good and a bad circuit of migration across the Atlantic. Joining the good circuit of migration facilitated emancipation from a desolate situation of hunger and disease and offered a chance to build a better future overseas. Only in the New World was it possible to realize many contemporary ideals, such as land ownership, early marriage, and a large family. Some of these ideals may differ from present-day expectations in Western Europe with respect to improved quality of life. These aspirations did, however, help increase the population considerably, enabling one generation to double its size within two or three decades. In French Canada, which was an extreme example, children under the age of fifteen accounted for half the population, and the average number of surviving children per woman was higher than eight![10]

Participants in the second migration circuit faced completely different conditions. Moving from Africa and Europe to the tropical parts of the New World tended to shorten rather than lengthen the lives of the migrants and slaves, who usually had fewer rather than more children. Numerous factors

---

8. On the volume of intercontinental migration before 1800: Eltis, "Free and Coerced Transatlantic", pp. 252-255; Emmer, "European Expansion and Migration", pp. 1-13; Eltis, *Economic Growth* pp. 64-71.
9. Eltis, "Free and Coerced Transatlantic", pp. 251-255.
10. Davies, *The North Atlantic World*, pp. 63-80; and Fogel, *Without Consent or Contract*, p. 115.

underlie this discrepancy. The ill treatment of the migrants in the second circuit (who were mainly forced migrants) was an obvious culprit for blame. Also, scholars have suggested that the female slaves in the New World were unwilling to have children because their babies would be born into slavery; no wonder, many black women in the New World had abortions. Other researchers stress the imbalance between the sexes as the main cause for the decline in the African population of the New World.[11]

Unfortunately, none of these explanations solves all the demographic riddles. This fact can easily be demonstrated by considering the relatively small group of enslaved migrants from Africa (about 6 percent of those 9 million) who had the demographic good fortune to land in North America and by considering the half million Europeans (or about 17 percent of the total of 3 million before 1800) who had the bad fortune to go or to be shipped to the British, French, or Dutch parts of the Caribbean as indentured labourers, planters, or prisoners of war. The demographic growth of the Africans in North America hardly deviated from that of the European immigrants: women bore their first child relatively young, and far more children survived than would have been the case in Africa. Europeans who travelled to the British, French, and Dutch parts of the Caribbean died quickly and had relatively few children, much like the African slaves in those regions. These two groups – both exceptions – prove that neither bad treatment, nor abortions, nor the numerical imbalance between the sexes fully explain the difficulties of Africans and Europeans in adjusting to the conditions of tropical America.[12]

Much additional research will be necessary to ascertain the cause of this major demographic gap between the two migration circuits across the Atlantic. The answer may lie in the medical statistics of the military from the nineteenth century. These statistics are an excellent source of information on the medical effects of intercontinental migration for both European and non-European soldiers. They also contain information about the heights and weights of soldiers and recruits and thus indirectly shed light on their nutritional status.[13]

These data lead to the following conclusions:
a) Europeans and Africans could migrate to the temperate regions of North and South America without the risk of encountering many new diseases. Both groups improved their nutritional condition, and the Europeans lived in much

11. Kiple, *Caribbean Slave*, and Eltis and Engerman, "Was the Slave Trade" argue that the share of women among African slaves destined for the New World was relatively large compared with other intercontinental streams of migrants.
12. Emmer, "Immigration into the Caribbean", pp. 245-250; and Fogel, *Without Consent or Contract*, pp. 123-126.
13. Fogel *et al.*, "Exploring the Uses of Data".

less densely populated areas than at home. These factors explain why there were far fewer epidemics in the New World than in Europe and Africa.[14]

b) Migrating to the tropical parts of the New World entailed a considerably greater health risk, both for Europeans and for Africans. While the two groups might have been able to obtain healthier food than at home, they were exposed to many unknown, new, and lethal diseases. Europeans suffered more than Africans in the Caribbean: when relocating to the West Indies their mortality rate was four times as high as among slaves brought from Africa to the Caribbean.[15]

c) Last but not least, the medical statistics show that all immigrant groups were able to build up resistance to new diseases, albeit over time and provided that no new pathogens arrived. Reviewing the various migration flows suggests that migration to North and South America initially involved only a limited number of migrants, who arrived mainly in waves rather than in constant numbers. The same holds true for the migration of Europeans and Africans to the Spanish Caribbean. All these areas experienced demographic growth. Migration by Europeans to the British, French, and Dutch Caribbean, however, continued unabated over an extended period, as was the case for the migration of African slaves to the British, French, and Dutch Caribbean as well as to Northeastern Brazil. No demographic growth occurred in these parts of tropical America because they maintained a permanent, strong, and growing link between Europe and West Africa and their pathogens, which were the most dangerous in the world.[16]

Intercontinental Migration Circuits During the Nineteenth Century: Asia Enters the Picture

In view of this evidence it seems remarkable that only three million Europeans migrated to the moderate zones of the New World before 1800. Once some of the technical impediments to long-distance migration had been removed, however, traffic to the New World increased explosively. Transportation by train improved access to European ports of embarkation and facilitated departure from American ports of debarkation. Steamships made crossing the Atlantic more

14. Sokoloff and Villaflor, "Early Achievements"; McCusker and Menard, *Economy of British America*, pp. 211-235; Fogel, *Without Consent or Contract*, p. 133 (Table 21); Curtin, "African Health at Home", p. 392; and Curtin, "Nutrition in African History", pp. 181-184.

15. Fogel, *Without Consent or Contract*, p. 131; Curtin, *Death by Migration*, p. 33; and Kiple, *Caribbean Slave*, pp. 104-119.

16. Eltis, "Free and Coerced Transatlantic", p. 253 (Spanish Caribbean); Kiple, *Caribbean Slave*, p. 112.

comfortable and more affordable. The first migration circuit to the New World was twenty times as large as the combined preceding migration from the Old World: more than 41 million Europeans went to North America and about 6 million to South America. Again, the European migrants managed – on the average – to attain a higher standard of living in the New World than they did at home. In addition to the areas beyond the frontier in the New World, new settlements arose in Australia, New Zealand, and the Maghreb, as well as in South and East Africa.[17]

Strange as it may seem, even the second migration circuit continued during the nineteenth century. This process persisted after the discontinuation of the slave trade, which had been abolished by an increasing number of nations. Nevertheless, operations that were mostly illegal brought another 2 million slaves across the Atlantic after 1815. Without the international campaign to abolish the slave trade, many more millions of Africans would undoubtedly have been shipped across the Atlantic to satisfy the demand for labour on the growing tropical plantation economies over and above the 11 million slaves already there. During the period 1800-1880, both the slavery trade and slavery itself were gradually abolished for a variety of reasons despite the usual economic disadvantages connected with slave emancipation. The continuing urgent need for labour explains the constant efforts of the plantation owners (the main employers of workers arriving through the second migration circuit) to improve the working and living conditions on their plantations. Their motives were both economic and political, as the supply of plantation labour was scarce, and public opinion in the West showed a keen interest in conditions among enslaved and migrant labourers during transportation and on the plantations. Abolitionists kept a close watch on the situation. Long before employers in Western Europe (let alone in Eastern Europe) felt any responsibility for the living and working conditions of their workers, plantation owners in the New World had been forced by law to apply minimum standards for housing, medical care, and wage levels. Many plantation owners could afford to increase their expenditure on labour because of the dramatic rise in the efficiency of the production of cotton and sugar.[18]

These changes eliminated many of the drawbacks that distinguished the second migration circuit across the Atlantic from the first one. In addition to the advanced labour and housing laws, transportation of migrants to the plantation areas of the New World became subject to more rules and regulations than the transportation of migrants along the first circuit (mainly Europeans moving to North America and Australasia). Of course, one important difference between the two migration circuits remained immune to any change in legislation.

17. Woodruff, *Impact of Western Man*, pp. 60-113.
18. Ward, *British West Indian*, pp. 261-263 (sugar); and Fogel, *Without Consent or Contract*, pp. 72-80 (cotton).

Whereas participants in the second migration circuit mainly obtained employment in agriculture, migrants in the first circuit were able to settle in areas where
the economy offered many more possibilities.

Why did so few Europeans participate in the second migration circuit after so
many of its disadvantages disappeared? The unwillingness of the Europeans (even
the very poor ones) to enter the second migration circuit and to settle in the
plantation areas may be attributed to the balance between the dangerous disease
environment of the tropics and the opportunity to earn more there than elsewhere. The various military statistics, which have been addressed above, indicate
that the mortality rate among British and French troops in the Caribbean was
three and a half times as high as at home. Even troops from the North of the
United States who were employed in the South suffered from a mortality rate
double that of their counterparts deployed in the North.[19] These figures reveal
that the European migrants jeopardized their health by moving to the tropical
and subtropical destinations of the second migration circuit. Nevertheless, around
180,000 Europeans migrated to the Caribbean during the nineteenth century.

The African migrants derived little benefit from the improvements in the
second migration circuit. The number of voluntary labour migrants from Africa
(both temporary and permanent) remained exceedingly small. Paradoxically,
when individual African migrants were finally able to negotiate the price of their
intercontinental migration, migration out of Africa virtually came to a standstill.
Of course, the average living and labour conditions in Africa may have been
better than elsewhere. Most likely, however, Africa never developed a system
of free labour migration. Until 1900 migration within Africa was economically
unattractive because of the relatively high land to labour ratio.[20] Despite the
abolition of slavery in the Americas, the practice persisted in Africa and prevented migrants from remaining free labourers for long. The demand for labour
in African export agriculture was met by the migration of slaves to areas where
ground nuts, palm kernels, and palm oil were produced.[21]

The halt in the supply of migrants from Africa left plantation owners with the
labour reserve from Asia, the single untapped continent. From 1840 onward
about 1½ million Asians were brought to the plantation areas in the New World,
Africa, and the Pacific. About one sixth of the migrants came from China, but
the majority came from India.[22] Many of the existing descriptions and analyses
of this migration movement depict the arrival of Asian migrants indentured to

19. Curtin, *Death by Migration*, pp. 17 and 25-28.
20. Schuler, *Alas, Alas Kongo*, pp. 18-29. Labour migration within Africa began only in 1900.
    Hopkins, *Economic History of West Africa*, p. 218. I am indebted to David Eltis for his
    suggestions on this matter.
21. Eltis, *Economic Growth*, pp. 227-232.
22. Emmer, "Immigration into the Caribbean", p. 251.

labour on the plantations as a continuation of the slave trade out of Africa. Recent research, however, has yielded a different impression. Moreover, the available data on Indian mortality and natality overseas and on return migration indicate that emigration from India had more in common with nineteenth-century emigration from Europe than with the slave trade from Africa. Intercontinental migration from China, on the other hand, shared many characteristics with the African slave trade.

Hunger and loss of land forced many Indians to move away from their native soil. They migrated mainly within their own subcontinent. Relatively few Indians managed to migrate to other countries. Estimates suggest that about twenty million Indians or 6.7 percent of the Indian population (estimated at 300 million) participated in long-distance migration during the nineteenth century. Only 1.25 million of these twenty million Indians went overseas as part of government-supervised programmes.[23]

The history of the Indians in Suriname and Fiji reveals a considerable reduction in the demographic differences between the first and second migration circuits. In several tropical host societies the Indians achieved a higher rate of demographic growth than at home. The Indians were the first group of intercontinental migrants who could migrate to tropical areas without experiencing a prolonged decrease in numbers. Around 1850 the two migration circuits remained in place, both enabling their participants to improve their living conditions.[24]

Labour Migration Within Nineteenth-Century Europe, Africa, and Asia: A Third Migration Circuit?

In addition to the intercontinental migration from Europe, Africa, and Asia, large-scale migration movements within these continents preceded and continued alongside intercontinental migration.

The European manifestations of these intra-continental movements have been studied extensively. The research indicates that the internal and external migration movements of Europeans were closely interconnected and contradicts any assumption that migration within Europe constituted a separate, third circuit different from the first intercontinental migration circuit discussed above. Recent investigation has disproved the idea that European populations hardly moved before the onset of the Industrial Revolution. A relatively large share of England's rural population was undoubtedly on the move in search of employment

---

23. Engerman, "Servants to Slaves", p. 272.
24. Shlomowitz, "Fertility and Fiji's"; Emmer, "Great Escape"; and Shlomowitz's contribution to this volume.

outside their native villages and indeed outside the region in which they were born. The relatively high percentage of England's population on the move within the British isles was directly linked to the relatively high propensity to migrate from the United Kingdom to North America during the same period. Similarly, the high percentage of non-Dutch sailors and soldiers from Germany and Scandinavia among the personnel of the Dutch East India Company must be attributed to the larger framework of seasonal, temporary, and permanent labour migration from Scandinavia and Germany to the coastal areas of the North Sea.[25]

These internal migration movements within Europe did not differ from migration within the first intercontinental circuit and require no revision in the theory that only two migration circuits existed. On average, all Europeans on the move undoubtedly benefitted from their relocation, albeit to varying degrees. Migrants looking for work within Europe had several options. Their employment opportunities probably constituted a continuum in the labour markets of Western Europe during the period of the *Ancien Régime*. They might find employment as farmhands, as apprentices in one of the urban manufacturing trades, or as maids in rural or urban households. Usually, these positions entailed a contract spanning one or several years. Men had the additional option of obtaining employment as soldiers or sailors in the various armies, navies, and merchant marines. These jobs were available only on the basis of contracts for the duration of a voyage or military campaign. Employment agreements with the Dutch East India Company usually covered at least the three years required for sailing back and forth to Batavia. The labour markets in the United Kingdom (and to a lesser extent in France and the Netherlands) also offered long-term contracts for service as agricultural labourers in North America and the Caribbean. The conditions of these contracts changed over time and generally spanned a period of 2 to 7 years, depending on the supply of labour.[26]

Before 1800 internal migration also occurred in Africa and Asia. As in the case of Europe, it is questionable whether the conditions of internal migration within Africa and Asia differed from the conditions of the second migration circuit discussed above. In Africa, internal migrants were mainly slaves. Before the arrival of the Europeans on the West coast, the slave trade from tropical Africa was directed towards the Maghreb, to the plantations in East Africa, and to the Middle East. These slave trades predated the trans-Atlantic slave trade, lasted through the duration of this trade, and continued after it had ended.[27]

25. Wrigley and Schofield, *Population History of England*; and Lucassen, *Migrant Labour in Europe*.
26. McCusker and Menard, *Economy of British America*, pp. 242-243; Watts, *West Indies*, pp. 149-152.
27. Renault and Daget, *Traites négrières*.

In Asia the slave trade was also considerable. This market was partly tapped by the Europeans to provide labourers for the various enclave economies around the European forts and castles. In addition, important movements of non-slave labourers existed both within Moghul India and in China, as well as from China to Southeast Asia.[28] During the nineteenth century the propensity to migrate increased among Europeans and Asians alike. As a result, the volume of both the internal and the external migration flows within and from Europe and Asia during a single decade of the nineteenth century exceeded the volume of all internal and intercontinental migrations during the entire *Ancien Régime*. Africa was the sole exception. As mentioned previously, the abrupt halt to the external slave trade seemed to leave Africans with few opportunities for migration.

Several signs indicate that the percentage of internal and external migrants was highest in Europe. Obviously, the economic growth of this continent and the resulting infrastructure for long-distance transportation and travel had facilitated moving and thus allowed large numbers of Europeans to exploit the considerable regional, national, and international differences in social and economic opportunities by relocating permanently or temporarily. While new capitalist enterprises emerged rapidly in the West, their distribution was very uneven.

In Asia and Africa the distribution of the growth of capitalist enterprises was even more unbalanced than in Europe and in North and South America. Quite possibly, this uneven development instigated a drastic increase in the volume of external and internal migration movements. At the same time, the economies and the transportation infrastructure of Africa and Asia probably prevented the internal and external migratory movements from growing at the same rate as in contemporary Europe and the New World.

Much of the literature on Asian and African migration supports the argument that internal migration within Africa and Asia constituted a separate migration movement because the conditions of this migration were even worse than those of the second intercontinental circuit. Many analyses reveal that these internal migrations were highly detrimental to the migrants and to society at large. Migrants within Asia and Africa would have been better off staying at home. Increases in the propensity to migrate are usually attributed to the penetration of Western colonialism, which is believed to have upset the traditional economies. Some arguments hold that labour migration did not provide the migrants from South and Southeast Asia or their counterparts from the Pacific islands with an increase in income. The employers of these migrant labourers paid only subsubsistence individual wages, and the costs of reproduction and unproductive periods of the migrant labourers were the responsibility of their home communities. No wonder many labour recruiters in Asia and the Pacific resorted to force

28. Reid, *Slavery, Bondage and Dependency.*

and kidnapping. Some researchers intimate that the migrant labourers became permanent prisoners of their employers after arriving at their place of employment. Draconian measures prevented them from running away. Any migrant labourers who survived this ordeal usually returned home penniless. The period of such employment was brief, as the management of the Asian and Australian plantations, gardens, and mines preferred to change its migrant labour force as often as possible.[29]

Colonial governments played an important role in providing the new capitalist enclaves in Asia with an abundant supply of cheap labour. Some researchers argue that these governments were heavily biased against the labourers and intervened only on behalf of the employers in the event of labour disputes. The colonial authorities helped employers enforce the labour contracts. Employers and colonial authorities alike promoted the idea that Asia was populated by masses of poor, unruly, lazy, and stupid but nevertheless dangerous savages, who could be exploited only in a system of public administration radically different from that of civilized Europe and North America. Despite individual protests and some collective rebellions, the bulk of Asian labour migrants were moulded into the system devised by the European colonialists. They had no bargaining power, given the growing supply of poor migrants.[30]

Jan Breman and E. Valentine Daniel have advanced the thesis that the expanding European penetration into Asia gave rise to a large circular labour migration circuit within Asia that was composed of "proto-proletarians". They assume that the majority of these perpetual and circular labour migrants had not been marginal peasants. A considerable share of these migrants might have come from the cities and were doomed to continuous participation in the migratory labour circuit because of the impossibility of returning to agrarian life. The intra-Asian migrants were also kept on the move by the attitude of the employers, who were keen on constant change and made no attempt to re-indenture their migrant labourers, as they were not interested in creating an experienced labour force. Indentured migrants could be disposed of at will and at any moment. Other bleak characteristics of this system included a high rate of suicide, a ban on pregnancies, encouragement of prostitution, and efforts to hire women and children to reduce the total expenditure on labour.[31]

In addition to the analysis by Breman and Daniel, a host of other researchers suggest that intra-African and intra-Asian migration flows differed from the two circuits mentioned above. It therefore questionable whether the expansion of European colonialism in Asia and Africa actually produced a third migration

---

29. *Journal of Peasant Studies*, 19 (1992), 3/4; Alatas, *The Myth of the Lazy Native*; and Tinker, *New System of Slavery*.
30. Breman, *Taming the Coolie Beast*; and Breman, *Imperial Monkey Business*.
31. Breman and Daniel, "Conclusion: The Making".

circuit that held no improvements in store for its migrants and served only to foster the growth of Western capitalist enclaves in Africa and Asia.

The assumption of such a third circuit, however, seems premature. Topical literature is mainly based on assumptions and ideas, rather than on extensive quantitative archival research. The actual existence of a separate, third migration circuit is unlikely for three reasons.

First, new research concerning the government-supervised, long-distance migration movements of indentured Indians has clearly revealed that the considerable improvements achieved over time in living and working conditions made this migration stream a small but important escape hatch for migrant labourers from India. These improvements must have affected migration within India as well, as no researcher has ever contended the existence of a clear-cut distinction between India's internal and external migration circuits. The new research findings depict a situation that is virtually a mirror image of the circumstances described by Breman and Daniel. The large majority of the recruits for indentured migration to Suriname, for example, were not "proto-proletarians" but farmers. Despite the provision of a free return passage, few returned to India after the expiration of their contracts if they were given a plot of land. Over time, the suicide rate among the migrants declined and hardly differed from the corresponding rate in India. Mortality was considerably lower and natality only slightly lower than in India. Accordingly, the Indian indentured and non-indentured populations in Suriname and Fiji experienced rapid demographic growth. Other evidence indicates such growth among the communities of Indians indentured in Guyana, Trinidad, Mauritius, and South Africa as well. Both the government of British India and the governments of the receiving areas ensured strict adherence to the labour contracts and prevented random dismissal of indentured labourers. Obviously, no ban on pregnancies existed, and most employers in the Caribbean were inclined to release indentured females from their contracts during the final years if they so wished. Last but not least, government regulations inflated the number of indentured women and children that joined long-distance migration out of India. Neither the employers nor the prospective migrants would have insisted on a ratio of 40 women to every 100 men indentured.[32] The early unregulated migration of Indian indentured labourers to Mauritius shows that women would have accounted for less than 20 percent of the migrants if left to the forces of the market.[33] All these improvements were enacted some time before the nationalists in India started to criticize the system of indentured labour migration.

Another argument against a third, "bad" migration circuit in South and Southeast Asia lies in the rapid abolition of intercontinental migration by

32. Emmer, "The Meek Hindu".
33. Tinker, *New System of Slavery*, pp. 88-89.

Chinese indentured labourers, which took place between 1847 and 1874. The majority of Chinese indentured migrants probably compromised their earning potential and life expectancy by moving to destinations such as Cuba and Peru. Ample evidence indicates inadequate supervision of the recruitment and transportation of Chinese migrant labourers by the Chinese, British (Hongkong), and Portuguese (Macao) authorities. An important point concerning this situation is that the strong pressure to stop the emigration of Chinese indentured labourers came from North America and Europe and not from the employers on Cuba or in Peru, not from the indentured individuals, and not even from the Chinese imperial government. Abuses in international labour migration obviously attracted a powerful audience in the West, which was still imbued with the values of the abolition campaign against the Atlantic slave trade and against slavery. Anyone who had fought the many shortcomings of the second migration circuit would have objected to the creation of a new migration circuit characterized by conditions worse than the ones experienced by the enslaved Africans.[34]

Both these arguments, however, provide only circumstantial evidence. Determining whether the European settlers in Africa and Asia had created or facilitated a new circuit of labour migration requires tedious quantitative research on the various intra-African and intra-Asian labour migration movements to uncover serial data on mortality, morbidity, natality, incomes generated before and after migration, rates of return migration and of re-indenture, sex ratios, and the position of women and children.

Fortunately, studies have covered some intra-Asian migration movements in greater detail: i) the migration of indentured Pacific islanders to Queensland, Fiji, Samoa, Hawaii, and Papua New Guinea; ii) the migration of indentured Indians to Assam and Malaya; and iii) the migration of Javanese indentured labourers to North Sumatra. In all these studies most of the available data allow the analysis of death rates among these groups of migrants.

With respect to Pacific islanders, Adrian Graves has attributed the origin of the supply of indentured labourers to the destruction of the indigenous economies as a result of the penetration of European capitalism. The growth of European enclave economies forced Pacific islanders onto less fertile land. Harsh treatment on the plantations and gardens overseas supposedly caused very high death rates among the migrant labourers.

In a recent critique of this view, Ralph Shlomowitz has mentioned that the incorporation of most of the Pacific islands in the world economy did not take place until well into the twentieth century. By indenturing himself, the desire to obtain more Western products therefore appears to have played a greater role

---

34. Meagher, "Introduction of Chinese Laborers", pp. 307-346.

than the urge to survive for the group of Pacific islanders (which was mostly male). Second, careful analysis of the death rates reveals that mortality was highest in Queensland and Fiji, where the Pacific islanders had the most contact with European and Indian pathogens. When plantation owners on Fiji hired indentured labourers from India rather than from the Pacific islands, the death rate dropped from 108 to 19 per 1,000 without any indication that the Indian plantation labourers were treated differently from their counterparts from the Pacific islands.[35]

The decrease in the death rates among Indian indentured labourers during their voyage to Assam and Malaya and during their period of indenture there leads to a similar conclusion. In the frequent references to the relatively high death rates among these migrants, Western enclave capitalism has immediately been identified as the cause of the poor treatment received by these migrant labourers. Shlomowitz and Lance Brennan have analyzed the death rates and the various diseases that affected the migrants en route and in Assam. They concluded that the mortality rate in the tea gardens would have remained within average proportions, given a fairly constant percentage of new recruits over time. Absolutely no evidence indicates, however, that groups with many new recruits received different treatment from groups with many re-indentured labourers.[36]

Third, the debate regarding the plight of indentured labourers from Java on the tobacco plantations in North Sumatra merits attention. Breman has un-earthed a government report on the extremely bad living and working condi-tions of these indentured labourers that was prepared in 1904 (although it was never published). To prove that the workers received excessively bad treatment, Breman mentions that the death rate among these migrants reached 110 per 1,000.[37] In a recent study Vincent Houben shows that death rates averaged 12.5 per 1,000 between 1913 and 1917. Adaptation by the migrants to the new disease environment is the only explanation available for the reduced death rate, given the absence of any signs indicating a major change in living and working conditions. Javanese labourers who migrated to destinations other than Sumatra suffered considerably higher death rates than the mortality among their counter-parts employed in Sumatra's plantation belt.[38] This evidence re-emphasizes the unlikelihood that changes in the kind of work, the type of housing, or the amount of food were responsible for any decline in the death rate. Instead, growing immunity and greater attention to hygiene account for the drop in the

35. Graves, "The Nature and Origins"; and Shlomowitz, "Epidemiology and the Pacific".
36. Shlomowitz and Brennan, "Mortality and Migrant Labour in Assam"; and Shlomowitz and Brennan, "Mortality and Migrant Labour en route to Assam".
37. Breman, *Koelies, planters*, p. 85.
38. Houben, "'Menyang Tanah Sabrang'".

death rate among the overseas Javanese, among the Indian indentured labourers in Assam and Malaya, and among the Pacific islanders in Queensland and Fiji.

Much detailed research regarding the migration of labourers within Africa and Asia lies ahead. Because of the present status of this investigation, the conclusion that a third circuit of labour migration came into existence during the nineteenth century would be premature. Rather, new research regarding the causes of death and declining death rates among the indentured labour migrants within Asia suggests that no such circuit existed and that only during the initial period these migrants reduced their life expectancy by entering an intra-Asian migration circuit. Second, the research shows that both colonial governments and private enterprises were interested in reducing mortality among migrant labourers in Asia. Additional research is needed to determine whether the statistical data support the other negative aspects of nineteenth-century labour migration within Asia and Africa.

For the moment, the available evidence does not appear to support the hypothesis that the expansion of Europe in the nineteenth century gave rise to a migration circuit that precluded social, economic, and demographic advancement. Obviously, labour migration within Asia initially entailed problems similar to the ones that characterized the early decades of the first and second intercontinental migration circuits, such as kidnapping, excessive death rates, low birth rates, and abnormally high or low rates of return migration. After this initial period, however, migrants in Asia experienced some major improvements, as had been the case in other migration circuits.

Nevertheless, findings suggest that the colonial migration circuits remained different from the migration circuits within Asia (and perhaps also within Africa) in certain respects. "Colonial" labour migration was subject to better regulations and closer supervision than internal migration movements. Also, recruitment practices were more selective than among migrants intending to remain in Asia.

Conclusion: Research That Remains To Be Done

Migration has increased economic growth and has reduced income differences all over the world. The majority of the migrants increased their standard of living, even the African slaves. The average incomes of the descendants of Europeans, Asians, and Africans who migrated overseas exceed the incomes of the descendants of those who remained behind. Given this outcome, the question as to why people migrated should be replaced by the question as to why so few people took such action.

The answer is not easy. Comparing the relative and absolute volume of the migrating Europeans, Africans, and Asians suggests the 80 percent lead of

Europeans with respect to participation in intercontinental migration is attributable to the availability of an infrastructure for mass transportation and the rise in income beyond the subsistence level. While Africans and Asians have seemed to be catching up over the past two decades, their share in the post-World War II migration flows was smaller than that of Europeans until 1970. The majority of the migrants moving to Europe after the decolonization process were descendants of Europeans, rather than Africans and Asians.[39]

As with every opportunity, the choice to migrate entailed certain costs. Observations in the previous sections noted that migration from one disease environment to another sometimes involved several demographic drawbacks. Most Europeans opted to move to an area with a less dangerous disease environment than the one they faced at home. For more than three centuries, however, a minority of European migrants insisted on moving to the tropical regions of the New World, Africa, and Asia, where their mortality was much higher than at home. The motivations of the Europeans who continued to choose these destinations remains to be explored.[40]

African and Asian intercontinental migrants had a far more restricted choice of destinations. Africans were forced to migrate to the most dangerous regions of the New World. Only a small minority was sent elsewhere. At first, the circumstances of Asian migrants appeared similar to those of the enslaved Africans. After a few decades, however, the Asian intercontinental migrants overcame the demographic dangers of their host societies. More research is needed to explain this important breakthrough.

In addition to intercontinental migration, large migratory movements existed within Europe, Africa, and Asia. Unfortunately, scholars have devoted far less work to some of these intra-continental migration movements than to their intercontinental counterparts. Various similarities between the inter- and intra-continental migration movements indicate that the intra-continental movements were not a separate migration circuit. Nevertheless, some research has revealed that the socio-economic and demographic improvements of the intra-continental migrants were less significant than those of their intercontinental counterparts.

The explanation for this discrepancy is deceptively complicated. According to the easy answer, the investment in the costs of migration, and the compensation awarded to migrants in return for their initiative increased in proportion to the distance. This explanation is generally satisfactory in cases where the migrants were not slaves or prisoners or indentured workers.

---

39. Miège, "Migration and Decolonisation".
40. Grubb, "Fatherless and Friendless", suggests the existence in Europe of a small and inelastic supply of indentured labourers willing to go to the plantations, which remained relatively unaffected by the transition to slave labour in British America.

Enslaved and indentured migrants sometimes faced the opposite situation. Higher investments in these migrants by the employers coincided with harsher conditions during their voyage and their period of employment in an effort to maximize the return on their investment. Accordingly, slaves and indentured labourers overseas could expect worse treatment and higher mortality rates than their counterparts who migrated within their own continent. The available evidence, however, does not support this hypothesis. The scarce information about the labour conditions of slaves in Africa suggests that mortality rates among slaves being moved across the Sahara were higher than mortality rates among slaves shipped across the Atlantic. Similarly, mortality rates among indentured labourers travelling within India were higher than among their counterparts moving to other continents.

Selection of the migrants provides the first explanation for the difference in mortality. Slaves and indentured labourers who were bought or selected for migration overseas had to pass a more rigorous medical examination than their counterparts who were selected or who volunteered for migration inside their own region or subcontinent. All migrants, however, were probably younger and in better physical health than the general population.

Reversing the investment argument submitted above offers the second explanation for the relatively low mortality and good nutrition among intercontinental slaves and indentured labourers. The harshness of transportation, living, and working conditions of these long-distance migrants should not jeopardize the return on investment by leading to high mortality rates and frequent rebellions and escapes. The same line of reasoning also suggests that transporters and employers of slaves and indentured labourers remaining in Africa and Asia could afford to treat migrant labourers for the internal market more harshly because replacement of these labourers was relatively cheap. The implications of this hypothesis seem more compatible with the available data than the explanation that high investments in slave and indentured migrant labour lead to harsh labour conditions.

This hypothesis does not explain the reasons for the miraculous improvements over time. Some scholars have noted the dramatic increase in the value of the marginal product of virtually all labourers (both enslaved and free individuals) in sectors of manufacturing and agriculture where new technology was being introduced. These changes made labour more valuable and thus enabled employers to spend more on their workers. The available evidence, however, does not always support this theoretical observation. Labour in Europe during the Industrial Revolution seems to have obtained lower rewards than before this era, despite the dramatic increase in the value of its marginal product.[41] This

---

41. Eltis, *Economic Growth*, pp. 187-190.

state of affairs calls for a reconsideration of the role of the colonial government and a re-examination of the dialectical assumption that colonial governments were always inclined to support Western enterprises and to harm the interests of their colonial subjects.

The evidence currently available supports the contention that shipping firms and employers improved transportation and employment over time under pressure from the colonial governments, which had to answer to public opinion in Western Europe and North America. From the mid-eighteenth century, plantation owners in the Americas were under government pressure to improve living and working conditions for their slaves. Nothing indicates that these improvements increased the profits of the Western investors. The slave trade and slavery were completely abolished, despite the growing economic viability of these institutions. In fact, conclusive data prove that the abolition of the slave trade and the emancipation of the slaves increased the cost of labour considerably. After the mid nineteenth century stronger legislation governed the conditions of recruitment, transportation, employment, and return of intercontinental indentured labour on more solid legal ground without any apparent decrease in the costs of recruiting or employing indentured labourers overseas. Finally, the working and living conditions of some groups of labour migrants within Asia and the Pacific improved without any intended increase in the financial benefits to the employers from this type of migrant labour.

These changes imposed by the government considerably affected the balance between the advantages and drawbacks of all migration circuits. Accordingly, a more appropriate title for this contribution would be "Migration Was *Made* Economically Beneficial".

Coerced and Free Migration from the United Kingdom to Australia, and Indentured Labour Migration from India and the Pacific Islands to Various Destinations: Issues, Debates, and New Evidence

Ralph Shlomowitz

Introduction

In the preface to this conference, Jan and Leo Lucassen have urged scholars to develop "a comprehensive theory on migration and settlement", "a migration paradigm that encompasses both free and coerced, European and non-European migration", and the role of the state. This paper does not attempt to develop such a theory or paradigm; rather, it attempts to survey the recent historiography of a number of state-financed and/or state-regulated migration streams, which may assist scholars in constructing models of, and developing wider perspectives on, migration.

Four state-financed and/or state-regulated migration streams are surveyed: two of the streams (United Kingdom convicts and government-assisted free emigrants to Australia) were financed and regulated by the British imperial and colonial Australian governments, while the other two streams (Indian and Pacific Island indentured labour to a variety of destinations) were financed by private enterprise but extensively regulated by various imperial and colonial governments. There are, of course, many other differences among these four migrant streams: (1) convict transportation was forced migration while the other streams were (largely) voluntary; (2) the United Kingdom forced and free migrants to Australia and Indian migrants to various destinations were, in large measure, settlers, while Pacific Islander migrants generally returned to their home communities; and (3) there were important age and sex differences among these streams: Pacific Islander migrants were nearly entirely young adult males; United Kingdom convicts transported to Australia included women, but not children; while the UK government-assisted free migrant stream and the Indian indentured labour migrant stream included a relatively high proportion of women and young children.

The paper addresses issues and debates relating to the social origins of these migrants, and for the voluntary streams, the motivations of the migrants and the forces shaping their decision to migrate. The paper also uses new bodies of quantitative evidence to analyse the market for the shipping of these migrants to their destinations. New bodies of quantitative evidence are also used to measure some of the consequences of migration. Two indicators are presented on the costs and benefits of relocation: one measure of relocation costs is the increased mortality associated with migration while *en route* or soon after arrival at their destination; a measure of relocation benefits taking a longer time perspective, is the increased height of the descendants of the migrants, human stature being a sensitive indicator of nutrition and morbidity during the growing years, and so of economic well-being more generally.

Convicts Transported to Australia

In the historiography of the transportation of roughly 163,000 British and Irish convicts to Australia between 1788 and 1868, the central issue which continues to be debated is the degree of criminality of the convicts: Were they mostly professional criminals who had committed relatively serious offences, or were they mostly casual criminals who had committed relatively petty offences on a part-time basis while in regular employment? During the 1950s, 1960s, and 1970s, a broad consensus was reached by scholars: while the social origins of the convict transportees were diverse, most were transported for relatively serious offences and they were usually repeat offenders. They were criminals of some standing.[1] In reaching this conclusion, an earlier view that the convict transportees were mostly petty offenders who were forced into committing offences by adverse economic conditions, was overturned.[2]

More recently, an attack on the scholarship of Manning Clark, Alan Shaw, Lloyd Robson, and John Hirst has been mounted by Stephen Nicholas.[3] Convict transportees, according to Nicholas, were not professional criminals. Rather than living by crime, it is argued, they usually held regular employment but on occasion stole articles of small value. The publication of *Convict Workers*, accordingly, can be interpreted as bringing to a close a historiographic circle that began with the work of George Wood earlier this century.

There are two props to Nicholas's argument. The first prop is the information contained in the official government records – the convict indents – on the convict's previous occupation, number of previous offences, and the nature of the offence. Taking this information *at face value*, the following portrait is drawn: most convicts were first offenders found guilty of petty theft. Furthermore, as some 95 per cent of the convicts had an occupational status recorded in the

---

1. Clark, "Origins of the Convicts"; Robson, *Convict Settlers*; Shaw, *Convicts and the Colonies*; Hirst, *Convict Society and its Enemies*.
2. Wood, "Convicts".
3. Nicholas, *Convict Workers*, pp. 7, 74.

indents, it is inferred that nearly all had been in regular employment in British and Irish (non-criminal) labour markets prior to conviction. The second prop of Nicholas's argument is his inference from recent scholarship on the social history of crime in nineteenth century England, that nearly all crime was committed by ordinary working class men and women while in regular employment, so that convict transportees can be considered a random sample of the entire population of offenders in England.[4]

Nicholas's revisionism, however, lacks substance.[5] He can be faulted for not acknowledging the strictures of previous scholarship at taking information in the convict indents at face value: scholars have repeatedly warned that the indents alone cannot tell us about the criminality of the convicts; this can only be gathered from the trial records. Through a thorough analysis of these trial records, Shaw has shown that even though the offence listed in the indents may often be petty theft, the decision whether the offender should be transported to Australia was based on the offender's character and reputation, whether the offender had a bad record and was "known" to the judge or magistrate.[6]

Nicholas can also be faulted for not accurately representing the views of Jones, Philips, and Rudé on the social origins of English offenders. Although these scholars suggest that most crime should not be ascribed to professional criminals, they do not dispute that many offenders, particularly in London, were professional criminals.[7] And what is emphasized in this literature is that convict transportees were not a random sample of all offenders. Consider the distribution of punishments relating to 226,499 offences committed in England between 1806 and 1833: 12 per cent were for capital sentences, 22 per cent for transportation (2 per cent for life, 3 per cent for 14 years, and 17 per cent for 7 years), 63 per cent for imprisonment in England (0.1 per cent for 3-5 years, 8 per cent for 1-2 years, and 55 per cent for less than one year), and 3 per cent for whipping and fines.[8] In reporting the distribution of 14,686 sentences in the Black Country of England between 1835 and 1860, Philips similarly shows that transportation to Australia was mainly reserved for offenders who had committed serious crimes and for offenders whom the judges and magistrates considered to be particularly hardened criminals, while the less serious offences by first offenders not known to the judges and magistrates, were mainly punished by relatively short-terms of imprisonment in England.[9]

4. Jones, *Crime, Protest, Community*; Philips, *Crime and Authority*; Rude, *Criminal and Victim*.
5. Shlomowitz, "Convict Workers: A Review Article"; and exchange between Nicholas and Shlomowitz in *Australian Economic History Review*, XXXI (1991), pp. 95-109.
6. Shaw, *Convicts and the Colonies*, pp. 151-154.
7. Jones, *Crime, Protest, Community*, p. 170; Philips, *Crime and Authority*, pp. 126-127, 205-206, 210, 235, 242, 287; Rude, *Criminal and Victim*, pp. 80, 124-126.
8. Rusche and O. Kirchheimer, *Punishment and Social Structure*, p. 103.
9. Philips, *Crime and Authority*, pp. 171-173. See also McLynn, *Crime and Punishment*, p. 314.

Despite this challenge by Nicholas then, it can be suggested that the conclusion reached by Clark, Shaw, Robson, and Hirst remains intact: convict transportees were usually guilty of serious offences, were repeat offenders, or were known to the Courts as hardened criminals. They were not a random sample of all offenders in the United Kingdom, let alone a random sample of ordinary British and Irish working class men and women.

Free Emigration to Australia

A review of the historiography of nineteenth century British emigration suggests that the two main issues which continue to be debated are: (1) the extent to which the timing of emigrant flows are associated with fluctuations in labour market conditions in Great Britain and in overseas destinations, particularly the United States (the so-called "push-pull" debate), and (2) the social origins of the emigrants. According to the leading authority, Charlotte Erickson, during the first half of the nineteenth century push factors predominated with most emigrants being farmers and artisans travelling in family units, while after the Civil War, pull factors predominated with most emigrants being urban labourers travelling on their own, unaccompanied by family members. These findings, however, have recently been modified by Raymond Cohn who argues that labourers were the dominant group of migrants in the period of his study, 1836-1853.[10]

During the nineteenth century, about one and a half million emigrants from the United Kingdom came to Australia, the passage of about 47 per cent of whom were financed in full or in part by the governments of the various Australian colonies.[11] Initially, in 1831, the first government-assisted emigrants were *selected* by government agents, but from 1848, emigrants could also be *nominated* by their friends or relatives in the colonies. Both the selected and nominated government-assisted emigrants had to be of specified occupations and of good health and character. Between 1848 and 1900, about 30 per cent of all government-assisted migrants were brought out under the nominated system, with the Irish being, in particular, extensive users of this "chain-migration" system.[12]

There has been little controversy on the explanation of the timing of the flows of government-assisted emigrants to Australia. As the stream was financed by Australian colonial governments, pull factors predominated: during times of

---

10. Thomas, *Migration and Economic Growth*; Baines, *Migration in a Mature Economy*; Baines, *Emigration from Europe*; Erickson, "Who were the English and Scots Emigrants"; Erickson, "Emigration from the British Isles to the USA in 1831"; Erickson, "Emigration from the British Isles to the USA in 1841"; Cohn, "Occupations of English Immigrants".
11. Haines and Shlomowitz, "Nineteenth Century Government-Assisted and Total Immigration".
12. Shlomowitz, "Nominated and Selected Government-Assisted Immigration".

economic depression in the 1840s and 1890s in Australia, for example, these migration schemes were largely discontinued. There has, however, been considerable debate on the social origins of the government-assisted emigrants. In contrast to an earlier view which held that these emigrants were from the lowest strata of United Kingdom society shovelled out to Australia, a new view has been put in recent scholarship. In her pathbreaking dissertation, Robin Haines has documented the mainly rural origins of the government-assisted emigrants; though they were mostly farm labourers, artisans, and domestic servants, they were rarely the most impoverished members of rural society. She argues that they were enterprising, self-selecting individuals who took advantage of a scheme which allowed them to improve their prospects abroad.[13]

Indian Indentured Labour Migration

Between 1834 and 1917, about one and a quarter million Indians, principally from the United Provinces and Bihar in north India and the Madras Presidency in south India were recruited as indentured labourers for work on the sugar cane estates of Fiji, Malaya, Mauritius, Reunion, Natal, and the Caribbean, while nearly two million north Indians, principally from the United Provinces, Bihar, and Bengal, were recruited as indentured labourers for work on the tea estates of Assam in northeastern India. In addition, other south Indians worked under more informal arrangements on the coffee and tea estates of Sri Lanka, the coffee and rubber estates of Malaya, and in construction and the rice mills of Burma.

In the historiography of Indian indentured labour, three key issues have been debated: (1) Were the recruits free agents with sufficient information to enable them to choose whether to recruit, or were they coerced into recruiting? (2) What motivated the recruits to enlist? (3) What were the social origins of the recruits?

In contrast to an earlier viewpoint which held that the recruits were generally kidnapped or deceived into enlisting, a new view has emerged with the scholarship of Brij Lal and Pieter Emmer. After reviewing the evidence relating to kidnapping and deception in the recruiting process, they concluded that coercive practices mostly occurred in the early decades of the system, but with the British gradually setting in place a reasonably effective administrative structure to protect the recruits from unfair practices and with information about the system increasingly becoming available to prospective recruits, the system settled down

13. Haines, "Government-Assisted Emigration"; Haines, "'Shovelling out Paupers'?". On British emigration to Australia, see also the many publications of Eric Richards. For recent contributions, see Richards, "Annals of the Australian Immigrant"; Richards, "British Poverty and Australian Immigration"; Richards, "Return Migration and Migrant Strategies".

to an orderly business arrangement with most recruits making a deliberate choice to migrate. They conclude that the Indian indentured labour system cannot be regarded as forced migration.[14]

While emphasizing that prospective recruits had decision-making power over their lives, it is also recognized that the choice to migrate was subject to severe economic constraints. There is large agreement among scholars that emigration was induced more by push than pull factors. Good evidence in support of this conclusion is the positive correlation between economic distress (and famine) in India and the number of prospective recruits offering to enlist. The nature of the push factors, however, are debated. Some scholars argue that British intrusion led to the dislocation and distress of a wide cross-section of Indian society, while other scholars stress the pressure of population in the main recruiting areas and that this increase in the man-land ratio was largely independent of British intrusion.[15]

For purposes of identification, the name of the indentured labour emigrant and his or her age, place of origin, social group (caste, religion, or tribe), and physical character (such as height) were recorded on departure from India, and these emigrant passes are extant for emigrants departing for Mauritius, Natal, Fiji, Jamaica, and Trinidad. Brij Lal has pioneered the quantification of these records in his pathbreaking study of north Indian emigration to Fiji. More recently, Surendra Bhana, for Indian emigrants to Natal, and a team of researchers at The Flinders University of South Australia, for Indian emigrants to Jamaica, Mauritius, and Fiji, have followed Lal's lead. In contrast to an earlier literature which held that the emigrants of the Hindu religion were nearly entirely from the lower castes, these new studies show that the social origins of the emigrants were diverse, covering a wide-cross section of Hindu society. Although high, middling, and low castes were represented, it can be suggested, however, that as emigration was mainly prompted by economic distress and famine, it was only the most impoverished of the high and middling castes who enlisted. Muslims, christians, and tribals were also represented among the recruits, but the emigrant passes yield no clues whether the emigrants were typical of their social/religious groups in India.[16]

---

14. Lal, *Girmitiyas*; Emmer, "Great Escape"; Emmer, "Meek Hindu"; Emmer, "Immigration into the Caribbean".

15. See Kumar, *Land and Caste in South India*; Kumar (ed.), *Cambridge Economic History of India, Vol. 2*; Baker, *Indian Rural Economy*; Guha, *Agrarian Economy of the Bombay Deccan*, especially pp. 199-200.

16. Lal, *Girmitiyas;* Bhana, *Indentured Indian Emigrants to Natal*. For a critique of Bhana's study, see Shlomowitz, "Indentured Indian Emigrants to Natal: A Review Article". The papers of the Flinders University group are focused on the height of the emigrants and will be cited below.

Pacific Islander Indentured Labour Migration

Between 1862 and the late 1940s, Pacific Island workers from the Solomon Islands, Vanuatu, Papua New Guinea, Kiribati, and other island groups were recruited on (usually) three year indenture contracts for employment on the sugar cane and copra plantations, and gold, nickel, and phosphate mines of Queensland (Australia), Fiji, New Caledonia, Samoa, Hawaii, Tahiti, Nauru, and Ocean Island. In addition to this inter-island recruitment of workers, migrant workers, from Papua New Guinea, the Solomon Islands, and Vanuatu, were also recruited for employment under indenture contracts within their own territories.

During the past three decades, the historiography of this so-called Pacific labour trade has taken a number of new directions. Up until the 1960s, research on the labour trade was generally conducted within the larger framework of British imperial history and was largely concerned with British or colonial government policies to stop abuses in the trade. With the seminal work of Deryck Scarr and Peter Corris and the more recent study by Clive Moore, however, the focus of research has shifted to the islanders themselves. In contrast to the earlier literature which treated the islanders as helpless victims of historical forces, easily kidnapped or manipulated by more powerful whites, the new literature treats the islanders as active participants, or even as protagonists, in the historical process.

The new literature, which is focused on the Queensland and Fiji labour trade between 1863 and 1911, recognises that there was an initial period in which episodes of kidnapping and deception are well documented, but from the mid-1880s the labour trade settled down to an ordinary, albeit often dangerous, business arrangement due to an understanding of the islanders what the trade involved, to the ability of island communities to retaliate against those recruiters using unfair practices, and to the active policing of the trade by the British imperial government and the colonial governments of Queensland and Fiji. According to this new literature, recruits signed on of their own free will, or following directions from their parents or community leaders, and were generally not forced by economic circumstances to enlist. Islanders were willing recruits with a variety of motives: to obtain western goods (such as guns, cloth, tools, utensils, and tobacco); to travel and seek adventure; and, for some, to escape punishment for the breaking of community taboos.[17]

17. Scarr, *Fragments of Empire*; Corris, *Passage, Port and Plantation*; Moore, *Kanaka*. For a recent wide-ranging survey of the labour trade, see Moore *et al.*, *Labour in the South Pacific*. And for two recent historiographic surveys, see Moore, "Revising the Revisionists"; Munro, "Pacific Island Labour Trade".

More recently there has been a number of challenges to this new literature by scholars who have attempted to draw fresh perspectives to the labour trade from models which were developed to explain circular labour migration in other parts of the world. Adrian Graves, for example, argues that capitalist penetration undermined indigenous rural economies, leading to rural impoverishment. Lacking adequate land to provide for their subsistence, workers, according to Graves, became proletarianized, forced by necessity to enter the labour trade. Scarr and other Pacific historians, however, have dismissed Graves's argument as simply not fitting the facts of the Pacific: throughout the period of the labour trade, capitalist penetration in the main recruiting areas was exceedingly slight, so islanders were not proletarianized, forced to recruit due to economic necessity.[18]

A number of scholars have also challenged the new literature by applying a model developed by Claude Meillassoux to explain circular labour migration in Africa to the Pacific labour trade. Male migrant workers, in Meillassoux's model, are only paid a "bachelor's wage" to cover their subsistence during the contract, because their home communities support their parents, wife, children, and the workers themselves in their old age. As much of the cost of the care and reproduction of the labour force was borne by their home communities, the home communities, according to this view, subsidize the capitalist economy, and so the colonial state attempts to preserve these recruiting areas for the use of the capitalist economy. Underlying this model then are three key assumptions: (1) male migrant workers are only paid a "bachelor's wage" covering the worker's subsistence, so there was no return flow of goods to the worker's home community; (2) employers preferred the circular labour system to a settled labour force at their place of employment as it was the cheaper option; and (3) the choice of labour system was determined solely by employers.[19]

A review of these propositions, however, shows that this model does not fit the facts of the Pacific. First, in the Pacific labour trade, the recruit's subsistence was met by various payments in kind, and their money wages represented savings which were usually spent at the end of the contract on various goods to be taken back to their home islands. There was, accordingly, a considerable flow of goods to the home communities of the recruits, so it is not at all obvious that the home communities subsidized the capitalist sector. Second, although wage rates appeared to be low, the migrant labour system was not necessarily a provider of cheap labour. As compared to a settled labour force, the migrant labour system was costly due to heavy recruiting and repatriation costs, the lack of skill of new recruits, and the heavy losses, as will be shown below, through mortality. And third, for a full explanation of the emergence and persistence of the circular

18. Graves, "Nature and Origins of Pacific Islands Labour Migration"; Scarr, "Review".
19. Meillassoux, "From Reproduction to Production".

labour system as compared to developing a more settled labour force at the place of employment, consideration must be given not only to the employer's demand for cheap and tractable labour, but also to the side of supply. The access of islanders to land usually adequate for subsistence, meant that the decision of what system was adopted was influenced by the islanders themselves. And their preference was not for settled labour as few females were prepared, or were allowed by their communities, to recruit, and the vast majority of male recruits wanted to eventually return to their home communities.[20]

A consideration of recent scholarship on British government-assisted emigration to Australia, and Indian and Pacific Islander indentured labour migration to various destinations suggests a common thread: in contrast to earlier literatures which were mainly concerned with issues of government policy, the new literatures focus on the migrants themselves, on their social origins, and on their aspirations, perceptions, and contributions. A second novelty in the new literatures, as has been alluded to in the above discussion of the social origins of the migrants, is the use of quantification as a research tool. Some illustrations will follow of other uses of quantification in migrant studies.

The Market for Shipping Passengers

The shipping of British and Irish convicts and government-assisted free emigrants to Australia, and Indian indentured labour to Mauritius, Natal, Fiji, and the Caribbean was organized by the British government. In general, these groups were conveyed in privately-owned sailing vessels, which were chartered by the British government. The charter prices were usually determined following a tendering process, a separate tender being called for each voyage. For over 2,500 sailing voyages between 1816 and 1904, data are extant on the charter price, tonnage of the vessel, the number of passengers embarked, the length of the voyage, and the date of departure of each voyage.

In modelling this bulk passenger shipping market, the real charter price (that is, the nominal charter price corrected for inflation or deflation) was made a function of demand and supply forces, as the shipping market for sailing vessels was one of the best examples of a freely competitive market. The main finding of the resulting regression analysis is that despite the marked fall in the real freight rate for shipping commodities in sailing vessels during the second half of the nineteenth century, the real charter price for the bulk shipping of passengers on sailing vessels did not exhibit a long-term decline. One possible explanation for the failure of the real contract price to decline in the second half

20. Shlomowitz, "Pacific Labour Trade and Super-Exploitation"; Shlomowitz, "Marx and the Pacific Labour Trade".

of the nineteenth century following cost-reducing improvements in the efficiency of shipping, is that such improvements were offset by changes in the quality dimension of the passage, such as better victuals being provided. The other findings are as expected: the contract price was influenced by demand conditions, being bid up during the Australian gold rushes (1852-1854), the Crimean War (1854), and the Indian Mutiny (1857), and by cost considerations such as the length of the voyage, the size of vessels, and the extent to which they were crowded. The contract price was not, however, influenced by seasonal variations in demand.

When the transition was made from sail to steam, the charter prices offered for steamers and sailing vessels were comparable. In the bulk shipping of British and Irish government-assisted emigrants to Australia, sailing vessels were displaced in 1884, while in the bulk shipping of Indian indentured workers, steamers first displaced sailing vessels in the relatively short routes from India to Mauritius and Natal (in 1889), and it was only later that sailing vessels were displaced on the longer routes to Fiji (in 1905) and the Caribbean (in 1908).[21]

The transport of Pacific Islanders from their home communities to their place of employment in Queensland, Fiji, and elsewhere in the Pacific was performed by privately-owned sailing vessels, and the passage rates that were charged by recruiters on hundreds of these voyages are also extant. These data, however, cannot be incorporated in the modelling and analysis of the market for the overall bulk shipping of passengers in sailing vessels, because the recruiting voyages in the Pacific labour trade relate to a round-trip voyage in which workers were recruited from their home villages, and the passage rate was primarily dependent on expectations of the ease or difficulty in eliciting workers to enlist.[22]

Relocation Costs

Philip Curtin has introduced the term "relocation cost" to refer to the increased mortality associated with the movement of migrants from the disease environment of their childhood to a new disease environment.[23] Exposure to infectious diseases, usually in a mild form, in childhood, gives the survivors either lifelong

---

21. McDonald and Shlomowitz, "Cost of Shipping Convicts"; McDonald and Shlomowitz, "Passenger Fares on Sailing Vessels"; McDonald and Shlomowitz, "Fares Charged for Transporting Indian Indentured Labour"; McDonald and Shlomowitz, "Contract Prices for the Bulk Shipping".
22. Shlomowitz, "Markets for Indentured and Time-Expired Melanesian Labour"; Shlomowitz, "Fiji Labor Trade in Comparative Perspective"; Shlomowitz, "Internal Labour Trade in Papua"; Shlomowitz and R. Bedford, "Internal Labour Trade in New Hebrides".
23. Curtin, *Death by Migration*.

immunity (in the case of diseases such as smallpox and measles) or partial immunity (in the case of diseases such as malaria and cholera) to a further attack. Movement of people exposed the migrants to new diseases to which they had no immunity, so placing them at great risk.

The process of migration also brought together people with differing immunities and susceptibilities, and the congregation of migrants while in departure depots and on board vessels, often under unsanitary conditions, facilitated the spread of infectious diseases. Furthermore, for indentured labourers, the congregation of workers on plantations under unsanitary conditions, and harsh working and living conditions placed them under additional risk.

In order to evaluate this relocation cost, it is necessary to provide estimates of (1) mortality rates of the various populations from which the migrants originated, and (2) mortality rates suffered by the migrants while *en route* to their destination, and, for indentured labourers, during their contracts of employment.[24]

As age-specific death rates of the populations of the United Kingdom and India are not available for the nineteenth century, these rates will be inferred from life tables. On this basis, the annual death rates of United Kingdom infants (up to age one), children (from one to 19 years), and young adults (from 20 to 39 years) were about 250 per 1,000, 13 per 1,000 and 8 per 1,000, respectively, while the annual death rates of these age groups in India were about 300 per 1,000, 50 per 1,000, and 30 per 1,000, respectively. Although information is not available on the mortality suffered by Pacific Islanders in their home communities, it can be assumed that it was lower than in India. The disease environment of the main recruiting areas (Solomon Islands, Vanuatu, Papua, and New Guinea) - other than for endemic malaria -was benign, being free of most of the infectious diseases that afflicted the populations of Europe and Asia.[25]

The "excess" mortality associated with migration (as compared to remaining in their home communities) can be reported in two stages: (1) for forced and free United Kingdom emigration to Australia, and Indian and Pacific Islander indentured labourers, the mortality suffered *en route* to their destination, including comparisons with the mortality of other seaborne populations, is shown in

---

24. In terms of their health, it can be assumed that the migrants were very roughly typical of the populations from which they originated: though United Kingdom convict and government-assisted free emigrants to Australia and Indian indentured workers came from the lower strata of their respective societies, they – as did Pacific Islander recruits – had to pass a medical examination attesting to their good health before embarking.

25. See McDonald and Shlomowitz, "Mortality on Immigrant Voyages", p. 96; Shlomowitz, "Infant Mortality", p. 301; Shlomowitz and Brennan, "Mortality and Migrant Labour in Assam", p. 102.

Table 1, while (2) for Indians and Pacific Islanders, the mortality suffered during their periods of employment is shown in Tables 2 and 3.[26]

Although these results are discussed in detail elsewhere, the following findings are germane to the theme of the excess mortality associated with migration in this paper. First, the average death rates of seaborne populations were generally higher than those of equivalent land-based populations; the first seaborne population for which the average death rate at sea approached that of the comparable land-based death rate was that of government-assisted United Kingdom emigrants to Australia, but then only from the 1850s, and only for adults. Second, the average death rate of (non-slave) seaborne populations declined in the nineteenth century due to a series of administrative reforms which included the better screening of passengers on embarkation to prevent the sailing of sick passengers, the establishment of an adequate system of sanitation on board the vessels, reduced crowding, and the provision of adequate and uncontaminated food and water. Third, Pacific Islanders were much more at risk of death during their contracts of indenture than Indians and Chinese in the Pacific, due to their lack of prior exposure to infectious diseases such as measles, influenza, pneumonia, tuberculosis, and bacillary dysentery. Fourth, the average death rate of Pacific Islanders gradually declined over time as infectious diseases were introduced into recruiting areas, in part by returned workers on the conclusion of their contracts, so building up immunities to these diseases. Administrative reforms, such as effecting an improved sanitation regime on plantations, also helped in reducing death rates.

Fifth, the variation in average death rates of Indian workers in different territories is explained, at least in part, by epidemiological factors. Assam and Malaya had a most hostile disease environment as cholera and malaria were endemic in Assam and malaria was endemic in Malaya, while Natal and Fiji had most benign disease environments, generally free of cholera and malaria. The lower average death rates of Indian workers in the Caribbean, with its endemic malaria and epidemic yellow fever, than in Malaya is more difficult to explain. It appears that Indians were seldom exposed to yellow fever in the Caribbean, and when exposed did not suffer high fatality rates. And it appears that malaria in the Caribbean was less intense and virulent than malaria in Malaya and Assam.[27]

26. Death rates on ocean voyages are usually presented as rates per 1,000 per month. Multiplying these rates by 12 give the more conventional annual death rates. The use of annual death rates are not thought appropriate for the study of mortality at sea as it may be taken to imply that the high level of mortality suffered by shipborne populations was sustained for 12 months when most voyages were completed in only a few weeks or months.

27. In their childhood disease environment, many Indians were exposed to malaria and developed some degree of immunity. But immunity to malaria is strain specific, and so Indian migrants were at risk when encountering different strains of malaria in the Caribbean, Assam, Malaya, and Mauritius (after malaria was introduced into Mauritius in 1866).

There is also a literature on Indian indentured labour emigration which suggests that not only was migration associated with excess mortality but also with reduced fertility, due to the fragility of the institution of marriage on plantations and harsh working and living conditions leading to an "excess" number of abortions, miscarriages, and stillbirths.[28] Quantitative appraisals of this proposition for Indians going to Surinam and Fiji, however, show that fertility on overseas plantations was not lower than in contemporary India.[29]

Relocation Benefits

In considering the consequences of migration, attention must also be paid to the benefits of relocation. Viewed in long-term perspective, descendants of United Kingdom and Indian settler migration have benefited in terms of various indicators of well-being. One quantitative measure of their increased well-being is a secular increase in human stature.

Although the cross-section variation in the height of any population reflects both genetic and environmental factors, the secular change in the height of a closed population (that is, a population not subject to immigration or emigration) largely reflects environmental factors, in particular nutrition and morbidity during the growing years. Recent studies have shown that the descendants of both free European and coerced African migrants to the Americas were considerably taller than their progenitor populations.[30] Similarly, the descendants of United Kingdom migrants to Australia were taller than their progenitor population (see Table 4).[31] And although the average height of the inhabitants of the Indian sub-continent has shown no secular increase during the past century, the average height of the descendants of Indian indentured workers has increased markedly, at least in Fiji and the Caribbean for which data are available (see Table 5).

One of the most interesting findings in the study of Indian stature is the greater responsiveness of males than females to environmental improvement or adversity, and this finding is replicated in the study of other populations. The finding is

28. Tinker, *New System of Slavery*, pp. 201, 202, 206.
29. Emmer, "Great Escape", p. 264; Shlomowitz, "Fertility and Fiji's Indian Migrants". On the fertility of United Kingdom government-assisted emigrants to Australia, see Shlomowitz and McDonald, "Babies at Risk on Immigrant Voyages".
30. Fogel *et al.*, "Secular Changes in American and British Stature"; Steckel, "Stature and Living Standards".
31. The gap between the average height of the Australian-born and United Kingdom-born in Table 4 is only a lower bound on the gap between Australian and United Kingdom heights, as some of the United Kingdom-born would have come to Australia as children and so benefitted from the higher standard of living and lower levels of morbidity in Australia.

shown in the cross-section relationship of height-by-caste: the differential in height between high and low caste Hindus is much greater for males than females. And the finding is also shown in time-series relationships: the sex differential in height increases *pari passu* with the increase in average height over time: in the Caribbean and Fiji, the ratio of male to female height increased from 1.079 to 1.095 and from 1.082 to 1.098 between 1905-1913 and the 1960s, and between 1879-1916 and 1982, respectively (see Table 5). The explanation for the greater responsiveness of male than female heights appears to be that females are more protected from the ill effects of environmental adversity than males. It times of such adversity, the height of males falls relative to females, while in times of environmental improvement, the height of males increases relative to females.

The overall costs and benefits associated with the process of migration, of course, go far beyond the objective and quantifiable demographic and bio-medical variables discussed in this paper. For a more complete analysis of these costs and benefits, historians of various migrant flows have to include other objective and quantifiable variables (such as changed income levels), and also they have to evaluate the subjective experience of the migration process.

Conclusion

The paper has attempted to introduce to a wider audience some of the issues, debates, and new bodies of evidence used in the literature of four govern-ment-financed and/or government-regulated migrant streams from the United Kingdom, India, and the Pacific Islands. The development of the literatures on these migration streams illustrates well the changes that have taken place in the way history is being researched. In contrast to earlier literatures which were mainly political and administrative histories of migration concerned with issues relating to government policy, recent literatures are mainly socio-economic histories of migration, placing emphasis on the migrants themselves, their social origins, motivations, and aspirations, and employing quantitative techniques and computers to investigate large bodies of individual-level socio-economic data.

Appendices

Table 1: Comparative Death Rates on Ocean Voyages, 1620-1917

Ages of Passengers and Nature of Voyage	Period	Number of Voyages	Average Voyage Length (in days)	Death Rate per 1,000 per month
All Ages Combined:				
Slaves to the Americas[a,b]	1680-1807	728	67	50.9
	1811-1863	741	–	65.3
Indians to the Caribbean, Natal, Mauritius, and Fiji[c]	1850-1873	382	88	19.9
	1873-1917	876	65	7.1
Adults:				
Dutch to Batavia[d]	1620-1780	3,914	218	14.5
Convicts to North America[e,f]	1719-1736	38	c60	56.5
	1768-1775	12	c60	12.5
Convicts to Australia[g]	1788-1814	68	174	11.3
	1815-1868	693	122	2.4
Immigrants to Philadelphia[h]	1727-1805	14	c68	15.0
Immigrants to New York[i]	1836-1853	118	c45	4.5
Immigrants to Australia[j]	1838-1853	364	109	2.4
	1854-1892	1,036	92	1.0
Indians to Fiji[k]	1879-1916	87	53	4.0
Chinese to Peru and the Caribbean[l]	1847-1874	343	116	25.5
African Indentured Labour to the Caribbean[m]	1848-1850	54	29	48.7
	1851-1865	54	29	12.3
Pacific Islanders to Fiji[n]	1882-1911	112	117	3.6
Pacific Islanders to Queensland[n]	1873-1894	558	111	3.0
Children:				
Immigrants to New York[i]	1836-1853	118	c45	13.7
Immigrants to Australia[j]	1838-1853	89	109	18.2
	1854-1892	628	92	7.9
Indians to Fiji[k]	1879-1916	87	53	17.8
Infants:				
Immigrants to New York[i]	1836-1853	118	c45	97.7
Immigrants to Australia[j]	1838-1853	89	109	66.1
	1854-1892	627	92	40.1
Indians to Fiji[k]	1879-1916	87	53	54.7

Sources:

[a] R.L. Cohn, "Deaths of Slaves in the Middle Passage", *Journal of Economic History*, XLV (1985), p. 689.

[b] D. Eltis, "Mortality and Voyage Length in the Middle Passage: New Evidence from the Nineteenth Century", *Journal of Economic History*, XLIV (1984), p. 303.

[c] R. Shlomowitz and J. McDonald, "Mortality of Indian labour on Ocean Voyages, 1843-1917", *Studies in History*, VI (1990), pp. 42-43, 47-48.

[d] J.R. Bruijn, F.S. Gaastra, and I. Schoffer, *Dutch-Asiatic Shipping in the 17th and 18th Centuries* (The Hague, 1987), vol. 1, derived from data on pp. 67, 72, 163.

[e] A.R. Ekirch, *Bound for America: The Transportation of British Convicts to the Colonies, 1718-1775* (New York, 1987), pp. 104-105.

[f] K. Morgan, "The Organization of the Convict Trade to Maryland: Stevenson, Randolph and Cheston, 1768-1775", *William and Mary, Quarterly*, XLII (1985), p. 213.

[g] J. McDonald and R. Shlomowitz, "Mortality on Convict Voyages to Australia, 1788-1868", *Social Science History*, XIII (1989), p. 288.

[h] F. Grubb, "Morbidity and Mortality on the North Atlantic Passage: Eighteenth-Century German Immigration", *Journal of Interdisciplinary History*, XVII (1987), p. 571.

[i] Cohn, "The Determinants of Individual Immigrant Mortality on Sailing Ships, 1836-1853", *Explorations in Economic History*, XXIV (1987), p. 376.

[j] McDonald and Shlomowitz, "Mortality on Immigrant Voyages to Australia in the Nineteenth Century", *Explorations in Economic History*, XXVII (1990), p. 90.

[k] Shlomowitz, "Infant Mortality and Fiji's Indian Migrants, 1879-1919", *Indian Economic and Social History Review*, XXIII (1986), p. 298.

[l] McDonald and Shlomowitz, "Mortality on Chinese and Indian Voyages to the West Indies and South America, 1847-1874", *Social and Economic Studies*, XLI (1992), p. 213.

[m] Shlomowitz, "Mortality and Voyages to Liberated Africans to the West Indies", *Slavery & Abolition*, XI (May 1990), p. 36.

[n] Shlomowitz, "Mortality and the Pacific Labour Trade", *Journal of Pacific History*, XX (1987), pp. 41-42, 47, 49.

Note: The Dutch and Chinese voyages are inclusive of a few children. Information on voyage length of slaves to America from 1811 to 1863 was not reported in the cited paper. For European immigrant voyages to New York and Australia, infants were defined as under one year, and children from their first birthday; for Indian voyages, infants were defined as under two years, and children from their second birthday.

Table 2: Comparative Death Rates of Asian and Pacific Islander Indentured Labour in the Pacific, 1879-1953

Population Group, territory	period	Average annual death rate per 1,000	Average population at risk
Asians:			
Indians in Fiji:	1879-1919	19	6,474
Chinese in Nauru:	1913-1940	7	811
Pacific Islanders:			
Queensland:	1879-1887	82	8,916
	1888-1892	53	8,812
	1893-1906	35	8,239
Fiji:	1879-1886	82	4,997
	1888-1892	66	579
	1893-1906	33	231
	1907-1913	38	578
Papua:	1902-1909	32	2,157
	1909-1921	27	7,243
	1921-1941	17	7,311
	1947-1953	9	6,023
New Guinea:	1921-1940	19	30,606
	1947-1953	5	12,038
Vanuatu:	1909-1919	28	570
	1920-1929	29	392
Solomon Islands:	1913-1919	29	3,770
	1920-1929	26	3,698
	1930-1940	12	2,466
Nauru:	1913-1926	72	258

Sources: R. Shlomowitz, "Epidemiology and the Pacific Labor Trade", *Journal of Interdisciplinary History*, XIX (1989), p. 597; R. Shlomowitz, "Differential Mortality of Asians and Pacific Islanders in the Pacific Labour Trade", *Journal of Australian Population Association*, VII (1990), pp. 123-124.

Note: There was considerable variation in the lengths of indenture contracts among population groups and territories: Indians in Fiji served five years, Pacific Islanders in Queensland and Fiji served three years, while Chinese in Nauru and Pacific Islanders in Papua, New Guinea, New Hebrides, Solomon Islands, and Nauru generally served shorter contracts. For Queensland, the data relate to the combined indentured and time-expired (who worked on shorter contracts) population.

Table 3: Comparative Death Rates of Indian Indentured Labour, 1868-1920

Territory	1868-70	1871-80	1881-90	1891-1900	1901-10	1911-20
Death Rate per 1,000:						
Assam Province		77	59	50	41	55
Wellesley (Malaya)		57	40	50	57	
Perak (Malaya)			57	74	86	
Fiji			31	21	15	11
Surinam		54	21	17	14	14
Guyana		23	24	23	18	
Trinidad	45	31	23	18	20	
Jamaica		30	32	21	24	24
Natal				14	20	16
Average Population at Risk:						
Assam Province		43,701	73,899	127,472	71,269	7,031
Wellesley (Malaya)		2,078	3,588	3,749	2,283	
Perak (Malaya)			986	1,493	3,499	
Fiji			3,836	4,508	8,975	12,510
Surinam		2,435	3,966	4,854	3,448	1,849
Guyana		22,331	17,931	17,789	14,234	
Trinidad	8,236	9,119	10,161	9,827	7,519	
Jamaica		4,573	1,138	2,013	2,024	3,471
Natal				14,617	26,143	15,983

Sources: Shlomowitz and L. Brennan, "Epidemiology and Indian Labor Migration at Home and Abroad", *Journal of World History*, V (1994), p. 56; Emmer, "The Great Escape: The Migration of Female Indentured Servants from British India to Surinam, 1873-1916," in D. Richardson (ed.) *Abolition and Its Aftermath: The Historical Context* (London, 1985), pp. 262-263.

Note: There was some variation in the lengths of indentured contracts among territories. Indians in Fiji, Surinam, Guyana, Trinidad, Jamaica, and Natal served five years, while Indians in Assam and the two Malayan provinces of Province Wellesley and Perak served shorter contracts. The data for Jamaica included the children of indentured workers; in the other territories, the data related to adult workers, exclusive of their children.

Table 4: Average Height of Adult Males in Australia

Group Measured	Australian-Born		U.K.-Born	
	number of observations	average height (in inches)	number of observations	average height (in inches)
West Australian Miners [a]	2,555	67.1	729	66.4
South Australian Prisoners [b]	2,024	66.83	1,050	66.47
South Australian Police [c]	357	70.54	705	69.53

Sources:

[a] J.H.L. Cumpston, *Health and Disease in Australia: A History.* Edited by M.J. Lewis (Canberra, 1989). The source does not specify when the goldminers were measured, but as this volume was completed in 1928, the data probably relate to the 1920s.

[b] Yatala Prisoners' Register, Convict Department, 1866-1877, 1883-1928, Public Record Office, Adelaide.

[c] Records of Ex-Members of the South Australian Police Force, Police Service Reports, Vol.1-12, 1839-1920, Public Record Office, Adelaide.

Note: The sample of South Australian prisoners and police were restricted to the age group 20-40 years; Cumpston did not specify the ages of the goldminers who were measured.

Table 5: Secular Change in Average Height of Indo-Caribbeans and Indo-Fijians

Population Group and Age	Males		Females	
	number of observations	average height	number of observations	average height
Indo-Caribbeans:				
(1) Born in India, aged 25-40, measured 1905-1913	902	64.4	267	59.7
(2) Born in the Caribbean, aged 35-44, measured in the 1960s	115	65.5	111	59.8
Indo-Fijians:				
(1) Born in India, aged 20-40, measured 1879-1916	33,163	64.2	12,836	59.4
(2) Born in Fiji, aged 20-40, measured in 1982	124	66.5	246	60.6

Sources: Brennan, McDonald, and Shlomowitz, "Trends in the Economic Well-Being of South Indians under British Rule: The Anthropometric Evidence", *Explorations in Economic History*, XXXI (1994), pp. 225-260; Brennan, McDonald, and Shlomowitz, "The Heights and Economic Well-Being of North Indians under British Rule", *Social Science History*, XVIII (1994), pp. 271-307; Brennan, McDonald, and Shlomowitz, "Secular Change in the Height of Fijians and Indo-Fijians," *Journal of the Australian Population Association*, 11 (1994), pp. 159-169; Brennan, McDonald, and Shlomowitz, "Secular Change and Sex Differences in the Height of Afro-Caribbeans and Indo-Caribbeans", *Social and Economic Studies*, 44 (1995), pp. 73-93; M.T. Ashcroft, H.M.S.G. Beadnell, G.J. Miller, and R. Bell, "Anthropometric Measurements of Guyanese Adults of African and East Indian Race Origins", *Tropical and Geographical Medicine*, XXI (1969), p. 173; J.S. Johnson and J.N. Lambert, *The National Food and Nutrition Survey of Fiji*, (Suva, 1982), Table 3B.

Note: Unfortunately, no other data on the height of these population groups are available.

Migration to Colonial Australia: Paradigms and Disjunctions

Eric Richards

Paradigms and Australia

The search for explanations of international migration is almost as old as the phenomenon itself. Whenever people have moved beyond their national boundaries, contemporaries have sought diagnoses, often investing the act of migration with special significance, even regarding emigration as an index of the condition of the society from which people depart. But the collective quest for "a comprehensive theory of migration and settlement", for "paradigmatic patterns and structural factors in the history of international migration", involves a much larger intellectual challenge.

In western historiography the search has been framed mainly in terms of questions about connections between historical circumstances in Europe and the flow of people to various destinations, usually under European hegemony. The boldest and most provoking thoughts of this sort came from Frank Thistlethwaite's celebrated paper on European emigration first published more than thirty years ago.[1] He postulated structural shifts in the processes of European industrialization and demographic change out of which issued great waves of migration within and beyond the European continent. More recently, and on a similarly heroic scale, have been the speculations of Bernard Bailyn who conjures up a series of stunning metaphors to dramatise what he terms the "centrifugal Volkerwanderung" affecting European societies since the 18th century. He suggests that there was "some latent torque or twist or turn in the foundations of society", resulting in an "elemental movement of the world". Bailyn believes that there must have been some great and comprehensive seismic convulsion to account for the subsequent oceanic movements of population across the Atlantic world of the late 18th and 19th centuries.[2]

We do not yet possess an agreed paradigm in the history of international migration. But the prevailing wisdom, at least in the minds of non-specialist historians, is perhaps well captured in the recent book by the global strategist-cum-futurologist, Paul Kennedy. In his influential survey of the modern world, Kennedy works with a general paradigmatic assumption about 19th century

---

1. Frank Thistlethwaite, "Migration from Europe".
2. Bailyn, "1776. Year of Challenge", p. 446; and Bailyn, *Peopling of British North America, passim.*

migration. He sees international migration in the late 18th and early 19th centuries as one of the main responses to "the growing mismatch between people and resources", that is an approaching Malthusian crisis which threatened "a gigantic inevitable famine". International migration was a means by which European societies responded to the danger of demographic catastrophe. Migration was also an alternative to social instability, poverty and crime. The interesting aspect of Kennedy's interpretation is that it is entirely mechanical, and interprets migration as a negative element in the context of population growth, a simple reaction.[3] It is a view which contrasts with (though does not necessarily contradict) the idea that "European commercial and colonial expansion created the demand for intercontinental migration via the sea routes."[4]

Australia is, by geography only, a case peripheral to this wider search for systematic relationships in international migration. Australia was the most distant theatre of international migration in the nineteenth century. It was much further from the main sources of European migrants than American or African destinations. For that reason alone Australia, the great southern continent, was a latecomer in the history of European migration. Australia entered the arena at a time when voluntary mass migration from Europe was already launched.

Though remote from Europe, Australia was much closer to the newly emergent Asian and Pacific sources of international migrants in the mid-nineteenth century. Yet Australia drew relatively little on those ostensibly cheaper and more convenient supplies of labour and settlers. Indeed the vast majority of Australia's immigrants, from the start of colonial settlement in 1788 down to the second world war, came not simply from far-distant Europe but from a particular corner of Europe, namely the British Isles.

In the nineteenth century about 1.6 million people emigrated from the British Isles to Australia, the longest-distance migration known in human history. For purposes of general speculation we need to consider the degree to which these people were simply respondents to structural shifts in the relationships between the different parts of the world economy and the emergent global system of mobility. In particular the key question is whether there was an identifiable functional relationship between phases of emigration and those of industrialization and empire. We seek, in the process, a systematic connection between the operation of emigration to Australia and the "condition of Britain". In Kennedy's exposition, emigration is a kind of hydraulic machine, gigantic in proportions, which channelled the surplus human residues of Britain's industrialization to suitable colonial sumps. There they could be recycled into useful labour for the peripheral zones of the world economy, in this case the Australian

3.   Paul Kennedy, *Preparing for the 21st Century* (1993), as extracted in the *Australian*, 10-11 April 1993, p. 29.
4.   Boogaart and Emmer, "Colonialism and Migration: an Overview", p. 3.

colonies. And such a view is not distant from some contemporary diagnoses of the situation. At the end of the 1820s, for instance, there were many leaders in Britain who warned of the current crisis in Britain's affairs and, under direct Malthusian advocacy, prescribed emigration to Australia (among other places) as the vital safety valve by which to divert the pressures. Nevertheless few historians today would accept such a mechanical rendition of the 1.6 million lives transferred from Britain to Australia in the 19th century.

The history of Australian immigration is a distant and paradoxical expression of the global story of European migration in the nineteenth century. Its extreme homogeneity in terms of its almost exclusively British origins suggests a remarkable continuity in its immigration history, a simple case of population transfer among complicated and overlapping diasporas which characterised most of the story of global migration in the nineteenth century. In reality the Australian narrative carries of series of shifts and disjunctions (in the sense of the succession of one immigration system by another), which expose a more interesting evolution bearing directly on all the problems we face when constructing a paradigm of international migration.

In the Australian experience, for instance, there was a series of sequential shifts in its immigrant intakes – analogous to the salient "transitions in labour flows" identified in the European-originated international system by Stanley L. Engerman.[5] The Australian case involved also a massive intervention by the State in the organisation of immigration and in the selection of migrants; it entailed ambiguities and paradoxes similar to those of other sectors of the global system. The best known disjunction in Australian immigration history – the so-called "White Australia" policy – was formalised in 1901 (though it was anticipated by racially-exclusionist policies from the 1850s) and was dismantled with little ceremony in the 1970s, neither departure being particularly consistent with the prevailing primary economic needs of the island continent.

This programmatic survey examines the main streams of migration into Australia in terms of their alignment with general patterns in the history of international migration. It also demarcates the principal continuities and structural disjunctions in the account of Australian immigration in the 19th century. Most of all, the Australian case provides some antipodean, long-distance tests of our common propositions about the structure of international mobility in the age of *laissez-faire*. Australia in the nineteenth century attracted about 5 per cent of the migrants leaving Europe which, given the difficulties of distance, was a remarkable achievement which owed as much to governmental as to private enterprise. Paradigms of migration need to cope with continuities and disjunctions in the course of historical change. Australia has enough of both to test our emergent theories.

5. Engerman, "Servants to Slaves", p. 264.

The Convict Stream

The first immigration system into Australia in modern times was unambiguously coerced. Convict transportation from Britain began in 1788 and remained practically the only source of incoming population for the first forty years of Australian colonisation. After 1830 transportation continued but was then accompanied by a parallel flow of voluntary migrants from the British Isles. Convict transportation was retained in some parts of Australia until the 1860s but was of rapidly diminishing significance from the 1840s. In all, about 160,000 convicts were transported from Britain to Australia in the century after 1788. Most of them stayed on after the expiry of their sentences: the convicts provided the basic population stock of the colonies for more than half a century. They and their children provided most of the labour and free citizenry of Australia before 1850. There was a surprisingly smooth passage from convictism to the civilian society and economy that emerged as transportation declined in significance in the middle decades of the century.

The coerced immigration of convicts to colonial Australia was not, at least at the start, designed as a specific labour force for an economic function, apart from its own maintenance. Botany Bay, in New South Wales, was meant to be self-supporting, and it functioned essentially as an overflow for the British gaol system which was in crisis at the end of the 1780s. The American colonies, which had performed this role in the 18th century, no longer accepted Britain's criminal refuse after the Declaration of Independence. Britain's main answer was Botany Bay. The timing was partly determined by the American War, partly too by the perceived crisis in crime and incarceration in Britain itself, the belief that Britain was in danger of being deluged by crime, and that its gaols were unable to cope with the results. This perception did not diminish during industrialization; modern analysis tends to confirm the notion that the practical problems associated with the management of crime grew even faster than population growth in this period.[6] Hence the first phase of Australian immigration leans towards the idea of specific disequilibria in the source country as the simple propellent of migration.

The process was, of course, highly artificial. The convict immigration was instituted entirely at the behest of the British and was financed and directed by British government agencies – it was a severely autocratic system. It was a

---

6. See Beattie, "Pattern of Crime in England"; Gatrell and Haddon, "Criminal Statistics"; Hartwell, *Industrial Revolution and Economic Growth*, ch. 4. On the "intensified" anxiety about crime and order, see Gatrell, "Crime, Authority". There is a continuing debate about the original motives for the first convict settlements in Australia (including prospects of wider commercial and naval stategies). Minding convicts, however, remained the primary economic function of the colonies for the first thirty years.

coerced immigration within a command economy. No alternative form of immigration or colonisation was given consideration until the late 1820s. Slavery was never contemplated and voluntary immigration was discouraged except in one category, namely the introduction of capitalist farmers who could employ convicts and reduce the costs of the penitentiary.

Eventually – as New South Wales discovered effective staple exports – the balance of economic activity in the colony shifted decisively. By the 1820s the market sector of the colonial economy generated autonomous growth and began to call heavily upon local supplies of convict and ex-convict labour. In effect, the colonies of New South Wales and Van Diemen's Land began generating their own labour needs beyond their penitentiary function as laid down in London. It was at this point that a change in the immigration system became imperative for the further development of the Australian colonies. In the third decade of the century there were intensifying labour shortages and it was becoming evident that convictism was inadequate, on its own, to service the rapidly growing demands of the the pastoral industry and its connecting activities.[7]

The Australian convict system was virtually the exclusive labour supply until 1831 and dominant for a further fifteen years. It provides an example of the flexibility of our distinctions between free and unfree migration systems. Recent quantitative research has argued powerfully that the stream of convicts directed to Australia was remarkably consistent with the general socio-economic and occupational character of the British population at large. Nicholas and his colleagues, in their analysis of a large sample of the incoming convicts, conclude that the convicts (apart from their defining criminality) were hardly distinguishable from the working-class population from whom they came. (Indeed the explicit purpose of their work was to analyse the convicts "as migrants"). The convicts' skill levels were fairly typical of levels prevailing in the British working population in general. Though the legal system operated in a highly selective fashion, the people transported to Australia were nevertheless representative of the working population in general. In their view many of the convicts were pressed into crime (and therefore into emigration) by difficult economic circumstances. Moreover, in a methodological leap, Nicholas claims that the convicts were so typical of the working-class at large that they can stand as proxies for the British working population as a whole, and that the excellence of the nominal data on transported convicts may be used to settle much wider questions about British living standards and mobility.

Adopting a human capital approach, Nicholas and his colleagues argue explicitly for the congruence and complementarity of "the transportation system to the free migration system that succeeded it." "The convicts were not drawn

7.   See Nicholas, *Convict Workers*, pp. 15 *et seq.*; and Price, *Great White Walls*, p. 39.

from a criminal class but were ordinary working class people, from a variety of occupations with a variety of skills." The convicts were essentially "ordinary British and Irish working class men and women" – and were excellent migrants despite their criminal pasts. They were in the prime of life, with no dependents, and (though mainly labourers and domestic servants) were more literate and skilled that the population from which they had been ejected. They were already experienced in the process of migration too.[8] Moreover within Australia the convicts were relatively well-off compared with wage-labour in Britain – in terms of health, height, standards of living, education and skills. Nicholas portrays the convicts as "migrant workers" and argues that the convict system in general complemented free European migration. It was a half-way house between the slave and the free labour system.

The more we accept the essential "ordinariness" of the Australian convicts, the fainter becomes the line distinguishing the convicts, at least in socio-economic terms, from the subsequent assisted immigrants from the British Isles who are also sometimes represented as close to a cross-section of the common folk of the islands. The convict emigration to Australia was clearly coerced, dominated by the needs of the State which, in its turn, was responding to the disproportionate increase of anxiety about crime in early industrial Britain. In the next phase the colonies themselves generated autonomous pressures for immigration which began to transcend the specific needs of the metropolitan centre.

The new options

The first disjunction in the immigration systems of Australia was the substitution of free un-coerced migration for convictism, a process underway by the end of the 1820s. It was the product of several forces, some in Britain, others in the colonies, not all working in the same direction nor necessarily simultaneously. Though economic elements were critical to the transition from coerced to un-coerced immigration, the change was accompanied by important ideological shifts in both Britain and Australia.

8.   The authors argue ingeniously from the transportation indents that the convicts were typical of the general population in terms of their pre-transportation mobility. Employing birth and court data they claim evidence of greater mobility over longer distances among the convicts and, by extrapolation, among the general population of Britain in the years 1780 to 1860. Their thesis, contentious though it is, bears upon general propositions relating to internal and external migration out of 18th and 19th century Britain and Ireland. Many of the convicts had migrated across English counties "to maximise their economic returns" contingent on their relatively high skill and literacy levels. Nicholas argues that though they were mostly labourers and domestic servants, "that there was a fair range of skills which were often employed by the colonial authorities". Nicholas, *Convict Workers*, pp. 8-9.

Within Australia, though the convict inflow was strong and, when settled, prolific in terms of its net reproduction, the signs in the 1830s were that the effective supply of labour from this source alone (convicts and ex-convicts and their offspring) was inadequate to the rising needs of the New South Wales economy.[9] Export-oriented enterprise, notably the emergence of a highly successful wool-growing industry, over-stretched the capacity of the old system (reinforced by the growth of urban and agricultural activity too). The convict economy was not necessarily inefficient or uneconomic – indeed recent research emphasises its contribution to the early development of the colonial economy and that it was more efficient than generally assumed. But the supply of convict labour was not expandable at a rate required in the colony. Employers were already complaining of labour shortages in the late 1820s; wages rose rapidly; all the signs were that the convict system was insufficient for the demands of the emergent colonial economy. In strictly labour terms neither the demand for, nor the supply of convicts in Britain (where crime continued was seen as to growing faster than population), was in question. In reality the flow was blocked by non-economic considerations.

The responses to colonial labour shortages were varied. The most obvious solution – which many employers continued to advocate for several decades – was simply to maintain and extend the supply of convicts from Britain. This however was a restricted solution and was eventually terminated entirely by the tide of opinion – ideology indeed – against the continuation of transportation. Within the metropolitan country, in London, humanitarian and penal reform movements mounted increasingly successful agitation against the system. In Australia there was a home-grown campaign (in diametrical opposition to the interests of many employers) to terminate the import of criminals from Britain – in part on humanitarian grounds but partly also on the argument that convict transportation spoiled Australia's reputation and dissuaded respectable free emigrants from choosing Australia as a destination. By the 1830s opinion-makers regarded convict and free immigration as antipathetic and it was widely believed that transportation deterred a free flow of spontaneous emigration to Australia. The new colony of South Australia, established in 1836, set its face completely against convicts. The weight of colonial opinion helped to terminate transportation to New South Wales in 1840 despite its extreme labour shortages. During the following decade most convicts were transported to the overcrowded gaols of Van Diemen's Land, almost entirely at London's behest. Western Australia, which faced severe developmental problems, continued to import small numbers of convicts until the 1860s.

9. This applied especially to the new growth of the colonial economy around Port Phillip (later Victoria) and the more so to the new colony of South Australia established in 1836 on explicitly anti-convict lines.

The West Australian variant suggests that Australia's immigration systems were, at the margin, negotiable wherever economic conditions appeared to require imperative exceptions to be made. In the outcome transportation ceased in the rest of Australia at the very time the employers could not get enough convicts and were complaining of labour shortages. On the whole, however, neither the labour needs of Australia nor the convict pressure from Britain, determined the cessation of convict immigration. There was an authentic disjunction in the provision of labour to Australia and this altered radically the character of Australia's immigration. This disjunction was driven by ideological factors and was uncontrolled by the levers of capitalism. It was not a response to the revealed needs of the economy. The main British opposition to convictism came from humanitarian quarters, from penal reformers, evangelicals, systematic colonisers and utilitarians. Within Australia there were equivalent groups much aided by popular opinion at large, and by the nascent labour movement in particular. Transportation was regarded by many working people as a threat to wage levels in the colonies: this indeed was a recurring argument in Australian history and commonly invoked during periods of high unemployment against both European and Asian immigration, though not necessarily with equal strength. The switch out of convictism does not appear to have been determined by the requirements of capitalism which, in Australia, could have been met by a continuing expansion of convictism. Instead added urgency was invested in the search for a substitute form of labour importation.

The first shift to free or voluntary migration was generated by different and newly-perceived pressures within Britain which (in the late 1820s) seemed to connect in a mutually beneficial way with the labour needs of the colonies. The first step came in the form of British schemes to export paupers to Australia, at parish expense. In 1831 several consignments of this sort were dispatched. This transition coincided with the crisis in British political life at the end of the 1820s which, in retrospect, was a logical extension of Britain's original conception of the Australian colonies as a receptacle for the human refuse engendered by its own economic and social problems.

Such was the the labour-scarcity in New South Wales in the late 1820s that this new solution was welcomed by many employers. In reality the channelling of British paupers to Australia was merely a short-term transition to a much larger and more radical shift towards voluntary mass migration which occurred over the following two decades. The colonies soon exerted their own influence over the selection of immigrants and counteracted the British policy which was framed originally on the idea of simply channelling paupers and the unemployed to Australia. The Australian colonies soon sought entry into the global market for international migrants at a critical, perhaps climacteric moment, in the late

1820s and 1830s, when the propensity to migrate was shifting structurally in Britain and western Europe.[10]

Two other solutions were canvassed at the time. One was a resort to the practice of white contract or indenturing methods. The contract system looked backwards to the 18th century when it had been the mainstay of white labour recruitment to North America before Independence, but which was virtually defunct by 1815. Serious efforts were made in several parts of Australia in the 1820s to resurrect the system and to generate a consistent supply of white immigrants by indenture. Several agricultural and mining companies invested in this system from the 1820s,[11] but they never constituted more than a small percentage of total labour recruitment. There were legal problems and, though Masters and Servants Acts operated in the Australian colonies, there was great difficulty in their actual enforcement. There was probably resistance in the source areas in Britain to the idea of indenture which, by 1815, rendered the system inoperable in terms of long-distance migration. Indenturing white labour in Australia was confined mainly to the provision of key skilled personnel on particularly favourable contracts. But, it must be said, the relative failure of white indenturing in Australia is not well-explained in the current literature though it probably relates to the weakness of legal provisions for contracts and the greater attraction of alternative modes of employment. Certainly the failure of white contracting in Australia paralleled its decline in North America.

Another possible solution to the labour supply needs of Australia was to seek labour from Asia, the so-called "coolie solution". This certainly had many proponents and was, of course, widely employed in other parts of the British colonial world (including Mauritius with which New South Wales had many connections). The idea of "tapping the vast reservoir of labour in Asia" had been supported by a succession of distinguished advocates from Sir Joseph Banks in the 1780s through to E.G. Wakefield in the 1820s and by many prominent settlers in the 1830s.[12] India, a potential source of supply, was a long-standing trading partner with the Australian colonies. Australia received a steady flow of Anglo-Indians throughout the 19th century – often men with capital accumulated in India, seeking opportunities in the new colony, or to rescue their

10. The idea of an increase in European propensities to emigrate seems to lurk in Boogaart and Emmer's version of the the transition out of slavery in the Atlantic theatre. Thus Brazil and the United States coped with the end of slavery "from the massive exodus of Europeans at the time when slavery disappeared" – "but these phenomena were by no means always connected with one another"; Boogaart and Emmer, "Colonialism and Migration: an Overview", p. 9. This suggests an autonomous rise of European migration, not itself contingent on the decline of slavery as such, though the incentive for emigration may have been enhanced by that decline.

11. For example, the Van Diemens Land Company, the South Australia Company, and the Australian Agricultural Company.

12. Price, *Great White Walls*, pp. 38-39.

social status on retirement. Private employers had imported small numbers of coolie labourers into several parts of Australia and the idea was revived during labour shortages in, for instance, 1839-40. But there was political resistance to the coolie solution in official circles in both London and Sydney, and private enterprise was not sufficiently vigorous to force the issue. Apart from the era of the gold-rushes, contract labour was insignificant until later in the century when plantation production opened up the sugar fields of Queensland, then utilising contract labour from the Pacific Islands but very little from Asia.

The assisted immigrants

The idea of Britain exporting to Australia the human wreckage derived from agricultural depression, cyclical downturn in the new industrial economy, and "overpopulation" – approximates closest to the "crisis model of emigration". The inmates of the Poor Houses certainly included "casualties" of industrialization and economic change. Their subsidised removal abroad was strongly advocated by political and economic figures in the years 1825-35. Yet the pauper solution (which was indeed the effective start of free Australian immigration) proved to be a temporary and relatively insignificant component in the streams of migration to Australia. In Britain itself the Poor Law Unions were not prepared to fund the large-scale emigration of their paupers[13]; and the Australian colonies harboured increasing doubts about the economic and social qualities of pauper migrants. Moreover in both Australia and Britain public opinion recoiled from the notion of "shovelling out paupers". Indeed Australia (and the north American destinations) had little recourse to pauper immigration and this weakens the arguments for the "expulsive model" of emigration from industrialising Britain.

Pauper migration to Australia, even within five years of its start, was clearly an inadequate solution to colonial labour needs. In neither quantity nor quality could British Poor Law mechanisms satisfy colonial requirements. The colonies were in a position in which they had little alternative but to generate their own flows of immigrants which transcended the market and acted on behalf of employers collectively. Distance and cost effectively rendered Australia out of the reach of migrants in the normal course of events. Hence the colonies could not rely simply on spontaneous immigration, even after the 1850s.

In the outcome the state (ostensibly metropolitan but mainly responding to colonial authorities) entered the arena and developed a system of comprehensive subsidised emigration which initiated and propelled much of the flow of people

---

13. For those that did assist the emigration of their paupers, Canada was a cheaper and therefore more popular outlet than Australia.

from Britain to Australia over the long period from 1831 to the mid-20th
century. The state took unto itself this great function, and in the process
absorbed a large proportion of colonial resources to finance emigration from
the other side of the globe. It did this (in the middle decades of the 19th
century) by appropriating revenue derived from the sale of colonial land which
was ear-marked for immigration. Though this received imperial blessing (indeed
the fiat) of the Colonial Office in London, Australia was one of the few countries which systematically taxed its economy on this scale.[14] It was the Australian
solution to distance and, though private shipping interests in Britain found
lucrative ways of working the subsided system to their own advantage,[15] it was
essentially a State enterprise in long-distance and long-term population management. Its success could be measured in the numbers transmitted to Australia,
the relative cost-efficiency of the schemes in per capita terms, and the excellence
of the low voyage mortality rates achieved in the middle decades of the 19th
century.

Of the 1.6 million immigrants reaching nineteenth century Australia, almost
half were assisted by fully- or partially-subsidised passages. Assistance was most
significant before the period of the gold-rushes of the 1850s and also in the later
decades of the century. The provision of assisted passages made the Australian
colonies competitive with the North American destinations, especially in certain
years, such as 1841 and 1853/4, though mostly Australia continued to receive
far fewer migrants than the closer competitors. Assistance allowed the colonies
to exercise a selective policy which undoubtedly affected the composition of
the immigrations. Generally Australia sought young couples qualified as agricultural labourers or domestic servants, though the intakes varied with conditions
of supply in Britain and also with those of demand in Australia. The colonies
also sought to replicate national and religious proportions as they existed in the
British Isles, mainly to avoid "excessive" inflows from catholic Ireland.

In the outcome the Australian colonies were relatively successful in recruiting
rural labour though difficulties arose at several times in the century. In 1841 the
colony of New South Wales recruited more than 20,000 assisted immigrants.

14. See Eric Richards, "Emigration to the New Worlds". The subsidized migration system was
     actually devised in Britain and coincided with the re-definition of Britain's own needs –
     notably in its changed attitude to the facilitation of emigration. In the process the British
     government imposed a land sales policy on the Australian colonies which many in the colonies
     regarded as repugnant and unnecessary. Many influential colonists in New South Wales
     preferred the idea of coolie and convict labour. The combination of radical and Wakefieldian
     opinion in London and humanitarian opinion in the colonies defeated the economic
     rationalists in the colony. The last group, as Hirst remarks, were "deprived of convicts and
     coolies". (Hirst, Convict Society, p. 204.)
15. See Broeze, "Cost of Distance Shipping". This may connect with the arguments that carriers
     operated as a quasi-independent force in the emigration process.

Their characteristics were well recorded in the shipping lists[16] – regarding occupation, literacy, origins, religion, age and familial status. Since their assistance was generous but selective, the Australian colonies were able to exert a quality control over its immigrants, most notably in terms of sex balance. Most of its selections were in the prime of life and were better-off and more educated than the average of the British working-class. Though there were recurrent complaints about the unreliability of the selections, on the whole the immigrants were generally from those echelons of the working classes somewhat above the worst off. No strings were attached to the immigrants and they were free to choose any employment they wished Assistance to immigrants departing for Australia was generous but was rarely enough to reduce the actual cost of the passage to Australia below the lowest transatlantic fare. Nevertheless the assisted passage undoubtedly opened more choice to prospective migrants.

In terms of the significance of the Australian assisted immigration schemes for our general model of migration, a striking feature was the recurring difficulty which the Australian recruiters encountered in activating flows of labour from some of the lowest echelons of British society. The unresponsiveness of the poor – especially the rural poor in England (the most desired category of emigrant), and the sheer difficulty of channelling them on to the emigrant ships is one of the most enduring impressions in the operation of the Australian assisted schemes. Since some of the worst standards of life in Britain were in rural areas and since Australia's needs were primarily rural also, one might have expected that the flow between them to have been both smooth and copious. In reality the recruitment of agricultural labourers in Britain was often slow and expensive. Sometimes farmers in Britain resisted the loss of any part of their reservoir of cheap labour (notwithstanding the burden of seasonally redundant labour on the Poor Law). Rural labour was notoriously immobile and also more distant from the ports of embarkation. Much of the Australian story required an actual seeking out of migrants in remote and rural parts of Britain, prising people out of their rural inertia.[17] Sometimes the prospective migrants were

16. The shipping lists provide excellent nominal data which can sometimes be linked with other behavioural data for complex purposes. In the first place, however, they offer evidence of the way in which British people reacted to the offer of assistance to a distant destination, and of the pattern of recruitment. A current exercise is being directed to a particular year – 1841 in New South Wales – to provide the basis of comparison with the convict intake, with the British and Australian populations in that census year, and more specifically, with the results of Charlotte Erickson's study of US immigrants from Britain in that same year, 1841. It should be possible to extend the analysis over time, to select further years in the century and other colonies, to expose trends in the composition of Australian immigration, and for more ambitious comparisons with other flows of international migration in other parts of the world.

17. Unfortunately, in contrast with the convict materials, the immigrant records generally give little evidence of the pre-emigration mobility or post migration mobility. One would expect an above average degree of mobility among migrants in the time prior to their emigration.

eager for assisted passages; but the scale and urgency of the propaganda at certain times suggests that emigration agents could not rely on mere population pressure or rural poverty to procure a reliable flow of migrants either to Australia or America. It required the positive activation of "latent" migrants. As Britain became increasingly urbanised Australian recruitment necessarily reflected the changes in the donor country. Nevertheless Australian recruitment was sufficiently successful to skew the relative rates of recruitment – Australia took a higher proportion of agricultural labourers and domestic servants than the American destinations in the 1870s and probably at other times too.[18] Most immigrants to Australia were not migrating under duress, they had the option of staying in Britain if they wanted to. The major exception to this rule is the apparent alacrity with which the Irish took up assisted passages to Australia, though even among the Irish there appears to have been a bias towards the better off strata of the population.[19]

The great majority of assisted immigrants to Australia, therefore, appear to have been relatively sturdy and independent members of the working classes and not visibly the casualties of specific economic crises in Britain. But within the mainstream of this immigration there were small groups of people who arrived in Australia from very poor backgrounds and they may be regarded as "economic refugees" if we accept a broad definition. It was a paradox of the generous, voluntary assistance afforded in the Australian schemes of migration that the arrangements gave rise to some significant blurring of the distinctions between coerced and un-coerced migration. There was indeed a cluster of categories of "refugee" migrants, varying according to the degree of overtness by which duress was exerted. Some migrants were in such difficult economic or tenurial circumstances that any offer of free expatriation left them with Hobson's choice in the matter. For example, a convict's wife stranded in Britain without a breadwinner perhaps, when offered a passage with her children, was under severe moral compulsion. A juvenile convict offered immediate release if he accepted a passage to Australia was also under pressure. The poor of the West Highlands, facing famine or debt or eviction, were evidently economic refugees. So were many Irish emigrants, when offered a choice between passage or eviction. An agricultural labourer with a big family in depressed Wiltshire – a classic victim of post Napoleonic War depression and the New Poor Law –

So far we have few ways of establishing a systematic check on this proposition. On the question of the pre-emigration mobility of the assisted migrants, Australian historians have not yet made significant progress. Individual cases, however, suggest considerable mobility and one educated guess indicates that, as early as the 1830s, many of the emigrants to South Australia were country folk who, before their emigration, had moved already into urban places or to the ports. On this see Pike, *Paradise of Dissent*, p. 183.

18. See Richards, "How Did Poor British Emigrants".
19. See Fitzpatrick, "Irish Emigration".

saw only opportunity and release in a free passage to Australia. Unemployed lacemakers were in the same state – they grabbed at the chance but had little alternative. Charity was sometimes added to the assisted passage to lubricate the exodus of the indigent.

The Australian migration experience therefore provides numerous examples of "free" immigrants departing Britain under pressure or even force.[20] Some of them were identifiable as the victims of agricultural decline and depression, of cyclical and structural decline in new and old industries, and social disruption. They almost invariably required assistance far beyond that normally offered in the assistance schemes. These cases (which are relatively well documented among the immigrants which itself creates its own bias) undoubtedly blur the distinction between the categories of free and coerced migration and reduce the sense of disjunction between the convict phase and that of voluntary assisted immigration in Australia.

The best-founded impression of the spectrum of immigration is that the quasi-coerced elements in the intake (including the so-called victims of economic change) were a small fraction of the total number of immigrants recruited by the Australian colonies among the British working classes. Current analysis of the shipping lists of assisted immigration tends to confirm the idea that these were overwhelmingly sturdy young people who were located somewhat above the most depressed strata of the British proletariat. The Australian evidence suggests that the barriers to international migration were usually too high for most of these latter categories. The poorest were able to make the journey only where extraordinary help was available, sometimes by way of family networks.

In terms of our general search for a paradigm, the evidence suggest that long distance oceanic migration tended to exclude the lowest strata of European societies. Emigration was expensive and needed complicated mechanisms. The Australian case has particular salience because it contained a special characteristic to test the mobility and suggestibility of the worst-off sections of the British population. That is to say, some of the most deprived and disadvantaged people were offered unprecedented and direct assistance to extricate themselves from their distress. The fact that the colonies experienced recurrent difficulties in filling their quotas of migrants suggest that there existed a greater degree of inertia and resistance than "the expulsion hypothesis" would appear to allow. Population pressure and poverty are often seen as the goad to emigration but they often acted as impediments and this was certainly true of parts of Britain. Moreover population pressure did not always work in the same direction. In some parts of Britain a *decline* of population was itself a propellant of further emigration. In one microscopic Hebridean example of collective migration to

---

20. See Richards, "How Did Poor British Emigrants".

Victoria in the 1850s it may be argued that the exodus was associated more with a declining than an increasing population.[21]

The metropolitan State determined the flows of Australian immigration for the first fifty years – expelling convicts, restricting voluntary immigration, and then (briefly) disposing of paupers to the colonies. Each of these early streams was determined by perceptions of the needs of the mother country – Australian immigration was indeed structurally related to the condition of the metropolitan economy. The idea that the condition of Britain made mass emigration imperative reached a crescendo in the 1820s But by the 1830s the process reversed itself: the Australian colonies began to exercise their independent influence over the recruitment of immigrants within Britain. The British State began to retreat from the game. To an unprecedented extent, the Australian colonies found it necessary to intervene in the process and foster the flows on behalf of its own labour market. The salient point, however, is that very soon the Australian colonies exerted great influence in the recruitment of the immigrants within Britain, and the British State itself adopted a minimalist position in the process. Indeed though a substantial mechanism – the Colonial Land and Emigration Commission – was established in 1840 to supervise the emigrant trade – its function was primarily humanitarian and bureaucratic. It established minimum standards of shipping and conditions for British emigrants, but was essentially a conduit for colonial (and especially Australian) interests and determined by colonial priorities. There was a withdrawal of the British State from the active promotion of emigration, at a time when the colonies were increasing their functions in this sphere. This change in the balance of interest applied even more to "spontaneous" emigration which, as far as the imperial British State was concerned, had become almost entirely a private matter. The tune was now called, not by the British government at the behest of British capitalists, but by colonial governments acting under the influence of their own independent parliaments.

In terms of the general historical paradigm this transition may reflect the diminution of the structural necessities deriving from the industrialization of Britain; or it may have been contingent on the emergence of spontaneous mass migration on a sufficient scale to be seen to be solving the structural difficulties created in the course of industrialization.

In Australia, therefore, the colonial State was in a position to exert strong centralised control over the composition of its immigrant population during the long periods during which spontaneous migration was inactive or insufficient. This was ultimately reflected in the sex balance and age composition of the incoming population.[22] It seems likely that the skill levels of the convict- and

21. See Richards, "Decline of St Kilda", and Richards, "St Kilda and Australia".
22. The impact of the state selection on the incoming population could best be seen in the

the assisted-immigrant were both close to the average of British labour and some of the "refugee" elements among the free immigrants were probably as poor as many of the convicts. And although the recruitment of immigrants in Britain sometimes became unsynchronised with conditions in the colonies and led to unemployment among newly arrived immigrants at the quayside, mostly the governments in Australia were able to turn the immigration tap on and off in response to colonial labour market requirements.

The unassisted immigrants

Though the government-organised subsidised system of immigration (successor to the government-operated convict system) was vital in initiating mass migration to Australia, it did not prevent market-oriented spontaneous systems operating in parallel, eventually to account for slightly more than half of all colonial immigrants. At the start – in 1788 – there was no realistic likelihood of obtaining free migrants from Britain – even apart from the problem of distance, there were strictly limited supplies in Britain and these were directed entirely to North America. In any case this flow was sporadic and highly regionalised.[23] Self-financed private immigration to Australia did not emerge in significant proportions until special circumstances erupted which dramatically enhanced the power of the magnet attracting common people to this continent. Until the late 1830s the reputation of the Australian colonies in Britain was very low. As a recent historian has put it, "No banana republic of the present day stands as low in our esteem as New South Wales did in English eyes."[24] Free, self-financing migration to Australia was fitful until the 1850s though it seems probable that substantial numbers of middle-sized farmers and land investors were attracted, especially to the growing pastoral industry and to the new colony of South Australia in the late 1830s. Favourable propaganda, a new "scientific" theory for a plan of colonisation developed in the name of Edward Gibbon Wakefield, and most of all, the rising profits of Australian enterprise and good access to land, increased the flow of "respectable" immigration. (In 1830 less than 500 self-financing immigrants arrived in New South Wales, but more than 3,600 in 1841, and at least 10,000 unassisted arrived in Australia in 1849).

Amid this gradual growth of spontaneous immigration occurred the greatest discontinuity in Australian immigration history. The discovery of gold in 1852/3 shifted the perceptions and attractive power of eastern Australia into a new phase

---

changes wrought during the gold-rushes when the proportion of males among the immigrants shot up, one effect of the rise in the proportion of unassisted in the intake.

23. See Bailyn, *Voyagers to the West.*
24. Hirst, *Convict Society*, p. 191.

which swiftly altered the entire structure of immigration. Gold created labour shortages in all sectors of the Australian economy especially in the gold-bearing regions; wages were driven up and schemes for subsidising immigration continued right through the decade of the gold rushes. Gold opened up Australia to a much larger potential catchment area for self-financing migrants, including people from its own hemisphere. The ability of the Australian colonies to attract assisted immigrants was, naturally, massively enhanced by the glamorous publicity associated with the gold-rushes. Within a decade the population of Australia nearly trebled – from 405,000 in 1850 to 1.145m in 1860. The impact of gold was decisive because the massive labour-intensive demands of gold-mining were imposed on a relatively small and slow-moving colonial economy. The discovery of gold was like a random shock to the economy – a great disjunction which was accommodated by the system of international labour in several different ways – by free, assisted and Chinese immigration. /

The main impact of gold, however, was to generate a sudden switch of spontaneous migration to eastern Australia. Within a couple of years the size and composition of the unassisted flow grew at an extraordinary rate. One of the recurrent themes in the descriptions of the goldfields was the multinational character of the miners – including interesting minorities from Europe and America. The gold-rushes also created great labour shortages within Australia and generating large internal movements of population into the goldfields from adjacent colonies and from New Zealand. There was a much higher proportion of English among the unassisted than in the assisted immigration system, and this itself offers hints about the selectivity of different migration systems. Indeed the gold-rushes brought to Australia a much more heterogeneous body of immigrants. Britain remained the largest supplier of immigrants but the catchment area widened significantly. There is a substantial argument which says that the immigration of the 1850s brought to Australia better-off immigrants than before.[25] It is likely that the unassisted streams attracted to Victoria and New South Wales during the gold-rushes contained a higher proportion of young single men who also entertained a greater intention of returning to Britain. Australia was able to tap into the newish phenomenon – the existence by then of the freewheeling, youthful, more mobile and risk-taking male products of industrialising Britain.

These new flows of immigrants, both during and after the gold-rushes, are poorly documented. Unassisted migration was a private activity which did not pass through official bureaucracies. We do not even know, with any confidence, the total numbers entering Australia. These immigrants are mainly known through their later careers and through the survival of many of their letters back to Britain. They paid the high cost of passage to Australia without governmental

25. See Jupp, *Immigration*, pp. 14-15; and Serle, *Golden Age*, pp. 47-48.

assistance and it is likely that they were drawn from a more affluent and wider band of British society than the assisted immigrants. Their relationship to conditions in the British economy is not well-known though it is likely that they migrated in a more speculative frame of mind than, for instance, family migrants. They were risk-takers to a greater degree than other migrants. They appear to have responded spontaneously to conditions reported of the Australian economy. They mainly exemplified the new ethos of mobility among of the better off and younger elements of the British population in the age of *laissez-faire*, willing and able to undertake vast journeys in search of adventure, fortune and higher living standards. They perceived the world of migration – even that of remote Australia – as safer and less fearful than in earlier times. And the more free emigration took place the lower the risks became in the minds of the migrants. But it was nevertheless a private activity which statistical analysis cannot yet reach.

In terms of the historical paradigm it is unlikely that the unassisted migrants to Australia – who constituted the majority of all immigrants – were ever direct victims of capitalism or industrialization in Britain. The costs of private emigration to Australia operated against such people. It is substantially more likely that the self-financing immigrants were internationally mobile precisely because they had benefitted from the greater economic and physical freedoms generated in the the process of economic growth in the British Isles. It is also likely, but not proven, that these migrants had a higher propensity to return to Britain and a higher rate of travel in the international system.[26] In many respects the voluntary migration of "ordinary" people is more difficult to explain than that of coerced or sponsored migrants, precisely because their emigrations were essentially private.

Non-British streams

A significant new flow of migrants during the gold-rushes was that from China, organised by private enterprise on a contract basis, mainly through Hong Kong and Shanghai. There had been very little Chinese migration before the gold rushes; from the 1850s the flow sprang forth and an estimated 60,000 reached Australia in the following four decades, mostly to return to China after a period of work in Australia. Almost entirely male, and under indenture-like agreements of one sort or another, the Chinese were treated both as inferior and as a threat to other immigrants. It was Chinese immigration during and after the gold-rushes that precipitated the first steps towards the White Australia policy which marked immigration for the following century.[27]

26. See Richards, "Return Migration and British Emigrant Strategies".
27. Price, *Great White Walls*, p. 23.

High wages and the lure of possible fortune on the gold fields quickly established a well organised system of Chinese immigration in the 1850s. In a larger sense Chinese immigration was a symptom of the inadequacy of European immigration in the 1850s The very high level of wages was the necessary condition to overcome previous impediments to oriental migration to Australia.

The history of the Chinese in Australia was one of mobility, harassment, and overwhelmingly, of return migration. The Chinese were involved in successive mining developments in the years 1850 to 1890 in many different parts of Australia; they were adaptable and competitive. But they were regarded as interlopers and as undermining the income and morals (sic) of the white workforce in all parts of Australia. Political demagoguery and the labour movements in colonial Australia combined to restrict Chinese immigration, effectively from the early 1860s which, together with high return rates, reduced the Chinese proportion in the Australian population to insignificance by 1901.

In this it is difficult to avoid a racial and ideological interpretation of their exclusion – the rejection of non-white labour was clearly against the interests of many employers in Australia. It is also plain that the economic development of particular parts of Australia was delayed by the exclusion of the Chinese in the process. Instead of recruiting self-financing labour from China and India, the Australian colonies continued to scout the villages of Ireland and the back streets of London for labour which was, even in the best light, in no way superior to that of the Orient which was also closer and much cheaper. In order to preserve their racial and cultural homogeneity the colonies denied themselves not only Asian labour supplies but were reluctant to recruit in continental Europe.

There were eventually significant exceptions to British homogeneity. Thus small numbers of Italians became indispensable in certain parts of late19th century Queensland, and Pacific Island labour was employed widely in the sugar plantations of the tropical north, both demonstrating the inadequacy of British immigration to supply the labour for some of the the most arduous tasks of colonisation in Australia.

The Pacific island labour trade brought 62,000 migrants to Australia between 1863 and 1904 . Mostly they were temporary and many were counted twice in this figure. Like the Chinese they were overwhelmingly male, on contract, with high return rates and were treated as unassimilable.[28] The Pacific island trade was eventually closed off partly in response to external humanitarian protest, but more particularly responding to trade union opposition and the strengthening politics of White Australia at the end of the century. The islander trade was terminated at a time when, despite technological change, the demand

28. *Ibid.*, p. 44.

for such labour remained buoyant.[29] It was essentially a political decision. As agitation against the trade grew, Queensland turned increasingly to southern Europe for its tropical labour force – notably to Italy and Malta. The policy of reserving Australia for free white British migrants was an ideology which, in certain circumstances, was negotiable – thus the extreme labour difficulties of Western Australia persuaded this colony to accept convicts for 30 years beyond the rest of the continent; and the revulsion against contract 'coloured' labour was overcome for 40 years in Queensland despite adverse publicity and public opinion not only in Britain but also in the rest of the Australian colonies. The ideology of controlled immigration was, to this small degree, malleable.

Australia continued to turn its back on non-British immigration until the 1940s, such was the power of xenophobia and ideology. The decline of gold and the relative modesty of Australian economic development (and its labour needs) in much of the late 19th century, meant that Britain was able to satisfy most of its immigrant needs. In any case it seems that the resurgent propensity to emigrate from Britain converged with Australia's own immigrant require-ments, except for short-term shortfalls which led to special recruitment drives in the British labour catchment zones (e.g. in the 1870s). To argue thus, however, is to come dangerously close to circular reasoning. In hypothetical terms it is not unlikely that greater transfusions of cheaper immigrants from Asia and the Pacific could have accelerated the development of Australia and, more certainly, could have widened its cultural base.

It is, of course, important to relate the Australian response to Asian immigration to concurrent developments in immigration restrictions in other parts of the international mining world in the late 19th century. Comparable restrictions were imposed in California, Oregon, British Columbia and New Zealand which suggests a form of international copycat behaviour.[30] Resistance to non-white contract labour was at least partly prompted by a genuine fear of a recrudescence of semi-slavery and of a downward pressure on wage levels among labour unions (which also opposed ordinary immigration for much of the time). The hostility to cheap labour was a recurrent factor in Australian labour organisations which often acted in effective opposition to the periodic attempts of pastoralists, cotton-growers, and sugar planters to find efficient and cheap labour over the period 1830 to 1900.[31] It is clear however that ideology and government intervention distorted the patterns of immigration into this continent, for otherwise a spontaneous growth of Asian migration to Australia would have been highly likely. Recurrent labour shortages sent the colonies searching for labour, not in Asia, but in the British Isles, sometimes with poor results, especially in the 1880s.

---

29.   This point is most vigorously pursued by Shlomowitz, in "Marx and the Queensland Labour".
30.   See Price, *Great White Walls*, ch. 6.
31.   *Ibid.*, p. 30.

The imposition of the ideology of White Australia was comprehensive and swift because there was little resistance to the policy within (nor little pressure from outside) and this remained so until the mid 20th century. Indeed the Australian story is one of quite sudden alterations in the modes of labour migration, the velocity and shape of which need to be accommodated in any international paradigm which may emerge. It may be argued that capitalism in Australia was not always "well-oiled" by immigration, that non-British immigrants were ghetto-ised or sent home, and inadequately utilised in terms of economic development.

Volition

Structural factors operate as in a vacuum and rarely inter-connect with the more proximate causes shaping either collective or individual behaviour. If we are to consider questions of volition in the actual circumstances surrounding migration we have no other resource than to listen to the migrants directly. So far the most fruitful historical source has been the correspondence of the migrants between home and abroad. It is from their own words that we can begin to divine their fear for the future, the wrench of departure, the horizons of their own lives.[32] In practical terms few of those who departed for Australia before about 1850 had plausible expectations of a return to Britain. Equally, in these personal testimonies, one senses the enterprise and risk entailed in the emigrations, the prospect of betterment, allied with the danger of misfortune and the falsity of promise. More especially one can feel the strength of kinship – as exposed in the working links required in chain migration (re-inforced by official polices of assistance to nominated migrants) and in the practical organisation involved in the effort to re-unite kin over 13,000 miles apart. Among Australian immigrants the Irish were most able to transact these complicated trans-oceanic family reunifications and this was expressed in their letters in a manner which shows that emigration was like second nature, undertaken without fuss and with great trust.

Part of the general argument is that we may find out more about the dynamics of emigration by considering the ways that migrants were able to overcome inertia and finance their great leaps across the globe, especially by analysing the means by which they emigrated. Moreover as prospective emigrants calculated the benefits and costs of migration, the question of risk-taking was undoubtedly uppermost in their minds. One of the continuities exposed in this type of evi-

---

32. Much of the Australian discussion drawn from such sources has been directed to the ambiguities of perception in the interpretation of personal documents – especially about the notion that emigration was mainly regarded as exile rather than as an extension of home. See especially the work of David Fitzpatrick and Patrick O'Farrell in Fitzpatrick, *Home or Away?*

dence is the sustained reduction over time of fear and risk in the individual act of emigration, as the facilities and normalization of migration evolved. The calculation of risk involved a much wider range of factors than merely the expectation of increased individual income. The fear of the voyage, of the death of family members *en route,* the loss of contact with the wider family, the maintenance of social status and the normal supports of social life, especially of religion – all this entered the matrix of considerations in the minds of the intending or prospective migrant. These matters relating to decisions and motives were, by definition, less significant in coerced systems of migration. But as voluntary migration developed – in its various forms – there was a high degree of subjective calculation along a broad scale. The psychology was variable from case to case and it may be impossible to generalize across an entire population of emigrating people.

In this context there occurs an interesting intersection of migration and family history – which invests the family with a central function in the migration system. As Tamara Hareven has pointed out in relation to internal mobility, "Most of the migration to industrial centres was carried out under the auspices of kin",[33] and this applies *a fortiori* to emigration. Kinship was not necessarily eroded by emigration and in some ways may have been strengthened. Kinship was certainly one of the main carriers of voluntary migration in the Australian case, reinforcing and supplementing in varying measures, assistance offered by the State. The networks of support, the extraordinarily sophisticated understandings which kept the contacts intact, were vital. One of the most striking impressions derived from this literary data is the dispersed nature of family contacts and the balancing of possible destinations in the mind of the prospective migrant prior to emigration. Many Australian immigrants from modest backgrounds had relatives and friends in several places in different hemispheres, usually though not only North America. Often it was the case that such barely-literate people exercised genuine choice in the widest context of inter-continental migration. But the general youthfulness of the emigrant tended to tell against a full articulation of life plans in the decision to emigrate. Chain migration to Australia was partly intertwined with the official systems of assistance and created some powerful and persistent links between certain areas of the British Isles and locations in Australia (for example, between Clare in Ireland and Clare in South Australia, the south west Highlands of Scotland and parts of New England in New South Wales, and between Cambridgeshire and Victoria) But none of these spontaneous associations created exclusive ethnic pockets of immigrants. Australian immigrant society rarely produced ghetto mentalities.

At the level of the individual there is evidence among Australian immigrants, of the operation of a U-shaped curve relating to the impact of emigration on their

33. Hareven, "History of the Family", p. 117.

living standards. The costs of departure, emigration and the adjustments on arrival often left an emigrant family with reduced capital and income in the first phase. Eventually the benefits of emigration and relocation began to accrue and living standards rose above levels experienced before the emigration. The initial sacrifice entailed a personal investment in the act of emigration (that is some degree of deferred utility). In a substantial way the Australian State assisted and, to a certain extent, insured (sometimes by guarantees of employment and sustenance for a period after first arrival), the fulfillment of emigrant expectations.

There were contrasting psychologies about the migrational future – possibly varying systematically with age and generation, even within an individual family. And some migrants were clearly less fastidious than others, that is less critical of the terms of the assistance they received or the arrangements for their future. Thus a peasant from the north of Scotland, or from southern Ireland during the famine years, saw emigration to Australia as an escape from current distress and looming privation and danger to his or her children. The risk of the voyage and the uncertainty of the Australian future loomed smaller for such people than those who were more comfortably placed in other parts of Britain. There were others who were inconsequential by temperament – possibly a particular charac-teristic of youth – people who saw mainly adventure and excitement in the idea of emigration. For these people the lottery of goldmining made the lure of emigration virtually irresistible.

It is not unconceivable that these spectra of responses to risk in the decision to emigrate were influenced by more overarching considerations of a structural sort. Undoubtedly the improvement in shipping technology and information about destinations diminished risk both in reality and in the minds of the migrants. The rise of living standards in the source and the destination places also placed all decisions on a safer plane as the century wore on. Ultimately, however, the greater historical question remains, that is whether the larger structural forces, operating on a global scale, subsumed the myriad acts of individual volition, or were themselves transformed by the exercise of individual decision-making in contexts only partially geared to the specific needs of economic advancement.

Australian immigration and the general model of migration

As far as the periodisation of migration is concerned, the Australian case lends itself to certain propositions which stress the evolution of conditions at both ends of the migrations:

a) Convict migration was powerfully related to the contemporary perception that crime in Britain was growing even faster than population and urbanisation.

b) The onset of assisted migration coincided with a perceived crisis in British economic and political life and was widely advocated as a safety valve for the tensions of the period 1825-35. The direction of policy is easily connected with structural conditions in the exit country. But it may be reasonable to emphasise the overlay of cyclical conditions upon the longer term structural conditions.

c) More significant as a structural component of the Australian intake was the growth in the demand for labour in this continent – as expressed in the dissatisfaction with the convict supply, in high wages, in the small experiments with Asian labour supplies, and the flow of Australian money into the assisted system. The imperative labour needs of the Australian economy were the engine of immigration and they brought into existence the sophisticated mechanism for channelling mass migration to this part of the globe.

d) In structural terms it is not difficult to regard the labour demands generated in Australia primarily as backward linkages of industrialization in Britain. In some cases – for example, in the wool-growing industry, the linkage is obvious. Colonial planning required the development of "vents for export", and the magnetism of the British market guaranteed a close reciprocal relationship. To connect the shaping and rate of growth of the Australian economy and immigration with the process of British industrialization is not contentious, but it may be banal. The connecting argument in this paradigm is that the colonial demand for labour itself was functionally related to the expansion of the world economy (which, some would argue, was in the thrall of the British economy anyway).

e) Less easily accommodated in this thesis are two phenomena: the gold rushes which caused a sudden and radical shift in the patterns of Australian immigration; and, second, the ideology which restricted and later prohibited convict and Asian immigration. The former was ostensibly a random factor; the latter is probably best related to simultaneous restrictions elsewhere in the newly settled regions of the anglo-centric world from the mid-19th century.

It is more difficult to identify systematic connections between the selection of migrants for Australia and the condition of Britain itself. Australian assistance schemes may have altered the terms on which people migrated, but we do not know by how much. There appears to have been some re-channelling of rural folk and domestics to Australia through the assistance schemes – people who perhaps might otherwise have stayed at home or gone to America.

That Australia might have taken the casualties of the British industrial revolution (for example, as the result of demographic imbalance or some form of economic or political disruption) is unlikely in that these people were not normally in the sights of the assisted passage systems (except perhaps those in the agricultural sector) and such people could not meet the entry costs even of the assisted schemes and still less the expenses of private emigration. The recruitment by Australian colonies in Ireland stands as a partial exception to these generalisations. Australia entered this market in the 1830s, coinciding with the emergence of mass Irish catholic emigration, most of which went to Britain and America. The Australian colonies recruited disproportionately in the better-off regions of Ireland and this remained true for the rest of the century.

Beyond the convicts, and arguably some of the Pacific Islanders and a small proportion of the assisted immigrants, it is difficult to sustain the notion that ineluctable expulsive forces propelled migrants to Australia. Much more important for the reciprocal connection between Australia and Britain was the operation of the international price mechanism which transmitted economic signals between the two economies and created opportunities for labour and capital in both places. Eventually the signals reached into the British labour market and, with substantial support from colonial governments, prompted emigration. At the British end the suggestibility and the mobility of the potential emigrants was itself changing – and Australia benefitted from the rising propensity of British workers to emigrate – which of course, coincided with the rise of living standards in both Britain and Australia.[34] The *sine qua non* of almost all voluntary international migration was the existence of an economic differential between the despatching and the receiving countries. But it is within this shifting calculus of economic opportunities that we need to accommodate the less-measureable considerations affecting individual and collective psychologies.

Among the continuities of Australian immigration history should be counted the relatively constant factor of living standards. Almost continuously through most of the 19th century Australia could claim, with some small room for argument, the highest average standards of living in the world. This was a decisive factor in the maintenance of flows of immigrants to such a remote corner of the European world. Australia was also, by 1860, one of the most urbanised societies[35] and this eased the psychological transition involved in the migration of an increasing proportion of urban immigrants from Britain. Within Australia mobility is more difficult to account. There is clear evidence of inter-colonial migration during mining booms and during agricultural depressions. It is also likely that second and third generation rural settlers tended to move outwards from their original settlements, pressing forth to the Australian farming frontier – similarly to the American-Scandinavian model proposed by Jan Gjerde.[36] The general homogeneity of the immigrant population probably made for a society which experienced relatively little inter-communal conflict. There

34. See Baines, *Emigration from Europe*, esp. p. 53.
35. See Butlin, "Shape of the Australian Economy".
36. See Richards, "Paths of Settlement".

was, moreover, surprisingly little aggravation between the Irish and the rest of the British population (most tension was expressed in inter-religious rivalry). The Irish were relatively poorer than most of the other immigrants but neither their Irishness nor their original poverty seems to have restricted for long their upward mobility through colonial society. Much more significant was the widening gap between the Europeans and the Aboriginal society which certainly experienced enduring discrimination in the process of colonisation.

Australia's role in international mobility was essentially that of recipient of people from Britain with a a certain amount of interchange with New Zealand and some reciprocating migration between the mining booms in Australia and North America. There was some interesting secondary migration, on a small and selective basis, from Australia into the Pacific which provided much of the personnel for the extension of Australian and British colonisation to the oceanic islands, most notably, but not only, to Fiji.

More surprising are the data (fragmentary and still inconclusive) of mobility, including return migration, from Australia to Britain, despite the distance and expense. Return migration at the end of the 19th century was somewhat complicated by the growing quantum of international travel which was contingent on the accumulated effects of rising living standards both in Britain and Australia. The movements of visitors and travellers between Australia and Britain by the turn of the century became so large that they caused serious confusion in the statistics of permanent migration. Compared with the total colonial population, the movement both ways between Britain and Australia in the second half of the 19th century was extraordinary.[37] The evidence serves to emphasise the continuum of mobility from the first origins in Britain prior to migration to Australia, through migration to Australia, to permanent and temporary return to Britain. Eventually it may have eroded the sense of finality in the minds of emigrants sailing for the antipodes.[38]

37. See Richards, "Return Migration and British Emigrant Strategies".
38. I am grateful to my colleague Ralph Shlomowitz for his comments though he does not necessarily agree with my interpretations.

The "Yellow Peril" and the "Chinese of Europe": Global Perspectives on Race and Labor, 1815-1930[*]

Donna Gabaccia

Historians rightly approach global studies with trepidation. While our discipline requires us to respect culture, context, and chronology and to pursue research in primary sources, global approaches more often demand broad structural comparisons and methodologies that point us instead toward quantitative data and secondary literatures. Still, the histories of international migration and the development of labor internationalism in the nineteenth century seem particularly appropriate topics for historical interpretation at a global level.[1] Carefully formulated and historically specific comparisons of migrant groups should allow historians to make a unique contribution to global analysis. As Nancy Green argues in her contribution to this volume, "mezzo" level comparison of human groups in particular times, places, or economic structures allow historians to bring discussions of global or world systems "down to earth".

This paper compares the experiences of Italian and Chinese migratory laborers around the world in the nineteenth and early twentieth centuries. The choice may seem a surprising one to many readers who think of European and Asian patterns of work and migration as fundamentally different or who simply view Italians and Chinese as representatives of incomparably different races or cultures. For historians of migration, the nineteenth century marks the end of the slave trade (albeit, only after the transportation of an additional 2 million Africans to the Americas after 1800[2]) and the migration of 35 million Asians toward colonial plantations and what Hugh Tinker has termed the "new slavery" of coolie labor.[3] During the same years, European international migrants followed capital flows either (as settlers and administrators) to newly revitalized colonial empires (circa 4 to 7 million) or (as laborers) to the industrializing "core" of the world

[*] In addition to Jan and Leo Lucassen and to Marcel van der Linden, I would like to express my thanks here to colleagues who read an earlier version of this paper and who saved me from several errors: Alex DeGrand, Randy Dodgen, Bill Douglass, Evelyn Hu-DeHart, Lyman Johnson, Walter Nugent, Fraser Ottanelli, Dave Roediger and Scott Wong. The mistakes that remain are my own.

1. Baily, "Cross-Cultural Comparison"; Gabaccia, *Militants and Migrants*; Ramirez, *On the Move*.
2. Boogaart, "Colonialism and Migration: An Overview", p. 4.
3. Tinker, *New System of Slavery*.

economy. Circa 10 million laborers migrated internationally within Europe and another 41 million traveled to the Americas before World War I.[4]

Viewed from the perspective of historians today, the characteristically blunt and unapologetic racism of the nineteenth century defined very different migratory patterns and labor experiences for the Chinese and the Italians by forcing nonwhites into unfree systems of labor. In the work of Lydia Potts, for example, the Chinese (and other Asian) coolies appear as the new slaves of the colonized world, with its plantation production, while Italians appear as a particularly large and important component of the new, and international, industrial proletariat.[5] Italians appear as forgers and beneficiaries of labor movements' defense of free labor, while Chinese appear as their victims.

This is not how contemporaries saw the two, however. Instead, in many places around the world, Chinese and Italians (along with some other European migrants) occupied an ambiguous, overlapping and intermediary position in the binary racial schema common in the countries where they worked. Nineteenth century labor activists in Europe and North America, for example, typically viewed both Chinese and Italians as neither black nor white, but as something else- "yellow," "olive," or "swarthy". They expressed the similarities of the two in telling language, calling Italians "European coolies," "padrone coolies" or (most frequently) "the Chinese of Europe". Typical was the radical Australian activist who argued in 1891, "We resisted the wholesale immigration of Chinese [...] and when we are in danger of the Chinese of Europe flowing onto our shores we must again give a note of warning of no uncertain sounds [...]".[6] Historians have found native-born workers' reference to the Italians as "the Chinese of Europe" in the U.S., France, Canada, and several European nations, but not in Latin America, where both Chinese and Italians also migrated in substantial numbers.[7]

Why did Italian and Chinese migrants seem racially similar to some observers in the nineteenth century yet not to others? This paper finds a partial answer to those questions in the labor systems that developed hand-in-glove with both migrations. Significant proportions of both Italian and Chinese migrants left their homelands in debt to those who financed their travels; many traveled the globe as laborers under various forms of contracts; others fell into new forms of debt-created peonage or dependency when they began work abroad. Their ambigu-

---

4. Moch, *Moving Europeans*; Nugent, *Crossings*; Hoerder, "Introduction to Labor Migration"; or Vecoli and Sinke, *Century of European Migrations*; Gould, "European Intercontinental Emigration".
5. Potts, *World Labour Market*, ch. 3; Kloosterboer, *Involuntary Labour Since the Abolition*; Gabaccia, "Worker Internationalism and Italian Labor Migration".
6. Douglass, *From Italy to Ingham*, pp. 49-50.
7. Foerster, *Italian Emigration of Our Times*, p. 142; Ragionieri, "Italiani all'Estero ed Emigrazione", p. 654; Vecoli, "Italian Immigrants in the United States Labor Movement".

ous and intermediary racial status reflected their involvement in labor systems that also fell, according to most western observers, somewhere between slave and free labor. Feared in many lands as unfree laborers, Chinese (and to a lesser and less successful degree) Italian migrations sparked explicitly racial campaigns for their exclusion or (once they had entered) their containment. Given the confluence of understandings of race and labor systems during these years, it is scarcely surprising that the labor movements of Australia, the United States, and Canada played especially crucial roles in enacting racially discriminatory legislation – first against the Chinese; later (and less effectively) against Italians and other "swarthy" Europeans.[8]

We know of course, from our own racial understandings, that the "race" attributed to Italian and Chinese immigrants subsequently mutated. Latin Americans had welcomed Italians as white Europeans throughout the nineteenth century, even when they came as impoverished laborers. In other countries, however, Italians and their children "became white" only after discriminatory legislation diminished their migrations. The Chinese, by contrast, continued to occupy a shifting and ambiguous racial territory – neither white nor black – in those western nations that had made the greatest efforts to exclude them. The diverging trajectories of racial classification of Italian and Chinese migrants in the twentieth century – itself a compelling topic – is beyond the scope of this paper.[9] A comparison of the two in the previous century nevertheless uncovers how little we know about the interaction of class, race, and ethnicity in the world economy.[10]

Italian and Chinese Laborers in the International Market for Labor

Together, Chinese and Italian migrants made up about one-third of total international world migrations in the years between the Napoleonic Wars and the Great Depression of the 1930s. Roughly 27 million Italians left their

8. The Italians were by no means the only European group so labelled; they were, however, the largest such group and the only one associated so extensively with labor systems disparaged as "unfree" in the nineteenth century. See pp. 186-189 below for further development of this argument.

9. Unfortunately so are racial understandings of the Chinese in the many Asian lands where they also migrated. This is a topic that requires far greater attention but that my unfamiliarity with Chinese language sources does not allow me to pursue adequately. It is, quite simply, a missing piece in my analysis.

10. For an exciting, early effort to sort out class, nationality and race from an international perspective, see Prato, *Protectionnisme ouvrier*. Prato wrote as a labor activist determined to convince labor movements of the futility of protectionist responses to migrant labor. An Italian reviewer of Prato's (earlier) Italian edition titled his remarks "Why the Japanese and the Italians should form an alliance".

homeland during those years; somewhere between 2 and 10 million Chinese did so. Viewed from the perspective of the sending or home nation, the Italian migrations seem of greatest significance. Italian migrants between 1870 and 1920 constituted a third of Italy's population in 1911; Chinese migrations never totalled more than two percent of China's much larger population.[11] Switching focus to the impact of the two migrant groups on receiving nations, however, their relative significance reverses: the arrival of Chinese most often provoked fundamental change in state policy toward migration, and these changes targeted not only the Chinese, but ultimately other immigrant groups as well.

One of the common, and most distinctive, characteristics of these two migrations is that Italian and Chinese migrants found their way to almost every corner of the earth. Unlike most migrant groups (e.g. Indians moving within the British Empire; Mexicans heading for the U.S.) Chinese and Italian migrants went everywhere, including to Mexico and to India. Chinese men labored in France, England and the Netherlands,[12] while Italian men went to China itself looking for work.[13] Both groups sought work in Africa, Europe, Asia, and Australia, as well as in North and South America. Only rarely, however, did Chinese and Italians migrate to precisely the same destinations at the same time; only rarely did they compete directly with each other for the same jobs.

The national histories of China and Italy provide few easy clues to their peculiarly extensive, yet rarely overlapping, migrations. Chinese migration – long a clandestine tradition among traders to southeast Asia – expanded in the nineteenth century against the prolonged resistance of its Ch'ing rulers. Mass Chinese migration toward the west dates to Great Britain's "opening" of China in the Opium war of 1840-42 and to the discovery of gold in the United States, Australia and Canada shortly thereafter. Chinese migration continued, with increasing imperial toleration at home but with rising national barriers imposed abroad, until after World War I.[14]

Until the turn of the century, Chinese emigrants came almost exclusively from two southern provinces – Kwangtung and Fukien; thereafter northerners' presence among migrants increased.[15] The shift in migrants' home regions reflects the spread of foreign capital, markets, and political influence in China,

11. Perkins, *Agricultural Development in China*, pp. 207-214. Estimates of Chinese emigration vary widely; compare, e.g. Wu, "Chinese Immigration in the Pacific Area"; Tan, *Your Chinese Roots*, p. 4; Willcox and Ferenczi, *International Migrations*, Vol. 1, pp. 148-159.
12. Stegen, "Chinois en France"; Summerskill, *China on the Western Front*; Benton and H. Vermeulen, *Chinezen*.
13. Audenino, *Mestiere per Partire*, ills 17-18.
14. General studies include MacNair, *Chinese Abroad*; Pan, *Sons of the Yellow Emperor*; Wang, *Organization of Chinese Emigration*.
15. Perkins, *Agricultural Development in China*, p. 213; Richardson, *Chinese Mine Labor in the Transvaal*, p. 267.

and – at the same time – the contracting hegemony of China's emperors over their rural provinces. Foreign capital and foreign merchants first made inroads into the peripheries of coastal and southern China. This was more than historical accident: Kwangtung and Fukien provinces had long resisted incorporation into Chinese dynasties centered in the north. In the south by the 1840s (and sixty years later in the north), foreign-financed railroads, western imports, and new export routes for local grains threatened traditional habits of subsistence in the Chinese countryside. Economic change and the vagaries of centralized state control provoked the devastating Taiping revolts in the inland region bordering Kwangtung and Fukien in the 1850s, and unrest in the countryside had spread to other regions of China by the twentieth century, setting the stage for a series of Chinese revolutions.[16]

Migration from Italy, too, had a long history, and it too emerged from Italians' early modern importance as traders and explorers. A newly independent nation state, by 1870, however, Italy no longer counted among the "core" economies of the world; industrialization had scarcely begun in 1900, and then only in a small number of northern provinces. With a few notable exceptions (e.g. Sardinia), a mix of commercial and subsistence agriculture prevailed. The products of Italy's diverse agricultural regions circulated on world markets. Exports and imports linked northern Italian regions closely to continental Europe, while the *mezzogiorno*'s (Italian south's) integration into the world economy tied it most closely to northern Africa and to the Americas.[17]

Italian emigration was a by-product of complex and interacting economic forces unleashed by the political changes of unification. These included the new demands of the nation state for peasant taxes, the continued proletarianization of a rapidly growing peasant population, the formation of a national market and the opening of that market to foreign imports (resulting in collapsing native industries), the end of feudalism, and – finally – falling world prices for important Italian exports, from wheat, wine and oil, to sulfur. Predictably, perhaps, Italy's countryside exploded periodically throughout the century: peasant rebellion preceded, accompanied, and followed unification. The real threat of revolution threatened during each decade from 1870 until fascist dictatorship under Mussolini.[18]

The Italians and Chinese who migrated in the nineteenth century were quite typical of nineteenth century migrants in leaving rural homelands rocked by economic and political turmoil. The manner in which they left home, however,

---

16. Wolf, *Peasant Wars of the Twentieth Century*, ch. 2.
17. Still enormously useful is Foerster, *Italian Emigration of Our Times*. Recent studies of Italian emigration worldwide include Assante, *Movimento Migratorio Italiano*; Ciuffoletti, *Emigrazione nella Storia d'Italia*; Rosoli, *Secolo di Emigrazione Italiana*.
18. C., L. and R. Tilly, *Rebellious Century*, p. 94.

set them apart from some other mass migrations during these years, especially those from India and from much of Europe. The recruitment of Chinese and Italian men as laborers for foreign employers began differently but nevertheless developed through strikingly parallel structures.

The Chinese, unlike the Italians, found themselves, along with Indians, in demand as indentured, "coolie" laborers as early as the 1840s. Plantation owners in European colonies began recruiting coolies when the British Empire set a new standard for modern empires by emancipating its African-origin slaves during the course of the 1830s. Great Britain sought to repress the slave trade but it also looked (along with Spain, Portugal, and France) with growing interest toward India and China as new sources of labor. From the 1840s until World War I the British sought to regulate international coolie traffic (at the expense, especially of Portuguese traders) and to guarantee that it not become "the moral equivalent of the slave trade".[19]

Historians hotly debate how many Chinese migrants should be considered coolies.[20] Part of the confusion originates in the complex meaning of the term "coolie".[21] Evidence of widespread ensnarement, trickery, and involuntary migration and for long-term and exploitative indenture contracts is quite strong for early Chinese migrations to Cuba[22] and Peru,[23] weaker for Chinese migrations to Australia[24] and Hawaii[25] and weaker still for the U.S.[26] The Chinese laborers who went to work in South Africa, France, and Great Britain after 1900, while indentured, enjoyed conditions of labor and terms of servitude far superior to those in earlier decades.[27]

My own reading of this debate is that scarcely more than a third of Chinese migrants were coolies in the narrowest and most pejorative sense of the term (e.g. ensnared to work under conditions bordering on slavery). At the same time, *most* Chinese migrants either left their homes to pay off debts or became

19. The relative importance of Chinese and British efforts to regulate the coolie trade can be explored in Campbell, *Chinese Coolie Emigration*; Irick, *Ch'ing Policy Toward the Coolie Trade*; Tsai, "Reaction to Exclusion".
20. Contrast Potts, *World Labour Market*, ch. 3, to Arensmeyer, "British Merchant Enterprise", pp. 23-38.
21. Breman and Daniel, "Making of a Coolie".
22. *Report of the Commission Sent by China to Ascertain the Conditions of Chinese Coolies in Cuba* (Taipei, 1970); Corbitt, *Study of the Chinese in Cuba*; Hu-DeHart, "Chinese Coolie Labor in Cuba"; Powers, "Chinese Coolie Migration to Cuba".
23. Stewart, *Chinese Bondage in Peru*; Real de Azua, "Chinese Coolies in Peru".
24. Saunders, "The Workers' Paradox"; also Saunders, *Workers in Bondage*.
25. Takaki, *Pau Hana*.
26. Zo, *Chinese Emigration into the United States*.
27. Besides Richardson, *Chinese Mine Labor in the Transvaal*, Summerskill, *China on the Western Front*, and Stegen, "Chinois en France", see Richardson, "Chinese Indentured Labour in the Transvaal".

indebted in order to migrate and to find work abroad. Persia Crawford Campbell, in one of the earliest systematic studies of Chinese coolies, distinguished indentured migrants from the larger group of Chinese who migrated under what she termed "the credit-ticket system", whereby laborers fell into a kind of debt peonage to the labor agent or merchant who paid for their passages.[28] In this paper I (unlike most contemporaries who used the term indiscriminately) reserve the use of the term coolie for indentured labor. Campbell's distinction between indenture and "credit ticket" as competing auspices of migration is a useful one. It points to institutions common to migrations from both China and Italy.

Italians rarely migrated under formal contracts of indenture, but – much like the Chinese – they often left home to pay off existing debts or went into debt in order to migrate and find work. Sparked by foreign-born labor recruiters, native-born middlemen "merchants in flesh" became intimately involved in financing and delivering migrants from both places to workplaces around the globe. In Italy, the native middlemen were the infamous *padroni*. In China, the middlemen were the "crimps", sometimes called also "pig traders". Padroni and crimps linked illiterate Italian and Chinese peasants, and ex-peasants, to the shipping companies, labor agents, and employers of the capitalist world economy.[29]

Both crimps and padroni worked within agricultural worlds accustomed to limiting individual workers' control over both their own persons and their labor power. Just as the European slave trade in West Africa had exploited native traditions of slavery, foreign employers of migrant labor found in Italy and in China cultures accustomed to parents, employers, and patrons controlling, bartering and even selling their dependents. In Italy, elements of feudal banalities and corvee survived the transition to commercial agriculture and speculative land ownership. Italian parents bound children into long-term indentures and apprenticeships to migratory tradesmen; the plight of the "little slaves of the harp" in Europe and the Americas first led to the outraged identification of Italian padroni as organizers of migration.[30] In China the sale of poor girls into sexual work, concubinage and marriages continued into the twentieth century.[31] Chinese boys, too, could be sold into a form of permanent and transmittable domestic bondage.[32]

In neither Italy or China, however, had adult men's labor commonly been sold through indenture contracts. In Italy, adult male sharecroppers more commonly fell into debt bondage. In China, kinship, too, tied many adult men

---

28. Campbell, *Chinese Coolie Emigration*, p. xvii. See also Zo, "Credit Ticket System".
29. Iorizzo, *Italian Immigration and the Impact of the Padrone System*; Harney, "Padrone and the Immigrant"; Harney, "Commerce of Migration", pp. 37-38.
30. Zucchi, *Little Slaves of the Harp*.
31. Jaschok, *Concubines and Bondservants*.
32. Watson, "Chattel Slavery in Chinese Peasant Society"; Watson, "Transactions in People".

in servitude to lineage head-men. As economic change and population growth forced increasing numbers of Italian and Chinese peasants out of family-based agriculture to search for cash incomes, local strong men moved to bind newly mobile men into new forms of patronage and dependency replacing kin and lineage affiliations with various kinds of "secret societies".

Manipulating credit, kinship, religious and personal or charismatic ties, padroni and crimps built organizations that blended self-help, mutual aid, profit-seeking, crime, and politics. Historians might best view padroni and crimps as entrepreneurs seeking their fortunes along the fine line that separated legal from illicit business: their businesses included gambling, prostitution, extortion, harassment, and illicit services like "protection".[33] Padroni developed in and alongside the same social milieu that produced Italy's rural mafiosi; China's crimps are unimaginable outside of a world in which secret societies functioned as quasi governments far from centralized Manchu power and authority. It is true that secret societies and mafia cliques exploited poor, marginal and ignorant peasants. But it is also true that both offered group affiliation to marginal men in societies where unaffiliated individuals had few options for survival.[34]

Through social or financial dependency on padroni and crimps, Italian and Chinese migrants entered an international market for workers, and they found work in a roughly similar range of jobs. Chinese migrants gained notoriety mainly as coolie gang laborers on tropical sugar and tobacco plantations, but Italians also replaced slave laborers after emancipation – most noticeably on Brazil's coffee plantations and on the sugar plantations of Louisiana.[35] Similarly, although Italians became best known as human steam shovels on railroad construction sites around the globe, the Chinese too earned reputations for their construction in the western U.S. and Canada, and on construction sites in Panama, Java, and the Philippines.[36] Both groups also found niches in mining.[37]

33. A case study from Italy is Angelini, "Suonatori ambulanti e 'garzoni'", pp. 477-485.
34. On the Italian case, see Blok, *Mafia of a Sicilian Village*; Arlacchi, *Mafia, Peasants and Great Estates*. On the Chinese case, see Wolf, *Peasant Wars of the Twentieth Century*, pp. 106, 111-113; Chesneaux, *Secret Societies in China*; Chesneaux, *Popular Movements and Secret Societies*.
35. Studies of Italian agricultural and plantation labor include Trento, *Dov'é la Raccolta del Caffe*; Scarpaci, *Italian Immigrants in Louisiana's Sugar*; Holloway, *Immigrants on the Land*; Solberg, *Prairies and the Pampas*, pp. 89-110, passim; Dean, *Rio Claro*. On the Chinese and plantation labor, see Anders, "Coolie Panacea"; Lasker, *Human Bondage in Southeast Asia*; Meagher, "Introduction of Chinese Laborers to Latin America"; Mookerjii, *Indenture System in Mauritius*.
36. See Roy, *White Man's Province*; Montgomery, *Fall of the House of Labor*, p. 67; Faith, *World the Railways Made*, pp. 193-194; Mon Pinzon, "Century of Chinese Immigration"; Potts, *World Labour Market*, pp. 92-94, 213. Italians' work in construction is best documented for Canada, although Foerster's early study established its importance in every nation where Italians settled: see especially Harney, "Padrone System and Sojourners"; Avery, *"Dangerous Foreigners"*, pp. 26-33.
37. Richardson, *Chinese Mine Labor in the Transvaal*; Gittins, *Diggers from China*; Bonnet et al.,

The sizeable minorities of petty merchants who migrated alongside these laborers served their needs, joined in their exploitation, and documented real possibilities for upward mobility.

Although both the Italian government and many receiving nations hoped to encourage Italian cultivators to settle on the land – and indeed Italian statesmen regularly referred to Italian enclaves abroad as "colonies", conjuring wishful images of demographic imperialism – most Italians left home initially in the hopes of "making a successful campaign" and returning with cash to shore up peasant subsistence production at home. Considerable evidence suggests that the Chinese, too, left hoping to return. Often used as an indirect measure of the permanency of migration, sex ratios in the two groups were strongly unbalanced. Ninety percent or more of Chinese migrants were male – as were 60 to 90 percent of Italian migrations.[38]

Because of their continued orientation toward the homeland, Wang Gungwu has labelled Chinese migrants "sojourners", and he has differentiated sojourning (Huaqiao) from coolie migration (Huagong).[39] In doing so he follows a long, if also much-debated, scholarly tradition. But historians of Italian migrants have also used this same terminology, sometimes substituting "bird of passage" for "sojourner".[40] This is scarcely surprising: about fifty percent of all Italian migrants eventually returned home. Return rates are harder to estimate in the Chinese case but they seem to have considerably exceeded fifty percent.[41] (The significance of Chinese return is also harder to assess as some coolies remained contractually obligated to return at the end of their indentures.) Final evidence of emigrants' continued connection to the homeland comes from their remittances – they were considerable in both cases.[42]

A comparison of Chinese and Italian migrations thus highlights some problems inherent in forcing the past into the racial categories of the present. The Chinese were not pushed passively into colonial agriculture and a new system of slavery, while Italians found easy welcome in the industrial core as a free proletariat of wage-earners. In fact, nowhere outside of Argentina and a few Brazilian cities did more than a quarter of migrant Italian men find work as industrial wage-earners. Instead, both Chinese and Italians occupied ambiguous occupational areas, somewhere between agricultural and industrial work. As assisted migrants furthermore, they both rapidly found themselves castigated as nonwhite "slaves".

Homme du Fer, Notarianni, "Italian Involvement in the 1903-04 Coal Miners' Strike"; Boyd Caroli, "Italians in the Cherry".

38. Gabaccia, "Women of the Mass Migrations".
39. Wang, *China and the Chinese Overseas*, pp. 4-5.
40. Harney, "Padrone System and Sojourners".
41. Willcox and Ferenczi, *International Migrations*, Vol. I, p. 152; Tan, *Your Chinese Roots*, p. 47.
42. Cinel, *National Integration of Italian Return Migration*; Yen, "The Overseas Chinese and Late Ch'ing".

Fearing slavery, nascent labor movements in the developing world pioneered in developing racialized terminology as weapons for their own defense. One of those defenses was discriminatory immigration policy.

Free Migration. Unfree Labor?

The organization of Chinese and Italian migration limited migrants' ability to find work for wages, and thus to claim for themselves the primary marker of free labor in the nineteenth century. Although undeniably part of a capitalist world economy, the plantations, mines, and construction sites employing Chinese and Italian workers rarely compensated them exclusively with cash wages. Instead, indenture, other varieties of labor contracts, and debt bondage of various kinds characterized Chinese and Italian work around the globe. Contemporaries described all these labor systems as continuations of slavery; they viewed all as threats to free, white laborers. Defense of free labor often degenerated into campaigns against racially disparaged sojourners. Indeed, it sometimes seems that nineteenth-century observers *had* to label migrants as unfree *in order to* exclude them as racially undesirable.

The spread of the terms "coolie" and "slave" to describe a wide range of capitalist labor systems employing unskilled wage-earners[43] suggests how central racial terminology became to nineteenth-century understandings of free labor. It appears that heated debates about Chinese migration between 1850 and 1900 helped shape definitions of race and of free labor around the world. Significant numbers of adult Chinese men did, in fact, migrate as formally indentured coolies. Some faced lengthy indentures (7-8 years for Asian coolies in the Caribbean 1845-1870; 3-5 years on Asian plantations later in the century).[44] Furthermore, crime and coercion did fuel the recruitment of much labor in China, especially in the 1840s, and death rates of coolies during transportation matched those of the slave trade (20 percent) until 1860.[45] Plantation owners purchased coolies dockside as they had slaves as late as 1900 in parts of Asia; they could also sell their coolies at will. In Cuba Chinese coolies labored beside African slaves and suffered the same harsh discipline and miserable living conditions. Even escape from indenture might not always mean freedom: Cuban contracts required Chinese coolies to either re-indenture themselves or to return home.

---

43. See, e.g., Cunliffe, *Chattel Slavery and Wage Slavery*.
44. Engerman, "Servants to Slaves to Servants".
45. Steckel and Jensen, "New Evidence on the Cause of Slave and Crew Mortality". Mortality among adult voluntary immigrants, by contrast was under 1 percent, see McDonald and Shlomowitz, "Mortality on Immigrant Voyages".

But not all, or even most, Chinese coolies migrated involuntarily – the exact numbers will remain the object of debate because they cannot be precisely known.[46] The act of contracting oneself had distinguished voluntary migration under indenture from the involuntary African slave trade in England's eighteenth century Atlantic colonies,[47] and it might have continued to do so in nineteenth century colonies. Admittedly, options for poor landless men in south China in the nineteenth century had become extremely limited – but that only explained men's willingness to indenture themselves. Chinese coolies risked death and unbelievable mistreatment if sold into a shipment headed for Peru[48] or Cuba.[49] If they headed for Africa or Hawaii, however, their future proved brighter. Remaining at home already carried high risks for marginal men with few dependable social ties. The world that produced coolies was very much a culture of gambling.[50] Binding oneself as a coolie was, in betting terms, playing a "long-shot" – but it could be a voluntary one.

By the end of the century, furthermore, even coolie labor had evolved toward free wage labor.[51] Under the indentures of the British Empire, coolies earned fixed daily wages for fixed hours of work; their costs of passage and of daily subsistence (when this was provided) were subtracted on a regular schedule. In some places coolies bought their own food and housing with the wages they earned. Indenture contracts bringing Chinese laborers to South Africa's mines in 1904 and to France and England's armies during World War I specified days of rest, medical care, and cash payments to families left behind.[52] Their lives foreshadowed those of "guest workers" in Europe in the twentieth century.

Plantation demand for coolie labor also diminished after 1870, especially in older areas of cultivation. While new tobacco, cocoa, and rubber plantations in Europe's Asian colonies generated new demands for indentured labor, sugar and coffee planters in older areas of cultivation began experimenting with new systems of employing immigrant labor – sharecropping, tenancy and seasonal wage labor. As they did so, planters in North and South America and in Australia increasingly recruited Italian as well as Chinese workers.[53] Nevertheless charges of unfree labor on plantations persisted even under these newer labor systems.

46. Cloud and Galenson, "Chinese Immigration and Contract Labor".
47. Steinfeld, *Invention of Free Labor*; see also Galenson, "Rise and Fall of Indentured Servitude".
48. Stewart, *Chinese Bondage in Peru*.
49. Walton, *Indentured Labor. Caribbean Sugar*; Powers, "Chinese Coolie Migration to Cuba"; Meagher, "Introduction of Chinese Laborers to Latin America".
50. Davis, *Primitive Revolutionaries of China*, p. 83; see also Chao, *Chinese Kinship*, p. 183.
51. Engerman, "Coerced and Free Labor", p. 13.
52. Richardson, *Chinese Mine Labor in the Transvaal*; Summerskill, *China on the Western Front*; Stegen, "Chinois en France".
53. Douglas "The Swarthy Alternative"; Scarpaci, *Italian Immigrants*; Trento, *Dov'é la Raccolta del Caffe*; Vangelista, *Braccia per la fazenda*.

And they extended as well to Chinese and Italian migrants who were neither indentured nor plantation-bound, but merely indebted or contracted laborers.

"Coolie slave" and "padrone slave" labelled as unfree even those Chinese and Italian men who had borrowed money to migrate, or who had depended upon a labor agent to find them work during or after migration. These men (or in some cases, their families) had received cash advances from crimps, padroni, and kinsmen; they intended to work off the debt abroad.[54] Others had incurred debts against labor contracts or gone into debt to the ticket agent or labor contractor, for padroni and crimps and secret societies also sold tickets and recruited laborers. They remained labor agents once migrants reached "the other side". Debts rose further as Italians paid a "bossatura" (payment for the boss's services) to the man who handled contacts with steamship company, state bureaucracy or employer.

Illustrative are the migrants who, recruited by and indebted for passage money to a kinsman patron in Europe, traveled to Canada to build railroads in the west. There, they signed simple contracts with a padrone railroad contractor; the contract gave them free transport to the construction camp but only if they stayed on the job for six months. Thus they arrived at the construction camp – $100 in debt. If they quit before six months had elapsed, they carried away no cash wages at all, for these were held in reserve to pay their transport costs to and board in the camps. And, even if they ran away penniless, they still owed their patron for their passages.[55]

In somewhat parallel fashion, fazenda owners in Brazil advanced cash for supplies and subsistence until the first coffee harvest, indebting newly arrived Italian sharecroppers for several years and, thereafter in times of poor harvests. (In this case, the Brazilian government had paid Italians' transatlantic passages and rail transport to the countryside.[56]) Mines, railroad contractors, and plantation agents in Asia, Africa, and the U.S. paid Chinese, Italian and other workers in scrip, limiting their freedom to leave in protest with the wages they had earned.[57] Fazenda owners forbad Italian sharecroppers to leave their plantations, and they threatened them with physical violence when sharecroppers contested crop divisions at harvest time.[58] In the U.S., plantation owners could count on sheriffs or vigilantes to intimidate indebted foreigners.[59] At construction and mining camps, as on many isolated plantations around the globe, contractors and supervisors carried guns to prevent laborers from escaping. Padroni, labor

54. Such cash advances, to lure seasonal laborers, had a long history in Italy: see J. Lucassen, *Migrant Labour in Europe*, p. 118.
55. Bradwin, *Bunkhouse Man*, p. 74.
56. Dean, *Rio Claro*, pp. 179-181.
57. Daniel, *Shadow of Slavery*, ch. 5; LaSorte, *Merica: Images of Italian Greenhorn*.
58. Trento, *Dov'é la Raccolta del Caffe*, p. 47.
59. Whayne, *Shadows over Sunnyside*.

agents, and crimps sometimes manacled or confined their migrants before and during transport.[60]

The labor experiences of Italian and Chinese workers in the nineteenth century reveal how often capitalist labor systems combined elements of physical discipline and debt dependency with wage labor in the nineteenth century.[61] The long shadow of slavery was most obvious in Chinese coolie plantation labor, but not limited to it. Many nineteenth century observers seemed unable to notice that differing degrees of restraint characterized Italian and Chinese migratory labor or that differing types of restraints shaped the lives of coolie, contract laborers or debt peons. They viewed coolies, contract laborers, and debters alike as slaves; all in turn, appeared to threaten free wage laborers and their labor movements when Chinese and Italian migrants came ashore looking for work.

"I'm no Dago: I'm a Blacksmith": Class, Race, and the Restriction of Migration

Clearly, nineteenth century observers, including those who worked as free – that is waged – laborers in developing industries often conflated labor systems and racial terminology. Thus did Italians become the "Chinese of Europe" and both Chinese and Italian laborers appear as threats to the freedom of wage-earners in developing nations around the globe.

Acknowledging that race is a social construction rather than an objective category, historians have noted recently many cases of European workers failing to qualify automatically as white in the nineteenth century.[62] In one case, a study of railroad laborers in the early twentieth century Canada noted only two races among bush camp workers – "whites" and "foreigners".[63] The former did skilled work; the latter were laborers. In Queensland, Australia, when public opposition forbad sugar planters from recruiting Chinese and Kanaka (Pacific) laborers, and when they attempted instead to recruit Italians, debate about the racial character of the Italian nation immediately emerged. Planters urged recruiters to avoid "swarthy" southerners, and – if forced to recruit south of Rome – to examine carefully the cuticles of potential recruits in order to guarantee they were not too dark.[64]

Similarly, nowhere in the world did Chinese find themselves labelled as "black", like the African slaves who had preceded them as plantation laborers. Observers thus distinguished Chinese from colonized peoples of the Pacific,

60. Daniel, *Shadow of Slavery*, p. 95.
61. For early essays on this topic, see Lasker, *Human Bondage in Southeast Asia*.
62. Roediger, *Wages of Whiteness*.
63. Bradwin, *Bunkhouse Man*, p. 92.
64. Douglass, *From Italy to Ingham*.

India, Africa or even Ireland, all of whom were called "blacks" or "niggers" on occasion.[65] Free workers and plantation owners agreed in disparaging the origins of blacks in a primitive Africa while noting (and fearing) a Chinese empire and civilization viewed as both inscrutable and cunning. Observers contrasted the meticulous and incessant labor of the emigrant Chinese to the "laziness" of Africans and other tribal peoples, whose recourse to subsistence allowed them to withdraw from waged labor when not coerced.

Racial terminology, informed by perceptions of imperial and national hierarchies, thus provided explanations for what were, at base, class differences created by colonialism and capitalist expansion. In such a world a "dago" or a "coolie" could not be a blacksmith, nor a blacksmith anything but white. Still, references to "the Chinese of Europe" and direct comparisons of Chinese and Italians did not occur everywhere. I have yet to find even a single reference to the "Chinese of Europe" from Latin America or from Great Britain itself. Instead, racial equations of Chinese and Italians appear most frequently in Anglo-American labor movements outside of Great Britain (notably Canada, the U.S., and Australia) and to a lesser extent in the labor movements of France, Switzerland, Germany, and Austria.

Why was this so? One sensible hypothesis might be that racial construction differed around the globe in ways that reflected both class dynamics and prior systems of racial terminology. The conflation of class and race, and battles over racial boundaries were both sharpest where free laborers had no recourse to traditions of racial subordination through plantation agriculture or colonial rule. Thus, as long as unfree labor remained isolated on colonial plantations, modern labor movements in Europe and the U.S. took but cursory note of coolies' potential threat to free laborers, and did not concern themselves extensively with workers' racial status or maltreatment. Within the British Empire and the U.S., opposition to coolie abuses came more often from moralizing Protestant elites and from the Colonial office or Congress than from laborers' organizations. Jan Breman has even documented the collusion of labor's representatives in covering up studies of coolie abuse in Dutch colonies in Asia.[66]

Pulling free of colonialism generated a different dynamic of racial construction – one which made fears of Chinese and "the Chinese of Europe" both more central to and far stronger in emerging labor movements in the U.S., Canada, South Africa, New Zealand, and Australia. These five nations struggled to create national identities by claiming the racial superiority of their original European colonizers ("whites") for themselves. All inherited a British legacy of dividing colonized peoples (blacks) from colonizers (whites). Yet all had also inherited from British imperial policy a tradition of granting citizenship to children born

65. Drost, "Forced Labor in the South Pacific"; Huttenback, *Racism and Empire*.
66. Breman, *Taming the Coolie Beast*.

within their territories and of accepting immigrants without regard to nationality or race. In each case, greater national autonomy generated racially exclusionary practices in regulating labor migrations. The U.S., for example, had denied naturalization rights to non-Europeans already in 1790 (although it later revised its laws to allow naturalization of those of African descent). Between 1870 and 1930, the U.S., Canada, and Australia all enacted laws to privilege immigrants most like the colonizer/original settlers (British or northern Europeans) over newer arrivals – be they Chinese, the "Chinese of Europe" or other "unfree" laborers from Eastern or Southern Europe. In all these cases, labor movements initiated and built legislative coalitions to exclude the Chinese, contract laborers generally, and also "swarthy" Europeans. The legal barriers erected against "the yellow peril" exceeded in every respect those imposed later on Italians and other foreign laborers; but restriction originated with racial assumptions in all three cases.[67]

As this suggests, Canada, Australia, and the U.S. drew racial boundaries at the entrance gate only when migrants threatened to compete successfully for waged work with British or other Anglo or white workers. Although the U.S. and Australia both experimented briefly with indentured laborers, most Chinese seeking work in these countries had not come as coolies. Studies of the reception of Chinese adventurers in gold rushes on both sides of the Pacific show how racial stereotyping of them intensified as native-born and/or European workers in Australia, California, and British Columbia recognized their capability and willingness to compete for industrial and construction jobs.[68] Similarly Italians menaced native-born workers not when they took jobs on Louisiana's sugar plantations (as they did in large numbers in the 1880s) but when they sought work in mines, construction sites, and factories.

U.S. trade-unionism within the American Federation of Labor offers the clearest case of a labor movement that tried to protect the privileges of free from unfree labor by excluding migrant and contract laborers (those who had been recruited and promised jobs before emigrating) from the labor movement, often with explicitly racist arguments.[69] California's labor movement developed initially as an anti-Chinese movement; the state's labor activists (including Irish and some German immigrants) organized and led the campaign in order to stop Chinese entrance into industry.[70] The exclusion of Chinese laborers (but not merchants,

67. The best-studied case remains the U.S. one: see Sandmeyer, *Anti-Chinese Movement in California*; Miller, *Unwelcome Immigrant*; Saxton, *Indispensable Enemy*.

68. Chan, *Entry Denied*; Cronin, *Colonial Casualties*; Gittins, *Diggers from China*; Markus, *Fear and Hatred*, ch. 5.

69. On labor attitudes toward contract labor itself, see Erickson, *American Industry and the European Immigrant*, and Erickson, "Why Did Contract Labour Not Work". On the increasing relevance of race in labor's arguments against free migration, see Mink, *Old Labor and New Immigrants*.

70. The special role of Irish workers – colonized peoples themselves – in claiming the privileges

professionals, or students) in 1882 was followed by the exclusion of all contract laborers, regardless of background in 1885. In 1921 the exclusion of all Asians and the imposition of small quotas to reduce drastically immigration from southern and eastern European nations followed.[71] All these restrictions – while the product of broad legislative coalitions – had the strong support of the American Federation of Labor and its almost five million members. (They did not, however, enjoy support from the much smaller Socialist Party or the syndicalist Industrial Workers of the World – both of which not only welcomed immigrant and black members in sufficient numbers to attract considerable, negative attention from more conservative Americans.) The demise of S.P. and I.W.W. during the post-war "red scare", with its imprisonment and deportation of foreign-born radicals, left labor's support for racially restrictive immigration policies unchallenged. Prohibitions against Asian migrations and naturalizations were suspended only in the 1940s, and discriminatory quotas aimed at both Asians and southern and eastern European remained in place in the U.S. until 1965.

In Australia the Labor Party became the moving force behind immigration restriction.[72] Labor organizations had argued for restrictions against the Chinese since the 1860s; by the 1880s and 1890s they often argued as vehemently against Italian immigration. Some Australian labor men claimed even to prefer "black" (that is, Kanaka or Pacific Islander) to Italian labor since blacks "could be controlled" while Italians, like the "insidious" Chinese, "could erupt and spread like lava".[73] Australia's Labor Party had been founded by internationalists (an Italian among them), but by the 1880s it pursued greater political autonomy for Australia in order, in part, to guarantee that Australia stayed white.[74]

When the new Australian federation passed its first significant piece of legislation in 1901 – a restrictive immigration law with strong labor support – it shrank from the unapologetically racist categories of exclusion and quota laws in the U.S. Bending to Great Britain's distaste for overt racial discrimination within its empire, Australia's law required only that immigrants write out fifty words in a European language selected by an immigration officer. By giving immigration officers considerable discretion to interpret law, it excluded Chinese immigrants along with illiterates from Europe.[75] Canada, in similar deference to British custom, required substantial landing fees of immigrants, but (like Australia) gave individual immigration officers considerable leeway in setting

of the British race as immigrants needs careful analysis in all three countries. Markus, *Fear and Hatred*, p. 100; Roediger, *Wages of Whiteness*; Shumsky, *Evolution of Political Protest*.

71. Chan, *Entry Denied*; LeMay, *From Open Door to Dutch Door*.
72. The fullest account, is Huttenback, *Racism and Empire*, ch. 5.
73. Douglass, *From Italy to Ingham*, p. 49.
74. Gabaccia, "Clase y Cultura".
75. Huttenback, *Racism and Empire*, p. 168.

and changing fees for immigrants of varying backgrounds. In a bizarre Australian case, a German citizen whose father was Egyptian found himself excluded after being forced to attempt a passage in Greek – a telling comment on slippery racial boundaries in a British settler colonies.[76]

That prior understandings of race also mattered is most evident in the Latin American case. When they became independent, both Argentina and Brazil possessed sizeable populations of colonized indigenous peoples and African slaves. Long generations of intermarriage had produced large mestizo populations in both places, too. Argentina and Brazil sought immigrants to spur economic development, and both hoped consciously to "whiten" mestizo populations which, to the creole elite, seemed to bear the mark of colonialism and its early modern labor systems.[77] Although both countries initially sought northern European settlers, their limited success in attracting German, Irish and British farmers encouraged them to change focus in their immigration policies.[78]

In Brazil, where plantation elites held considerable power, the nation supported plantation agriculture as the motor for economic development. Brazil initially attempted to import Chinese coolies to work alongside of, and eventually to replace Afro-Brazilian slaves, but failing at this experiment, planters then convinced the Brazilian government to subsidize European migration to the coffee fields. Thus, even though Italians entered Brazil as indebted migrants, and for about fifteen years worked alongside slaves on some coffee plantations, resulting in further restraints on their freedom, Italians remained firmly European and firmly white in Brazilian eyes. Native-born peoples of mixed or African descent tried to stigmatize them as foreigners (when asked to perform a task, a servant and former Afro-Brazilian slave taunted her employer, "What do you take me for? An Italian?"[79]), but their power to influence both racial terminology and national migrations policies was slight.

In Argentina, Italian (and other immigrant) traders and refugees who had settled in the country's cities soon after independence, argued for (and invested in) industry as the quickest route to prosperity and power. Argentina showed little interest in recruiting coolie labor of any sort, but it welcomed Europeans of all backgrounds as desirable, white, and potentially "modernizing" influences. By welcoming Italians quite explicitly as racially superior Europeans, Argentina too closed off the possibility of Italians ever becoming "the Chinese of Europe". By 1910, Italians formed the largest immigrant group in both Brazil and Argentina. Chinese immigrants, by contrast, were present in only very small numbers in both nations. European immigrants – Italians among them –

76. Ibid., p. 307.
77. Graham, Idea of Race in Latin America; Solberg, Immigration and Nationalism, p. 19.
78. Browne, "Government Immigration Policy in Imperial Brazil".
79. Holloway, Immigrants on the Land, p. 105.

dominated the urban working and middle classes of both countries. Spanish, Portuguese, Italian, German and Jewish immigrants also created the modern labor movements of both countries. Multi-ethnic, although rarely welcoming to rural people of African descent, the small syndicalist labor movements and Socialist parties of Argentina and Brazil were sometimes hailed by European radicals as uniquely "international".[80] These labor movements never supported the restriction of migration. When Argentina finally closed its doors partially in 1931, it was in response to demands of nationalists among the landed native-born and creole elite, not of socialist or anarcho-syndicalist labor activists.

Racial construction in the European nations employing Italian and Chinese (and other) migrant workers is hardest to interpret. Neither Chinese nor Italian suffered complete or even partial exclusion as racially disparaged migrants as they did in the U.S., Canada, and Australia. Unlike these settler ex-colonies, European nations neither needed immigrants in order to develop demographically nor had to fear the racial legacy of colonization. But neither were Italians simply welcomed as white, fellow Europeans. European labor movements had invented the concept of worker internationalism: Socialist activists within the Second International regularly rejected U.S. and Australian initiatives to gain labor support for restrictive immigration policies. Still, migratory workers – Italians, Poles, and Chinese – remained "the other" according to one student of the Second International.[81]

With the possible exception of the French, European labor movements failed to view Italians or Chinese as free workers. And even the French aired some of the earliest complaints about Italian threats to free labor at the very first meeting of the Second International.[82] Swiss charges against Italians as the "Chinese of Europe" accompanied Italians' move from seasonal harvest labor into construction and some industrial jobs after 1880. Rather than prohibit the entrance of laborers working seasonally for construction contractors or to exclude racially undesirable laborers as the U.S. did, however, most European nations instead experimented with state regulation of foreign labor through what – much later – would be called "guest worker" programs.[83]

European labor movements attempted to pursue their own interests with foreign laborers. German and Swiss trade unions, for example, cooperated with Italian trade unions to educate migratory workers about the importance of trade union membership while abroad.[84] By accepting the regulation of migration

80. Gabaccia, "Worker Internationalism and Italian Labor Migration".
81. Weil, *Internationalisme et l'Autre*.
82. Joll, *Second International*, p. 37.
83. Herbert, *Geschichte der Ausländerbeschäftigung in Deutschland*; Potts, *World Labour Market*, ch. 5.
84. Decleva, *Etica del Lavoro*; Punzo, "Societa Umanitaria e l'Emigrazione"; Forberg, "Foreign Labour, the State and the Trade Unions".

through seasonal work permits, trade union movements even became involved in a number of innovative experiments in international labor organizing.[85]

Ultimately, however, labor's acceptance of seasonal labor by foreigners working for labor contractors helped institutionalize labor markets segmented along national lines. Labor did not challenge the laws of nationality that (outside France) granted citizenship rights through blood lines rather than residence. By regulating foreign labor in this way, native-born laborers certainly enjoyed protection from the worst competition of both the Chinese and the Chinese of Europe, and they also prevented outrageous abuse of foreign workers by exploitative employers. At the same time, the institutionalization of labor in temporary guest worker programs guaranteed that foreigners could not settle, or become either citizens or skilled white workers. Only in the past 30 years have the racial dimensions of guest worker programs come under scrutiny among critical labor activists.[86] Just as British regulation of the coolie trade within the British Empire guaranteed that coolie labor remained in its proper place – as a temporary labor reserve of carefully regulated workers – so, too, guest worker programs relegated foreign workers to the status of temporary sojourners within the developing economies of Europe.

Conclusion

By the third decade of the twentieth century, the mass international migrations ended, the victim of restrictive migration policies, most of them overtly or implicitly racist. Some of these restrictions had been proposed and enacted with the support of modern labor movements fearful of unfree laborers like the Chinese "yellow peril" and the "Chinese of Europe". To defend free labor, labor activists had curtailed free migration. Immigration restrictions in turn helped to replicate under capitalism some of the inequalities of colonialism.

Labor movements' participation in these developments are inseparable from the varying ways wage workers constructed racial categories in the nineteenth century. While many students of social construction trace the tenacity of racial and other social categories to the power of paired dichotomies, an analysis of Chinese and Italian migrants revealed a more complex dynamic. The dichotomy of "free" and "unfree" labor remained a powerful influence as native-born laborers confronted new groups of migratory laborers in the nineteenth century, enabling them to collapse a wide variety of labor systems into the racially

85. Milner, "International Labour Movement and the Limits"; Gabaccia, "Worker Internationalism and Italian Labor Migration".
86. Potts, *World Labour Market*; pp. 210-213; Castles and Kosak, *Immigrant Workers and Class Structure*.

charged category of "slavery". At the same time, however, the racial categories
that emerged from "slavery" failed to transform all unfree workers into "blacks"
although they reserved the label "white" for those few workers who performed
free, waged labor. The creation of a third and overlapping "yellow/olive/
swarthy" category existed uneasily in a world divided simplistically between
"free" and "unfree" labor.

With hindsight, of course, it is easy to see that labor movements in Europe,
Australia and North America had alternatives to discriminatory immigration
policies to defend free labor. International organization of migratory workers
existed as a theoretical ideal. The same internationalist ideals that prevented
Europeans from following the lead of Australia's or the United States' labor
movements also encouraged Europeans to experiment with labor organizing
across national boundaries. But given the influence of racial thinking on both
labor and nation-state policies toward migration, these experiments in internationalism – tied as they were to the institutionalization of contract labor – left
Europe's labor movements, along with those of Canada, the U.S., and Australia
unable to manoeuvre effectively in a rapidly internationalizing world economy.
Labor in Europe, Australia and North America would face the collapse of
colonialism and the new internationalization of capital in the postwar world
handicapped by the legacy of race.

Migration on the Border of Free and Unfree Labour: Workers in Calcutta's Jute Industry, 1900-1990[*]

Arjan de Haan

Introduction

Eastern India comprised an integrated network of trade and circulation of labour in the nineteenth century. At the end of the century, a number of migration streams existed. For many years, labour from the Western areas (Uttar Pradesh, Buhar) had been migrating to the fertile areas in the East for seasonal work. A stream of indentured labour migration arose through the recruitment of people from the Western areas prior to their transportation via Calcutta to overseas plantations. Finally, the growth of industries and plantations in the second half of the century gave rise to new large-scale movements of labour. Each of these activities targeted certain areas of recruitment, attracted specific social groups, and applied different methods of recruitment. Around the beginning of the twentieth century, free labour migration overtook unfree migration: indentured labour was declared illegal, and a surplus of labour gradually developed. Yet, during this period, different methods of recruitment co-existed with respect to free and unfree migration. In describing the various forms of labour recruitment, this paper focuses on migration to the industrial area of Calcutta.

Earlier migration studies portray migrants as victims of economic development. Migration was thought to result from economic and ecological crises, from a population surplus, and from poverty in rural areas. In this context, migrants were considered isolated individuals desperate for an income and vulnerable to labour recruiters and other middlemen. The historiography of Europe has disproved this image, as the contributions by Fertig, Hoerder and Moch, in this volume show. Migration is now regarded as normal in most societies, rather than as the result of sudden crises. In Indian historiography, however, the image of the migrant

[*] This paper is based on information collected for my doctoral dissertation, *Unsettled Settlers. Migrant Workers and Industrial Capitalism in Calcutta*, published by Verloren Publishers, Hilversum, 1994. My research focused on migration towards the jute mills. In addition to archival research, I carried out field work in Titagarh (an industrial neighbourhood in Calcutta) and collected the histories of eighty families. Most were families of current and former workers in the jute industry, some worked in the paper mill, and a number held jobs in the so-called informal sector. The research was funded by the Erasmus University Rotterdam and WOTRO of the NWO, the Dutch Organization for Scientific Research. My field work would have been impossible without the assistance of Gautam Sanyal.

as a victim still exists. Authors like Ranajit Das Gupta and Dipesh Chakrabarty stress that migrants in Bengal were recruited to replace local labour, that migrants were forced to leave their village of birth, unable to settle in the city because of low wages and bad living conditions, and victims of various forms of deceit by labour recruiters. They stress the lack of freedom in a labour market that, while purportedly free, continues to resemble the system of indentured labour.

In my opinion, these studies ignore the perspective of the migrants, their reasons for migrating, for taking a certain job, and for returning to their village. This paper contributes to the Indian historiography by stressing the choices of the migrants who came to the jute industry in Calcutta. The first section describes the context of this migration by showing that the tradition of migration considerably predated the effort to recruit labour for the jute mills, which emerged as a new opportunity for workers. The second section discusses the replacement of local labour and shows that these workers were not forced out of the industry. The third section presents the principal method of recruitment in the jute industry while emphasizing its reliance on personal contacts. The fourth section sketches the predominant mode of migration (which has always been circular) and lists the reasons of the workers for retaining a link with their villages. The concluding section examines the usefulness of the theoretical distinction between free and unfree labour.

Migration within Eastern India: a segmented labour market

At the end of the nineteenth century, an intricate network of migration existed within Eastern India. The migrants worked in agriculture in Bengal, entered contracts as indentured labour, and moved to Calcutta, to the coal mines, and to the tea plantations. The large numbers of workers who migrated to Bengal before 1880 increased considerably during the following decades. "Nearly 2,000,000 persons of all classes and races were enumerated in 1921 as coming from outside Bengal, including other provinces in India and other countries, and the great majority of the immigrants came from the areas which supply labour to Bengal industries and plantations."[1] In 1881, the largest stream of migrants came from Uttar Pradesh (UP). This particular stream did not grow in the two decades that followed. Migration from Bihar increased continuously until 1911.[2]

1. Royal Commission on Labour in India, *Report of the Royal Commission on Labour in India* (Calcutta, 1931), Vol. 5, pt. 1, p. 5 (hereafter "RCLI"). "By the early twentieth century, Bihar, Bengal, and coastal Burma (Arakan) had become joined together in a single system of interlocking labour migration [...] The literature suggests that almost anyone hired labour at one time or another [...]" Van Schendel, *Three Deltas*, pp. 107-108.
2. A map showing the main recruiting districts for the jute industry appears at the end of this article (p. 222). Bihar has remained the area that supplies most Indian migrants to West

At the beginning of the century, immigration reached a saturation point. Between 1921 and 1951, inter-rural migration decreased. Population growth reduced the demand for migrant rural labour. At the same time, rural-urban migration increased because of the expansion of employment opportunities in the cities. With the partition of India, migration to the Eastern parts of Bengal came to a standstill. While the number of migrants within Bengal remained high – due to migration from East Pakistan – long-distance migration within Eastern India continued to drop.

Many of the two million migrants came to work in industries and plantations. In 1921, the large-scale industries (including the coal mines and tea gardens) employed 770,000 people, about a quarter of all the migrants. The 1921 Census noted that many of the migrants, however, "ply their traditional caste trades in the industrial area as they do also in towns in other parts of Bengal". Almost half the two million migrants in Bengal came to the industrial area around Calcutta. This city has been a nodal point in the migration streams. For the past hundred years, the majority of Calcutta's inhabitants have been born outside the city.

Migration by wealthier classes to Calcutta has been very important throughout its history. Its status as a capital and its cultural and educational prestige attracted a great many affluent people. Zamindars migrated to Calcutta or sent their children there to be educated. The city also attracted large numbers of merchants, such as the Marwaris, a moneylending and trading Jain community from Rajasthan in West India. Migration by the elite sometimes paves the way for other migrants. Das writes that some brighter, higher-caste boys were the first to migrate from the village of Changel in Bihar to attend schools in a town or village at the end of the nineteenth century. Some of the servants who accompanied these boys did not return and sought alternative employment in the city and established "a regular channel of seasonal migration of agricultural labourers to distant parts".[3] Migration by the affluent has opened channels of migration by workers to urban areas.

Labour migration was far from a new phenomenon. Before the expansion of the capital and industrial area, migration had been a common practice, and the stream of migration from West to East predates the colonial period. In the seventeenth century close ties existed between the areas in Bihar and Bengal. Bihar supplied goods to Bengal, and indigo for example was exported through Bengal's port. In the eighteenth and nineteenth centuries, Bihar and UP became major labour-supplying areas. In the second half of the nineteenth century, workers flocked to the fertile rice fields of Bengal. "Precisely when these patterns

Bengal. In 1971 and 1981, data from the Census of India indicated that over 1,300,000 people living in West Bengal had been born in Bihar. During this century, an increasing part of the migrants began to work in tertiary activities.

3.   Das, "Longue Durée", p. 44.

of migration developed cannot be determined, but there have always been people from the Indian countryside who have moved elsewhere in response to better opportunities."[4] During the colonial period a significant part of these "up-country" labourers in Bengal worked in agricultural occupations.[5] In 1881, for example, almost 200,000 people (predominantly men) migrated from the district of Saran in Bihar. Migration from Saran increased to 360,000 in 1891 and stagnated in the first two decades of this century. The stream of migration to rural Bengal seems to have been diverted towards urban destinations. Sources suggest that rural-rural migration was linked with migration toward the cities[6] and note that migrants carried out different occupations and took up all kinds of labour.[7]

The abolition of slavery led to a search for new sources of labour for plantations all over the world. India was among the areas where such a supply was found. The medium for recruiting labour has been termed a "new system of slavery" and existed between the 1820s and 1917.[8] Villagers were drafted by licensed recruiters, who employed unlicensed local recruiters able to find people interested in migrating. The migrants entered a contract of about five years duration and were brought to "depots" before boarding the ships.

Whereas most studies about indentured labour have focused on the process of recruitment or the situation at the point of destination, Carter's research on indentured migrants from Mauritius examines the role of returning migrants. During the first decades of the indentured system, recruitment was controlled by agency houses located in India's ports. To deflect the criticism of this system,

4. Yang, Limited Raj, p. 191.
5. "These people [up-country labourers] travelled to Bengal during the winter months and returned home in the spring or early summer. Often they travelled in groups [...] and they could be found all over Bengal [...] They worked as general labourers, taking whatever work came their way. Most of them found employment as harvesters of Bengal's main paddy crop (amon), but they also took other cold-weather jobs such as coolie, earthworker or palanquin bearer [...]" Van Schendel and Faraizi, Rural Labourers in Bengal, p. 47.
6. "Throughout our period [1880-1980] migrant labour combined income from agricultural activities with that from non-agricultural activities; although its base remained the countryside, it accepted urban employment whenever this presented itself. To labour migrants, boundaries between economic 'sectors' are meaningless beyond the fact that some may offer more employment or better wages than others." Ibid., p. 57.
7. Yang, Limited Raj, p. 203. The 1921 Census concluded: "The diversity of occupations plied by the immigrants from all directions is very remarkable indeed" (Census 1921, Vol. 6, pt. 1, p. 26).
8. Tinker, New System of Slavery. Piet Emmer (in this volume) disputes the thesis that indentured labour represents a "system of slavery". He submits that indentured labour was not such a bad option: the majority of the recruits were not proletarians but farmers, and conditions overseas were not as bad as claimed by many authors. Research shows, according to Emmer, that suicide rates declined after an initial period, and that mortality in indenture was lower than back home in India. For a point of view similar to Tinker's, see e.g. Breman and Daniel, "Conclusion: The Making of a Coolie".

planters sought alternative strategies, which they found in the migrants returning to India. By 1860, the role of returnees in recruitment had become an established custom.[9]

Tinker writes that during the 1820s and 1830s, prospective migrants for overseas destinations were recruited in the metropolis, although most came from the Chota Nagpur plateau, the "aboriginal borderland" that had established contact with Bengal in the early nineteenth century. The "hill people" descended to the plains to work for the indigo planters of Bihar. They were also attracted to Calcutta for seasonal employment and were often lured onto ships with overseas destinations. From the 1850s, the numbers of this migrant group dwindled, both because of bad conditions on the ships and because of alternatives arising in Bengal. In the 1870s, emigration agents began to focus their efforts on the more distant areas to the Northwest. They started recruiting Biharis, who had a reputation for being stable, accustomed to hard labour, and docile.[10] Bhojpur, or Shahabad, was the main recruiting district for overseas migration. At the turn of the century, most indentured labourers came from UP and only a small portion from Bihar.

From the 1860s, tea plantations in the Duars and Assam created new opportunities for migrants. In 1870, 8,000 labourers were employed in Darjeeling district. By 1901 this figure had increased to 64,000. In Jalpaiguri, employment rose from 235 in 1876 to 90,000 in 1901.[11] Two main streams of migration developed, one from Nepal to Darjeeling and the other from Chota Nagpur and the Central Provinces to the Duars. The "hill coolies", who had previously been recruited as indentured labourers, were attracted to the tea plantations. In 1921, 750,000 people born in Chota Nagpur lived outside the region, mostly in the tea districts of Assam and Rajshahi.[12] Ranchi was the centre of the labour supply. In 1921, 126,000 persons born in Ranchi were counted in Jalpaiguri. In the first decades of the century, recruitment was extended to areas in Central India.[13]

According to Das Gupta, the method of recruitment for tea plantations resembled the indentured system in terms of the restrained freedom of movement among labourers. Indentured recruitment for the plantations started in 1859 with the Workmen's Breach of Contract Act, which remained in effect in a modified form until 1926. Labourers were bound by penal contracts that varied from three to five years and were liable to be arrested by the planter if they absconded from work. Licensed contractors, often Europeans, recruited labour through a large number of professional *arkattis*. According to Das Gupta,

9. Carter, "Strategies of Labour Mobilisation".
10. Tinker, *New System of Slavery*, pp. 52-53.
11. Iftikhar-ul-Awwal, *Industrial Development of Bengal*, p. 68.
12. Schwerin, "Control of Land and Labour", p. 23.
13. RCLI, *Report*, Vol. 5, pt. 1, pp. 7-8.

they used all the forms of deceit, intimidation, and violence reminiscent of the slave trade. From the 1870s, unregulated migration became more commonplace, albeit through middlemen. The system of *sardari* recruitment emerged: "Even the non-indentured labour was subject to various kinds of unfreedom, dependency relations and servitude [...] the so-called 'free' or 'voluntary' labour for all practical purposes lived and worked in a state of bondage."[14]

At the end of the nineteenth century, the rise of the coal industry in the Manbhum and Burdwan districts led to a new stream of migration.[15] This labour force expanded from about 29,000 in the 1880s to over 229,000 in 1939. According to the 1911 Census, less than two-thirds of the workers in the mines in Manbhum and Burdwan were born in these districts. The majority of the first labourers were tribals (Santhals and Bauris from Chota Nagpur, traditionally the area for recruiting labour for the tea plantations), and the coal and tea industries competed for labour. Later, attempts were made to recruit labour from Bihar and UP. Until the prohibition of women from underground employment, a system of production by families prevailed.

Various methods were applied for recruiting labour for the coal fields. The first was the *zamindari* method, which was used in the larger collieries. Colliery owners purchased large plots of land around the mines, with a view to pressuring tenants to work there. As with the tea plantations, the migrants were offered plots of land. According to so-called *nokarni* or service tenancy arrangements, workers were granted land either free of charge or at nominal rates in return for working in the mines a certain number of days. Many original inhabitants were reportedly deprived of their occupancy rights and replaced with *nokarni* tenants. The system remained intact until the late 1930s and began to diminish when a labour surplus developed. Smaller companies had to resort to a variety of other methods to recruit workers. As the managers rarely did the actual recruitment, the middlemen played a crucial role. Workers were told to bring people from their village. In other cases, labour was recruited through a *ticcardar* (contractor), who established links with village chiefs and was responsible for labour at the workplace.

The colonization of Burma initiated a new demand for labour, and the government encouraged migration to Burma. Nolan, who wrote a "report as to the measures which may be adopted with advantage for the purpose of facilitating migration from the over-populated districts of Bengal to Burma", noted that 174,000 people had migrated from Upper India in 1881, including a large number of women. A considerable share had settled in Burma. Nolan estimated that 250,000 people born in India lived in Burma in 1888, and that 150,000 were there to stay.[16] In the period 1908-1929, more than 6.5 million

14. Das Gupta, "Structure of the Labour Market", p. 1785.
15. The following is based on Simmons, "Recruiting and Organizing".
16. Nolan, *Report on Emigration from Bengal*.

people immigrated, mainly adult males.[17] The migrants came from six divisions in India, and each group performed specific occupations. According to Andrew, Indian labourers obtained employment through two systems of recruitment. One share could be classified as "free labour" and another share as "contract labour". The prevalent system of recruitment was the "maistry system". When labourers were recruited, they began their work with a debt, an advance of Rs.400 in some cases. Their wages were about Rs.20 per month. Labour was under direct control of the maistry, who controlled the disbursement of wages and made "false deductions from this".

This brief description of different migration streams shows that the hinterland of Bengal (the labour-catchment area) has not been an undifferentiated unit, and that the migration streams have been dynamic processes. During certain periods, people from specific areas were recruited for particular occupations, and this practice changed as new alternatives arose. While many references mention these forms of segmentation in the migration streams and note groups of people who concentrated on specific activities, few studies examine how this segmentation operated. Migrants were not bound to one single occupation. Nevertheless, the life histories of the migrant workers we interviewed in Calcutta show little mobility between economic sectors. Accordingly, I conclude that linkages with streams of migration to other areas have been rare. Although the migrants who went overseas came from the same districts, nobody knew of relatives who had travelled to such destinations. Generally, the migration streams seem clearly separated. Indigo plantations employed hill people. Recruitment for colonial emigration initially comprised mainly the tribal areas of Chota Nagpur. The tea plantations obtained their labour supply from the same areas. Later, emigrants came from the Gangetic plain, Eastern UP, and Western Bihar. This stream originally migrated to the rice fields. Slowly, more people started going to the industries in Calcutta. The jute industry began by employing local Bengali labour. Around the turn of the century, however, these workers were replaced by migrants from UP and Bihar. The next section describes this course of events.

Replacement of local labour

In 1855, the first Indian jute mill was founded to the north of Calcutta. After 1870, the industry expanded rapidly and easily surpassed its predecessor and competitors in Dundee. The jute mills were concentrated around Calcutta, close to the jute-growing districts in Bengal and the port of Calcutta. The industry expanded till the late 1920s. During the first decades of the jute industry, the

17. The following is based on Andrew, *Indian Labour in Rangoon.*

workers were predominantly locals from the surrounding countryside. Labour was in short supply during the explosive growth of the industry, and Ranajit Das Gupta has shown that local labour was replaced by immigrant labour, mainly from the Northwestern part of Bihar and the Eastern part of Uttar Pradesh.[18] Surprisingly, a few decades later, the refugees from East Bengal did not go to work in the mills, despite the evidence that this option was available.[19] In the 1940s, the bombings by the Japanese air force and the Hindu-Muslim riots created a shortage of workers, and the government unsuccessfully encouraged industrial employment among the refugees.[20] Up until the present, jute-mill labour, like most unskilled industrial labour, has been dominated by non-Bengalis. Around 1970, 87 per cent of the jute workers came from outside Bengal,[21] and my field research confirms that the labour force is still predominantly non-Bengali. This section offers various explanations for the situation.[22]

Many authors have stressed the strategies and recruitment policies of employers in their efforts to explain the predominance of labourers from outside Bengal in the jute industry. Little evidence is available, however, of any active policy among employers.[23] Foley, who wrote the most extensive report on the recruitment of labour, noted that migrant labour had been found to be more regular, stronger, and steadier. Nevertheless, he concluded:

> "One naturally asks what recruiting agency is used to supply this constantly increasing enormous demand, and it is somewhat astonishing to find that no recruiting on any systematic method is done at all."[24]

18. Das Gupta, "Factory Labour in Eastern India". See the evidence in the report of the Indian Industrial Commission 1916-18 [hereafter referred to as "IIC"], Minutes of Evidence, Vol. 6, Confidential Evidence, pp. 95 ff. (the volumes of evidence appear in the Parliamentary Papers 1919, House of Commons, Vol. XVIII (II), Cmd 235, India Office Library and Records).
19. The partition caused huge waves of migration. Between 1947 and 1970, an estimated one million refugees entered Calcutta. Laxmi Naranyan, "Growth of Metropolitan Cities".
20. Evidence from the company archive of Thomas Duff and Co., Managers' Reports to Directors, 1930-1974, at the University of Dundee, Archive Department, MS 86/V/8; reports Samnuggur South, 1950, pp. 57-58, and Victoria Mill, 1950.
21. Bhattacharya and A.K. Chatterjee, "Some Characteristics of Jute Industry Workers".
22. See also my "Jute Industry and its Workers".
23. I have come across only two references to such policies. In 1881 Finlay Muir of Champdany Jute Mill requested the Government of India for assistance in the recruitment of labour in Bihar and UP (Das Gupta, "Factory Labour in Eastern India", p. 285). Basu concluded that the Indian Jute Mills Association preferred migrants because Bengalis would not respond to cash incentives, and because migrant labour was more steady and regular in attendance. Basu, "Labour Movement in Bengal", p. 12.
24. Foley, *Report on Labour in Bengal*, p. 9.

Prentice, the Magistrate of 24-Parganas, wrote in 1919:

"Local labour is insufficient for mill requirements. All offering is accepted and *none is displaced* by imported labour. Indeed the mills can usually employ more labour than is available, whether local and imported, and ordinarily there is no surplus though this year labour is comparatively easy to obtain owing to high prices and general scarcity."[25]

Few references indicate complaints by mill owners that local labour was too expensive, unwilling to work, or frequently absent. Opinions differed as to which type of labour was better.[26] Bengali labourers, whose villages were close to the mill, left regularly throughout the year. Up-country labourers, on the other hand, left en masse during the hot season, thus causing a dearth of labourers in the period from March till July.[27] The introduction of electric light and the subsequent extension of the working day in the first decade of this century played a role in changing the composition of labour: the up-country hands were said to prefer the long hours and the local Bengali weavers the shorter hours.[28] Clarck, a manager of two jute mills, firmly believed they would get a great deal more local labour with a ten-hour day: "The Bengali would not come at 5 A.M. [...]" The weavers in a mill south of Calcutta with a fairly large share of Bengalis said that they would be more satisfied with a lower wage and shorter working hours.[29] The extended working hours made the industry less attractive to local labourers living near the mill with their whole families and more attractive to single migrants who came to the mill for a specific period. Even in such cases, however, employers did not show any preference: Bengalis left the mills that had extended the working days and were replaced by migrant labour. They were not pushed out.

Perhaps the oldest explanation for the absence of Bengalis in the industry is the relative affluence of Bengal and the relative prosperity of the Bengali peasants, which made joining the industry unnecessary for them. Foley concluded that labour could not be recruited from districts like Darjeeling, Murshidabad, Jessore, and Khulna because "the natives of these districts are too prosperous to leave their homes in search of work".[30] The Indian Industrial Commission (IIC) noted in 1918:

25. West Bengal State Archive (hereafter "WBSA"), Commerce Department, Commerce Branch, 1W-15, A 1-15, May 1919 (emphasis added).
26. See in particular the Indian Factory Labour Commission (Morison Committee), *Report of the Indian Factory Labour Commission*, Government Press, Simla, 1908, 2 vols. (hereafter "IFLC").
27. See for example the evidence from the manager of Champdany Jute Mill (in Foley, *Report on Labour in Bengal*, Appendix, p. viii).
28. IFLC, "Inspection Notes", p. 126; see also Chakrabarty, *Rethinking Working-Class History*, p. 104.
29. IFLC, oral evidences, nos 170 and 192.
30. Foley, *Report on Labour in Bengal*, par. 82.

"Not only do the inhabitants multiply and thrive, but large numbers of people have to be imported from other provinces to assist in the cultivation and marketing of the crops. In many of the districts of Bengal, according to the 1911 Census Report 'the people are so prosperous that they can afford to look down upon menial work and leave most of it to immigrants from Bihar and the United Provinces who serve as earth-diggers, palki-bearers, domestic servants, boatmen and general labourers'."[31]

The idea of the prosperity of Bengal has drawn criticism. While Bengal as a whole may have been relatively prosperous, current assertions hold that this situation did not apply among the total agricultural population.[32] The Dufferin Report of 1888[33] shows that labour was the sole source of income for a considerable portion of the population in the late nineteenth century. Throughout Bengal, 26 per cent of all households depended entirely on labour, and this share was considerably higher in the Western districts. Another 13 per cent of households relied on labour as a supplementary source of income. Agricultural wage-labour increased with commercial investment in land and cash crops (jute, opium, sugar). In 1888, about 13 million Bengalis lived off wages derived from labour. The proportion of rural labourers remained the same until the middle of the twentieth century.[34]

At the end of the nineteenth century, an intricate network of migration that was mainly seasonal and circular existed within Bengal. During the first half of the nineteenth century in Birbhum, labour was said to be so cheap that a native would carry a box to Calcutta.[35] Migration to the neighbouring districts also continued. Foley noted that Nadia had a high population density, and that people migrated away from the area because the land tenure was bad, the climate unhealthy, and the wages of unskilled labour low. While some migrated to Calcutta, more went to East Bengal and the Sunderbans. From Murshidabad, migrants travelled to Malda for the paddy harvest, and some made their way to Jessore and Khulna. Bankura also had a sufficient supply of local labour and even

---

31. IIC 1916-18, *Report*, Vol. 6, Confidential Evidence, p. 103. The District Magistrate of Howrah wrote: "People of this district do not go out to other places in quest of labour; they have their own lands to till and it appears from the reports of the mill managers that they cannot have these people during the tilling and reaping season when up-country and Orissa people take their places, but this is only for [a] short time." WBSA, Comm., Comm., 1W-15, A 1-15, May 1919.

32. Greenough describes the "prosperity of Bengal" as a cultural construct (an ideal formulated by Bengalis) and contrasts this perception with the material situation under colonial rule. Greenough, *Prosperity and Misery*.

33. Quoted in Schendel and Faraizi, *Rural Labourers in Bengal*.

34. Schendel and Faraizi, *Rural Labourers in Bengal*, p. 46. In 1900, about 7 per cent of the rural population reported labour as their primary occupation; in 1970 this figure was 27 per cent (Census figures; in: *ibid.*, p. 6).

35. Tinker, *New System of Slavery*.

a surplus in the winter months. Many people migrated from Midnapore, mainly to the 24-Parganas, Calcutta, and Hooghly districts.[36]

Thus, although these migrants covered shorter distances than up-country labourers (who travelled as far as 600 kilometres, more than three times the distance of the migration within Bengal), circulation between districts was considerable and was probably even greater at the beginning of the twentieth century than around 1950.[37] During the period of industrialization, when local labour was replaced, Bengal as a whole was more prosperous than other provinces. Within Bengal, however, large income discrepancies prevailed. The Western districts were clearly poorer, and a significant part of the population depended on wage labour and migrated. Migrants from the poorer Bengali districts generally travelled to destinations other than Calcutta and the industrial occupations in the area.

Racial and cultural grounds have also frequently been submitted (not only by colonial authorities) as explanations for the small numbers of Bengalis that joined the jute industry. Characteristics commonly associated with Bengalis include an unwillingness to abandon agricultural work and a preference for work in open fields over factories. Foley, for example, noted that inhabitants from different districts were not suitable for jute work. The people who migrated from Santal Parganas refused to go to Calcutta: they were said to be afraid of diseases and were "recommended" only for coal mines. People from Hazaribagh went to Assam, and people from Bankura and Sambalpur were reportedly "too jungly".[38] Indeed, "tribals" were rare in the industry. According to the 1921 Census, four major tribal groups constituted only 0.7 per cent of the jute labour force.[39]

These explanations, which often reflect stereotypes, persist and have emerged in many interviews. A migrant labourer from Benares told us that very few Bengalis joined the migration process, as they were more interested in agriculture. Because they owned land, he said, Bengalis came for work only two to four months per year, when there was no work on their own land. A *bara sardar* (head supervisor) from Burdwan (in West Bengal) reported that many people from his village had migrated for work, but that few went to the jute mills. The people from his village whom he had taken and helped find work returned to the village because they came from the "open field" and could not adjust to factory work.

Another explanation asserts that Bengalis were unwilling to do manual labour. The Royal Commission on Labour (RCLI) in India stated:

36. Foley, *Report on Labour in Bengal*.
37. Schendel and Faraizi, *Rural Labourers in Bengal*, pp. 50 ff.; Census 1951, Vol. 6, pt. 1a, p. 298.
38. Foley, *Report on Labour in Bengal*.
39. Tribals are sometimes considered to be India's original population. They are neither Hindus nor Muslims, and a considerable number of tribes have converted to Christianity. Nowadays, tribes ("scheduled tribes") form an official category, and "reservation" policies exist to improve the position of these generally disadvantaged groups.

"The [river] Hooghly [...] is surrounded by the heavily populated districts of Bengal, but does not draw the bulk of its factory workers from them. The Bengalis have *less inclination for factory work than other Indian races*; when the industries of the Hooghly were being built up, their economic position was not such as to make the terms offered by industry attractive [...] they, more than most Indian peoples, have been realising the possibilities which industry offers to skill [...]".[40]

Bengalis worked in jute mills, but only in skilled, mechanical, and administrative areas of employment. Mitra, the Chief Census Officer for the 1951 Census, discarded the myth of the affluence of Bengal, only to put another one in its place:

"The latter [Bengali] is more a precision worker, an artisan, a craftsman with a sense and gift of individual design, a sense of freedom of fabrication, than a mass producer."[41]

These stereotypes were "common knowledge" among the inhabitants of the industrial area. "Unsuitability" is clearly a myth, albeit possibly an effective one: once certain patterns of migration and employment are established, they do not change easily. My argument is that if we free the myths from their racial connotations, they reveal information about existing divisions of labour that define the segmentation in the labour market. Interpreting the descriptions of the character of the Bengali as sociological categories indicates why certain groups joined the industries while others did not.

Thus, different groups of Bengalis had different reasons for their disinterest in the industry. The local elite could hardly bear the sight of up-country labour and the sound of the factory whistle. The sons of the local landholders neither needed nor wanted to join the industry, except in clerical jobs. Because of the expanding economy, artisans could afford to forego the industry. Demand for labour and for the products of small-scale industries was sufficient.[42] Accordingly, the lower classes were not forced to join the industry. Presumably, this economic expansion enabled Bengalis to shun industrial work. During this period, jute work also came to be viewed as *chhoto kaj* or low-status work. Even today, Bengalis have a reputation for not wanting to join the jute industry for status reasons, as it might, for example, reduce their dowry. In contrast to Bengalis, Biharis began to take different kinds of work in Bengal. While they replaced Bengali labourers, they did not push them out: Bengalis left of their own accord. The next section examines the methods of recruitment for migrant workers in the industry in more detail.

---

40. RCLI, Vol. 1, p. 11, emphasis added. A recent study argues that there "was, besides, the general disinclination of the labouring class in Bengal towards undertaking labour involving much physical strength and exertion and also such labour as was looked upon as degrading in a caste-ridden society". Chattopadhyaya, *Internal Migration in India*, p. 252.
41. Census 1951, Vol. 6, pt. 1a, p. 433.
42. Morris, "Growth of Large-Scale Industry", p. 657.

Methods of recruitment in the jute industry

Few subjects relating to Indian labour have stirred ideas and imagination as much as the role of the *sardar*, who was the labour recruiter and foreman.[43] Sardars are generally seen as individuals who exploit workers and serve the purposes of the mill owners. Adams, the Chief Inspector of Factories, told the IIC:

> "At the present time, especially in textile factories, the labour is almost entirely in the hands of the sirdars and time-keepers, who systematically extort money from the workers and are not only the direct agents in causing strikes but are also responsible for the continuous shifting of labour from one factory to another [...] The shifting of labour from one factory to another is arranged with a view to extortion of money before re-employment."[44]

He thought both employers and labourers would benefit if this system were discontinued. While mill owners also complained about this system, they claimed they were unable to alter matters: it was "essential to Indian labour".[45] The 1921 Census and the Royal Commission of 1931 attributed an important role to the sardar, both in the process of labour recruitment and as a foreman. According to the Royal Commission, the sardars not only controlled labour, but also lent money to the workers, had a say in their housing, and often owned or controlled shops. The Commission attributed the ease of outsiders in persuading workers to go on strike to the presence of the sardars.[46]

Upon closer inspection of the available evidence, the role of the sardar appears to have been less important than often suggested. As mentioned above, active recruitment in the jute industry was infrequent. The oral evidence in the report of the Royal Commission, which contains brief life histories for 20 jute workers, does not indicate that the sardars were of overriding significance. For example:

43. Sardar (or sirdar) literally means headman. Scholars have created the image of the powerful sardar, a headman from the village who, in addition to recruiting labour, also controlled the workers in the mill and the town. See Chakrabarty, *Rethinking Working Class History*, pp. 109 ff.; Das Gupta, "Structure of the Labour Market"; and Goswami, "Multiple Images", pp. 558-560.
44. IIC, Vol. 2, p. 327. The Chief Inspector thought that the sardars had an interest in keeping the labour force unstable, since they collected bribes from the workers who obtained jobs. I think that the sardar's power has been exaggerated; as I will describe below, the workers had their own reasons to change between mills.
45. IIC, Vol. 1, p. 11. Illegal practices were often attributed to the existence of the system of multiple and overlapping shifts in the mills: "in some mills at 22 different times of the day workers were coming in or going out of the mill". Sub-Divisional Officer, Barrackpore, in: WBSA, Comm., Feb. 1933, 1A-21, Progs. A 5-37. Dummy names entered in the daily employment register may have meant an excess employment of 10 per cent. Goswami, "Multiple Images"; RCLI, Vol. 5, pt. 2, pp. 119 and 143; and pt. 1, p. 280.
46. RCLI, Vol. 5, pt. 1, p. 152.

"A worker, born in Puri in Orissa "[...] was obliged to seek work outside of his native place some time after his parents died. He had married in the meantime. Work was hard to get and food scarce. Having heard of the good wages paid to workers in the mills in Bengal he decided to come here. Borrowed money to pay his fare. On arrival he was lucky enough to find work almost at once in the Howrah Jute Mill [...]"[47]

Nor do my interviews show that the sardar played a central role in recruitment. The most common pattern of migration and recruitment was through the contacts of families, husbands, neighbours, or, more generally, people from the same village.[48] Until around 1960, finding employment for one's relatives was fairly easy. Older workers told us that much of the recruiting happened at the railway station, where sardars, as well as babus, asked incoming migrants about their place of origin and invited them to work in their mills. Many migrants did not need to pass through this channel, as they already had relatives in the city.

In one case involving a group of migrants from South Orissa, I have been able to trace the person who started a new stream of migration towards Calcutta. In the first decade of the twentieth century, Patro and his two wives paid a religious visit to Calcutta. They were not the first persons arriving from Orissa, and they heard from other Orissa people that work was available. Patro opened a tea shop, and the two women started working in a jute mill. After a year or two, he returned to the village and brought back a group of 10 or 20 workers. Later he repeated this process and went back to the village again, thus bringing a total of about 30 workers. Patro initiated a migration stream which continues to this day. People from the area received information from family and relatives about work opportunities. According to an educated and English-speaking member of this community, "birds of a feather flock together".

"Anyone can become a sirdar", said the Chief Inspector of Factories in 1919.[49] The older workers we interviewed confirmed this statement. The sardar in the jute mill had little authority and was generally an ordinary worker who (after he had got more experience) was put in charge of a few machines and assigned supervision of a relatively small group of workers (15 to 50). Sardars were neither powerful nor rich; they were mere foremen. The wages of sardars – excluding the "bribes" and earnings through writing more labour on the register than actually employed – were not exceptionally high: a weaver might have earned as much as a line sardar. While some sardars were home owners or moneylenders, most of the ones we interviewed were not.

47. RCLI, Vol. 11, p. 355-365. Only 4 of the 20 cases refer to recruitment through a sardar.
48. This pattern of migration was by no means specific to this kind of large industry and probably differed little from migration to the rice fields or from the methods for recruiting rickshaw pullers. See e.g. Shah, "Rural-Urban Networks". Literature on migration in other areas and historical periods also emphasizes the importance of personal networks; see Baud, "Families and Migration".
49. Oral Evidence for the IIC, Vol. 2, pp. 329-334.

Without a doubt, bribery was common but the notion of bribe is a problematic one.[50] In the past, some money or food was paid to get a job. Women and children were more likely to have to pay. The workers told us, however, that this practice had not been enforced in former days. Giving a senior person some tea or money was a socially accepted practice. A union leader told us that when he wanted to obtain permanent employment in 1958, the English sahib required Rs.100 for himself and Rs.40 for the babu. The union leader did not regard such payments as bribes. He saw them as a gift to please someone in exchange for a favour. Nowadays, he said, people are obligated to pay bribes. Most workers claimed they had not paid a *ghush* or bribe in the past. While they did offer something, such initiatives came from the workers themselves; the sardars and babus did not demand gratuities.

Since the 1930s, attempts have been made to limit the influence of the sardars. Labour exchanges have been set up and labour officers employed to improve communication between the management and the employers and to abolish the practices of sardars. Employment and reorganization of workers has also become subject to increasing regulations. For example, redundancies and reorganizations must be reported to the Labour Commissioner, and vacancies should be submitted with a list of the reorganized workers eligible for the vacancies. In cases of reorganization and re-employment, the seniority principle prevails. Recruitment procedures have become more formal, and the role of sardars has been reduced. But these policies have not always been successful.[51] Some sardars tried to resist the introduction of new systems of registration. Struggles might pitch trade unions against sardars, head sardars, or babus.

Although the role of the sardar changed, the individualized nature of recruitment persisted. The very fact that one labour officer in a mill was responsible for recruiting more than 3,000 workers already suggests the continuation of informal practices of recruitment. Most interviewees reported having obtained employment through personal connections. Permission from the labour office appears to have been merely a formality. I perceive the labour office as little more than a cog in the employment network and an additional party that expected bribes.[52] Trade unions, which emerged in the 1920s seem to have

---

50. Goswami ("Multiple Images") notes that the word corruption should be taken in context to signify power as well as duties.

51. Govt. of India, Labour Investigation Committee (S.R. Deshpande), *Report on an Enquiry into Conditions of Labour in the Jute Mill Industry in India* (Delhi, 1946); Mukherjee, *Indian Working Class*.

52. In the study of a large factory in New England, Hareven describes how overseers retained the right to request a specific worker through the employment office following the establishment of a centralized personnel system, which shows that the influence of personal contacts is not exclusively an Indian or pre-capitalist phenomenon. Hareven, *Family Time and Industrial Time*, p. 89.

served a similar function. They did not really alter the system. Despite official statements to the contrary, unions try to obtain employment for their people and distribute the vacancies among themselves. As far as recruitment is concerned, unions are merely an additional intermediary agent.

Interpretations of the role of the sardar in Indian historiography appear rather one sided. Historical studies have emphasized the influence of the sardar as an instrument of the power of management. The sardar's traditional ties (i.e. his personal connections with people from his village) have been construed as means of control. The very existence of the sardars may, however, signify a lack of control on the part of employers, as well as their power. The existence of migration streams during the nineteenth century meant that little active recruitment was needed for the jute industry. Rather than stressing the role of the sardar, I submit that recruitment proceeded mainly through personal relations. For the workers, personal connections were crucial for obtaining employment. Sardars were not powerful lackeys of management. Various channels led to work, and the presence of a middleman in the personal network of relations provided an additional opportunity. The position of the middleman arises primarily from his background within the community, and employers did not invent the institution of intermediation. Several intermediaries have always been involved in the recruitment procedure, with the sardar accounting for a small share of the entire process.

Circular migration and the resilience of the rural structure

Hazari Pal, the rickshaw puller in Lapierre's *City of Joy*, left his village in West Bengal after a harvest failure and came to Calcutta with his family. He knew no one in the city, where he had to start by finding a place to live and, inevitably, wound up being cheated. This story does not resemble the dominant pattern of migration. As described above, Biharis, rather than people from rural Bengal, have dominated labour migration to Calcutta. Second, migrants who come without knowing anyone in the city are the exception rather than the rule; in general people come through personal connections. Third, the dominant pattern of migration does not result from sudden economic or ecological crises. Rather, it reflects a more regular pattern of single male migrants travelling back and forth between their villages and rural or urban destinations. This section describes this pattern of circular migration and the reasons of the migrants for departing from and returning to their villages.

As described above, the migrants came from specific areas of Eastern India. Economic conditions in the districts of recruitment were invariably bad, and the West to East stream of migration is attributable to the lower wages for agricultural labourers in the West. In Saran in Bihar, the main recruiting district for the jute mills, about one fifth of the population lived below subsistence level at the beginning of this century.[53] The wage of an unskilled labourer was two to three annas per day. The rate of pay was closer to five annas around Calcutta and even higher towards the East. Old industries, like weaving, indigo, and opium, had declined during the nineteenth century. The districts were densely populated, and new arable land was not available. Nevertheless, the area remains characterized by the proliferation of small-landownership, although the number of people who are landless or who own plots of land that are too small for subsistence has increased over time.

While Saran may have been exceptional with respect to its high population density, the characteristics of recruitment in this area differ little from the ones in most other recruiting regions. The districts from which many people migrated were poor, but not necessarily the poorest. General explanations for the large-scale migration from some of the agricultural areas are insufficient to elucidate the specific patterns involved here. Saran's status as one of the poorer districts with a high population density is not the whole story. First, I believe its high population was probably largely possible because of the income from migrant labour. Second, I disagree with the depiction of Saran as a victim. Rather, people from Saran were able – for reasons that remain to be determined – to take better advantage of the opportunities available within the regional context.

Were the migrants the poorest residents? Contemporary writings on Bengal have depicted the labour force as the poorest segment, who came to industry as a last resort. The Census and the Royal Commission assert that they were "pushed, not pulled". This image reappears in the writings of historians.[54] My research has convinced me that the impression that migrants were victims of economic development merits rectification. As a starting point, consider the mixed social and caste background of the migrant labour force, as noted for example in the 1911 and 1921 Censuses. While certain groups did not migrate, the migrant population generally seems to have come from all strata of rural society.[55] Data on the measure of land ownership of migrants are scarce and

---

53. The following is primarily based on Yang, *Limited Raj*.
54. According to Das Gupta: "*ruined artisans, labourers failing to get adequate employment and subsistence in the rural economy, agriculturalists unsettled by the sort of changes taking place in the agricultural economy, unskilled of all trades, and peasant, artisans and labourers turned into destitutes and paupers were the most numerous* among the working mass employed in the jute mills" (Das Gupta, "Factory Labour in Eastern India", p. 315, italics in original). "The push was felt particularly by persons of low economic and social status because 'this class of population had little inducement to stay at home for agricultural wages are notoriously low, and (they) will be ready to go abroad in order to earn a fair wage'" (Yang, *Limited Raj*, p. 196; the quote is from a 1906 report by S.H Fremantle).
55. "The emigration from North India represented an average sample of the rural population,

unreliable. Nevertheless, the available information reveals a highly diverse pattern of land ownership. At the end of the 1940s, a survey found that 59 per cent of the mill workers were landless, and that 21 per cent owned less than two bigha (two thirds of an acre).[56] The last large survey among the jute workers, which was held around 1970, showed that 42 per cent of the families of workers did not own any land, and that 29 per cent owned less than 1 acre.[57] In the 1980s, a survey taken in Bihar showed that 39 per cent of the migrants were landless, and that 38 per cent owned less than 2.5 acres. This distribution does not differ substantially from the distribution observed for the total sample population.[58] My field study confirmed the diversity in the pattern of land ownership: the migrants included both land owners and landless individuals. For example, some migrants from the area in South Orissa are landowners and are not the poorest inhabitants of their village. When the first migrant left, he owned a few acres of land. His family was able to increase this land significantly, and their well-built houses are now a formidable presence on the village market. Other people we interviewed also possessed land, and their families generally did not farm this land themselves. Renting out land to sharecroppers is a common practice. The examples indicate that the migrants are not necessarily the poorest residents of the rural area. People with land migrate almost as often as landless individuals.

Decisions to migrate ...

The majority of the people interviewed said that problems in their village had motivated their departure. In most cases, these statements refer to land shortages. Half the people interviewed said they did not own any land, and many mentioned that the growth of their family forced them to migrate. Four families from Andhra Pradesh had been weavers and reported that they had come to the city because the income from this trade was insufficient to support the family. Although land shortage is the main reason for people to come to the city, the decision is generally more complex. Many of the people interviewed referred not only to the "push" of land shortages, but also to the "pull" of the industrial area. A person from Bihar improved his status by moving to the city. Migrants enjoyed a higher standard of living and were regarded with respect.[59] According to a Bhojpuri proverb: "One who gets a job in the East, can fill his house with

excluding the trading, clerical and priestly castes – and also excluding many of the really downtrodden, the sweeper-folk, the lowest of the Untouchables." Tinker, *New System of Slavery*, p. 267.

56. Chattopadhay, *Socio-Economic Survey of Jute*, pp. 29 ff.
57. Bhattacharya and Chatterjee, "Some Characteristics of Jute".
58. Oberai *et al.*, *Determinants and Consequences*, p. 36.
59. Yang, *Limited Raj*, pp. 198-199.

gold." The departure of the men was not always welcome, however, and another proverb says: "Railways are not our enemy. Nor are the steamships. Our real enemy is nokari [service]."[60]

Family situation is an important factor in the decision to migrate, although its influence can be quite complex. While men migrated with a view to providing an income for the family, the number of brothers that went varied. The need to work the land did not necessarily prevent migration by additional brothers. Changes in family composition might be crucial as well. Deserted women and widows constituted an important part of the labour force, and division of the family or quarrels between brothers were other important reasons for migration. In addition, certain stages in individual and household cycles are more conducive to migration than others. Young men can sometimes afford the luxury of not taking any job available and are able to look and move around; only from a certain age are they expected to settle down.

Definitions of need are not fixed, but vary from person to person. For example, a fairly educated man from Arrah who now owns a bookshop said that serious poverty in the family had driven him to the city, where he began to work as a cleaner. Two brothers were already "in service" and had started a moneylending business. Upon returning to his village after five years, his family's circumstances had certainly improved. Somebody else mentioned that if he had owned land, he would not have worked in the city. Nevertheless, his work in Calcutta has enabled him to acquire three acres of land, and he continues to live in the city.

... and to return

Thus, the decision to migrate results from a complex of factors. Such moves do not conclude the story, however, since decisions to migrate are not final acts. Many migrants have retained their links with their home villages and move back and forth between the urban-industrial and the rural sectors.

The evidence seems to leave little doubt that the jute industry's labour force was unstable and characterized by a high turnover.[61] Foley concluded in 1906: "The mill employees are not as a whole attached to the mills in which they started working, but if they see a chance of making more money in any other

60. Pandey, Gyanendra, "Community Consciousness and Communal Strife", unpublished manuscript; quoted in Chakrabarty, *Rethinking Working Class History*, p. 187.
61. This problem was one of the most important themes in the government reports from the beginning of the twentieth century. Industrialization was thought to be socially difficult because the Indian "native" did not adapt easily to the capitalist work discipline. This idea has been criticized, especially by Morris, who revealed that the idea was an employer's concept without any empirical basis. Morris, "Labor Market in India". I have presented part of the following argument in De Haan, "Migrant Labour in Calcutta Jute Mills". For Bombay, see the recent book by Chandavarkar, *The Origins of Industrial Capitalism in India*, pp. 124 ff.

mill, they will at once leave."[62] The Royal Commission estimated that the whole factory population was replaced within less than two years, and that over 60 per cent was employed less than five years.[63] In 1946, according to the LIC,[64] more than half the labourers had worked for their current employer for less than five years. The following life stories (one from the RCLI and one from my field research) illustrate that the workers had indeed changed. The story of a Madrasi sardar runs as follows:

"On the death of his father his mother came to Serampore with him when he was 12 years old. His mother secured a job in the Serampore Cotton Mill while he got a job as a spinning shifter in the India Jute Mill. He worked there for two years and then left the place in order to secure some better job at Titaghur.. Both of them remained at Titaghur for four years, then went home. His mother got him married and he then returned from his home with his mother and wife to Shamnuggur where he got a job as a rover.. he associated with bad company and thereby got into bad habits of drinking and gambling [...] He worked five years in his present job as a rover and was then promoted to assistant drawing sirdar [...] Being unable to clear the debt (which he accumulated due to drinking and the ceremony at his mother's death) he was compelled to leave this place and went to Jagatdal where he worked as a rover... He came back again to Shamnuggur and got drawing sirdar's job [...]"[65]

While many labourers today have had the same employment for most of their working life, many have also changed jobs often. Workers said changing work by leaving and returning to the same mill used to be possible. The following story is an extreme example of this practice. Ali is a retired worker of 75 years, a Bengali Muslim. He started in Standard Jute Mill in Titagarh when he was 20 years old, as a mechanic. After five years he left for the neighbouring Kinnison Mill where he also worked for about 5 years. Then he went to EMCO Jute Mill, where he left after a quarrel. He joined Laxmi Jute Mill but left after two weeks because he was not satisfied with the wage. He left the area and went to the western parts of Bengal and Bihar, and worked in a Jute Mill for one year. Back in Titagarh he joined a friend as a radio mechanic. Finally he joined the Paper Mill in Titagarh, in the fire service, and worked there for 44 years.

---

62. Foley, *Report on Labour in Bengal*, p. 9. See also the IFLC, pp. 19-20; Curjel, Dagmar F., "Enquiry into the Conditions of Employment of Women before and after Childbirth, in Bengal Industries. Report", unpublished, West Bengal State Archives, 1923.

63. RCLI, Vol. 1, p. 26 (cited in Mukherjee, *Indian Working Class*, p. 35); RCLI, Vol. 5, pt. 1, pp. 262-279.

64. *Labour Investigation Committee (Government of India), Report on Enquiry into Conditions of Labour in Jute Mill Industry in India*, Manager of Publication, Delhi, 1946.

65. RCLI, Vol. 10, p. 359. Foley wrote about a weaver: "He had worked in four or six jute mills; he had come home now because of his family. He left one mill for another when he found he could make more at another; he preferred a new mill [...]" Foley, *Report on Labour in Bengal*, p. 16.

The reasons for this movement of labourers between mills varied. First, the proximity of the mills enabled such mobility. Second, wage rates were not standardized, and differences in wages allegedly induced workers to try their luck in other mills. The introduction of electric light also played a role. In 1908, employers told the Indian Factory Labour Commission (IFLC) that workers preferred the mills with electric light and longer working hours because they could earn higher wages. Workers and their representatives felt otherwise.[66] Sardars and time-keepers also encouraged movement of labour between factories with a view to extorting money before re-employing the workers.[67] Labour laws were another cause of movement by workers. Employers said that children worked in different mills after working hours were reduced[68] and made the same statement about women following the legislative provision for maternity leave and benefits.[69]

Over time, the workforce has become more stable. Workers say that finding a job is very difficult nowadays, and that choosing a mill is impossible. The average number of years of employment has clearly increased. In 1972, the estimated average period of employment among permanent workers was almost 15 years.[70] My computations based on figures from one jute mill show that the trend towards longer employment continues. When the supply of labour began to exceed the demand, and part of the labour force became permanent, changing jobs between mills decreased.

In another respect, however, the workforce has remained unstable: workers continue to return to their villages. Foley noted that the shortage of labour had virtually disappeared from the 25 jute mills he visited and concluded:

"There was a general complaint, however, that there had been deficiency of labour during the months of April, May and June [...] The bulk of hands, it is said, are immigrants from the United Provinces and Behar: they make more money than they require, and a larger number than can be spared take a three months' holiday every year, because it is their cultivation and marriage season and because they wish to avoid the heat. Nothing will prevent them from going away at this time: they would not stay for an increase of wages, and the provision of excellent quarters and various kinds of comforts has no effect in restraining them."[71]

My field-work shows that almost one hundred years later, many workers still return to their villages regularly. A large share of the labourers leaves the mill

---

66. IFLC, Vol. 1, witness 126; Vol. 2, witnesses 176, 181, 182, 183 and 184.
67. Witness 126 of the IIC, Minutes of Evidence, Parl. Papers.
68. RCLI, Vol. 5, pt. 1, p. 298.
69. For example, the Oral Evidence of Adams in IIC, Minutes of Evidence.
70. Bhattacharya and Chatterjee, "Some Characteristics of Jute".
71. Foley, *Report on Labour in Bengal*, p. 7. This pattern also emerged from the answers by some of the workers to the Indian Factory Commission in 1890. *Report of the Indian Factory Commission*, IOL&R, Parliamentary Papers V/4/59, 1890-91, pp. 69 ff.

area each year, especially in the hot months (April and May) until the outbreak
of the monsoon. About half the workers interviewed still had a link with the
village from which they had come and returned there regularly.

A number of explanations have been submitted with respect to this regular
leave. Higher wages were thought to reduce stability among the work force,
although little relation exists between the level of the wages and the leave taken.
Work stoppages and seasonal production in industry have played little role in
the patterns of yearly return, unlike in many other activities attracting migrant
labour. The continuous complaints by employers of shortages of experienced
weavers and spinners show that this slack cannot be the reason that workers
leave. Available figures show constant production in the period April till June,
although the number of absent workers, and therefore also the number of *badlis*
(substitute labourers) employed, increases significantly.[72] Likewise, leaving in
this period has little to do with labour demand in agricultural areas either, as
already mentioned by Foley and the Royal Commission.[73]

These explanations do not account for the pattern of circular migration and
the moment of leave. I believe that the arguments raised by the workers (both
economic and socio-cultural) reflect their motives for their repeated returns to
their villages. The predominance of men among the migrants has resulted not
from the preferences of employers, but from cultural restrictions on the mobility
of women.[74] Among the different reasons for return migration, I consider the
separation between workers and their families to be the most important factor.
The workers say they go back to their villages because of obligations there. Most
return during *tana time* (the hot months in which marriages and other festivals
take place) and meet their families and friends. Although many migrants have
worked in the city for decades, most regard their villages as their home. Despite
the economic problems that forced them to migrate, they may have enjoyed
life in the village: the weather is nice there, goods are cheap, and they feel an
emotional attachment to their birthplace. People say that they work in the town
to maintain or improve their position in the village. They take pride in having

---

72. Figures on the Labour Complement of Titaghur No. 2 Mill, 1969-70. The continuity of the
      regular leave, notwithstanding reduced working hours and improved conditions, shows that
      the pattern of circular migration had little to do with the organization of the industry. While
      poor housing conditions were a cause for returning, they were also a consequence: workers
      invested their savings in the village, not in the city.
73. The only agricultural activity in May is the wheat harvest. The number of people required
      for this activity, however, bears no relation to the droves of migrants returning to their
      villages. For a description of agricultural cycles in Bihar see Yang, *Limited Raj,* pp. 99 ff. Foley
      already noted that the workers did not return for agricultural work, thereby contradicting
      the opinions of the managers (see the quote above).
74. I have described the perceptions of female labour and the changes during this century, in
      "Towards a Single Male Earner".

purchased some land. Overstatements with respect to the amount of land they own are said to be commonplace, and one worker said that he works to invest in his land. Many workers own property in their villages, although the value varies considerably from just a house or a few *katha* of land (1/27 of an acre) to several acres that are rented out to sharecroppers. Possession of property was often mentioned as the main reason for the workers to return at any time they deemed necessary.

Most migrants return periodically for one or two months every year (occasionally more, as mills grant unpaid leave), after retirement, and in times of crisis and unemployment. The way many of the migrants talked about their leave was most enlightening. We asked them whether it was possible to leave for longer than the statutory one month's holiday (14 days with pay). It appeared to be a public secret that this practice was quite easy, either with permission from the management or through the purchase of a medical certificate from a doctor indicating that the worker had been unable to return in time. Equally illuminating were their responses to the question about the loss of wages that accompanied their extended leaves: many workers laughed and said: "what to do", we have family in the village, some work or duty there. One worker replied: would you be able to return after 14 days (the official holiday with pay) when you have not seen your family for a year?

Thus, the industrial growth in this area has not led to a unidirectional movement of proletarians to the city. The migrants were not only the poorest and the landless. Rather, they came from many sections of rural society. Migration was not a last remedy in the fight for survival or a decision of last resort. Rather, migration was a conscious strategy to maintain the family's position in the village, a decision influenced by a complex of factors. The pattern of circulation was not caused by seasonal production, as in the case of rural migrants in India (described by Breman)[75] and the migrants to the coast of Holland in the seventeenth century (as described by Lucassen).[76] The circular pattern of migration to the industrial area of Calcutta arose from the situation in which men migrated to the city individually while leaving their women behind and thus wished to retain a link with their villages.

Conclusion: between free and unfree migration

Completely different migration scenarios exist. At one extreme, migrants are portrayed as the upper crust in their area of origin, the young men with money

75. See the collection of his articles in *Wage Hunters and Gatherers*.
76. J. Lucassen, *Migrant Labour in Europe*.

and contacts who took advantage of the opportunities offered. The other extreme presents the picture of the forced migrant, a destitute individual with no alternative. An obvious variety of this practice involves slave labour, which has been extended to indentured labour ("a new system of slavery") and to the even broader field of "colonial migration", including recruitment for large-scale enterprises under colonial rule.

From 1850 onwards in Eastern India, the dominant pattern of migration seems to have shifted from forced colonial migration to free migration. Abolition of indentured labour and contract labour in large-scale enterprises and the appointment of labour officers and labour-exchange agencies to replace sardars seem to have led to the establishment of a free labour market. At the same time, however, the supply of labour has grown faster than the demand, and land has become increasingly scarce. Rising numbers of migrants have been forced to accept jobs whenever and wherever they were offered.

Such a uni-linear pattern from unfree to free migration is not, however, entirely accurate. In the first place, different forms of migration and labour recruitment persisted throughout the period. Around 1900, indentured migration overseas and the movement to the tea plantations near Darjeeling existed alongside migration for seasonal agricultural work and towards the new industrial centres. The tradition of migration predated the search for labourers by the colonial enterprises. Uprooting Indian villagers was quite unnecessary. The different streams of migration were clearly segmented. For example, migrants from one village might tend to go to Calcutta, while most people leaving a village a few miles away might travel to the tea plantations near Darjeeling. Nevertheless, attributing this segmentation exclusively to force would be unjustified. While we are very often unable to trace the origin of this segmentation, several causes are possible. More importantly, certain patterns of migration do not change easily once they have come into existence.

Second, we need to use the theoretical opposition of free versus unfree with caution.[77] Migration in India tends to be classified as unfree, as opposed to the free migration believed to exist in the neo-classical labour market model. The existence of middlemen (like *sardars* and *arkattis*) and the segmentation of the labour market are often interpreted as the absence of a free market. My main criticism of these kinds of interpretations is that they reflect an outsider's perspective. My research shows that the workers do not believe they are controlled by the sardar. They are certainly not bonded labour. The migrants regard work in the jute mills as *naukri*, or service. The meaning of this term is somewhat ambiguous, as service also means being tied to an employer – a

---

77. In his study of bonded labour in India, Prakash discusses the free versus unfree opposition encountered in historiography as well as in colonial records: he relates this opposition to the "hegemonic rise of the western conception of history as progress". Prakash, *Bonded Histories*, p. 8.

situation that many people say they try to avoid. Most migrants, however, experienced naukri as an improvement. Industrial labour was more prestigious than agricultural labour, and the migrants returned with savings from their relatively high incomes and impressed their fellow villagers with presents. Understanding the labour market requires far closer examination of the local meanings of different forms of labour recruitment and their individual interpretations among workers. In most cases, local people were responsible for recruitment, and little is known of their methods. While coercion and force were important elements, they were not the only mechanisms used. The middleman usually originated from the areas where he was recruiting. Accordingly, some measure of legitimacy was involved.

This paper has illustrated the recruitment issue with regard to migration to the jute mills. It has shown that the strategies of employers did not force the replacement of local labour. The local population did not need to join the industry, and many considered the work beneath their status. Moreover, this paper has stressed the importance of personal networks, rather than the unlimited power of the middleman as an instrument of the employer; this chain in migration is a general feature and is not specific to the Indian labour market. Finally, migration has been portrayed as a strategy of the rural population (and not only of the poorest people), to maintain its position in the village; migration was not the last option after proletarianization. For the migrants, the jute industry was one of many options that emerged in Bengal. They did not view the jute industry as the worst option available. The wages were relatively high, and the work was stable and increased the status of migrants in their villages. Hence, this migration was more voluntary than suggested by Indian historiography, which is hindered by a lack of evidence written by workers.

While my research has focused on the industrial area, some of the arguments may also apply to other migration streams. Studies about migration to coal mines, tea plantations, and overseas destinations stress the unfree element and the role of the middlemen. They also note, however, that the actual recruitment was carried out by local people. Again, little information is available about the local manifestations of this process. We know much more about what happened in the depots, aboard the ships, and at the points of destination. As said above, we have little knowledge about the segmentation of the migration streams and the reasons why certain areas provided the indentured labourers, while others supplied the workers for the industries. We do not know the causes of the popularity of migration in certain villages as opposed to others. We do know, however, that the indentured migrants, like the industrial workers, came from almost all segments of rural society. In addition, the emphasis on the role of the returning migrants indicates a similar process of chain migration. Although migrants may return to their villages with exaggerated stories and glorified stories about their work abroad, the persistence of chain migration cannot be the result of deceit alone. Likewise, the miserable conditions aboard the ships cannot be equated directly with coercion in the recruitment process; even the deplorable conditions may have been a welcome escape for the migrants. Without writing an apology for colonialism, understanding the process of migration requires examining the perceptions among the migrants of these conditions and the process of recruitment.

Eastern India. Recruitment Districts of the Jute Industry.

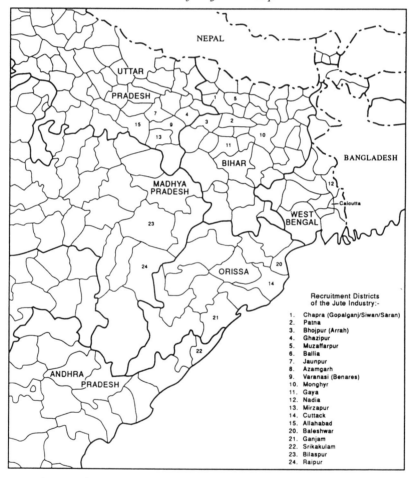

Recruitment Districts
of the Jute Industry:-

1. Chapra (Gopalganj/Siwan/Saran)
2. Patna
3. Bhojpur (Arrah)
4. Ghazipur
5. Muzaffarpur
6. Ballia
7. Jaunpur
8. Azamgarh
9. Varanasi (Benares)
10. Monghyr
11. Gaya
12. Nadia
13. Mirzapur
14. Cuttack
15. Allahabad
20. Baleshwar
21. Ganjam
22. Srikakulam
23. Bilaspur
24. Raipur

Source: the map is based on Joseph E. Schwartzberg, *A Historical Atlas of South Asia* (New York, 1992) and has been processed by Mrs. Catherine Lawrence, SOAS. Note: the districts have changed during this century; therefore the present names and areas do not correspond exactly with those used in earlier reports (especially the source district of the jute industry).

Eternal Vagrants? State Formation, Migration, and Travelling Groups in Western-Europe, 1350-1914[*]

Leo Lucassen

Introduction

Historical studies of migration and migrants reflect many different methods and perspectives. Research on one striking case of migrants, however (known as itinerant or travelling groups), has been marginal at best. The migratory behaviour of groups such as gypsies, tinkers, travellers, and nomads, who all characteristically travel in families and lack a permanent sedentary base, is not regarded as part of normal migration. The few references to such people usually label them as vagrants or marginals and hardly ever analyse their migration *patterns* or the functionality of their itinerant lifestyle. The existence of itinerant groups is generally viewed as a sign of crisis and social degradation.[1] This perception surfaces not only in migration studies, but also in literature focused especially on these groups. The emphasis lies on their cultural features, such as births, marriages, deaths, languages, and physical appearance. Their travelling lifestyle is either taken for granted or interpreted in a negative way (the well-known idea of *dolce far niente*).[2] Only in the last decades have a few historians, sociologists, and anthropologists started to stress the economic functions of the travelling lifestyle and to offer some criticism of the prevailing school of thought.[3] Itinerancy as such has also proven to extend beyond travelling groups and should be studied in the light of more general migration patterns (such as peddling and circular migration). Almost all the trades practised by gypsies and others (including fortune-telling) also existed among sedentary people. Finally, the essential characteristics of the travelling lifestyle (the family as a working unit, mobility,

---

[*] I thank Jan Lucassen, Wim Willems, and Florike Egmond for their thorough and stimulating critique of an earlier draft of this paper.

1. See for example Clark, *Migrant in Kentish Towny*, pp. 144-145; Clark and Souden, "Introduction", p. 36; Whyte, "Migration in Early-Modern Scotland", pp. 96-98; Moch, *Moving Europeans*, pp. 88-89. Notable exceptions are Samuel, "Comers and goers", and Angelini, "Suonatori ambulanti". For a critical historiographical review, see my article "A Blind Spot".
2. For an analysis of this stereotyping in the case of gypsies, see Willems and Lucassen, "Church of Knowledge"; and Willems, *Op zoek naar de ware zigeuner*.
3. Okely, *Traveller-Gypsies*; Gmelch, "Groups that Don't Want In"; Rao, *Other Nomads*; Mayall, *Gypsy-Travellers*; Fricke, *Zwischen Erziehung und Ausgrenzung*; L. Lucassen, *"En men noemde hen zigeuners"*; and L. Lucassen, "Under the cloak of begging?".

and self-employment) are widespread phenomena and therefore explicable on the basis of reference to a group culture.

In this paper I will try to explain the repressive policy of European societies (especially the authorities) towards travelling groups, whom they assigned labels such as gypsy or vagrant from the Middle Ages onwards. I will also explore the process of stigmatization that these groups underwent. I will focus both on stigmatization and on the economic functionality of migration in the various Western European states and the process of state formation.

Until now, travelling groups have been studied from four major angles: criminality, marginality, poverty, and, only recently, labour migration.[4] As the more recent studies within these angles already show, the answer to the main question formulated above should primarily be sought within the attitude of authorities who have labelled people as vagrants, gypsies, and the like and who propagate a negative image of these categories.[5] My basic assumption is that the impression that these people are rogues and vagabonds is generally unjustified.[6] Admittedly, some criminal vagrants may have existed in the past, and a functional economic model is not necessarily applicable to all travelling groups. Examples abound of stealing, cheating, and begging gypsies or vagrants. In the case of gypsies in particular and of travelling groups overall, however, this image has been generalized to encompass the whole category, thereby neglecting the many individuals who do not live up to their stereotype.

Although the emergence and development of the stigma is indeed an important subject of analysis, this paper will not study this process in terms of ideas and images.[7] Instead, it will highlight the policies adopted by authorities and the more general role of the state. State officials initiated the repressive policy and thus propagated the negative ideas that otherwise would have been restricted to a small literate elite. Understanding these ideas in terms of their implementation by the authorities and influence on state policy is therefore more important.

The assumption that the attitude of the authorities and the state towards migration in general and itinerant groups in particular is pivotal in explaining the co-existence of a strong and ongoing stigmatization of these groups as social misfits and their simultaneous functional economic role is not enough. State formation is not the sole factor. To avoid a circular argument and to gain clear

---

4. L. Lucassen, "Blind Spot".
5. On the labelling question, see L. Lucassen, *"En men noemde hen zigeuners"* and L. Lucassen "The power of definition", and especially L. Lucassen, *Zigeuner*.
6. Based on the historical research from among others Schubert ("Mobilität ohne Chance"), Mayall (*Gypsy-Travellers in Nineteenth-Century*), and L. Lucassen (*"En men noemde hen zigeuners"*).
7. For an analysis of the ideas on vagrants, see Geremek, *Les fils de Cain*. An excellent study on the stereotyping of gypsies in Western Europe from the eighteenth century onwards is Willems, *Op zoek naar de ware zigeuner*.

insight into the interaction between authorities and travelling groups, an *economic* approach – the function of migration for the labour market – is indispensable.[8] The economic nucleus of the accusation is the main indicator for this approach: working under the guise of begging and stealing or the refusal to work. Understanding this stigmatization therefore requires linking the ideas about travelling groups to the structural economic developments from the Middle Ages onwards.

Changing conceptions about vagrancy and labour migration, 1350-1550

According to Bronislaw Geremek, who wrote a number of fundamental and influential studies on the changing attitude in Europe towards the poor in general and vagrants in particular, the stigmatization of travelling groups originated during the fourteenth century. Following the sociologist Vexliard, Geremek places the first use of the term vagabond (a term with an unmitigated pejorative connotation[9]) in France around 1350.[10] Its negative connotation signified undesirable wandering behaviour. Vagrancy soon came to be considered a crime in itself.[11] The negative stereotyping, which had started in the 1340s, culminated around the turn of the sixteenth century in popular books, such as *Das Narrenschiff* (1494), the *Liber Vagatorum* (about 1510), and publications on the secret language of rogues.[12] These works depicted vagabonds and beggars as professional thieves, robbers, and cheats. This image strongly influenced public opinion and was supported by state and church alike. Martin Luther, for example, wrote an introduction to one of the editions of the *Liber Vagatorum*. The Catholic Church and the Humanists did not lag behind their Protestant counterparts in this respect.[13] As a result, people lacking a fixed abode and labelled as beggars or vagabonds were increasingly stigmatized as lazy and prone to criminal behaviour.

The literature primarily attributes this stigmatization to economic circumstances, namely the transition from a feudal to a market-oriented capitalist system, which entailed a change from bound to free labour. Such texts also stress the serious labour shortage that arose due to the dramatic plagues in the fourteenth century (which almost halved Western Europe's population) and that

8. As is made clear by the work of J. Lucassen, *Migrant Labour in Europe* and Moch, *Moving Europeans*, among others.
9. Geremek, "Criminalité, vagabondage, paupérisme", p. 346.
10. Vexliard, *Introduction à la sociologie du vagabondage*, pp. 13-14.
11. Geremek, *Truands et misérables*, p. 71. See also Woolf, *Poor in Western Europe*, pp. 17-18, and Sachße and Tennstedt, *Geschichte der Armenfürsorge*, p. 36.
12. Geremek, *Les fils de Caïn*, p. 53.
13. At the council of Trent (1545-1563), the start of the counter-reformation, begging and vagrancy were condemned outright (Cataluccio, "Avant propos. Les vagabonds", p. 18).

led to rising wages and a short-lived golden age for workers. Many stood to benefit from leaving their masters to search for another job at a better wage. Employers joined forces with the authorities in trying to prevent this practice by enlisting as many workers as possible. People who preferred different ways of earning their living (for example as self-employed itinerants) were increasingly regarded with suspicion and stigmatized as vagabonds. Two measures taken to bind labour to capital and fix wages were the *Statute of labourers* issued in England in 1351 and a similar act that became effective two years later in France.[14]

These structural ideological and economic changes gave rise to a repressive policy towards people looked upon as vagrants and an attempt to control labour migration. Migration was only admitted within institutionalized frameworks: pilgrims, emigrants, compagnonnage, colonists, seasonal labourers, and others. People who travelled without such an "alibi" risked being stigmatized and treated as vagrants, *gens sans aveu* or masterless men. Travelling groups were especially afflicted by these prejudices because being on the move with one's family without any apparent intention to settle down symbolized a preeminently undesirable lifestyle. The appearance of the first "Egyptians" (travelling in family groups) in Western Europe (1419) fits well within this categorization. As they claimed to be pilgrims from Little Egypt, they were tolerated and sometimes supported. Doubts about their pilgrim status (they were suspected of being spies for the Turks) rapidly led to stigmatization. Their presumed conduct came to symbolize lazy and criminal vagrancy, and the travelling "Egyptians" suffered the brunt of a severely repressive policy from 1500 onwards.

The practicability of the general vagrant policy depended both on the power and organization of the states and on the local interpretation of the term vagrant. I disagree with Vexliard and Geremek, who assert that this category consisted mainly of people lacking ties to normal society who had retreated from the conventional public.[15] This image of vagrants, which resembles views of homeless people today, ignores their ongoing economic functioning (even after stigmatization) and further suggests that they were to a large extent a constructed category. Closer examination of government policy, however, reveals that the label was quite flexible and could encompass all sorts of mobile people, including seasonal labourers and self-employed peddlers.[16] More or less the same holds true for the gypsy label.

14. Geremek, *Truands et misérables*, p. 71. For the 1351 act see also Miskimin, *Economy of Early Renaissance Europe*, pp. 45-46.
15. Geremek, "Criminalité, vagabondage, paupérisme", p. 349.
16. Lis and Soly, *Poverty and Capitalism*, p. 82.

The rise of commercial capitalism and the slow shift to direct rule: 1550-1815

The "long sixteenth century" was a period of economic expansion in Western Europe that led to the concentration and commercialization of the agricultural and trading sectors. The labour shortage disappeared due to population growth, and wages became relatively stable.[17] The stigmatization of labour migration, which had been so prominent in the former period, might therefore have been expected to subside following the loss of its functionality. This effect seems to have occurred in general terms. The expanding economies needed seasonal labour and peddling middlemen, and repressing them would have been economically imprudent. As we know from the economic history of Western Europe, however, important regional differences persisted. This expectation is best exemplified in the sea provinces of the Dutch Republic, where a capital intensive economy developed that depended on migrant labour from low capital regions in the eastern part of the Republic and in the western part of Germany.[18]

The situation in England, however, where commercial capitalism proliferated almost a century later than in the Dutch Republic, differs markedly. Commercialization and the emergence of capitalistic farmers, who increasingly replaced the small peasants, led to considerable proletarianization. Moreover, the early development of the English state was characterized by far greater integration of local and central authorities than the loosely connected provinces of the federal Dutch Republic. The combination of these economic and political forces gave rise to another outcome in England. Perceiving the growing numbers of landless and sometimes masterless men as a threat, the state associated such individuals with uprooted and disorderly circumstances[19] and tried to control their movements and to bind them to capital through a sandwich formula of vagrant and poor laws aimed at curbing migration. The period 1560-1640 can therefore aptly be characterized as the "peak of state activity against vagabonds".[20]

For a third type of relationship between economic and political developments, consider France and Germany west of the Elbe. Here, low capital existed alongside high coercion, to borrow Tilly's analytical tools. The countryside maintained its fragmented character, with the mass of the "peasants" (in contrast to the commercial "farmers" in the Northwest) bound to their land. Population growth, however, led to smaller and smaller parcels of land, forcing many to combine their farm work with activities that in many cases stimulated migration. One means for retaining land and earning a living at the same time involved seasonal labour. Others, mostly young people without land, often became

17. Vries, *Economy of Europe*, pp. 184-187.
18. J. Lucassen, *Migrant Labour in Europe*.
19. Beier, *Masterless Men*, p. 9.
20. *Ibid.*, p. xix.

servants. The role of this process of partial proletarianization in producing a structural vagrancy problem (as Hufton and Lis & Soly argue[21]) is unclear. More importantly, the extensive local and circular migration worried local and regional authorities.[22] Their fear was not altogether unfounded. Poor vagrants could cause financial and security problems in this age of religious wars, of which the Thirty Years War is an outstanding example with large groups of plundering and marauding mercenary soldiers. Their concern did not, however, curtail migration, as Fertig's study on the southern part of Germany has made clear:

> "Regulations were not intended to prevent migration; or if they were, they achieved but little success. Regulations did not function as a floodgate against mobility, but rather as channels for it. Spatial mobility was possible for everybody. However, from the authorities point of view, it had to be justified, and it had legal consequences."[23]

According to a preliminary conclusion of this still very rough typology,[24] despite the fundamental change in the economic circumstances that had produced the stigmatization of migrant labour as a result of the economic expansion from about 1450 onwards, the interplay between capital and coercion in the process of state formation justifies (with the Dutch Republic forming a notable exception) the continued concern for migration among the authorities.

Up to this point, the focus has been on the general attitude towards labour migration. This background has paved the way for the main topic of this paper: travelling groups and the fear for vagrancy. At first glance, travelling groups do not fit the vagrancy pattern because the changing negative attitude towards beggars and vagrants was a general Western European phenomenon since the fifteenth century. The main explanation for this development is the major change in the organization of poor relief.[25] The initiative came from urban authorities, who took over the coordination of the poor relief from the various private and religious bodies. This reorganization not only led to a more rational and bureaucratic distribution of alms, but also to the exclusion of alien beggars (whose stay in cities was officially forbidden from the sixteenth century onwards). These prohibitions did not imply that their entrance could be stopped. Alien beggars were difficult to distinguish from indigenous beggars, and many

21. Lis and Soly, *Poverty and Capitalism*; Hufton, *Poor of Eighteenth-Century France*.
22. Moch, *Moving Europeans*.
23. Fertig, "Transatlantic migration from the German-speaking", pp. 203-204.
24. Future research requires differentiations between levels of "authorities" (local, regional, central) and their interests in and view on migration and vagrancy.
25. Woolf, *Poor in Western Europe*, pp. 17-20; Sachße and Tennstedt, *Geschichte der Armenfürsorge*; Schubert, *Arme Leute*; Jütte, *Obrigkeitliche Armenfürsorge*; Lis, Soly and Van Damme, *Op vrije voeten?*, pp. 53-55; Jütte, *Poverty and Deviance*, pp. 100-102.

citizens tolerated them and thus frustrated the official policy.[26] Furthermore, Woolf shows that the transition was very gradual:

> "The wanderer or errant remained welcome; nor indeed in societies in which migration performed so central a function would anything else have been conceivable."[27]

Nevertheless, the progressive attempts by the cities (and later by the villages as well) to restrict poor relief to their own residents made life more difficult for those unable to prove that they belonged in a certain place and stimulated a kind of local aliens policy *avant la lettre*. One of the aims of the reorganization of the poor relief was to improve regulation and control over the labour reserves. As the demand for labour fluctuated strongly, relief offered by employers during bad times was very important.[28] In Germany, the main pillar of the policy for excluding allegedly poor aliens was the *Heimat* principle. Every city or village was given the right to send aliens back to the place where they were supposed to have some sort of citizenship,[29] mostly the place of their birth. The frequent inability of travelling individuals to assert their rights thus gave rise to a class of wandering and illegal (to use the modern term) people.[30]

Few readers will be surprised that the reorganization of poor relief was soon followed by acts and regulations aimed at repressing these vagrants. The definition of the vagrant category was expanded and equated with criminals.[31] The intention, however, of banning poor aliens from the cities was not put into practice in general. Widespread beggary persisted, and the centralization of poor relief remained a utopia.[32] The implementation of this legislation, enacted at the state rather than at the Reich level in Germany from the seventeenth century onwards, therefore proved to be quite difficult. Not only did these weak states have to rely on local authorities and cooperation from their citizens, but the distinction between the good and the bad was more complex than assumed by the acts. The group of itinerant people was very heterogeneous. To start with, a number of migrants had an alibi (in the sense of Geremek's work) against stigmatization, such as seasonal labourers, comfortable peddlers, and showmen and apprentices who served as a flexible working force.[33] Their mobility was

26. Clasen, "Armenfürsorge in Augsburg", pp. 109-114.
27. Woolf, *Poor in Western Europe*, p. 19.
28. Lis and Soly, *Poverty and Capitalism*; for a good overview of this and other motives, see van Leeuwen, "Logic of charity".
29. In Germany, three different types of status prevailed: *Bürger* (full citizens), *Hintersasse* (denizens with limited rights) and *Aufenthalt* (legal sojourners) (Fertig, "Transatlantic migration", p. 204).
30. Sachße and Tennstedt, *Geschichte der Armenfürsorge*, p. 31.
31. Lis, Soly, and Van Damme, *Op vrije voeten?*, p. 57.
32. Schubert, *Arme Leute*. See also Lindemann, *Patriots and Paupers*, p. 84 on Hamburg.
33. Reith, "Arbeitsmigration und Gruppenkultur", p. 2.

fairly controlled and condoned. The level of acceptance was considerably lower among all kinds of itinerants performing a variety of services, such as catching mice and rats, mending kettles, playing music, and peddling. In general, their socio-economic functions were also indispensable to pre-modern society and therefore cannot be regarded as a symptom of crisis, as Fertig and others rightly argue.[34] Many authorities nevertheless regarded their mobility as a problem because they tended to be poorer and were therefore suspected of begging and stealing. The third category consisted of people denounced – rightfully or otherwise – as beggars and vagrants, who were often equated with the "Egyptians". This group was considered the most dangerous, and the legislation in Western Europe was mainly aimed at repressing their mobility. In their capacity as the unwanted itinerants, gypsies symbolized *ultimate aliens*. Their way of living and of travelling with their families seemed to indicate a permanent state of wandering. Their status as aliens complicated any efforts to return them to their places of birth. Accordingly, the legislation simply forbade their stay in the country and aimed at expelling them. Although these "Egyptians" were described in ethnic terms (having a dark complexion, wearing a distinctive costume), the edicts clearly attributed the core of the accusation to their way of life. These accusations were, incidentally, very similar to the accusations levelled against vagrants. Soon the category of "Egyptians" therefore came to encompass all kinds of other "travellers", such as vagrants and people with certain itinerant professions, especially entertainers and peddlers. The edicts also warned against counterfeits, who were people disguised as Egyptians. This new label ("counterfayte Egyptians") did not clearly apply to the native-born offspring of the original immigrants. As in England, this extension was probably also aimed at indigenous travellers who joined or imitated the "Egyptians".[35]

What were the consequences of this stigmatization of gypsies and people associated with them? While the poor research in this field does not allow definitive statements, the results indicate that part of this category did indeed become engaged in organized crime in the course of the seventeenth century.[36] This process is discernable both among gypsies and among some of the itinerant Jews (known as *smousen*) who migrated from Poland to Western Europe in the seventeenth and eighteenth centuries. Although the economic transformation in the sixteenth century did produce a growing mass of poor and wandering people (and may have led to a rise in criminality),[37] the stigmatization cannot

---

34. Schubert, "Mobilität ohne Chance", p. 128; Fertig, *Migration from the German-speaking parts*, p. 4. See also L. Lucassen, "Blind Spot", and Riis, "Poverty and Urban Development", pp. 12-14.
35. Mayall, "Making of British Gypsy", pp. 25-26.
36. Egmond, *Underworlds*.
37. See also Clark, "Migrant in Kentish towns", p. 149.

be explained mainly by objective factors. Bandits and professional criminals, so prominent in the negative stereotyping, formed only a small part of the groups designated as the vagrant class. Recent research has disproved the idea – essential to the nineteenth-century rogue literature – that the social problems of the early modern period may be attributed to the vagrants.[38] The emergence of stigmatized categories (vagrants, "Egyptians", etc.) and the discriminatory regulations aimed at them, however, combined with the resulting individual and organized criminality to produce a self-fulfilling prophecy. The increasing coincidence of these labels with criminality seemed to confirm the ideas of people and authorities alike through selective perception and thus reinforced the stigmatization.

While poor relief may be the general propelling force behind the exclusion of the alien poor and most of the travelling groups, this service does not explain the wide discrepancies between the repressive policies pursued in Western Europe. This situation is best demonstrated by taking a closer look at the persecution of gypsies in the seventeenth and eighteenth centuries. In all western European states, the authorities increasingly criminalized their life style in the course of the sixteenth century. The edicts forbade their stay in the country and threatened them with torture and death in the end, from the German Diets in 1497, 1498, and 1500, Charles V and Philip II in the Netherlands in 1524, 1537, and 1560, François I in France in 1539, and Henry VIII and Elizabeth I in England in 1530 and 1562, respectively.[39] In the course of the seventeenth century, and especially during the first decades of the eighteenth century, legislation towards gypsies and other vagrants grew more radical and actually made their mere presence a crime punishable by death. Again, enforcement of these acts – all issued by the central authorities – was quite a different story. Locating these cases on the map of Western Europe reveals that the gypsy hunts (which authorized killing gypsies without any ground or trial) took place in a rather restricted area.

First, *Germany* appears as the centre of these hunts, which extended from the southern area of the Palatine (immediately west of the French Lorraine, where hunts were also organized) through Baden, Württemberg, and Bavaria to Thüringen and Saxony.[40] The traditional explanation for this geographical concentration invokes the political fragmentation into many tiny states and separate legislative entities, as well as the inaccessible terrain full of hills and woods. Both characteristics made this area attractive for bandits, vagrants, and gypsies.

---

38. Beier, *Masterless Men*; Slack, "Vagrants and Vagrancy".
39. Based on Vaux de Foletier, *Tsiganes dans l'ancienne France* and Kappen, *Geschiedenis der zigeuners.*
40. Based on Schubert, "Mobilität ohne Chance", p. 136; Küther, *Räuber und Gauner*, pp. 24–25; Gronemeyer and Rakelmann, *Zigeuner*, p. 56; Vaux de Foletier, *Mille ans d'histoire*, p. 78; and Hohmann, *Geschichte der Zigeunerverfolgung*, p. 35. More general see Danker, *Räuberbanden im Alten Reich*, p. 15.

Although plausible, these arguments are less than convincing. First, vagrancy and banditry were general phenomena in an age when the state was unable to maintain its monopoly on violence. These practices were not restricted to certain areas.[41] More important, however, are the insights that can be derived from the body of literature on recruitment of the poor for the galleys and the army in general. In both cases, the demand for soldiers and rowers in the galleys clearly exceeded the supply, especially in the second half of the seventeenth century. This shortage was attributable not only to the warmongering tendencies of Louis XIV between 1672 and 1714, but also to an absolute and relative increase of the men under arms in Europe in the course of the seventeenth century, particularly during the second half.[42] As the increased demand for soldiers taxed the recruitment network, the responsible agents turned to the poor and vagrant classes. Redlich has shown that after 1675 a number of German states, where the authorities increasingly took the recruitment process into their own hands, forced people whom they considered unwanted to enlist. The rulers of states such as Prussia, Brandenburg, and Saxony ordered their districts to supply them with enough recruits, who were to be gathered by means of hunts on vagrants.[43] As a result of the rapid development of this system:

> "By 1700 it was common practice for state governments to advise local authorities to arrest able-bodied men, who for one reason or another were considered un-desirables, and to deliver them as recruits to the next regiment."[44]

The number of regulations in Germany ordering local authorities to ban and round up vagrants and gypsies understandably reached an all time high in the period after 1675.[45]

A similar situation arose in the South around the same time. Here, the demand for soldiers was less. Instead, rowers were needed at the galleys of Venice, Genoa, and Marseille. The galleys had already become an alternative to the death penalty during the sixteenth century. By the middle of this century, however, these states had difficulty finding enough volunteers and followed the example of the Turkish navy by turning to slave labourers captured during raids in the Balkans.[46] A small part of these rowers was bought from prisons in northern

---

41. See e.g. Danker, *Räuberbanden im Alten Reich*, whose study concentrates on the North of Germany.
42. C. Tilly, *Coercion, Capital*, p. 79: except for Spain, the armies of France, England/Wales, the Netherlands, Sweden, and Russia grew from some 180,000 in 1600 to 1,062,000 in 1700. On the average, the share of the national population increased from 0.8 to 4.2 percent. See also Chandler (*Art of Warfare*, p. 65), who notes the increase in numbers after 1688.
43. Redlich, *German Military Enterpriser*, pp. 173-174.
44. *Ibid.*, p. 173.
45. L. Lucassen, *Zigeuner*, ch. 2.
46. J. Lucassen, *Dutch Long Distance Migration*, pp. 30-31 and J. Lucassen, "No golden age", p. 786.

states, such as the Austro-Hungarian Empire, Bavaria, Württemberg, and Baden.[47] Again, the demand for slaves and the raids on vagrants are remarkably coincidental, both peaking during the second half of the seventeenth century and ending quite abruptly – due to a change in naval technique – around 1730.[48]

Combining the modes of recruitment in the North and the South of Germany leaves an interesting outlaw-corridor in the middle and adds an entirely new angle to the traditional explanation. The hypothesis is basically as follows: the demand for soldiers and rowers met by the increasing rounding up of "unwanted elements" in Germany led to a concentration of vagrants in the Palatine-Saxony corridor, which was too far away from either the Prussia-Brandenburg recruitment area or from the Mediterranean (transport costs to the Mediterranean exceeded the price per slave). The states in the corridor were therefore confronted with a double problem: they could not get rid of vagrants and moreover faced immigration by individuals seeking to evade recruitment from other areas of Germany. In some cases, these hunted groups joined forces as bandits and threatened the physical safety and property of the inhabitants. The authorities reacted by issuing regulations that became more severe every year and culminated in draconian measures outlawing gypsies and other vagrants. As a result, in a number of cases (for the corridor some 100 are documented[49]) people were killed without a trial.

The policy towards vagrants and gypsies in *France* also seems to fit very well in the military-recruitment hypothesis. The repressive policy in France began to increase around the middle of the seventeenth century. The most important act was the royal decree of 1682 against the "Bohemians", which stated that all gypsies and vagrants had to be rounded up and sent to the galleys. For the enactment of this decree the central government in this age of "brokerage", as Tilly called it, had to rely on intermediary groups, such as the nobility. According to Vaux de Foletier, many of these intermediaries, however, were not inclined to help in any way. Some even protected the "Bohemians", as most gypsies were *not* criminals and performed services that were wanted by this group, especially dancing (by the women) and making music and the like.[50] This lack of local cooperation may have motivated the central government five years later to establish the first fully centralized police force in Western Europe (the maréchaussée) whose most important task involved enforcing the policy towards

47. Schubert, *Arme Leute*, p. 292; Bog, "Über Arme und Armenfürsorge", p. 1001.
48. Zysberg, *Galériens. Vies et destins*. See also Frauenstädt, "Bettel- und Vagabundenwesen", p. 534 and p. 538 and Schubert, *Arme Leute*, p. 292.
49. L. Lucassen, *Zigeuner*, ch. 2. This observation implies that the idea that the gypsy hunts led to a massive extermination is therefore untenable. The state was simply too weak.
50. Vaux de Foletier, *Tsiganes dans l'ancienne France*, pp. 152-160. Based on an analysis of the policy in the Languedoc, De Foletier concludes that most gypsies were arrested *not* because of crimes, but because of their wandering way of life (p. 160).

vagrants and gypsies. In the last years of the seventeenth century, the *maréchaussée* mainly arrested people considered to be vagrants and gypsies. Unlike in Germany and the eastern provinces of the Dutch Republic this campaign did not lead to gypsy hunts (except in Lorraine in 1723).[51] Also in contrast to Germany with its hundreds of autonomous areas, France as a whole was much more centralized, notwithstanding local and regional autonomy. This situation enabled the state, represented by the *maréchaussée*, to round up vagrants throughout the country. With the possible exception of the newly formed region of Alsace Lorraine on the periphery – which was integrated into the French state only from about 1780 onwards – outlawing and killing did not take place. The course of events after capture is not entirely clear. Although France also sent more than one thousand persons to the galleys in the period 1680-1715, few of these individuals were categorized as "bohesme" (gypsy). Rapidly increasing numbers of gypsies and other vagrants were, however, rounded up between 1716 and 1748.[52]

The *Dutch Republic* resembled Germany in some respects. In the eastern provinces of Gelderland and Overijssel, the outlawing of vagrants and gypsies coincided with gypsy hunts during the first decades of the eighteenth century. According to Egmond, this process reflects the reaction of local – and later also of regional – authorities to rising criminality among certain organized groups of gypsies and people who had joined them, including former mercenaries. Furthermore, Egmond argues that strong indications reveal that many were recent arrivals from France and from German states.[53]

The map on the following page offers a graphic explanation for the process and scale of rounding up vagrants and gypsies. The persecution may have been far less severe and ubiquitous than some authors assert (not in the least because of the limited coercive means).[54] Nevertheless, it marks an important break with the former period in the sense that the power of authorities in different states, such as France, the German principalities, and the eastern provinces of the Dutch Republic, proved capable of organizing such general repression.[55] Moreover,

---

51. Liégeois, *Gypsies. An Illustrated History*, pp. 95-97.
52. Zysberg, *Galériens. Vies et destins*, pp. 65-67. In the period 1680-1715 only about 50 "gypsies" were sent to Marseilles, compared to 137 in the subsequent period 1716-1748. Including vagrants and beggars, the numbers for the respective periods were 698 (5.9%) and 1,323 (13%).
53. Egmond, *Underworlds*.
54. Kenrick and Puxon even characterize this policy as "slow genocide" (*Destiny of Europe's gypsies*, p. 46). This idea, which I have also endorsed (L. Lucassen, *"En men noemde hen zigeuners"*, ch. 2) is debunked in L. Lucassen, *Zigeuner: Die Entstehung*, ch. 2.
55. For Germany, see especially Danker, *Räuberbanden im Alten Reich* (p. 86), who criticized Küther's (*Räuber und Gauner*) idea that German authorities in the eighteenth century were virtually powerless against organized crime. A similar argument is made for the Netherlands by Egmond, *Underworlds*.

Regions in Germany where vagrants and gypsies were outlawed and killed without a trial, combined with the regions with the greatest demand for soldiers and rowers (1675-1730)

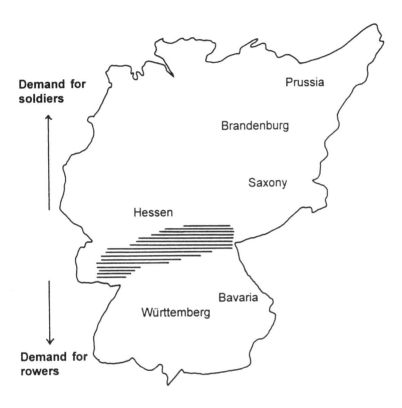

Source: Lucassen, *Zigeuner*, ch. 2.

this repression reinforced the existing stigma by connecting gypsies with criminality more firmly than ever. The shift in policy ties in well with the change in state formation in Western Europe from brokerage to centralization. A decisive switch took place from the traditional private to the public domain. The growing power of the state was embodied in the emergence of a police apparatus and effective criminal justice procedures. State institutions gradually took over the prosecution of crime and curtailed the rights of privileged groups (guilds, nobility, etc.).[56] This process marked the beginning of the transition from indirect to direct rule and from a reactive to a proactive policy, which was firmly established in the nineteenth century.

How did the gradual change to direct rule together with growing coercive power on the part of the state influence the general attitude towards vagrants and people regarded as poor migrants in general during the long eighteenth century we are dealing with here? To start with, Great Britain differed remarkably from the other states. On the British Isles, the policy can be circumscribed as a system of control. While the *central* government may not have been as strong as in France or in absolutist principalities in Germany, Great Britain was the only state capable of implementing acts and regulations locally. The settlement act (1662) and the old poor law (1601-1834) are of particular interest. According to Snell, the poor law created miniature welfare states and thus helped reduce vagrancy and slowed migration by providing relatively generous relief and by mobilizing the local poor for temporary labour.[57]

Both France and the German principalities lacked any such facilities. There, the state resorted to *repression* instead of *control*, notwithstanding efforts to create a system of work houses (which could not hold a candle to the systematic English approach), prisons, and *dépôts*.[58] As we already saw, the best example of the repression model was the *maréchaussée* in France. In the eighteenth century, this force was expanded and became the foremost state instrument in the offensive against the mobile poor.[59] Schwartz has argued that, due to their specialization with respect to vagrants and their success in repressing banditry, people living in the countryside began to trust the maréchaussée during the last decades of the eighteenth century and gradually changed their conception of the state. The purely parasitical image, manifested especially in the French state, gave way to a certain extent to the idea of the state as a protector of property

---

56. Lenman and Parker, *Crime and the Law*, p. 42; Gatrell, "Crime, Authority", pp. 243-244.
57. Snell, *Annals of the Labouring Poor*, p. 107. See also Beier, *Masterless Men*, pp. 171-175.
58. As Petit and others (*Histoire des galères*, pp. 75-76) make clear, the great "renfermement" à la Foucault did not actually take place in the eighteenth century. Only a fraction of the criminals and vagrants could be put away. See in this respect also Perrot, *Impossible prison*, pp. 9-56.
59. Gutton, *Société et les pauvres*, p. 13. See also Schwartz, *Policing the Poor* and Norberg, *Rich and Poor in Grenoble*, ch. 9.

and a guard of the peace.[60] The *maréchaussée* was concerned not only with crime, but with all kinds of disorderly behaviour and allegedly suspect forms of migration as well. Although many officials recognized the functionality of migrant labour, this perspective did not alter the image of the *maréchaussée*:

> "[...] from the standpoint of law and order, migration and the mobile poor were readily identified with acts of begging, vagrancy, and crime – with disruptive and dangerous acts that needed to be controlled."[61]

During the most severe repression in France, the maréchaussée therefore focused its efforts on vagrants and gypsies. The occasional arrests of peddlers and seasonal labourers are not entirely unexpected.[62] Like in England and Germany, the interpretation of the term vagrant was very broad and encompassed all suspected perpetrators of crimes and misdemeanours when the evidence was insufficient to secure conviction by trial.[63] Although this policing seems to have been quite effective (at least in France) and made the countryside a safer place by indiscriminately lumping together bandits with all kinds of migrant people, the stigmatization of the mobile poor in general and travelling groups in particular deepened.[64] In addition to the association with organized crime, the growing gulf between the sedentary population and the vagrants exacerbated this effect.

In the other continental states, local and regional authorities with very limited means shouldered the main responsibility for enforcing the policy of repression. The state intervened and assumed control very gradually. Notwithstanding the general absolutist rhetoric,[65] the attempts by Western European states to monopolize the use of violence and to establish a state police force were embryonic and did not truly get under way until the end of the eighteenth

---

60. Schwartz, *Policing the Poor*, pp. 250-251. His conclusions at this point are somewhat weakened by Adams, *Bureaucrats and Beggars*, p. 119.
61. Schwartz, *Policing the Poor*, p. 153.
62. Gutton, *État et la mendicité*, pp. 180-181; Norberg, *Rich and Poor in Grenoble*, pp. 223-224. This observation also refutes to a certain extent the conclusions of Hufton (*Poor of Eighteenth-Century France*), who treats all migrants as poor and vagrants. For a more elaborate criticism, see L. Lucassen, "Blind Spot", pp. 218-220.
63. Schwartz, *Policing the Poor*, p. 169; Finzsch, *Obrigkeit und Unterschichten*, pp. 2 and 23; Depauw, "Pauvres, pauvres mendiants", p. 408 and 416. See also Woolf, *Poor in Western Europe*, p. 28; Donovan, "Changing Perceptions of Social Deviance", p. 37; and Egmond, *Underworlds*.
64. The English Vagrancy Act of 1744 grouped all the categories that had been condemned in the seventeenth century: "Beggars, strolling actors or gamblers, gypsies, peddlers, and all those who refused to work for the usual and common wages." (Ignatieff, *Just Measure of Pain*, p. 25.)
65. For a critique of the idea of the absolutist state as a police state, see Nitschke, *Verbrechensbekämpfung und Verwaltung*, pp. 190-194. See also Wettmann-Jungblut on the weakness of state control over the police in the eighteenth century and on the emergence of the gendarmerie in nineteenth-century Baden ("'Stelen inn rechter Hungersnodtt'", pp. 169-171).

century. The German states (and the Netherlands) took over the French gendarmerie system only after the Napoleonic wars.[66]

Modern state formation in an age of industrialism and urbanization, 1815-1914

From the end of the eighteenth century onwards internal migration in Western Europe increased. Proletarianization continued, and the combination of progressive commercialization within the agricultural sector and the unstable course of industrialization made jobs less secure. These trends led to rising mobility. In agriculture, contracts spanning a year were replaced by irregular demand,[67] and in industry much work was still seasonal (construction), while factory work was often temporary as well. The lack of stability that characterized the labour market kept many workers perpetually on the move.[68]

Given the traditional ideas on migration and mobility, the growing concern on the part of the authorities with respect to this situation is understandable. While migration may have been the rule (as it had been in pre-industrial Europe), a sedentary state remained the norm. The fear of a great mass of rootless and wandering paupers was widespread. At the same time, the rapid urbanization that attracted many people from the countryside gave rise to similar ideas. This sentiment is well illustrated in the work of Chevalier on Paris and of Stedman Jones on London.[69] In both cities, the ruling classes saw the poor immigrants as "pathological nomads" who eschewed work and who lived from theft and begging alone. The image of these "new barbarians"[70] differed little from the perceptions of vagrants. Often, the central authorities did not differentiate poor immigrants from vagrants.

Apart from political disturbances, the fear of the mobile poor, especially those labelled as vagrants, seems to have been one of the major reasons for professionalizing the police in Western Europe. This situation was especially true in Great Britain:

---

66. Most German states, including Prussia and Bavaria, established their gendarmerie between 1809 and 1812 (Nitschke, *Verbrechensbekämpfung und Verwaltung*, p. 183). See also Emsley, "Peasants, Gendarmes and State Formation", p. 70. Some states, such as Nassau, already had precursors as early as 1767, like the Husars (Plaum, *Strafrecht, Kriminalpolitik und Kriminalität*, p. 137).

67. In England this process started already around 1770 and accelerated after 1810 (Snell, *Annals of the Labouring Poor*, pp. 73-80).

68. Moch, *Moving Europeans*, ch. 4.

69. Chevalier, *Classes laborieuses et classes dangereuses*, and Stedman Jones, *Outcast London*.

70. Chevalier, *Classes laborieuses et classes dangereuses*, p. 596. For Germany see Lüdtke, *Police and State in Prussia*, p. 79.

"So central was the question of vagrancy in discussions surrounding the emergence and development of the Scottish rural police, that it would have been no exaggeration to conclude that these early police forces were in most instances an extension to the highly defective local machinery for handling Scotland's poor."[71]

In other parts of the realm the motives were similar.[72] From 1840 to 1850, the discussion on the professionalization of the police stressed the repression of vagrancy and associated crime mainly with migrants.[73] According to Steedman, the *County and Borrow Police Act* (1856) resulted directly from the wish to repress vagrancy.[74] The most important means for the police was the *Vagrancy Act* of 1824, characterized as "the most pernicious piece of legislation against gypsies and travellers in the nineteenth century".[75] The definition of the term vagrant had become so wide and the discretionary power of the police so extensive that all obnoxious behaviour could be labelled as vagrancy.[76] In practice, however, the designation primarily applied to migrants. Although this policy was in some cases neutralized by the protective effects of other acts,[77] it complicated life for migrant labourers and travelling groups considerably and frustrated their economic functioning. Nevertheless, no evidence attributes a disproportionate share of the responsibility for theft in the countryside to these groups. Vagrants did not constitute the core of the property criminals, and:

"His appearances in court [...] were in part a tribute to the deliberate economic and social policies of authorities."[78]

In France, the professionalization of the police was not linked to vagrancy alone, but served first of all to stabilize the insecure political situation and to alleviate the fear of revolutions and disturbances of the public order.[79] After 1850, however, criminality also emerged as a dominant theme. Like in Great Britain, the

---

71. Carson and Idzikowska, "Social Production of Scottish Policing", p. 273.
72. Davis, "Urban Policing", p. 4; Jones, *Crime, Protest, Community*, pp. 178-209; Jones, "Welsh and Crime", pp. 83-84; Leigh, "Vagrancy and the Criminal Law"; Roberts, "Public and Private", p. 282; Storch, "Policing Rural Southern England", pp. 218-219.
73. Emsley, *English Police*, p. 49.
74. Steedman, *Policing the Victorian Community*, p. 57.
75. Mayall, *Gypsy-Travellers in Nineteenth-Century*, p. 147. Jones issues a similar judgement: "One of the most flexible, useful and criminal-making statutes of the century." (*Crime, Protest, Community*, p. 207).
76. Roberts, "Public and Private"; Leigh, "Vagrancy and the Criminal Law", p. 108.
77. Cottaar, Lucassen and Willems, "Justice or Injustice?" p. 57.
78. Jones, *Crime, Protest, Community*, pp. 206-207. For Germany see Wettmann-Jungblut, "'Stelen inn rechter Hungersnodtt'", p. 165: "Vieles deutet darauf hin, dass trotz der weitverbreiteten Furcht vor Vaganten und "Jaunern" die meisten Diebstähle von Ortsansässigen ausgeführt wurden." [Much indicates that despite the widespread fear of goliards and "Jaunern", most thefts were committed by locals.]
79. Roach, "French Police"; Forstenzer, *French Provincial Police*, p. 109.

causes were primarily sought among the poor (i.e. the unskilled, unemployed paupers and vagabonds), whose personal defects were thought to be underlie their criminal behaviour. The vagabond was depicted as the prototype of the criminal because of his alleged refusal to work and to accumulate possessions.[80] According to Wright, the vagabond question engendered an atmosphere of paranoia on criminality in general. In 1885, a law was passed enabling the transportation of backsliders (who included many vagrants) to the colonies.[81] In this respect, England had also pursued this policy a century earlier by sending criminals (who were regarded as cancerous tumours in the national body) first to the Americas and – after the war of independence – to Australia. The practice supported the argument advanced in previous paragraphs that the English state formation was way ahead of the developments on the continent. In Germany, at least before the unification, the situation was more complicated and differed from state to state. In general, however, Tilly's characterization of nineteenth-century police policy as proactive seems to be confirmed by our knowledge of the professionalization of the police. This preventive activity is especially well illustrated by the emergence of police journals containing all kind of descriptions of people wanted, missing, or expelled.[82] These journals were preceded by the so-called *Steckbriefe* or *Gaunerliste* (warrants), which were already issued in the eighteenth century by certain police functionaries with the aim of tracking down vagrants and criminals (the criminals were mostly accused of banditry). Comprehensive individual information was given and sometimes included the labels assigned to them (Jew, gypsy, vagrant). The proactive element involved establishing the status of people to enable other authorities to take appropriate action in the future. The persons concerned had greater difficulty getting rid of the label they had been assigned. After the Napoleonic wars, these incidental warrants were slowly replaced by police journals that appeared regularly.

These journals devoted considerable attention to the *gemeinschädliche Umhertreiber*.[83] Although such individuals rarely committed crimes (and hardly ever serious offences), the police tried to establish constant supervision and control by spreading detailed information about the *Umhertreiber* throughout the local police forces.[84] As Lüdtke observed, the tenor of executive police conduct was directly influenced by the increase in population and migratory movements:[85]

---

80. Davis, "Urban Policing", pp. 5-6; Perrot, "Delinquency and the Penitentiary System", p. 220.
81. New Caledonia, Guiana, Indochina and the Marquesas Islands (Wright, *Between the Guillotine and Liberty*, pp. 144-145).
82. For the Dutch research this type of source proved to be very rich and useful. Regarding the results of the analysis of the *Algemeen politieblad* ("General Police Journal") in the period 1852-1921, see L. Lucassen, *"En men noemde hen zigeuners"*, pp. 323 ff.
83. "harmful vagrants" (L. Lucassen, *Zigeuner*, ch. 4).
84. See for this general process also Lüdtke, *Police and State in Prussia*, p. 70.
85. *Ibid.*, p. 82.

"The main victims of administrative hostility towards 'itinerants' [...] house searches and the observation of taverns, the introduction of travel and employment registration books and work tickets for railway navvies, were not 'criminals' or foreign, or revolutionary, 'emissaries', but those considered 'fully able to work, but lacking the willingness to do so'."[86]

The dissolution of the guilds and the breaking up of the patriarchal relations in agriculture forced the state to assume its responsability.[87] At the same time, the national state began to define its citizens, and the attention of the emerging gendarmerie forces on the continent was foremost aimed at preventing alien vagrants from entering the country and monitoring the indigenous migrant population.[88] This was not a straightforward process. For a long time the state tried to delegate the control to the estates.[89] The erosion of the old order proved to be final, however, and once the state took responsibility the process was irreversible.

The process of state formation and economic change alone does not fully explain the ongoing stigmatization in the nineteenth century. Again, poor relief merits consideration as well. From the end of the eighteenth century, the state became more involved in the locally organized system. One of the consequences of the centralization that took place in all countries of Western Europe,[90] but especially in the Netherlands and Germany, was that the state clearly became responsible for all its citizens and therefore also for its poor. In Prussia – and in other states as well – a similar development took the form of the *Allgemeines Landrecht* (1794),[91] which laid down the principle that the state would take care of the poor who lacked a *Heimat* or who required special treatment.[92] This safety net was intended especially for people without a fixed place to stay, a category that increased steadily after 1820 because of the successful restrictive policy of municipalities with regard to granting citizenship to newcomers.

---

86. *Ibid.*, p. 87. See also Funk, *Polizei und Rechtsstaat*, p. 250.
87. On the replacement of private and informal modes of control with public and legal methods, see also Wiener, *Reconstructing the Criminal*, p. 260.
88. Jessen, *Polizei im Industrierevier*, pp. 35-36; Haupt, "Staatliche Bürokratie", pp. 228-230; Becker, "Vom 'Haltlosen' zur 'Bestie'", p. 119; Wirsing, "'Gleichsam mit Soldatenstrenge'", p. 67.
89. This was the case with the "Handarbeiterverordnung" (regulation concerning manual labour) of 1846, which left supervision and punishment to private building companies Jessen, Polizei im Industrierevier, p. 36. This situation is in line with the Funk's conclusion that the professionalization of the police took place in the period after 1848.
90. See in this respect; Noiriel, *Tyrannie du national*; Hobsbawm, *Nations and Nationalism*; Brubaker, *Citizenship and Nationhood*; and Moch, *Moving Europeans* (ch. 5).
91. Nassau (Blum, *Staatliche Armenfürsorge*, p. 69) and Hannover (Henning, *Deutsche Wirtschafts- und Sozialgeschichte*, p. 933).
92. Hattenhauer, *Allgemeines Landrecht*, p. 663-664 (§ 1 and 16). See also Dorn, *Öffentliche Armenpflege*, p. 133.

This increasing state involvement in the distribution of poor relief necessitated a definition of who was and who was not a Prussian citizen. As Brubaker argues, the codification of citizenship in 1842 and the economic liberalization ("Freizügigkeit") suddenly made the importance of nationality acute:

> "The connecting link was migration, more precisely the migration of the poor. Prussian state-membership was codified as a means of shielding the state against foreign poor, while preserving freedom of movement within the state."[93]

The conflicts about the responsibility for the poor shifted from municipalities to states. As Germany was divided into some 39 states before 1870, this change easily led to a rise in the consciousness of "foreigners".

In other countries, the concern for the poor wandering foreigners (or the people regarded as such, as in the case of the gypsies) also played a pivotal role in the enactment of aliens legislation. Dutch representatives, for example, devoted the lion's share of their debate on the very liberal Aliens Act of 1849 to the category of the destitute aliens, personified among others by the gypsies. Together with the politically dangerous aliens, they were the only people to be denied entry into the Kingdom. The circulars against foreign showmen, musicians,[94] and peddlers reveal the following profile of the unwanted alien:

> "[...] self-employed itinerant people, who depend for their earnings on the population. Their activities [...] were mistrusted by the authorities and in many cases considered as a cloak for begging."[95]

In the period until 1914, when a coherent aliens policy was lacking, the destitute aliens and, from 1868 onward, the gypsies were the official targets. In France, travelling groups also served as a test case for general legislation towards aliens. With the act on nomads of 1912 the French government initiated an obligatory identity card for people (indigenous as well as aliens) who travelled with their families and had no fixed abode. In addition to listing the holder's marital status and profession, this *carnet anthropométrique* contained details about physical appearance, fingerprints, and two photographs. Although the act was not

---

93. Brubaker, *Citizenship and Nationhood*, p. 63.
94. Instructions against foreign musicians and showmen were also issued in other countries, although not only motivated by concern about vagrancy. Especially in France, these prohibitions also had political overtones in that the authorities were afraid of inflammatory songs. Most instructions therefore date from revolutionary periods (1830, 1848, etc.) (Zucchi, *Little Slaves of the Harp*, pp. 47-51; and Bernard, "Surveillance des itinérants", p. 245). For Belgium see Tiggelen, *Musiciens ambulants*, pp. 9, 32-35.
95. L. Lucassen, *"En men noemde hen zigeuners"*, p. 33. A more detailed analysis of Dutch aliens policy can be found in Leenders, *Ongenode gasten*.

specifically aimed at aliens, the promoters had this category in mind.[96] Within five years, this card became obligatory for all aliens.[97]

The consequences of the growing state interference for the stigmatization of itinerants and travelling groups were far-reaching. The growing concern about criminality in Western Europe illustrates their scope. In the nineteenth century, the first crime statistics showed an alarming increase in crime rates. Contemporaries attributed this rise to the socio-economic changes mentioned above. In fact, the increase lay not so much in the number of crimes committed as in the improved registration of crimes *and* in the extension of criminal law to previously untrodden areas (prostitution, drunkenness, poaching, etc.), as we saw with the Vagrancy Act of 1824. According to Gatrell, the process of problematizing of crime from 1780 onwards illustrates mainly the public fear about the changes and disorder caused by urbanization, democratization, and the industrial revolution.[98] As traditional limitations disappeared, the menace of an anarchistic individual freedom became acute:

> "Crime was a central metaphor of disorder and loss of control in all spheres of life. [...] As the brutality of the law was lessened, its reach was extended to cover more persons and more forms of behavior. Vagrants, drunkards, and other 'immoral' and 'disorderly' persons [...]"[99]

The changing ideas about foreigners and criminality hardened the stigmas about migrants and travelling groups, as illustrated both by the emergence of a specialized policy towards gypsies and by the more general attitude towards alien immigrants and migrants, such as the Irish navvies in England[100] and foreign peddlers in Belgium and France.[101]

This tendency was reinforced by the specialization within police forces that took place in the last decades of the nineteenth century. In the wake of the general bureaucratization that accompanied state formation in Western Europe, special branches were established for the surveillance of social problems, such as prostitutes, aliens, vagrants, and, in some countries, gypsies.[102] Strongly

---

96. Bernard, "Surveillance des itinérants", p. 247.
97. Noiriel, *Creuset français*, p. 89.
98. Gatrell, "Crime, Authority", pp. 245-252.
99. Wiener, *Reconstructing the Criminal*, p. 11.
100. Jones, "Welsh and Crime", p. 83. See also Dennis, *English Industrial Cities*, p. 35.
101. Jaumain, "Métier oublié", pp. 314-318; Chatelain, "Lutte entre colporteurs", p. 375. In Paris foreign peddlers were unable to obtain licences after 1851 (Baruch-Gourden, "Police et le commerce ambulant", p. 254).
102. This process was linked to the emergence of a criminological school that, stimulated by the ideas of Lombroso among others, defined the "nomadic tendency" as an atavistic and pathological and therefore incorrigible nucleus (Wiener, *Reconstructing the Criminal*, pp. 12

influenced by prevailing negative ideas on travelling groups, the sections that dealt with these categories could acquire some measure of autonomy and the power to define the problems according to their own perception and interest, if only to justify their existence. In the late nineteenth and early twentieth centuries, the achievement of a sedentary state and regular work were two main thriving policy objectives with respect to travelling groups (as well as expulsion in the case of foreigners).[103] As a result, the dividing line between nationals and foreigners on the one hand and normal and anti-social citizens at the other was increasingly stressed. Such a process acquired its own momentum following activation[104] and could be described as a form of infrastructural power (closely connected to the emergence of the modern nation state[105]) according to Michael Mann's definition:

> "Any state that acquires or exploits social utility will be provided with infrastructural supports. Those enable it to regulate, normatively and by force, a given set of social and territorial relations, and to erect boundaries against the outside. [...] In this sense the state gives territorial bounds to social relations whose dynamics lies outside of itself."[106]

Germany provides a good example of this specialization.[107] Already from the beginning of the nineteenth century onwards, police authorities in the various states regarded wandering people (especially the ones whose identity was unclear) as one of the greatest threats to an orderly and safe society. The problems with identification, however, were to a great extent the result of the system of poor relief. The *Heimat* principle led municipalities to avoid settlement by people whom they suspected of being or of becoming poor. One method involved restricting marriages, since the place of the marriage was also responsible for any poor relief needed by the new couple.[108] This practice resulted in growing numbers of people without a *Heimat* and in illegitimate children. Especially travelling groups had major difficulties obtaining valid passes and thereby an official identity as a result of these restrictions. Many did not know the exact date and place of their birth. Police officials, who from 1820 onwards started to issue police journals full of information on the "dangerous vagrant

---

and 90; Nye, *Crime, Madness, and Politics*, p. 175; Stedman Jones, *Outcast London*; and Becker, "Vom 'Haltlosen' zur 'Bestie'", p. 106).

103. Haupt, "Staatliche Bürokratie", p. 230, "Durchsetzung der Arbeit als Normalität und der bürgerlichen Ordnung als Norm war Inhalt der polizeilichen Tätigkeit."

104. With respect to the first discriminatory acts in the 1880s, Noiriel incisively comments: "[...] c'est la solution qui créait le problème. La question de l''identité des étrangers' ne faisait que commencer." Noiriel, *Creuset français*, p. 87.

105. See also Giddens, *Nation-State and Violence*, ch. 7.

106. Mann, *States, War and Capitalism*, p. 26.

107. This paragraph is based on the conclusions of L. Lucassen, *Zigeuner*.

108. Kraus, "'Antizipierter Ehesegen'".

people"[109] (including travelling journeymen and servants) in several German states,[110] interpreted the homelessness and unclear identity as deliberate attempts by these people to hide their real identity for less than honourable reasons. Although an analysis of these journals shows that only a minor part of the "vagrants" was involved in crime, the innocence of the majority did not prevent criminalization of the whole category. The suspicion invariably aroused by the lack of a clear identity led the police to search for the real identity of these groups. From about 1840 onwards, these journals began to label some of the individuals grouped under the vagrants category (especially people travelling with their families and lacking a clear identity) as gypsies. Their intricate family relations – the result of the specific system of poor relief – puzzled many police authorities, and some of them started to devise genealogical tables and registrations to tackle this "problem".

After the unification of Germany in 1870, the need for identification became even more urgent because all states tried to restrict people from wandering about in family groups by denying them permits for itinerant trades (*Wandergewerbeschein*). Notwithstanding numerous acts and regulations, many "gypsies" managed to obtain such permits anyway. The police also faced the problem of distinguishing between foreign and indigenous "gypsies", as the "homelessness" of the "gypsies" often prevented them from getting official papers. In many cases, they had to resort to forged papers. Their custom of obtaining false papers aroused even greater suspicion in the eyes of the German police, who understandably designed a special category for registering "gypsies" during the phase of specialization (from about 1885).

Studies by Strauss and others show that most states soon developed their own specialized anti-gypsy policy extending this label beyond foreigners (except for the Netherlands) after 1870 (the German unification).[111] In 1899 in Bavaria, a specialized police service was even established (a gypsy station) for the purpose of registering *all* persons (both with and without a criminal record) considered gypsies. In 1905, this effort led to a "gypsy directory" containing 3,350 entries, with extensive information on some 613 persons.[112] In the course of the twentieth century, this database was expanded and transformed into a federal centre (*Reichszentrale*) in 1938. The number of people labelled as gypsies increased accordingly: from 3,350 in 1905 to about 33,524 in 1938. Their nomadic lifestyle, rather than any violations of the law, motivated the practice of registering these people. The German example, which to some extent resembles other

109. "Gemeinschädliche Umhertreiber".
110. First in Prussia, followed by Saxony, Baden, Hannover, and Bavaria.
111. Strauss, "Zigeunerverfolgung in Bayern". For a review of the German historiography, see L. Lucassen, "'Zigeuner' in Deutschland".
112. Dillmann, *Zigeunerbuch*.

Western European countries, further illustrates the discretionary power of semi-autonomous police forces. In addition to deciding who was to be labelled as a gypsy, the police also pioneered the criminalization of this category by deliberately interpreting existing general acts and regulations in a negative way. They also promoted new legislation to curtail the travelling lifestyle. One of the best examples is the interdiction on travel in "hordes", which defined a "horde" as a group of more than two persons without family ties.[113]

Conclusion

This paper deals with the paradox surrounding the effort to explain the repressive policy toward travelling groups from the fourteenth century onwards in spite of their clearly useful and necessary function. How could states and their officials have remained blind in this respect for such a long time? As a matter of fact, they were not entirely ignorant. This historical overview began by noting that authorities have constantly upheld distinctions within the migrant population between the good and the bad, the honest and the dishonest, or – in Geremek's words – between migrants with and without an alibi. This information shifts the question, but does not explain why travelling groups have usually been depicted as bad. The traditional answer is that these groups, especially the "gypsies" among them, *were* parasites. Therefore, we cannot speak of stigmatization or prejudices. Although much research lies ahead, recent studies indicate that the parasite image is generally false. As a rule, many gypsy or travelling groups had genuine professions and earned their own living, apart from periods of general crisis. Many people labelled as vagrants had not retreated from society, but were temporarily without a job or – in the case of circular migrants – on their way to work. The opposite explanation, à la Lis and Soly, which is not convincing either, interprets the repressive policy as a way of disciplining and controlling people who did not fit the ideal of the dominant classes and views the social problems (poverty, banditry, etc.) as social constructions serving as an excuse. Although this approach has valuable elements and is not to be rejected in its entirety, it does not help us much further, unless we settle for conspiracy theories. Moreover, the debate on social control ("the most overworked piece of jargon in the critical historian's vocabulary"),[114] has, especially in Great Britain, made clear that this way of thinking does not account for the autonomous position of the so-called lower classes and the strength of their own culture.[115] Finally, maintaining that control agents

---

113. Cottaar, Lucassen and Willems, "Justice or Injustice?", p. 52.
114. Gatrell, "Decline of Theft and Violence", p. 256.
115. A thorough criticism was offered by Thompson, "Social Control in Victorian Britain". A recent useful overview appears in Wiener, *Reconstructing the Criminal*, pp. 4–10.

served exclusively repressive functions would be naive and overlooks the valued protection that police forces offered.[116]

So far, the matter has only become more complicated. If neither the actual groups, nor the dominant society are to blame, are we then stuck with an unsatisfactory middle of the road explanation? Not necessarily. This paper has made clear that the key to our problem lies in the development of *poor relief* in Western Europe.[117] The practice of restricting poor relief from the fifteenth century onwards to the local poor and of simultaneously refusing citizenship rights to poor immigrants created a category of "vagrants" and "gypsies". Although much research remains necessary (especially local studies revealing the enforcement of this policy), the poor relief system based on the restriction of the relief to local inhabitants and the exclusion of aliens (known as the *Heimat* principle in Germany) clearly had far-reaching effects for the stigmatization of travelling groups who (rightfully or otherwise) were suspected of being reduced to beggary. By the nineteenth century, the final transition, which linked poor relief to people's domicile, changed little for travelling groups.[118] On the contrary, now every municipality risked incurring liability for their support and thus had an added incentive to prevent them from staying, let alone from settling. The history of poor relief is of special relevance and interest in a broader context as well because the same mechanisms can be detected that characterize nineteenth and twentieth-century aliens policy. In the sixteenth century, the restriction of the poor relief by the cities formed a prelude to the national aliens policy of later days.[119]

Explaining the ongoing stigmatization of travelling groups in the nineteenth and twentieth centuries, especially in Germany and France, requires linking the poor relief with the process of *state formation*. Both states became increasingly dependent on migrant labour (this statement applies to a lesser extent to Great Britain as well), but nevertheless pursued the most repressive policy towards vagrants and gypsies. Although their policy may still be influenced by their anti-migration tradition in the ancien régime, this argument alone is not convincing. I hope this paper has demonstrated the incipient role of the process of modern state formation. The modern state, which is characterized by direct rule, has an interest in controlling migration and needs to know the locations of its citizens for general purposes (conscription, taxes etc.). Moreover, the growing fear for

---

116. Gatrell, "Decline of Theft and Violence", p. 245; Schwartz, *Policing the Poor*, pp. 239-245.
117. As the Dutch historian Van Leeuwen wrote recently: "To suggest that the social history of Europe is unintelligible without an understanding of poor relief is only a slight exaggeration." Van Leeuwen, "The logic of charity", p. 589.
118. In Germany the "Unterstützungswohnsitz".
119. This comparison was made by Catherine Lynch during the round-table discussion on Moch, *Moving Europeans*, at the Social Science History Association conference in Atlanta in October 1994.

the criminality of the underclasses (especially with respect to people on the move) increased the desire to establish a permanent system of supervision. The primary control mechanism for performing this task was the police.

This trend reflects the general development in Western Europe. Understanding the differences in repression requires a new typology linked with the *type* of state formation. States with a strong central government, such as Germany and France, were much quicker to form a centralized and specialized police force than more decentralized states, such as the Netherlands and Great Britain. The early professionalization and specialization of the police within the centralized states reinforced the existing stigmatization of travelling groups. This process was manifested not only in a quantitative sense (by the increase in the number of policemen), but also in the *specialization* of the police with respect to types of crime or allegedly dangerous groups (anarchists, anti-socials, aliens, gypsies, etc.). This professionalization and specialization created a certain autonomous space for police forces and at the same time stimulated the act of labelling potential criminals, who had to be watched carefully and arrested if possible.[120] While many groups experienced the criminalizing effects, the example of the vagrants and gypsies (especially in Germany) is the most instructive in our case.[121] The far-reaching power of definition and its consequences was facilitated by new techniques for tracing and identifying people. This process of labelling, involving the attachment of stigmatizing labels as vagrant or gypsy to individuals through registration and supervision, typifies the modern state. Whereas in the ancien régime the labelling methods were quite primitive, modern techniques combined with a proactive policy (registration, fingerprints, photographs) made escaping registration and stigmatization far more difficult.

This specialization of the police affected both travelling groups and migrants and aliens. The policy toward the first category therefore has to be analysed in terms of this more general development. As shown by Noiriel and Moch, among others, the expansion of central government profoundly influenced control over migration (internal as well as between states) and practices for defining citizenship. The combined processes of democratization, nationalism, and the expansion of the central government afforded citizens more rights and thus rendered the definition of the individuals who did or did not belong to the state more important. The establishment and control of boundaries coincided with a more negative attitude toward migration and a desire to discourage the practice if possible and opportune. For travelling groups (especially people who had to cross national boundaries for their work), this trend further aggravated their way of living. They faced difficulties at borders (not only between states, but also

---

120. Becker, "Vom 'Haltlosen' zur 'Bestie'", p. 119.
121. See in this respect Zimmermann, "Ausgrenzung".

between smaller territorial units).[122] Perhaps more importantly, the new alien status of these people increased their visibility to the authorities and subjected them to general aliens policy as well. The specialization of the aliens police, which gained momentum in Western Europe after World War I, therefore increased the stigmatization.

Finally, the *stigmatization process* that came about at the end of the Middle Ages entailed a *psychological angle* as well. As we have seen, a process of selective perception and self-fulfilling prophecies deepened the negative perceptions. Once the image and category of parasitic and work-shy vagrants and travelling groups has been established, people will not only be stigmatized as such. In addition, individuals who conform (or who seem to conform) to this image contribute involuntarily to the hardening of the stigma. Examples of stealing and begging vagrants start to ignite the stigmatization engine. However simple and familiar this mechanism may be, its influence cannot be underestimated. The self-fulfilling prophecy is the final stage in attaching of the stigma. People treated as riffraff in some cases start to behave as such and to develop their own subculture. Although little information is available about this process, and many questions remain unanswered (e.g. the manner of selection) the process was clearly not linear or necessarily the result of the preceding steps. The expanse of any emerging underworlds must not be exaggerated. They contributed inversely to the stigma by serving as a justification for this policy. Perhaps the best example is the repression of gypsies and banditry in the eighteenth century. Clues indicate that a number of these organized criminal bands had a vagrant background. More important, however, is that the authorities associated these people with vagrants and travelling groups and viewed the emergence of these bands as a logical and inevitable outcome of a travelling way of life. Until late in the nineteenth century, when these bands had long become extinct, these associations remained alive.

---

122. In many countries, including Germany, Great Britain, and the Netherlands, even municipalities tried to ban travelling groups.

Moving Around and Moving On:
Spanish Emigration in the Sixteenth Century

Ida Altman

Emigration from the realms of the crown of Castile in the sixteenth century constituted the first major, sustained movement of people to the Americas from Europe. Beginning with the second voyage of Columbus (1493), this movement, initially directed to the islands of the Caribbean and numerically fairly small, gained momentum in the 1520s and 1530s with the conquests of Mexico and Peru; they would become the main centres of the Spanish empire in the Americas. The growing numbers of migrants meant greater complexity as individuals from an increasingly large geographical area headed for a number of possible destinations. By the middle decades of the sixteenth century patterns such as chain migration, growing participation of women, departure of nuclear family units, forms of labour migration, and return migration (often a stimulus for further emigration from the returnee's place of origin) emerged clearly.

I will discuss here the context in which the transatlantic movement of Spaniards took place. All too commonly emigration has been treated as if it were marginal not only to early modern Spanish society but even to the new societies of Spanish America. Until recently the topic failed to attract much attention from scholars working in the field of either Spanish or Spanish American history, although in the past decade and half scholarly study of Spanish migration to the Americas has increased notably.[1] On the whole, however, not only has Spanish emigration failed to find a place within the mainstream of the historiography of Spanish settlement of the Americas, it also has remained largely on the margins of the more general history of European expansion.

---

1.   The main published sources for Spanish emigration are the *Catálogo de pasjeros de Indias durante los siglos XVI, XVII y XVIII*, Vols 1-7 (Seville, 1940-46, 1980-86), and Boyd-Bowman, *Indice geobiográfico*, Vols 1-2. The Fondo de Cultura Económica has republished the first volume as the *Indice geobiográfico de más de 56 mil pobladores de la América hispánica* (1985) and is due to publish volumes 3-5. Another important source for information on emigrants is Otte, *Cartas privadas*. Articles written by Peter Boyd-Bowman, James Lockhart, Woodrow Borah, Theopolis Fair, and Magnus Mörner – the last including a useful bibliography – that appeared in Chiapelli (ed.), *First Images of America* serve as a good summary of research on emigration to that point. Mörner's "Migraciones a Hispanoamérica durante la época colonial", is an excellent guide to current scholarship and trends in the field.

The context of Spanish emigration was a complex one that encompassed varied societies and cultures as well as periods of time that, while not necessarily coinciding, might have embraced congruent stages of development. Spanish migration to the Americas preceded English migration by a full century, yet the similarities between the movements appear to outweigh the differences that might have resulted primarily from the discrepancy in timing. In fact comparison of migration from Spain with other early modern European movements points to so many parallels that it would appear that factors such as timing, the relative attractiveness of possible destinations, and the availability of labour for establishing commercial enterprises all played a much greater part in determining the size, direction, and composition of emigrant groups than did national identity or policy as such.[2] Rather than being homogeneous, cohesive phenomena, migration movements from any one country really were aggregates of differentiated migrant groups – servants, entrepreneurs, artisan or farming families. Such groups, whether defined by their socioeconomic and occupational status or by motivation, in some cases overlapped with one another and in others were fairly sharply delineated (although they were always, of course, at least indirectly connected). Certainly what we now know about Spanish migration indicates that it was no different in this regard.

Rather than offer a broad discussion of statistics and national histories I instead will consider certain groups or individuals, chosen mainly because there is sufficient detail regarding at least some of their activities that by scrutinizing them one gains a basic understanding of some of the mechanisms that governed transatlantic migration overall. These same mechanisms not only helped to convey people from one place to another but at the same time worked to reinforce cultural continuity as well as transference and change.

I begin with the story of a marriage in which one partner emigrated and the other would not. Benito de Astorga, a man from the town of Astorga in León in north central Castile, first went to Hispaniola in 1502 as part of the large group that accompanied the new royal governor of the island, Frey Nicolás de Ovando. Apparently he continued to travel back and forth between the islands and Spain as a merchant, so it is not entirely surprising that in 1512 he married a woman named Isabel de Mayorga, who lived in his home town in León. Probably he intended to return there permanently to live once he had accumulated sufficient capital. These plans went awry in 1521, however, when he returned to Hispaniola from a visit to Castile intending to sell off all his property there and leave the island for good. Initially he sold a herd of cattle but was

---

2.   See, for example, the studies in Altman and Horn, *"To Make America"*, and the discussion in the "Introduction" by Altman and Horn (pp. 1-30). The bibliography on early modern emigration by now is substantial, although the scholarly work on British migration still dwarfs the remainder of the field.

unable to divest himself of the rest. Astorga wrote to his wife telling her he had decided to stay and asking her to join him; he also began to invest in a sugar estate and purchased and rented African slaves.[3]

What might have seemed to Benito de Astorga a reasonable enough request – that his wife come to live with him in Santo Domingo – encountered strong and continued resistance on the part of his wife and her family. Notwithstanding visits from a series of Astorga's acquaintances and numerous letters not only from him but from male and female friends of his in Santo Domingo, his wife proved unwilling to commit herself to leaving her home and family for married life in the Indies. Certainly the means to have done so existed in abundance. On three different occasions she was to have travelled with another woman who was accompanying or going to join her own husband. Benito de Astorga made arrangements for her to stay in the house of a man named Luis Fernández de Alfaro when she arrived in Seville. Astorga sent money for all her travel expenses to this resident of Seville, who himself might have been in Hispaniola at some time and whose son Juan de Alfaro was living there in the 1520s. At Christmas time in 1526 she, along with two of her brothers, was to have met Astorga's friend Melchor de Castro (who had visited Isabel de Mayorga in Astorga) in Seville, but she failed to do so. Subsequently Isabel wrote to her husband saying that if Benito's cousin Hernando de Ponferrada, who was married and living in La Palma (in the Canaries), would come for her she would make the journey to Hispaniola with him and one of her brothers. Ponferrada left Palma for Seville and from there went to Astorga in León for Isabel. Once again, however, she and her "mother and relatives" decided she should not leave. As of 1533, the latest that records were found for this case, she still had not joined her husband.

One observes a notably high degree of physical mobility on the part of many of the participants in this domestic drama, both within Spain and back and forth across the Atlantic. Astorga himself made numerous trips between Spain and Hispaniola, his friend Melchor de Castro returned to Spain at least twice (travelling not just to Seville, of course, but all the way north to Astorga), and several of Astorga's other acquaintances on the island visited there at least once during the 1520s. Astorga's cousin Hernando de Ponferrada travelled from La Palma to Seville and north to Astorga and then home again, but he had been ready and willing to accompany Isabel de Mayorga all the way to Hispaniola.

The frequency and seeming ease with which individuals moved from place to place – within Castile, to Seville, the Canaries, or the Caribbean – suggests how quickly in the early sixteenth century the expanding Spanish empire came to be viewed as one arena in which people could move around to pursue

3.   Benito de Astorga's deposition for the Audiencia regarding his efforts to get his wife to join him and the testimony of his friends in the case appear in Archivo General de Indias (AGI) Santo Domingo 9, ramo 2, no 18; see also AGI Santo Domingo 9, ramo 2, nos l9A and l9B.

opportunities. Just as remarkable was the rapidity with which networks of contact and communication developed to facilitate this movement. The affected parties in this case maintained intense, continuous communication through letters and by word of mouth. The thrust of this constant communication was to underscore and ensure the primacy of the bonds of kinship and friendship, in which individuals looked first to friends and relatives to see to their affairs in their absence and help safeguard their interests, often reaching decisions on the basis of collective, not individual, welfare and advantage.

None of these observations are of much help, unfortunately, when it comes to deciphering Isabel de Mayorga's motivations. Her voice is heard only very indirectly through the comments and reactions of others, who are mostly men (Melchor de Castro, for example, complained on his return to Santo Domingo that she and her brothers had made a fool of him). Assuming that she had no strong objections to the general notion of conducting married life with her husband, one might conclude that her (and her family's) decision that Isabel should not join him in Hispaniola hinged on a negative answer to the most basic question posed by the possibility of emigrating: Will I (or my family) be better off? Apparently she – or they – thought not.

The story of this marriage suggests two topics which, while seemingly unrelated, actually were closely connected. These are the role played by Seville in channelling emigrants to the Indies, and the migration patterns of women. The connections between the two are largely circumstantial; but then it is those circumstances that to a great extent shaped and defined the nature of mobility in Castilian society and hence formed an essential part of the context in which emigration took place.

Seville dominated the "Indies enterprise", acting as virtually the sole port of embarkation in the sixteenth century and sending large numbers of emigrants all through the period; in the early years, up to 1519, one in six emigrants came just from the city itself. While its share (and the share of Andalucía) diminished somewhat over time (although still remaining high), Sevillian women continued to figure especially prominently in the movement. In the years between 1560 and 1579 Seville sent one-third of all women migrants to the Indies.[4] But Seville not only funnelled people to the Indies. As a flourishing centre for trade, industry, and commercial agriculture the port city was a major source of attraction for Spaniards, doubling in size to over 100,000 inhabitants by the end of the sixteenth century.[5] A number of individuals (all men!) living in the

---

4. Boyd-Bowman, *Patterns of Spanish Emigration*, pp. 5, 17, 44, 72, 75.
5. The population figures compiled by Molinie-Bertrand, *Siècle d'or: L'Espagne et ses hommes*, show that many Castilian towns, both large and small, doubled in size during the sixteenth century, a pattern that appears somewhat different from the one identified by Jan de Vries for the Netherlands in the same period, where most urban growth was in the largest cities

Extremaduran town of Cáceres, some 250 kilometres distant from Seville, testified in the 1560s that they had travelled there several times.[6] Young men from villages of the distant northern Cantabrian region would spend a few years working in Seville before returning home with sufficient savings to establish themselves.[7]

By necessity most Spanish emigrants passed through Seville, regardless of whether they had any previous connections with the city or not. In the case of emigrants from Extremadura (and elsewhere) contacts with people in Seville, especially people from their own home towns who were living there temporarily or permanently, formed a vital link in the chain connecting them to the Indies and facilitated their move there.[8] The process of obtaining a license and preparing for the journey usually involved a stay of weeks, or more likely months, in Seville.[9] Seville's monopoly over emigration meant that some experience of life in the cosmopolitan port city was shared by virtually all emigrants, not just those who were from there. The existence of this common denominator might have mitigated the differences between Sevillian emigrants and others and doubtless played a part in the decision of some returnees (admittedly a minority, but a fairly conspicuous one) who established themselves in Seville rather than in their home towns after leaving the Indies.

Consideration of the role and significance of Seville in emigration thus brings us to the topic of internal migration and its relationship to the transatlantic movement. Clearly a high degree of physical mobility existed in early modern Spanish society. The evidence for this moving around is considerable, and the lack of any special comment it seems to have elicited (recall all the moving about

(the phenomenal growth of Lisbon compared to all other Portuguese towns is an even more extreme case); see De Vries, *European Urbanization*, pp. 62 and 28-29 on the general phenomenon of urban growth in Europe in the sixteenth century. Thus while the nature of the transatlantic movement from Seville suggests that in some ways it might have functioned somewhat as did London in the seventeenth century (both in attracting people and sending them on), there are also significant differences in the two cases. London grew from a population of 60,000 in the early sixteenth century to 575,000 in 1700, as internal migration brought an estimated one million migrants to the city between 1550 and 1750; see Bailyn, *Peopling of British North America*, pp. 24-25, also 40, 12. While, as was true for Seville, there was substantial movement out of London across the Atlantic – suggesting that the move to the city often was a first step (whether intentional or not) of the transatlantic move (Bailyn, in fact, calls this movement a "spillover") – it is also true that sixteenth century departures to the Indies from Spain overwhelmingly were concentrated in Seville, while Bailyn has suggested that British emigration essentially consisted of two movements – one from London and the other from the northern British provinces.

6. Altman, *Emigrants and Society*, p. 207.
7. Vassberg, "Mobility and Migration". Cited with permission of the author (work in progress).
8. See discussion in Altman, *Emigrants and Society*, pp. 205-208 on the important role played by prospective emigrants' compatriots living temporarily or permanently in Seville.
9. Jacobs, "Legal and Illegal Emigration".

in Castile of Benito de Astorga's various agents) seems to attest to its utter normality.[10] Much of the movement was, of course, essentially local or cyclical – i.e., from smaller places to larger ones, or conversely from central to more outlying parts of municipal jurisdictions where more land was available,[11] connected with marketing activities, or seasonally in conjunction with such employment as transport and peddling or herding or other agricultural work.[12] There also was movement over longer distances, directed perhaps in particular toward the fastest-growing urban centres – Toledo in the first two-thirds of the sixteenth century and, of course, Seville[13] – but affecting many cities in this period.[14]

One very common form of internal migration resulted from the apparently widespread practice of childhood and adolescent service. Both boys and girls commonly left their Castilian villages to work for families elsewhere, usually (although not invariably) in neighbouring villages. While the total period of service could last for years, there often was much turnover, and young people commonly served in more than one household before reaching adulthood. Although most boys and girls went to nearby places within the province, some moved much greater distances.[15]

We still lack detailed knowledge of the demographic, socioeconomic, or even regional composition of internal migratory movements that would permit meaningful comparison with the transatlantic movement;[16] nonetheless one

10. See Moch, *Moving Europeans*, especially chs 1 and 2, on the frequency of migration in pre-industrial Europe. Although she begins her discussion in the seventeenth century and devotes little attention to the Iberian peninsula, many of her observations apply to sixteenth-century Castile as well.

11. See Nader, *Liberty in Absolutist Spain*, on the establishment of new settlements and municipalities.

12. See Vassberg, "Mobility and Migration", pp. 2-3.

13. See Martz, *Poverty and Welfare in Habsburg Spain*, on the growth of Toledo.

14. See Molinie-Bertrand, *Siècle d'or: L'Espagne et ses hommes*, on the population growth of towns and cities. Reher, *Town and Country in Pre-Industrial Spain*, examines rural to urban mobility in some detail, although most of his data are for the nineteenth century. Both Jan de Vries's work on European urbanization and Leslie Page Moch's on migration suggest a number of similarities between early modern Castile and other parts of Europe.

15. Vassberg, "Mobility and Migration", pp. 4-7. He cites (n. 37) a study by María del Carmen García Herrero, "Mozas sirvientas en Zaragoza durante el siglo XV", in: Angela Muñoz Fernández and Cristina Segura Graiño (eds), *El trabajo de las mujeres en la Edad Media hispana* (Madrid, 1988), in which the author found cases of girls in domestic service in Zaragoza from Navarre, Castile and even Mallorca (pp. 276-277). See also Reher, *Town and Country in Pre-Industrial Spain*, ch. 7 ("Mobility and migration in pre-industrial Cuenca"). His data for the nineteenth century indicate rapid turnover and a high incidence of return of young people to their villages following periods of domestic service in the city (see pp. 255-256).

16. Vassberg comments on the abundance of anecdotal evidence of mobility as compared to the paucity of data on age, sex, place of origin, return migration, geographical distribution, sex-

discerns some connections between these migration movements. Here we return to the question of distinctive migration patterns for men and women. While fairly localized moves probably were as likely to involve girls or young women, couples, and families as single men, longer distance migration seems to have been more preponderantly male. Childhood service, which may have included equal numbers of boys and girls, under normal circumstances doubtless conveyed young people to known destinations. Relatives and acquaintances helped to arrange children's entrance into household service, and better-off families often took in poorer relatives on this basis.[17] Men, especially single young men, seem to have been more likely to undertake the dangers and uncertainties both of travel and of relocation in little known or unknown destinations than were women; likewise cyclical and seasonal employment that required mobility – hauling, peddling, herding, migratory farm labour – probably mainly involved men.

It appears likely, then, that within Spain women and girls principally moved to prearranged destinations where they would marry or be received in a specific household (of an employer, relative), or else they moved with their husbands, fathers, or other male relatives. How does this pattern correlate with the transatlantic movement? Very few women of any social rank travelled alone to the Indies; they moved to America under circumstances similar to those under which they relocated within Spain itself. Among the emigrants from Trujillo for whom it was possible to determine modes of travel, only 7 women appear to have undertaken the journey alone (none of them before 1530); in contrast 14 travelled as *criadas* (servants), nearly 60 with husbands or children, 82 with parents, siblings, or other relatives, and 13 went to join relatives.[18]

Notwithstanding the growing participation of women migrants to the Indies – women's share in the movement increased from 5.6 percent in the period up to 1519 to 28.5 percent in the decades between 1560-79[19] – the prospects of extensive overland travel within Spain itself, with its attendant risks and uncertainties, might have continued to discourage potential women emigrants.[20] This reluctance to travel is hardly surprising, given the estimated time required to reach Seville from various points of departure. Whereas travellers leaving Córdoba

and job-specific mobility, and the like that would allow more complete analysis of internal migration ("Mobility and Migration", p. 14).

17. Vassberg, "Mobility and Migration", p. 5; Reher, *Town and Country in Pre-Industrial Spain*, pp. 270, 296. Reher writes that "much of the migration and mobility in Cuenca was a function of family interests and needs, or received the support of kin networks" (p. 303).

18. See Altman, *Emigrants and Society*, Table 9 (p. 177).

19. Boyd-Bowman, *Patterns of Spanish Emigration*, pp. 25, 49, 72.

20. According to Boyd-Bowman, *Patterns of Spanish Emigration*, pp. 49-50, 75, over half of the female emigrants in the period 1540-1559 were from Andalucía (accounting for 30 percent of the emigrants from Seville itself), and in the period 1560-1579 the city of Seville sent 34 percent of all the women migrants.

could reach Seville in a few days, the trip on foot from Cáceres or Granada could take three weeks, from Madrid a month, and from León over six weeks.[21] The stay in Seville before embarking for the Indies could last another two or three months. Hence emigrants from outside Seville's hinterland might be on the road and away from home three or four months or more before departing on a transoceanic journey which, although tedious and uncomfortable, might not have appeared to entail nearly the risk and insecurity of the journey up to that point (and could be considerably shorter). There is perhaps little reason to wonder why Seville and Andalucía continued to supply the largest numbers of women willing to travel to the Indies, or why Isabel de Mayorga decided to stay home.

But stay home she did, perhaps because the journey was unappealing, perhaps because she and her family decided that her husband's prospects looked less than rosy. The stimulus to most early modern migration was, of course, real or perceived opportunity, particularly when access to potential opportunities was enhanced by the existence of networks of kinship and acquaintance that provided needed information and assistance. In the largest sense the most important connection between internal mobility and transatlantic migration lay in the predisposition of people at practically all levels of society to relocate temporarily or permanently, principally in conjunction with the search for economic opportunity and security, whether this meant going off to study at the university or to enter a religious order or the army, going to work as an artisan, innkeeper, or entrepreneur in a booming port city like Seville, or moving to another town or village where access to land appeared promising or to marry. This willingness to move, and the means to do so afforded by networks of communication and personal ties, affected people's decisions and activities after they arrived in the Indies as well, so that the entire leapfrogging and interconnected process of settling one area after another reflected the interplay between the rapid consolidation and stabilization of Spanish society, on the one hand, and the predisposition to move on in search of other opportunities on the other.

Consider the example of Diego Guerra of Cáceres, who went to the Indies in the 1530s, ostensibly seeking his father, Alonso Guerra. Alonso Guerra was in Peru, where he had received an *encomienda* from Francisco Pizarro and by 1537 was sitting on the city council of San Miguel de Piura. His son Diego first arrived in the Indies in Puerto Rico, then moved on to Hispaniola, where he helped put down an attempted slave revolt. After a couple of years he departed for the isthmian region (Tierra Firme) and subsequently for Peru. Although by then he had heard his father was living in San Miguel, he did not find him there, only finally encountering him, apparently fortuitously, while participating in

21. Jacobs, "Legal and Illegal Emigration", pp. 66-67.

a military expedition; his father met the expedition with supplies. In addition to Diego, who became his father's principal heir, four other sons of Alonso Guerra, two of them Dominican friars, made their way to Peru; one left Peru for Chile and died there with Pedro de Valdivia. Last, Alonso Guerra's brother Diego Guerra de la Vega went to New Spain, where he served as a secret royal envoy and produced chronicles of the conquest of Mexico. Subsequently he entered the priesthood. He too eventually ended up in Peru and died in San Miguel. The careers of these six members of the Guerra family known to have emigrated to the Indies, then, virtually covered the Spanish empire, encompassing the Caribbean, Mexico, Tierra Firme, Peru and Chile.[22]

The mobility of Spanish immigrants tied the developing societies of Spanish America together in ways that are only now attracting some attention.[23] Such movement bound these societies to one another just as transatlantic migration tied Spanish America to Spain.[24] Furthermore in the Indies the mobility of Spaniards and other Europeans was but one element in a complex of migratory movements. These included the migration of indigenous groups and individuals, which encompassed movements that predated the arrival of Europeans as well as new, altered, or accelerated forms; and the movements of Africans and people of African descent which, since they involved both slaves and free people, also showed variety in their direction and causation.[25]

The Caribbean, the first arena of Spanish activity in the Indies, in a sense epitomizes how these various migratory movements interacted, while at the same time the outcome was unique. Francisco Manuel de Landa's "Relación de la isla" of Puerto Rico, compiled in 1530-31,[26] showed that the island had undergone radical transformation in the generation following its conquest. The two towns, San Juan and San Germán, between them had 415 free adult

22. For the Guerra family see Altman, *Emigrants and Society*, pp. 230-231. For a detailed examination of how kinship ties and family strategies functioned to convey members of one noble family from Cáceres to Peru, see Altman, "Spanish Hidalgos and America".

23. Cook, in "Migration in Colonial Peru", comments that "There is probably a significant, although as yet an under-studied link between commercial and plantation families on Hispaniola and coastal Peru" (p. 49). See also comments on connections between Spanish activities in the Caribbean and early Mexico in Altman, "Spanish Society in Mexico City".

24. Doubtless the same was true for the movements of British and French migrants within their respective colonial empires. See, for example, Dunn, "English Sugar Islands" on the relocation of British settlers from Barbados to South Carolina.

25. See Robinson, *Migration in Colonial Spanish America*, especially Robinson's "Introduction: towards a typology of migration in colonial Spanish America".

26. AGI Justicia 106, no. 3. Francisco Manuel de Landa, as *teniente de gobernador* of Puerto Rico, collected the information in this account which was not, strictly speaking, a census but rather a listing of all African and Indian slaves and servants held by Puerto Rico's Spanish residents. Since probably virtually every Spaniard held at least an Indian slave or two (including the most humble *estancieros* and criados in the countryside), the compilation comes close to being a census of the island's population.

residents, mainly Spanish men and women but including a few free blacks or mulattos and probably some mestizos. There were 2287 African slaves and around 1000 Indian slaves. About a fifth of the Spanish and African residents were women, although women might have constituted a majority of the Indian slaves. Nearly all these people were migrants. Europeans and Africans came from across the Atlantic or from Hispaniola, and the Indian slaves generally were presumed to have come from elsewhere ("de fuera"). Occasionally this was noted specifically; in one case four were said to have been brought from Yucatan. Only 486 people were listed as "free" Indians in repartimiento, or *naborías,* in service to Spaniards. Apart from the small number of indigenous women ("de la tierra") married to Spaniards, they apparently were the only remaining native inhabitants of Puerto Rico.

By 1530, then, migrants from Europe, Africa, and other parts of the Caribbean collectively outnumbered the indigenous people of Puerto Rico by more than seven to one. Their presence underscored not only the drastic demographic changes that had taken place on the island but also the speed with which people were moving or being moved around and coming into contact with one another. The rapid and seemingly unstoppable reduction of the native popula-tions of the large islands where Spaniards first settled led to the importation of labour from other islands on a considerable scale; population decline, combined with a shift from gold mining to sugar cultivation, which Europeans already associated with the use of African labour, stimulated the importation of African slaves. These new migratory patterns set off by Spanish activities did not entirely displace preexisting ones, however. Residents of Puerto Rico, for example, complained in the 1520s about the periodic raids of Caribs;[27] most likely these raids represented a continuation of an older phenomenon, although perhaps new kinds of plunder made the Spanish settlements particularly attractive targets.[28] A high degree of transience characterized Spanish society itself in the Caribbean. Yet despite economic decline and the existence of more promising opportunities on the mainland in the 1520s and 30s, a coherent and fairly stable Spanish society took hold in many places.

The story of Benito de Astorga and consideration of Spanish society in the Caribbean suggests that most of the basic patterns associated with sixteenth century emigration existed virtually from the outset.[29] People followed their

---

27.   See the description of a raid by 150 Caribs in 1520 in AGI Patronato 176, ramo 6.
28.   Boucher, *Cannibal Encounters,* p. 49, notes that from the sixteenth century Caribs carried off Africans from Puerto Rico and kept them as "highly prized" slaves.
29.   For Castile to date these patterns have been most systematically analyzed and discussed in Altman, *Emigrants and Society,* which focuses on two small cities in Extremadura in the middle decades of the sixteenth century. My work on Castilian emigration has shown that the six kinds of migratory movements that Frank Bovenkerk identified for the nineteenth and

friends and relatives, and emigrants already in the Indies sent back for or returned to get family members and others; they maintained their connections through letters and other networks of communication; they returned home, temporarily or permanently. Such patterns, present as they were from the earliest years, over time did not so much demonstrate real changes in form but rather underwent a gradual process of elaboration which in large degree was the natural outgrowth of the increasing size, and therefore complexity, of the movement, as well as of the development and consolidation of society in the Indies.

The choices of emigrants with regard to destinations, careers, business associations, and marriages probably reflected the strength of two kinds of important connections: first, their ties with a specific point of origin and with other emigrants from that place (with all that would imply for preexisting ties of kinship, friendship, patronage and the like); and second, bonds arising from experiences in the Indies, perhaps most particularly early experiences, even including the journey itself. The interaction of those two sets of connections, both of which were as much emotional as practical, played an important part in shaping associations and preferences of Spaniards in the Indies.

The two kinds of bonds did not function at odds but rather appear largely to have complemented and reinforced each other. The word "amigo" seems to have carried much the same authority and moral weight as terms expressing kinship. Cacereno Lorenzo de Aldana left his houses, lands, and slaves in Peru in his will of 1562 to Diego Hurtado, whom he called "my friend and brother who has been in my house and company".[30] Aldana and Hurtado had no familial relationship, nor did they share a common place of origin in Spain. One of the most striking elements in the story of Benito de Astorga and his wife Isabel de Mayorga is the cohesiveness of the Spanish community in Santo Domingo, which in this case again apparently resulted more from long-term association and friendship than from kinship or common origin. In all at least thirteen people in Santo Domingo, including judges of the Audiencia, the prior of the Dominican monastery, and the treasurer of Hispaniola and his wife, became involved in Astorga's efforts to convince his wife to come, whether through letters or actual visits to her and her family in northern Spain. Only one of these individuals was from Astorga's home town in León and knew his wife before going to Santo Domingo. This witness testified that the person who made the

---

twentieth century – emigration, return migration, transient migration, re-emigration, second-time emigration, and circulation – all apply to the movement of people from Spain to the Indies in the sixteenth century; see Bovenkerk, *Sociology of Return Migration*. See also C. Tilly, "Migration in Modern European History", pp. 50-55, who identifies four basic forms of migration – local, circular, chain, and career; and Moch's discussion of the applicability of these in *Moving Europeans*, pp. 16-17 and 59.

30. See Zarama, *Reseña histórica*, app. 1, pp. 189-196.

greatest efforts on Astorga's behalf, Melchor de Castro, did so because he and Astorga were close friends – "eran y son muy amigos".[31] Castro, like Astorga, had lived for many years on Hispaniola.

Perhaps the classic example in which the close bonds forged by friendship and shared experience substituted for, and finally were transformed into, ties of kinship and common origin was that of two men who were present at Cajamarca, Lucas Martínez Vegaso and Alonso Ruiz. Lucas Martínez was from Trujillo, and although there is no evidence that Alonso Ruiz was, the two were partners from at least the time they arrived in Peru. In 1540 Ruiz left Peru for Martínez's home town of Trujillo with the intention of marrying his partner's sister. Both contributed to Isabel Martínez's dowry, and each held the other's power of attorney during their years of separation, which turned out to be permanent, although they might not have foreseen that when Ruiz left Peru. Ruiz became not only a member of Martínez's family but a prominent trujillano as well, holding a seat on the city council in the 1550s and purchasing señorío of the village of Madronera close to Trujillo.[32] Their story points to a perceived equivalence between bonds based on kinship and common origin and others that developed from new experiences and circumstances that generated loyalty and trust. This enlargement of the circle of personal association based on activities and choices connected with moving to the Indies contributed to the forging of new allegiances, hence laying the basis for the construction of new communities while simultaneously allowing preservation of older ties that kept the connection with relatives and friends at home alive.

The tendency of Spaniards in the Indies to move around and move on, while crucially important in shaping societies there, nonetheless should be understood within a context that also was characterized by a fair degree of stability. Even if people eventually moved on or returned home, they frequently stayed in one place long enough to contribute to the cohesiveness and consolidation of the evolving American societies while at the same time they generated contacts and connections that might prove enduring. One sees this in the case of that minority of emigrants who returned to Castile. Half of the returnees (for whom length of absence can be determined) to Trujillo and three-quarters of the returnees to Cáceres stayed away from home at least ten years.[33]

A small number of returnees stayed in Spain long enough that their eventual decision to leave again for the Indies would place them in the category of

---

31. The testimony in this case is in Archivo General de Indias (AGI) Santo Domingo 9, ramo 2, no. 18. The man from Astorga was Abel Meléndez, who apparently went to the island in the early 1520s, by which time Benito de Astorga had been there many years.
32. For Lucas Martínez see Arestegui, *Lucas Martínez Vegazo*; and Lockhart, *Men of Cajamarca*, pp. 300-305, and *ibid.* for Alonso Ruiz, pp. 343-346.
33. See Altman, *Emigrants and Society*, pp. 250-251.

re-emigrants or second-time emigrants (rather than temporary visitors).[34] Textile entrepreneur Cristóbal de Ribas, part of a group of Brihuega emigrants that settled in Puebla in the second half of the sixteenth century, spent such long periods at a spell in Spain and in Mexico that he might plausibly be considered as participating fully in society in both places during his adulthood. Born around 1530, he arrived in Puebla de los Angeles by 1561, possibly already married. He returned to Brihuega in 1572, having sold his textile manufacturing business for 10,000 pesos. His brother Alonso de Ribas, with whom he might originally have travelled to Mexico, apparently stayed on, at least for a while. Twenty years later, when Cristóbal would have been at least sixty, he returned to Puebla with an entourage consisting of at least twenty-four people, including his wife, nine children, seven grandchildren, and the in-laws of one daughter.[35] Careers such as his that involved one or more moves – whether back and forth between two places or from one to another and then perhaps a third – entailed considerable mobility that affected many members of a kin group while at the same time they fostered continuity and helped to maintain the ties between an individual or family and a specific place (or places).

The increasing size and complexity of the sixteenth-century transatlantic movement meant the fairly early appearance of labour migration – people going to the Indies in response to specific business or employment opportunities.[36] This is a phenomenon that has not been commonly associated with Spanish emigration in this period. Yet some time ago Boyd-Bowman pointed to a case of what surely was labour migration from the mining town of Guadalcanal in the Sierra Morena. He noted the great "exodus" of some 150 people in the mid-1530s after the discovery of silver in Taxco, apparently following a group of ten men who went to Mexico in 1527 and became involved in mining there. One of these men, a miner in Taxco, returned to Spain and then went back to Mexico in 1536.[37]

A number of individuals left Trujillo for the Indies to work in a specific capacity there. Several members of two generations of the Valencia family, for example, went to Peru to work for Lucas Martínez Vegaso, who very likely was their relative.[38] In individual cases of this kind, however, it often is difficult to

34. See Bovenkerk, *Sociology of Return Migration*, p. 5. According to his definition re emigration refers to emigration to the same destination after having returned, while second-time emigration refers to emigration to a new destination.

35. AGI Indiferente General 2054; *Catálogo de pasjeros,* Vol. 3, no. 3415, and Vol. 7, nos. 2427, 2428, 2573, 2575.

36. For comparison see, for example, Dirk Hoerder's comments on labor migration from Europe to America in the nineteenth and early twentieth centuries in his introductory chapter to Hoerder and Rössler, *Distant Magnets*, especially, pp. 11-17, and other articles in the volume.

37. Boyd-Bowman, *Patterns of Spanish Emigration*, p. 21.

38. See Altman, *Emigrants and Society*, p. 227; and Trelles, *Lucas Martínez Vegazo*, pp. 174-177.

distinguish between what could be called labour or employment recruitment and other types of personal and private recruitment. This ambiguity arises particularly in connection with the people who travelled to the Indies as "criados". The term criado encompassed a variety of statuses. A criado or criada made a contract with an employer on an individual basis, and the term of service often did not outlast the journey itself. Obviously there is a considerable difference between this kind of employment contract – the purpose of which often was to secure license or passage to the Indies with no subsequent continuing obligation – and the terms by which British or French indentured servants took passage; on arriving in America they were required to perform a standard number of years of obligatory service. Since only a minority of Spanish criados arrived in the Indies under obligation to fulfil a work contract with a specific employer (slaves brought to the Indies, of course, normally remained slaves), criado status did not necessarily equate with labour recruitment or migration.

There were, however, clear examples of labour recruitment, such as the movement of people, many of them involved in textile manufacture, from the Castilian town of Brihuega (and other towns nearby, like Fuentelencina and Pastrana) to Puebla de los Angeles in the second half of the sixteenth century.[39] Examination of this group to date shows that perhaps 1000 people left Brihuega for Mexico. The great majority settled in Puebla, although some moved out to nearby but connected places such as Cholula and the valley of Atlixco, and a handful were based in Mexico City.[40] More than a third of the emigrants left Brihuega in the 1570s, and the number of departures in the 1580s and 90s continued to be high. The group as a whole, while it included individuals and families of varying wealth and status, consisted mostly of commoners; few claimed hidalgo status.

The impetus for the movement lay in the establishment in Puebla in the 1550s and 60s of members of several families that would play a key and even dominant role in the development of Puebla's textile industry in the latter part of the sixteenth century. Chief among this first generation of Brihuega emigrants were five members of the Anzures family, four sons and a daughter of Diego de Anzures, who was both an *obraje* (textile factory) owner and *escribano* (notary) in Brihuega. In Puebla two of his sons served as escribanos and in other offices

---

39. The connection between Brihuega and Puebla first came to the attention of scholars when Enrique Otte published "Cartas privadas de Puebla del siglo XVI", (many of these letters were destined for Brihuega they also appear in Otte, *Cartas privadas de emigrantes a Indias*), and Albi-Romero published "Sociedad de Puebla de los Angeles en el siglo XVI", based on research in the Archive of the Indies.

40. Discussion of the Brihuega emigrants is based primarily on Otte, "Cartas privadas"; Albi-Romero, "Sociedad de Puebla"; the *Catálogo de pasajeros de Indias*, Vols. 4-7; and records in the following: AGI (primarily the Indiferente General and Contratación sections); the Archivo General de Notarías in Puebla; and the Archivo General de la Nación in Mexico.

as well as establishing obrajes. Owing principally to their success, eventually at least fifty of their relatives, in-laws, and their in-laws' relatives went to Puebla. The success of other individuals like Cristóbal de Ribas (discussed above), Juan de Brihuega, and Juan de Pastrana, all of whom were in Puebla by the mid 1560s, had a similar impact. Ribas, who had sold his obraje to Juan Barranco (a relative of the Anzures family) and returned to Brihuega by 1573, was related by marriage to the Angulo family, which also became prominent in textiles and office-holding in Puebla. Andrés de Angulo returned to Brihuega in 1578 after spending fourteen years in Puebla. His sons Pedro and Gabriel went back to Puebla in 1582 and owned obrajes there in the 1580s and 90s.[41] The large Pastrana and Brihuega clans also were related to each other.

The Brihuega group exhibited patterns frequently associated with labour migration: initial establishment of men, who subsequently returned for or sent for wives and children; direct recruitment for specific kinds of employment (fullers, cloth cutters and the like); temporary and permanent return migration; and the continuing departure of single young men all through the period. Despite the increasing presence of women and children (28 percent of the adult migrants were women, and of the total group including children, at least 35 percent were female), in the 1570s, for example, 40 percent of the emigrants were single men. Many of these men, of course, went with other relatives or as criados or joined someone already in Puebla. There also are indications among the migrant group of moves connected with the search for employment and economic opportunity that preceded emigration to Puebla. Members of the Pliego family, for example, were living in the Alpujarras in the 1570s before moving on to Mexico.

The patterns discerned among the emigrants to Puebla suggest that while the nature and direction of the Brihuega movement was distinctive – linked as it was to the part played by the Brihuega entrepreneurs and artisans in developing Puebla's textile industry- nonetheless the movement as a whole resembled others that were not necessarily conditioned by recruitment for a specific enterprise. A comparison between emigrant groups from two quite different localities in the 1570s – Brihuega and Trujillo – is suggestive. The Brihuega group of approximately one hundred included fourteen family groups (twelve families of two parents and at least one child, and two men returning to Mexico with their families), two married couples with no children, and two men whose families joined them within the same decade; as mentioned, 40 percent of the group consisted of single men. A group of around the same size that left Trujillo

41. See AGI Indiferente General 2054, and the *Catálogo de pasajeros*, 4, no. 3726 for Andres de Angulo, who went to Mexico with his wife Isabel de Ribas, five sons and three daughters in 1565. See Albi-Romero, "Sociedad de Puebla", pp. 132, 135-136 for activities of sons Pedro and Gabriel.

for New Spain in the same decade included twenty-two family groups (fourteen families consisting of two parents and at least one child and eight of one parent and children), and two married couples with no children. In this group, however, there were only seven single men and one single woman.[42]

Timing may in large part account for the differing composition of the groups. Emigration from Trujillo got underway much earlier, and the departure of single young men seems to have reached its peak in the 1530s, when nearly 130 left for the Indies. By the 1570s the Trujillo movement might be said to have reached its mature period, and the migrant group had become much more familial in nature.[43] Migration from Brihuega barely got started in the 1550s and only reached sizeable proportions in the 1570s. The group of slightly over one hundred people who went to Puebla from Brihuega in the 1590s, however, resembles more closely the "mature" pattern of the 1570s Trujillo group that went to Mexico. This 1590s group included seven married couples, seventeen families of parents and at least one child, two women with children going to join their husbands, and two pairs of siblings. There were eleven criados and two other "solteros", a considerably smaller proportion of single men than in the 1570s Brihuega group.

It is possible, then, that more detailed analysis of the make-up of migrant groups from various localities and of the timing of departures will tend to show that the apparent phenomenon of "labour migration" may be subsumed, at least in the sixteenth century, within more general migratory trends, by which a movement usually began with the departure mainly of young men and only after some time became essentially familial in nature. The existence of such a pattern also suggests that in many cases the "rhythm" and trajectory of transatlantic migration from any particular locality might reflect more strongly (although doubtless not exclusively) the influence of local circumstances and considerations rather than the changing attractions of society in the Indies. By the mid-sixteenth century Spanish society in central Mexico already had achieved a notable level of consolidation;[44] nonetheless the timing of the Brihuega migration reveals that, notwithstanding the coincidence of its early stages with increasing stability and prosperity in Mexico, the initial phase of the movement resembled earlier movements to destinations in the Indies during periods of formation and development.

The movement from Brihuega to Puebla and other examples that have been briefly discussed here suggest that sixteenth-century emigration from Castile to

---

42. See Altman, "New World in the Old", pp. 40-47 for discussion of this group.
43. See Altman, *Emigrants and Society*, p. 175, Table 8 and pp. 180-184, Table 10 for a listing of the 1570s group.
44. See Altman, "Spanish Society in Mexico City"; Hirschberg, "Social History of Puebla de los Angeles"; and Albi-Romero, "Sociedad de Puebla".

the Indies must be considered in several distinct but related contexts. Strong parallels between Castilian migration and other early modern European movements show that the Castilian movement was not so distinctive or peculiar as to form an entirely separate phenomenon; rather it clearly represented the first phase of modern European migration to the Americas, foreshadowing much of what would take place later and elsewhere. The Castilian movement, while fitting well within European transatlantic migration, also can be seen to have consisted of an aggregate of movements from separate localities where particular economic, social, and familial circumstances functioned to determine who might depart (and return), with whom, and to what destinations. The similarities among these local movements in timing, composition, and organization, together with the connections that existed among them, make it possible to discuss Castilian emigration at some level of generality; yet it also is clear that real understanding of the nature of the movement, and of its impact on local society in Spain and on the formation of society in the Indies, requires more detailed study of particular migrant groups and the contexts in which they functioned.

At the outset I suggested that within Spanish American history migration, somewhat inexplicably, has been treated as marginal. In fact it was the indispensable factor that, operating in conjunction with the huge reduction in indigenous populations and simultaneous introduction of large numbers of African slaves, made the Americas what they became after European contact – societies that remained culturally diverse but were increasingly Hispanicized and creolized.

Eighteenth-Century Transatlantic Migration and Early German Anti-Migration Ideology

Georg Fertig

In the spring of 1817, Friedrich List, a young Württemberg bureaucrat who later became one of Germany's most seminal economic theorists, was sent to the city of Heilbronn to enquire about the causes of emigration to North America. Both his results and his general perspective on migration reflected the interpretations of migration to America that had prevailed among German bureaucrats throughout the preceding century of German transatlantic mass migration. List's task was the prevention of emigration, both by warning the emigrants he was to interview and by investigating such "causes of emigration that the government might be able to remove". In Heilbronn, the young bureaucrat encountered vehement protest against high taxes and abusive civil servants. He concluded that the "fundamental cause of the emigration" lay in "discontent, i.e. pressure, [and] lack of freedom in their present condition as state and local citizens".[1] This view was, of course, rather conventional. In the late eighteenth century, it was common wisdom that "frequent emigrations" like those to North America "usually require severe defects of policy (*Policeyfehler*)".[2] The fundamental logic of this view implies that normally (or under a successful government) people would not emigrate, and that they departed only because of specific causes of tremendous sociopolitical significance.

In German social history, the paradigm of "causes of emigration" has enjoyed extended popularity. While some authors – mostly local historians and genealogists – have compiled long laundry lists of the causes that mobilized potential migrants,[3] more theoretically-oriented scholars have identified overpopulation as both the fundamental cause of emigration and the single sociopolitical problem that the contemporary governments were unable to resolve.[4] The model that focuses on overpopulation as an insoluble sociopolitical problem

1. The List interviews have been edited by Moltmann, *In Aufbruch nach Amerika*. Quotations from Doc. 14 and 19.
2. (Andreas Böhm) s.v. Colonien, *Deutsche Encyclopädie oder Allgemeines Real-Wörterbuch aller Künste und Wissenschaften* (Frankfurt, 1782).
3. See e.g. the list given by Hacker, *Auswanderungen aus Baden*, pp. 31-42.
4. Marschalck, *Deutsche Überseewanderung im 19. Jahrhundert*; Köllmann, "Versuch des Entwurfs"; Hippel, *Auswanderung aus Südwestdeutschland*.

serves to explain both emigration and nineteenth to twentieth century internal migration and asserts that an original state of society would not even manifest a "latent propensity to migrate". Overpopulation then loosened the links people had to their homelands and instigated the sociogenesis of such a propensity. More ephemeral "push and pull factors" could then influence the atomized and mobilized members of the formerly stable traditional society. We might label this model of migration through destabilization as revolutionary because it confronts two utterly different states of society.

The revolutionary overpopulation model has the advantage of being a rather explicit theory and should therefore be considered preferable to the vague laundry list approach that attributes emigration to all kinds of destabilizing push and pull factors. Indeed, the revolutionary model has informed some of the best migration studies we possess. This paper argues, however, that the revolutionary model is inadequate to explain both the early movement of Swiss and Germans to British North America (which has been labelled the "prototype of a transatlantic mass migration"[5]) and migration in German-speaking central Europe in general during the early modern period. In the first section of this paper, I shall try to place the revolutionary model in the context of some proportions of migration on the one hand and some empirical observations on the problem of overpopulation in the eighteenth century on the other hand.[6] In the second section, I shall discuss the relation between the channels or modes of internal migration that were available to potential migrants in the eighteenth century and the spectacular transatlantic migration of the time.[7] In the third section, I will attempt to reconstruct the perspectives of migrants and territorial bureaucracy in the discourse on causes of emigration that emerged during the early modern period and that continues to exert a formative influence on our present understanding of migration.

1. Proportions of migration and the problem of overpopulation

If overpopulation was indeed the decisive cause of emigration in the eighteenth century, emigration might be expected to be a relatively surprising and unusual phenomenon during that age and to involve significant numbers. Indeed, contemporary observers tended to view emigration as a mass phenomenon

5. Wokeck, "German Immigration to Colonial America".
6. The paper summarizes the findings of my dissertation "Wanderungsmotivation und ländliche Gesellschaft im 18. Jahrhundert: Vom Oberrhein nach Nordamerika". See also my article "'Um Anhoffung besserer Nahrung willen'".
7. This section is a severely shortened and revised version of section 2 of my article "Transatlantic Migration from the German-speaking Parts of Central Europe, 1600-1800: Proportions, Structures, and Explanations".

comprising surprisingly large numbers. Moreover, the principle that "the population of the absolutist state was sedentary" was common wisdom in social history until the 1980s.[8] These views enabled the study of emigration without addressing the topic of internal migration, which was considered irrelevant to the population movement.[9]

Close examination of the proportions of migration reveals, however, that internal migration was in fact far more widespread in eighteenth-century Germany than the revolutionary model suggests. According to a conservative (if rather rough) estimate, approximately one third of all adults changed their place of residence during their lifetime in seventeenth and eighteenth century Germany. In addition, even changes of residence that involved only short distances had far greater consequences for everyday life in those days than they would today. No "sociogenesis of a latent propensity to migrate"[10] seems to have been necessary before the movement from the Rhine lands to Pennsylvania and the other British colonies in America began: German villagers and townspeople had manifested a strong propensity to migrate for many generations, although not necessarily over very large distances. Also, the numbers of long distance migrants (especially to North America) have been grossly exaggerated, both by contemporary observers who viewed emigration as sensational and by filio-pietistic migration historians. While the migration of German speakers to North America prior to 1800 has traditionally has been placed at roughly 200,000, recent estimates reduce this figure to around 100,000. Regardless of the exact numbers and their importance in the process of populating British North America with Europeans, German emigration to American destinations is insignificant when considered (as in Table 1) in the context of total German migration of the eighteenth century. Germans who went to North America did not come from a spatially static, traditional German society. Rather, departure from the home community seems to have been almost the norm for individuals born in eighteenth century Germany.[11]

If departure from home was normal, overpopulation is not a necessary explanation for the occurrence of this practice. Also, stating that central Europe suffered from a fundamental overpopulation crisis during the eighteenth century that uprooted no more than 1.3 % of the population seems rather awkward.

8. Tennstedt, *Sozialgeschichte der Sozialpolitik*, p. 18.
9. See e.g. Hippel, *Auswanderung aus Südwestdeutschland*, p. 27.
10. For the term, see Bade, "Sozialhistorische Migrationsforschung", p. 66.
11. For sources and a more elaborate discussion, see my "Transatlantic Migration", pp. 193-203.

Table 1. German Empire and Swiss Confederacy in the eighteenth century: rough estimates of adult population and migration

	Number	Percentage
Adult population, several generations	46,000,000	100
Adult migrants to all destinations	15,000,000	33
to Eastern Europe	516,000	1.1
to North America	70,000	0.2

Apart from these basic proportions of migration, the concept of overpopulation as the cause of emigration might be challenged from a second perspective. Were the places of origin of the migrants to North America indeed overpopulated? Answering this question requires defining overpopulation in the first place. The term overpopulation usually describes a population increase that exceeds the capacity of the area in question. While estimating the actual population of a given village or town is not very difficult, measuring its capacity is rather complicated. Most population biologists approach this problem by defining "carrying capacity" as a function of the population development itself, namely as the maximum attained by a sigmoid growth process of the population, a phenomenon which Markus Mattmüller has termed the "*plafond*" (ceiling).[12] Overpopulation thus signifies reaching or briefly exceeding this *plafond*. The population of southwestern Germany, however, had clearly not reached such a *plafond* when emigration to North America set in during the first half of the eighteenth century. Indeed, most population growth was still to come. Göbrichen, a small village in the margravate of Baden-Durlach for which I have calculated a yearly estimate of the families residing there, did not reach a *plafond* between the late sixteenth and late eighteenth centuries. Still, several dozen people left Göbrichen for America between 1742 and 1754.

Another definition of carrying capacity (and thus overpopulation) is based on the amount of food that was available in the given area. This usage is widely accepted in the Malthusian tradition. However, the output of food in a specific area depends to some extent on the labour input. Accordingly, fixed estimates of the amount of food that can be produced in (or exchanged for other products from) a given place is impossible. Rather, the Malthusian Law should be understood as a version of the Law of Diminishing Returns. *Ceteris paribus*, an increase in population of a given proportion yields a food increase of a smaller proportion. Thus, the *per capita* income would fall as a consequence of popula-

---

12. Vogel, "Populationsdichte-Regulation und individuelle Reproduktionsstrategien", p. 17; Mattmüller, *Bevölkerungsgeschichte der Schweiz*, Vol. 1, pp. 425-427.

tion growth, despite the increase in overall production.[13] In any case, overpopulation in a Malthusian sense might be conceived as a low *per capita* income caused by population growth. Emigration would then result not directly from population growth, but rather from low income.

Indeed, both contemporaries and historians have frequently asserted that poverty was the main cause of emigration. Wolfgang von Hippel, for instance, has stated that the existence of a large group of *Grenzexistenzen* (individuals leading an economically marginal existence) in the eighteenth century was a necessary precondition for the "latent propensity to emigrate".[14] Nevertheless, migrants to America seem to have been no poorer than the average Swiss or Germans in the eighteenth century.[15] My own attempt to use genealogical and tax list data to compare emigrants and non-emigrants in the village of Göbrichen around 1740 has also revealed that agrarian property had virtually no influence on out-migration.[16] The low percentage of the very poorest individuals among migrants has frequently been attributed to their inability to finance their translocation. Even the poorest migrants, however, frequently received credit toward their translocation costs to British North America in the eighteenth century. If overpopulation causing poverty and poverty causing a "propensity to emigrate" formed the basic dynamics of migration in the case of German-language "redemptioner" migration to British North America, the people who decided to emigrate might be expected to come from the most marginalized classes. This, however, was not the case.

Another problem with defining overpopulation as low *per capita* income caused by population growth is the *ceteris paribus* clause that assumes that aside from labour, all other input factors (e.g. land, knowledge, and capital) are constant. In 1701 in Göbrichen for instance, only a small percentage of the fields were cultivated. Surely, the local food production was hardly sufficient, even for the relatively few inhabitants. In the decades until 1720, the rate of increase in cultivated acreage exceeded population growth. Even when emigration set in around 1740, the villagers seem to have enjoyed a far higher *per capita* income than at the beginning of the century. In addition to land, German peasants had new crops and agricultural techniques at their disposal, although they did not utilize these assets on a large scale. As the underproductivity of traditional agriculture constituted a significant reserve for additional production, identifying the point where the capacity of a given area was exceeded seems virtually impossible.[17]

13. Gordon, "Basic Analytical Structure".
14. Hippel, *Auswanderung aus Südwestdeutschland*, pp. 56, 59.
15. Häberlein, *Vom Oberrhein zum Susquehanna*, pp. 55-57; Blocher, *Die Eigenart der Zürcher Auswanderer*.
16. For results of a rank correlation analysis on the household level, see my dissertation.
17. On underproductivity see Groh, "Strategien, Zeit und Ressourcen". The Göbrichen data corroborate the findings of Pfister and Kellerhals, who state that in a Swiss rural area around

Most German population theorists espousing the tradition of Johann Peter Süßmilch favour a third operationalization of capacity. This concept of "scope of nourishment"[18] is based on the socially defined and controlled availability of *Stellen* (full family positions). The concept of a limited number of family positions in each village, however, is appropriate only in areas where virtually no land market existed, and where marriages between peasants required consent from the lords (e.g. in the serf countries east of the Elbe river). Emigration to British North America came from the western German territories, where the position of the manorial lords had weakened since the Middle Ages in favour of both peasants and the territorial state. In a broader sense, the "principle of *Stellen*" might be understood as the ability of a society to control the reproductive behaviour of its members according to the perceived economic scope by restricting marriage chances among the poor.[19] In this context, overpopulation can be defined as the process by which society loses this controlling ability and thereby becomes destabilized. The existence of such a destabilizing process is open to question simply because the effectiveness of the previous control is doubtful. In southwest Germany, some scarcely successful attempts were made to prevent marriages between poor subjects, although not before the seventeenth century. In Göbrichen, children's chances for marriage, indeed the reproductive opportunities of families in general, were increasingly (and not decreasingly) influenced by the resources of their parents. While economy obviously did influence demography in that village, social control was ineffective in this process. Rather, the improved reproductive opportunities of the wealthy may be attributed to the growing importance of land in the calculations of the individual potential marriage partners as the village became more crowded, and additional land grew increasingly scarce and expensive. A similar argument might explain the rather small influence of acreage on out-migration. As possession of land became increasingly significant for an individual's chances in life, moving to places where land was presumed to be easier to acquire seemed more rational to people who did not own much land. We would then expect the decision to out-migrate to prevail not among the "surplus population",[20] but simply among the residents who expected to benefit from this action. Poverty and overpopulation are hardly prerequisites for such sentiments. This line of reasoning obviously leads to a reinterpretation of the decision to emigrate. The revolutionary model holds functional necessities (overpopulation) responsible

---

    1760, the "theoretical carrying capacity" (in the Malthusian sense of overall food production)
    was far from exhausted: "Verwaltung und Versorgung", pp. 170-215.

18. *Nahrungsspielraum*, as opposed to the frequent Malthusian concept of *Nahrungsmittelspielraum*
    or "scope of food production". Unfortunately, many authors confuse these two concepts.

19. For a critique of this concept, see Ehmer, *Heiratsverhalten, Sozialstruktur*.

20. Hippel, *Auswanderung aus Südwestdeutschland*, p. 107.

for the change in mentality ("sociogenesis of a latent propensity to migrate") that initially enabled individuals to decide to move – a decision that many authors consider of dubious rationality. This interpretation minimizes the active role of the migrants. My interpretation in this article emphasizes the active part of the German-speaking population in a traditional society and their ability to reach fairly rational, "utility-maximizing" decisions to move or stay. As any beginning of geographic mobility is impossible to locate in time, assuming an immobile and non-rational attitude towards migration for any period of German history seems equally unnecessary.

2. Channels of mobility and the evolution of transatlantic migration

Although the gross numbers of people who moved and stayed in their places of residence preclude any characterization of German premodern society as geographically stable, the old view of a fixed society before the industrial revolution contained an element of truth. The population did not roam about freely, and both spatial and social mobility were regulated. These regulations were not, however, designed to prevent migration, or, if they were, their intentions achieved little success. Regulations functioned not as floodgates against mobility, but rather as channels for such displacement. Spatial mobility was possible for everybody. The authorities, however, required that this process be justified. Also, legal consequences often ensued. I shall now discuss some of the most important channels of spatial mobility before addressing the extension of these patterns to British North America.

Seven major channels of mobility can be distinguished. First, the legal system provided both for people arriving and departing. Villeinage was compatible with migration. In fact, the institution of *Leibeigenschaft* (villeinage) was a consequence of medieval mobility: villeins were originally subjects living outside the *Zwing und Bann* (the territory of their lord's jurisdiction). Theoretically, lords were entitled to prevent their villeins from moving. In practice, however, they exercised this right only to extract taxes from out-migrants. Networks of mutual agreements between lords allowed their subjects to move freely between huge interconnected regions. Not all immigrants were fully accepted as citizens of the southwest German towns and villages. Nevertheless, most migrants could obtain the status of a *Hintersasse* or denizen with limited rights and obligations.

Second, exit from and entry into labour contracts was well institutionalized in preindustrial German society. Many authors have described the *Ganzes Haus* (integrated household) as the basic unit of production, reproduction, and consumption. This institution certainly played an important role both ideologically and as the basis for the fiscal system. From the perspective of the people living there, however, the household was not an encompassing functional unit. Although cameralist theory propagates such a family model, south and west German families were based not on unpaid family labour, but rather on norms of equality and reciprocity, and, of course, on the amount of work that was performed by the day labourers who lived in their own households anyway.[21] No artificial dichotomy should be made between family values on the one hand and the labour market with its implications of mobility on the other hand: departure from families was permitted, and many households were fragmented or even dispersed. Servitude was a common form of exit from the household. Unmarried young women and men travelled considerable distances in search of work as servants. The authorities tried to use *Gesindedienst* (servitude) to control the labour market. Unlike day labourers, servants had fixed contracts of six or twelve months and were not permitted to stop working even if they had earned sufficient pay to satisfy their needs. In areas with a strong demand for labour, the yearly markets were a common forum for arranging employments, and some developed into proper servant markets. In the cities, servant brokers who traded in young women were also common.[22] Independent of formal systems, seasonal migrant labour emerged in many regions where short-term workers were needed for hay or grain harvesting, sometimes crossing distances of several hundred miles.[23]

   Third, professional specialization created other channels of mobility. Specialists of any kind were not very likely to find work for their entire lifetime in a single village or town. Some professional and artisan groups required that people travel away from home for formal education or forced people to leave because of guild restrictions on the number of masters in a particular trade in a given area.[24] Even the mobility of the vagrant marginal classes should not be interpreted as a symptom of crisis. To a large degree, these individuals served an indispensable function within society. Many people within this category were specialists; they made their living by performing a wide variety of tasks ranging from killing rats and cleaning chimneys to selling books and almanacs to the peasants. Official efforts to prevent mobility struck a serious blow to such occasional workers. Many were *herrenlos*, people without a lord and thus without protection. Their position became increasingly precarious during the early modern period, when the authorities tried to create a closed territory.[25]

21. On the "ideology of the house" see Sabean, *Property, Production and Family*, pp. 88–123.
22. Engelsing, "Arbeitsmarkt der Dienstboten".
23. For the "North Sea System" which existed since the seventeenth century, see J. Lucassen, *Migrant Labour in Europe*.
24. For many forms of preindustrial mobility, see the bibliography by Müller and Matschinegg, "Migration – Wanderung – Mobilität in Spätmittelalter und Frühneuzeit".
25. Schubert, "Mobilität ohne Chance"; L. Lucassen, "Blind Spot".

Also, the mobility option was built into the practice of giving alms, which – apart from its ritual meaning – functioned as an informal and only partially localized insurance against fire, unemployment, the death of husbands and fathers, sickness, and many other risks. Although every village or larger territorial entity was expected to care for its own poor, municipalities unable to fulfil this obligation used to send these people away, relying on universal Christian solidarity. Foreign beggars could expect at least some travelling money when they were sent on and were sometimes transported for free. At least in cameralist theory, the increasing interpretation of the territorial state as a functional and closed entity eroded the role of the universal level of Christian solidarity. Far from being mobilized, central European society became more and more localistic during the formation of the modern territorial state.

The fifth type of migration resulted from the reformation and its consequences. The right to emigrate was granted to Lutherans, Catholics, and Calvinists. People affiliated with denominations other than the ones recognized by the state, however, had nowhere to settle where they might enjoy full legal rights. Voluntary and forced migration were especially frequent among such marginalized groups. Continuous religious migration and large-scale, long-distance migrations triggered by confessional considerations occurred during the seventeenth and eighteenth centuries. Church leadership of emigrant groups was not limited to cases of expulsion. In Zurich, for instance, pastors organized emigrations to Brandenburg and to North America.[26]

The sixth type of migration came into being because of the military ambitions of the emerging territorial states. To supply their armies, officials recruited hundreds of thousands of soldiers, including many from beyond the confines of their own territories. This practice increased mobility and mortality, both among the soldiers themselves and among the civilians they drove away in flight, killed, or infected with diseases. Contemporaries have even described the recruitment of soldiers as kidnapping in some cases.

Finally, the populationist doctrine that the wealth of a state depended on the number of its inhabitants gained considerable acceptance among European leaders after the devastations of the Thirty Years' War. Territories inside and outside the Holy Roman Empire recruited Germans, as did the numerous newly founded cities of the absolutist age. Officials even tried to populate parts of their territories that seemed to have fewer inhabitants than they deemed appropriate by inducing immigration from more densely populated areas of the same state.

Reviewing all these varieties of migration suggests that socially accepted and well-known forms of spatial mobility were almost universally available in early-modern central Europe. The option of exiting, a hallmark of a capitalist market society, was an integral part of the preindustrial world. Although the concepts

---

26. Pfister, *Auswanderung aus dem Knonauer Amt*, pp. 117-120, 144-145.

and the descriptions I have provided of these channels of mobility are largely based on normative and bureaucratic sources, they were not actually products of early modern bureaucracy (e.g. by restricting certain categories of persons from moving except in the line of duty as servants). Rather, I should like to interpret these channels as structures of the collective knowledge available to potential migrants in the sense that any child in southwest Germany knew the ramifications of leaving the parental household, for example to enter domestic service.

As Bernard Bailyn has suggested, emigration to British North America should be understood within the context of such domestic mobility patterns.[27] Mass migration from the Rhine lands to British North America evolved as an extension and modification of the traditional channels of mobility. This evolution occurred in three partly parallel phases. Prior to the foundation of Germantown by Francis Daniel Pastorius in 1683, German migration to North America was little more than a spillover. Mobility was so characteristic of German society that some persons were certain to find their way to America, even if only through other countries that had established contacts with British North America. Pastorius's separatist and quasi-nationalistic project deserves to be seen as a form of the mobility by religious minorities. The project should also be counted among a second type of transatlantic migrations, which we might label trial-and-error migrations. Such endeavours served ambitious if not necessarily realistic intentions that were organized by official institutions, private entrepreneurs, and religious groups. A similar situation applied with respect to the huge emigration wave of 1709, when over 13,000 Palatines migrated to England, hoping in vain to be transported to Carolina. This migratory experiment had started as a successful combination of pastors' mobility, religious emigration, and collective alms-seeking. Only a small fraction of these migrants, however, managed even to reach New York. As a consequence of this disappointment, German migration to the Carolinas and to New York never became a continuous stream in the eighteenth century. Nevertheless, the trend described by Marianne Wokeck as a pattern of "unsustained flows" continued throughout the century. Wokeck uses this phrase to describe an initial strong lure to settle in a particular place that subsequently "failed for some reason to generate direct immigration over the long term".[28] Some of these projects involved the recruitment of non-agrarian labour by entrepreneurs, a practice that was of course far from unusual in Europe as well. Colonies and private investors repeatedly tried to attract Swiss or Germans to settlements that had been founded upon rather questionable assumptions. One example was climate theory.[29]

27. Bailyn, *Peopling of British North America*, p. 20.
28. Wokeck, "Harnessing the Lure", p. 225.
29. During the seventeenth and eighteenth centuries, it was believed that the climate of a given

Another involved the beliefs of the founders of Broad Bay, Massachusetts, who thought that German migrants had a desire to "know who will be their loving and helpful lord in America". Although the Broad Bay founders tried to brand the transport of emigrants to Pennsylvania as materialistic and disorderly, they failed to convince large numbers of German subjects (who turned out to have little need for *Obrigkeit*). All in all, we might see these trial-and-error migrations as a process of collective exploration. While until 1709 many Germans thought of Pennsylvania and Carolina as islands, the subsequent restriction of this misconception to occasional bureaucratic documents suggests that Germans were learning from experience after 1730.

Although the appeal of the various European and American options to the emigrants concerned during the eighteenth century remains unknown, Pennsylvania established a name for itself as "the best poor man's country". Farm sizes, soil fertility, wages, and opportunities for demographic reproduction differed dramatically between Germany and Pennsylvania. Before the 1740s, immigrants who left Europe and had some money of their own had especially strong prospects of upward mobility. Topical German historiography fails to emphasize the advantages of conditions in Pennsylvania over those in Germany, partly because these benefits did not figure in the perspective of German bureaucrats on emigration.

Two additional factors were crucial in producing the "self-generating momentum" (Wokeck) that enabled migration to Pennsylvania – as opposed to other North American destinations – to enter the third phase, one of mass migration. These factors were the existence of a network of informal connections to the Rhine lands and the availability of credit.[30] The network resulted from the small but steady stream of religious groups moving into Pennsylvania.[31] By the 1730s, this number been insufficient to turn Pennsylvania into a country where everybody lived up to the spiritual ideals of the area's first New Christian inhabitants. Instead, the German pietists had helped their more materialistic compatriots explore the worldly opportunities available in North America. Thus, the "prototype of a transatlantic mass migration" developed out of increasingly routine contact and more accurate information. Such a process was, in a European context, far from unique. Some migration movements that began as highly experimental and controlled operations turned into more spontaneous and self-generating streams after their first successes.

Travel to Pennsylvania, however, was far more expensive than travel from Switzerland to the Palatinate. Turning the occasional spillover of individual

---

place primarily depended on its degree of latitude. Victims of this theory included the settlers of Jamestown, Virginia and Purysburg, South Carolina.

30. Wokeck, "Harnessing the Lure", p. 219.
31. Fogleman has estimated that between 3,077 and 5,550 German-speaking radical pietists and anabaptists immigrated to the thirteen colonies. See Table 4.1, p. 103 of his *Hopeful Journeys*.

migrants and the movement of small organized groups into a migration involving considerable numbers required means for financing the passage. "Redemptioner" migration solved the problem by transporting passengers on credit with the understanding that they would serve a variable term with a Pennsylvanian master who would pay off their debts. About half of all German immigrants entered servitude for terms between two and five years.[32] From a British point of view, such agreements were a modification of indentured servitude. From a German perspective, however, they were similar to *Gesindedienst* and servant markets.

The consequences of this innovation for the passage market are reflected in the absolute numbers of immigrants arriving in Philadelphia, which increased sharply between 1727 and 1754. Also, the development of transport fares shows how credit made mass transport possible. Passengers travelling from Rotterdam to Philadelphia consistently paid about five or six pounds sterling throughout the period before 1770 (with higher prices during wars than in times of peace). The prices payable by the merchants of Rotterdam to the ship owners, however, declined sharply to one or two pounds per freight after 1730. This change may be attributable to the increased tonnage of the ships used in this traffic. They also carried larger numbers of passengers and were more densely packed than in the early years. Rotterdam sources support Farley Grubb's assertion that the passage market was not monopolized. The British merchants of Rotterdam, frequently accused of selfishness in the older literature, are therefore unlikely to have had any chance to cheat their poor German passengers systematically. Rather, the merchants passed at least part of the diminished costs of transatlantic transport that they enjoyed as a result of operating on a larger scale after 1730 on to the passengers. They accepted more and poorer passengers on credit, even at the increased risk of never being paid. Thus the merchants enabled more sections of the German population than before to migrate to North America.[33] The risk of carrying poorer Germans and Swiss to Philadelphia, however, only paid off as long as Pennsylvania masters contracted the services of large numbers of German redemptioners. During the French and Indian War, many indentured servants were recruited and replaced by slaves. This unique type of transatlantic labour brokerage did not resume in the recession that followed the war.[34]

The everyday character of German migration to Pennsylvania in this third phase is also apparent from the processes of cultural transfer and the integration of Germans in North America. Although the legal system was different in the

32. Grubb, "Incidence of Servitude"; Grubb, "Auction of Redemptioner Servants".
33. Wokeck, "Tide of Alien Tongues"; Wokeck, "Harnessing the Lure"; Grubb, "Market Structure of Shipping", p. 46. Only after 1770 did fares increase to approximately fifteen pounds per freight. Prices at Rotterdam: Gemeentelijke archiefdienst Rotterdam, ONA.
34. For the consequences of the economic recession of the 1760s on the Philadelphia labour market, see Salinger, *"To Serve Well and Faithfully"*, pp. 134-135.

new environment, Germans could apply their own sense of justice to settle their inheritance matters.[35] Germans preserved their separate domestic customs, language, and religion, while adapting successfully to the needs of economic and legal-political interaction with the English-speaking people. German-American networks of communication, maintained by pastors, merchants, and printers, ensured both preservation and adaptation. The occasional spillover migration of the seventeenth century and the organized trial-and-error migration of the early eighteenth century seem to have brought German transatlantic migrants into a puzzling, possibly dangerous, and adventuresome new environment. By the mid-eighteenth century, however, the mass migration to Philadelphia can best be understood as yet another migration option that was available to most people who lived in the Rhine lands.

3. The double discourse on "causes of migration"

The evolutionary interpretation of migration to North America presented on the preceding pages would not have appealed to all observers of the time. State and church authorities considered transatlantic migration sensational in scale, hardly comprehensible in motivation, irresponsible, dangerous, and generally deplorable. This negative value judgement was not confined to transatlantic migration – authorities had tried to prevent or to curtail migration since the Middle Ages. The peasants, on the other hand, clearly took a different view of migration. Their interpretations of their decisions to migrate are not easily apparent in the extant sources. The migrants did not frequently participate in the discourse on "causes of emigration" that developed during the early modern period. Discussions of "why I decided to emigrate" simply do not appear in their letters. Migrants tended to emphasize that everybody was free to reach his own decision whether to emigrate or not; they did not go beyond the "free will" of a given person to elucidate deeper causes of that person's decision. Most contemporary explanations of the reasons for the decision of a given person or of people in general to migrate occurred either in a normative context or in discussions about whether a particular destination could be recommended. Both discussions were not about the circumstances that induced otherwise immobile men and women to move and that should be changed if a happy state of sedentariness was to be restored, but about arguments for or against migration – not about causality but about justification, not about causes but about reasons.[36]

35. Roeber, "The Origins and Transfer".
36. The latter distinction would be hard to convey in eighteenth century language because the German word most frequently used for "reason" or "argument" at the time was *Ursache* (cause). Officials might, for example, reach the conclusion that "the applicants do not have

The discussions pro and contra emigration to North America that were printed in Switzerland and Germany reveal that the criteria for the acceptability of emigration could be either religious or economic. Religious arguments invoked either persecution or clear signs from the Lord that one had to leave.[37] As only about 4 percent of the German emigrants to British North America belonged to the Pietist and Anabaptist groups, however, these arguments were not overly relevant. The economic arguments were more important. Supporters of emigration emphasized the advantages of migration, adversaries stressed the risks. Especially the German bureaucrats who habitually argued against migration manifested an almost paranoid obsession with the risks of spatial mobility. In 1628, for instance, Württemberg officials were ordered to warn prospective emigrants about the "obvious danger" to which they were exposing themselves.[38] In Baden-Durlach, officials claimed that emigrants to Pennsylvania would be led on a "long and arduous way to a rough, stony, mountainous, cold, and barren country" – an utterly incorrect statement that can be traced to a pro-emigration pamphlet on Virginia read by a member of the government, who overlooked dozens of pages with favourable descriptions of Virginia and Pennsylvania until he finally found two totally disjointed negative remarks, one of which referred to the odyssey of some emigrants to South Carolina, the other to the unsettled hinterlands of Pennsylvania.[39] In 1748, a Hanau official showed an equally strong inclination to selective perception when he suggested to some emigrants to Pennsylvania "that only a minority of such emigrants reach their destinations, but they are mostly kidnapped on their way and either forced to serve on ships, or they are abducted to the Indian plantations". The emigrants themselves proved to be better informed: "According to the news they have received, all these emigrants have been transported to their correct destination", as their spokesman stated.[40] In any case, the logic of such anti-migration propaganda implies that the potential migrants were thought to act according to a subjective rationale by weighing possible advantages and disadvantages to reach a sound and economic decision.

The same logic underlies behind the most usual pro-emigration arguments. Not every advantage, however, was an acceptable reason for emigration. The encouragement two emigrants from Bern gave ("Here one can subsist by working two months a year, so if you like wealth, come and join us") met with

a justified cause to leave the country". Even today, the reason-cause distinction is not firmly rooted in everyday German usage. *Grund* ("reason") is now frequently used as a synonym for *Ursache* (cause).

37. Reference was usually made to the exile of Abraham (Genesis 12, 1).
38. Hippel, *Auswanderung aus Südwestdeutschland*, p. 96.
39. Generallandesarchiv Karlsruhe 74/84, 4 November 1737.
40. Freeden and Smolka, "Deutsche Auswanderung im 18. Jahrhundert", p. 118.

the scepticism of emigration critics, who held that "most people who move to that place [...] think the new country is a Cockaigne where everything you wish will come to your house while you are sleeping, or where it falls into your open mouth".[41] Both the wish "to become rich and grand" and the desire to avoid work were unacceptable to early modern moralists. The distinction between acceptable and unacceptable gains, however, was far from clear-cut. Economic justifications for migration were acceptable as long as the expected advantage did not exceed a certain limit. The intention to "improve one's luck", to look for "better nourishment", or for a "better living" have been stereotype formulas for both internal and for external migrations. "Nourishment", indeed, had been the standard justification for spatial mobility in German society since the Middle Ages.[42] This value served a function similar to the concept of virtue for social mobility: while German society was, in fact, far from immobile in either social or spatial respects, the idea that people should remain satisfied with their station in life was commonplace in legal and religious discourse. As Winfried Schulze has shown, virtue legitimized upward mobility. Likewise, nourishment – or the lack thereof – could justify physical movement.[43]

The concept of nourishment will be very familiar to any German sociologist. Since Werner Sombart's often-quoted description of the spirit of pre-capitalist economy, nourishment has been understood as a traditional principle that adjusted consumption to the fixed needs of the different social ranks and that was opposed to the capitalist principle of acquisitiveness.[44] The statements above about the Süssmilchian "principle of *Stellen*", however, also apply to this concept of fixed and limited needs. No socially defined level of subsistence existed for everybody in southwest Germany. The accumulation of wealth over a lifetime was the rule, as children were frequently allowed to leave the parental household without much property. While the Christian idea that everybody should be content with life's necessities was of course propagated in the early modern period, it was an almost utopian concept. Accordingly, it is not surprising that the Pietist emigrant Christopher Sower, discontented with the economic orientation of his fellow Germans, believed he had observed a perfect state of subsistence orientation among the Amerindians of Pennsylvania: "They do not gather more than they expect to eat. If a man's wife dies between seed-time and

41. *Der nunmehro in der Neuen Welt vergnügt und ohne Heimwehe Lebende Schweitzer* (Bern, 1734).

42. See, for example, the *Weistum* (codification of rural local law) of Helfant (1600): "When a poor man (i.e. a subject) is not able to nourish himself here and wants to move away, he shall settle up with his lord and neighbours in all matters and move wherever he wants to" (Grimm, *Deutsche Rechtsalterthümer*, Vol. 1, p. 137).

43. On virtue, see Schulze, "Ständische Gesellschaft des 16./17. Jahrhunderts". On nourishment, compare Blickle, "Nahrung und Eigentum".

44. Sombart, *Bourgeois*, pp. 11-25.

harvest, he gathers only for himself; the remainder is left standing."[45] No Rhenish peasant would ever have exhibited such behaviour. The "principle of nourishment" was accepted as a limitation of the extremes of the economic order: nobody should be "rich" (i.e. nobody's possessions should exceed the level appropriate to his position), and nobody should have less than he needed and live in *Nothdurfft* (deprivation). Within these limits, better nourishment was preferable to worse; and *reichliches Auskommen* (an ample living) was certainly better than *nothdürfftiges Auskommen* (a meagre living).[46] Also, assuming that the average peasant ever wasted much thought about reaching a maximum of desirable wealth is rather pointless. Acquiring the minimum necessary for subsistence was difficult enough.

During the early modern period a second discourse on the *Ursachen* of emigration developed – a discourse that comprised Friedrich List's task in 1817. This discourse has given rise to the view that emigration must have causes (which should be removed so that emigration can be prevented); this view is one of the constituent elements of the revolutionary model of emigration history because the causes of emigration in this sense are meant to explain why a presumably fixed society turned mobile. One important root of this discourse seems to be the political connotation of outmigration. Leaving a territory implied the termination of a contract-like relationship between lord and subject; it therefore offered a code for protest against any perceived deficiency in this relationship. This quality of emigration as a means for expressing discontent through symbolic behaviour appears even in texts with medieval origins. Disappointment among villagers could lead to collective and conspicuous *Austreten* (leaving).[47] Even in the context of smaller conflicts, peasants made clear that they would have to emigrate if their demands were not met. For emigrants, such protest arguments offered two advantages. On the one had, these claims enabled them, by attributing their emigration to pressure from their lords or the state, to shift the responsibility for their decisions to the authorities and to justify a decision considered morally problematic, at least by the authorities. On the other hand, emigrants could thus demonstrate their disapproval of the bones of contention between peasants and lords. By confronting their emigrating subjects, authorities both recorded and generated this discourse of protest.[48] Johannes Kleinefeller, for instance, a wealthy peasant from Lohrhaupten in Hessia, was asked by the official *Amtmann* Wannemacher, "what moved him to his intended

---

45. Christoph Saur, 1.12.1724, in Kelsey, "Early Description of Pennsylvania", p. 248.
46. Johann H. Zedler, *Großes vollständiges Universallexicon* (Halle/Leipzig, 1732-1754), s.v. "Alimentum", "Nahrung", "Nöthiges Auskommen", "Nothdurfft", "Reichliches Auskommen", "Reichthum", "Subsistentz", "Unterhalt".
47. Schulze, *Bäuerlicher Widerstand*, pp. 93-95.
48. On emigration and protest, compare Moltmann, "German Emigration to the United States".

emigration, and what causes had he to give for it?". Kleinefeller complained about the calculation of taxes, forest laws, and irrigation rules.[49] He obviously accepted the official's negative value judgement on emigration, but blamed his decision to emigrate on the policies of the government. Implicitly, both Kleinefeller and Wannemacher thought of emigration as something that could be averted through prudent policy – which may have been feasible for emigration out of protest, but certainly not in general.

Most contemporary political theorists subscribed to the same inadequate view. The early modern German states were led by bureaucrats who adhered to eudaemonistic doctrines and developed utopian ideologies of reform intended to form a closed territory, a closed set of competences, and a closed body of subjects who would stay happily at home.[50] Of course, few German cameralists would have agreed with the nationalist philosopher Johann Gottlieb Fichte, who stated that "any intercourse with the foreigner must be forbidden to the subject and must be made impossible".[51] According to the generally accepted doctrine, however, common happiness was the purpose of the territorial state and depended on the number of its inhabitants. While immigration should be encouraged, emigration was seen both as harmful and as proof of a fundamentally bad state of affairs. Interpretations of the causes of emigration as a result of unfortunate circumstances differed.

"Overpopulation" was a very popular interpretation in the early eighteenth century. The *Amtmann* of Steinau argued in this fashion in his report on emigration from Schlüchtern to Lithuania: "The general causes why it looks so bad at Schlüchtern, that even the better sort has to suffer, are due to the fact that [...] the number of inhabitants is too high."[52] Both officials and subjects tended to see population increase as threatening. Although, as I have argued above, society did not actually regulate the demographic reproduction of its members by restricting this practice to a limited number of positions, the view seems to have been widespread that all good was limited, that consumption by additional persons would diminish the consumption of the others, and that "overpopulation" was the necessary consequence of population increase. In emphasizing "overpopulation", modern theorists thus repeat a traditional world view, which, as the ethnologist George M. Foster argued in 1965, is universal in peasant societies.[53]

While officials subscribing to the overpopulation approach used to accept emigration as a necessary evil, population optimists objected to this view. In

49. Staatsarchiv Marburg, Bestand 80 Hanauer Geheimer Rat, XII A 7, 1 February 1751.
50. On bureaucratic eudaemonism, see Maier, *Ältere deutsche Staats- und Verwaltungslehre.*
51. Fichte, *Der geschloßne Handelsstaat*, pp. 58-59.
52. Staatsarchiv Marburg, Bestand 80 Hanauer Geheimer Rat XII A 1 17, 6 August 1740.
53. Foster, "Peasant Society".

Baden-Durlach, for instance, a shift in population theory gave rise to a change in migration policy during the 1760s. Traditionally, poor emigrants to North America were seen as superfluous in their original area of residence. Migrants of some means were also allowed to leave the margravate, provided they paid their departure tax. Only occasionally did officials exhort emigrants to "stay in the country and make an honest living" or make sarcastic remarks about their aspirations. These policies changed when the government adopted the population optimism of the influential Prussian cameralist Johann H. von Justi.[54] Justi mainly attributed emigration to bad government, lack of religious freedom, or lack of "nourishment" in the Süssmilchian sense and advocated that the governments attempt to determine the causes for the emigration in question and that they avoid depopulation by eliminating these factors.[55] At the same time, physiocracy gained influence in Baden-Durlach, and Johann A. Schlettwein (the leading German physiocrat) joined the government. These developments indicated that agrarian conditions were thought of as appropriate for and in need of radical change by a wise government. Consequently, research on causes of emigration became a powerful instrument for the endeavour to diagnose reform necessities. In February 1769, the government denied permission to emigrate to Pennsylvania to Michel Weisenbacher (a poor bricklayer) and the widow Ebelin, two residents of the village of Dietlingen who wished to follow the example of a dozen of their neighbours before them.[56] Instead, their applications set off a chain reaction of government concern. "What are the causes of this disaster?" Minister Reinhard asked. Thorough investigations were subsequently held in the village and revealed, not surprisingly, that Dietlingen was in desperate need of agrarian reform. Therefore, a single tax system was introduced in the village, cows and grain were donated to the poor peasants, and the place was given freedom of trade. This physiocratic reform experiment, which may have had other merits, did not, however, prove able to keep Michael Weisenbacher's family at home, who finally emigrated in 1771.

Better arguments for the reform experiment of Dietlingen may have existed. All the same, the Baden-Durlach government decided to use emigration as the main indicator of the need for reform. I should like to suggest that the government's perspective on emigration was highly ideological, and, in fact, inappropriate. The ideological quality did not reflect the government's idea (like all German governments of the time) that emigration was against its own interest. The more subjects stayed in the country, the more workers, soldiers, and tax

---

54. Johann Jacob Reinhard, the most influential member of government, has described the change in Durlach policy in his "Versuch einer pracktischen Betrachtung", Ms. ca. 1769, Generallandesarchiv Karlsruhe 65/1030.

55. Justi, *Grundfeste zu der Macht*, Vol. 1, pp. 256-259.

56. Generallandesarchiv Karlsruhe 171/2791, 229/18955

payers were indeed available. Rather, the idea that the prevention of migration served not only the interest of the government, but also the needs of the migrants themselves, and that therefore the prevention of migration could be a realistic strategy of a benevolent government manifested profound ideological convictions. This scenario, however, was not the case in reality. The Baden-Durlach government pursued two strategies of migration prevention, both grounded on the incorrect assumption that it was in the migrants' interest to stay. The first strategy consisted of warning potential emigrants and informing them of the horrible fate that awaited them in North America. The problem with this strategy was that the government's information was wrong and that the emigrants were better informed than the officials. The second strategy consisted of the attempt to remove anything labelled as "causes of emigration". Nevertheless, as long as Baden-Durlach was not the "best poor man's country" in the world – which it never managed to become – and as long as the subjects viewed migration as a normal option open to everybody, a society where everybody would happily stay at home remained a Utopia.

From Justi, List, and the other enlightened bureaucrats, the historiography of German migration has inherited some important if implicit attitudes and assumptions. First, migrants have frequently been looked upon as victims. Migration seemed to be a bad thing – not only for the power-maximizing states they left, but also for the migrants themselves. The cameralist school of thought, did not allow for a distinction between the true interest of the state and the individual. Even though the resulting tragic school of migration historiography is now surrendering to historical revisionism, the bureaucratic stereotype that migrants usually cherished false hopes persists. Second, it was held that migration was a bad thing, but that the world was good. Therefore, a harmonious, functional, and encompassing society without exit must have existed at some point in history. Both a pessimistic and an optimistic version of this concept can be traced to early modern political thought and still inform much of migration historiography. The pessimistic or traditional bureaucratic version holds that this happy and sedentary society existed in the past (e.g. before the industrial revolution, or before medieval society lost cohesion) and has decayed since. According to the optimistic, late cameralist or early liberal version, society is actually designed as a closed entity that can and must be placated by the state, and people will remain in their proper places in the absence of any mistakes. Migration therefore reflects sociopolitical imperfections or causes. As society is designed wisely, however, migration is not exclusively bad. Rather, migration also has a balancing or safety valve function – people will migrate until no more migration is necessary. Third, because in the Justi and List tradition we are primarily interested in the alleged alarm function of migration, historians and social scientists have frequently neglected aspects that could not be translated into defects of policy – most importantly the autopoietic and uncontrollable dynamics of networks. Some have assumed that the justifications migrants give for their decisions reflect the dynamics of the process; others have identified the ill-defined phenomenon of overpopulation as a generic "defect of policy". Nevertheless, the benevolent state and its ability to make its subjects happy can not provide an adequate framework for the interpretation of human mobility. No physiocratic reform experiment could keep the inhabitants of Dietlingen at home, and no development – let alone anti-overpopulation – policy will exempt us from sharing our world with migrants.

The Great Wall Against China: Responses to the First Immigration Crisis, 1885-1925

Aristide R. Zolberg

Introduction

Since human migrations generally "reflect the world as it is at the time",[1] it stands to reason that the conjunction of epochal changes that took place in the final decades of the long nineteenth century, which Geoffrey Barraclough identified as the beginning of "contemporary history", also constituted a turning point in the history of population movements.[2] Most visibly, these changes induced a vast increase in the numbers of people on the move world-wide, and in the distances they covered; concomitantly, there was a diversification of the cultural composition of the pool of migrants and a linking up of hitherto isolated currents into a single interconnected global stream. But ironically, the very states that stimulated the expansion of the migration system came to view the masses on the move as posing an unprecedented "immigration crisis", to which they reacted by erecting a great wall. Hence the specificity of the epoch arises precisely from the emergence of an unprecedented and growing gap between *potential* and *actual* international movement, which contributed to a sharpening of the boundary between "internal" and "external" realms, and ultimately between "us" and "them".

This paper highlights the crucial role of states in shaping the history of international migration, especially in the form of regulation of immigration in the countries of potential destination. The reference to China in the title is meant to indicate that the reactions to the onset of a substantial migration of Chinese to the Pacific-rim white settler countries (the United States, Canada, Australia) constituted a prelude for the more comprehensive change of immigration policy that followed. It was in the course of dealing with the issue of Chinese immigration that the United States developed the legal rationale for barring the entry of certain groups, as well as the administrative organization for doing so. Widely commented on in Europe, these measures were subsequently invoked in both the overseas countries and in Europe to support restrictions directed at other groups, notably a variety of Asians, Jews and non-Jews from eastern Europe, and ultimately mass migrants of any kind. Conversely, the proliferation of anti-

---

1. Davis, "Migrations of Human Populations".
2. Barraclough, *Introduction to Contemporary History*.

Chinese measures alerted American and European Jews to the fact that they might be similarly targeted, and prompted them to undertake preventive action. This challenges standard historiography, which has tended to treat responses to Asian immigration among the countries in question as a special case.

Although it would be too much to speak of explicit concertation among the states involved, there is no doubt that the new policies were highly *interactive*, in that decision-makers in each of the individual states were aware of the global situation, and viewed enhanced border control as necessary because of increased "migration pressure" occasioned by the closing of doors elsewhere. Given the growing interconnectedness of disparate migratory flows, they perceived the situation as a constant sum game; the fear of being subjected to increasing pressure and of acting too late to keep out unwanted immigrants triggered anticipatory moves, and thereby determined an upward spiral of restriction. The dynamics involved were thus simultaneously national and international. In this manner, parallel actions by individual states – with some variation in timing and degree of closure – resulted in the emergence of a *restrictive international migration regime*, with *zero immigration* as its normative baseline. This was rationalized on a dual basis: on the one hand the economic welfare of the receiving society, particularly employment conditions; and on the other its spiritual and political welfare, focusing on the undesirability of changes in the existing culture and established ethnic composition. In keeping with prevailing norms, this was usually expressed in the form of xenophobic and racialist ideologies.

Until very recently, the historiography of the turn to restriction was entirely American. Nowhere was the change more dramatic than in the United States, then the single most important receiving country, where within the span of one generation, arrivals were reduced from over one million a year to about 150,000, and immigration was in effect eliminated as a significant factor of social change. Since this was attributable almost entirely to the adoption of restrictive legislation, the nascent historiography of immigration in the post-World War II period focused largely on "restrictionism" as a social and political movement. This reflected the efforts of self consciously "liberal" historians – the word is used here in its American sense, akin to a mildly social-democratic position – who sympathized explicitly with attempts to reform the immigration laws in the direction of greater openness. Hence the leading explanation for restriction, as set forth notably in the works of Oscar Handlin and in John Higham's classic *Strangers in the Land*, was psychological, a paranoid response to anxiety induced by accelerated modernization. This was in keeping also with the broader interpretation of American political character set forth by Richard Hofstadter in such works as *The American Political Tradition*.[3]

---

3.   Hofstadter, *The American Political Tradition*.

However, a U.S.-centered "internalist" explanation fails to account for parallel contemporaneous developments in other countries, and this fact in turns suggests an explanation might be found at the *global* rather than the national level. This is indeed the major theme developed here. The starting point is a conjunction of world-wide changes, which resulted in a suddenly much enlarged pool of potential international migrants, and also much more heterogeneous with regard to cultural composition. As will be detailed later on, these changes pertained primarily to the world-wide expansion of market forces, which created a forceful "push"; and to this were added forced population movements generated by the transformation of empires into states.[4] Although this does not in itself account for restrictive responses, there is no denying that potential receivers did face an unprecedented challenge in the sphere of immigration, for which existing regulatory institutions were inadequate. A number of concomitant factors, spanning the global and the national levels, account for their generally negative reaction. Overall, the prospect of a vastly increased influx of foreigners occurred at a time of increasing concern with national integration and social control in the receiving societies, in response to political democratization, the emergence of the welfare state, as well as increasing international tensions.[5] It should be noted also that an increasing proportion of the immigrants belonged to groups that were undesirable according to *preexisting* norms in the receiving societies.

1. Epochal Changes

It was only in the final decades of the nineteenth century that the capitalist market economy and the national state, long in gestation within a limited group of countries, became truly worldwide forms of social organization. Somewhat paradoxically, while this was manifestly an age of acute nationalism, it was also a moment of perceptible globalization of the economic, strategic, and cultural spheres. The globe was linked by way of transcontinental railroad networks and transoceanic steamship lines into a single web of mass transportation; and the combination of rapidly spreading literacy with cheap printing, enhanced by the telegraph and photography, concurrently produced an integrated sphere of world-wide communication, fostering the emergence of rudimentary elements

---

4. Regarding the uprooting effects of the economic transformation, the seminal work is Polanyi's *Great Transformation*. For a theoretical argument regarding the transformation of empires, see Zolberg, "Formation of New States". The relevant history is detailed by Marrus in *The Unwanted: European Refugees*.
5. Within the vast literature on the development of nationalist ideologies, see especially Anderson, *Imagined Communities*. For the military dimension in European state-formation, see C. Tilly, *Coercion, Capital, and European States*. For an investigation of the effect of "nationalization" on immigration policy in France, see Noiriel, *Tyrannie du national*.

of a genuinely global culture. But at the same time, the unevenness of world conditions was accentuated, with a growing gap between a small group of capital-rich, technologically advanced, and concomitantly strategically powerful countries, European or of European origin plus Japan, and the rest. Internal conditions among the latter were henceforth largely determined by the transnational economic, social, cultural, and political processes generated by the leading countries, all of which also engaged in colonial expansion.[6]

Although the leading countries were becoming liberal democracies, with governments accountable to broadly-based representative bodies, this was combined with an expanding and more centralized state apparatus, giving the state a much greater capacity for internal and external intervention.[7] Economic competition among the leading states in a worldwide arena, under conditions of accentuated economic fluctuations whose effects were concomitantly worldwide, resulted in the reorganization of the global economy into neomercantilist segments. These rivalries interacted with the evolution of three of the world's states – the United Kingdom, the Russian Empire, and the United States – into a new breed of superpowers, either by virtue of continental size and commensurately large population, or by virtue of an extensive maritime empire. The strategic chess-board expanded as well to encompass hitherto marginal regions, particularly the Pacific. Undermining the century-old Concert of Europe, these developments rendered international conflict more likely; and once it erupted, the processes it unleashed further exacerbated global dislocations.

There were also epochal changes in the demographic sphere, aptly summarized by Barraclough's phrase, "the dwarfing of Europe".[8] After a period of rapid population growth occasioned by a drop in the death rate, the industrialized countries experienced a fertility decline, which afforded them a population structure that was more efficient in relation to the new economic dynamics. Consequently, whereas in the previous century and a half western populations had grown at a more rapid rate than the rest, the difference was now reversed, and subsequently widened further. This development attracted considerable attention because it entailed a dramatic shift in the relative importance of white and colored populations, at a time when "racial" differences were being essentialized. For contemporaneous elites, this ominous phenomenon reenacted at the international level the inability of European ruling strata to maintain their demographic strength within their own societies. In a world sharply divided between haves and have-nots, and a time when population size was reckoned

6. For a good overview, see Hobsbawm, *Age of Empire*.
7. This analysis, which contests the conventional notion whereby greater liberalism is assumed to entail lesser state power, is founded on Michael Mann's distinction between "despotic" and "infrastructural" power.
8. Barraclough, *Introduction to Contemporary History*, p. 65.

as a vital component of international power, the decreasing fertility of the haves came to be viewed as a dangerous form of unilateral disarmament.[9]

Rapid population expansion in the world at large was expected to produce a Malthusian crisis of subsistence, for which the only remedy would be migration. By 1900, Barraclough suggests, there was an "almost neurotic awareness of this process", expressed most egregiously by way of warnings regarding "the yellow peril".[10] Although this was attributable in large measure to a projection of widespread racist fantasms regarding Asia, the belief that economic development occasioned massive uprooting was hardly irrational, but rather a sound extrapolation of ongoing western experience, which was consecrated by E.G. Ravenstein in his classic 1885 presentation to the fellows of the Royal Statistical Society as one of the fundamental laws of migration.[11]

The world was indeed very much more on the move, as ever more people were propelled from their native localities in search of work. Whereas over the long term, the transformation of agrarian societies unto industrial ones might enable them to sustain a much larger population, and at a higher standard of living, the catastrophic impact of the "great transformation" on the countryside left many people with no alternative but to leave home.[12] Since the larger population resulting from improvements in the production and distribution of food shared finite land resources, the proportion of landless laborers increased. As land became more concentrated and production more specialized, particularly with the introduction of sugar beet as a leading crop of northwestern Europe, farmers found the traditional system of service based on an annual contract providing for housing as well as wages economically burdensome; and with the shift to short-term wage work, social ties and shared interests binding landlords to workers were severed, leaving large numbers without housing or sustenance. The presence of a greater rural population also rendered crop failures more devastating. And finally, as capital moved to urban sites and fled some regions altogether, the European countryside was deindustrialized; chances for village work disappeared and the pay rates for rural goods declined, reducing the ability of country workers to get by in the local cottage economy.

In the classic formulation, these "push" forces were combined with the "pull" of demand generated by the vigorously growing agro-industrial and industrial

---

9. Teitelbaum and Winter, *Fear of Population Decline*. The role of population in relation to international power was emphasized by the "geopolitical school" of international relations that flourished around the turn of the century, and was revised in the United States (in opposition to "Wilsonian idealism" after World War II). See, for example, early editions of Hans Morgenthau's foundational textbook, *Politics Among Nations*.

10. Barraclough, *Introduction to Contemporary History*, pp. 80-81.

11. Ravenstein, "Laws of Migration".

12. Moch, *Moving Europeans*, pp. 104-160. For the process of transformation more generally, see the classic work by Polanyi, *Great Transformation*.

sectors. Eschewing traditional craftsmen and women, they were eager for less skilled, less expensive, more docile, and more disposable labor. Migrants from less developed regions, within the state itself – as in the case of Ireland in relation to the United Kingdom, or Bretons in France – or from outside – as with Russian Poles in Germany, Flemish Belgians in France, Swedes in Denmark and later Finns in Sweden – were especially *convenient* for these purposes.[13]

An important contributing factor to the expansion of transnational movement was the easing of legal and administrative barriers to *emigration* among the latecomers. This marked a major turn in policy, since during the period of absolutism and mercantilism, which coincided by and large with an epoch of slow population growth (or even of decline), subjects and the services they were capable of performing were in effect part of the sovereign's domain; unauthorized departure was a form of treason, and punishable as such – including often retaliation against relations who remained behind. In this vein, most European states reacted to the emergence of an independent overseas republic that welcomed immigrants by reinforcing measures against exit.[14] The turning point came in the late 1820s, when in keeping with the principles of the new political economy, Britain relinquished prohibitions against the emigration of skilled subjects. Moreover, emigration was discovered to be a cost-effective solution to the mounting burden of poor relief, as well as a safety-valve for social unrest, particularly in the troublesome Irish periphery. Within a few decades, the Swiss cantons, the German principalities, and the Scandinavian kingdoms followed suit. Similarly among the latecomers, for example, legal restrictions on exit from Spain remained very tight up the 1850s, then relaxed, and by 1903 passports and governmental permission were no longer required at all.[15]

In the last third of the nineteenth century, physical travel between regions, countries, and even continents, was vastly facilitated by the development of an integrated world-wide network of rapid and inexpensive mass transportation based on steam power. Railroad development was especially dramatic among the late developers in Europe, as well as overseas. In Austria-Hungary the total numbers of kilometers of track soared from 6,112 un 1871 to 22,981 in 1913, in Russia from 10,731 to 62,300, in Norway from 359 to 3,085, and in Italy from 6,429 to 18,873.[16] On the receiving side, the U.S. total grew from 85,170 in 1870 to 386,714 in 1910; Canada experienced an even more dramatic growth, from a mere 4,211 in 1870 to 39,799 in 1910; and that rate of expansion was

13. Given its familiarity, there is no need to rehearse the vast literature on the subject, beginning with Marx and Engels's analysis of the use of the Irish in Britain. For a brief discussion of recent theoretical developments, see Zolberg, "Next Waves".
14. For the historical background, see Zolberg, "International Migration Policies".
15. Nugent, *Crossings*, p. 103.
16. Mitchell, *European Historical Statistics*, table G1, pp. 583-584.

in turn surpassed by latecomers such as Argentina (from 732 to 27,713) and Brazil (from 745 to 21,326). Similar processes were taking place in Asia and somewhat later in parts of Africa.

The major turning point in the economics of ocean-crossing occurred in the 1860s, as the result of the replacement of sail by steam, then of the wheel by the screw, and of wood by iron – lighter, more lasting, and easier to repair – which together facilitated the building of much larger and faster ships, and thereby vastly increased the total capacity for passengers.[17] The change occurred very fast: in 1860 steam accounted for 31.5 percent of passenger traffic arriving in New York, by 1865 over half, and in 1870 over 90 percent. In 1856, transatlantic sailing vessels carried on the average 247 passengers, as against 232 for steam; but in 1870 the relationship was reversed, 153 as against 385; and by the 1880s, as many as 1,500 persons were occasionally packed into a single vessel.[18] The shipping industry expanded spectacularly: As of 1873, seventeen companies were operating 173 ships totalling over 500,000 tons between New York and Europe, with the largest ship around 4,000 tons: but by 1914, Hamburg-America alone operated 442 ships with 1.4 million tons, and the largest ship was over 50,000 tons.

Although the expansion of shipping capacity was a response to growing demand, it also contributed to the expansion of emigration, in that the companies actively promoted their services and recruited passengers, much as was the case earlier with regard to northwestern Europe, but on a commensurately much larger scale. In particular, the Hamburg-America Line developed a network of agents in Russia and Eastern Europe from the 1870s, and helped stimulate the great Jewish emigration. In the fall of 1894, in collaboration with the city of Hamburg, they built new port facilities, complete transient facilities for emigrants arriving by rail from neighboring regions of the Tsarist and Austro-Hungarian empires, including churches and synagogues. Altogether, of the 1.8 million who left Austria between 1870 and 1910, 1.3 used Hamburg or Bremen.[19] Shipping lines, like railroads, also helped to develop markets by moving closer to places of origin, for example by embarking passengers in Ireland, obviating the need to first sail to Liverpool. In many regions ships and railroads were integrated into well-established itineraries.

The cost of travel went down as well. On the New York run, the steerage price was about $40 in 1870, but down around $20 at the turn of the century, dipping even lower in years of depression such as 1894, when the fare from

17. Heffer, *Port de New York*, pp. 48, 160.
18. Nugent, *Crossings*, p. 31.
19. *Ibid.*, pp. 41, 85.

Ireland fell to $8.75.[20] As before, much of this was financed by remittances and prepaid tickets sent home from overseas, but the enlargement and diversification of the overseas immigrant communities had further amplifying effects.

Overall, the nexus of factors considered induced an expansion of international migrations to unprecedented and hitherto inconceivable levels. In the Atlantic region as a whole (including both within Europe and overseas) the combined international flows grew fourfold within a forty year period, from 2.7 million for the 1871-80 decade to over 11 million in 1901-10.[21] Overseas migration to the major receivers alone (Argentina, Brazil, Canada. and the U.S.A.) expanded in the same time period by an even more dramatic fivefold factor, from 2.6 million to 17.9 million. Although return migration increased as well, and probably constituted a growing share of the total, this matters little for present purposes, in that the perception of the receivers regarding the magnitude of immigration was governed, then as now, entirely by gross immigration figures.

What disturbed the receivers was not only that there were so many more immigrants, but that they were increasingly *strange*. There were objective grounds for this perception: since cultural differences tend to broaden as a function of distance, the steady geographical expansion of the pool meant that it encompassed an ever-growing proportion of groups that diverged markedly from accustomed norms. With regard to overseas Atlantic movement, at the beginning of the period under consideration the leading contributors were Britain (27 percent of the total), Germany, Ireland, and the Scandinavian group; but on the eve of World War One Britain had fallen to second place (23 percent of the total), with Italy now well ahead of the pack (33 percent), and Austro-Hungary and Spain in the lead quartet. On the basis of their relative contribution to overseas movement (decennial intercontinental emigration in proportion to national population), in 1871-80, the first four European emigration countries were Ireland, Britain, Norway, and Portugal, whereas in 1913 they were Italy, Portugal, Spain, and Britain; and while the annual rate of emigration for first-place Ireland in 1871-80 was 661 per 100,000 inhabitants, for Italy in 1913 it was nearly three times higher, 1,630 per 100,000. In fact, all four leaders at that time had an emigration rate above 1,000 per 100,000.[22]

20. Heffer, *Port de New York*, graph 19, p. 169; Nugent, *Crossings*, p. 51.
21. Computed from Nugent, *Crossings*, table 1, p. 12 (based on B.R. Mitchell, *European Historical Statistics*). Actual figures were undoubtedly somewhat higher because the table in question omits some of the lesser European contributors (notably Belgium and the Netherlands, Greece and others in the Balkans).
22. Nugent, *Crossings*, table 9, p. 43.

2. The Coming of the Chinese

Similar forces were already at work in various parts of what would later be called the "Third World" as well, largely as the result of more intrusive penetration by the industrializing countries, which between 1876 and 1915 appropriated one quarter of the globe's land surface, but also as a consequence of indigenous attempts to catch up. Some of the flows were entirely new, other followed well-established paths. After the extinction of the African slave trade, the two largest sources were India and China; but whereas Indians were largely confined to the tropical and sub-tropical colonies of the British Empire, the Chinese also migrated to the independent countries of the New World as well as to the "white" dominions. Hence they figured much more prominently in the "immigration crisis" that erupted at the turn of the century.

Southeast Asia had long been the domain of Chinese trading colonies and concomitant migrations.[23] Although the Chinese state's decision in the fifteenth century to throttle foreign commerce and create an unpopulated no man's land along the coast to prevent foreign contact with the Han population stemmed out-migration, labor continued to be exported by the Portuguese through Macao, and the Dutch East India Company captured Chinese along the China coast in order to populate its headquarter plantation in Batavia. Eager to procure labor for their expanding plantations (Malaya, Dutch East Indies) producing tropical commodities for the world market, at the end of the "Opium Wars" (1839-42, 1856-60), the Europeans insisted on including in the treaties they dictated provisions removing barriers to emigration, and allowing foreign entrepreneurs to operate freely in the "Treaty ports". This facilitated the launching of a "coolie" trade, which combined Chinese and European entrepreneurs into an extensive network of labor recruitment and shipping.[24] The supply was assured by growing rural poverty, attributable on the one hand to a spurt of population growth, leading to competition for scarce land and hence higher rents – as in Ireland or in India; and on the other to an increase in the size of the Chinese upper class, leading to a greater squeeze on the peasantry.[25]

Long the center of trade with Southeast Asia, Quanzhou, in Fujian (Fukien) province, was also the fountainhead of nineteenth century emigration to Malaya and neighboring countries. Most of the America-bound Chinese originated instead around Guangzhou (Canton), the capital of Guangdong (Kwangtung) province, which had a long history as China's main port open to foreign commerce. Bearing the brunt of the concessions China was forced to make in the wake of the "Opium Wars", the region's population experienced dramatic

23. Chan, "European and Asian Immigration".
24. Chan, "European and Asian Immigration", p. 43; Foster, "Chinese Coolie Trade".
25. Bastid-Bruguiere, "Currents of Social Change".

downward mobility, with many driven to accept labor contracts abroad, both as free passengers and as "credit-ticket" indentured labor. Over the next decades emigration was further stimulated by a series of violent political upheavals including the Taiping Rebellion, the Bendi-Keija [Hakka] ethnic conflict, and the Red Turban uprisings.[26]

Availing themselves of these opportunities, in the late 1840s British and American entrepreneurs organized new Chinese migrations across the Pacific to South and North America. Given subsequent development, it is noteworthy that at the time, U.S. diplomats in China were concerned over competition resulting from the increased use of Chinese labor on West Indian plantations; hence they advocated presidential intervention to prevent the use of American shipping in furthering such emigration, and in keeping with this, in 1858 the Congress called for a condemnation of the "coolie trade" as "a matter of humanity and policy".[27] However the Attorney General ruled the following year that the United States did not have that authority; accordingly, a law was enacted in 1862 merely prohibiting the coolie trade by American citizens in American vessels. The measure was ambiguous, however, because it was not designed to block voluntary emigration, nor to prevent American vessels from carrying "voluntary" emigration, most of which was in fact founded on debt bondage.[28]

Indeed, six years later, Washington actively intervened to further expand the traffic. This episode is worth considering in some detail, because it highlights the determinative role of the United States in fostering a migration which even then evoked considerable opposition, and which was widely viewed as a malevolent "invasion" engineered by Oriental cunning. It will be remembered that throughout the first half of the century, ongoing dynamics provided the United States with an ample supply of European immigrants, with no need for positive policy intervention; however, in the face of a manpower shortage induced by the Civil War, Secretary of State Seward (of Alaska fame) secured the enactment of a law designed to facilitate the recruitment of labor from hitherto untapped regions by financing their transportation, and concomitantly authorizing labor contracts, enforceable in U.S. courts, that would make such ventures profitable. The measure led to the establishment of the quasi-official American Emigration Company. Although the company was oriented mostly to Europe, an attempt was also made to import Chinese. However, this was discouraged by the U.S. Commissioner for Immigration on the grounds it was contrary to the true interests of the United States to introduce "new races bound to service and labor", and as contrary to established laws.[29] As it was, when an

26. Chan, "European and Asian Immigration", p. 44.
27. Henson, Jr., *Commissioners and Commodores*, p. 83.
28. Cohen, *Chinese in the Post-Civil War South*, p. 35.
29. *Ibid.*, p. 50.

attempt was made to enhance profitability by imposing penal sanctions on workers who violated their contract, the law was denounced as licensing a new form of bondage. Opponents explicitly charged that European contract workers would be no better off than Chinese "coolies". Accordingly, it was repealed in March, 1868.

At this very time, Seward was in the course of imposing on a reluctant China a treaty designed explicitly to facilitate the massive procurement of Chinese labor, which was signed on behalf of the Emperor by Anson Burlingame, the former U.S. Ambassador to China, but now in Washington as head of a *Chinese* mission, despite any specific mandate to that effect and without consulting the Chinese government.[30] The document asserted the right of the Chinese to expatriate themselves and to immigrate freely into the United States, but specified that the right of entry should not be construed to entail the right to acquire American citizenship by way of naturalization. Hence it is reasonable to infer that Seward envisaged future arrivals as temporary sojourners – in today's parlance, guestworkers – rather than immigrants; moreover, the linkage Seward provides suggests that visionary capitalists envisaged Chinese labor not merely as a solution to California's short-term problem, but as a device for augmenting the nation's manpower more generally, since the forthcoming completion of the transcontinental railroad (1869) would make it possible to move the Chinese inland. The treaty's effectiveness was reflected in a rapid escalation of recorded Chinese arrivals, from an annual average of 4,300 for the 1861-67 period to successive highs of 15,740 in 1870, 20,292 in 1873, and 22,781 in 1876.

Southern planters were familiar with West Indian experiments in using East Indians and Chinese for slave or emancipated blacks. An Augusta, Georgia, newspaper noted in 1854 that Asian labor in the West Indies was cheaper than slaves purchased from the slave-surplus states such as Maryland or Virginia, and had the advantage of returning home at the end of their term. However, the balance of opinion still leaned toward a reopening of the African slave trade, albeit under "just, humane, and equitable laws".[31] But as early as 1853, in the face of apparent reluctance of European immigrants to settle in the south, the Eddyville Iron Works in Kentucky engaged twenty Chinese "coolies" as iron workers. After the Civil War, when reconstruction afforded blacks unprecedented rights, of which many availed themselves by deserting the fields, the Chinese were touted by entrepreneurs as "docile and thrifty" substitute; the one drawback, however, was that they would not go in debt to the proprietor, and hence could not be retained after their contract expired.[32] A number of Chinese

---

30. Hsu, "Late Ch'ing foreign relations", pp. 73-74; Davids, *American Diplomatic and Public Papers*, I, pp. xxiii-xxiv, 49.
31. Cohen, pp. xii, 26.
32. Cohen, *Chinese in the Post-Civil War South*, p. 45.

were imported from Cuba when their contracts expired, others from San Francisco and New York, or even from China itself, by way of a French "immigration agency". In the wake of the Burlingame treaty, the promoters of a Chinese Labor Convention held in Memphis in July, 1869, spoke of bringing up to several hundred thousand workers to the cotton fields; and the following year several hundred Chinese were recruited for work on the Alabama-Chattanooga railroad. However, the importers were hampered by prohibitions on the coolie trade, and further failed to raise the needed capital; moreover, to impede competition, in 1870 the British authorities in Hong Kong prohibited the export of Chinese labor outside the British colonies. More fundamentally, in the absence of effective instruments of coercion, the system could not get off the ground; the Chinese turned out to be much less "docile" than anticipated; and southern planters soon discovered that under prevailing circumstances, the most efficient form of exploitation was the sharecropping system.[33]

There were thoughts of using the Chinese as industrial labor as well. For example, after initially deriving the Burlingame treaty, the editor of *The Nation* subsequently welcomed it, explaining in July 1869 that prejudice and prohibitory legislation notwithstanding, American capital would continue to seek Chinese workers because they "will work harder and for less wages, and are more tractable" than Irish or Germans.[34] Within California, tensions between white and Chinese workers were exacerbated when the transcontinental railroad was completed in 1869, as this brought about a massive influx of white workers from the East – mostly recent Irish immigrants – while surplus Chinese railroad workers were dumped on the labor market, facilitating the rapid industrialization of the mining sector.[35] East Coast employers were remarkably quick in availing themselves of the Chinese as a weapon in industrial disputes, thanks once again to the transcontinental railroad. In 1870, only one year after its completion, a contingent of 75 Chinese shoemakers were brought all the way from San Francisco to North Adams, Massachusetts, under a three-year contract, to break a strike staged by mostly Irish and French Canadian Knights of St. Crispin; later in the year, two carloads were brought for the same purpose to the Passaic Steam Laundry in New Jersey; and a similar episode was reenacted two years later at a cutlery in Beaver Falls, Pennsylvania.[36] Although the practice remained limited because of its high cost, and was abandoned altogether following the crash of 1873, it propelled Chinese immigration to the tore as a central grievance of organized labor.

---

33. *Ibid.*, p. 107.
34. Armstrong, "Godkin and Chinese Labor".
35. Young, *Bismarck's Policy Toward the Poles.*
36. Barth, *Bitter Strength*, pp. 203-207.

Although the Chinese migrations undoubtedly constituted the largest of all the extra European flows during this period, there are no reliable comprehensive estimates, and no synthesis is available. Immigration data are available for the United States; however, they are ambiguous because successive prohibitions on the landing of Chinese "coolies" drastically reduced immigration early on, but by all accounts fostered substantial surreptitious landings and border-crossings, particularly from Mexico. With these qualifications in mind, recorded arrivals from Asia reached a first peak of 39,629 in 1882, of whom 39,579 originated in China; the following year, following the enactment of restrictive legislation, admissions fell to 8,031, and never rose above 3,363 again for the remainder of the period.[37] As of the early 1870s, although the Chinese constituted only about 9 percent of California's total population, as nearly all of them were adult males, they amounted to one-fifth of the economically active, and one-fourth of all wage earners.[38] Sucheng Chan has pointed out that, contrary to the conventional historiography which contrasts Chinese "sojourners" with European "immigrants". the crude rate of return of Chinese during the period of free movement (1848- 1882) was 47 percent, comparable to many European groups such as Italians (albeit for a slightly later period).[39] Arrivals from Asia reached a second peak of 40,424 in 1907, of whom 30,226 originated in Japan and 8,053 in "Turkey in Asia", but only 961 from China. Altogether, 322,000 Chinese arrivals in the United States were recorded for the 1848-1882 period.

Some 90,000 Chinese were shipped to Peru in 1849-1874, mostly by way of Macao, to replace Hawaians; others by way of Hong Kong to British Columbia to build the Canadian Pacific. But over the same period, some 15 million Chinese migrated to Southeast Asia, mostly by way of Singapore, both as contract workers and as permanent settlers. For the region as a whole, the population of Chinese descent currently numbers over 12 million.[40]

Whereas Chinese trans-Pacific migrations illustrate the consequences of that country's dependent status within the global economy, the case of Japan illustrates how a successful attempt by a late developer to catch up also stimulated massive emigration. In short, the Japanese government's modernization from above after the Meji Restoration (1868) fostered conditions similar to those of the European "Great Transformation", which similarly led the government to lower barriers against emigration, and instead encourage it as a safety valve and source of public income.[41] By the turn of the century, Japanese workers constituted two-thirds of the sugar plantation work force in Hawai. But when

---

37. *Historical Statistics of the United States*, 1961, C 88-114, pp. 58-59.
38. Saxton, *The Indispensible Enemy*, p. 10.
39. Chan, "European and Asian Immigration", p. 38.
40. Wolf, *Europe and the People*, p. 175.
41. Chan, "European and Asian Immigration", p. 50.

they engaged in strikes, the Sugar Planters' Association took advantage of the American missionary network to organize the recruitment of Korean substitutes. However, when Japan gained the upper hand in Korea, emigration was severely restricted so as to maintain an adequate supply of labor locally for Japanese enterprises. Some 400,000 Japanese arrivals were recorded in the United States, including Hawaii, between 1885 and 1924, when they too were excluded along with all other Asians.

3. Building the Great Wall

Despite the profitability of Chinese labor, in the face of what was perceived as an "invasion" the overseas countries governed by populations of European descent quickly adopted draconian measures to prevent the further procurement of Asian workers. Although this was done on an ad hoc basis, in the course of pursuing their objective they generated institutional innovations in the sphere of immigration control that rendered further regulation much easier to achieve. Moreover, there are some indications to suggest that the successful exclusion of one group encouraged those who were disturbed by the changing character of immigration more generally to envisage the exclusion of others as well. In the United States, attempts to drastically reduce immigration from eastern and southern Europe were launched as early as the 1890s; and both the advocates and the targets of exclusion saw the Chinese experience as a relevant precedent. This was echoed not only in the overseas dominions, but also in Europe.

How did exclusion come about? From the perspective of capitalist entrepreneurs, cheap labor from China or the less-developed countries of Europe was undoubtedly profitable; yet ultimately they did not get their way. On the other hand, although the restrictionist outcome accorded with the wishes of white workers, by and large they lacked the power to determine legislation. Hence the explanation cannot be found in the sphere of economic rationality alone. In short, the emerging immigration policies were determined by the interplay of two distinct sets of considerations, the one essentially economic, but the other "moral" or political, arising from "scientific" and popular understandings of demography, economic, and psychology, shaped by nationalism and imperial rivalries.

In the United States, the struggle to exclude the Chinese originated in California. Although white immigrant workers succeeded in launching a radical labor movement which quickly gained considerable political power in San Francisco and at the state level, its substantial achievements in the economic sphere were jeopardized by the availability to employers of the Chinese alternative. Because it required overhead capital, the use of Chinese labor gave larger industry an edge over small operations; and because Chinese entrepreneurs were

more efficient than American in exploiting their countrymen within the confines
of an enclave economy, they competed successfully in certain mass-production
sectors, particularly the manufacture of cheap cigars and of inexpensive garments.
Small white businessmen thus joined the exclusionist camp, leaving the railroad
and mining "monopolists" as the only advocates of the Chinese. However, they
were soon joined by agricultural entrepreneurs who discovered California's
vocation as the cornucopia of fruit and vegetables for the expanding nation-wide
consumer market. Organized from the outset as an up-dated version of the
colonial plantation system. Agro-industry required a massive supply of cheap
"stoop" labor, which was provided initially by Chinese already in the state, or
introduced surreptitiously; as of 1886, they constituted seven-eights of California's farm labor. In the 1890s the state's farmers steadfastly opposed exclusion.[42]

Nevertheless, anti-Chinese sentiment was making rapid strides at the level of
general opinion, rooted in the soil of traditional Christian prejudice, now
exacerbated by well-publicized events such as the massacres of American
missionaries in Tientsin (1868), a coolie revolt in Peru (1870), and the outbreak
of a famine (1879). Given China's enormous population of four hundred
million, this raised the specter of America being swamped by a tidal wave of
starving humanity vastly larger even than the Irish of the preceding generation.[43]
Within this climate, the advocates of Chinese labor were clearly pushed to the
defensive, and it became much easier for the exclusionists to achieve their
objective. In 1875, at the initiative of President Grant, the United States enacted
a law to exclude Chinese brought by "headmen" against their will, singling out
women imported for "lewd and shameful purposes" as the worst segment. This
constituted a major turning point in American immigration policy, because it
was the first national measure to control admissions directly. In 1880, a mere
twelve years after imposing on China a treaty to foster the export of labor, the
U.S. dictated the terms of a modification of that treaty whereby it could decide
one-sidedly to restrict Chinese immigration; and two years later the importation
of Chinese contract labor was prohibited for a ten-year period, subsequently
renewed several times and eventually extended to encompass the new American
possessions in the Pacific.

Beyond its deterrent effect, the 1882 law established a presumption that any
Chinese seeking to enter the United States were "coolies", and that those who
were in the United States were there illegally. All persons of Chinese origin,
including those who were American citizens by virtue of birth, were henceforth
subject to harassing identity checks, and liable to deportation unless able to
produce a certificate that they were *not* coolies, or proof of U.S. birth. There
were also half-hearted efforts to return Chinese workers to their homeland,

42. Coolidge, *Chinese Immigration*, p. 370.
43. Miller, *The Unwelcome Immigrant*, pp. 151, 159.

paralleling efforts earlier in the century to return freed slaves to Africa, as persons who were not fit for membership in the American political community. This was reflected also in discriminatory laws "that aimed to deprive them of their means of livelihood, restrict their social mobility, and deny them political power".[44] Besides the exclusion from the possibility of acquiring citizenship by naturalization, which was upheld by the Supreme Court as applying also to Japanese in 1922 and Asian Indians in 1923, Asians faced obstacles such as the California prohibitions on the use of certain types of nets for commercial fishing and on establishing laundries in wooden buildings, and its 1913 land law which prohibited "aliens ineligible to citizenship" (i.e., Asians) from buying agricultural land or leasing it more than three years.

The movement to exclude the Chinese from the United States was highly successful, and reduced Chinese immigration much below the level it would have reached otherwise. Paradoxically, however, it failed to reduce the flow of peoples of color into the country, because as the Chinese waned from the scene, others were solicited to take their place. A contemporaneous observer remarked in 1909 that "The history of general labor in California since about 1886 is the story of efforts to find substitutes for the vanishing Chinese".[45] Unable to secure additional Chinese hands, farmers and ranchers recruited Japanese and Filipinos, whose experience as groups initially wooed and later excluded largely parallels that their predecessors.[46] But as Mary Coolidge noted in 1909, California had already begun to tap the abundant population pool south of its border.

Around the turn of the century, a steady flow of disposable and cheap unskilled labor, ethnically distinct from indigenous workers – mostly the descendants of earlier waves of immigrants – accorded well with the requirements of the manufacturing sector, which was rapidly shifting from craft methods toward mass production, while simultaneously doing the utmost to prevent labor from improving its bargaining position in the labor market by way of collective action. Given the apparently inexhaustible pool of immigrants, the business community no longer objected to state action to screen out those unable or unwilling to function in a mature capitalist society; indeed, such screening might even be welcome as reducing the wastage occasioned by unregulated laissez-faire. In any event, federal laws enacted in the 1880s with regard to European immigration were merely culled from the existing corpus of state and local measures directed against the entry of persons deemed incapable of supporting themselves by reason of physical or mental disability, or morally unfit as indicated by a previous criminal record. In 1885, organized labor gained sufficient strength to secure the prohibition of immigration under pre-arranged contract, which was notoriously

44. Chan, "European and Asian Immigration", p. 62.
45. Coolidge, *Chinese Immigration*, p. 384.
46. Boyd, "Oriental Immigration", pp. 49-51.

used to procure strikebreakers; but by all reports this had little impact on labor recruitment because employers recruited workers after landing instead.

As had been the case with the Irish in an earlier generation and with the Chinese more recently, however, the very attributes that rendered the newcomers suitable as cheap labor were viewed by many as rendering them unfit for membership in the receiving society. Their linguistic and religious distance from the hegemonic anglo-germanic, Protestant culture, was expected to make their assimilation into the mainstream more difficult; and it was reckoned that the difficulty of Americanizing them would be compounded by the sheer mass of newcomers, as well as by that fact that many of them saw themselves as temporary migrants, who had little incentive or opportunity to adopt American ways.

The movement to restrict immigration was thus initiated by traditional social elites of the East Coast, and quickly gained widespread support among what would be termed in a later age the "silent majority". Concurrently, however, restriction was also advanced as a *sine qua non* for improving the situation of the American working class by organized labor itself as well as an emerging group of sympathetic professional economists. Thus, as immigration moved to the fore as a political issue around the turn of the century, the battle was fought by two coalitions of strange bedfellows, cutting across the right-left continuum: organized capitalists together with the Catholic Church, Jewish organizations, and urban political machines sought to keep the door open in the face of a growing movement to close it, which included organized labor, WASP social and intellectual elites, and populist political forces that encompassed the South as a whole and rural constituencies throughout the country. The basic reorientation of U.S. immigration policy can be dated to 1896, when both houses of Congress approved a proposal imposing a literacy requirement, designed to reduce total incoming numbers and effect an ethnic selection by barring the bulk of arrivals from southern and eastern Europe, where schooling was rarely available. However, the measure was vetoed by President Cleveland, and the tug-of-war was reenacted several times until the law was finally passed in 1917 over Woodrow Wilson's two successive vetoes. Although war-induced xenophobia was undoubtedly a contributing factor, by this time there was a consensus, shared by the most politically progressive groups, regrading the undesirability of a continued massive inflow of poor strangers.

In the event, the measure's effectiveness could not be immediately tested because the war drastically reduced trans-Atlantic movements. As soon as shipping returned to normal, however, it was evident that the literacy act provided little or no deterrent; given the large stock of deferred family reunions and many additional departures stimulated by post-war economic difficulties and political upheavals, numbers rapidly escalated and gave every indication of soon exceeding pre war peaks. On the American side, the anti-immigration camp was now reinforced by the fear of revolutionary contagion and a yearning for a return to "normalcy", as well as post-war economic doldrums. In this context, the widely-supported determination to close the door must be understood as an instrument of regime maintenance that interfaced with other reactionary trends of the period: repression of radicalism, national prohibition of alcoholic beverages, adoption of mandatory segregation throughout the South, systematic social discrimination against Catholics and Jews in elite institutions (including leading universities), and adoption of a firmly assimilationist stance toward recent immigrants and their descendants.

Given these favorable circumstances, the restrictionists expanded their objectives to include a ban on all immigration from Asia, as well as first a temporary, and subsequently a *permanent* annual limit on the number of admissions from Europe, and an allocation of these numbers in a manner designed to restore the ethnic profile that prevailed *before* most of the latest wave arrived.

From the perspective of migration history, the mechanisms devised to implement the new American policies are as significant as the policies themselves. In short, they amounted to the elaboration of a administrative system whereby the receiving country regulated admission not merely at the physical point of entry, but rather at the *point of embarkation* abroad. The process involved, which might be termed "remote border control", is now so familiar that we tend to underestimate its radically innovative character and its fundamental importance in regulating world-wide movement. This innovation was facilitated, of course, by the fact that access to the United States from Europe (or Asia) was possible only by ship, and that a vessel constitutes a closed container, which one cannot easily enter or leave once under way. Ever since the early part of nineteenth century, state and local authorities availed themselves of these elements to secure the cooperation of shippers in keeping out paupers and the like, by way of holding them financially liable for landing prohibited persons; but the shippers generally got around the regulations by ignoring them altogether, or making a market in the required bonds, or yet challenging them in the courts as unconstitutional impediments to commerce. Following the nationalization of immigration regulation, and as the categories of prohibited persons proliferated around the turn of the twentieth century, the authorities made some headway in integrated shippers into the border control apparatus by requiring them to return those rejected.

Yet the policing of immigration, as reflected in the construction of a huge processing station at Ellis Island, was still conceived of essentially in terms of an inspection at the border; it is noteworthy, for example, that the legislative history of the literacy test is replete with detailed prescriptions for administering it to the incoming masses at the moment of landing. However, the imposition of an annual quantitative limit on admissions, and their allocation in accordance with national origins, wreaked havoc with ongoing practices, creating not only considerable duress for the immigrants, who might find the quota filled by the time they arrived in the United States, but also for the shippers and the American authorities. It thus became quickly evident that efficient operation of the new system required distribution of entry permits in advance of embarkation. But this in turn necessitated the provision of an extensive American immigration bureaucracy abroad. This was achieved in 1924, by way of the Rogers Act, which professionalized the U.S. consular service, and charged it among other things with the task of attributing immigration visas, whose allocation could be centrally controlled. Once this bureaucracy was in place, the complex qualification procedures – which included in addition to the literacy test a variety of police checks, medical inspection, determination of financial responsibility, and a political interview – could be administered abroad, as prerequisites for obtaining the visa. Moreover, it also made it possible for the United States to impose notoriously demanding requirements on temporary visitors, thereby reducing the likelihood that such visits would constitute a significant source of illegal immigration by overstaying. These controls proved remarkably effective from the time of their institutionalization in the 1920s until well into 1970s – a half-century of success, which by any reasonable standard must be reckoned as a remarkable administrative achievement.

Once again, however, the efforts to stem one incoming flow were accompanied by actions that stimulated the onset of others. World War I enhanced the demand for American goods, but simultaneously occasioned a labor shortage, as transatlantic immigration ground to an abrupt halt, and subsequently because American males were drafted for military service. Even as the restrictionists were gaining ground, American employers secured the enactment of measures to facilitate the recruitment of workers from neighboring countries by exonerating them from the literacy requirements, and from the prohibition against contract labor. They included Mexico, where many were being uprooted by revolutionary upheavals; Quebec, which had long provided migrant labor for the New England lumber industry and its factories; and the English-speaking islands of the Caribbean. In the light of the racialist arguments that underlay the exclusion of Asians and the draconian restrictions imposed on southern and eastern Europeans, it is noteworthy that every one of these sources provided people who were considered undesirable, on the grounds of their low intelligence (French Canadians), racial inferiority (Caribbean blacks), or because they were of "mixed breed" (Mexicans). Moreover, these exceptional war-time arrangements were in effect institutionalized in the 1920s by exempting independent countries of the Western Hemisphere from the annual immigration ceiling and quota system that governed flows from Europe. Beyond this, in response to pressures from agricultural interests, American immigration authorities condoned the practice of unregulated movement across the U.S.-Mexican border, and cooperated with employers to insure an adequate supply of labor when demand was high, as well as to dispose of the workers when no longer needed. The resulting dualism of a well-regulated main gate, and an informally managed back door, became a permanent feature of U.S. immigration that still prevails today. Combined with renewed exceptional measures to tap neighboring parts of the "south" in wartime or to provide temporary workers for particular sectors, these practices contributed to the formation of extensive self-sustaining migratory networks throughout the region.

The experience of the other English-speaking overseas countries largely paralleled that of the United States. In relation to population size, on the eve of World War I immigration was much larger phenomenon in Canada than in the United States. Still the historical maximum for a single year, the 400,870 arrivals recorded in 1913 amounted to 5 percent of the country's population – over three times the highest level in relation to population achieved in the United States (1907). Unlike in the United States, until late in the nineteenth century immigration to Canada was tightly controlled by way of passenger regulations as well as land and settlement policies, designed in London to favor British immigrants of a class suited to the role of imperial guardianship. Immigration was seen as a critical mechanism for overcoming the demographic superiority of the French Canadians, and hence their political weight in the dawning democratic age. However, in the absence of industrial development, Canada functioned largely as a way station to the United States. Around the turn of the century, in the face of a continuing shortage of agriculturally-oriented immigrants from the United Kingdom as well as of French-Canadian demands for equal status as a "founding nation", the preference system was broadened to include French-speaking Europeans and other national groups committed to agriculture (e.g., Ukrainians), as well as economically qualified Americans; blacks, and eventually Asians, were firmly excluded. The Chinese were dealt with summarily; but Indians, who trickled into British Columbia around the turn of the century, were difficult to exclude because as British subjects, they had the right to travel freely to other parts of the empire. However, the restrictionists achieved their objectives in 1908 by devising a law that barred immigrants who did not come by "continuous journey" from their country of origin.[47]

Immigration from Europe finally soared in the 1890s, when U.S. migration to Canada briefly outweighed the southward movement. After World War I, the problem was no longer how to secure suitable immigrants, but how to keep out the mass of undesirables deflected toward Canada by U.S. restrictions. The solution here also included an annual cap on immigration, and a system of

47. Chan, "European and Asian Immigration", p. 55.

preferences that deterred southern and eastern Europeans. Consequently, in the period 1921-1931 the contribution of immigration to Canadian population growth was only half as large as that of births, and in the following decade, less than one-tenth. Similarly, Australia's positively encouraged British immigration, coupled with the restricted admission of eastern and southern Europeans, and outright exclusion of nonwhites.[48] The policy's success is reflected in the fact that as of 1947, 95 percent of the country's 7.6 million were of the preferred stock, of whom 88 percent were British or Irish; one percent was Aborigine, leaving only 4 percent as the contribution of less desirable immigration. Both countries also adopted the "remote control" system developed in the United States; and since potential immigrants could reach their destination only by boat (leaving aside for this purpose entry to Canada by way of the United States), neither experienced significant illegal immigration.

The specter of the Chinese presence was by no means limited to the Pacific rim. Other than diplomats and occasional visitors, some Chinese first came to Britain in the late 1860s, mainly as seamen employed by companies that traded with China. Although the number remained in the hundreds, responses to their presence were conditioned by negative reports on the situation in the empire; hostility to Chinese labor in the Transvaal became an issue in the 1906 general election campaign, and five years later a mob destroyed all of Cardiff's thirty-odd Chinese laundries.[49] But although Europeans were alarmed by the "yellow peril", which was also sounded by Kaiser Wilhelm at the time of the Boxer rising, they believed a similar but more directly threatening invasion was at hand – the massive westward exodus of the Jews from eastern Europe.[50] During the heated debates on legislation to restrict immigration that raged in England around the turn of the century, the Chinese were referred to as the truest of aliens, but the Jews differed only "as a matter of degree".[51]

Within the prevailing frameworks of racialist ideology, many parallels were drawn between the two groups. As the globe became more integrated and the world-wide stream of migration brought hitherto invisible men to its very center, both groups figured in mythical conspiracies such as are depicted in the "Protocol of the Elders of Zion" and Sax Rohmer's popular Fu Manchu novels. Having mastered mysterious mental processes or accumulated esoteric knowledge consigned in arcane texts, the Chinese and the Jews were thought to have the power to hypnotize ordinary beings into becoming subservient instruments of their will, or to enslave them with the bait of gold or opium, using them to operate malevolent transnational networks of illegitimate gain that national

48. Price, "Australia"; Zubrzycki, "International Migration in Australia".
49. May, "Chinese in Britain", p. 111.
50. Barraclough, *Introduction to Contemporary History*, p. 81.
51. Gainer, *Alien Invasion*, p. 112.

authorities were helpless to resist. Both groups were also associated with filth and contagious disease, particularly cholera, which still perennially reappeared in Europe by way of shipping routes, and hence was associated with migration.[52]

By and large, the massive migration of the Jews from eastern Europe was stimulated by economic factors associated with the "great transformation" already noted, which undermined their traditional roles as trade intermediaries, craftsmen, and small manufacturers; although this population was generally poor, philanthropic assistance from fellow-Jews in the receiving countries made it easier for them to emigrate. In newly independent Rumania and in the Tsarist Empire, the exodus was accelerated and magnified by new discriminatory measures and outright violence, in the face of which western-based Jewish organizations secured the lifting of prohibitions on exit. Although the preferred destination was the United States, there were also smaller streams to various European countries, Canada, and Latin America Everywhere, the arrival of East European Jews precipitated hostile reactions, manifested by way of a more political form of anti-semitism as well as efforts to bar their entry. That they were not excluded as quickly or as thoroughly as the Chinese, despite widespread fearful hostility, is attributable to the presence within the receiving countries of well-established Jewish communities that had managed to achieve relatively high status and wielded some economic and political power.

In England, for example, "immigrant" rapidly became synonymous with Jew, a group so undesirable that they were compared unfavorably with the despised Irish and, as noted, categorized as close to the Chinese.[53] As in France and Central Europe, anti-Semitism was readily exploited by the emerging nationalist Right. Invoking the 1882 American legislation against the Chinese and other "unfit", a spate of associations were launched in the mid-1880s for the explicit purpose of fighting the "alien invasion" which, it was argued, weakened the core of the Empire at a time of expanding responsibility. In his Unionist campaign of 1892, Joseph Chamberlain endorsed restriction with the expressed purpose of diverting working class support from the Home-Rule Liberals. Although the leading theme of the English campaign was the threat of "declining quality", immigration was also opposed on economic grounds, particularly during the 1894 depression, when the Trade Union Congress endorsed restriction on the grounds that the immigrant-based mass-production garment industry undermined the traditional trades. Later, however, the TUC reversed its stance

52. Cholera irrupted from eastern Europe in 1865-68; 737 died in Atlantic crossings or in
      quarantine in 1866, mainly from Hamburg; the following year another 133, again mainly
      Hamburg. There were severe outbreaks in 1873 and 1887 among passengers embarking in
      Marseille, and again in 1892, 132 deaths were recorded among passengers embarking in
      Hamburg, mainly Jews (Nugent, *Crossings*, p. 175). For the association of Chinese with
      disease, see Barth, *Bitter Strength*.
53. On the issue of "quality", see Teitelbaum and Winter, *Fear of Population Decline*.

on the grounds that the issue was a red herring designed to detract attention from the working class's real problems. Although an Aliens bill was first proposed in 1894, the Liberals opposed it steadily as an unwarranted interference with the free movement of labor, in keeping with their stalwart adherence to Manchesterian principles of free trade. Conversely, as the neo-mercantilist movement away from free trade and toward imperial preference gained ground, it provided a rationale for restricting the free entry of people as well.

Finally enacted by the Conservative majority in 1905 as the first immigration control measure since the era of the Napoleonic wars, the Aliens Act merely restricted the landing of poor immigrants who might constitute a public burden; but the context makes it quite clear that this was designed principally to reduce the ongoing flow of Russian Jews. Although the incoming Liberal government decided not to apply it systematically, the measure appears to have served as an effective deterrent, as indicated by the immediate decline of recorded immigration from 12,481 in 1906 to 3,626 in 1911, a period of rising immigration elsewhere.[54] Immigration was further restricted at the outbreak of World War I and again in the 1920s, when Britain experienced a protracted period of slow economic stagnation and unemployment. Consequently, around 1930, Britain had the lowest proportion of foreign-born of any industrial democracy.[55] It is thus appropriate to view Britain as the first country to achieve a "zero-baseline" immigration policy. However, it should be noted that did not entail any sort of sacrifice on the part of Britain's employers, since Ireland continued to provide a plentiful supply of migrant labor, as it does indeed to this day.

In Germany, the "immigration crisis" was precipitated by an influx of Polish workers from Tsarist Russia and the Austro-Hungarian Empire.[56] In short, in the course of the commercialization of agriculture in East Prussia, many of the emancipated serfs of German stock or assimilated Polish stock were driven by the processes noted earlier to migrate, either to America or, later on, the emerging industrial poles of western Germany. In the same vein as their counterparts elsewhere, the estate owners found it profitable to replace them with short-term workers, of which an ample supply was available in the neighboring regions of Poland. As with all temporary migrations, however, these flows produced a sediment of permanent settlement. From the perspective of Germany state-builders of the late nineteenth century, the increase in a Catholic and non-German speaking population constituted a major obstacle to national integration. In 1885, Bismarck dealt with the problem on an ad hoc basis by a massive expulsion; but the Prussian owners were adamant, and subsequently resumed their recruitment. Following the denunciation of these practices by

54. Gainer, *Alien Invasion*, p. 211.
55. Kirk, *Population in Europe*, p. 222.
56. Herbert, *History of Foreign Labor in Germany*; Dohse, *Ausländische Arbeiter und bürgerlicher Staat*.

Max Weber and his associates of the Society for Social Research in 1892 as contrary to the national interest, the German authorities devised a system combining the recruitment of temporary workers with draconian controls on border-crossings and on their stay in Germany, which anticipated twentieth-century guestworker programs.

Conclusion

In the final decades of the nineteenth century, the dynamics of the expanding market economy fostered a rapid quantitative and geographical expansion of the international migratory stream. While the older industrializers completed their demographic transition and acquired the capacity to absorb new age cohorts into their national labor markets, the economies most recently affected by the "great transformation" faced a growing "surplus population", reflecting the conjunction of declining demand for labor in the rural areas with accelerating population growth. The global stream was thus not only much larger but also more heterogenous, now sweeping along also migrants from southern and eastern Europe, as well as from various parts of Asia, including the Near East, India, and China. Leaving aside colonials whose movements were controlled and confined to particular destinations, a considerable proportion of the new proletarians driven out of their homes in search of work availed themselves of the new cheap long-distance transportation and of more permissive governmental regulations to move where opportunity beckoned most powerfully, the promising overseas countries as well as the more advanced industrial states of western Europe, which appeared to have an unlimited hunger for strong arms. It should be noted that some were escaping persecution as much as poverty, particularly Jews from the new states of eastern Europe and the Tsarist Empire

By any standard, this world on the move constituted a truly unprecedented phenomenon. From the perspective of the receivers, the increasing numbers of newcomers appeared as the vanguard of a massive wave of culturally heterogeneous settlers. For example, in both the United States and Canada, annual arrivals on the eve of World War I amounted to about 1.5 percent of the total population.[57] As of 1910, 14.6 of the U.S. population was foreign-born; and the proportion of new immigrants originating from the traditional sources, Northwestern Europe and Germany, had declined from about 95 percent in 1851-60 to around 20 percent in the first decade of the twentieth century.

Responses were differentiated along two distinct axes, economic interest and political concern, making for an alliance of "strange bedfellows" in support of

57. Simon, "Basic Data Concerning Immigration", pp. 17 and 19.

restriction. Along one axis, employers generally welcomed the migrants as additional cheap labor while workers – along with their intellectual supporters – saw them as a threat; along the other, the social and religious establishment raised the alarm regarding threats to national integrity, leaving only occasional Kantian cosmopolites and those related to the newcomers – where they existed – to fight off prejudice. Cutting across the class divide, the restrictionist coalition was broadly based and cast a multifarious appeal; its victory was only a matter of time. In the United States, anti-Chinese legislation was enacted very easily, with nearly unanimous legislative support; but industrialists and transporters successfully fought off more general restriction. Having stated their objectives as early as the 1890s, the restrictionists took nearly a quarter of a century to achieve their legislative objectives, so that many more millions were able to move in the intervening period. Both overseas and in Europe, World War I and the Soviet Revolution prompted a further reinforcement of controls and restrictions on grounds of national security. By the 1920s most states had erected solid walls. with narrow gates to let in specific categories.

Devised in an atmosphere of panic to stem the "alien tide", the new immigration regime, which prevailed for nearly a century from the early 1920s to the 1960s, was remarkably effective. Its most visible consequence was a drastic reduction of immigration into the world's affluent countries, and since this constituted a large part of ongoing flows, of international migration more generally. Beyond this, the adoption of the "zero baseline norm" contributed to the naturalization of nativism, that is, of a cultural construction whereby national societies are viewed as self contained population entities with a common and homogeneous ancestry, growing by way of natural reproduction alone. In relation to this, immigration came to be regarded as a pathogenic disturbance.

Another important consequence of the closing of borders was the impossibility for persecuted groups to secure asylum abroad, at a time when the need was escalating, and concomitantly the legitimation of their persecution as people who were demonstrably undesirable because nobody wanted them.[58] We would do well to remember this tragic sequel of the first immigration crisis as we respond the second.

---

58. This point was emphasized by Arendt in *Origins of Totalitarianism*, pp. 269-290.

Hostile Images of Immigrants and Refugees in Nineteenth- and Twentieth-Century Britain

Colin Holmes

Resnick [...] stopped at the first delicatessen for a pound of smoked sausage, a quarter of dried mushrooms [...] two ounces of dill and a slice of poppy seed cake; [...] and finally he bought pickled herring, horseradish and sour cream from the delicatessen near the exit. Here as at the first the salesman spoke to him in Polish, knowing that he understood and Resnick answered in English.

There were idle moments when he thought he should do more than sell his house, sell up altogether, apply for a transfer to another town (away from Nottingham).

He knew he could never do it: this was his life. Here.

John Harvey, *Rough Treatment* (Harmondsworth, 1991), p. 85.

Introduction

The demand for labour generated by industrialization has often acted as a powerful magnet, drawing workers away from the economic periphery towards an expanding core. Yet the most decisive industrial transformation in European history, that unprecedented surge of economic growth in Britain which became evident in the late eighteenth century and reached its fruition by the mid-nineteenth century, a process known today as the Industrial Revolution, exercised only a limited effect on the course of emigration from the continent. Long before the origins of that process Europeans had contributed to the course of commerce and industrialization in what we now call Britain.[1] However, in the late eighteenth and early nineteenth centuries a greater influence was exerted by the reserve army of labour lying in Ireland and the vast pool of colonial workers under British domination. Even so, the precise weight of those contributions remains uncertain.[2] But, to repeat, the influence of continental Europeans in the shape of say, the French, the Germans (and contemporaries referred

---

1. Kiernan, "Britons Old and New", on Europeans in Britain.
2. Hunt, *British Labour History*, pp. 172-173, which discusses Irish immigration.

to Germans long before the official creation of the German Empire), Italians, and other nationalities, was not pronounced.

However, a growing number of political exiles from Europe can be observed as the nineteenth century wore on and from the 1880s an increasing emigration got under way from Russia, some of which came to Britain. The focus of attention here will rest particularly upon these arrivals from the Tsar's Empire and then, moving into the twentieth century, upon the nationals of the newly-independent states of Poland, Hungary and Czechoslovakia. In short the focus is primarily upon immigration from Eastern Europe and the problems and difficulties faced by newcomers from this part of the world.

However, towards the end of the discussion we move towards a comparative perspective by placing the responses to these Eastern Europeans against the reception accorded to the Blacks and Asians who came to Britain in increasing numbers after 1945. The Irish also feature in this comparative discussion.

Let us begin however, at an earlier date, by way of an introduction. At the beginning of the nineteenth century Britain provided a temporary or permanent home for various groups from territories East of the Elbe. Among these were Polish émigrés who arrived after the failure of the 1831 Polish Revolt: "of all the refugee nationalities in Britain in the nineteenth century the Poles were the most numerous, the poorest, the most intractable and, as it turned out, the most permanent".[3] These refugees had their numbers swollen by later arrivals as Polish hopes of independence were dashed. At the same time these Poles were joined by refugees from the sprawling Austro-Hungarian Empire. History is to be seen as well as read and the observant can detect wall plaques, in London and elsewhere, which bear testimony to the procession of refugees.[4]

Among the political exiles from the Tsar's Empire, Alexander Herzen can be counted as an early arrival and he was followed by others, including Bakunin in 1861, Kropotkin in 1876 and Stepniak in 1883.[5] However, such individual Russian political exiles became overshadowed by the emigration from the Tsar's Empire which occurred in the late nineteenth century. It is this movement which has the first major claim on our attention.

From 1881 up to the outbreak of the First World War as a result of various influences the Jews in the Tsar's Empire faced a season of unremitting persecution. As a consequence of such hostility, compounded in some cases by economic pressures, large numbers of Jews emigrated westwards towards Germany, France, Great Britain, South Africa, Argentina and, above all, the United States,

---

3. Porter, *Refugee Question*, p. 13.
4. See for example the plaques in London to Joseph Conrad, Louis Kossuth and Thomas Masaryk.
5. Slatter, *From the Other Shore*.

the *Goldene Medina*. It would be myopic to claim that Jews alone migrated. Other ethnic minorities in the Tsar's Empire came under attack and these assaults also led to some emigration, even if on a less significant scale. The Lithuanians provide one example of this process of attack and subsequent migration, though their experiences in Britain have been dwarfed by the attention which has been paid to the Jewish immigration from Russian Poland.[6]

This Jewish immigration surpassed in its size the previous inflows from Europe. However, accurate statistics remain elusive. It can be estimated, tentatively, that between approximately 100,000 and 150,000 Jews settled in Britain.[7] Moreover, an uncertain number stayed briefly as transmigrants. The arrival of these Jews assumed historical significance in various ways. They exercised a major influence on the religious life of Anglo-Jewry. They made a contribution to the history of Anarchism and Socialism in Britain. But they also posed a test, a challenge, to the claim that Britain is a uniquely tolerant country. This is not the place to review the full history of such responses: in any case a fair amount of that ground is well-trodden already. The focus is more specific. It is to suggest that, in combination, pressures from the general public and also from Government, which might be described as popular and official opinion, respectively, led to changes in immigration legislation which, in effect, overturned a long-established laissez-faire tradition.

On the streets, in the major areas of settlement in London's East End, in Leeds, and in Manchester, responses were not uniformly hostile.[8] However, in the short term prominent strands of hostility appeared. In London this antipathy was related to competition for housing particularly, and also for jobs. At the same time fears became expressed regarding the instrusion of alien cultures.[9] In the major centres of settlement in London's East End, in the districts of Whitechapel and Stepney, this opposition became gathered together in February 1901 under the political umbrella of the British Brothers' League. But the BBL reflected more than a surge of popular sentiment. It could count upon the support of certain Tory MPs. Through this route popular opinion could be channelled to Westminster. Such overt support by MPs for grassroots' opinion became too

---

6. On the Jewish dimension see Gartner, *Jewish Immigrant in England*; Garrard, *English and Immigration*; and Gainer, *Alien Invasion*. A fair amount of general information on Lithuanians appears in: Lunn, "Reactions to Lithuanian and Polish Immigrants", and Rodgers, "Political Developments in the Lithuanian Community".

7. See Gartner, "Notes on the Statistics"; Garrard, *English and Immigration*, App. 1. In 1891 the instructions for the census returns contained for the first time guidance in Yiddish.

8. Garrard, *English and Immigration*, and Gartner, *Jewish Immigrant in England*, discuss the immigration to London. Buckman, *Immigrants and Class Struggle*, is focussed upon Leeds. The history of immigration into Manchester remains unwritten.

9. Royal Commission on Alien Immigration, British Parliamentary Papers, IX (1903), pp. 178, 286, 298.

much for Tory Party managers and, as a result, the politicians were encouraged to work more discreetly through the agency of Immigration Reform Association. Whatever the route, however, popular opinion had access to policy makers. The effects were significant.[10]

For much of the nineteenth century Britain had been free from any restrictions on alien immigration. However, the migration from the East led to a change in that laissez-faire approach. The 1905 Aliens Act stopped the automatic entry of aliens. Henceforth the prospect of restriction and official discretion had to be reckoned with. In part such legislation reflected an attempt by the Conservative Government to act tough against alien labour, to prevent it entering the country as a matter of course. Through their stance the Conservatives hoped to retain and attract working class support. In short, they made a political calculation. But that calculation needs to be viewed against the background of popular opposition, particularly within the areas of settlement, to the immigration from the Russian Empire. The 1905 Act, which reflected the interaction of such influences, affected all aliens – French, Germans, Italians, no matter – but its actual thrust was aimed at keeping out the newcomers from the Russian Empire, particularly the Jews.

Those Jews who arrived from Russian Poland also posed a problem for the Anglo-Jewish elite. The newcomers disturbed the peace of well-established Jews, many of whom feared that immigration from the Russian Empire would create a wave of antisemitism under which they too would become engulfed. As a result, Jewish agencies returned some of the newcomers to the Russian Empire. Some newly-arrived Jews were re-directed to other countries. Furthermore, pressure was exerted via sources in Eastern Europe to discourage immigration. If the view still persists that immigrants and refugees can automatically expect a welcome from their kinsmen this particular episode alone suggests that it needs to be reconsidered. Within the Anglo-Jewish elite it became recognized that the stream of immigration could not be fully diverted and that, consequently, a strategy had to be developed in order to guide those Jews who did gain entry to Britain. The resulting policy of the Anglo-Jewish elite can be summed up in the slogan: "Become Englishmen as soon as possible".[11] This policy, based on the assumption that the Jewishness evident in the Tsar's Empire was inappropriate within a British context, carries its own streak of intolerance.[12] However, a similar strategy was to be repeated later in different contexts by other agencies.[13]

---

10. See *East London Observer*, 18 January 1902, for a large meeting at the People's Palace. Holmes, *Anti-Semitism in British Society*. Ch. 6 has a full discussion of the BBL and IRA.
11. Porter, *Refugee Question*, p. 218.
12. Lipman, *Century of Social Service*, pp. 111-113 noted discreetly the elite's actions. Later younger historians have sometimes emphasized them.
13. See below, p. 326.

In considering the issues which swirled around the 1905 Act one is struck by the emergence of a number of emphases which set the tone for the later debates on immigration into Britain. In particular the interaction of popular and official opinion which led to the 1905 Act and the fears and subsequent policy initiatives pursued from within the Anglo-Jewish elite, revealed an early capitulation to the forces of intolerance.[14] Viewed from that position the concessions to racism which occurred in Britain with the imposition in the 1960s of immigration controls and the major codification of such controls in the 1971 Immigration Act, cannot be viewed historically as a new departure; the events surrounding the 1905 Act can be regarded as a dress rehearsal for later developments.[15]

As in the United States this immigration from Eastern Europe in the late nineteenth century raised especial tensions. But the impact on legislative developments of the movement into Britain did not end in 1905. With the outbreak of the First World War the presence of aliens assumed an increased significance. In such circumstances a new Aliens Act of 1914 tightened the measure of official control.[16] The authorities aimed to restrict the movement of the so-called enemy aliens, the Austrians and Germans, groups which also had to contend with the rigours of internment and deportation.[17] However, the Act did create problems for members of other groups, including some Poles.[18]

Important as this law was, the decisive piece of legislation affecting alien immigration came in 1919. Together with the annual Order in Council which renewed it, this later Act provided the state with considerable control regarding the entry, movement and deportation of aliens. It remained essentially unaltered until the passing of the 1971 Immigration Act. In short the 1919 Act is of pivotal significance in the history of immigration control. In effect, it converted the emergency legislation on aliens passed in the first year of the Great War into general law. Even so, despite its significance, it has not been exposed to much scrutiny.[19] To the extent that the legislation in Britain has received attention, we are brought into contact once more with the immigration from Eastern Europe. The 1919 Act has been treated in some recent literature as an attempt, building on the earlier legislation, to control the activities of Russian Polish Jews.[20] The tensions which developed in relation to the question of conscription after 1916, an issue which led to collective violence being directed against Russian Polish

---

14. For the wider issue of toleration: Holmes, *Tolerant Country?*
15. Lea, "Contradictions of the Sixties". See also Bevan, Development of British Immigration Law, pp. 75-84.
16. Bird, *Control of Enemy Alien Civilians*, is useful on administrative issues.
17. Panayi, *Enemy in Our Midst*.
18. Davies, "Poles in Great Britain".
19. Bevan, *Development of British Immigration Law*, p. 73; Holmes, *John Bull's Island*; and Cesarani, "Anti-Alienism in England", are the major sources.
20. Cesarani, "Anti-Alienism in England", pp. 9-18 particularly.

Jews in Leeds and London in the following year,[21] together with the image which some commentators painted of the Bolshevik Revolution as a Jewish Revolution, counted among the forces which propelled the Government towards legislation.[22] The 1919 Act helped to place Russian Jews further under the microscope of the Government and there is no doubt that the State wanted to engage in a tighter surveillance of this group and control its development.

However, any attempt to explain the introduction of the 1919 Act entirely in such terms would be flawed. That position could be defended only by a selective reading of the evidence. It is clear from the parliamentary debates that the Act, passed in an atmosphere of intense post-war xenophobia which threatened all things alien,[23] was also aimed at controlling German influences. In the words of one MP, "We do not want German blood any more in this country [...] we have had it in high places and we want it no more".[24] Doubtless some of the Germans whom parliamentarians had in mind were Jews but they were not the Jews who had recently arrived from Russian Poland. Moreover, it would be restrictive to view the introduction of the 1919 Act as an exclusive reflection of fears relating to European aliens. Some of the fiercest labour disputes before 1914 had taken place in the merchant shipping industry and, in particular, the National Sailors' and Firemen's Union had campaigned hard against the use of Chinese labour. Some of these Chinese were British but not all of them were. J. Havelock Wilson, the man who had led the NSFU in its post-war campaigns, was in the House of Commons by 1919 and he lost no opportunity to continue his battle against "The Yellow Peril".[25] In other words, a number of pressures came together in 1919 and exerted pressure to produce the act.

Two additional emphases underline the importance of the 1919 Act and reveal the extent to which its history cannot be confined to Russian Polish Jews. The Act was deployed against Bolshevik agitators and, consequently, a number of Jews from the Russian Empire found themselves deported from Britain.[26] This development has received some emphasis in the surrounding literature. But the Act also had a serious impact upon those Lithuanians who had fled to Britain from the Tsar's Empire. Some men who had left Britain during the First World War to fight in the Tsar's Empire could not persuade the British authorities to grant their re-admission to the country under the 1919 Act. In such desperate circumstances family life could be sustained only by the subsequent departure of women and children from Britain. The fate of the Lithuanians has been

21. Holmes, *Anti-Semitism in British Society*, pp. 125-137.
22. Kadish, *Bolsheviks and British Jews*.
23. Parliamentary Debates (Commons), Vol. 114 (1919), 15 April 1919, col. 2765.
24. Ibid., col. 2799.
25. Ibid., Vol. 120 (1919), 3 November 1919, col. 1196.
26. Cesarani, "Anti-Alienism in England", pp. 7, 9-14.

recovered only recently and it should not be allowed to slip out of sight when the Act is considered.[27] Nor should its other consequences. Apart from the NSFU's fears relating to Chinese seamen, the union campaigned in the early twentieth century against Blacks and Arabs of alien nationality who worked on British ships. The 1919 Act did not prevent this practice: a legal loophole existed which such seamen could exploit. In 1925, however, the Special Restriction (Coloured Alien Seamen) Order brought these seamen into line with other aliens.[28] In its implementation, though, the Order gave rise to enormous problems. To escape its restrictions, men had to prove that they were British. In many cases, however, owing to administrative problems, documents could not be produced even by those colonial seamen who did have British nationality. The problems became further exacerbated at the local state level in Cardiff by the particularly insensitive application of the Order by the police.[29] We are witnessing here an illustration of the fact that the tangled question of who was truly, clearly "British", a form of tension which the 1981 British Nationality Act attempted to resolve, had longer and deeper roots than is often recognized.

Where have we reached in the unfolding discussion? The arrival of Eastern Europeans in Britain in the half century or so before 1919 in the shape particularly of Russian Polish Jews assumed a central significance in bringing about a tightening of official immigration policy, even if it did not account for each and every development. In passing such legislation Governments were catching the prevailing wind of public opinion. There was indeed a pronounced interaction between official and public pressures. As regards the consequences of such legislation, we have noticed that it had an impact on a variety of groups. In the specific case of the Jews, the main focus of our attention, the legislation of 1905 to 1919 helped to guarantee an end to the relatively large immigration inflow from Russian Poland. The consequent world depression also placed a brake on all international movement during the inter-war years but, even so, various local pressures could still encourage an interest in migration. In both Hungary and Poland, for example, official anti-semitism became the order of the day. However, no easy exit to Britain was possible.[30] The legislation of 1905 and 1919 had effectively shut the door on unrestricted alien immigration. Stimulated chiefly by the arrival of Jews from the Russian Empire, the continuing impact of such restrictions became particularly evident at a later date when Jews attempted to flee from the Greater Germany which had been constituted by the Nazis between 1933 and 1939. The British Government insisted on a tight control of

27. Rodgers, "Anglo-Russian Military Convention". See also on this turbulent period: White, "Scottish Lithuanians".
28. S.R. and O. (No. 296), 1925.
29. Evans, "Regulating the Reserve Army".
30. One Hungarian émigré of the inter-war years, George Mikes, wrote the classic book *How to be an Alien*.

immigration. The days of laissez-faire policy which prevailed before 1905 had vanished out of sight. It was not only in Britain that doors had been more tightly shut. The Great War and its consequences resulted in Europe soon being awash with refugees and in such circumstances the 1919 Act found its parallel in other countries as well as in the United States to which many Europeans had looked as an ultimate refuge.

Later Arrivals

Notwithstanding the tight controls which had been thrown over alien immigration, some Eastern Europeans did arrive in Britain during the inter-war years and, more particularly, during the Second World War. The groups which can be identified between 1939 and 1945 consisted mainly of nationals from those countries which had joined with Britain in the fight against Nazism. Governments-in-exile representing Czech and Polish interests became based in London and military personnel from countries which had fallen under Nazi control became a regular sight. All such personnel were viewed as temporary additions to the population who would return home as soon as conditions allowed. However, interesting as these experiences might be, our attention jumps over their lives in order to focus upon the years following the Second World War when a new phase began in the history of Eastern European immigration.

Europeans in exile after 1945

Surveys of immigration into Britain since the end of the Second World War have concentrated particularly upon the arrival of groups from the Caribbean and the Indian sub-Continent. Newcomers from these countries arrived in larger numbers than in any earlier period and at the same time became the focus of considerable public attention. However, an exclusive attention to those groups who came from "beyond the oceans" does not tell us the whole story of immigration into post-war Britain.[31] The census returns reveal the continuing strength of an Irish presence. Moreover, and central to our developing theme, in the years immediately following the Second World War other European groups arrived in relatively large numbers. It is in this context that Eastern Europeans re-enter the picture and it provides a degree of perspective on these early postwar years to realize that their numbers exceeded the size of the immigration from the Caribbean.[32]

31. Holmes, "Historians and Immigration", pp. 192-194. The phrase "beyond the oceans" is from Kiernan, "Britons Old and New", p. 54.
32. Lunn, "Race Relations or Industrial Relations?", pp. 18-19.

At the close of the war a large number of Polish ex-servicemen stationed in Western Europe displayed a marked reluctance to return to Poland whilst the country remained under Soviet domination. At first the British Government revealed little enthusiasm for the Poles' position. However, eventually it allowed ex-servicemen who wished to stay in Britain to remain and to be later joined by their dependants.[33] An additional number of Polish nationals became added to this population when they were brought to Britain from DP camps in Europe along with a variety of other nationalities, including Latvians, Estonians, Lithuanians and Ukrainians.[34] These workers, both men and women, known collectively as the European Volunteer Workers, arrived between 1945 and 1951.[35] Shortly afterwards, in 1956, it has been estimated that 21,000 Hungarians came to Britain following the Soviet suppression of the revolution in Hungary. Altogether 14,000 of these people made a permanent home in Britain.[36] A much smaller number of refugees arrived from Czechoslovakia after Soviet intervention in 1968 dashed the hopes of the Prague Spring.[37] Finally, throughout the post-war years a small trickle of refugees came to Britain from various countries in Eastern Europe and the Soviet Union though numbers were never large.[38] Defectors from the USSR who had once been part of the state apparatus received particular publicity. The cumulative effect of the main movements into Britain can be revealed to some extent in the post-war census returns which indicate country of birth:[39]

33. "The Poles", Channel 4 TV ("Passage to Britain"), 16 May 1984. The well-known study of the post-war Poles is: Zubrzycki, *Polish Immigrants in Britain*.

34. Kay and Miles, *Refugees or Migrant Workers?*, is the last study of such groups. On camps see Wyman, *Europe's Displaced Persons*. For an early assessment of DPs, the camps and the psychological trauma affecting refugees see Murphy, *Flight and Resettlement*, Part Two.

35. Tannahill, *European Volunteer Workers*, is a useful early study.

36. Wilson, *They Came as Strangers*, pp. 241-245; Levin, *What Welcome?*, pp. 41ff. On re-emigration see Parliamentary Debates (Commons), Vol. 582 (1957-8), 20 February 1958, col. 172.

37. On which episode there is no accessible history.

38. Bradford Heritage Recording Unit Tape B0081. There is acknowledgement in Patterson, "The Poles", p. 216.

39. Based on "Census 1951, England and Wales. General Report" (London, 1958), p. 104; "Census of Scotland, 1951, Vol. III" (Edinburgh, 1954), p. 54; "Census of 1961, Great Britain, Summary Tables" (London, 1966), p. 10; "Census 1971, Great Britain. Country of Birth Tables" (London, 1974), p. 26; "Census 1981, Great Britain Country of Birth Tables" (London, 1983), p. 5. It is not always possible to identify the precise number of people of alien origin in the country of birth tables.

Date	Poles	Hungarians	Czechs
1951	140,149	3,970	4,482
1961	127,246	18,272	10,318
1971	110,925	15,910	n.a.
1981	88,286	14,005	9,541

Any comparison with earlier figures is fraught with difficulty. No census was compiled in 1941. And in the 1931 census some Poles, Hungarians and Czechs, hide elusively within broader categories which featured in the census returns. The changing boundaries of East-Central Europe could also lead to some uncertainty in replying to the question on country of birth. A further complicating factor is that not everyone born in, say Poland, was of alien nationality. Even so, with all these qualifications, the census figures provide the best source we have and they show that, cumulatively, in comparison with the pre-war period when the total population of Eastern European groups numbered no more than a few thousand, it increased in size in the years immediately after the Second World War. However, in more recent times these minorities have been reduced through natural wastage which has not been replaced by any continual influx from Eastern Europe. In terms of their settlement after 1945 the Poles tended to cluster in their old wartime centres and, in the case of Poles, Hungarians and Czechs, as well as other Eastern European émigrés, London acted as a magnet. However, other cities, such as Bradford, also assumed a general importance as a centre of settlement.

Against that background it is possible to turn to our central theme and consider public responses towards the Eastern Europeans, though venturing as before, wherever appropriate, into the wider landscape peopled by immigrants and refugees. In the specific case of these post-war Eastern Europeans the focus is upon the Poles and Hungarians.

In the aftermath of the Second World War it was the Government's drive to recruit labour which greatly influenced its change of policy and led to the Poles being allowed to stay. In such circumstances the establishment by the Government in 1946 of the Polish Resettlement Corps provided an administrative filter through which the Poles could be placed in employment. However, such developments generated some concern among British workers. In turn, trade union responses reflected these fears which surfaced particularly in organizations such as the Amalgamated Union of Foundry Workers (AUFW) and the NUM, the National Union of Mineworkers. This opposition needs to be set within the appropriate industrial relations framework and within the context of an aim to preserve the employment of British workers, although it did also include some strands of overt anti-Polish sentiment. In such circumstances the Government accepted as early as 1946 that foreign workers could not be allowed to displace British workers.[40] These fears relating to employment extended beyond the industrial sector to embrace agricultural workers, with some fierce anti-Polish sentiment appearing in their union's publication, *The Landworker*. Moreover, such concerns need to be set alongside other anxieties. The housing market provided another area of tension as Poles began to move away from the hostels in which they were initially accommodated.[41] Other forms of opposition echoed from the war. The Poles could be described as Fascists by some people on the political Left[42] and Polish men could be stereotyped as "a race of Casanovas"[43] who posed a threat to British women or, more accurately, to British men who regarded women as their own exclusive property. The Poles also stood accused of other forms of undesirable social behaviour including that of black marketeering.[44]

Tensions, then, undoubtedly surfaced. But responses displayed more complexity than has so far been suggested. In the trade union movement differences of opinion emerged at national and local level, with local branches proving more tolerant in some instances than the national leadership, a phenomenon which can be traced particularly in the AUFW.[45] And, at the grass roots, in the midst of opposition towards the Poles in Scotland, some of the émigrés captured public support as footballers: the role of entertainer has often served as a protective niche for immigrants and refugees.[46]

As we journey away from the early post-war years certain significant developments can be observed. In the shadow of the war the Poles regarded themselves as in temporary exile. But the dream of a return to Poland did not easily turn into reality. We are reminded once again of the poignant observation: "Many corners of English graveyards are for ever Poland, or Italy or Spain."[47] The grip which Communism exerted on Eastern Europe discouraged a return to Poland. In London that dream of return could still be contemplated over Wyborowa or Zubrowka in the Daquise but until the 1980s it was effectively off the agenda other than in exceptional circumstances.[48] Moreover, the original refugees became constrained by their children who had been born and brought up in Britain, even though younger people might have a sentimental attachment to

---

40. Economic Survey for 1947, Cmd 7046 (1947), pp. 27-28. Also Sword *et al.*, *Formation of the Polish Community*, p. 256.
41. TUC, Annual Report, 1946 (London, 1946), p. 357.
42. "No British Jobs for Fascist Poles" (London, 1946). A CPGB pamphlet in the University of Sheffield Archives.
43. Zubrzycki, *Polish Immigrants in Britain*, p. 82.
44. Sword *et al.*, *Formation of the Polish Community*, p. 347.
45. Lunn, "Race Relations or Industrial Relations?", p. 21.
46. Grant, "White Eagles of the North".
47. Kiernan, "Britons Old and New", p. 49.
48. "Alec the Pole", Channel 4 TV ("40 Minutes"), 17 October 1991.

Poland.[49] This myth of return, a sustaining but illusory belief, has featured in the lives of other minorities: the Poles are in no sense unique.

So the majority of Poles have remained in Britain. Yet tension and hostility in such circumstances have been less evident than in the early post-war years. Why? Partly because no significant flow of Polish migration has occurred: the toughness of Polish and British policies guaranteed that no fears of a Polish deluge would surface. Moreover, the Poles in Britain benefited from the growth of anti-Communist sentiment in the West. The authorities helped to massage public responses on that score and certain writers and publications helped to boost such sentiment. In this ambience the Poles could become regarded as the personifcation of good people sheltering in exile from an evil power. Other influences also had an input into the situation, including the strategies pursued by the Poles in their new environment. Their commitment to trade unions and also to their local communities smoothed the process of adjustment.[50] Not that in this improving situation the Poles were remarkable for their social mobility. Notwithstanding some success stories, the majority remained firmly locked in the working class even if they did not always remain in their original occupations.[51] Problems of adjustment, as with other East Europeans were not uncommon.[52] That lack of social mobility might also have assisted the toleration of the Poles; it was difficult to imagine the ever-decreasing remnant of Poland in exile as a significant threat. In such circumstances compensation for Poles was often gained through the progress made by their British-born children.[53]

Let us leave the Poles for a moment and turn to consider the Hungarians. Unlike the Poles they were not already in exile in Britain; they came in desperate flight from the Soviet repression of the 1956 uprising in Hungary. The Soviet response was condemned by the British Government. The attention thus focused upon Soviet repression diverted attention from the simultaneous Anglo-French invasion of Suez. Yet there is a world of difference between condemning developments in a faraway country and allowing those affected by such policies to enter Britain. The Government initially set a low ceiling on the number of refugees it was prepared to accept. However, some relaxation occurred in official policy, as a result of which, we have just noticed, 21,000

49. On the Poles born in Britain see Wojciechowska, "Generational Differences in Ethnic Consciousness".
50. Lunn, "Race Relations or Industrial Relations?", p. 24.
51. "Time Stands Still", Channel 4 TV ('10 X 10'), 9 October 1992; a study of Ilford Park Polish Home. See also the earlier report in *The Times*, 30 December 1987.
52. *The Times*, 21 May 1951, "Foreign Labour in Britain (1)", noted the problems which older officers and former professional groups had in adjusting to a new life. A literary treatment of the problem of adjustment is Gebler, *August in July*.
53. Kucewicz, "Immigrant Experience", and James, "Eagle in Exile", are excellent local studies of later trends.

Hungarians came to Britain, 14,000 of whom stayed in the country, with some refugees departing to pastures new in the Commonwealth and North America and others returning to Hungary.[54]

Compared with its involvement in the resettlement of the Poles the Government pursued a less vigorous policy, even if its hand can be detected at various points. It disseminated information to assist refugees; in addition, it provided funds for accommodation and eventually the Ministry of National Insurance became responsible for the various hostels in which the Hungarians were initially housed.[55]

As for popular opinion, it was characterized at first by a surge of sympathy for the uprising and the refugees. There was talk of an International Brigade of Students going to Hungary to fight side by side with the Hungarians against the Soviets. Shades of the Spanish Civil War. Students at Sheffield, London and Nottingham Universities stood at the forefront of this episode.[56] In the case of the refugees the extent of public sympathy can be gauged from the responses to the Lord Mayor of London's Fund and the various local equivalents in cities such as Sheffield and Manchester.[57] Charities such as the Women's Royal Voluntary Service, the Save the Children Fund, and the British Council for Aid to Refugees, also responded enthusiastically to the circumstances.

Even so, it would be wide of the mark to assume that public reponses assumed a one-dimensional shape, even if a situation of virtual full employment helped to keep initial hostility in check. As with the Poles some opposition developed towards the Hungarians from within the NUM.[58] The NCB was keen to attract workers but for its part the NUM placed difficulties in the path of this scheme. In the mining communities a strong inward-looking character told against the toleration of foreigners and memories of the unemployment which scarred the 1930s remained fresh in many minds. Not that such emphases always entered into the discourse of the public debate. A greater emphasis was often placed on the problems which language difference could create if Hungarian men went down the pits: this claim had a familiar ring: it had sounded when the Lithuanian Catholics had arrived from the Tsar's Empire[59] and it had also featured in the opposition encountered after the Second World War by the Poles.[60] This recognition of linkages serves as a reminder of yet another connection with

54. See above p. 327 on numbers.
55. On the dissemination of leaflets and publicity see PRO LAB 8/2345. Appendix to Council Minutes (City of Manchester) 1957-58, Vol. 17, pp. 1627-1633 notes the role of the National Assistance Board at Styal.
56. Donson, "British Responses to Hungarian Immigration", p. 40. On Hungarian students in Britain see PRO LAB 8/2346.
57. Ibid., p. 36 on Sheffield. On Manchester see *Manchester Evening News*, 27 November 1956.
58. Larner, "1956 Hungarian Refugees", ch. 3.
59. Lunn, "Reactions to Lithuanian and Polish Immigrants", p. 319.
60. Noticed in Holmes, *John Bull's Island*, p. 248.

earlier years. In the defence of its position the NUM continued to draw attention to the 1947 agreement it had concluded with the NCB which had governed the employment of foreign workers: it was an agreement used to powerful effect soon afterwards by pits in Yorkshire where the rejection of Hungarians appears to have been virtually total.[61]

A further link with earlier debates came in another strand of opposition which the Hungarians faced. Like the Polish refugees who remained after 1945 they were sometimes dismissed as a "bad lot", an observation which in the case of the Hungarians was often accompanied by the claim that the better type of refugee had gone to other countries such as the United States.[62] Finally, in this process of drawing backward links, the Hungarians like the Poles had at times to face the claim that they were stealing British women. It is an allegation which all male-dominated minorities entering Britain have faced at one time or another. In the specific case of the Hungarians, the tension was illustrated in Yorkshire by a number of fights in the Barnsley area between local men and refugees resident at the Broadway Miners' Hostel when "the Barnsley lads felt the refugees were stealing their girls".[63]

Forty years on, however, the tensions have evaporated. The Hungarians have become even more invisible than the Poles. It is always possible to spot an occasional Hungarian name: a Finta, a Bugner, a Varadi, a Killi, a Farkas, a Hegedus, but it needs particularly sensitive antennae to locate these peoples as Hungarian. Whereas Polish London can feature in guide books the Hungarian presence remains invisible.[64] In explaining this invisibility we need to begin with the question of numbers. Over the past thirty or so years the Hungarian population has gently declined. Part of this decline relates to natural causes, the deaths of Hungarians living in Britain. At the same time, the reduction has been assisted by the tight rein which the British Government has kept on alien immigration and also by the restrictions until recently on emigration from the former Soviet bloc. We are reminded once again of the Polish experience in exile in Britain and the lives of the various nationalities who constituted the European Volunteer Workers. Following the early post-war years none of these groups has shown any substantial increase in population. In the case of those Hungarians who did come to Britain in the shadow of the uprising and decided to stay, Government policy was based on the premise that they would soon have to stand on their own feet. They would have to "blend in". We can recall here the emphasis in the 1949 Royal Commission on Population on the desirability

---

61. Larner, "1956 Hungarian Refugees", pp. 19, 21.
62. Personal information on Hungarians; on the Poles see above, p. 329. EVWs also faced charges of black marketeering. See Tannahill, *European Volunteer Workers*, p. 72.
63. The Star, 13 December 1957.
64. See Davies, *New London Spy*, pp. 273-278 and McAuley, *Guide to Ethnic London*, pp. 69-82.

of newcomers "becoming merged" in to what was called "the host population".[65] The terms are revealing: an emphasis on hosts carries the implication of aliens as guests; an emphasis on "becoming merged" gives no concession to integration with its stress on mutual tolerance. But nevertheless the Hungarians have gone along the route which was expected of them. Hungarian Jewish refugees have filtered into local Jewish communities, in some cases strengthening the degree of religious observance just as some of the earlier refugees from Russian Poland heightened the practice of religious orthodoxy in Anglo-Jewry. Roman Catholics among the Hungarian refugees have also become absorbed. In general, therefore, a specific Hungarian presence in Britain is not especially visible. And, to repeat, in this context, earlier antipathies have evaporated.

General Comments

Are there any general observations which emerge from these episodes? Attention can be directed first of all to a number of similarities between these earlier and later immigrations from Eastern Europe.

In both cases the groups contained refugees who were intent on escaping from religious or political pressures rather than immigrants who came primarily to improve their economic prospects.[66] To be sure, some Jews moved westwards on account of economic pressures towards the end of the Tsarist autocracy but for others it was persecution which acted as the primary immediate stimulus to their flight, although the distinction between refugees and economic migrants is not always easy to delineate. In the case of the Poles, Hungarians and Czechs who settled after 1945 the Soviet presence and policies in Eastern Europe after 1945 and the consequent disappearance of Poland, Hungary and Czechoslovakia as independent national states acted as the key determinants influencing their westward movement. The British Government might have viewed the minorities from these countries primarily in terms of additional units of labour, as migrant workers rather than refugees, but these Eastern Europeans, like some of the EVWs who arrived contemporaneously, perceived themselves as exiled groups temporarily uprooted from their homelands.[67]

All these Eastern European groups in the late nineteenth century and after the Second World War were often hazily viewed by the British. At the former time distinctions were not always made between Lithuanian Catholics and Polish Jews and in the postwar years Eastern Europeans were often lumped together quite indiscriminately as "bloody Poles". These fuzzy images mirrored the perceptions

65. See "Royal Commission on Population Report", Cmd (1949), p. 124.
66. Kunz, "Refugee in Flight".
67. Kay and Miles, *Refugees or Migrant Workers?*

of Eastern Europe as a faraway part of the world about which little was known. But such haziness did not offer a shield against hostility even if the lives of the newcomers generally improved through their transfer from Eastern to Western Europe. Such improvements occurred, incidentally, in the absence of any specific infrastructure designed to reduce or eliminate antipathy and discrimination.[68] That kind of infrastructure appeared for the first time in the 1960s following the arrival of immigrants from the Caribbean and the Indian sub-Continent, a fact which some Eastern Europeans were not slow to point out whilst stressing that they had been required to make their respective ways in the absence of any such framework.

In addition to these similarities there are differences between the immigrations. A comparison of responses reveals that the hostility generated up to 1919 against the Russian Poles was fiercer and more pronounced than that which the Eastern Europeans encountered after the Second World War. There is a need to explain such differences.

In attempting to do so, one influence which needs to be emphasized it that the immigration from Russian Poland in the late nineteenth and early twentieth centuries consisted mainly of Jews.[69] This movement also occurred during one of the most significant periods in the history of recent anti-semitism and the fierceness of the debate surrounding the arrival of Jews from Russian Poland reflected the wider anti-semitism of that epoch.[70] Although Jewish survivors found it difficult to enter Britain after the Holocaust,[71] a fact which reveals the lingering significance of anti-semitism, there is no doubt that in the wake of the Nazi extermination programme and the horror it provoked, such sentiment had weakened.

A second factor which helps to explain the different level of responses relates to the legislation of 1905 and 1919 which had been introduced to control the entry of aliens. When the immigration from Russian Poland began to assume significant proportions, as it did in the late nineteenth century, immigration restrictions were not in place in Britain. However, this laissez-faire stance became reversed by the legislation of 1905 and 1919. As a consequence, with such controls in place, there was no prospect after 1945 of any continuity of large scale immigration from Eastern Europe even if departures to the West had been allowed by the various governments in the former Soviet bloc. Strict controls derived from the same legislation affected the early lives of those aliens who did gain admittance. Moreover, and of considerable significance, the British

---

68. Lunn, "Reactions to Lithuanians and Polish Immigrants", p. 107; Bradford Heritage Recording Unit Tape, M0006/01/22.
69. See above p. 321.
70. Higham, "Anti-semitism in the gilded age".
71. Cesarani, *Justice Delayed*, pp. 77-80.

Government had the necessary powers to deport those aliens who contravened the conditions of their residence. In short, after 1945 the State found itself in a position to exercise a greater control over aliens and alien immigration.

It had less control, however, over Irish immigration, and also that of Blacks and Asians, from the Caribbean and the Indian sub-Continent, respectively. A consideration of the experiences of these groups helps also to shed light on the postwar Eastern European experience.

The Irish remained the largest single immigrant group in postwar Britain and their entry remained unrestricted. Indeed, in the early years after the war it increased to levels which had last been witnessed in the nineteenth century. Yet the Irish encountered less hostility than the Blacks and Asians, notwithstanding the fact that "No Irish" signs in lodging houses were commonplace in the 1950s and, furthermore, as aliens they were exposed to the threat of deportation for contraventions of the law. Why then, had the Irish ceased to be regarded as a serious problem? After all, in the mid-nineteenth century, well before the big immigration of Russian Polish Jews and the fierce debates their presence created, the Irish had been widely perceived as an undesirable scourge on British society, its chief affliction through immigration. In part, the lower levels of anti-Irish hostility after 1945 compared with the group's experiences in the nineteenth century related partly to the declining influence of religion in Britain. In the nineteenth century the Roman Catholicism which clung to many Irish people had acted as a powerful condensing rod drawing antipathy towards them. In addition, it became less easy, though not impossible, to portray the Irish as a backward people. When they had lived under British domination such stereotyping became commonplace but whilst it still lingered on, stereotypes are often durable, it had lost some if its force. After all, the Irish in the Irish Free State had run their own affairs since 1922. But there is yet a further and indeed decisive consideration. By the postwar years the Irish, as Europeans, were regarded in influential quarters as having a greater potential to blend into postwar British society than workers from the Colonial and Imperial territories.[72] That last observation also helps to explain why Eastern Europeans encountered less hostility than Blacks and Asians from the Empire and Commonwealth.

In other words, if all migrants entering Britain have revealed through their experiences society's propensity for racializing such minorities, certain groups have been especially exposed at particular times. In the postwar years the Eastern Europeans and the Irish still had to contend with such hostility. However, the unwillingness displayed in influential and official circles to contemplate a noticeable influx of Blacks and Asians from the Empire, and the simultaneous

72. "Political and Economic Planning, Population Policy in Great Britain" (London, 1948), pp. 108-116.

overt preference for European workers, opinions which came on display in the 1949 Royal Commission on Population and in Cabinet discussions, ensured that images developed of such Black and Asian immigration, as an especially un-wholesome and dangerous process.[73] At the same time, as immigration from the Caribbean and the Indian sub-Continent nevertheless continued to increase, and Black and Asian communities increased their visibility, a policy dilemma persisted on how to exclude such immigrants, all of whom, until 1962, possessed a legal right of entry into Britain. Hence it was around these Blacks and Asian groups rather than European minorities, that tensions particularly developed and opposition became fiercely focussed, whether in private or in public, discreetly or overtly, and with strong popular hostility soon aligning itself with similar sentiment within elite circles.

This shifting of emphasis in the course of the nineteenth and twentieth centuries from the Irish to the Russian Poles and then towards Blacks and Asians as the major subjects of immigration controversy suggests a degree of flux and change in the history of attitudes towards immigrant and refugee groups. That observation is particularly apposite at present in view of the dramatic changes currently sweeping over Eastern Europe and the former Soviet Union. Problems in that part of the world might lead in the future to a build-up of pressure for another wave of emigration to the West, although at present no major move-ment has occurred. However, alerted to the possibility that in today's Eastern Europe there might be a disaster waiting to happen, Western countries have been involved in aid programmes whilst emphasizing the need for immigration control to prevent any significant westward movement.[74] At the moment it remains uncertain how the relationship between Western and Eastern Europe in this new phase of the Continent's history will be fully worked out. To claim otherwise would be to engage in speculation masquerading as history.

---

73. "Royal Commission on Population Report", Cmd (1949), p. 124.
74. "House of Commons Foreign Affairs Committee. First Report. Central and Eastern Europe. Problems of the Post-Communist Era", Vol. 1 (London, 1992), pp. XV, XXXIV-XXXV; Institute for European Defence and Strategic Studies, "After the Soviet Collapse: New Realities and Illusions" (London, 1992).

Immigration and Reaction in Britain, 1880-1950: Rethinking the "Legacy of Empire"*

Kenneth Lunn

Since many social analyses of contemporary "race relations" still perceive the starting point of the "problems" to be the influx of so-called "New Commonwealth" immigration into Britain after 1945,[1] it is therefore assumed that the process of "racialisation", of the identification of "race" as a social and political issue, began essentially with this post-war influx. Much of the existing literature on the various dimensions of the history of immigration into Britain before this time deals, therefore, with the events and circumstances as if they were some minor footnote to, or precursor of, the really significant phase of settlement after that date. By association, it is also suggested that a fully-fledged "race" dimension is absent from the attitudes and responses towards earlier dimensions of Britain's immigration history. This develops, therefore, into a paradigm which links racism and racialism in Britain with a significant "black" presence and thus historical concerns become fixed upon the establishment of black communities in Britain and responses to them. Other ethnic minorities, such as the Irish or Jews, are seen as relatively insignificant or even marginal to the inexorable move towards an institutionalized British racism focussed exclusively on blacks. Whilst there have been developments in the literature which challenge this basic approach, it still remains the dominant one within the literature, particularly where sociology seeks to appropriate a unilinear version of the history of immigration and reaction to explain the post-1945 "race relations" situation within British society.

Within the existing literature, too, there is a tendency to use a stock phrase to explain the development of racism in Britain, one which often appears to need no further explanation or analysis, the "legacy of empire". As a substitute for significant historical analysis and an evaluation of the processes of ideological construction and inheritance, this concept of "legacy" has been applied quite

* I would like to thank the participants in the conference "Migration and settlement in a historical perspective", held in Leiden and Amsterdam in September 1993 for the constructive debate which ensued. I am particularly grateful to Jan Lucassen and Leo Lucassen and to Marcel van der Linden for their comments on my original paper.

1. See the recent debate resulting from the remarks of Winston Churchill MP – summarized in *The Runnymede Bulletin*, no. 267 (July/August 1993).

randomly as a standard introduction to the study of post-war immigration. Yet, as has recently been argued by Gilroy, this approach fundamentally misunderstands the conceptual importance of the construction of "race".

> "Racism is not a unitary event based on psychological aberration nor some ahistorical antipathy to blacks which is the cultural legacy of empire and which continues to saturate the consciousness of all white Britons regardless of age, gender, income or circumstances. It must be understood as a process [...]"[2]

Such an analysis raises two perhaps obvious but not always related strands within the theoretical debate. One is concerned with what is now a fairly familiar notion of "race" as a social construct.[3] The other is the view of "race" as a dynamic, a construction which is constantly in the process of formulation and reformulation, according to particular historical circumstances. Again, as Gilroy notes,

> "'Race' has to be socially and politically constructed and elaborate ideological work is done to secure and maintain the different forms of 'racialization' which have characterized capitalist development. Recognizing this makes it all the more important to compare and evaluate the different historical situations in which 'race' has become politically pertinent."[4]

In what seems still to be a much-neglected work, published nearly twenty years ago, Banton and Harwood suggested that the meaning of the word "race" could only be understood through the study of its evolution and its historical usage. They also suggested that the relationship between what might be termed "the legacy of history" and "contemporary political affairs", which gave birth to popular imagery of race, required a recognition of a long and complex history of attitudes and processes for the transmission of values.[5] What is being suggested here is that not only should the history of British immigration and "race" be studied more analytically in order to better understand the present, vital though that task may be, but that it is also important to recognize the complexity of the past in order to make sense of the historical processes in their own right. Without such an analysis, we are in danger of also misunderstanding the present.

The aims of this study, then, are to suggest the need for a more sophisticated approach to the analysis of historical dimensions of immigration into Britain, following three major themes. The first is to identify the range of different migration experiences and patterns within Britain in the period under consideration. Noting Irish immigration as a continuous, if uneven, process throughout the period, we can also see an increase in Jewish immigration in the 1880s and

---

2.   Gilroy, *There Ain't No Black in the Union Jack*, p. 27.
3.   See, for example, Miles, *Racism*.
4.   Gilroy, *There Ain't No Black in the Union Jack*, p. 38.
5.   Banton and Harwood, *Race Concept*, p. 9.

1890s. Over a similar timescale, African and Asian seafarers settled or sojourned in Britain. After the end of the Second World War, Poles and other European labour were specifically engaged to solve some of the identified labour shortages. Even these few examples give some indication of the ethnic composition of British society before 1950. Each group operated in different circumstances, with varying degrees of state and employer control, differing levels of involvement with the labour movement and significantly different cultural "baggage" and images from within the "host" society.

The second theme is to challenge the focus on the nation state and "nation" as *the* significant entity in the formulation of atttitudes towards ethnic minorities and determining the immigrant experience. In the period under consideration, although it is possible to generalize about the emergent structures of the British state, and estimate the growing levels of state intervention upon its citizens, in matters of "race"and immigration, state involvement could be seen as relatively unimportant. Attitudes and cultures were often formulated in the local context, whether it was through the influence of the local state or community/workplace networks. This is not to argue for the absence of national input, politically, culturally or economically, but to suggest that this had to compete with a number of often oppositional forces, whose origins were from a more localized setting. In ideological terms, the national state has found it difficult to create a common voice.

> "As Hall *et al* (1978) and Downing (1980, ch. 7) have stressed there is no single monolithic ideology shared by all Britons. The interlocking imagery and values which dominate the experience of any one group defined by class, region, ethnicity or gender is not the same as that prevailing in another group. And the same image or value found to be present in two different groups does not necessarily have the same range of meaning [...] Hence Downing's insistence that there are many ideological elements in contemporary British society which cannot be reduced to a single core."[6]

If this can be seen as relevant for contemporary society, then it is equally appropriate for the study of the recent past. It is the particular conjuncture of circumstances, what Downing calls "the contradictory and dynamic interac-tions",[7] which is the concern of this study.

Finally, attention will focus more specifically on the relationship between immigrant or migrant workers and the labour movement. Existing work has tended to suggest a continuum of overt hostility both by the labour movement towards "foreign" workers and by immigrant groups towards the labour movement. Case-studies suggest a far more complex set of attitudes. These require an evaluation of local political cultures, social and economic contexts

---

6. Husband, "Introduction: 'Race'", pp. 19-20.
7. Ibid., p. 20.

and ideological concerns. By looking at a range of experiences, it should be possible to offer a more evaluative approach to this topic.

Immigration into Britain

It should not be necessary here to go into great detail about the ethnic diversity of British society in the period 1880-1950. The work of several historians, Colin Holmes in particular, has now provided a series of studies which should become part of a standard curriculum.[8] What perhaps still requires some emphasis is the degree of diversity *within* those ethnic groups who arrived in Britain. Contemporary commentators, as well as historians, have tended to assume a homogeneity about particular groups, whereas the social, economic and cultural differences within any ethnic group may well have been more significant. Here, writers such as Robert Miles, with an emphasis on "race" as a social construction, have done a valuable service in emphasizing the contextual dimensions for any study of ethnicity and immigration.[9] "Race" can often be a distraction in the analysis of particular sets of social relations, even if it can never be ignored. It is, therefore, important to comprehend the history of immigration into Britain as an uneven process and one which is multi-faceted rather than one-dimensional.

Work already done on aspects of Jewish immigration has indicated the value of identifying divisions within what is defined as "the Jewish community". Differences in class position, degrees of social mobility, variations in political and religious beliefs, all offer a very differentiated experience within what is defined as British Jewry and also in the responses of a wider society towards Jews.[10] No longer can we accept the Chicago school notion of assimilation, at least as the sole interpretation of the history of Jews in Britain. In turn, we should note that these internal divisions within the Jewish community may well have produced a range of responses from the "host" society, as will be suggested below.

Similarly, analysis of the Irish in Britain is increasingly suggesting the fragmentation of experience. Dispersal throughout Britain in the second half of the nineteenth century added to existing differences of origin, class, religion and gender.[11] As will be demonstrated here, differences could often help shape the everyday reception and reaction and produce very significant variations in the ways that Irish people were dealt with during their time in Britain.

---

8. See Holmes, *John Bull's Island*, and the same author, *Tolerant Country?*
9. See, for example, Miles, *Racism*.
10. See Williams, "Beginnings of Jewish Trade Unionism"; Buckman, *Immigrants and Class Struggle*; Kushner, "Jew and Non-Jew in the East End".
11. See, for example, Fitzpatrick, "Curious Middle Place".

Equally, the category of "alien" seamen includes a range of groups, from India, Africa, China and the Middle East. Concentration on their "foreign" origin may mask the often complex ties of kinship and tribe which drew together particular crews and which helped shape community structures in Britain.[12] To view them as an undifferentiated mass is to miss the cultural and economic expectations held by different groups and their very different experiences within British society.

Moving onto the immediate post-war period, there were two distinctive elements in the consequent wave of settlement which deserve attention and help highlight variations within the immigrant experience. At a superficial level, we might expect the reception of these two groups – Europeans and West Indians – to be very different, based on assumptions about cultural attitudes to skin colour. Although East Europeans, including the Polish Resettlement Corps and European Volunteer Workers, may have been perceived as closer culturally and "ethnically" to Britons, and West Indians regarded as "others", perceptions and attitudes were also determined by other factors.[13] Certainly, for the British government, distinctions were complicated by the different legal status of the groups. The Europeans were brought to Britain on very strict terms, were a far more controlled workforce and were not, at least until naturalized, British citizens with all the ensuing rights. West Indians were citizens, came as free labour and were thus, at least officially, beyond control by state agencies.[14] Thus, although for most Britons, the Europeans, by sheer weight of numbers, appeared to pose a threat to jobs and lifestyles, for the government, it was the West Indians who, in the long term, raised more difficult questions. Although , by 1950, the numbers were still relatively small, their status as British citizens seemed to promise a less controllable workforce and also raised fears at government and at a popular level about "race relations" within Britain. Thus, it is clear that the significance of these two groups depends not simply upon the "race" dimension, important as that may have been, but also on other dimensions of status and legal definition, which in turn helps to determine a more coherent view of their lives in Britain.

Collectively, then, as has been suggested, it becomes almost impossible to talk in any meaningful way about *the* immigrant experience from the perspective of the immigrants themselves. Historians have too frequently simply defined immigrants as objects of hostility, of opposition, without taking the time to look more carefully at the ethnic groups themselves, at their social, cultural and

12. The as-yet unpublished work of Richard Lawless on "Arab" seamen will be particularly valuable in this respect. See also Visram, *Ayahs, Lascars and Princes*; and the various publications of Neil Evans on South Wales.

13. See Kay and Miles, *Refugees or Migrant Workers?*, which argues a very powerful case for the "racialization" of attitudes towards these workers.

14. Jan and Leo Lucassen, "Preface to the Conference", p. 8.

political dimensions. The assimilation model is clearly no longer an acceptable one, although it may describe quite accurately the experiences of some immigrants. It does not fit for many others and we need a more differentiated approach to analyse and explain the variations encountered in this rich history.

Immigration and "Nation"

Any historical account of the immigration process and the interaction between an established "British" community and settler groups immediately raises more problems than it solves. We need to question the role and function of the state within such an historical relationship. We also need to recognize the diversity, the complexity of anything labelled "British culture" and therefore challenge any particular stereotype of host-immigrant attitudes and values.

The impact of the British state apparatus on the immigration process and on the construction of a discourse with regard to ethnic minorities is clearly important. It is possible to trace such influence in conventional ways, as for example through the introduction of legislation designed to control and limit immigration.[15] However, in the period under consideration (and in stark contrast to the 1960s onwards), much of the legislation appears retrospective, reactive rather than proactive, and constructed to deal very specifically with particular situations allegedly created by particular groups or phases of immigration. The first major piece of interventionist legislation, the Aliens Act of 1905, was directed specifically at the influx of Jews into Britain which had become more consistent from the 1880s onwards.[16] Legislation during the First World War has been described as a watershed in British immigration history,[17] in that it marked the shift of the British state away from a strategy of laissez-faire with regard to immigration. However, it could be argued that this change was marked more by other events and discourses than by national legislation. Looking beyond 1918, there is little evidence of a concerted drive by the state to establish a water-tight legal framework with which to control the influx of peoples into Britain. Specific legislation, such as the Aliens Restriction Order of 1925, dealt with identified "problems" (in this case, "coloured alien" seamen), often thrown up by localized "moral panics". The British Nationality Act of 1948, with its clarifications of status, particularly in regard to Commonwealth citizenship rights, can hardly be seen as a restrictive measure.[18] All this is not to argue, however, the marginality of the state in determining the immigrant experience – those

---

15. See Bevan, *Development of British Immigration Law.*
16. See Garrard, *English and Immigration.*
17. See, for example, Holmes, *John Bull's Island*, p. 95.
18. See Deakin, "British Nationality Act"; Holmes, *John Bull's Island*, p. 257.

Jews who sought shelter in Britain from Central Europe in the later 1930s could bear chilling testimony to the power of the British state in this respect. What is suggested is that the national state cannot be seen as inevitably the sole or dominant agent in the determination of the immigrant experience.

Thus, overall, whilst state-enacted legislation may have provided a framework for the control, restriction and administration of various phases of immigration into Britain, it could be argued that it was the enabling process, the administration and interpretation of the legal system by local authorities, the lobbying and persuasion which such authorities were able to enact which more frequently shaped the every-day lives of immigrants. Too often, within this history, the central state has been seen as the initiator. The reality is more likely that its actions were the final outcome of a long series of negotiations at a local level, reflecting particular aspects of local feelings, views and needs. A useful study of such a process is the inter-war period in Cardiff, where Neil Evans has very effectively identified the operation of local forces within the experience of "alien" seamen in the port. In assessing the ways of "regulating the reserve army",[19] Evans has analysed the role of local agencies, such as the police, the seamen's union and the local city council, in constant lobbying for restriction and control of so-called "aliens" living in and working through the port. This involved a web of some-times conflicting but always interactive pressures. As Evans puts it:

"The local authorities were not the only bodies to be confronted with the issue, for though they sometimes acted independently and at the behest of their racist urges, they were also enmeshed in a wider network of action and power, both local and national. Pressures exerted on them locally from non-conformist groups, the press, trade unions, shipowners and ratepayers. Some of these groups also acted through the central state, which in turn was a source of instructions and directives. Local bodies – the City Council, the police, immigration officers, Poor Law Guardians, the local Mercantile Marine Office – the agencies directly charged with regulating this reserve army, were the focus of converging pressures."[20]

Similarly, during the Second World War, ostensibly the British state was concerned to operate a flexible and smooth system for the recruitment of workers from Eire as part of the industrial effort. Considerable lengths were gone to by state agencies to ensure the effective running of this programme, particularly since it was the result of delicate negotiation with the Irish government because of its neutral status during the war. Any hostility, prejudice or racism directed at Irish workers was therefore dysfunctional in terms of the current needs of the British state and the war effort. However, there is ample evidence that the official culture of the national state did not coincide with that of local

19. Evans, "Regulating the Reserve Army".
20. Ibid., pp. 68-69.

officials or of popular consciousness. For example, without any apparent incident to spark off such a response, a Regional Welfare Office for the Ministry of Labour, based in Manchester, could draw upon the drunken Irishman stereotype in a directive to his local officials.

> "It should also be made as difficult as possible for them to obtain strong drink, particularly spirits, (including methylated spirits) on the journey or immediately upon arrival."[21]

Similarly, it was felt that it would be difficult to find lodgings for these Irish workers, due to popular hostility.

> "[...] the majority of householders in England are strongly unwilling to have Irishmen in their houses as lodgers and it may be very difficult to persuade Local Authorities to compel their citizens to accept Irishmen, even of the better type".[22]

Here we find illustrations of the clashes between the needs of the national state and the local structures. In the case of Irish employment during the war, evidence can be produced to show that the role of the state was to attempt to "de-racialize", albeit temporarily, the immigration process, to mediate against popular forms of hostility displayed at the local level. Its success in this is disputed but it does indicate the divergence of interests and, in this case, the lack of impact that the central state might have upon popular attitudes and actions.[23]

Nor should it be assumed that popular attitudes and actions within Britain were constant throughout the period. Immigration historians have often poured through the sources looking for evidence of hostility, discrimination, negative behaviour of any kind and linked these together into a continuum of opposition. Perhaps we have been less aware of what might be called the "significant silences" within immigration history. Recognizing these would not deny the existence of a consistent racism within British society but could also indicate the presence of more positive forms of response, ones which are not merely rehearsed or pre-ordained reactions. In addition, it would be important to argue that different political and social cultures within British society could produce significantly varied experiences: national agendas, if they existed at all, could be disregarded or be only one element within any ideological construction.

Illustrations of this can be found in the following discussion on the labour movement, particularly where it can be argued that, at least within certain sections, notions of internationalism and solidarity could overcome wariness of "foreign" competition within the labour market. More specifically, instances of solidarity, of acceptance, meant that some impact, however slight, was made

21. Cited in Lunn "'Good for a Few Hundreds'", p. 109.
22. Ibid.
23. Ibid.

upon the cultural baggage of negative images which often constituted such a dominant force and that the impact of these more positive experiences could operate beyond their immediate context. Thus, for example, it was something of a legend in the inter-war mining industry in Scotland that Lithuanians, who came to work in the pits before the First World War, had displayed a powerful commitment to the miners' union in the 1912 national strike. They had been at the forefront of a march to Tarbrax Colliery, the one pit left working during the strike, and which subsequently had its pithead gear burnt to the ground. Some of the Lithuanians were tried, convicted and deported as a result of the incident, despite a campaign by the union to save them.[24] Consequently, the example of solidarity across ethnic divides was used in the 1920s and 30s, when tensions between Protestant and Catholic re-emerged within the union, to indicate the futility, for both union and community, of such divisions. This could not, of course, eliminate the sectarian tensions within the workforce and the wider community but could provide a powerful argument for those who sought to challenge this kind of internal conflict. There is also some evidence that the experience of the Lithuanians helped to modify responses towards Poles and EVWs employed in Scottish pits after the Second World War.[25]

Equally, other regional and political responses could be positive, or at least displayed significant variations from the assumed outright and permanent hostility. Kushner's exploratory work on the East End of London takes as one of its themes the notion of "pessimistic" and "optimistic" schools of race relations[26] and he makes out a very good case for seeing Jewish-Gentile relations as supporting both of these perspectives. Whilst Kushner is keen to emphasize the continuity of racism within British society, and its unexceptional occurrence as part of a tradition of intolerance, he also wishes to identify "the anthropology of everyday ethnic relations in the East End [...]. (which indicates the British people's) ability to accept local and national plurality".[27] Kushner's explanation, in part, for the relative failure of fascism to make a significant impact in the East End is that it proposed an opposition "to the idea of an ethnically diverse neighbourhood which was widely accepted at the local level".[28] It might be even more useful to suggest an end to the notion of "optimistic" and "pessimistic" and make more specific reference to the particular circumstances which could construct a particular view of immigrants and ethnic minorities, one which still drew upon historical images but which reflected a specific conjunture of circumstances and a complex web of competing perspectives.

24. See Lunn, "Reactions to Lithuanian and Polish Immigrants".
25. See Lunn, "Employment of Polish and European Volunteer Workers".
26. See Kushner, "Jew and Non-Jew in the East End", pp. 33-34.
27. Ibid., p. 52.
28. Ibid.

We might illustrate this by looking again at the reception of Irish workers during and immediately after the Second World War. Although little detailed work has been done, the general conclusions have been that they faced much opposition and discrimination at a local level. The exception to this generalization appears to have been those women recruited into nursing. As Nancy Lyons, an Irish woman who came to Britain in the war years, explained, their experience was very different from that of their compatriots. They were provided with accommodation in nurses' homes, and followed a work and life-style which put them in a relatively privileged position vis a vis most British workers.

> "We weren't exposed to so much prejudice – not in the same ways as somebody who walked the streets looking for a room. We didn't have to live with a household like the chaps living in digs did."[29]

Here is provided an explicit illustration of the importance of an interplay between dimensions of "race", class, status and gender within the immigrant experience. The gender dimension alone cannot explain the kind of reception noted above: Irish women working in munitions factories in Britain in the same period often found a far more hostile response. What makes for the particular reaction described by Nancy Lyons is the blend of circumstances – gender, occupational status, protected position in the housing market, local context – all of which are significant elements in explaining the singularity of this situation. It is the identification of the particular combination of influences which is required by the historian of immigration.

Immigration and the labour movement

There still exists, within the scholarly literature and popular imagery, a notion of the British labour movement as essentially opposed to immigration and as displaying many of the characteristics of a general xenophobia or racism directed at ethnic minorities who came to compete in the labour market. As Jan and Leo Lucassen write:

> "A long-standing tradition in the European labour movement considers the immigrant not so much as a victim of capitalism as much as a threat to organized native labour. Migrants are a weapon in the hands of the capitalist, enabling him to decrease wages and to divide and rule."[30]

Thus, within the British context, it has been possible to identify a continuity of opposition by labour movement officials and from the rank and file. This

---

29. Cited in Lunn, "'Good for a Few Hundreds'", p. 108.
30. Jan and Leo Lucassen, "Preface to the Conference", p. 8.

history ranges from nineteenth century notions of the Irish as strike-breakers
– "there are three ways in which immigrants were thought to reduce living
standards: by taking work, by reducing wages, and by weakening trade unionism [...]",[31] images which were maintained into the twentieth century,[32] through
the well-documented dimensions of hostility towards Jewish immigration at the
turn of the century[33] and into the various manifestations of opposition towards
different groups in the twentieth century. For example, Tannahill could write
of the union views on the employment of Poles and European Volunteer
Workers in the immediate post-war period:

> "In most industries there was, no doubt, a background of suspicion of the foreign
> worker, arising partly from ignorance and partly from the old fear of unemployment.
> Foreign workers are, even now, sometimes told to 'go home and stop taking our
> jobs away from us'. There is a vague feeling that there is only a fixed quantity of
> money and goods to be shared, and anything given to the foreigner means less for
> the British."[34]

Clearly, there are aspects of such an analysis which could be said to be self-
evident. There is sufficient documentation of the degree of intolerance, hostility,
racism within British society which indicates its pervasiveness. There is no reason
to see the labour movement as exempt from such forces, nor not to have played
a part in the construction of institutionalized and popular racism. However, it
is the case that historians and social commentators have often approached the
general study of "race" and labour by looking simply for instances of opposition.
Thus, it has become something of a self-fulfilling prophecy.[35]

What needs to be offered is a far more complex view of the relationship
between the labour movement and immigrants. A more subtle and wide-ranging
re-examination of the empirical evidence alone would indicate the need for this.
It has been suggested that in any analysis of "British labour's responses to
immigration",[36] all three constituent elements need to be unpacked. The notion
of a *British* labour movement is one which inevitably forces us back to the major
institutional sources and pronouncements. A recognition of the regional diversity
of labour, of its very different cultural and political traditions within the general
framework of British society, of the significant variations within work processes
and experiences would help to identify a range of varying responses to immigrants.

31. Hunt, *British Labour History*, p. 167.
32. See Lunn, "'Good for a Few Hundreds'".
33. See Lunn, "Race Relations or Industrial Relations?"
34. Tannahill, *European Volunteer Workers*, pp. 63-64.
35. Historians of both right and left have followed these traditional stereotypes – see the recent
     work of Kay and Miles, *Refugees or Migrant Workers?* for illustration of this.
36. Lunn, "Race Relations or Industrial Relations?", p. 3.

Secondly, in dealing with *the* labour movement, as has been suggested above, we need to move beyond the institutional sources, beyond published statements from the Trades Union Congress and the major union leaders and to examine attitudes at a local level and within the workplace and community, not simply with labour officials. Thus, we need to take cognisance of the advances in labour and social history and to recognize a wider concept of much of what constitutes "labour" within the British context and thus identify a diversity of views towards immigrant workers.

Finally, as has already been emphasized, we cannot accept a perspective which categorizes all immigrants as a homogeneous mass. Ethnicity cannot be seen as the sole and permanent determinant of immigrant behaviour, nor of "host" responses. Yet, still far too frequently, this is the tenor of the literature. In a path-breaking study some years ago, Bill Williams wrote of the tendency to "ghettoize" immigrant history.[37] He was particularly concerned with the way in which the involvement (or non-involvement) of Jewish immigrants in trade union activity had often been explained in terms of ethnically-defined patterns of behaviour.

Little or no attempt had been made to contextualize such responses by Jewish workers or to identify patterns of behaviour which would appear to challenge such stereotypes. Williams argued that responses by Jewish workers should sometimes be seen as those of a particular class or group, rather than those determined or defined by ethnicity. This is not necessarily to suggest that "class" always supercedes "ethnicity" as *the* determining characteristic in any relationship – to pursue such a line would be to take the methodology which Gilroy has so neatly categorized as "[...] some of the most anachronistic strands in Marxian thought", which he sees as living on "[...] like residual dinosaurs in the lost valley of 'race relations' analysis".[38] What is being suggested here is the need to identify and analyse a more complex pattern of interaction than has previously been provided.

Thus, for example, whilst the pages of labour and immigration history are filled with detail of opposition to the various waves of incomers into the labour market, they rarely note the positive and/or conflicting images which could be presented. They therefore fail to recognize the circumstances under which such "different" views could be constructed. Two brief studies highlight such cases. The first concerns the reactions towards Jewish immigrants in the period 1880-1914. Here, it was frequently suggested that Jewish "alien" status was not simply a legal definition but marked out an inevitable and perpetual gap between their so-called values and those of a British labour culture. Their part in strike-breaking, in under-cutting of wages and conditions, in weakening any

37. Williams, "Beginnings of Jewish Trade Unionism", p. 298.
38. Gilroy, *There Ain't No Black in the Union Jack*, p. 18.

impact which trade unions had made within particular industries was therefore a natural corollary of that "alien" status.

Yet, Jews could be, and were, active in the labour movement, either in separate unions, in political organizations or in general solidarity. Local studies show just how different their commitment could be from the much-trumpeted stereotype of non-involvement. Bill Williams's work on Manchester shows considerable militancy at particular times in certain industries, like that of waterproof garments.[39] Joe Buckman's study of Leeds indicates what was at times a radical Jewish tailors' union.[40] Both cities have examples of cooperation between Jews and Gentiles at these moments of labour consciousness. Even in London, often deemed to be the archetypical illustration of labour conflict over Jewish immigration, the evidence suggests a far more diverse picture. Bill Fishman's study of Jewish radicalism in the East End provides ample evidence of militant politics and of cooperation. As one recent commentator put it:

> "Ethnic divisions existed at the level of local politics and trade union activities, yet did not preclude cooperation between Jewish and non-Jewish workers as at the time of strikes in 1889 and 1912. Indeed, Bill Fishman has written concerning the latter, when Jewish tailors associated with the Jewish anarchist movement led by the non-Jew, Rudolph Rocker, provided help to the striking dockers including taking in some 300 children."[41]

Equally, labour movement responses to the proposed employment of members of the Polish Resettlement Corps and of the various groups generally classified as European Volunteer Workers display a similar pattern. Initial union responses were often hostile but were often based on union perceptions of threats to jobs, conditions of work and the ideological concerns of the movement.[42] To deal with these fears, employment was eventually arranged by careful agreement between the Ministry of Labour and the unions concerned, mostly in agriculture, coal-mining and textiles. Most agreements, particularly those concerned with Polish workers who were most likely to become naturalized British citizens and permanent members of the labour force, required full union rates of pay, union membership and a clause which stated that foreigners would only be employed in the absence of suitable British labour. Disputes over employment usually occurred at a local level, often provoked by the insensitivity of local employment officials and employers, who failed to consult union branches or check that the agreed conditions were being enforced. Many local confrontations over apparently "racial" objections were, in fact, part and parcel of a

39. Williams, "Beginnings of Jewish Trade Unionism".
40. Buckman, *Immigrants and Class Struggle.*
41. Kushner, "Jew and Non-Jew in the East End", p. 40.
42. For details, see Lunn, "Employment of Polish and European Volunteer Workers", pp. 384-385.

broader industrial relations framework, sometimes racialized but often based on other economic and/or political issues.[43]

A study of the Scottish coalfield indicates that there were also positive views about those Poles who came to work in the area. Disputes over housing and hostel accommodation, a particularly sensitive issue, were dealt with by careful negotiation and once the Poles had "proved" themselves, they were often championed by the union. For example, in July 1949, Polkemmet branch protested at the action of the local NCB Labour Relations Officer in trying to sack some Poles and replace them with Scots miners being transferred from Shotts in Lanarkshire. The local branch claimed that the sacking was unnecessary, detrimental to the smooth working of the colliery and requested the Scottish Executive to prevent the Poles' dismissal. This was agreed without dissent and the Poles were allowed to remain at the pit. The situation was summed up well by Walter Kobak, a Polish miner, who talked of the initial pressures and the changing response:

> "To start with it was really very hard physically and mentally. Mentally because I went into a pit that was a closed shop, meaning that all the people who worked in that pit came from that particular village. And of course there was resentment of me coming in and probably taking away (someone's) job [...] I was a hard worker and I was gradually being accepted as a good worker, not as a Pole [...] Down below we were all black, dirty, and you couldn't recognise a Pole from – from a Chinaman."[44]

Such a process of adaptation was significantly aided by the union leadership, who, subsequent to the initial opposition, sought to inform its members of Polish culture and of the problems of assimilation to life in Scotland in order to aid the process of transition.

Both positive and negative stereotypes of these "foreigners" existed and were employed as seemed appropriate by different elements within the labour movement. It does seem that the hostile views were not necessarily, except in a few cases, fixed or permanent. Certainly, from a union perspective, the commitment of many Poles and EVWs to the labour movement (particularly important in an areas such as the Fife coalfield where the union still played a central role in many aspects of community life[45]) helped to ease the process of resettlement, adaptation and acceptance.

It may well be that the Scottish coal industry provides the most positive of examples. Kay and Miles's work on European Volunteer Workers generally offers a less sympathetic view of trade union attitudes. However, what has been argued above is that historians should not have to follow one or other of these

---

43. See Kay and Miles, *Refugees or Migrant Workers?*, for the most useful discussion of this.
44. Quoted in Addison, *Now the War is Over*, pp. 182-183.
45. For a still-significant overview of this phenomenon, see McIntyre, *Little Moscows*.

models. What they indicate are two particular processes of ideological construction, different from each other, but equally rooted within the context of
particular aspects of the labour movement and of labour culture. Labour history,
like many other kinds of history, cannot be quite so neatly compartmentalized
as many historians might wish.

Conclusion

In attempting to rethink the existing orthodody about British immigration
history, it is inevitable that some of the suggestions are tentative, seeking to
explore possible avenues to open up the debate. In the main, the arguments have
been against the construction of monolithic models but not theoretical analysis.
What seems to emerge from this approach is that, despite the apparent unilinear
development of the history of British immigration, it represents a series of
complex interrelationships, with different forces shaping its outcomes. Whilst
it is clear that the dominant experience of opposition to immigrants and the
construction of cultural and institutional racist ideologies are very significant
dimensions of any British experience, this cannot be assumed to be a universal
occurrence. Within the dominant perspective, there were (and perhaps still are?)
oppositional forces, or different conjunctures of events, which could produce,
at a local and perhaps national level, a variety of responses and experiences.

Thus, in attempting to mould this diversity into a single model, we are in
danger of losing track of the "making" of particular forms of immigrant history.
This is not to declare the triumph of empiricism over theory, nor to claim
naively that every case is different. What is required is a more flexible theoretical
approach to the analysis of particular situations, where the strands of "race", of
class, of gender, of culture and ideology, have worked together in different
combinations to construct concrete historical reality. After all, if historians of
immigration are concerned with the analysis of this reality, they should not be
hampered by a framework which seeks to reduce the diversities of human
experience to rigid formulae often divorced from any significant recognition
of those everyday lives.

Shaping the Nation, Excluding the Other:
The Deportation of Migrants from Britain

Robin Cohen

In recent years, historians, social theorists and literary scholars have developed an impressive theoretical armoury with which to penetrate the question of how a national identity is formed and how it becomes distinguished from other national entities. Traditional discussions of racism, xenophobia and nationalism have now been complemented by notions of "Otherness and difference", "boundary formation" and "identity construction". Though there are important differences in nuance between contemporary thinkers, since the publication of Anderson's influential book, Imagined Communities,[1] in a sense we are all "constructionists" now – in that it is difficult to imagine any contemporary scholar insisting on the biological determinacy of race, the immutability of national character or the primordiality of ethnicity. After providing a brief exegesis of some of the more recent theory, I use the case of expulsions and deportations from Britain to show how immigration policy was deployed, both in a metaphorical and more literal sense, to give shape and meaning to the emerging British national identity.

Theory

Notions of "Otherness" and "difference" though often vague, have been used with dramatic effect by literary theorists and cultural anthropologists to show how Eurocentric views of the world came to be dominant. For example, Pratt,[2] a scholar of comparative literature, showed how travellers' descriptions of the San of southern Africa (called "Bushmen") codified difference and fixed "the other" in a timeless present. All actions and reactions of the "native" were thought to be habitual and predictable. The ethnographic present gave a history

---

1. Anderson, *Imagined Communities: Reflections on the Origins and Spread of Nationalism* (1983). See also Jackson and Penrose, *Constructions of Race*, for a useful synthesis of cognate work over the previous decade.
2. Mary Louise Pratt, "Scratches on the Face of the Country; or, What Mr. Barrow Saw in the Land of the Bushman", in: Gates, *"Race", Writing and Difference*, pp. 139-162.

to the observer (characteristically the European, the insider, the Self), but denied coevalness to the observed (the outsider, the alien, "the Other"). By suggesting that members of the Other were incapable of change, they become unamenable to reason, and incapable of change, adaptation or assimilation.

Useful in showing how non-Europeans were denied an historical consciousness, notions of the Other have also been used to portray how Europe distanced itself from the rest of the world's regions. This process was probed notably by Edward Said, who argued that the Orient had a special place in Europe's experience as its main cultural contestant and a source of rival civilisations, languages and cultures. The Orient was the source of Europe's "deepest and most recurring images of the Other. [...] European culture gained in strength and identity by setting itself off against the Orient as a sort of surrogate and even underground self."[3] If the Orient represented a redoubtable yet ultimately subordinated enemy, Africa and the indigenees of the Americas were so easily enslaved, conquered or infected with European diseases, that their inhabitants (and descendants) became lodged in the European consciousness as inferior beings placed on the lowest rungs of a static hierarchy of racial excellence.

Despite their allusive, metaphorical and literary quality, discussions of Otherness have undoubtedly helped in understanding the general processes of identity formation at national and international levels. A closely-related strand of theory looks at how boundaries are formed between peoples. Again I will start with Said's observation that a group of people living on only a few acres of land will set up boundaries between their land, its immediate surroundings and the territory beyond, often designated as "the land of the barbarians". It is not required that the barbarians accept the "us – them" label for the distinction to work. The difference may be arbitrary or fictive: it is enough that "we" have set up the boundaries of "us", for "them" to become "they". "They" have a culture or an identity incompatible with ours. As Said reasons, "To a certain extent, modern and primitive societies seem thus to derive a sense of their identities negatively." [4]

Said's contention can be greatly extended by reference to an established and more complex anthropological debate started by Frederick Barth's discussion of ethnic boundaries.[5] For Barth, boundaries could be real or symbolic, visible or invisible. The markers that divide could include territory, history, language, economic considerations, or symbolic identifications of one kind or another. In addressing the question of which markers the social actors would use, Barth used the metaphor of a boundary "vessel". The contents of the vessel would

3. Said, *Orientalism: Western Conceptions*, pp. 1-2.
4. Ibid., p. 4.
5. Barth, *Ethnic Groups and Boundaries*.

determine the firmness or weakness of the boundary and the significance of the diacritica which differentiated the "us" from the "them".

The literary scholars and the tradition pioneered by Barth essentially considered group identity formation without reference to nationality and state formation. The attempt to make the boundaries of nationality, identity and territory coincide is, of course, the central political project of all nationalists. Despite the nationalists' claims, Anderson emphasised that the nation remained an imaginary identity-construct, as real in people's minds as it is in the world. The nation is an "imagined community" with four principal qualities: It is *imagined* because the members of even the smallest nation will never know the most of their fellow members, yet in the minds of each is the image of their commonality. The nation is imagined as *limited* "because even the largest of them has finite, if elastic boundaries beyond which lie other nations". (No nation claims to be coterminous with humankind.) It is imagined as *sovereign* in that it displaces (or at least severely undermines) the legitimacy of organised religion or the monarchy. Finally, it is imagined as a *community* because regardless of actual inequality, the nation is conceived of as a deep horizontal comradeship.[6]

While I share the view that identity boundaries are more indeterminate, malleable and variable than is commonly surmised, national identities differ from other group identities by involving the achievement of, or aspriation to, statehood. However, once the state is brought back in, the extent to which national identities can be reshaped, reformed and recombined simply through a form a "cultural politics" becomes far more problematic. I argue, therefore, for a greater historical specificity, a more exacting focus on the different diacritica used to define the Self and the Other and an appreciation of the key role of major political and social actors in selectively constructing the walls that separate, or selectively permitting access through the turnstiles and gateways linking the inner and outer worlds. In the case of the boundary between the British and the Others, I suggest that immigration policies and practices (and, in particular, deportations) can be used to tell which forms of distinction (religion, language difference, economic competition, fear of dangerous political ideas, assumed racial difference, imperial arrogance or whatever) were associated with the growth of the English (and, more diffusely, the British) national identity.

A second limitation of recent theory (particularly of the literary variety) is that much of it grew up as a critique of colonialism and imperialism and consequently centres on the relations between European and non-European societies. By correcting the monochromatic view of the latter, Said and others fell into the error of falsely assuming an historical, moral and practical unity among Europe-

6. Anderson, *Imagined Communities*, pp. 15-16.

ans. As I show below, the level of official British suspicion and hostility to European continental immigrants makes this assumption far from accurate.

Despite these two limitations on recent theory, the core insight remains. This I would summarise as follows: "We know who we are by who we reject". Or – to be more pertinent to my current argument – "we know who we are by who we eject".

Beginnings of State Control

When did the English state's right to control entry and exit become established? T.W.E. Roche, the historian of the Immigration Service, argued that immigration control commenced with William the Conqueror who, in the wake of his successful invasion, set up castles along the south coast to prevent somebody else emulating what he had just done. The five key control points, "the Cinque Ports", were at Hastings, Romney, Dover, Hythe and Sandwich: the process of passing through these ports gave birth to the word "passport". The policing of the frontier became an important aspect of royal power to be executed by the monarch's most trustworthy vassals. William the Conqueror and Henry I were particularly preoccupied with excluding Papal delegates and with threats to their own power from rivals who had taken refuge abroad. The assassination of Henry at Canterbury by Becket's four knights only arose because they were not successfully intercepted at Hythe. In the second year of Henry II's reign, all "aliens" were abruptly banished on the grounds that "they were considered to be becoming too numerous".[7]

The early thirteenth century showed the first signs of the shaping of an exclusive English identity. With the seizure of Normandy in 1204 by the French king, Philip Augustus, some of the English magnates were in the uncomfortable position of having to chose between two liege lords on either side of the Channel. The ex-Norman baronage were now sufficiently indigenised to see Normans as "foreigners". One illustration can be found in the attempted invasion of Dover by Louis the Dauphin. When this was threatened in 1216, the port's custodian, with the decidedly Gallic name of Herbert de Burgh, provided a ringing declaration of early nationalism: "As long as I draw breath I will not surrender to French aliens this castle, which is the key in the lock of England."[8]

---

7. Roche, *Key in the Lock*, pp. 13-15.
8. Ibid., pp. 17-18.

Middlemen Minorities

The notion of a "French alien" was especially innovative in that (though they had lost Normandy) Poitou still remained under the control of the English Crown and many officials and nobles of continental origin sought and found preferment in England under Henry III's rule (1216-72). For much of his reign, Henry was tolerant of continental merchants, money-lenders and foreign wool-workers. He afforded them protection so long as they made suitable contributions to the Crown. However, as W. Cunningham cynically remarked, "they were protected only to be plundered".[9] Even this conditional haven did not last. The final years of Henry's reign were marked by increasing hostility to three groups – the Flemish, some of whom were granted a "denizen" (resident alien) status, but most of whom were deported; the Caorsine "usurers" who were expelled at the insistence of the Church; and the Jews.

We respect to the last, in the first half of the twelfth century anti-Jewish riots had occurred in Westminster (on the day of Richard the Lionheart's coronation), in Dunstable, Stamford, York and Norwich. However, the full force of royal disapproval was to await Edward I's rule. Within two years of his accession, Jews found guilty of usury had to wear a placard around their necks. Then in 1290, the entire resident Jewish population, some 15,660 people, were deported. They were not allowed to return until 367 years later during the Cromwellian period.

The Jewish role as the classical "middleman minority" (as the sexist sociological term has it), was supplanted by the Lombards, the Hansards and the Flemish who fared little better at the hands of the rapacious Crown or mobs manipulated by City magnates who owed money to their creditors. In a particularly excruciating test of political correctness, members of the Flemish colony at Southwark were enjoined to pronounce the words "Bread and Cheese" in the proper London pronunciation. Those who failed were summarily executed.

But deportations and expulsions were rare in the fourteenth and fifteenth centuries. The Lombards were protected by the Pope, the Black Death meant that Edward III needed to rebuild the population of England and, at the end of the period (when the unsettling Wars of the Roses had finally ended), a new era of international trade between England and Flanders had been opened up.

Religion

The liberalism of movement that followed trade liberalisation was, however, short-lived. The religious oppression and intolerance that started in the mid-

---

9. Cunningham, *Alien Immigrants to England*, p. 70.

sixteenth century over much of Europe soon ramified at the English Court and in the Privy Council. At the accession of Mary (1553), all "strangers"[10] were commanded to leave the realm. These included Walloon weavers who professed a Calvinist faith and were returned to the Continent. Another example can be found in the Privy Council papers of 1562, which refer to the expulsion of an unfortunate "Dutch heretic", one Hadrian Hamslede, who is described as "being found obstinat in dyvers erronious opinions".[11]

Although Elizabeth (1558-1603) allowed the return of the weavers expelled by Mary, she used the royal prerogative to expel other religious dissenters fearing, in particular, a pro-Catholic revival. For the same reason, she also restricted movement out of England by her own subjects – in case they might be schooled at the Catholic seminaries in the Netherlands, Reims and Rome which were dedicated to training missionaries for the English field. In 1585 alone, fourteen Catholic priests were deported; some were suspected of preparing the ground for an invasion by Philip II. Three years later when the long-feared Spanish Armada finally materialised, Elizabeth again used her power to expel Jesuits and "Spanish agents".[12]

In the seventeenth century, the power to deport seems to have been progressively conceded to the Privy Council, though the notion of a royal prerogative still survived.[13] The principal targets remained religious dissenters, especially Jesuits. For example, in 1618, "by letters patent of comission", James I (James VI of Scotland) gave the power to six or more Privy Councillors "to exile and bannish out of and from his Majesty's realmes of Englaund and Irelaund [...] so manie jesuits, seminarie priests and other eccelesiasticall persons whatsoever made and ordayned accordinge to the order and rites of the Romish Church".[14] The Lord Chancellor, Lord Treasurer, Lord Privy Seale and others set about their task with determination, the Acts of the Privy Council recording no less than 49 Jesuit priests so expelled in the 1620-1 session alone. The Privy Council also formalised the procedure. A deportation order issued in December 1620 was issued in the recognisably modern form of a warrant to constables and other officers.

---

10. The category "strangers" did not, presumably include the "denizens "– privileged aliens who had been granted the right to live and conduct their business in England by royal agreement.
11. Dasent, *Acts of the Privy Council of England*, p. 127.
12. Bindoff, *Tudor England*, pp. 235-236; Roche, *Key in the Lock*, p. 39.
13. The barrister and legal expert in immigration law, Andrew Nicol (*Illegal Entrants*, pp. 9-10), pointed out that, as recently as 1971, section 33(5) of the Immigration Act stated: "This Act shall not be taken to supersede or impair any power exercised by Her Majesty in relation to aliens by virtue of Her prerogative." In practice, the royal prerogative seems not to have been exercised since Elizabeth I, though Nicol is wrong in saying that the last occasion was in 1575. As indicated earlier, Elizabeth signed deportation orders at least as late as 1588.
14. Lords Commissioner of His Majesty's Treasurer under the direction of the Master of the Rolls, *Acts of the Privy Council of England* (London, HMSO, 1930), p. 338.

Revolutionaries & the "Alien Menace"

In his history of the Home Office, Sir Edward Troup suggested that "in the eighteenth century the right to exclude had fallen into abeyance".[15] However, an important legal landmark was initiated by the British government's apprehensive reaction to the French Revolution. In 1793, Grenville's Aliens Act was passed, which gave parliamentary sanction for the expulsion of aliens for the first time. The Act provided, *inter alia*, for the transportation of an alien who returned after being expelled. If the alien were so impudent as to return yet again, the Act allowed capital punishment.

The most prominent victim of the Grenville's Act was the French politician and diplomat, Tallyrand, who had been elected President of the French Assembly in 1790. When the Revolution debouched into the period known as "The Terror", he had swiftly fled to England. Tallyrand was deported to the US in 1793, but argued in his memoirs that he was expelled so as to show that the Aliens Act was no dead letter. Under Clause XVII of the Act, all principal secretaries of state were empowered to issue a deportation under specified conditions. This provision was strengthened in 1803 when expulsion was allowed on "mere suspicion"; this sweeping power prevailed until 1836.

Lord Loughborough's speech in defence of the 1793 Act was instructive in alluding to the crisis that had faced Elizabeth in 1588 when the country was threatened by "religious fanaticism". Now, he opined, England was threatened by "the fanaticism of infidelity". This referred to the progress of French revolutionary ideas including "atheism" and "anarchism". In the Act there is a clear legal distinction made between an alien and a denizen (privileged foreigner), its provisions not being applicable to "foreign ambassadors" or to an "Alien who shall have Letters Patent of Denization".

The 1793 Act was only rarely deployed and intermittently re-enacted (in 1816, 1826 and 1836). Indeed, the evaporation of the tensions that followed the defeat of Napoleon, led Troup to consider that the measures against aliens, "fell into desuetude".[16] However, powers of deportation were renewed in 1848 in readiness for another "alien menace" from continental revolutionaries. The Removal of Aliens Act of 1848 gave the home secretary and the lord lieutenant of Ireland the right to expel foreigners if it was deemed that they threatened the "preservation of the peace and tranquillity of the realm". Nine years later, Palmerston insisted on the repeal of the 1848 Act on the liberal grounds that deporting aliens on this vague basis would lead to an abuse of power.

The relaxed attitude of the period 1815-90 came to an abrupt end with another "alien menace" – the influx of Russian and eastern European Jews. The

15. Troup, *Home Office*, p. 125.
16. Ibid., p. 125.

discriminatory May Laws in Russia (1882) had precipitated the first big wave of migrants to the UK. Press and popular opinion was not slow to respond, albeit with contradictory arguments. According the *Manchester City News* (2 April 1887), "Jews [were] advanced socialists who sympathise with the Paris Commune and Chicago martyrs". On the other hand, English trade unionists and socialists frequently represented all Jews as wicked capitalists. A Royal Commission on Alien Immigration which reported in 1903 accepted the force of various popular accusations against the Jewish immigrants. For example, the Commission regarded it as an "evil" that "immigrants of the Jewish faith do not assimilate and intermarry with the native race".[17] Fierce controls were proposed. In fact when the Aliens Act of 1905 was passed in parliament the restrictionists did not have it all their own way. The Act limited the powers of expulsion granted to immigration officers to the exclusion of "undesirables". These were defined as previous deportees, fugitive offenders, the mad and the destitute. Moreover, those refused admission had the right to appeal to an immigration board whose members were often surprisingly sympathetic.

Potential "undesirables" were thought to be exclusively found among the steerage passengers. The restrictionists in the Home Office were unhappy – not at the stunning demonstration of class justice that allowed those who could afford cabin fares to escape examination – but at their limited powers to stop what they saw as mass immigration. That noses were out of joint in the Home Office can be discerned in Sir Edward Troup's history of the department. The permanent under-secretary of state at the Home Office over the period 1908-22, Troup was probably the most important of the what might be termed the "hidden frontier guards" in the first quarter of this century. He claimed the 1905 Aliens Act was disliked on the purely pragmatic grounds that it was difficult to administer, but it is clear that he and his immediate colleagues identified fully with the restrictionists. Competition from the "aliens from eastern Europe", he asserted, "lowered the wages in some of the unorganised trades to starvation point and their habits had a demoralising effect in the crowded areas in which they settled".[18]

While other minorities including Indians, Africans and Gypsies were all victims to restrictionist attitudes, there is little doubt that the main targets of animosity just before the First World War were the Jews. The term "alien" was effectively the turn-of-the-century newspeak for "Jew". Chamberlain campaigned on an anti-alien platform, the anti-semitic British Brother League was established, while the journal, *The Alien Immigrant*, thought it "scarcely necessary to labour the point that the first generation of children of Russian Jews in the East End

17. Roche, *Key in the Lock*, p. 66.
18. Troup, *Home Office*, p. 143.

are only English by legal fiction".[19] The Jews also had no friend in court, as W. Haldane Porter, the chief inspector under the Aliens Act and "the founding father of the Immigration Service" was covertly associated with Major Evans Gordon, one of the most vocal of the anti-alien agitators.[20] One commentator on the "alien invasion" dropped all restraint and penned this verse offering the alternatives of voluntary departure or death:

> "Be he Russian, or Pole, Lithuanian or Jew
> I care not, but take it for granted
> That the island of Britain can readily do
> With the notice: "No aliens wanted".
> I would give them one chance – just one week to clear out
> And if found in the land one hour later
> Then – death without trial or fooling about
> Whether Anarchist, banker or waiter."

A curious gentility surrounded these odious sentiments. They were published in *The People* in February 1909 over the *nom de plume* of "a lady" and described by the columnist "Mr Will Workman" as "a rousing patriotic stanza".

War-time Expulsions and the Aftermath

Administrative discretion and popular agitation, however, had their limitations. The frontier guard, Sir Edward Troup, was clearly a great deal happier with the logic of the military mind. In 1914, the Committee of Imperial Defence discussed the issue of aliens in Britain. The Aliens Act of that year – which placed rigid controls over the registration, movement and deportation of all aliens – was rushed through in a single day, 5 August. It was introduced in the House of Commons at 3.30 p.m. and gained the Royal Assent by 7 p.m. Troup had no doubts as to its efficacy and justification[21]:

> "[...] the base was laid for the effective control of aliens which was maintained throughout the war [...] [before the war] all attempts on the part of the Home Office to exclude persons who had not identified themselves with English life and remained in sentiment *really* foreigners proved abortive [emphasis added]."

Troup saw no difficulty in bureaucratically separating "the real foreigners" from "the English" (he ignored the rest of Britain). Modern historians have shown that it was not quite so easy in practice to segregate the sheep from the goats, due to the almost hysterical levels of Germanophobia that the outbreak of the

---

19. Landa, *Alien Problem and its Remedy*, p. 137.
20. Kaye and Charlton, *United Kingdom Refugee Admission*, p. 6.
21. Troup, *Home Office*, pp. 143, 152.

First World War had generated.[22] George V felt constrained to drop all German family titles and adopt the name "Windsor". German Knights of the Garter were struck off the roll, grocers with German names were accused of poisoning the public, while *The Times* ran a series of "loyalty letters", in which German or German-Jewish public figures were enjoined to declare themselves. (Those who refused found themselves cold-shouldered.) Another telling example, in the light of Britain's international reputation for the care of domestic animals (the RSPCA was founded as early as 1824), was that dachshunds were stoned in the streets of London. Spy stories also abounded.

After the sinking of the Lusitania off the coast of Ireland in May 1915 with the loss of 1,201 lives, all restraints on the frontier guards of British identity were off. In the previous autumn, the repatriation of women, children, elderly men, invalid men of military age, ministers of religion and medical doctors of German origin had been initiated by the government. Henceforth, German-background women and men over military age were obliged to show why they should not be expelled – a stunning administrative diktat significantly reversing the tradi-tional burden of proof. According to Holmes over the period 1914-1919, 28,744 aliens were repatriated, of whom 23,571 were Germans.[23] Cesarani offers even higher figures: 30,700 Germans, Austrians, Hungarians and Turks over the 1914-18 period, together with 7,000 Russians, probably all Jews.[24]

The xenophobia of the war years no doubt helped in recruitment and in manufacturing a patriotic consensus in support of the increasing costly, blood-drenched and futile war. But no amount of jingoism could keep pace with the losses at the front. In January 1916, the British government introduced conscrip-tion. Conscription placed particular pressures on three minority groups: the Belgians, the Russian Poles and the Lithuanians. The Belgians on the whole took up an offer for repatriation worked out jointly between the Belgian and British governments. The Russian Poles, who were mainly Jewish, split three ways. Established Anglo-Jewry persuaded some of their co-religionists to show their gratitude to their country of settlement by enlisting. But many Russian aliens, a substantial number of whom had not taken out British nationality, saw no good reason to support Britain's anti-Semitic ally, the Tsar – whom they considered responsible for their enforced flight. A third group, with socialist views, simply saw the war as a capitalist conspiracy which any self-respecting internationalist should denounce.[25] The frontier guards in the Home Office and War Office pressed the issue: the Russians and Lithuanians either should serve in the British army or in the armies of their original citizenship. The Lithuanians became

---

22. See for example Holmes, *John Bull's Island*, and the same author's, *Tolerant Country?*
23. Holmes, *John Bull's Island*, p. 66.
24. Cesarani, "Anti-Alienism in England", p. 5.
25. Holmes *John Bull's Island*, pp. 101-106.

wedged in a particularly tight vice. The conscripts split into two bodies: in 1917, 700 joined the British army, while 1,100 returned to serve in Lithuania, then part of the Tzar's empire. With the Russian revolution came another turn of the screw. Only 300 of the Lithuanian returnees were permitted to come back to Britain, on the grounds that the remaining 700 could not prove they had fought on the side of the allies, or had not fought for the Bolsheviks. The small allowances made to their families in Britain were withdrawn by the Treasury and 600 dependents (all women and children) of the Lithuanian returnees were deported.

The aftermath of the extensive war-time expulsions and repatriations saw the frontier guards riding high. The ejection of "enemy aliens" became an election pledge for Lloyd George in 1918 and some 19,000 Germans were repatriated by April of the following year. Given the fanning of popular sentiment, it was no surprise that the emergency war-time powers over aliens were largely retained in the Aliens Restrictions (Amendment) Act of 1919. An Order-in-Council in 1920 reserved the home secretary's right to deport someone if he considered it "conducive to the public good", a phrase that still echoes through the corridors of the Home Office. Home Secretary Shortt also insisted on additional clauses to exclude or deport aliens who encouraged sedition in the armed forces or promoted industrial unrest.

These clauses reflected the general apprehension of the ruling élite immediately after the war. The Bolsheviks were triumphant in Russia and the rot looked like spreading to Germany. Anti-British riots had occurred in a number of colonies. Socialist political organisations were making great headway in the US. And in Britain itself, suffragettes chained themselves to the railings of Buckingham Palace, a Soviet was briefly established in Glasgow and the first major race riots had broken out in Liverpool and Cardiff against a background of a police strike. Truly, hands must have wobbled in the gentlemen's clubs as they reached out to grab the port.

The frontier guards lashed out. Eighty "Bolshevik sympathisers" were deported in May 1919. The Labour MP for Whitechapel complained that the Home Office were sending out Russian Jews almost weekly. Excluding dependents, 31 were expelled in November 1920, 49 in December 1920, 58 in March 1921. Some of the 1917 conscripts who had elected to serve in the Russian Army illegally returned to Britain: 40 were found and deported, 29 others were sent to Brixton jail.[26]

As home secretary, Shortt's administrative powers included, but also transcended, the enforcement of a court's recommendation for deportation following conviction. This form of dual power (impossible in any country where a written constitution separates administrative and judicial powers) allowed the home

26. Cesarani, "Anti-Alienism in England", pp. 7, 13.

secretary to order a deportation even when the court had not made such a recommendation or, indeed, had acquitted an alien defendant. The home secretary saw no problem. He maintained that deportation need not be treated as a judicial issue, "but rather as a matter of administration". Deportation was not punishment for a particular offence, but "administrative action taken on behalf of the public".

During the 1920s and 1930s, the 1919 Act was extended on an annual basis, despite an attempt in 1927, thrown out in parliament, to have the powers accorded to the home secretary made permanent. Reformers and pressure groups, notably the British Board of Deputies (the representative body of Jewry), managed to establish an independent Aliens Deportation Advisory Committee in 1930. The Home Office held to its old line of "administrative discretion" in the cases of illegal entry and overstaying (beyond the time allowed at the port of entry), but the home secretary agreed to refer all other cases to the Committee on the basis of a "private understanding" and after "radicals" like Harold Laski (a politics lecturer at the London School of Economics) were dropped from its membership. When the Committee had the temerity to question the home secretary's judgements in 33 cases, the Committee was quietly side-tracked then discontinued.

That the Committee was batting on a sticky wicket can be deduced from the attitudes of the top civil servants at the Home Office. For example, in a departmental memo to the home secretary in 1924,[27] Troup's successor as permanent under-secretary of state at the Home Office, Sir John Pedder, explained why he systematically delayed looking at some classes of applications for "far longer" than the statutory minimum time of five years' residence. This was because his experience suggested

> "that different races display very different qualities and capabilities for identifying themselves with this country. Speaking roughly, the Latin, Teuton and Scandinavian races, starting some of them, with a certain kinship with British races, [are] prompt and eager to identify themselves with the life and habits of this country and are easily assimilated. On the other hand, Slavs, Jews and other races from Central and Eastern parts of Europe stand in quite a different position. They do not want to be assimilated in the same way and do not readily identify themselves with this country. Even the British-born Jews, for instance, always speak of themselves as a 'community', separate to a considerable degree and different from the British people."

While Sir John wrestled with his comparative studies of the differential rate of assimilability of various "races", another committee of the Home Office planned for future encounters with other alien beings. In the light of the negative Isle of Man experiences with internment during the 1914-18 conflict, the Committee of Imperial Defence concluded in 1923 that there was no point in depriving

---

27. Ibid., p. 17.

the enemy of its able-bodied men if it took a large number of your own to look after them. It was thus agreed (with the exception of a limited provision for exactly 5,490 internees) that in any future conflict, expulsion would be far better than detention.[28]

As the Second World War loomed this policy looked dangerously simplistic. Thirty thousand German-Jewish refugees had been admitted, while other Germans had put down roots, hoping to be naturalised. In 1938, the Home Office still clung to the 1923 ruling suggesting that all enemy aliens who came to Britain after 1 January 1919 should be "required to return to their own countries". Clearly forcible repatriation of the Jews would be politically indefensible, so the Home Office, rather than abandon its expulsion plans, proposed a system of appeals against deportation. But what if these appeals were successful and the individuals concerned were still considered a security risk? Surely internment, the rejected policy, was bound to be reinstated?

In fact some repatriations were effected: 110 women and eight children were sent back to Germany between December 1939 and January 1940. Later, the policy and practice of detention and internment during the Second World War paralleled, then soon exceeded, the hopeless mire of detentions during the First World War.

The Racialisation of Immigration: Deportations, 1945-78

After the Second World War the state's powers of deportation (in the Aliens Acts of 1905, 1914 and 1919) were supplemented by the British Nationality Act of 1948, the signing of the European Convention on Establishment and the Immigration Acts of 1962, 1968 and 1971. With the single exception of the European Convention, which gave rights to proposed deportees in certain categories to make representations to the courts, the effects of all this legislation were to extend the reasons for deportations and to widen the categories of people who could be expelled. In particular, Commonwealth citizens, especially black Commonwealth citizens, were gradually legally "reduced" to the status of aliens.

The succession of immigration measures was harsh by any standards, but they were made more odious by the virtually-naked appeal to "race" as a key differentiating category between those who were immune from deportation and those who were subject to this state power. In particular, the 1971 legislation gave a right of abode to "patrials" (nearly all of whom were white) and denied that right to "non-patrials" (nearly all of whom were black, brown or yellow).[29]

---

28. Gillman and Gillman, "Collar the Lot!", p. 23.
29. The legislation fell just short of an explicitly racial classification scheme (along, say, the lines of the apartheid regime), by allowing the notion of "patriality" to include marginal numbers

The moment in the post-1945 period that has come to symbolise the racialisation of the "immigration issue" was Enoch Powell's infamous speech in Birming-
ham in April 1968. Powell developed the theme of "an alien wedge" which
threatened the notion of legality that had hitherto informed the British national
culture. While the numbers in the alien wedge were important, more pertinent
were the character and effects of black settlement. Powell continued, "[...] in
fifteen or twenty years' time the black man will hold the whip hand over the
white man". As Paul Gilroy comments, this image inverts the customary roles
of master and slave, thereby accepting historical guilt, but immediately counter-
acts guilt with fear.[30] Later in the speech, the masculine black remains (either in
the form of "charming wide-grinning piccaninnies" or "negro workers") but the
white is transformed into a vulnerable little old lady. She is taunted by the cry of
"racialist"[31] by the blacks, who also push excreta through her letter-box. Powell
is distraught; he is "filled with foreboding". Like the ancient Roman he sees "the
River Tiber foaming with much blood". Moreover, all of this is a "preventable
evil" visited upon the UK "by our own volition and our own neglect".

What effects did this curious speech and the enormous row it provoked, have
on the question of deportations and removals? First, and most important, it lent
force to the gathering view that black Commonwealth citizens were as "alien"
as the foreigners and aliens of old. Instead of evoking the Empire and Commonwealth, or common military service against the Nazis, the differences between
white Britons and non-white Commonwealth citizens were now stressed. This
extended also to the East African Asians who as UK and Colonies passport-
holders had the untrammelled right of entry. Many believed they had been
promised protection by successive colonial secretaries should their situation in
independent African countries become intolerable. Powell, however, angrily
denounced these historic rights and denied any suggestion that Britain had any
responsibilities. Suddenly, the East African Asians were India's responsibility,
despite their UK citizenship. Notice below how the notion of "belonging" was
used by Powell to elide the force of international law and separate the "them"
from the "us"[32]:

> on a non-racial basis. Thus patrials were those citizens of the UK and Colonies who had been
> ordinarily resident for five years or more, or acquired their citizenships through naturalisation
> or registration (a small number of non-white citizens were so qualified), as well as those whose
> birth, adoption, parenthood or grandparenthood made them citizens through descent
> (overwhelmingly a white category).

30. Gilroy, *"There Ain't No Blacks"*, pp. 85–88.
31. "They cannot speak English, but one word ['racialist'] they know." Powell's well-known
     pedantry is a dead give-away here. Even in 1968, it stretches all credulity to imagine that the
     verbally-inadequate "piccaninnies" would "chant" the linguistically-proper but passé term
     "racialist", rather than the more common form "racist".
32. Enoch Powell cited in Goulbourne, *Ethnicity and Nationalism*, p. 117.

"When the East African countries became independent there was no suggestion, let alone undertaking, in parliament or outside, that those inhabitants who remained citizens of the UK and Colonies would have the right of entry into this country [...] the practice of international law which requires a country to re-admit or admit its own nationals applies in our case only to those who belong to the UK and not to other Commonwealth countries, whether classified as citizens of the UK and Colonies or not."

In short, the first effect of Powell's intervention was to draw the frontiers of identity more tightly around the British Isles and to try to renounce any responsibilities inherited from empire. Next, despite his phantasm of a foaming river of blood, like all good politicians, Powell did not project a message of complete fatalism. The "evil" was "preventable". For his supporters, the problem was how. The 1971 legislation probably went as far as it could in explicitly diminishing the former privileges of Commonwealth citizens. To play with "Powellism" more openly was both unrespectable and possibly dangerous, with unpredictable outcomes in the politics of the streets and perhaps open racial violence.

Table 1. Alleged illegal entrants removed, 1973–86

Year	Foreign	Commonwealth	Total
1973	35	44	79
1974	33	80	113
1975	76	78	154
1976	127	137	264
1977	184	312	496
1978	275	263	538
1979	330	255	585
1980	589	319	908
1981	357	283	640
1982	223	208	431
1983	179	195	374
1984	188	237	425
1985	n.a.	n.a.	528
1986	246	458	704

Source: Correspondence with the Home Office Research and Statistics Department (1992).

But Powell had touched a nerve of popular sentiment (across party lines) which sanctioned tougher action by the frontier guards. This is most dramatically evidenced in the use of the powers the home secretary was given (in practice exercised by immigration officers) to "remove" alleged "illegal entrants" by administrative fiat. Whereas the power to "remove" was conditional and very

rarely used in the case of Commonwealth citizens prior to the 1971 Act, once
the Act had come into force (on 1 January 1973) the numbers of alleged illegal
entrants removed from the Commonwealth were soon comparable to the
number of aliens removed (Table 1).

Cultural Swamping: Conservative Governments, 1979-92

While the Labour party is fearful of appearing "soft" on immigration, there is
little doubt that there is a qualitative distinction in immigration matters between
the two major parties, one which turns on the Conservative's more intimate
association with the ideas that Powell's 1968 "rivers of blood" speech brought
to the surface. For example, in her much-quoted television speech in February
1978, Mrs Thatcher linked herself firmly to that tradition. Referring to trends
in New (the official code name for "non-white") Commonwealth and Pakistani
immigration, she said:

> "That is an awful lot, and I think it means that people are really rather afraid that
> this country might be swamped by people of a different culture. The British
> character has done so much for democracy, for law, and done so much throughout
> the world that if there is any fear that it might be swamped, then people are going
> to be rather hostile to those coming in."

This was precisely the message that a large part of the British electorate wanted
to hear. Paradoxically, however, for a politician whose popularity lay in the
claim that she always did what she promised, Mrs Thatcher was already making
an anachronistic appeal. The immigration legislation of 1961 and 1971 had
already throttled off all primary ("breadwinner") immigration from so-called
New Commonwealth countries and the British-Caribbean population, including
their descendants, was actually declining. All that was left in respect of controlling the inflow, was making it as a difficult as possible for Indian, Bangladeshi
and Pakistani spouses and dependents to join their breadwinners in the UK. The
Home Office, the British visa officials in Asia and the immigration officers at
Heathrow obliged with a series of petty, vindictive and obstructionist measures.

Some of the unrequited hostility of Mrs Thatcher's supporters was slaked by
these actions, while xenophobia directed against asylum-seekers provided a
second outlet. Finally, however, a series a highly-publicised deportation cases
provided much symbolic satisfaction to the anti-foreigner and anti-black brigade.
The increased use of deportations can in some measure also be seen as a sop to
the Tory right who had demanded "voluntary repatriation" at a noisy intervention at the Tory conference in October 1983.[33]

33. The demand for a national programme of repatriation was strongly resisted by David

How were expulsions carried out the post-1979 period? It may be useful first to provide some quantitative data on deportations during the three Thatcher terms of office (1979-90) and for the first two years under the leadership of Mr Major, which commenced in November 1990 after her enforced resignation (Table 2).

Table 2. Removals and Deportations under the Conservative Governments, 1979-92

1979	1,382	1986	1,880
1980	1,872	1987	2,700
1981	946	1988	2,961
1982	863	1989	4,500
1983	1,365	1990	4,330
1984	1,545	1991	5,600
1985	1,665	1992	6,100

Sources: Home Office Statistical Bulletins (various years); reports of the Immigration and Nationality Department, Home Office (various years); correspondence with the Home Office.

A cursory examination of the statistics shows that there has been a strong and increasingly propensity to use the powers of removal and deportation during the successive Conservative administrations commencing in 1979, the total more than doubling over the period. The number of deportation orders served (and the much small number ultimately enforced) also went up dramatically. According to figures provided by the Joint Council for the Welfare of Immigrants, in the period 1979-1983, orders made went up by 145 per cent and those enforced by 64 per cent, compared to the previous Labour Party government's period.

The quantitative data, however, tell only a part of the story. As pertinent at the figures themselves, were four more qualitative changes in the policy of expulsions: first an increased propensity to deport and detain asylum-seekers requesting refuge in the UK; second, a greater determination in the Home Office to see through highly-publicised and often controversial cases "to the end"; third, an attempt to restrict the role of MPs to intervene in deportation cases; finally, the passing of additional legislation tightening the powers of deportation even further.

Waddington, the Home Office minister responsible for immigration: "The government is not in the business of telling people who have made their lives here, who perhaps have even become British citizens: You are unwelcome. Here is some money. Clear off!" (*Financial Times*, 14 Oct. 1983). But behind this public reaction, there in fact existed modest government support for at least two repatriation schemes.

Home Office Attitudes

The proliferating use of deportation orders by the immigration authorities triggered determined opposition by the church, by newly-formed pressure groups, by left-wing fringe parties and amongst friends and neighbours of those threatened. This took the form of a sanctuary and anti-deportation movement. Let me provide just one example of this phenomenon, chosen on the one hand not to provoke automatic sympathy with the victims, but on the other to demonstrate the hardening of attitudes at the Home Office.

First some background. Roughly one-third of deportation orders follow a drugs conviction. The courts have the power to recommend deportation and in anything from one-third to one-half of drugs-related cases, they do so. Almost invariably the Home Office complies, but even where the court does not recommend deportation, the Home Office can still proceed with a deportation order. This is what happened in the case of Andy Anderson and Farida Ali, whose campaign against deportation was taken up by the Greater Manchester Immigration Aid Unit. According to the campaigners, Mr Anderson arrived in the UK from Jamaica in 1976 and was given permanent residence in 1978. He married a British citizen and had two children born in the UK. All his family were in the country. In 1987 the couple were convicted for the possession and supply of cannabis. Ms Farida Ali (his spouse) was given a twelve-month sentence, her husband – who had one previous conviction for supplying – was imprisoned for four years. In September 1988, while in prison, he was served with a Home Office notice that his presence in the UK "was not conducive to the public good". His appeal was rejected at an Immigration Tribunal (with one out of three members, who happened to be black, strongly dissenting) and by the High Court.

In this case the trial judge had not ordered deportation, but the home secretary decided to deport, despite very favourable reports from the prison governor, the prison education officer, the probation officer, the prison chaplain and even an immigration officer sent to interview Ms Ali. The campaigners argued that the mass of positive evidence was ignored because Mr Anderson was black and a Rastafarian. The relevant minister at the Home Office, Mr Peter Lloyd, refused to withdraw the deportation order, but offered to pay the fares for Ms Ali and the children to join him in Jamaica! As the campaigners contended, it was extraordinarily that the government of the day was prepared to pay a British citizen to go into exile.

Although it is more than likely that a convicted drug dealer does not constitute most people's idea of a good citizen, this case illustrates several general features. First, any residual notion that Commonwealth origin provided a privileged status was firmly disabused. Second, the hidden frontier guards at the Home Office considered their own assessment of the case for deportation superior to the advice of prison officers, care workers close to the individual and even to the court itself. Third, in their determination to proceed with deportation, the fates of three British-born citizens (the wife and two children) counted for little.

The Restriction of MPs' Rights

Members of Parliament have a right (indeed a responsibility) to represent their constituents in immigration matters where a they, or a constituent's relative or friend has fallen foul of the immigration authorities. The principal forms of intervention available to MPs are two: first, the "stop" procedure, initiated in the 1960s, whereby a removal direction is delayed pending representation by a MP and the further consideration given to the case by the relevant minister of state at the Home Office. Second, MPs can ask the minister to allow a person entry "outside the immigration rules", a power of administrative discretion allowed in the 1971 Immigration Acts. Taking these forms of representation together, Table 3 indicates the number of representations made.

Table 3. Representations by MPs on immigration cases

1979	10,395	1984	13,164
1980	10,029	1985	16,024
1981	8,945	1986	17,511
1982	9,931	1987	11,842
1983	11,456		

Source: Parliamentary reply to Mr Jeremy Corbyn MP, 12 April 1988.

There is no doubt that many of these representations were conscientious responses to genuine cases of distress at the ports of entry. On the hand, some MPs became well-known as sympathetic to deportation cases and they often pursued cases even where there was no obvious constituency connection. Again, the power to ask for a "stop", particularly if a number of members made this request, delayed matters for long-enough for an ordinary visitor – perhaps without the necessary visa – to see their families.

By July 1983, the minister of state at the Home Office, David Waddington, had had enough. He wrote to all MPs stating that he would only consider the first representation and that this should be made by an MP with a constituency interest. Then in May 1985, he initiated a brief experiment which only lasted two weeks, requesting that MPs should intervene in port-of-entry cases within

24 hours. With the assistance of the Tamil Refugee Action Group and the United Kingdom Immigration Advisory Service, the MPs swung into action to beat the deadline, only to find the Home Office was not able to respond equally as quickly. The experiment was abandoned.[34]

Rattled by this fiasco and the continuing flow of correspondence, in October 1985 Waddington accused MPs of "abusing their right to make representations" and during the course of 1986 he issued four successive sets of "guide-lines" with which he asked MPs to comply. He failed in his attempt to get the chief immigration officers at the ports of entry, rather than his own office, to be responsible for giving reasons for refusal. But he succeeded in halting the grant of an automatic "stop" in cases where visas had been required and where there was "a clear attempt to seek entry through clearly bogus application for asylum". The minister's mailbag was lighter by nearly 6,000 letters (see Table 3) in the year following this new ruling. He also was able to press the ruling that removal would be deferred only by twelve days if an MP intervened. Subsequently this period was reduced to eight days.

Further Immigration Legislation

The Nationality Act of 1981 which was not so much an immigration act, as a way of reconciling (and multiplying) definitions of nationality to conform to the evolving practice of immigration law, in particular, the determination of who had the right of abode in the UK. With respect to my current concern with deportations, it is worth drawing attention to the difficult (though thankfully rare) situation that, after the Act, could result for those who are deported without having gained a *jus soli* status, a citizenship derived from their birthplace.

On such case concerned a London-born baby, Sidrah Syed, who happened to be born just four months after the implementation of the 1981 Act on 1 Jan. 1983. His father, Shahid Syed, had come to the UK as a student in 1975 and worked for British Gas as an accountant after graduation. When his work permit was not renewed in 1983, he, his wife and baby Sidrah were faced with deportation to Pakistan, a country that Sidrah had no formal right to enter. In essence, the 1981 Act has created the possibility of statelessness for minors and may continue to generate great complexity at the level of international relations in sorting out the consequences of deporting a stateless minor.

Seven years later, the Conservative government passed the Immigration Act of 1988. Lord McNair in the House of Lords lambasted this legislation as "another mean-minded, screw-tightening, loophole-closing concoction imbued

---

34. Morgado, *Role of Members of Parliament*, p. 14.

with the implicit assumption that almost everybody who seeks to enter this demi-paradise of ours has some ulterior, sinister, and very probably criminal motive and the sooner we get rid of him the better".

In truth, the justification for another round of national legislation did seem rather thin. The government could not detect widespread abuse of the system or the influx of large additional numbers demanding entry. (According to the Home Office's own figures, 1986 was "the lowest calendar year since Commonwealth citizens first became subject to control in 1962".) So it appears that, once again, the legislation was directed to the ideological right who, like the hydra-headed Cerberus of classical times, needed continual supplies of honey-cake to quieten them. One small example which reinforces this interpretation is the abrupt insistence in the Act that polygamous wives should no longer have the right of abode in the UK. This is both a demonstration of cultural arrogance and an illustration of the mean-mindedness Lord McNair referred to, as there were only perhaps 25 such claims each year.

On the other hand, with respect to deportation the 1988 Act did contain some real teeth. Clause 4 severely limited the availability and scope of appeals for all those without UK citizenship and also constrained the right to appeal against deportation for those seeking refugee status. In the case of an overstayer who had been in the UK for less than seven years, no appeal would be allowed. In effect, the government appeared to be viewing the courts as getting in the way of the running a smooth immigration control system and in interfering in the minister's discretionary powers. This impression was strongly reinforced by the speech of Mr Renton in the House of Commons who referred to the courts as a "thicket within which the immigrant [sic] is well-protected. He goes from one appeal to the next while the years drag on, at the end, after eight or nine years it is almost inevitable that he will be given leave to remain in Britain".

The Act was also interpreted by the home secretary as having allowed changes at the administrative level, so that deportation orders could be made by immigration officers at the inspector level (instead of by staff at the Immigration and Nationality Department). Under the "supervised departure" power accorded to them, immigration officers were allowed to offer the alleged offender a speedy exit, rather than waiting 14 days in jail for all the formalities to be completed. Some 70 per cent of deportees in 1989 took this option.

Three immediate effects of the increased power granted to the immigration officers were visible. First, the number of deportations went up dramatically – nearly 1,000 people were deported in the first months of 1989 alone; in one court case the judge alluded to a three-fold increase since the Act came into force. Second, the police got involved to a much greater extent on the grounds that, as a Home Office spokesperson claimed: "It is useful for immigration officers to have police along for their expertise. They attend in an advisory capacity" (*Standard*, 29 November 1989). Joint raids by the police and immigration service also increased. One, on British Petroleum's headquarters in London, turned up 39 allegedly illegal cleaners, who were served with deportation orders. Finally, a number of cases appeared where immigration officers exercised their newly-assigned powers with such indecent haste that they deported British citizens. One instance concerned the unfortunate Mr Koyobe Alese, a 25 year-old British citizen, born and educated in Britain and whose parents live in north-west London. Stopped for a driving offence, he gave a false name which the police could not find on their computers. They tipped off immigration officers who refused to believe him even after he had given his correct name. Somewhat distressed and bemused, he found himself at Lagos airport the next day (*Independent*, 29 April 1989).

These high-handed actions by immigration officers showed a scandalous disregard by the Home Office for the decision of Lord Justice Woolf in the High Court on 21 February 1990 that the home secretary had no right to delegate the power to issue deportation orders to immigration officers and that consequently 500 deportation orders were legally invalid. Individual immigration officers and the Home Office itself appeared to ignore this decision even though their own lawyers (in a confidential memo leaked to a newspaper in April 1989) had anticipated the judgement.

Conclusion

Who, historically, have the British authorities vomited out, ejected from the body politic? As I've skipped through the centuries, the cast list has grown quite bloated. Former French allies, Jews, Lombards, Hansards, Flemings, Calvinists, Catholics, Spanish agents, continental revolutionaries, Jews (again), Germans, Gypsies, Bolsheviks, black Commonwealth citizens, illegal entrants, overstayers, drugs-dealers; finally, a black Briton who had committed a driving offence – all these have been deported by executive authority, judicial recommendation or administrative decision.

The very diversity of the deportees' backgrounds questions any mono-focused characterisation of the character of the state and the motivations of its agents. At various times their fears were structured by appeals to national security, economic competition, religious uniformity, ideological rigidity, cultural distinctiveness and racial purity. In short the Other is a shifting category. We need greater historical specificity to distinguish between Herbert de Burgh's refusal to surrender Dover to the "French aliens" in 1216 and (say) Enoch Powell's classification of black Commonwealth citizens as "an alien wedge" more than 500 years later. Who becomes the alien, who the Other, who has to be feared, despised and deported, varies greatly. But all are victims of a nasty version of the old game of "pass the parcel". The parcel gets dumped into the lap of that group that the Self, or more exactly the defining agents and agencies of the British identity, most need at that time to distance themselves from and repulse.

Before the last war all manner of people fell victim to this horrid game. From the 1950s to the 1980s the victims have primarily been black and brown people from the Commonwealth. Unfortunately, they are still subject to the most disgraceful forms of racial discrimination within Britain, which I in no way wish to discount or minimise. However, it became apparent in the late 1980s that a new alien menace was being constructed by the frontier guards. These are the "undeserving asylum-seekers", from the Middle East, Turkey, Asia, eastern Europe or the New Commonwealth. Colour is now less relevant. These are not "genuine refugees" but disguised "economic migrants" – we are told. The history, characterisation and uncertain future of asylum-seekers and refugees indicate that they are being framed for their role as the Other of the *fin de siècle*.

Collective Bibliography

Adams, Thomas McStay, *Bureaucrats and Beggars. French Social Policy in the Age of Enlightenment* (New York and Oxford, 1990).

Addison, P., *Now the War is Over: A Social History of Britain 1945-51* (London, 1985).

Alatas, H.S., *The Myth of the Lazy Native: A Study of the Image of Malays, Filipinos and Javanese from the 16th to the 20th Century and its Function in the Ideology of Colonial Capitalism* (London, 1977).

Albi-Romero, Guadalupe, "La sociedad de Puebla de los Angeles en el siglo XVI", *Jahrbuch für Geschichte von Staat, Wirtschaft und Gesellschaft Lateinamerikas*, 7 (1970) pp. 77-145.

Alderman, Geoffrey and Colin Holmes (eds), *Outsiders and Outcasts* (London, 1993).

Altman, Ida, "Spanish Hidalgos and America: The Ovandos of Cáceres", *The Americas*, 43 (1987), pp. 323-344.

Altman, Ida, *Emigrants and Society. Extremadura and Spanish America in the Sixteenth Century* (Berkeley and Los Angeles, 1989).

Altman, Ida, "Spanish Society in Mexico City After the Conquest", *Hispanic American Historical Review*, 71 (1991) pp. 413-445.

Altman, Ida, "A New World in the Old", in: Altman and Horn, *"To Make America"*, pp. 30-58.

Altman, Ida and James Horn (eds), *"To Make America": European Emigration in the Early Modern Period* (Berkeley, 1991).

Anders, Steven E., *The Coolie Panacea in the Reconstruction South: A White Response to Emancipation and the Black Labor "Problem"* (Oxford/Ohio, 1973).

Anderson, Benedict, *Imagined Communities: Reflections on the Origins and Spread of Nationalism* (London, 1983).

Anderson, Michael, *Population Change in North-Western Europe, 1750-1850* (London, 1988).

Anderson, Virginia DeJohn, *New England's Generation: The Great Migration and the Formation of Society and Culture in the Seventeenth Century* (Cambridge, 1991).

Andrew, E.J.L., *Indian Labour in Rangoon* (Oxford, 1933).

Angelini, Massimo, "Suonatori ambulanti e 'garzoni' a Manchester nel 1857: due contratti d'ingaggio", *Ventesimo Secolo*, 1, 2-3 (May-December 1991), pp. 85-87.

Angelini, Massimo, "Suonatori ambulanti all'estero nel XIX secolo: considerazioni sul caso della valle Graveglia", *Studi Emigrazione*, XXIX (1992), no. 106, pp. 309-318.

Antin, Mary, *Promised Land* (Princeton, 1969[2]).

Appell, John J., "American Negro and Immigrant Experience: Similarities and Differences", *American Quarterly*, 18 (1966), pp. 95-103.

Appleby, Joyce Oldham, *Economic Thought and Ideology in Seventeenth Century England* (Princeton, 1978).

Archdeacon, Thomas, *Becoming American: An Ethnic History* (New York, 1983).

Archdeacon, Thomas, "Problems and Possibilities in the Study of American Immigration and Ethnic History", *International Migration Review*, 19 (1985), pp. 112-134.

Archer, Ian W., "Responses to Alien Immigrants in London c. 1400-1650", in: Cavaciocchi, *Migrazioni in Europa*, pp. 755-774.

Arendt, Hannah, *The Origins of Totalitarianism* (New York, 1973³).

Arensmeyer, Elliott C., "British Merchant Enterprise and the Chinese Coolie Trade: 1850-1874" (Unpublished Ph.D. Dissertation, University of Hawaii, 1979).

Arestegui, Efraim Trelles, *Lucas Martinez Vegazo: Funcionamiento de una encomienda peruana inicial* (Pontificia Universidad Católica del Peru, 1982).

Arkel, Dik van, "The Growth of the Anti-Jewish Stereotype. An Attempt at a Hypothetical-Deductive Method of Historical Research", *International Review of Social History*, XXX (1985), pp. 270-300.

Arlacchi, Pino, *Mafia, Peasants and Great Estates: Society in Traditional Calabria* (trans. Jonathan Steinberg, 1980; reprint Cambridge, 1983).

Armengaud, André, "Population in Europe, 1700-1914", in: Cipolla, *Fontana Economic History of Europe*, vol. 3.

Armstrong, William, "Godkin and Chinese Labor: A Paradox in Nineteenth-Century Liberalism", *The American Journal of Economics and Sociology*, 21 (1961/62), pp. 91-102.

Assante, Franca (ed.), *Movimento Migratorio Italiano dall'Unita Nazionale ai Giorni Nostri*, 2 vols (Geneva, 1978).

Atsma, Hartmut and André Burguière (eds), *Marc Bloch aujourd'hui. Histoire comparée et sciences sociales* (Paris, 1990).

Audenino, Patrizia, *Un Mestiere per Partire: Tradizione Migratoria. Lavoro e Comunita in una Vallata Alpina* (Milano, 1992).

Avery, Donald, *"Dangerous Foreigners": European Immigrant Workers and Labour Radicalism in Canada, 1896-1932* (Toronto, 1979).

Bade, Klaus J., *Auswanderer, Wanderarbeiter, Gastarbeiter. Bevölkerung, Arbeitsmarkt und Wanderung in Deutschland seit der Mitte des 19. Jahrhunderts*, 2 vols (Ostfildern, 1984).

Bade, Klaus J., "Sozialhistorische Migrationsforschung", in: Hinrichs and Van Zon, *Bevölkerungsgeschichte im Vergleich*, pp. 63-74.

Bade, Klaus J. (ed.), *Deutsche im Ausland, Fremde in Deutschland; Migration im Geschichte und Gegenwart* (München, 1992).

Bade, Klaus J., "Fremde Deutsche: 'Republikflüchtige', Übersiedler, Aussiedler", in: Bade, *Deutsche im Ausland*, pp. 401-410.

Baily, Samuel L., "The Italians and the Development of Organized Labor in Argentina, Brazil and the United States, 1880-1914", *Journal of Social History*, 3 (1969), pp. 123-134.

Baily, Samuel L., "The Adjustment of Italian Immigrants in Buenos Aires and New York, 1870-1914", *American Historical Review*, 88 (1983), pp. 281-305.

Baily, Samuel L., "Cross-Cultural Comparison and the Writing of Migration History: Some Thoughts on How to Study Italians in the New World", in: Yans-McLaughlin, *Immigration Reconsidered*, pp. 241-253.

Bailyn, Bernard, "1776. A Year of Challenge – the World Transformed", *Journal of Law and Economics*, 15 (1976), pp. 437-466.

Bailyn, Bernard, *The Peopling of British North America: An Introduction* (London, 1987).

Bailyn, Bernard, *Voyagers to the West* (New York, 1987).

Baines, Dudley E., "European Labor Markets, Emigration and Internal Migration, 1850-1913", in: Hatton and Williamson, *Migration and the International*, pp. 35-54.

Baines, Dudley E., *Migration in a Mature Economy. Emigration and Internal Migration in England and Wales, 1861-1900* (Cambridge, 1985).

Baines, Dudley E., *Emigration from Europe, 1815-1930* (London, 1991).

Baker, C.J., *An Indian Rural Economy 1880-1955: The Tamilnad Countryside* (Delhi, 1984).

Balsdon, J.P.V.D., *Romans and Aliens* (London, 1979).

Bamyeh, Mohammed A., "Transnationalism", *Current Sociology*, 41 (Winter 1993), pp. 1-101.

Bandhyopadhyay, S., A. Dasgupta and W. van Schendel (eds) *Bengal. Development, Communities and States* (Delhi, 1994).

Banton, M. and J. Harwood, *The Race Concept* (Newton Abbot, 1975).

Barbour, Violet, "Marine Risks and Insurance in the Seventeenth Century", *Journal of Economic and Business History*, 1 (1929), pp. 561-596.

Barbour, Violet, "Dutch and English Merchant Shipping in the Seventeenth Century", *Economic History Review*, 2 (1930), pp. 261-290.

Barraclough, Geoffrey, *History in a Changing World* (Oxford, 1955).

Barraclough, Geoffrey, *An Introduction to Contemporary History* (Harmondsworth, 1967).

Barrett, James R., "Americanization from the Bottom Up: Immigration and the Remaking of the Working Class in the United States, 1880-1930", *Journal of American History*, 79 (1992), pp. 997-1020.

Barth, Frederick, *Ethnic Groups and Boundaries* (Bergen, 1969).

Barth, Guenther, *Bitter Strength. A History of the Chinese in the United States, 1850-1870* (Cambridge, MA, 1964).

Barton, H. Arnold (ed.), *Letters from the Promised Land. Swedes in America, 1840-1914* (Minneapolis, 1975).

Barton, Josef, *Peasants and Strangers: Italians, Rumanians, and Slovaks in an American City, 1890-1950* (Cambridge, MA, 1975).

Baruch-Gourden, Jean-Michel, "La police et le commerce ambulant à Paris au XIXe siècle", in: Vigier *et al.*, *Maintien de l'ordre*, pp. 251-267.

Bastid-Bruguiere, Marianne, "Currents of Social Change", in: Fairbank and Liu, *Cambridge History of China*, II, Part 2, pp. 582-586, 591-593.

Basu, Subho, "Labour Movement in Bengal. From Community Consciousness to Class Consciousness: A Case Study of the Jute Mill Worker (1881-1909)" (Ph.D., Jawaharlal Nehru University, Delhi, 1988).

Baud, Michiel, "Families and Migration: Towards an Historical Analysis of Family Networks", *Economic and Social History in the Netherlands*, 6 (1994), pp. 83-109.

Bayor, Ronald, *Neighbors in Conflict: The Irish, Germans, Jews, and Italians of New York City, 1929-1941* (Baltimore, 1978).

Beattie, John M., *Crime and the Courts in England, 1660-1800* (Princeton, 1986).

Beattie, John M., "The Pattern of Crime in England, 1660-1800", *Past and Present*, 62 (1974), pp. 47-95.

Becker, Peter, "Vom 'Haltlosen' zur 'Bestie'. Das polizeiliche Bild des 'Verbrechers' im 19. Jahrhundert", in: Lüdtke, *"Sicherheit" und "Wohlfahrt"*, pp. 97-132.

Beckert, Sven, "Migration, Ethnicity and Working Class Formation. Passaic, New Jersey, 1889-1926", in: Hoerder and Nagler, *People in Transit*, pp. 347-377.

Beckles, Hilary McD., *White Servitude and Black Slavery in Barbados, 1627-1715* (Knoxville, 1989).

Beier, A.L., *Masterless Men. The Vagrancy Problem in England 1560-1640* (London etc., 1985).

Benton, G. and H. Vermeulen (eds), *De Chinezen* (Muiderberg, 1987).

Berger, John and Jean Mohr, *A Seventh Man: Migrants Workers in Europe* (New York, 1979).

Berkner, Lutz and Franklin Mendels, "Inheritance Systems, Family Structure, and Demographic Patterns in Western Europe, 1700-1900", in: C. Tilly, *Historical Studies of Changing Fertility*, pp. 209-223.

Bernard, Daniel, "Surveillance des itinérants et ambulants dans le département de l'indre au XIXe siècle et au début du XXe siècle", in: Vigier *et al.*, *Maintien de l'ordre*, pp. 235-250.

Berrier, Robert, "The French Textile Industry: A Segmented Labor Market", in: Rogers, *Guests Come to Stay*, pp. 51-68.

Bethell, Leslie (ed.), *The Cambridge History of Latin America*, II (Cambridge, 1985).

Bevan, V., *The Development of British Immigration Law* (London, 1986).

Bezza, Bruno (ed.), *Gli Italiani fuori d'Italia. Gli Emigrati Italiani nei Movimenti Operai dei Paesi d'Adozione 1880-1940* (Milan, 1983).

Bhana, S., *Indentured Indian Emigrants to Natal, 1860-1902: A Study based on the Ships' Lists* (New Delhi, 1991).

Bhattacharya, N. and A.K. Chatterjee, "Some Characteristics of Jute Industry Workers in Greater Calcutta", *Economic and Political Weekly* vol. VIII (February 1973), pp. 297-308.

Bindoff, S.T., *Tudor England* (Harmondsworth, 1961).

Bird, J.C., *The Control of Enemy Alien Civilians in Great Britain, 1914-1918* (New York, 1986).

Blickle, Renate, "Nahrung und Eigentum als Kategorien in der ständischen Gesellschaft", in: Schulze, *Ständische Gesellschaft*, pp. 73-93.

Bloch, Marc, "Pour une histoire comparée des sociétés européennes" [1928], in: Bloch, *Mélanges historiques*, 1, pp. 16-40.

Bloch, Marc, *Mélanges historiques*, 2 vols (Paris, 1983).

Blocher, Andreas, *Die Eigenart der Zürcher Auswanderer nach Amerika 1734-1744* (Zurich, 1976).

Blok, Anton, *The Mafia of a Sicilian Village. 1860-1960. A Study of Violent Peasant Entrepreneurs* (New York, 1974).

Blum, Peter, *Staatliche Armenfürsorge im Herzogtum Nassau 1806-1866* (Wiesbaden, 1987).

Bodnar, John, *Immigration and Industrialization: Ethnicity in an American Mill Town, 1870-1940* (Pittsburgh, 1977).

Bodnar, John, *The Transplanted. A History of Immigrants in Urban America* (Bloomington, 1985).

Bodnar, John, Roger Simon and Michael P. Weber, *Lives of their Own: Blacks, Italians, and Poles in Pittsburgh, 1900-1960* (Urbana, 1982).

Bog, Ingomar, "Über Arme und Armenfürsorge in Oberdeutschland und in der Eidgenossenschaft im 15. und 16. Jahrhundert", *Zeitschrift für Fränkische Landesforschung*, 34-35 (1975), pp. 983-1002.

Bonacich, Edna, "A Theory of Ethnic Antagonism: The Split Labor Market", *American Sociological Review*, XXXVII (1972), pp. 547-559.

Bonnet, Serge, Etienne Kagan and Michel Maigret, *L'Homme du Fer, Mineurs de Fer et Ouvriers Sidérurgistes Lorrains. 1889-1930* (Nancy, 1975).

Boogaart, E. van den and Pieter C. Emmer, "Colonialism and Migration: an Overview", in: Emmer, *Colonialism and Migration*, pp. 3-11.

Boucher, Philip P., *Cannibal Encounters. Europeans and Island Caribs, 1492-1763* (Baltimore, 1992).

Bouvier, Pierre, "Différences et analogies", in: Bouvier and Kourchid, *France-U.S.A.*, pp. 11-17.

Bouvier, Pierre and Olivier Kourchid (eds), *France-U.S.A.* (Paris, 1988).

Bovenkerk, Frank, *The Sociology of Return Migration: A Bibliographic Essay* (The Hague, 1974).

Bowden, Peter J., *The Wool Trade in Tudor and Stuart England* (London, 1962).

Boyd, M., "Oriental immigration: The experience of the Chinese, Japanese, and Filipino populations in the United States", *International Migration Review*, 5 (1971), pp. 48-61.

Boyd Caroli, Betty, "Italians in the Cherry, Illinois, Mine Disaster", in: Pozzetta, *Pane e Lavoro*, pp. 67-79.

Boyd-Bowman, Peter, *Indice geobiográfico de cuarenta mil pobladores españoles de América en el siglo XVI*, vols 1-2 (Bogota, 1964 and Mexico, 1968).

Boyd-Bowman, Peter, *Patterns of Spanish Emigration to the New World (1493-1580)* (Buffalo, 1973).

Boyd-Bowman, Peter, "Patterns of Spanish Emigration to the Indies until 1600", *Hispanic American Historical Review*, 56 (1976), pp. 580-664.

Bradwin, Edmund W., *The Bunkhouse Man: A Study of Work and Pay in the Camps of Canada 1903-1914* (Toronto, 1972).

Brass, Tom, Marcel van der Linden and Jan Lucassen, *Free and Unfree Labour* (Amsterdam, 1993).

Braudel, Fernand, *L'identité de la France* (Paris, 1986).

Braudel, Fernand, *The Identity of France*, 2 vols (New York, 1988), transl. by Sian Reynolds.

Braun, Rudolf, "Early Industrialization and Demographic Change in the Canton of Zurich", in: C. Tilly, *Historical Studies of Changing Fertility*, pp. 289-334.

Breen, T.H. (ed.), *Shaping Southern Society* (New York, 1976).

Breman, Jan, *Taming the Coolie Beast: Plantation Society and the Colonial Order in Southeast Asia* (Delhi, 1987).

Breman, Jan (ed.), *Imperial Monkey Business; Racial Supremacy in Social Darwinist Theory and Colonial Practice* (Amsterdam, 1990).

Breman, Jan, *Koelies, planters en koloniale politiek; het arbeidsregime op de grootlandbouw-ondernemingen aan Sumatra's Oostkust in het begin van de twintigste eeuw* (Leiden, 1992).

Breman, Jan, *Wage Hunters and Gatherers. Search for Work in the Urban and Rural Economy of South Gujarat* (Delhi, 1994).

Breman, Jan and E. Valentine Daniel, "Conclusion: The Making of a Coolie", *Journal of Peasant Studies*, 19 (1992), 3/4, pp. 268-296.

Brenner, Robert, "Agrarian Class Structure and Economic Development in pre-Industrial Europe", *Past and Present*, 70 (1976).

Brettell, Caroline B., "Is the Ethnic Community Inevitable? A Comparison of the Settlement Patterns of Portuguese Immigrants in Toronto and Paris", *The Journal of Ethnic Studies*, 9 (Fall 1981), pp. 1-17.

Brettell, Caroline B., *Men Who Migrate, Women Who Wait: Population and History in a Portuguese Parish* (Princeton, 1986).

Briggs, John W., "Fertility and Cultural Change among Families in Italy and America", *American Historical Review*, 91 (1986), pp. 1129-1145.

Briggs, John W., *An Italian Passage: Immigrants to Three American Cities, 1890-1930* (New Haven, 1978).

Broeze, F.J.A., "The Cost of Distance Shipping and the Early Australian Economy, 1788-1850", *Economic History Review*, XXVIII (1975), pp. 582-597.

Browne, George F., "Government Immigration Policy in Imperial Brazil, 1822-1870" (Unpublished Ph.D., The Catholic University of America, 1971).

Brubaker, Rogers, *Citizenship and Nationhood in France and Germany* (Cambridge, MA, and London, 1992).

Bruser Maynard, Fredelle, *Raisins and Almonds* (Toronto, 1985).

Buckland, P. and J. Belchem (eds), *The Irish in British Labour History* (Liverpool, 1993).

Buckman, J., *Immigrants and Class Struggle: The Jewish Immigrant in Leeds, 1880-1914* (Manchester, 1983).

Burawoy, Michael, "The Functions and Reproduction of Migrant Labor: Comparative Material from South Africa and the United States", *American Journal of Sociology*, 81 (March 1976), pp. 1050-1087.

Burke, Peter, "French Historians and their Cultural Identities", in: Tonkin *et al.*, *History and Ethnicity*, pp. 157-167.

Butlin, N.G., "The Shape of the Australian Economy, 1861-1900", *Economic Record*, 34 (1958), pp. 10-29.

Caestecker, Frank, "Het vreemdelingenbeleid in de tussenoorlogse periode, 1922-1939, in België", *Belgisch Tijdschrift voor Nieuwste Geschiedenis*, 15 (1984), no. 3-4, pp. 461-486.

Caestecker, Frank, *Vluchtelingenbeleid in de naoorlogse periode* (Brussels, 1992).

Caestecker, Frank, *Ongewenste gasten. Joodse Vluchtelingen en migranten in de dertiger jaren* (Brussels, 1993).

Campbell, B.M.S. and M. Overton (eds), *Land, Labour, and Livestock: Historical Studies in European Agricultural Productivity* (Manchester, 1991).

Canny, Nicholas (ed.), *Europeans on the Move. Studies on European Migration, 1500-1800* (Oxford, 1994).

Carr, Lois Green and Russell R. Menard, "Immigration and Opportunity: The Freedman in Early Colonial Maryland", in: Tate and Ammerman, *Chesapeake in the Seventeenth Century*, pp. 206-242.

Carson, Kit and Hilary Idzikowska, "The Social Production of Scottish Policing 1795-1900", in: Hay and Snyder, *Policing and Prosecuting*, pp. 267-297.

Carter, Marina, "Strategies of Labour Mobilisation in Colonial India: The Recruitment of Indentured Workers for Mauritius", in: Daniel *et al.*, *Plantations, Proletarians*, pp. 229-245.

Carus Wilson, E.M., "Trends in the Export of English Woollens in the Fourteenth Century", *Economic History Review*, 3 (1950), pp. 162-179.

Castles, Stephen, "Migrants and Minorities in Post-Keynesian Capitalism: The German Case", in: Cross, *Ethnic Minorities and Industrial Change*, pp. 315-339.

Castles, Stephen (with Heather Booth and Tina Wallace), *Here for Good. Western Europe's New Ethnic Minorities* (London and Sydney, 1984).

Castles, Stephen and Godula Kosak, *Immigrant Workers and Class Structure in Western Europe* (London, 1973).

Castles, Stephen and Mark J. Miller (eds), *The Age of Migration. International Population Movements in the Modern World* (Basingstoke and London, 1993).

Cataluccio, M., "Avant propos. Les vagabonds et les pauvres dans l'oeuvre de Bronislaw Geremek", in: Geremek, *Les fils de Cain*, pp. 7-32.

Cavaciocchi, Simonetta (ed.), *Le migrazioni in Europa secc. XIII-XVIII* (Prato, 1994).

Cedronio, Marina (ed.), *Méthode historique et sciences sociales* (Paris, 1987).

Cesarani, David, "Anti-Alienism in England after the First World War", *Immigrants and Minorities*, 6 (1987), pp. 5-29.

Cesarani, David, *Justice Delayed* (London, 1992).

Chakrabarty, Dipesh, *Rethinking Working-Class History. Bengal 1890-1940* (Delhi, 1989).

Chambers, J.D., "The Vale of Trent, 1670-1800", *Economic History Review*, Supplement no. 3 (1957).

Chan, Sucheng, "European and Asian Immigration into the United States", in: Yans-McLaughlin, *Immigration Reconsidered*, pp. 37-78.

Chan, Sucheng (ed.), *Entry Denied: Exclusion and the Chinese Community in America, 1882-1943* (Philadelphia, 1991).

Chandavarkar, Rajnarayan, *The Origins of Industrial Capitalism in India. Business Strategies and the Working Classes in Bombay, 1900-1940* (Cambridge, 1994).

Chandler, David, *The Art of Warfare in the Age of Marlborough* (London, 1976).

Chao, Paul, *Chinese Kinship* (London, 1983).

Chatelain, Abel, "Lutte entre colporteurs et boutiquiers en France pendant la première moitié du XIXe siècle", *Revue d'histoire économique et sociale*, XLIX (1971), pp. 359-384.

Chatelain, Abel, *Les migrants temporaires en France de 1800 à 1914*, 2 vols (Lille, 1977).

Chattopadhyaya, Haraprasad, *Internal Migration in India. A Case Study of Bengal* (Calcutta, 1987).

Chattopadhyay, K.P., *A Socio-Economic Survey of Jute Labour* (Calcutta, 1952).

Chesneaux, Jean, *Secret Societies in China in the Nineteenth and Twentieth Centuries* (Ann Arbor, 1971).

Chesneaux, Jean, *Popular Movements and Secret Societies in China, 1840-1950* (Stanford, 1972).

Chevalier, L., *Classes laborieuses et classes dangereuses à Paris, pendant la première moitié du XIX siècle* (Paris, 1978).

Chiapelli, Fredi (ed.), *First Images of America* (Berkeley and Los Angeles, 1976).

Christiansen, John B., "The Split Labor Market Theory and Filipino Exclusion: 1927-1934", *Phylon*, XL (1979), pp. 66-74.

Cinel, Dino, *The National Integration of Italian Return Migration. 1870-1929* (Cambridge, 1991).

Cipolla, C. (ed.), *The Fontana Economic History of Europe*, 4 vols (New York, 1976).

Ciuffoletti, Zeffiro, *L'Emigrazione nella Storia d'Italia, 1868/1975. Storia e Documenti* (Florence, 1978).

Clark, C.M., "The Origins of the Convicts transported to Eastern Australia, 1787-1852", *Historical Studies, Australia and New Zealand*, VII (1956), pp. 121-135, 314-327.

Clark, Gregory, "Yields per Acre in English Agriculture, 1250-1860: Evidence from Labour Inputs", *Economic History Review*, 44 (1991), pp. 445-460.

Clark, Peter A., "The migrant in Kentish towns 1580-1640", in: Clark and Slack, *Crisis and Order*, pp. 117-163.

Clark, Peter A., "Migration in England during the Late Seventeenth and Early Eighteenth Centuries", *Past and Present*, 83 (1979), pp. 57-90.

Clark, Peter A. and Paul Slack (eds), *Crisis and Order in English Towns 1500-1700. Essays in Urban History* (London, 1972).

Clark, Peter A. and Paul Slack, *English Towns in Transition, 1500-1700* (London, 1974).

Clark, Peter A. and David Souden (eds), *Migration and Society in Early Modern England* (London, 1987).

Clark, Peter A. and David Souden, "Introduction", in: Clark and Souden, *Migration and Society*, pp. 1-48.

Clarkson, Leslie, *Proto-Industrialization: The First Phase of Industrialization?* (London, 1985).

Clasen, Claus-Peter, "Armenfürsorge in Augsburg vor dem Dreißigjährigen Kriege", *Zeitschrift des historischen Vereins für Schwaben*, 78 (1984), pp. 65-115.

Cloud, Patricia and David W. Galenson, "Chinese Immigration and Contract Labor in the Late Nineteenth Century", *Explorations in Economic History*, 24 (1987), pp. 22-42.

Coats, A.W., "Changing Attitudes to Labour in the Mid-Eighteenth Century", *Economic History Review*, 11 (1958-59), pp. 35-51.

Cohen, Lucy, *Chinese in the Post-Civil War South: A People Without a History* (Baton Rouge, LA, 1984).

Cohn, R.L., "The Occupations of English Immigrants to the United States, 1836-1853", *Journal of Economic History*, LII (1992), pp. 377-387.

Coldham, Peter Wilson, *The Complete Book of Emigrants, 1607-1660* (Baltimore, 1988).

Coldham, Peter Wilson, *The Complete Book of Emigrants, 1661-1699* (Baltimore, 1990).

Coldham, Peter Wilson, *Emigrants in Chains: A Social History of Forced Emigration to the Americas of Felons, Destitute Children, Political and Religious Non-Conformists, Vagabonds and Other Undesirables, 1606-1776* (Baltimore, 1992).

Cole, Donald B., *Immigrant City: Lawrence, Mass., 1845-1921* (Chapel Hill, 1963).

Cook, Noble David, "Migration in Colonial Peru: an Overview", in: Robinson, *Migration in Colonial Spanish America*, pp. 41-61.

Cook, Tim (ed.), *Vagrancy. Some New Perspectives* (London etc., 1979).

Coolidge, Mary, *Chinese Immigration* (New York, 1909).

Corbitt, Duvon C., *A Study of the Chinese in Cuba. 1847-1947* (Wilmore, KY, 1971).

Corris, P., *Passage, Port and Plantation: A History of Solomon Islands Labour Migration, 1870-1914* (Melbourne, 1973).

Cottaar, Annemarie, *Kooplui, kermisklanten en andere woonwagenbewoners. Groepsvorming en beleid, 1875-1945* (Amsterdam, 1996).

Cottaar, Annemarie, Leo Lucassen and Wim Willems, "Justice or Injustice? A Survey of Government Policy Towards Gypsies and Caravan Dwellers in Western Europe in the 19th and 20th Centuries", *Immigrants and Minorities*, 11 (1992), pp. 42-66.

Cottaar, Annemarie and Wim Willems, *Indische Nederlanders* (Den Haag, 1984).

Courgeau, Daniel, "Recent Conceptual Advances in the Study of Migration in France", in: Ogden and White, *Migrants in Modern France*, pp. 60-73.

Crawford Campbell, Persia, *Chinese Coolie Emigration to Countries within the British Empire* (London, 1971).

Cronin, Kathryn, *Colonial Casualties: Chinese in Early Victoria* (Singapore, 1982).

Cross, Gary S., *Immigrant Workers in Industrial France. The Making of a New Laboring Class* (Philadelphia, 1983).

Cross, Malcolm (ed.), *Ethnic Minorities and Industrial Change in Europe and North-America* (Cambridge, 1992).

Cross, Malcolm, "Black Workers, Recession and Economic Restructuring in the West Midlands", in: Cross, *Ethnic Minorities and Industrial Change*, pp. 77-93.

Cunliffe, Marcus, *Chattel Slavery and Wage Slavery; The Anglo-American Context 1830-1860* (Athens, 1979).

Cunningham, W., *Alien Immigrants to England* (New York, 1969; first published in London, 1897).

Curtin, Philip, *The Atlantic Slave Trade. A Census* (Madison, 1969).

Curtin, Philip D., "Nutrition in African History", in: Rotberg and Rabb, *Hunger and History*, pp. 173-185.

Curtin, Philip D., "African Health at Home and Abroad", *Social Science History*, X (1986), pp. 369-398.

Curtin, Philip D., *Death by Migration; Europe's Encounter with the Tropical World in the Nineteenth Century* (New York, 1989).

Daniel, E. Valentine, Henry Bernstein and Tom Brass (eds), *Plantations, Proletarians and Peasants in Colonial Asia* (London, 1992).

Daniel, Pete, *The Shadow of Slavery: Peonage in the South. 1901-1969* (Urbana, 1972).

Daniels, Roger, "On the Comparative Study of Immigrant and Ethnic Groups in the New World: A Note", *Comparative Studies in Society and History*, 25 (1983), pp. 401-404.

Daniels, Roger, "Chinese and Japanese in North America: The Canadian and American Experiences Compared", *Canadian Review of American Studies*, 17 (1986), pp. 173-187.

Daniels, Roger, *Coming to America* (New York, 1990).

Danker, Uwe, *Räuberbanden im Alten Reich um 1700. Ein Beitrag zur Geschichte von Herrschaft und Kriminalität in der frühen Neuzeit* (Frankfurt am Main, 1988).

Das, Arvind, *The "Longue Duree": Continuity and Change in Changel. Historiography of an Indian Village from the 18th towards the 21st Century* (Rotterdam, 1986).

Das Gupta, Ranajit, "Factory Labour in Eastern India: Sources of Supply, 1855-1946. Some Preliminary Findings", *Indian Economic and Social History Review*, XIII (1976), pp. 277-329.

Das Gupta, Ranajit, "Structure of the Labour Market in Colonial India", *Economic and Political Weekly*, XVII (1981), November, special number, pp. 1781-1806.

Dasent, J.R., *Acts of the Privy Council of England, New Series, Vol. VII AD 1558-1570*, (London, 1890).

Davids, J. (ed.), *American Diplomatic and Public Papers. The United States and China*. Series II, vols 12 and 13 (Wilmington, 1979).

Davies, H. (ed.), *The New London Spy* (London, 1966).

Davies, Kenneth Gordon, *The Royal African Company* (London, 1957).

Davies, Kenneth Gordon, *The North Atlantic World in the Seventeenth Century* (Minneapolis and Oxford, 1974).

Davies, N., "The Poles in Great Britain, 1914-1919", *Slavonic and East European Review*, 50 (1972), pp. 63-85.

Davis, Fei-Ling, *Primitive Revolutionaries of China; A Study of Secret Societies in the late Nineteenth Century* (Honolulu, 1971).

Davis, J., "Urban Policing and its Objects: Comparative Themes in England and France in the Second Half of the Nineteenth Century", in: Emsley and Weinberger, *Policing Western Europe*, pp. 1-17.

Davis, Kingsley, "The Migrations of Human Populations", *Scientific American*, vol. 231 (1974), pp. 92-105.

Davis, Ralph, "English Foreign Trade, 1660-1700", *Economic History Review*, 7 (1954), pp. 150-166.

Davis, Ralph, *The Rise of the English Shipping Industry* (London, 1962).

Deakin, N., "The British Nationality Act of 1948: A Brief Study of the Mythology of Race Relations", *Race*, XI (1969), pp. 77-83.

Dean, Warren, *Rio Claro. A Brazilian Plantation System. 1820-1920* (Stanford, 1976).

Deane, Phyllis and W.A. Cole, *British Economic Growth, 1688-1959* (Cambridge, 1967).

Decleva, Enrico, *Etica del Lavoro. Socialismo, Cultura Popolare: Augusto Osimo e la Società Umanitaria* (Milan, 1985).

Denholm, A.F., Susan Marsden and Kerrie Round (eds), *Terowie Workshop: Exploring the History of South Australian Country Towns* (Adelaide, 1991).

Dennis, Richard, *English Industrial Cities of the Nineteenth Century* (Cambridge, 1984).

Depauw, J., "Pauvres, pauvres mendiants, mendiants valides ou vagabonds? Les hésitati-ons de la législation royale", *Revue d'histoire moderne et contemporaine*, 21 (1974), pp. 401-418.

Deprez, Paul (ed.), *Population and Economics: Proceedings of the Fourth Congress of the International Economic History Association, 1968* (Winnipeg, 1970).

Deslé, E., R. Lesthaeghe and E. Witte (eds), *Denken over migranten in Europa* (Brussels, 1993).

Deyon, Pierre, "Fécondité et limites du modèle protoindustriel: Premier bilan", *Annales ESC* 39 (1984), pp. 868-882.

Dignan, Don, "Europe's Melting Pot: A Century of Large-Scale Immigration Into France", *Ethnic and Racial Studies*, vol. 4 (1981), pp. 137-152.

Dillmann, Alfred, *Das Zigeunerbuch* (München, 1905).

Diner, Hasia R., *Erin's Daughters in America. Irish Immigrant Women in the Nineteenth Century* (Baltimore, 1983).

Doesschate, Jan-Willem ten, *Asielbeleid en belangen. Het Nederlandse toelatingsbeleid ten aanzien van vluchtelingen in de jaren 1968-1982* (Hilversum, 1993).

Dohse, Knuth, *Ausländische Arbeiter und bürgerlicher Staat. Genese und Funktion von staatlicher Auslanderpolitik und Ausländerrecht. Vom Kaiserreich bis zur Bundesrepublik Deutschland* (Königstein, 1981).

Donovan, Bill M., "Changing Perceptions of Social Deviance: Gypsies in Early Modern Portugal and Brazil", *Journal of Social History* 26 (1992), pp. 33-53.

Donson, J., "The British Responses to Hungarian Immigration, 1956-1957: The Response in Sheffield. A Case Study" (BA Dissertation, University of Sheffield, 1989).

Doomernik, Jeroen, "The Institutionalisation of Turkish Islam in Germany and The Netherlands: a Comparison", *Ethnic and Racial Studies*, 18 (1995), no. 1, pp. 46-63.

Dorn, Ulrike, *Öffentliche Armenpflege in Köln von 1794-1871* (Wien, 1990).

Douglas, William, "The Swarthy Alternative: Italian Sugar Canecutters in North America's Deep South and Australia's Far North" (Unpublished paper, University of Nevada, Reno).

Douglass, William A., *From Italy to Ingham* (St. Lucia, Queensland 1995).

Drost, Richard, "Forced Labor in the South Pacific, 1850-1914" (Unpublished Ph.D. Dissertation, State University of Iowa, 1954).

Dülmen, Richard van (ed.), *Verbrechen, Strafen und soziale Kontrolle. Studien zur historischen Kulturforschung* (Frankfurt am Main, 1990).

Dunn, Richard S., *Sugar and Slaves: The Rise of the Planter Class in the English West Indies, 1624-1713* (New York, 1972).

Dunn, Richard S., "The English Sugar Islands and the Founding of South Carolina", in: Breen, *Shaping Southern Society*, pp. 48-58.

Dupaquier, J. (ed.), *Histoire de la Population Française*, 4 vols (Paris, 1988).

Durckhardt, Heinz, "Glaubensflüchtlinge und Entwicklungshelfer: Niederländer, Hugenotten, Waldenser, Salzburger", in: Bade, *Deutsche im Ausland*, pp. 278-287.

Duwidowitsch, L. and V. Dietzel, *Russisch-Jüdisches Roulette. Jüdische Emigranten erzählen ihr Leben. 21 Gespräche* (Zürich, 1993).

Dyos, H.J. and Michael Wolff (eds), *The Victorian City. Images and Realities*. 2 vols (London, 1976).

Egmond, Florike, *Underworlds* (Oxford, 1993).

Ehmer, Josef, *Heiratsverhalten, Sozialstruktur, ökonomischer Wandel: England und Mitteleuropa in der Formationsperiode des Kapitalismus* (Göttingen, 1991).

Elsner, Lothar, "Ausländerbeschäftigung und Zwangsarbeitspolitik in Deutschland während des Ersten Weltkrieges", in: Bade, *Auswanderer, Wanderarbeiter, Gastarbeiter*, Vol. II, pp. 527-557.

Eltis, David, "Free and Coerced Transatlantic Migrations: Some Comparisons", *American Historical Review*, 88 (1983), pp. 251-280.

Eltis, David, *Economic Growth and the Ending of the Transatlantic Slave Trade* (New York and Oxford, 1987).

Eltis, David, "Europeans and the Rise and Fall of African Slavery in the Americas: An Interpretation", *American Historical Review*, 98 (1993), pp. 1399-1423.

Eltis, David, "Labour and Coercion in the English Atlantic World from the Seventeenth Century to the Early Twentieth Centuries", *Slavery and Abolition*, 14 (1993), pp. 207-226.

Eltis, David, "The British Transatlantic Slave Trade Before 1714: Annual Estimates of Volume and Direction", in: Paquette and Engerman, *Lesser Antilles in the Age of European Expansion*.

Eltis, David, "The Relative Importance of Slaves in the Atlantic Trade of Seventeenth Century Africa", *Journal of African History*, XXXV (1994), pp. 237-249

Eltis, David, "New Estimates of Exports from Barbados and Jamaica, 1665-1701", *William and Mary Quarterly*, 52 (1995), pp. 631-648.

Eltis, David and Stanley L. Engerman, "Was the Slave Trade Dominated by Men", *Journal of Interdisciplinary History*, XXIII (1992), pp. 237-257.

Eltis, David and David Richardson, "Productivity in the Transatlantic Slave Trade", *Economic History Review*, 32 (1995), pp. 465-484.

Emerson Smith, Abbott, *Colonists in Bondage: White Servitude and Convict Labour in America, 1607-1776* (Chapel Hill, NC, 1947; revised ed., 1966).

Emmer, Pieter C., "The Great Escape; The Migration of Female Indentured Servants from British India to Surinam, 1873-1916", in: Richardson, *Abolition and its Aftermath*, pp. 245-266.

Emmer, Pieter C. (ed.), *Colonialism and Migration; Indentured Labour Before and After Slavery* (Dordrecht, 1986).

Emmer, Pieter C., "The Meek Hindu; The Recruitment of Indian Labourers for Service Overseas, 1870-1916", in: Emmer, *Colonialism and Migration*, pp. 188-195.

Emmer, Pieter C., "European Expansion and Migration: The European Colonial Past and Intercontinental Migration: An Overview", in: Emmer and Mörner, *European Expansion and Migration*, pp. 1-13.

Emmer, Pieter C., "Immigration into the Caribbean; The Introduction of Chinese and East Indian Indentured Labourers Between 1839 and 1917", in: Emmer and Mörner, *European Expansion and Migration*, pp. 245-276.

Emmer, Pieter C. and Magnus Mörner (eds), *European Expansion and Migration. Essays on the International Migration from Africa, Asia and Europe* (New York and Oxford, 1992).

Emmons, David M., *The Butte Irish: Class and Ethnicity in an American Mining Town, 1875-1925* (Urabana and Chicago, 1990).

Emsley, Clive, *The English Police. A Political and Social History* (New York, 1991).

Emsley, Clive, "Peasants, Gendarmes and State Formation", in: Fulbrook, *National Histories and European History*, pp. 69-93.

Emsley, Clive and James Walvin (eds), *Artisans, Peasants and Proletarians 1760-1860* (London etc., 1985).

Emsley, Clive and B. Weinberger (eds), *Policing Western Europe* (New York, 1991).

Engelhardt, Ulrich *et al.*, *Soziale Bewegung und politische Verfassung* (Stuttgart, 1976).

Engels, Friedrich, *The Condition of the Working Class in England* [1845] (Oxford, 1971).

Engelsing, Rolf, "Der Arbeitsmarkt der Dienstboten im 17., 18. und 19. Jahrhundert", in: Kellenbenz, *Wirtschaftspolitik und Arbeitsmarkt*, pp. 159-237.

Engerman, Stanley L., "Servants to Slaves to Servants: Contract Labour and European Expansion", in: Emmer, *Colonialism and Migration*, pp. 263-294.

Engerman, Stanley L., "Coerced and Free Labor: Property Rights and the Development of the Labor Force", *Explorations in Economic History*, 29 (1992), pp. 1-29.

Engman, M. (ed.), *Ethnic Identity in Urban Europe. Comparative Studies on Governments and Non-Dominant Ethnic Groups in Europe, 1850-1940* (Aldershot, 1992).

Erickson, Charlotte, *American Industry and the European Immigrant. 1860-1885* (Cambridge, MA, 1957).

Erickson, Charlotte, "Who were the English and Scots Emigrants to the United States in the Late Nineteenth Century?", in: Glass and Revelle, *Population and Social Change*, pp. 347-382.

Erickson, Charlotte, "Emigration from the British Isles to the USA in 1831", *Population Studies*, XXXV (1981), pp. 175-197.

Erickson, Charlotte, "Emigration from the British Isles to the USA in 1841", *Population Studies*, XLIII (1989), pp. 347-367, and XLIV (1990), pp. 21-40.

Erickson, Charlotte, "Why Did Contract Labour Not Work in the Nineteenth-Century United States?", in: Marks and Richardson, *International Labour Migration*, pp. 34-56.

Erickson, Charlotte, *Leaving England. Essays on British Emigration in the Nineteenth Century* (Ithaca, N.Y., 1994).

Etzioni, Amitai and Frederick L. Du Bow (eds), *Comparative Perspectives: Theories and Methods* (Boston, 1970).

Evans, Neil, "Regulating the Reserve Army: Arabs, Blacks and the Local State in Cardiff, 1919-45", *Immigrants and Minorities*, 4 (1985), pp. 68-115.

Evans, Neil, "Regulating the Reserve Army: Arabs, Blacks and the Local State in Cardiff, 1919-1945", in: Lunn, *Race and Labour*, pp. 68-116.

Ewen, Elizabeth, *Immigrant Women in the Land of Dollars* (New York, 1985).

Fairbank, John K. and Kwang-Ching Liu (eds), *The Cambridge History of China*, II, Part 2 (London, 1980).

Fairchild, Henry, *The Melting Pot Mistake* (Boston, 1926).

Faith, Nicholas, *The World the Railways Made* (London, 1990).

Farnsworth MacNair, Harney, *The Chinese Abroad. Their Position and Protection. A Study in International Law and Relations* (Shanghai, 1924).

Feinstein, H. (ed.), *Socialism, Capitalism and Economic Growth: Essays Presented to Maurice Dobb* (Cambridge, 1967).

Fertig, Georg, *Migration from the German-Speaking Parts of Central Europe, 1600-1800: Estimates and Explanations*. Working paper no. 38 (1991) of the John F. Kennedy-Institut für Nordamerikastudien in Berlin.

Fertig, Georg, "'Um Anhoffung besserer Nahrung willen': Der lokale und motivationale Hintergrund von Auswanderung nach Britisch-Nordamerika im 18. Jahrhundert", *Beiträge zur historischen Sozialkunde*, XXII (1992), pp. 111-120.

Fertig, Georg, "Wanderungsmotivation und ländliche Gesellschaft im 18. Jahrhundert: Vom Oberrhein nach Nordamerika" (Diss., Free University Berlin, 1993).

Fertig, Georg, "Transatlantic Migration from the German-speaking Parts of Central Europe, 1600-1800: Proportions, Structures, and Explanations", in: Canny, *Europeans on the Move*, pp. 192-235.

Fichte, Johann Gottlieb, *Der geschloßne Handelsstaat* (Tübingen, 1800).

Finzsch, N., *Obrigkeit und Unterschichten. Zur Geschichte der rheinischen Unterschichten gegen Ende des 18. und zu Beginn des 19. Jahrhunderts* (Stuttgart, 1990).

Firmin, T., *Some Proposals for the Imploying of the Poor Especially in and about the City of London* (London, 1678).

Fisher, F.J., "London's Export Trade in the Early Seventeenth Century", *Economic History Review*, 3 (1950), pp. 151-161.

Fitzpatrick, David, "Irish Emigration in the later Nineteenth Century", *Irish Historical Studies*, 22 (1980), pp. 126-143.

Fitzpatrick, David, "A Curious Middle Place: the Irish in Britain, 1871-1921", in: Swift and Gilley, *The Irish in Britain*, pp. 10-59.

Fitzpatrick, David (ed.), *Home or Away? Immigrants in Colonial Australia* (Canberra, 1992).

Foerster, Robert F., *The Italian Emigration of Our Times* (New York, 1968; orig. published 1919).

Fogel, Robert William *et al.*, "Secular Changes in American and British Stature and Nutrition", *Journal of Interdisciplinary History*, XIV (1983), pp. 445-481.

Fogel, Robert William, *Without Consent or Contract; The Rise and Fall of American Slavery* (New York, 1989).

Fogel, Robert William, *Economic Growth, Population Theory, and Physiology: the Bearing of Long-Term Processes on the Making of Economic Policy*. Working paper 4638 of the National Bureau of Economic Research (Cambridge, MA, 1994).

Fogel, Robert William, Stanley L. Engerman and James Trussell, "Exploring the Uses of Data on Height; The Analysis of Long-Term Trends in Nutrition, Labor Welfare, and Labor Productivity", *Social Science History*, VI (1982), pp. 401-421.

Fogleman, Aaron, *Hopeful Journeys. German Immigration, Settlement and Political Culture in Colonial America* (Philadelphia, 1991).

Foley, Ben, *Report on Labour in Bengal* (Calcutta, 1906).

Foner, Eric, *Free Soil, Free Labor, Free Men: The Ideology of the Republican Party Before the Civil War* (New York, 1970).

Foner, Nancy, "West Indians in New York City and London: A Comparative Analysis", *International Migration Review*, 13 (1979), pp. 284-297.

Fontaine, Laurence, "Solidarités familiales et logiques migratoires en pays de montagne à l'époque moderne", *Annales ESC*, 45 (1990), pp. 1433-1450.

Forberg, Martin, "Foreign Labour, the State and the Trade Unions in Imperial Germany, 1890-1918", in: Lee and Rosenhaft, *State and Social Change in Germany*, pp. 99-130.

Forstenzer, Thomas R., *French Provincial Police and the Fall of the Second Republic* (Princeton, 1981).

Forster, R. and O. Ranum (eds), *Deviants and the Abandoned in French Society* (Baltimore, 1978).

Foster, Farley Mn., "The Chinese Coolie Trade, 1845-1875", *Journal of Asian and African Studies*, III (1968), 3-4, pp. 257-270.

Foster, George M., "Peasant Society and the Image of Limited Good", *American Anthropologist*, LXVII (1965), pp. 293-315.

Franchomme, Georges, "L'évolution démographique et économique de Roubaix dans le dernier tiers du XIXe siècle", *Revue du Nord*, 51 (1969), pp. 210-247.

Frauenstädt, P., "Bettel- und Vagabundenwesen in Schlesien vom 16. bis 18. Jahrhundert", *Zeitschrift für die gesamte Strafrechtswissenschaft* (1897), pp. 712-736.

Fredrickson, George M., "Comparative History", in: Kammen, *Past Before Us*, pp. 457-473.

Freeden, Hermann and Georg Smolka, "Deutsche Auswanderung im 18. Jahrhundert", first publication 1937, reprinted in: *Hessisches Auswandererbuch*, edited by Hans Herder (Frankfurt, 1984²), pp. 111-132.

Freeman, Gary P., *Immigrant Labor and Racial Conflict in Industrial Societies: The French and British Experience, 1945-1975* (Princeton, 1979).

Fricke, Thomas, *Zwischen Erziehung und Ausgrenzung. Zur württembergischen Geschichte der Sinti und Roma im 19. Jahrhundert* (Frankfurt am Main, 1991).

Friedrichs, Christopher R., *Urban Society in an Age of War: Nördlingen, 1580-1720* (Princeton, NJ, 1979).

Fuchs, Rachel G., *Poor and Pregnant in Paris* (New Brunswick, 1992).

Fuchs, Rachel G. and Leslie Page Moch, "Pregnant, Single and Far From Home: Migrant Women in Nineteenth-Century Paris", *American Historical Review*, 95 (1990) pp. 1007-1031.

Fulbrook, Mary (ed.), *National Histories and European History* (London, 1993).

Funk, A., *Polizei und Rechtsstaat. Die Entwicklung des staatlichen Gewaltmonopols in Preussen 1848-1914* (Frankfurt, 1986).

Furniss, Edgar, *The Position of the Laborer in a System of Nationalism* (New York, 1921).

Gabaccia, Donna R., *From Sicily to Elizabeth Street* (Albany, 1984).

Gabaccia, Donna R., *Militants and Migrants. Rural Sicilians Become American Workers* (New Brunswick and London, 1988).

Gabaccia, Donna R., "Clase y Cultura: Los Migrantes Italianos en Los Movimientos Obreros en el Mundo, 1876-1914", *Estudios Migratorios Latinoamericanas*, 7, 22 (1992), pp. 425-451.

Gabaccia, Donna R., "Women of the Mass Migrations: From Minority to Majority, 1820-1930", in: Hoerder and Moch, *European Migrants*, pp. 90-111.

Gabaccia, Donna R., "Worker Internationalism and Italian Labor Migration, 1870-1914", *International Labor and Workingclass History*, 45 (1994), pp. 63-79.

Gainer, Bernard, *The Alien Invasion* (London, 1972).

Galenson, David W., *White Servitude in Colonial America: An Economic Analysis* (Cambridge, 1981).

Galenson, David W., "The Rise and Fall of Indentured Servitude in the Americas: An Economic Analysis", *The Journal of Economic History*, 44 (1984), pp. 1-26.

Gallman, R.E. and J.J. Wallis (eds), *American Economic Growth and Standards of Living before the Civil War* (Chicago, 1992).

Gans, Herbert J., "Symbolic Ethnicity: the Future of Ethnic Groups and Cultures in America", *Ethnic and Racial Studies*, 2 (1979), pp. 1-20.

Garrard, J.A., *The English and Immigration 1880-1910* (London, 1971).

Gartner, L., *The Jewish Immigrant in England, 1870-1914* (Detroit, 1960; and London, 1973).

Gartner, L., "Notes on the Statistics of Jewish Immigration to England, 1870-1914", *Jewish Social Studies*, XXI (1960), pp. 79-102.

Gates, Henry Louis, Jr. (ed.), *"Race", Writing and Difference* (Chicago, 1986).

Gatrell, V.A.C., "Crime, Authority and the Policeman-State", in: Thompson, *Cambridge Social History of Britain*, Vol. 3, pp. 243-310.

Gatrell, V.A.C., "The Decline of Theft and Violence in Victorian and Edwardian England", in: Lenman and Parker, *Crime and the Law*.

Gatrell, V.A.C. and T.B. Haddon, "Criminal Statistics and their Interpretation", in: Wrigley, *Nineteenth Century Society*, pp. 336-396.

Gebler, C., *August in July* (Harmondsworth, 1987).

Gemery, Henry A., "Emigration from the British Isles to the New World, 1630-1700: Inferences from Colonial Populations", *Research in Economic History*, 5 (1980), pp. 179-231.

Gemery, Henry A., "Immigrants and Emigrants. International Migration and the US Labor Market in the Great Depression", in: Hatton and Williamson, *Migration and the Internation Labor Market*, pp. 175-199.

Geremek, Bronislaw, "Criminalité, vagabondage, paupérisme: la marginalité à l'aube des temps modernes", *Revue d'histoire moderne et contemporaine*, XXI (1974), pp. 337-375.

Geremek, Bronislaw, *Les marginaux parisiens aux XIV et XVe siècle* (Paris, 1976).

Geremek, Bronislaw, *Truands et misérables dans l'Europe moderne (1350-1600)* (Paris, 1980).

Geremek, Bronislaw, *Les fils de Caïn. L'image des pauvres et des vagabonds dans la littérature européenne du XVe au XVIIe siècle* (Paris, 1991).

Giddens, Anthony, *The Nation-State and Violence* (Berkeley and Los Angeles, 1987).

Gillman, Peter and Leni Gillman, *"Collar the Lot!" How Britain Interned and Expelled its Wartime Refugees* (London, 1980).

Gilroy, Paul, *"There Ain't No Black in the Union Jack": The Cultural Politics of Race and Nation* (London, 1987).

Gittins, Jean, *The Diggers from China. The Story of the Chinese on the Goldfields* (Melbourne, 1981).

Glass, D.V. and R. Revelle (eds), *Population and Social Change* (London, 1972).

Glazer, Nathan and Daniel Moynihan, *Beyond the Melting Pot* (Cambridge, MA, 1963).

Gleason, Philip, "The Melting Pot: Symbol of Fusion or Confusion?", *American Quarterly*, 16 (1964), pp. 20-46.

Gmelch, Sharon Bohn, "Groups that Don't Want In: Gypsies and Other Artisan, Trader, and Entertainer Minorities", *Annual Review of Anthropology*, 15 (1986), pp. 307-330.

Goldin, Claudia, "The Political Economy of Immigration Restriction in the United States, 1890 to 1921". Working paper 4345 of the National Bureau of Economic Research (Cambridge, MA, 1993).

Gordon, David M., Richard Edwards and Michael Reich, *Segmented Work. Divided Workers. The Historical Transformation of Labor in the United States* (Cambridge, 1982).

Gordon, Scott, "The Basic Analytical Structure of Malthusian Theory", in: Malthus, *Essay on the Principle*, pp. 167-168.

Goswami, Omkar, "Multiple Images: Jute Mill Strikes of 1929 and 1937 Seen Through Other's Eyes", *Modern Asian Studies*, 21 (1985), pp. 547-583.

Goulbourne, Harry, *Ethnicity and Nationalism in Post-Imperial Britain* (Cambridge, 1991).

Gould, J.D., "European Inter-Continental Emigration, 1815-1914: Patterns and Causes", *Journal of European Economic History*, 8 (1979), pp. 593-679.

Grafmeyer, Yves and Isaac Joseph (eds.), *L'Ecole de Chicago: Naissance de l'écologie urbaine* (Paris, 1984, republished in 1990).

Graham, Richard (ed.), *The Idea of Race in Latin America 1870-1940* (Austin, 1990).

Grant, R., "White Eagles of the North", *The Press and Journal*, 23 December 1986 – 11 February 1987.

Graves, Adrian A., "The Nature and Origins of Pacific Islands Labour Migration to Queensland, 1863-1906", in: Marks and Richardson, *International Labour Migration: Historical Perspectives*, pp. 112-139.

Green, Nancy L., *The Pletzl of Paris. Jewish Immigrants in the Belle Époque* (New York, 1986).

Green, Nancy L., "Immigrant Labor in the Garment Industries of New York and Paris: Variations on a Structure", *Comparative Social Research*, 9 (1986), pp. 231-243.

Green, Nancy L., "Leçons d'octobre – 1929, 1987, La presse française et américaine face aux deux crises boursières", *Esprit* (October 1988), pp. 91-110.

Green, Nancy L., "Diversité et unité dans les études immigrées: Les juifs étrangers à Paris", in: Kaspi and Marès, *Paris des étrangers*, pp. 106-118.

Green, Nancy L., "L'histoire comparative et le champ des études migratoires", *Annales ESC*, (1990), no. 6, pp. 1335-1350.

Green, Nancy L., "L'immigration en France et aux États-Unis, Historiographie comparée", *Vingtième Siècle*, no. 29 (January-March 1991), pp. 67-82.

Green, Nancy L., *Ready-to-Wear and Ready-to Work: A Century of Industry and Immigrants in the Women's Garment Trade in Paris and New York* (Durham, 1997).

Greenfeld, Liah and Michael Mertin (eds), *Center: Ideas and Institutions* (Chicago, 1988).

Greenough, Paul R., *Prosperity and Misery in Modern Bengal. The Famine of 1943-1944* (New York, 1982).

Grew, Raymond, "The Case for Comparing Histories", *American Historical Review*, vol. 85 (October 1980), pp. 763-778.

Gribaudi, Maurizio, *Itinéraires ouvriers: Espaces et groupes sociaux à Turin au début du XXe siècle* (Paris, 1987).

Grimm, Jacob, *Deutsche Rechtsalterthümer*, 2 vols (4th edition 1899; reprint East Berlin, 1956).

Grönlund Schneider, Aili, *The Finnish Baker's Daughters* (Toronto, 1986).

Groh, Dieter, *Anthropologische Dimensionen der Geschichte* (Frankfurt, 1992).

Groh, Dieter, "Strategien, Zeit und Ressourcen: Risikominimierung, Unterproduktivität und Mußepräferenz – die zentralen Kategorien von Subsistenzökonomien", in: Groh, *Anthropologische Dimensionen*, pp. 54-113.

Gronemeyer, Reimer and Georgia A. Rakelmann, *Die Zigeuner. Reisende in Europa* (Köln, 1988).

Grubb, Farley, "The Incidence of Servitude in Trans-Atlantic Migration, 1771-1804", *Explorations in Economic History*, XXII (1985), pp. 316-339.

Grubb, Farley, "The Market Structure of Shipping German Immigrants to Colonial America", *Pennsylvania Magazine of History and Biography*, CXI (1987), pp. 27-48.

Grubb, Farley, "The Auction of Redemptioner Servants, Philadelphia, 1771-1804: An Economic Analysis", *Journal of Economic History*, IIL (1988), pp. 583-603.

Grubb, Farley, "Servant Auction Records and Immigration into the Delaware Valley, 1745-1831: The Proportion of Females among Immigrant Servants", *Proceedings of the American Philosophical Society*, 133 (1989), pp. 154-169.

Grubb, Farley, "Fatherless and Friendless: Factors Influencing the Flow of English Emigrant Servants", *Journal of Economic History*, 52 (1992), pp. 85-108.

Guerin-Gonzales, Camille and Carl Strikwerda (eds), *The Politics of Immigrant Workers. Labor Activism and Migration in the World Economy Since 1830* (New York and London, 1993).

Guha, S., *The Agrarian Economy of the Bombay Deccan 1818-1914* (Bombay, 1985).

Gullickson, Gay, *Spinners and Weavers of Auffay: Rural Industry and the Sexual Division of Labor, 1750-1850* (Cambridge, 1986).

Gutman, Herbert and Ira Berlin, "Natives and Immigrants, Free Men and Slaves: Urban Workingmen in the Antebellum American South", *American Historical Review*, 88 (1983), pp. 1175-1200.

Gutmann, Myron, *Toward the Modern Economy: Early Industry in Europe, 1500-1800* (New York, 1988).

Gutmann, Myron and Etienne van de Walle, "New Sources for Social and Demographic History: The Belgian Population Registers", *Social Science History*, 2 (1978), pp. 121-143.

Gutton, Jean-Pierre, *La société et les pauvres. L'exemple de la généralité de Lyon 1534-1789* (Lyon, 1971).

Gutton, Jean-Pierre, *L'état et la mendicité dans la première moitié du XVIIIe siècle. Auvergne, Beaujolais, Forez, Lyonnais* (n.p., 1973).

Haan, Arjan de, "Migrant Labour in Calcutta Jute Mills: Class, Instability and Control", in: Robb, *Dalit Movements*, pp. 186-224.

Haan, Arjan de, "The Jute Industry and its Workers: Changes in Stratification in Eastern India", in: Bandhyopadhyay et al., *Bengal. Development*, pp. 255-295.

Haan, Arjan de, *Unsettled Settlers. Migrant Workers and Industrial Capitalism in Calcutta* (Hilversum, 1994).

Haan, Arjan de, "Towards a Single Male Earner: Decline of Child and Female Employment in an Indian Industry", *Economic and Social History in the Netherlands'*, 6 (1994), pp. 145-169.

Hacker, Werner, *Auswanderungen aus Baden und dem Breisgau: Obere und mittlere rechtsseitige Oberrheinlande im 18. Jahrhundert archivalisch dokumentiert* (Stuttgart, 1980).

Häberlein, Mark, *Vom Oberrhein zum Susquehanna: Studien zur badischen Auswanderung nach Pennsylvania im 18. Jahrhundert* (Stuttgart, 1993).

Haines, R., "'Shovelling out Paupers'?: Parish-assisted Emigration from England to Australia, 1834-1847", in: Richards, *Poor Australian Immigrants in the Nineteenth Century* pp. 33-68.

Haines, R., "Government-Assisted Emigration from the United Kingdom to Australia, 1831-1860: Promotion, Recruitment, and the Labouring Poor" (Ph.D., Flinders University of South Australia, 1992).

Haines, R. and Ralph Shlomowitz, "Nineteenth Century Government-Assisted and Total Immigration from the United Kingdom to Australia: Quinquennial Estimates by Colony", *Journal of the Australian Population Association*, VIII (1991), pp. 50-61.

Hall, Marie Ets, *Rosa. The Life of an Italian Immigrant* (Minneapolis, 1970).

Halter, Marilyn, *Between Race and Ethnicity. Cape Verdean American Immigrants, 1860-1965* (Urbana and Chicago, 1993).

Hammar, Tomas (ed.), *European Immigration Policy. A Comparative Study* (Cambridge, 1985).

Hammar, Tomas, *Democracy and the Nation State. Aliens, Denizens and Citizens in a World of International Migration* (Aldershot etc., 1990).

Handlin, Oscar, *The Uprooted; The Epic Study of the Great Migrations that Made the American People* (Boston, 1951).

Hansen, Marcus Lee, "The History of American Immigration as a Field of Research", *American Historical Review*, 32 (1927), pp. 500-518.

Hansen, Marcus Lee, *The Atlantic Migration, 1607-1860* (1940; reprint New York, 1961).

Hareven, Tamara K., *Family Time and Industrial Time. The Relationship Between the Family and Work in New England Industrial Community* (Cambridge, 1982).

Hareven, Tamara K., "The History of the Family and the Complexity of Social Change", *American Historical Review*, 96 (1991) pp. 95-124.

Harney, Robert F., "The Padrone and the Immigrant", *The Canadian Review of American Studies*, 5 (1974), 2, pp. 101-118.

Harney, Robert F., "The Padrone System and Sojourners in the Canadian North, 1885-1920", in: Pozzetta, *Pane e Lavoro*, pp. 119-140.

Harney, Robert F., "The Commerce of Migration", Canadian Ethnic Studies, 9 (1977), pp. 42-53.

Harrison, B., "Human Capital, Black Poverty and 'Radical Economics'", *Industrial Relations*, X (1971), pp. 277-286.

Hartwell, R.M., *The Industrial Revolution and Economic Growth* (London, 1971).

Hartz, Louis, "Comment", *Comparative Studies in Society and History*, 5 (1963), pp. 279-284.

Harzig, Christiane (ed.), *Peasant Maids, City Women. from the European Countryside to Chicago* (Ithaca, N.Y., forthcoming).

Hattenhauer, H., *Allgemeines Landrecht für den preußischen Staaten von 1794* (Frankfurt am Main, 1970).

Hatton, Timothy J. and Jeffrey F. Williamson (eds), *Migration and the International Labor Market 1850-1939* (London and New York, 1994).

Haupt, Heinz-Gerhard, "Staatliche Bürokratie und Arbeiterbewegung", in: Kocka, *Arbeiter und Bürger*, pp. 220-254.

Hay, Douglas and Francis Snyder (eds), *Policing and Prosecuting in Britain 1750-1850* (Oxford, 1989).

Head, Anne-Lise, "Quelques remarques sur l'émigration des régions préalpines", *Revue suisse d'histoire*, 29 (1979), pp. 181-193.

Heffer, Jean, *Le Port de New York et le commerce extérieur américain, 1860-1900* (Paris, 1986).

Heisler, Martin O. and Barbara Schmitter-Heisler (eds), *From Foreign Workers to Settlers? Transnational Migration and the Emergence of the New Minorities*. Annals of the American Academy of Political and Social Sciences, May 1986, no. 485.

Henkes, Barbara, *Heimat in Holland. Duitse dienstbodes 1920-1950* (Amsterdam, 1995).

Henning, Friedrich-Wilhelm, *Deutsche Wirtschafts- und Sozialgeschichte im Mittelalter und in der frühen Neuzeit* (Paderborn etc., 1991).

Henson, Curtis T., Jr., *Commissioners and Commodores. The East India Squadron and American Diplomacy in China* (Alabama, 1982).

Herbert, Ulrich, *Geschichte der Ausländerbeschäftigung in Deutschland, 1880 bis 1980: Saisonarbeiter, Zwangsarbeiter, Gastarbeiter* (Berlin, 1986).

Herbert, Ulrich, *A History of Foreign Labor in Germany, 1880-1980. Seasonal Workers/Forced Laborers/Guest Workers* (Ann Arbor, 1990).

Higham, J., "Anti-Semitism in the Gilded Age", *Mississippi Valley Historical Review*, XLIII (1956-1957), pp. 559-578.

Higham, John, *Strangers in the Land. Patterns of American Nativism* (New Brunswick, 1955).

Higham, John, "Immigration", in: Woodward, *Comparative Approach to American History*, pp. 91-105 (reprinted in Higham's *Send These to Me*).

Higham, John, *Send These to Me* (New York, 1975).

Higham, John, "The Strange Career of *Strangers in the Land*", *American Jewish History*, 76 (December 1986), pp. 214-226.

Hill, Alette Olin and Boyd H. Hill, Jr., "AHR Forum – Marc Bloch and Comparative History", *American Historical Review*, 85 (1980), pp. 828-857.

Hill, Christopher, "Pottage for Freeborn Englishmen: Attitudes to Wage Labour in the Sixteenth and Seventeenth Centuries", in: Feinstein, *Socialism, Capitalism and Economic Growth*, pp. 338-350.

Hinrichs, Ernst and Henk van Zon (eds), *Bevölkerungsgeschichte im Vergleich: Studien zu den Niederlanden und Nordwestdeutschland* (Aurich, 1988).

Hippel, Wolfgang von, *Auswanderung aus Südwestdeutschland* (Stuttgart, 1984).

Hirschberg, Julia, "A Social History of Puebla de los Angeles, 1531-1560" (Ph.D., University of Michigan, 1976).

Hirst, John B., *Convict Society and its Enemies: A History of Early New South Wales* (Sydney, 1983).

Hobsbawm, Eric J., *The Age of Empire, 1875-1914* (New York, 1987).

Hobsbawm, Eric J., *Nations and Nationalism since 1780. Programme, Myth, Reality* (Cambridge, 1990).

Hochstadt, Steve, "Migration and Industrialization in Germany, 1815-1977", *Social Science History*, 5 (1981), pp. 445-468.

Hochstadt, Steve and James Jackson, Jr., "'New' Sources for the Study of Migration in Early Nineteenth-Century Germany", *Historical Research/Historische Sozialforschung*, 31 (1984), pp. 85-92.

Hodson, Randy and Robert L. Kaufmann, "Economic Dualism: A Critical Review", *American Sociological Review*, XLVII (1982), pp. 727-739.

Hoerder, Dirk (ed.), *Labor Migration in the Atlantic Economies* (Westport, CT, 1985).

Hoerder, Dirk, "An Introduction to Labor Migration in the Atlantic Economies, 1815-1914", in: Hoerder, *Labor Migration in the Atlantic Economies*, pp. 3-32.

Hoerder, Dirk, "Labour Migrants' Views of 'America'", *Renaissance and Modern Studies*, 35 (1992), pp. 1-17.

Hoerder, Dirk, *People on the Move. Migration, Acculturation, and Ethnic Interaction in Europe and North America*. German Historical Institute Washington DC, Annual Lecture series no. 6 (Providence/Oxford, 1993).

Hoerder, Dirk, "Changing Paradigms in Migration History: from 'To America' to World-Wide Systems", *Canadian Review of American Studies*, 24 (1994), no. 2, pp. 105-126.

Hoerder, Dirk, "Migration in the Atlantic Economies: Regional European Origins and Worldwide Expansion", in: Hoerder and Moch, *European Migrants*, pp. 21-51.

Hoerder, Dirk, "From Immigrants to Ethnics: Acculturation in a Societal Framework", in: Hoerder and Moch, *European Migrants*, pp. 211-262.

Hoerder, Dirk and Leslie Page Moch (eds), *European Migrants. Global and Local Perspectives* (Boston, 1996).

Hoerder, Dirk and Jörg Nagler (eds), *People in Transit. German Migrations in Comparative Perspective, 1820-1930* (Cambridge, 1995).

Hoerder, Dirk and Horst Rössler (eds), *Distant Magnets. Expectations and Realities in the Immigrant Experience* (New York, 1993).

Hofstadter, Richard, *The American Political Tradition* (New York, 1948).

Hohenberg, Paul and Lynn Hollen Lees, *The Making of Urban Europe, 1000-1950* (Cambridge, MA, 1985).

Hohmann, Joachim S., *Geschichte der Zigeunerverfolgung in Deutschland* (Frankfurt etc., 1981).

Hollifield, James F., *Immigrants, Markets, and States. The Political Economy of Postwar Europe* (Cambridge, MA, 1992).

Holloway, Thomas H., *Immigrants on the Land: Coffee and Society in Sao Paulo. 1866-1934* (Chapel Hill, 1980).

Holmes, Colin (ed.), *Immigrants and Minorities in British Society* (London, 1978).

Holmes, Colin, *Anti-Semitism in British Society, 1876-1939* (London, 1979).

Holmes, Colin, "Historians and Immigration", in: Pooley and Whyte, *Migrants, Emigrants and Immigrants*, pp.191-207.

Holmes, Colin, *A Tolerant Country? Immigrants, Refugees and Minorities in Britain* (London, 1991).

Holmes, Colin, *John Bull's Island. Immigration and British Society, 1871-1971* (London, 1992; first edition 1988).

Holmes, Madelyn, *Forgotten Migrants: Foreign Workers in Switzerland before World War I* (Rutherford, NJ, 1988).

Hopkins, A.G., *An Economic History of West Africa* (London, 1973).

Horowitz, Donald L., "Europe and America: A Comparative Analysis of 'Ethnicity'", *Revue Européenne des Migrations Internationales*, 5 (1989), pp. 47-61.

Hotten, John Camden (ed.), *The Original Lists of Persons of Quality; Emigrants; Political Rebels; Serving Men Sold for a Term of Years; Apprentices; Children Stolen; Maidens Pressed; and Others who Went from Great Britain to the American Plantations, 1600-1700* (London, 1874).

Houben, Vincent, "'Menyang Tanah Sabrang'. Javanese Coolie Migration in- and outside Indonesia, 1900-1940". Paper for the Conference "The Malay Archipelago and the World Economy, 1700-1990" (Canberra, November 23-27, 1992).

Houston, R.A., *The Population History of Britain and Ireland 1500-1750* (London, 1992).

Hoyle, R.W., "Tenure and the Land Market in Early Modern England: Or a Late Contribution to the Brenner Debate", *Economic History Review*, 43 (1990), pp. 1-20.

Hsu, I., "Late Ch'ing foreign relations, 1866-1905", in: Fairbank and Liu, *Cambridge History of China*, II, Part 2, pp. 70-142.

Hu-DeHart, Evelyn, "Chinese Coolie Labor in Cuba in the Nineteenth Century: Free Labor or New Slavery?" (Unpublished paper, University of Colorado-Boulder).

Hufton, Olwen, *The Poor of Eighteenth-Century France* (Oxford, 1974).

Hunt, E.H., *British Labour History, 1815-1914* (London, 1981).

Husband, C. (ed.), *"Race" in Britain: Continuity and Change* (London, 1982).

Husband, C., "Introduction: 'Race', the Continuity of a Concept", in: Husband, *"Race" in Britain*.

Huttenback, Robert A., *Racism and Empire: White Settlers and Colored Immigrants in the British Self-Governing Colonies, 1830-1910* (Ithaca, 1976).

Iftikhar-ul-Awwal, A.Z.M., *The Industrial Development of Bengal. 1900-1939* (New Delhi, 1982).

Ignatieff, Michael, *A Just Measure of Pain. The Penitentiary in the Industrial Revolution 1750-1850* (New York, 1978).

Inikori, Joseph E. (ed.), *Forced Migration; The Impact of the Export Slave Trade on African Societies* (London, 1982).

Inikori, Joseph, "Slavery and the Development of Industrial Capitalism in England", in: Solow and Engerman, *British Capitalism and Caribbean Slavery*, pp. 79-101.

Inikori, Joseph E. and Stanley L. Engerman (eds), *The Atlantic Slave Trade; Effects on Economies, Societies, and Peoples in Africa, the Americas, and Europa* (Durham and London, 1992).

Inikori, Joseph E. and Stanley L. Engerman, "Introduction: Gainers and Losers in the Atlantic Slave Trade", in: Inikori and Engerman, *Atlantic Slave Trade*.

Iorizzo, Luciano John, *Italian Immigration and the Impact of the Padrone System* (New York, 1980).

Irick, Robert L., *Ch'ing Policy Toward the Coolie Trade. 1847-1878* (Taiwan, 1982).

Jackson, James H., Jr., "Migration and Urbanization in the Ruhr Valley, 1850-1900" (Ph.D., University of Minnesota, 1980).

Jackson, James H., Jr., and Leslie Page Moch, "Migration and the Social History of Modern Europe", *Historical Methods*, XXII (1989), pp. 27-36.

Jackson, James H., Jr. and Leslie Page Moch, "Migration and the Social History of Europe", in: Hoerder and Moch, *European Migrants*, pp. 52-69.

Jackson, Peter and Jan Penrose (eds), *Constructions of Race, Place and Nation* (London, 1993).

Jacobs, Auke Pieter, "Legal and Illegal Emigration from Seville, 1550-1650", in: Altman and Horn, "To Make America", pp. 59-84.

James, M., "The Eagle in Exile: The Polish Community in Manchester after 1945" (BA Dissertation, University of Sheffield, 1991).

Jaritz, Gerhard and Albert Müller (eds), *Migration in der Feudalgesellschaft* (Frankfurt etc., 1988).

Jaschok, Maria, *Concubines and Bondservants* (London and New Jersey, 1988).

Jaumain, Serge, "Un métier oublié: le colporteur dans la Belgique du XIXe siècle", *Revue Belge d'histoire contemporaine*, XVI (1985), pp. 307-356.

Jessen, Ralph, *Polizei im Industrierevier. Modernisierung und Herrschaftspraxis im Westfälischen Ruhrgebiet 1848-1914* (Göttingen, 1991).

Joll, James, *The Second International 1889-1914* (London, 1974; orig. publ. 1955).

Jones, David J.V., *Crime, Protest, Community and Police in Nineteenth-Century Britain* (London, 1982).

Jones, David J.V., "The Welsh and Crime, 1801-1891", in: Emsley and Walvin, *Artisans, Peasants and Proletarians*, pp. 81-103.

Jones, E.L., *The European Miracle; Environment, Economies and Geopolitics in the History of Europe and Asia* (Cambridge, 1987^2).

Jütte, Robert, *Obrigkeitliche Armenfürsorge in deutschen Reichsstädten der frühen Neuzeit. Städtisches Armenwesen in Frankfurt am Main und Köln* (Köln etc., 1984).

Jütte, Robert, *Poverty and Deviance in Early Modern Europe* (Cambridge, 1994).

Jupp, J., *Immigration* (Sydney, 1991).

Justi, Johann H. von, *Die Grundfeste zu der Macht und Glückseeligkeit der Staaten oder ausführliche Vorstellung der gesamten Polizey-Wissenschaft*, 2 vols (Königsberg, 1760).

Kadish, S., *Bolsheviks and British Jews. The Anglo-Jewish Community, Britain and the Russian Revolution* (London, 1992).

Kälvemark, Ann-Sofie, "The Country That Kept Track of its Population: Methodological Aspects of Swedish Population Records", in: Sundin and Soderlund, *Time, Space and Man*, pp. 221-243.

Kallen, Horace, *Culture and Democracy in the United States* (New York, 1924).

Kammen, Michael (ed.), *The Past Before Us: Contemporary Historical Writing in the United States* (Ithaca, 1980).

Kamphoefner, Walter D., Wolfgang Helbich and Ulrike Sommer (eds), *News from the Land of Freedom. German Immigrants Write Home* (Ithaca, 1991).

Kaplan, Marion, "Jewish Women in Nazi-Germany: Daily Life, Daily Struggles, 1933-1939", *Feminist Studies*, 16 (1990), pp. 579-607.

Kappen, O. van, *Geschiedenis der zigeuners in Nederland* (Assen, 1965).

Kaspi, Andre and Antoine Marès (eds), *Le Paris des étrangers* (Paris, 1989).

Katzman, David M. and William M. Tuttle, Jr. (eds), *Plain Folk. The Life Stories of Undistinguished Americans* (Urbana, 1982).

Katznelson, Ira, *Black Men, White Cities: Race, Politics and Migration in the United States, 1900-30, and Britain, 1948-68* (London, 1973).

Kay, Diana and Robert Miles, *Refugees or Migrant Workers? European Volunteer Workers in Britain 1946-1951* (London and New York, 1992).

Kaye, Ronald and Roger Charlton, *United Kingdom Refugee Admission Policy and the Politically-Active Refugee.* Research Papers in Ethnic Relations, no. 13, Centre for Research in Ethnic Relations, University of Warwick (Coventry, 1990).

Kaztauskis, Antanas, "From Lithuania to the Chicago Stockyards – An Autobiography: Antanas Kaztauskis", in: Katzman and Tuttle, *Plain Folk*, pp. 99-114 (first published in *Independent*, 57, 4 Aug. 1904, pp. 241-248).

Kellenbenz, Hermann (ed.), *Wirtschaftspolitik und Arbeitsmarkt: Bericht über die 4. Arbeitstagung der Gesellschaft für Sozial- und Wirtschaftsgeschichte in Wien am 14. und 15. April 1971* (Munich, 1974).

Kelsey, R.W. (ed.), "An Early Description of Pennsylvania", *Pennsylvania Magazine of History and Biography,* VL (1921), pp. 243-254.

Kenrick, Donald and Grattan Puxon, *The Destiny of Europe's Gypsies* (New York, 1972).

Kerr, Clark, *Markets and Other Essays* (Berkeley, CA, 1977).

Kertzer, David and Dennis Hogan, "On the Move: Migration in an Italian Community, 1865-1921", *Social Science History,* 9 (1985), pp. 1-23.

Kessner, Thomas, *The Golden Door: Italian and Jewish Immigrant Mobility in New York City, 1880-1915* (New York, 1977).

Kiernan, V.G., "Britons Old and New", in: Holmes, *Immigrants and Minorities*, pp. 13-59.

King, Russell (ed.), *Mass Migrations in Europe. The Legacy and the Future* (London, 1993).

Kiple, Kenneth F., *The Caribbean Slave; A Biological History* (Cambridge, 1984).

Kirk, Dudley, *Population in Europe* (Princeton, 1946).

Kisch, Herbert, *From Domestic Manufacture to Industrial Revolution: The Case of the Rhineland Textile Districts* (Oxford, 1989).

Klein, Herbert S., "The Integration of Italian Immigrants in the United States and Argentina: A Comparative Analysis", *American Historical Review,* 88 (1983), pp. 306-346.

Kloosterboer, W., *Involuntary Labour Since the Abolition of Slavery. A Survey of Compulsory Labour Throughout the World* (Leiden, 1960).

Kocka, Jürgen (ed.), *Arbeiter und Bürger im 19. Jahrhundert. Varianten ihres Verhältnisses im europäischen Vergleich* (München, 1986).

Köllmann, Wolfgang, "Versuch des Entwurfs einer historisch-soziologischen Wanderungs theorie", in: Engelhardt *et al.*, *Soziale Bewegung und politische Verfassung*, pp. 260-269.

Kornbluh, Joyce L. (ed.), *Rebel Voices. An I.W.W. Anthology* (Ann Arbor, 1972).

Kraus, Antje, "'Antizipierter Ehesegen' im 19. Jahrhundert. Zur Beurteilung der Illegitimität unter sozialgeschichtlichen Aspekten", *Vierteljahrsschrift für Sozial- und Wirtschaftsgeschichte,* 66 (1979), pp. 174-215.

Kraus, Otto (ed.), *Regulation, Manipulation und Explosion der Bevölkerungsdichte: Vorträge gehalten auf der Tagung der Joachim-Jungius-Gesellschaft der Wissenschaften Hamburg am 15. und 16. November 1985* (Göttingen, 1986).

Kriedte, P., H. Medick and J. Schlumbohm (eds), *Industrialization before Industrialization: Rural Industry in the Genesis of Capitalism* (Cambridge, 1981).

Kritz, M., C. Keely and S. Tomasi (eds), *Global Trends in Migration* (New York, 1981).

Kroes, Rob, *The Persistence of Ethnicity. Dutch Calvinist Pioneers in Amsterdam, Montana* (Urbana and Chicago, 1992).

Kubat, D. (ed.), *The Politics of Migration Policies* (New York, 1979).

Kucewicz, A.M., "The Immigrant Experience: The Perception of Polish Refugees and their Adaptation to a Life in Sheffield, post-1945" (BA Dissertation, Sheffield City Polytechnic, 1988).

Küther, Carsten, *Räuber und Gauner in Deutschland* (Göttingen, 1976).

Kuhlman, Tom, "Towards a Definition of Refugees". Research memorandum no. 36 (August 1990) from the Free University of Amsterdam.

Kumar, D., *Land and Caste in South India: Agricultural Labour in the Madras Presidency during the Nineteenth Century* (Cambridge, 1965).

Kumar, D. (ed.), *The Cambridge Economic History of India, vol. 2, c1757-c1970* (Cambridge, 1983).

Kunz, E.F., "The Refugee in Flight. Kinetic Models of Displacement", *International Migration Review*, 7 (1973), pp. 125-146.

Kushner, T., "Jew and Non-Jew in the East End of London: Towards an Anthropology of 'Everyday' Relations", in: Alderman and Holmes, *Outsiders and Outcasts*, pp. 32-52.

Kussmaul, Ann, *Servants in Husbandry in Early Modern England* (Cambridge, 1981).

Lacorne, Denis *et al.*, *The Rise and Fall of Anti-Americanism: A Century of French Perception* (New York, 1990).

Lal, B.V., *Girmitiyas: The Origins of the Fiji Indians* (Canberra, 1983).

Lamphere, Louise (ed.), *Structuring Diversity. Ethnographic Perspectives on the New Immigration* (Chicago and London, 1992).

Landa, M.J., *The Alien Problem and its Remedy* (London, 1911).

Larner, A., "The 1956 Hungarian Refugees in Britain" (BA Dissertation, University of Sheffield, 1985).

Lasker, Bruno, *Human Bondage in Southeast Asia* (Chapel Hill, 1950).

LaSorte, Michael, *La Merica: Images of Italian Greenhorn Experience* (Philadelphia, 1985).

Laxmi Naranyan, K., "Growth of Metropolitan Cities and their Migrants: A Historical and Demographic Profile", in: Rao, *Studies in Migration*, pp. 85-159.

Lea, J., "The Contradictions of the Sixties Race Relations Legislation", in: *National Deviancy Conference, Permissiveness and Control* (London, 1980), pp. 122-148.

Lee, E.S., "A Theory of Migration", *Demography*, 3 (1966), pp. 47-57.

Lee, W.R. and E. Rosenhaft, *The State and Social Change in Germany. 1880-1980* (New York, 1990).

Leenders, Marij, *Ongenode gasten. Van traditioneel asielrecht tot vreemdelingenbeleid* (Hilversum, 1993).

Leeuwen, M.H.D. van, "Logic of charity: poor relief in preindustrial Europa", *Journal of Interdisciplinary History* XXIV (Spring 1994), Nr. 4, pp. 589-613.

Lehmann, Albrecht, *Im Fremden ungewollt zuhaus. Flüchlinge und Vertriebene in Westdeutschland 1945-1990* (München, 1991).

Lehmann, Joachim, "Ausländerbeschäftigung und Fremdarbeiterpolitik im faschistischen Deutschland", in: Bade, *Auswanderer, Wanderarbeiter, Gastarbeiter*, vol. II, pp. 558-583.

Leigh, Leonard, "Vagrancy and the Criminal Law", in: Cook, *Vagrancy. Some New Perspectives*, pp. 95-118.

LeMay, Michael, *From Open Door to Dutch Door: An Analysis of U.S. Immigration Policy since 1820* (New York, 1987).

Lenman, Bruce and Geoffrey Parker (eds), *Crime and the Law. The Social History of Crime in Western Europe Since 1500* (London, 1980).

Lequin, Yves (ed.), *La mosaïque France: Histoire des étrangers et de l'immigration en France* (Paris, 1988).

Levin, M., *What Welcome?* (London, n.d.).

Levine, David, *Family Formation in an Age of Nascent Capitalism* (New York, 1977).

Levine, David (ed.), *Proletarianization and Family History,* (Orlando, FL, 1984).

Lévi-Strauss, Claude, *Anthropologie structurale* [1958] (Paris, 1974).

Licht, Walter, "Labor Economics and the Labor Historian", *International Labor and Working Class History*, XXI (1982), pp. 52-62.

Lieberson, Stanley, *A Piece of the Pie. Blacks and White Immigrants since 1880* (Berkeley etc., 1980).

Liégeois, Jean-Pierre, *Gypsies. An Illustrated History* (London, 1986).

Light, Ivan, *Ethnic Enterprise in America: Business and Welfare among Chinese, Japanese and Blacks* (Berkeley, 1972).

Lindemann, Mary, *Patriots and Paupers. Hamburg, 1712-1830* (Oxford, 1990).

Lipman, V., *A Century of Social Service, 1859-1959. The History of the Jewish Board of Guardians* (London, 1959).

Lis, Catharina and Hugo Soly, *Poverty and Capitalism in Pre-Industrial Europe* (Hassocks, 1979).

Lis, Catharina, Hugo Soly and Dirk van Damme, *Op vrije voeten? Sociale politiek in West-Europa (1450-1914)* (Leuven, 1985).

Lockhart, James, *The Men of Cajamarca: A Social and Biographical Study of the First Conquerors of Peru* (Austin, 1972).

Loescher, G. and J.A. Scanlan, *Calculated Kindness. Refugees and America's Half-Open Door 1945-Present* (New York and London, 1986).

Lovoll, O.S., *A Century of Urban Life. The Norwegians in Chicago before 1930* (Northfield, 1988).

Lowe, William J., *The Irish in Mid-Victorian Lancashire: The Shaping of a Working-Class Community* (New York, 1989).

Lubinski, Axel, "Die überseeische Auswanderung aus dem Großherzogtum Mecklenburg-Strelitz in der zweiten Hälfte des 19. Jahrhunderts" (Diss., Universität Osnabrück, 1992).

Lucassen, Jan, *Migrant Labour in Europe 1600-1900: The Drift to the North Sea* (London, 1987).

Lucassen, Jan, *Dutch Long Distance Migration. A Concise History 1600-1900.* Research paper of the International Institute of Social History (Amsterdam, 1992).

Lucassen, Jan, "The Netherlands, the Dutch, and Long-Distance Migration in the Late Sixteenth to Early Nineteenth Centuries", in: Canny, *Europeans on the Move*, pp. 153-191.

Lucassen, Jan, "No Golden Age Without Migration? The Case of the Dutch Republic in a Comparative Perspective", in: Cavaciocchi, *Migrazioni in Europa*, pp. 775-797.

Lucassen, Jan and Leo Lucassen, "Van incident tot structurele factor: Een historisch overzicht van de migratiegeschiedenis in Nederland", in: Rietbergen, *Migratie en vestiging in Nederland*, pp. 25-29.

Lucassen, Jan and Leo Lucassen, "Preface to the conference: *Migration and settlement in a historical perspective: old answers and new perspectives*" (Unpublished paper, International Institute of Social History, Amsterdam, 1992).

Lucassen, Jan and Rinus Penninx, *Nieuwkomers, nakomelingen, Nederlanders. Immigranten in Nederland 1550-1993* (Amsterdam, 1994; an English edition is planned for 1996).

Lucassen, Leo, *"En men noemde hen zigeuners". De geschiedenis van Kaldarasch, Ursari, Lowara en Sinti in Nederland: 1750-1944* (Amsterdam and Den Haag, 1990).

Lucassen, Leo, "The power of definition. Stigmatisation, minoritisation and ethnicity illustrated by the history of gypsies in the Netherlands", *Netherlands' Journal of Social Sciences*, 27 (october 1991) no. 2, pp. 80-91.

Lucassen, Leo, "A Blind Spot: Migratory and Travelling Groups in Western European Historiography", *International Review of Social History*, 38 (1993), pp. 209-235.

Lucassen, Leo, "Het onontkoombare nationaliteitsbeginsel. Een bespreking van enige recente literatuur over (im)migratie en natievorming", *Tijdschrift voor Sociale Geschiedenis*, 19 (1993), no. 4, pp. 489-505.

Lucassen, Leo, "Under the Cloak of Begging? Gypsy-Occupations in Western-Europe in the 19th and 20th Century", *Ethnologia Europaea. Journal of European Ethnology*, 23 (1993), pp. 75-94.

Lucassen, Leo, "Book Review of Leslie Page Moch's 'Moving Europeans'", *International Review of Social History*, 39 (1994), pp. 460-463.

Lucassen, Leo, "Het paspoort als edelste deel van een mens. Een aanzet tot een sociale geschiedenis van het Nederlandse vreemdelingenbeleid", *Holland, regionaal historisch tijdschrift*, 27 (1995), no. 4/5, pp. 265-285.

Lucassen, Leo, "'Zigeuner' in Deutschland 1870-1945: Ein kritischer historiographischer Ansatz", *1999. Zeitschrift für Sozialgeschichte des 20. und 21. Jahrhunderts* 10 (1995), Nr. 1, pp. 82-100.

Lucassen, Leo, *Zigeuner: Die Geschichte eines polizeilichen Ordnungsbegriffs in Deutschland, 1700-1945* (Köln etc. 1996).

Lucassen, Leo and Boudien de Vries, "Leiden als middelpunt van een Westeuropees textiel-migratiesysteem, 1586-1650", *Tijdschrift voor Sociale Geschiedenis*, 22 (1996) no. 2, pp. 138-167.

Lüdtke, Alf, *Police and State in Prussia 1815-1850* (Cambridge etc., 1989).

Lüdtke, Alf (ed.), *"Sicherheit" und "Wohlfahrt". Polizei, Gesellschaft und Herrschaft im 19. und 20. Jahrhundert* (Frankfurt am Main, 1992).

Lunn, Kenneth (ed.), *Hosts, Immigrants and Minorities* (Folkestone, 1980).

Lunn, Kenneth, "Reactions to Lithuanian and Polish Immigrants in the Lanarkshire Coalfield, 1880-1914", in: Lunn, *Hosts, Immigrants and Minorities*, pp. 308-342.

Lunn, Kenneth (ed.), *Race and Labour in Twentieth-Century Britain* (London, 1985).

Lunn, Kenneth, "Race Relations or Industrial Relations?: Race and Labour in Britain, 1880-1950", in: Lunn, *Race and Labour*, pp. 1-29.

Lunn, Kenneth, "Race Relations or Industrial Relations? Race and Labour in Britain, 1880-1950", *Immigrants and Minorities*, 4 (1985), pp. 1-29.

Lunn, Kenneth, "The Employment of Polish and European Volunteer Workers in the Scottish Coalfields 1945-1950", in: Tenfelde, *Towards a Social History of Mining*, pp. 582-592.

Lunn, Kenneth, "'Good for a Few Hundreds at least': Irish Labour Recruitment into Britain during the Second World War", in: Buckland and Belchem, *Irish in British Labour History*, pp. 102-114.

McAuley, I., *Guide to Ethnic London* (London, 1987).

McCusker, John J., *The Rum Trade and the Balance of Payments of the Thirteen Continental Colonies, 1650-1775* (New York, 1991).

McCusker, John J. and Russell R. Menard, *The Economy of British America, 1607-1789* (Chapel Hill and London, 1985).

McDonald, J. and Ralph Shlomowitz, "The Cost of Shipping Convicts to Australia", *International Journal of Maritime History*, II (1990), pp. 1-32.

McDonald, J. and Ralph Shlomowitz, "Mortality on Immigrant Voyages to Australia in the Nineteenth Century", *Explorations in Economic History*, 27 (1990), pp. 34-113.

McDonald, J. and Ralph Shlomowitz, "Passenger Fares on Sailing Vessels to Australia in the Nineteenth Century", *Explorations in Economic History*, 28 (1991), pp. 192-208.

McDonald, J. and Ralph Shlomowitz, "Fares Charged for Transporting Indian Indentured Labour to Mauritius and the West Indies, 1850-1873", *International Journal of Maritime History*, III (1991), pp. 81-99.

McDonald, J. and Ralph Shlomowitz, "Contract Prices for the Bulk Shipping of Passengers in Sailing Vessels, 1816-1904: An Overview", *International Journal of Maritime History*, V (1993), pp. 65-93.

MacFarlane, Alan, *Origins of English Individualism* (London, 1978).

McIntyre, S., *Little Moscows: Communism and Working-Class Militancy in Inter-War Britain* (London, 1980).

McLynn, F., *Crime and Punishment in Eighteenth-Century England* (London, 1989).

McNeill, William H., "Human Migration: a Historical Overview", in: McNeill and Adams, *Human Migration*, pp. 3-19.

McNeill, William H. and Ruth S. Adams (eds), *Human Migration: Patterns and Policies* (Bloomington and London, 1978).

Maier, Hans, *Die ältere deutsche Staats- und Verwaltungslehre* (Munich, 1980²).

Malthus, Thomas Robert, *An Essay on the Principle of Population* (1798¹), edited by Philip Appleman (New York, 1976).

Mann, Michael, *States, War and Capitalism. Studies in Political Sociology* (Oxford, 1988).

Manning, Patrick, *Slavery and African Life; Occidental, Oriental, and African Slave Trades* (Cambridge, 1990).

Marez, G. Des and F.L. Ganshof (eds), *Ve Congrès international des sciences historiques* (Brussels, 1923).

Marks, Shula and Peter Richardson (eds), *International Labour Migration: Historical Perspectives* (London, 1984).

Markus, Andrew, *Fear and Hatred: Purifying Australia and California. 1850-1901* (Sydney, 1979).

Marrus, M.R., *The Unwanted. European Refugees in the Twentieth Century* (New York and Oxford, 1985).

Marschalck, Peter, *Deutsche Überseewanderung im 19. Jahrhundert: Ein Beitrag zur soziologischen Theorie der Bevölkerung* (Stuttgart, 1973).

Martinez Montiel, Luz M. (ed.), *Asiatic Migration in Latin America* (Mexico City, 1981).

Martz, Linda, *Poverty and Welfare in Habsburg Spain: The Example of Toledo* (Cambridge, 1983).

Matschinegg, Ingrid and Albert Müller, *Migration – Wanderung – Mobilität in Spätmittelalter und Frühneuzeit: Eine Auswahlbiographie* (Krems, 1990).

Mattmüller, Markus, *Bevölkerungsgeschichte der Schweiz. Teil I: Die frühe Neuzeit, 1500-1700*, 2 vols (Basel, 1987).

May, J.P., "The Chinese in Britain, 1860-1914", in: Holmes, *Immigrants and Minorities in British Society*, pp. 111-124.

Mayall, David, "The Making of British Gypsy Identities c. 1500-1980", *Immigrants and Minorities*, 11 (1992), pp. 21-41.

Mayall, David, *Gypsy-Travellers in Nineteenth-Century Society* (Cambridge, 1988).

Meagher, Joseph Arnold, "The Introduction of Chinese Laborers to Latin America: the 'Coolie Trade', 1847-1974" (Unpublished Ph.D. Thesis, University of California, Davis, 1975).

Medick, Hans, "The Proto-Industrial Family Economy: The Structural Functioning of Household and Family during the Transition from Peasant Society to Industrial Capitalism", *Social History*, 3 (1976), pp. 291-315.

Meillassoux, C., "From Reproduction to Production: A Marxian Approach to Economic Anthropology", *Economy and Society*, IX (1972), pp. 93-105.

Menard, Russell R., "From Servants to Slaves: The Transformation of the Chesapeake Labor System", *Southern Studies*, 16 (1977), pp. 355-390.

Mendels, Franklin F. "Industrialization and Population Pressure in Eighteenth-Century Flanders" (Ph.D., University of Wisconsin, 1969).

Miège, J.L., "Migration and Decolonisation", *European Review*, I (1993), pp. 81-86.

Miers, Suzanne and Igor Kopytoff (eds), *Slavery in Africa: Historical and Anthropological Perspectives* (Madison, 1977).

Miers, Suzanne and Igor Kopytoff, "African Slavery as an Institution of Marginality", in: Miers and Kopytoff, *Slavery in Africa*, pp. 3-76.

Mikes, George, *How to be an Alien* (London, 1946).

Miles, Robert, *Capital and Unfree Labour; Anomaly or Necessity?* (London and New York, 1987).

Miles, Robert, *Racism* (London, 1989).

Miller, Mark J. (ed.), *Strategies for Immigration Control: an International Comparison*. Annals of the American Academy of Political and Social Sciences, no. 534 (1994).

Miller, Stuart Creighton, *The Unwelcome Immigrant: The American Image of the Chinese. 1785-1882* (Berkeley, 1969).

Milner, Susan, "The International Labour Movement and the Limits of Internationalism: The International Secretariat of National Trade Union Centres, 1901-1913", *International Review of Social History*, XXXIII (1988), pp. 1-24.

Minchinton, Walter E., *Naval Office Shipping Lists For Jamaica, 1683-1818* (Wakefield, 1977).

Mink, Gwendolyn, *Old Labor and New Immigrants in American Political Development: Union, Party, and State. 1875-1920* (Ithaca, 1986).

Miskimin, Harry A., *The Economy of Early Renaissance Europe, 1300-1460* (Cambridge, 1975).

Mitchell, B.R., *European Historical Statistics 1750-1970* (New York, 1976).

Moch, Leslie Page, *Moving Europeans; Migration in Western Europe since 1650* (Bloomington and Indianapolis, 1992).

Moch, Leslie Page and Louise Tilly, "Immigrant Women in the City: Comparative Perspectives". Working Paper, University of Michigan (Ann Arbor, MI, 1979).

Mörner, Magnus, "Migraciones a Hispanoamérica durante la época colonial", *Suplemento de Anuario de Estudios Americanos* (Seville, 1991), vol. 48, no. 2, pp. 3-25.

Mörner, Magnus and Herold Sims, *Adventurers and Proletarians: The Story of Migrants in Latin America* (Paris, 1985).

Molinie-Bertrand, Annie, *Au siècle d'or: L'Espagne et ses hommes. La population du royaume de Castille au XVIe siècle* (Paris, 1985).

Moltmann, Günter, "German Emigration to the United States during the First Half of the Nineteenth Century as a Social Protest Movement", in: Trefousse, *Germany and America*, pp. 103-110.

Moltmann, Günter (ed.), *Aufbruch nach Amerika* (Stuttgart, 1989²).

Mon Pinzon, Ramon Arturo, "A Century of Chinese Immigration to Panama", in: Montiel, *Asiatic Migration*, pp. 22-36.

Montgomery, David, *The Fall of the House of Labor. The Workplace, the State, and American Labor Activism, 1865-1925* (Cambridge, 1987).

Moogk, Peter, "Manon's Fellow Exiles: Emigration from France to North America before 1763", in: Canny, *Europeans on the Move*, pp. 263-283.

Mookerjii, S.B., *The Indenture System in Mauritius (1837-1915)* (Calcutta, 1962).

Moore, Bob, *Refugees from Nazi Germany in the Netherlands 1933-1940* (Dordrecht etc., 1986).

Moore, C., *Kanaka: A History of Melanesian Mackay* (Port Moresby, 1985).

Moore, C., "Revising the Revisionists: The Historiography of Immigrant Melanesians in Australia", *Pacific Studies*, XV (1992), pp. 61-86.

Moore, C., J. Leckie and D. Munro (eds), *Labour in the South Pacific* (Townsville, 1990).

Moore, W.E. and A.S. Feldman, *Labor Commitment and Social Change in Developing Areas*. Social Science Research Council (New York, 1960).

Morawska, Ewa, *For Bread with Butter: Life-Worlds of East Central Europeans in Johnstown, Pennsylvania, 1890-1940* (Cambridge, 1985).

Morawska, Ewa, "The Sociology and Historiography of Immigration", in: Yans-McLaughlin, *Immigration Reconsidered*, pp. 187-240.

Morawska, Ewa, "Return Migrations: Theoretical and Research Agenda", in: Vecoli and Sinke, *Century of European Migrations*, pp. 277-292.

Morelli, Anne (ed.), *Histoire des étrangers et de l'immigration en Belgique de la préhistoire à nos jours* (Brussels, 1992).

Morgado, Cosme, *The Role of Members of Parliament in Immigration Cases*. Policy Papers in Ethnic Relations, no. 14, Centre for Research in Ethnic Relations, University of Warwick (Coventry, 1989).

Morgan, Edmund S., "The Labor Problem at Jamestown, 1607-18", *American Historical Review*, 76 (1971), pp. 595-611.

Morgan, Edmund S., "Slavery and Freedom: The American Paradox", *Journal of American History*, 59 (1972).

Morgenthau, Hans, *Politics Among Nations* (New York, 1948).

Mormino, Gary R. and George E. Pozzetta, *The Immigrant World of Ybor City* (Urbana, 1987).

Morris, M.D., "The Labor Market in India", in: Moore and Feldman, *Labor Commitment and Social Change*, pp. 173-182.

Morris, M.D., "The Growth of Large-Scale Industry to 1947", in: *The Cambridge Economic History of India*, vol. 2 (Cambridge, 1983).

Müller, Albert and Ingrid Matschinegg, "Migration – Wanderung – Mobilität in Spätmittelalter und Frühneuzeit", *Medium Aevum Quotidianum*, XXI (1990), pp. 3-92.

Mukherjee, Radhakamal, *The Indian Working Class* (Bombay, 1945).

Munro, Doug, "The Pacific Island Labour Trade: Approaches, Methodologies, Debates", *Slavery and Abolition*, XIV (1993), pp. 87-108.

Murphy, H.B.M., *Flight and Resettlement* (Paris, 1955).

Muus, Philip, *Internationale migratie naar Europa. Een analyse van internationale migratie, migratiebeleid en mogelijkheden tot sturing van immigratie, met bijzondere aandacht voor de Europese Gemeenschap en Nederland* (Amsterdam, 1993).

Nadel, Stanley, *Little Germany: Ethnicity, Religion and Class in New York City, 1845-80* (Urbana and Chicago, 1990).

Nader, Helen, *Liberty in Absolutist Spain. The Habsburg Sale of Towns, 1516-1700* (Baltimore, 1990).

Nef, J.U., *The Conquest of the Material World* (Chicago, 1964).

Nelli, Humbert S., *From Immigrants to Ethnics: the Italian Americans* (Oxford and New York, 1983).

Nicholas, Stephen (ed.), *Convict Workers: Reinterpreting Australia's Past* (Melbourne, 1988).

Nicol, Andrew, *Illegal Entrants* (London, 1981).

Nitschke, Peter, *Verbrechensbekämpfung und Verwaltung. Die Entstehung der Polizei in der Grafschaft Lippe, 1700-1814* (Münster etc., 1990).

Noiriel, Gérard, *Le creuset français: histoire de l'immigration, XIXe – XXe siècles* (Paris, 1988).

Noiriel, Gérard, *La tyrannie du national. Le droit d'asile en Europe 1793-1993* (Paris, 1991).

Nolan, Philip, *Report on Emigration from Bengal to Burma and How to Promote it* (Calcutta, 1888).

Nonini, Donald M., "Popular Sources of Chinese Labor Militancy in Colonial Malaya, 1900-1941", in: Guerin-Gonzales and Strikwerda, *The Politics of Immigrant Workers*, pp. 215-242.

Nora, Pierre (ed.), *Les Lieux de Mémoire*, 7 vols (Paris, 1984-1993).

Norberg, Kathryn, *Rich and Poor in Grenoble 1600-1814* (Berkeley and London, 1985).

Notarianni, Philip F., "Italian Involvement in the 1903-04 Coal Miners' Strike in Southern Colorado and Utah", in: Pozzetta, *Pane e Lavoro*, pp. 47-65.

Nugent, Walter, *Crossings. The Great Transatlantic Migrations, 1870-1914* (Bloomington, 1992).

Nye, Robert A., *Crime, Madness, and Politics in Modern France. The Medical Concept of National Decline* (Princeton, 1984).

Oberai, A.S., P.H. Prasad and M.G. Sardana, *Determinants and Consequences of Internal Migration in India. Studies in Bihar, Kerala and Uttar Pradesh* (Delhi, 1989).

O'Brien, Patrick, Trevor Griffiths and Philip Hunt, "Political Components of the Industrial Revolution: Parliament and the English Cotton Textile Industry, 1660-1774", *Economic History Review*, 44 (1991), pp. 395-423.

Oeppen, J., "Back Projection and Inverse Projection: Members of a Wider Class of Constrained Projection Models", *Population Studies*, 47 (1993), pp. 245-267.

Ogden, Philip E., *Migration and Geographical Change* (Cambridge, 1984).

Ogden, Philip E., "Immigration to France since 1945: Myth and Reality", *Ethnic and Racial Studies*, 14 (1991), pp. 294-318.

Ogden, Philip E. and Paul E. White (eds), *Migrants in Modern France. Population Mobility in the Later 19th and 20th Centuries* (Boston etc., 1989).

Okely, Judith, *Traveller-Gypsies* (Cambridge, 1983).

Onody, Oliver, "Quelques traits caractéristiques de l'évolution historiques de la population de Brazil", in: Deprez, *Population and Economics*, pp. 335-364.

Oriol, Michel, *Bilan des études sur les aspects culturels et humains des migrations internationales en Europe occidentale, 1918-1979* (Strasbourg, 1981).

Otte, Enrique, "Cartas privadas de Puebla del siglo XVI", *Jahrbuch für Geschichte von Staat, Wirtschaft und Gesellschaft Lateinamerikas*, 3 (1966), pp. 10-87.

Otte, Enrique, *Cartas privadas de emigrantes a Indias* (Seville, 1988).

Pan, Lynn, *Sons of the Yellow Emperor: The Story of the Overseas Chinese* (London, 1990).

Panayi, Panikos, *The Enemy in Our Midst. Germans in Britain During the First World War* (Oxford, 1991).

Panayi, Panikos, *German Immigrants in Britain during the 19th Century, 1815-1914* (Oxford, 1995).

Paquette, Robert L. and Stanley L. Engerman (eds), *The Lesser Antilles in the Age of European Expansion* (Gainesville, 1996).

Patterson, S., "The Poles", in: Watson, *Between Two Cultures*, pp. 214-241.

Penninx, Rinus, J. Schoorl and C. van Praag, *The Impact of International Migration on Receiving Countries: the Case of the Netherlands* (Amsterdam and Lisse, 1993).

Perkins, Dwight H., *Agricultural Development in China, 1369-1968* (Chicago, 1969).

Perlmann, Joel, *Ethnic Differences: Schooling and Social Structure among the Irish, Italians, Jews, and Blacks in an American City, 1880-1935* (New York, 1988).

Perrot, Michelle, "Delinquency and the Penitentiary System in Nineteenth-Century France", in: Forster and Ranum, *Deviants and the Abandoned*, pp. 213-245.

Perrot, Michelle, *L'impossible prison. Recherches sur le système pénitentiaire au XIXe siècle* (Paris, 1980).

Petersen, W., "A General Typology of Migration", *American Sociological Review*, 23 (1958), no. 3, pp. 256-266.

Petit, Jacques-Guy *et al.*, *Histoire des galères, bagnes et prisons XIIIe-XXe siècles* (Toulouse, 1991).

Pfister, Christian and Andreas Kellerhals, "Verwaltung und Versorgung im Landgericht Sternenberg", *Berner Zeitschrift für Geschichte und Heimatkunde* LI (1989), pp. 151-215.

Pfister, Hans Ulrich, *Die Auswanderung aus dem Knonauer Amt 1648-1750: Ihr Ausmass, ihre Strukturen und ihre Bedingungen* (Zurich, 1987).

Pfister, Ulrich, "Proto-industrialization and Demographic Change: The Canton of Zürich Revisited", *Journal of European Economic History*, 18 (1989), pp. 629-662.

Philips, D., *Crime and Authority in Victorian England: The Black Country, 1835-1860* (London, 1977).

Phillips, Seymoor, "The Medieval Background", in: Canny, *Europeans on the Move*, pp. 9-25.

Phillips, William D., Jr., "The Old World Background of Slavery in the Americas", in: Solow, *Slavery and the Rise*, pp. 43-61.

Pierenkemper, Toni and Richard Tilly, *Historische Arbeitsmarktforschung. Entstehung und Probleme der Vermarktung von Arbeitskraft* (Göttingen, 1982).

Pike, Douglas, *Paradise of Dissent* (Melbourne, 1957).

Pinchemel, Philippe, *Structures sociales et dépopulation rurale dans les campagnes picardes de 1836 à 1936* (Paris, 1967).

Pinto, Diane, "Immigration: L'ambiguïté de la référence américaine", *Pouvoirs*, no. 47 (1988), pp. 93-101.

Piore, Michael J., *Birds of Passage: Migrant Labor and Industrial Societies* (New York, 1979).

Pirenne, Henri, "De la méthode comparative en histoire", in: Marez and Ganshof, *Ve Congrès international des sciences historiques*, pp. 19-23.

Plaum, Bernd D., *Strafrecht, Kriminalpolitik und Kriminalität im Fürstentum Siegen 1750-1810* (Siegen, 1990).

Poitrineau, Abel, "Aspects de l'émigration temporaire et saisonnière en Auvergne à la fin du XVIIIe siècle et au début du XIX siècle", *Revue d'histoire moderne et contemporaine*, 9 (1962), pp. 5-50.

Poitrineau, Abel, *Remues d'hommes: Essai sur les migrations montagnardes en France, aux 17e-18e siècles* (Paris, 1983).

Polanyi, Karl, *The Great Transformation* (Boston, 1957).

Pooley, Colin and Ian D. Whyte (eds), *Migrants, Emigrants and Immigrants. A Social History of Migration* (London and New York, 1991).

Porter, B., *The Refugee Question in Mid-Victorian Politics* (Cambridge, 1979).

Portes, Alejandro and Rubén G. Rumbaut, *Immigrant America. A Portrait* (Berkeley etc., 1990).

Portes, Jacques, *Une fascination réticente: Les Etats-Unis dans l'opinion française* (Nancy, 1990).

Posthumus, N.W., *Inquiry into the History of Prices in Holland*, 2 vols (Leiden, 1946-1964).

Postma, Johannes Menne, *The Dutch in the Atlantic Slave Trade, 1600-1815* (Cambridge, 1990).

Potts, Lydia, *The World Labour Market. A History of Migration* (London and New Jersey, 1990).

Poussou, Jean-Pierre, *Bordeaux et le sud-ouest au XVIIIe siècle* (Paris, 1983).

Poussou, Jean-Pierre, "Mobilité et migrations", in: Dupaquier, *Histoire de la Population Française*, vol. 2, *De la Renaissance à 1789*, pp. 99-144.

Powers, Marshall K., "Chinese Coolie Migration to Cuba" (Unpublished Ph.D. Dissertation, University of Florida, 1953).

Pozzetta, George E. (ed.), *Pane e Lavoro: The Italian American Working Class*. Proceedings of the Eleventh Annual Conference of the American Italian Historical Association (Toronto, 1980).

Prakash, Gyan, *Bonded Histories: Genealogies of Labor Servitude in Colonial India* (Cambridge, 1990).

Prana, G. la, "Foreign Goups in Rome during the First Centuries of the Empire", *Haward Theological Review*, 20 (1927), pp. 183-403.

Prato, Giuseppe, *Le protectionnisme ouvrier (l'exclusion des travailleurs étrangers)* (Paris, 1912).

Price, Charles A., *The Great White Walls are Built* (Canberra, 1974).

Price, Charles A., "Australia", in: Kubat, *Politics of Migration Policies*, pp. 3-18.

Priestley, Margaret, "Anglo-French Trade and the 'Unfavorable Balance' Controversy, 1660-1685", *Economic History Review* 4 (1951), pp. 37-52.

Przeworski, Adam and Henry Teune, *Logic of Comparative Social Inquiry* (New York, 1970).

Puckrein, Gary, *Little England: Plantation Society and Anglo-Barbadian Politics, 1627-1700* (New York, 1984).

Punzo, Maurizio, "La Societa Umanitaria e l'Emigrazione, dagli Inizi del Secolo alla Prima Guerra Mondiale", in: Bezza, *Gli Italiani fuori d'Italia*, pp. 119-144.

Puskas, Juliana, "Hungarian Overseas Migration: a Microanalysis", in: Vecoli and Sinke, *Century of European Migrations*, pp. 221-239.

Ragionieri, Ernesto, "Italiani all'Estero ed Emigrazione di Lavoratori Italiani: Un Tema di Storia del Movimento Operaio", *Belfagor*, 17 (1962), pp. 640-669.

Ramirez, Bruno, *On the Move: French-Canadian and Italian Migrants in the North Atlantic Economy* (Toronto, 1991).

Rao, Aparna (ed.), *The Other Nomads. Peripatetic Minorities in Cross-Cultural Perspective* (Köln etc., 1986).

Rao, M.S.A. (ed.), *Studies in Migration. Internal and International Migration in India* (Delhi, 1986).

Ravenstein, E.G., "The Laws of Migration", *Journal of the Royal Statistical Society*, 48 (1885), pp. 167-235; and 52 (1889), pp. 241-305.

Real de Azua, Mario Federico, "Chinese Coolies in Peru: The Chinca Islands", in: Martinez Montiel, *Asiatic Migration in Latin America*, pp. 37-52.

Redlich, F., *The German Military Enterpriser and his Work-Force. A Study in European Economic and Social History*, 2 vols (Wiesbaden, 1964-1965).

Reher, David Sven, *Town and Country in Pre-Industrial Spain. Cuenca, 1550-1870* (Cambridge, 1990).

Reich, Uwe, "Die Auswanderung aus dem Regierungsbezirk Frankfurt/Oder im 19. Jahrhundert" (Diss., Universität Potsdam, 1993).

Reid, Antony (ed.), *Slavery, Bondage and Dependency in Southeast Asia* (St. Lucia, London and New York, 1983).

Reith, Reinhold, "Arbeitsmigration und Gruppenkultur deutscher Handwerksgesellen im 18. und frühen 19. Jahrhundert", *Scripta Mercaturae*, 23 (1989), pp. 1-35.

Renault, François and Serge Daget, *Les traites négrières en Afrique* (Paris, 1985).

Reutlinger, Andrew S., "Reflections on the Anglo-American Jewish Experience: Immigrants, Workers, and Entrepreneurs in New York and London, 1870-1914", *American Jewish Historical Quarterly*, 66 (1977), pp. 473-484.

Richards, Eric, "Annals of the Australian Immigrant", in: Richards *et al.*, *Visible Immigrants*, pp. 1-19.

Richards, Eric (ed.), *Poor Australian Immigrants in the Nineteenth Century. Visible Immigrants: Two* (Canberra, 1991).

Richards, Eric, "British Poverty and Australian Immigration in the Nineteenth Century", in: Richards, *Poor Australian Immigrants*, pp. 1-32.

Richards, Eric, "Paths of Settlement in Colonial South Australia", in: Denholm *et al.*, *Terowie Workshop*, pp. 70-98.

Richards, Eric, "Return Migration and Emigrant Strategies in Colonial Australia", in: Fitzpatrick, *Home or Away?*, pp. 64-105.

Richards, Eric, "The Decline of St Kilda: Demography, Economy and Emigration", *Scottish Economic and Social History*, 14 (1992), pp. 55-75.

Richards, Eric, "St Kilda and Australia: Emigrants in Peril, 1852-3", *Scottish Historical Review*, LXXI (1993), pp. 129-155.

Richards, Eric, "How Did Poor British Emigrants Get to Australia in the Nineteenth Century?", *Journal of British Studies*, 32 (1993), pp. 250-280.

Richards, Eric, "Emigration to the New Worlds: Emigration Systems in the Early Nineteenth Century", *Australian Journal of Politics and History*, 44 (1995), pp. 391-408.

Richards, Eric (ed.), *Visible Women. Female Immigrants in Colonial Australia* (Canberra, 1996).

Richards, Eric *et al.* (eds), *Visible Immigrants: Neglected Sources for the History of Australian Immigration* (Canberra, 1989).

Richardson, D. (ed.), *Abolition and its Aftermath. The Historical Context, 1790-1916* (London, 1985).

Richardson, Peter, *Chinese Mine Labor in the Transvaal* (London, 1982).

Richardson, Peter, "Chinese Indentured Labour in the Transvaal Gold Mining Industry, 1904-1910", in: Saunders, *Indentured Labour in the British Empire*, pp. 262-279.

Richel, Arthur, "Armen- und Bettlerordnungen. Ein Beitrag zur Geschichte der öffentlichen Armenpflege", *Archiv für Kulturgeschichte*, 2 (1904), pp. 393-403.

Richmond, Anthony H., "Sociological Theories of International Migration: the Case of Refugees", *Current Sociology*, 36 (1988), no. 2, pp. 7-25.

Rietbergen, Louise (ed.), *Migratie en vestiging in Nederland: bronnenoverzicht en geselecteerde bibliografie*. Working paper of the International Institute of Social History, no. 25 (Amsterdam, 1994).

Riis, Thomas, *Aspects of Poverty in Early Modern Europe* (Alphen aan den Rijn etc., 1981).

Riis, Thomas, "Poverty and Urban Development in Early Modern Europe (15th-18th centuries) A general view", in: Riis, *Aspects of Poverty*, pp. 1-28.

Roach, John, "The French Police", in: Roach and Thomaneck, *Police and Public Order*, pp. 107-141.

Roach, John and Jürgen Thomaneck (eds), *Police and Public Order in Europe* (London etc., 1985).

Robb, Peter (ed.), *Dalit Movements, and the Meanings of Labour in India* (Delhi, 1993).

Roberts, M.J.D., "Public and Private in Early Nineteenth-Century London: the Vagrant Act of 1822 and its Enforcement", *Social History*, 13 (1988), no. 3, pp. 273-294.

Robinson, David J. (ed.), *Migration in Colonial Spanish America* (Cambridge and New York, 1990).

Robson, L.L., *The Convict Settlers: An Enquiry into the Origin and Character of the Convicts Transported to New South Wales and Van Dieman's Land, 1787-1852* (Melbourne, 1965).

Roche, T.W.E., *The Key in the Lock: The History of Immigration Control in England from 1066 to the Day* (London, 1969).

Rodgers, M., "The Anglo-Russian Military Convention and the Lithuanian Immigrant Community in Lanarkshire, Scotland, 1914-20", *Immigrants and Minorities*, 1 (1982), pp. 60-88.

Rodgers, M., "Political Developments in the Lithuanian Community in Scotland, c. 1890-1923", in: Slatter, *From the Other Shore*, pp. 141-156.

Roeber, A.G., "The Origins and Transfer of German-American Concepts of Property and Inheritance", *Perspectives in American History, New Series*, III (1987), pp. 115-171.

Roediger, David, *The Wages of Whiteness: Race and the Making of the American Working Class* (London and New York, 1991).

Rogers, James Thorold, *A history of Agriculture and Prices in England* (Oxford, 1887).

Rogers, J. (ed.), *Family Building and Family Planning in Pre-Industrial Society* (Uppsala, 1980).

Rogers, Rosemarie (ed.), *Guests Come to Stay: The Effects of European Labor Migration on Sending and Receiving Countries* (Boulder, CO, 1985).

Rogers, Rosemarie, "Post-World War II European Labor Migration", in: Rogers, *Guests Come to Stay*, pp. 1-28.

Rosenblat, Angel, *La Poblacion Indigena y el Mestizaje en America*, 2 vols (Buenos Aires, 1950).

Rosoli, Gianfausto (ed.), *Un Secolo di Emigrazione Italiana. 1876-1976* (Rome, 1978).

Rosoli, Gianfausto, "Italian Migration to European Countries from Political Unification to World War I", in: Hoerder, *Labor Migration in the Atlantic Economies*, pp. 95-116.

Rotberg, Robert I. and Theodore K. Rabb (eds), *Hunger and History; The Impact of Changing Food Production and Consumption Patterns on Society* (Cambridge, 1985).

Rothermund, Dietmar and D.C. Wadhwa, *Zamindars, Mines and Peasants. Studies in the History of an Indian Coalfield and its Rural Hinterland* (New Delhi, 1978).

Roy, Patricia E., *A White Man's Province: British Columbia Politicians and Chinese and Japanese Immigrants, 1858-1914* (Vancouver, 1989).

Rudé, G., *Criminal and Victim: Crime and Society in Early Nineteenth-Century England* (Oxford, 1985).

Rusche, G. and O. Kirchheimer, *Punishment and Social Structure* (New York, 1968; first published in 1939).

Sabean, David Warren, *Property, Production and Family in Neckarhausen, 1700-1870* (Cambridge, 1990).

Sachße, Christoph and Florian Tennstedt, *Geschichte der Armenfürsorge in Deutschland vom Spätmittelalter bis zum 2. Weltkrieg* (Stuttgart etc., 1980).

Said, Edward, *Orientalism: Western Conceptions of the Orient* (Harmondsworth, 1991).

Salinger, Sharon V., "'Send No More Women': Female Servants in Eighteenth-Century Philadelphia", *Pennsylvania Magazine of History and Biography*, 107 (1983), pp. 29-48.

Salinger, Sharon V., *"To Serve Well and Faithfully": Labor and Indentured Servants in Pennsylvania, 1682-1800* (Cambridge, 1987).

Salitan, Laurie P., *Politics and Nationality in Contemporary Soviet-Jewish Emigration, 1968-89* (Basingstoke and London, 1992).

Salo, M.T. (ed.), *100 Years of Gypsy Studies* (Cheverly, MD, 1990).

Samuel, Raphael, "Comers and Goers", in: Dyos and Wolff, *Victorian City*, vol. I, pp. 123-160.

Sánchez-Albornoz, Nicholás, "The First Transatlantic Transfer: Spanish Migration to the New World, 1493-1810", in: Canny, *Europeans on the Move*, pp. 26-38.

Sandmeyer, Elmer Clarence, *The Anti-Chinese Movement in California* (Urbana, 1939).

Sartorius von Waltershausen, A., *Die italienischen Wanderarbeiter* (Leipzig, 1903).

Sassen, Saskia, *The Global City. New York, London, Tokyo* (Princeton, NJ, 1991).

Sassen, Saskia, *The Mobility of Labor and Capital. A Study in International Investment and Labor Flow* (Cambridge, 1988).

Saunders, Kay, *Workers in Bondage: The Origins of Unfree Labour in Queensland 1824-1916* (St. Lucia, 1982).

Saunders, Kay (ed.), *Indentured Labour in the British Empire 1834-1920* (London, 1984).

Saunders, Kay, "The Workers' Paradox: Indentured Labour in the Queensland Sugar Industry to 1920", in: Saunders, *Indentured Labour in the British Empire*, pp. 213-259.

Saxton, Alexander, *The Indispensable Enemy: Labor and the Anti-Chinese Movement in California* (Berkeley, 1971).

Scarpaci, Jean Ann, *Italian Immigrants in Louisiana's Sugar Parishes: Recruitment, Labor Conditions, and Community Relations, 1800-1910* (New York, 1980).

Scarr, D., *Fragments of Empire: A History of the Western Pacific High Commission, 1877-1914* (Canberra, 1967).

Scarr, D., "Review", *Journal of Pacific History, Pacific History Bibliography and Comment*, XIX (1984), pp. 54-55.

Schendel, Willem van, *Three Deltas. Accumulation and Poverty in Rural Burma, Bengal and South India* (New Delhi, 1991).

Schendel, Willem van and Aminul Haque Faraizi, *Rural Labourers in Bengal, 1880 to 1980* (Rotterdam, 1984).

Schiffauer, Werner, *Die Migranten aus Subay. Türken in Deutschland: eine Ethnographie* (Stuttgart, 1991).

Schiller, Nina Glick, Linda Basch and Cristine Blanc-Szanton (eds), *Towards a Transnational Perspective on Migration. Race, Class, Ethnicity, and Nationalism Reconsidered*. Annals of the New York Academy of Sciences, vol. 645 (New York, 1992).

Schnakenbourg, Christian, "Statistiques pour l'histoire de l'economie de plantation en Guadeloupe et Martinique (1635-1835)", *Bulletin de la Société de la Guadaloupe*, 31 (1977).

Schnapper, Dominique, "Centralisme et fédéralisme culturels: Les émigrés italiens en France et aux Etats-Unis", *Annales ESC*, 29 (September-October 1974), pp. 1141-1159.

Schnapper, Dominique, "Quelques réflexions sur l'assimilation comparée des travailleurs émigrés italiens et des Juifs en France", *Bulletin de la Société Française de Sociologie*, vol. 3 (1976), pp. 11-18.

Schnapper, Dominique, "Jewish Minorities and the State in the United States, France, and Argentina", in: Greenfeld and Mertin, *Center: Ideas and Institutions*, pp. 186-209.

Schnapper, Dominique, "A Host Country of Immigrants that does not know Itself", *Diaspora*, 1 (1991), pp. 353-363.

Schubert, Ernst, *Arme Leute. Bettler und Gauner im Franken des 18. Jahrhunderts* (Neustadt a.d. Aisch 1983).

Schubert, Ernst, "Mobilität ohne Chance: Die Ausgrenzung des fahrenden Volkes", in: Schulze, *Ständische Gesellschaft*, pp. 113-164.

Schuler, Monica, *Alas, Alas Kongo: A Social History of Indentured African Immigration into Jamaica, 1841-1865* (Baltimore, 1980).

Schulze, Winfried, *Bäuerlicher Widerstand und feudale Herrschaft in der frühen Neuzeit* (Stuttgart, 1980).

Schulze, Winfried (ed.), *Ständische Gesellschaft und soziale Mobilität* (Munich, 1988).

Schulze, Winfried, "Die ständische Gesellschaft des 16./17. Jahrhunderts als Problem von Statik und Dynamik", in: Schulze, *Ständische Gesellschaft*, pp. 1-17.

Schwartz, R.M., *Policing the Poor in Eighteenth-Century France* (Chapel Hill and London, 1988).

Schwartz, Stuart B., *Sugar Plantations in the Formation of Brazilian Society* (Cambridge, 1984).

Schwartz, Stuart B., "Colonial Brazil, c. 1580-c. 1750: Plantations and Peripheries", in: Bethell, *Cambridge History of Latin America*, II, pp. 423-499.

Schwerin, Detlef, "The Control of Land and Labour in Chota Nagpur, 1858-1908", in: Rothermund and Wadhwa, *Zamindars, Mines and Peasants*, pp. 21-67.

Sée, Henri, "Remarques sur l'application de la méthode comparative à l'histoire économique et sociale", *Revue de synthèse historique*, 36 (1923), pp. 37-46.

Serle, Geoffrey, *The Golden Age* (Melbourne, 1963).

Sewell, William H., Jr., "Marc Bloch and the Logic of Comparative History", *History and Theory*, 6 (1967), pp. 208-218.

Shah, A.M., "The Rural-Urban Networks in India", *South Asia, Journal of South Asian Studies*, XI (1988), 2, pp. 1-27.

Shaw, A.G.L., *Convicts and the Colonies: A Study of Penal Transportation from Great Britain and Ireland to Australia and other parts of the British Empire* (London, 1966).

Shlomowitz, Ralph, "Markets for Indentured and Time-Expired Melanesian Labour in Queensland, 1863-1906: An Economic Analysis", *Journal of Pacific History*, XVI (1981), pp. 70-91.

Shlomowitz, Ralph, "The Fiji Labor Trade in Comparative Perspective, 1864-1914", *Pacific Studies*, IX (1986), pp. 107-152.

Shlomowitz, Ralph, "Infant Mortality", *Indian Economic and Social History Review*, 23 (1986), pp. 289-302.

Shlomowitz, Ralph, "The Internal Labour Trade in Papua (1884-1941) and New Guinea (1920-1941): An Economic Analysis", *Journal de la Société des Oceanistes*, LXXXII-LXXXIII (1986), pp. 177-188.

Shlomowitz, Ralph, "Fertility and Fiji's Indian Migrants, 1879-1919", *The Indian Economic and Social History Review*, 24 (1987), pp. 205-213.

Shlomowitz, Ralph, "Epidemiology and the Pacific Labor Trade", *Journal of Interdisciplinary History*, XIX (1989), pp. 585-610.

Shlomowitz, Ralph, "The Pacific Labour Trade and Super-Exploitation", *Journal of Pacific History*, XXIV (1989), pp. 238-241.

Shlomowitz, Ralph, "Convict Workers: A Review Article", *Australian Economic History Review*, XXX (1990), pp. 67-88.

Shlomowitz, Ralph, "Nominated and Selected Government-Assisted Immigration from the United Kingdom to Australia, 1848-1900", *Journal of the Historical Society of South Australia*, XX (1992), pp. 151-155.

Shlomowitz, Ralph, "Indentured Indian Emigrants to Natal: A Review Article", *Journal of Natal and Zulu History*, XIV (1992-3), pp. 113-122.

Shlomowitz, Ralph, "Marx and the Queensland Labour Trade: A Critique", *Journal de la Société des Oceanistes*, XCVI (1993), pp. 11-17.

Shlomowitz, Ralph and R. Bedford, "The Internal Labour Trade in New Hebrides and Solomon Islands, c1900-1941", *Journal de la Société des Oceanistes*, LXXXVI (1988), pp. 61-85.

Shlomowitz, Ralph and Lance Brennan, "Mortality and Migrant Labour en Route to Assam", *The Indian Economic and Social History Review*, 27 (1990), pp. 313-330.

Shlomowitz, Ralph and Lance Brennan, "Mortality and Migrant Labour in Assam, 1865-1921", *The Indian Economic and Social History Review*, 27 (1990), pp. 85-110.

Shlomowitz, Ralph and J. McDonald, "Babies at Risk on Immigrant Voyages to Australia in the Nineteenth Century", *Economic History Review*, XLIV (1991), pp. 86-101.

Shumsky, Neil Larry, *The Evolution of Political Protest and the Workingmen's Party of California* (Columbus, OH, 1991).

Silverman, Maxim, *Deconstructing the Nation. Immigration, Racism, and Citizenship in Modern France* (London and New York, 1992).

Simiand, François, "Méthode historique et science sociale" [1903], in: Cedronio, *Méthode historique et sciences sociales*, pp. 113-169.

Simmons, C.P., "Recruiting and Organizing an Industrial Labour Force in Colonial India: The Case of the Coal Mining Industry, c. 1880-1939", *Indian Economic and Social History Review*, XIII (1976), pp. 455-485.

Simon, Julian L., "Basic Data Concerning Immigration into the United States", in: R. Simon, *Immigration and American Public Policy*.

Simon, Julian L., "The Economic Effects of Immigration", *European Review*, I (1993), pp. 109-116.

Simon, Rita J. (ed.), *Immigration and American Public Policy*, vol. 487 of *The Annals of the American Academy of Political and Social Science* (1986).

Simonsen, Roberto C., *Historia Economica do Brasil (1500/1820)* (Sao Paulo, 1969⁶).

Singer-Kérel, Jeanne, "Foreign Workers in France, 1891-1936", *Ethnic and Racial Studies*, 14 (1991), no. 3, pp. 279-293.

Skocpol, Theda (ed.), *Vision and Method in Historical Sociology* (Cambridge, 1984).

Skocpol, Theda and Margaret Somers, "The Uses of Comparative History in Macrosocial Inquiry", *Comparative Studies in Society and History*, vol. 22 (1980), pp. 174-197.

Slack, P.A., "Vagrants and Vagrancy in England 1598-1664", in: Clark and Souden, *Migration and Society*, pp. 49-76.

Slatter, J. (ed.), *From the Other Shore. Russian Political Emigrants in Britain, 1880-1917* (London, 1983).

Smith, Judith, *Family Connections: A History of Italian and Jewish Immigrant Lives in Providence, Rhode Island, 1900-1940* (Albany, 1985).

Smout, Thomas Christopher, "Scots and Emigrants in Europe 1400-1700", in: Cavaciocchi, *Migrazioni in Europa*, pp. 659-669.

Smout, Thomas Christopher and T.M. Devine, "Scottish Emigration in the Seventeenth and Eighteenth Centuries", in: Canny, *Europeans on the Move*, pp. 76-112.

Snell, K.D.M., *Annals of the Labouring Poor. Social Change and Agrarian England, 1660-1900* (Cambridge etc., 1985).

Soboul, Albert, *La civilisation et la révolution française*, 3 vols (Paris, 1970).

Sogner, S., "Young in Europe around 1700: Norwegian Sailors and Servant-Girls Seeking Employment in Amsterdam", in: J.P. Bardet *et al.* (eds), *Mésurer et comprendre. Mélanges en l'honneur de Jacques Dupâquier* (Paris, 1991).

Sokoloff, Kenneth L. and Georgia C. Villaflor, "The Early Achievements of Modern Stature in America", *Social Science History*, VI (1982), pp. 453-481.

Solberg, Carl E., *Immigration and Nationalism. Argentina and Chile, 1890-1914* (Austin, 1970).

Solberg, Carl E., *The Prairies and the Pampas: Agrarian Policy in Canada and Argentina. 1880-1930* (Stanford, 1987).

Sollors, Werner, *Beyond Ethnicity: Consent and Descent in American Culture* (New York, 1986).

Solow, Barbara L. (ed.), *Slavery and the Rise of the Atlantic System* (Cambridge, 1991).

Solow, Barbara L. and Stanley L. Engerman (eds), *British Capitalism and Caribbean Slavery: The Legacy of Eric Williams* (Cambridge, 1987).

Soly, Hugo and Alfons K. Thijs (eds), *Minderheden in Westeuropese steden (16de – 20ste eeuw) / Minorities in Western European Cities (sixteenth – twentieth centuries)* (Brussels, 1995).

Sombart, Werner, *Der Bourgeois. Zur Geistesgeschichte des modernen Wirtschaftsmenschen* (1st ed. Munich, 1913).

Souden, David, "Movers and Stayers in Family Reconstitution Populations, 1660-1780", *Local Population Studies*, 33 (1984), pp. 11-28.

Steckel, Richard H., "Stature and Living Standards in the United States", in: Gallman and Wallis, *American Economic Growth and Standards of Living*, pp. 265-308.

Steckel, Richard H. and Richard A. Jensen, "New Evidence on the Cause of Slave and Crew Mortality in the Atlantic Slave Trade", *Journal of Economic History* 46 (1986), pp. 57-77.

Stedman-Jones, G., *Outcast London. A Study in the Relationship between Classes in Victorian Society* (London, 1971; reprint Harmondsworth, 1984).

Steedman, Carolyn, *Policing the Victorian Community. The Formation of English Provincial Police Forces 1856-1880* (London, 1984).

Steele, Ian K., *The English Atlantic, 1675-1740: An Exploration of Communication and Community* (Oxford, 1986).

Stegen, Judith van der, "Les Chinois en France, 1915-1924" (Unpublished Travail de Recherches de Maitrise, University of Paris X, Nanterre, 1974).

Steinberg, Stephen, *The Ethnic Myth* (Boston, 1981).

Steinfeld, Robert J., *The Invention of Free Labor: The Employment Relation in English and American Law and Culture. 1350-1870* (Chapel Hill, 1991).

Stewart, Watt, *Chinese Bondage in Peru, A History of the Chinese Coolie in Peru, 1849-1874* (Westport, 1951).

Storch, Robert D., "Policing Rural Southern England before the Police-Opinion and Practice, 1830-1856", in: Hay and Snyder, *Policing and Prosecuting*, pp. 212-266.

Stott, Ingrid, "Emigration from England, 1640-1680" (MA Thesis, Dept. of History, Queen's University, Kingston, 1993).

Stovall, Tyler, "Color-blind France? Colonial Workers during the First World War", *Race and Class*, 35 (1993), pp. 35-55.

Strauss, Eva, "Die Zigeunerverfolgung in Bayern 1885-1926" (MA Thesis on the Ludwig-Maximilians-University, Munich, 1985).

Strikwerda, Carl, "France and the Belgian Immigration of the Nineteenth Century", in: Guerin-Gonzales and Strikwerda, *The Politics of Immigrants Workers*, pp. 101-132.

Stuart Mill, John, "Two Methods of Comparison" (excerpt from *A System of Logic*, 1888), in: Etzioni and Du Bow, *Comparative Perspectives*, pp. 205-213.

Summerskill, Michael, *China on the Western Front: Britain's Chinese Work Force in the First World War* (London, 1982).

Sundin, J. and E. Soderlund (eds), *Time, Space and Man: Essays on Microdemography* (Atlantic Highlands, NJ, 1979).

Swift, R. and S. Gilley, *The Irish in Britain, 1815-1939* (London, 1989).

Sword, K. *et al.*, *The Formation of the Polish Community in Great Britain 1939-50* (London, 1989).

Tagliabue, John, "Europeans Fleeing West in Search of a Better Life", *New York Times*, 11 August 1991.

Takaki, Ron, *Pau Hana: Plantation Life and Labor in Hawaii. 1835-1920* (Honolulu, 1983).

Tan, Thomas Tsu-wee, *Your Chinese Roots: the Overseas Chinese Story* (Union City, 1987).

Tannahill, J.A., *European Volunteer Workers in Britain* (Manchester, 1956).

Tate, Thad W. and David L. Ammerman (eds), *The Chesapeake in the Seventeenth Century: Essays on Anglo-American Society* (Chapel Hill, 1979).

Tawney, R.H., *Religion and the Rise of Capitalism* (London, 1926).

Teitelbaum, Michael S. and Jay M. Winter, *Fear of Population Decline* (New York, 1985).

Tenfelde, K. (ed.), *Towards a Social History of Mining in the 19th and 20th Centuries* (Munich, 1992).

Tennstedt, Florian, *Sozialgeschichte der Sozialpolitik in Deutschland: Vom 18. Jahrhundert bis zum 1. Weltkrieg* (Göttingen, 1981).

Thernstrom, Stephan, *The Other Bostonians* (Cambridge, MA, 1973).

Thistlethwaite, Frank, "Migration from Europe Overseas in the 19th and 20th Centuries", *XIe Congrès International des Sciences Historiques. Rapports*, vol. 5, *Histoire Contemporaine* (Göteborg, 1960), pp. 32-60.

Thistlethwaite, Frank, "Migration from Europe Overseas in the Nineteenth and Twentieth Centuries", in: Vecoli and Sinke, *Century of European Migration*, pp. 17-49.

Thistlethwaite, Frank, "Postscript", in: Vecoli and Sinke, *Century of European Migration*, pp. 50-57.

Thomas, B., *Migration and Economic Growth: A Study of Great Britain and the Atlantic Economy* (Cambridge, 1954).

Thomas, William I. and Florian Znaniecki, *The Polish Peasant in Europe and America*, 5 vols (Chicago, 1920).

Thompson, F.M.L., "Social Control in Victorian Britain", *The Economic History Review*, XXXIV (1981), pp. 189-208.

Thompson, F.M.L. (ed.), *The Cambridge Social History of Britain 1750-1950*, vol. 3 (Cambridge, 1990).

Thornton, John, *Africa and Africans in the Making of the Atlantic World, 1400-1680* (Cambridge, 1992).

Thrupp, Sylvia, "Editorial", *Comparative Studies in Society and History*, 1 (October 1958).

Tiggelen, Ph.J. van, *Musiciens ambulants et joueurs d'orgue au XIXe siècle. Approche socio-historique du phénomène de la musique de colportage dans la région bruxelloise*. Special issue of the "The Brussels Museum of Musical Instruments, Bulletin", vols XII-XIII (1982-1983).

Tilly, Charles, "Migration in Modern European History", in: McNeill and Adams, *Human Migration*, pp. 48-74.

Tilly, Charles (ed.), *Historical Studies of Changing Fertility* (Princeton, 1978).

Tilly, Charles, "The Demographic Origins of the European Proletariat", in: Levine, *Proletarianization and Family History*, pp. 26-52.

Tilly, Charles, *Big Structures, Large Processes, Huge Comparisons* (New York, 1985).

Tilly, Charles, "Transplanted Networks", in: Yans-McLaughlin, *Immigration Reconsidered*, pp. 79-95.

Tilly, Charles, *Coercion, Capital, and European States A.D. 990-1990* (Oxford, 1990).

Tilly, Charles, Louise Tilly and Richard Tilly, *The Rebellious Century, 1830-1930* (Cambridge, MA, 1975).

Tilly, Louise A. and Joan W. Scott, *Women, Work and Family* (New York, 1978).

Tinker, H., *A New System of Slavery: The Export of Indian Labour Overseas, 1830-1920* (Oxford, 1974).

Todd, Emmanuel, *Le destin des immigrés. Assimilation et ségrégation dans les démocraties occidentales* (Paris, 1994).

Tonkin, Elizabeth, Maryon McDonald and Malcolm Chapman (eds), *History and Ethnicity* (London and New York, 1989).

Trefousse, Hans L. (ed.), *Germany and America: Essays on Problems of International Relations and Immigration* (New York, 1980).

Trento, Angelo, *La Dov'é la Raccolta del Caffe; l'emigrazione italiana in Brasile. 1875-1940* (Padova, 1984).

Trommler, Frank and Joseph McVeigh (eds), *America and the Germans: An Assessment of a Three-Hundred-Year History*, 2 vols (Philadelphia, 1985).

Troup, Edward, *The Home Office* (London, 1925).

Tsai, Shih-shan Henry, "Reaction to Exclusion: Ch'ing Attitudes toward Overseas Chinese in the United States, 1848-1906" (Unpublished Ph.D. Thesis, University of Oregon, 1970).

Valkenburg, F.C. and A.M.C. Vissers, "Segmentation of the Labour Market: The Theory of the Dual Labour Market – The Case of the Netherlands", *Netherlands Journal of Sociology*, XVI (1980), pp. 155-170.

Vandenbroeke, Christiaan, "Les formes protoindustrielles. Le cas flamand: Evolution sociale et comportements démographiques aux XVIIe-XIXe siècles", *Annales ESC*, 39 (1984), pp. 915-939.

Vandervelde, Emile, *Exode rural et le retour aux champs* (Paris, 1903).

Vangelista, Chiara, *Le braccia per la fazenda: immigrati e caipiras da formazione della mercato del lavoro paulista (1850-1930)* (Milan, 1982).

Vardi, Liana, *The Land and the Loom: Peasants and Profit in Northern France, 1650-1800* (Durham, NC, 1993).

Vassberg, David E., "Mobility and Migration in Sixteenth-Century Spanish Villages". Paper presented at the 1992 meeting of the American Historical Association.

Vaux de Foletier, F. de, *Les tsiganes dans l'ancienne France* (Paris, 1961).

Vaux de Foletier, F. de, *Mille ans d'histoire des tsiganes* (Paris, 1970).

Vecoli, Rudolph J., "The Contadini in Chicago: A Critique of The Uprooted", *Journal of American History*, LI (1964-65), pp. 404-417.

Vecoli, Rudolph J., "European Americans: From Immigrants to Ethnics", *International Migration Review*, 6 (1972), pp. 403-434.

Vecoli, Rudolph J., "Italian Immigrants in the United States Labor Movement from 1880 to 1929", in: Bezza, *Gli Italiani fuori d'Italia*, pp. 157-306.

Vecoli, Rudolph J., "Return to the Melting Pot: Ethnicity in the United States in the 1980s", *Journal of American Ethnic History*, 5 (Fall 1985), pp. 7-20.

Vecoli, Rudolph J. and Suzanne M. Sinke (eds), *A Century of European Migrations 1830-1930* (Urbana and Chicago, 1991).

Vexliard, A., *Introduction à la sociologie du vagabondage* (Paris, 1956).

Viazzo, Pier Paulo, *Upland Communities: Environment, Population and Social Structure in the Alps since the Sixteenth Century* (Cambridge, 1989).

Vichniac, Judith E., "French Socialists and *Droit à la Différence*: A Changing Dynamic", *French Politics and Society*, 9 (Winter 1991), pp. 40-56.

Vigier, Philippe, *et al.* (eds), *Maintien de l'ordre et polices en France et en Europe au XIX siècle* (Paris, 1987).

Visram, R., *Ayahs, Lascars and Princes: Indians in Britain 1700-1947* (London, 1986).

Vogel, Christian, "Populationsdichte-Regulation und individuelle Reproduktionsstrategien in evolutionsbiologischer Sicht", in: Kraus, *Regulation, Manipulation und Explosion*, pp. 11-30.

Vries, Jan de, *The Dutch Rural Economy in the Golden Age, 1500-1700* (New Haven, 1974).

Vries, Jan de, *The Economy of Europe in an Age of Crisis, 1600-1750* (Cambridge etc., 1976).

Vries, Jan de, *European Urbanization, 1500-1800* (Cambridge, MA, 1984).

Vries, Jan de and Ad van der Woude, *Nederland 1500-1815. De eerste ronde van moderne economische groei* (Amsterdam, 1995).

Waldinger, Roger and Robin Ward (eds.), "Cities in Transition: A Comparison of Ethnic Minorities in London and New York", *New Community*, 14 (Spring 1988).

Walton, Look Lai, *Indentured Labor. Caribbean Sugar: Chinese and Indian Migrants to the British West Indies* (Baltimore, 1993).

Wang, Gungwu, *China and the Chinese Overseas* (Singapore, 1991).

Wang, Sing-Wu, *The Organization of Chinese Emigration, 1848-1888: with Reference to Chinese Emigration to Australia* (San Francisco, 1978).

Ward, J.R., *British West Indian Slavery; The Process of Amelioration* (Oxford, 1988).

Watson, James L., "Chattel Slavery in Chinese Peasant Society: A Comparative Analysis", *Ethnology*, 15 (1976), pp. 361-375.

Watson, James L. (ed.), *Between Two Cultures* (Oxford, 1977).

Watson, James L. (ed.), *Asian and African Systems of Slavery* (Oxford, 1980).

Watson, James L., "Transactions in People: the Chinese Markets in Slaves, Servants and Heirs", in: Watson, *Asian and African Systems of Slavery*, pp. 223-250.

Watts, David, *The West Indies; Patterns of Development, Culture and Environmental Change since 1492* (Cambridge, 1987).

Weber, Adna, *The Growth of Cities in the Nineteenth Century* (Ithaca, NY, 1899, reprint 1965).

Weill, Claudie, *l'Internationalisme et l'Autre: les Relations interethniques dans la IIe Internationale (discussions et débats)* (Paris, 1987).

Wettmann-Jungblut, Peter, "'Stelen inn rechter Hungersnodtt'. Diebstahl, Eigentumsschutz und strafrechtliche Kontrolle im vorindustriellen Baden 1600-1850", in: Dülmen, *Verbrechen, Strafen und soziale Kontrolle*, pp. 133-177.

Whayne, Jeannie M., *Shadows over Sunnyside: An Arkansas Plantation in Transition. 1830-1945* (Fayetteville, 1993).

White, J.D., "Scottish Lithuanians and the Russian Revolution", *Journal of Baltic Studies*, 6 (1975), pp. 1-8.

White, Paul, "Internal Migration in the Nineteenth and Twentieth Centuries", in: Ogden and White, *Migrants in Modern France*, pp. 13-33.

Whyte, Ian D., "Migration in Early-Modern Scotland and England. A comparative Perspective", in: Pooley and Whyte, *Migrants, Emigrants and Immigrants*, pp. 87-105.

Wiener, Martin J., *Reconstructing the Criminal. Culture, Law, and Policy in England, 1830-1914* (Cambridge, 1990).

Willcox, Walter F. and Imre Ferenczi, *International Migrations*. 2 vols (New York, 1929).

Willems, Wim, *Op zoek naar de ware zigeuner. Zigeuners als studieobject tijdens de Verlichting, de Romantiek en het Nazisme* (Utrecht, 1995).

Willems, Wim, *In Search of the True Gypsy. Gypsies as Object of Study Durinf the Enlightenment, Romanticism and Nazism* (London, 1996).

Willems, Wim and Leo Lucassen, "The Church of Knowledge. The Gypsy in Dutch Encyclopedias and their Sources", in: Salo, *100 Years of Gypsy Studies*, pp. 31-50.

Willems, Wim and Leo Lucassen (eds), *Het onbekende vaderland. De repatriëring van Indische Nederlanders 1946-1964* (Den Haag, 1994).

Williams, B., "The beginnings of Jewish Trade Unionism in Manchester, 1889-1891", in: Lunn, *Hosts, Immigrants and Minorities*, pp. 263-307.

Williams, Eric, *Capitalism and Slavery* (Chapel Hill, 1944).

Wilson, F.M., *They Came as Strangers. The Story of Refugees to Great Britain* (London, 1959).

Wirsing, Bernd, "'Gleichsam mit Soldatenstrenge': Neue Polizei in süddeutschen Städten. Zu Polizeiverhalten und Bürgerwidersetzlichkeit im Vormärz", in: Lüdtke, *"Sicherheit" und "Wohlfahrt"*, pp. 65-94.

Wojciechowska, B., "Generational Differences in Ethnic Consciousness. A study based upon Post-Second World War Britain with Special Reference to Coventry and London" (MA Dissertation, Warwick University, 1976).

Wokeck, Marianne, "A Tide of Alien Tongues: The Flow and Ebb of German Immigration to Pennsylvania, 1683-1776" (Ph.D., Temple University of Philadelphia, 1983).

Wokeck, Marianne, "German Immigration to Colonial America: Prototype of a Transatlantic Mass Migration", in: Trommler and McVeigh, *America and the Germans*, vol. 1, pp. 3-13.

Wokeck, Marianne, "Harnessing the Lure of the 'Best Poor Man's Country': The Dynamics of German-Speaking Immigration to British North America, 1683-1783", in: Altman and Horn, *"To Make America"*, pp. 204-243.

Wolf, Eric R., *Peasant Wars of the Twentieth Century* (New York, 1969).

Wolf, Eric R., *Europe and the People Without History* (Berkeley etc., 1982).

Wolken, Simone, *Das Grundrecht auf Asyl als Gegenstand der Innen- und Rechtspolitik in der Bundesrepublik Deutschland* (Frankfurt am Main etc., 1988).

Wood, G.A., "Convicts", *The Royal Australian Historical Society, Journal and Proceedings*, VIII (1922), pp. 177-208.

Woodruff, William, *Impact of Western Man; A Study of Europe's Role in the World Economy, 1750-1960* (New York, 1967).

Woodward, C. Vann (ed.), *The Comparative Approach to American History* (New York, 1968).

Woolf, S., *The Poor in Western Europe in the Eighteenth and Nineteenth Centuries* (London and New York, 1986).

Wright, Gordon, *Between the Guillotine and Liberty. Two Centuries of the Crime Problem in France* (New York etc., 1983).

Wrigley, E. Anthony (ed.), *Nineteenth Century Society* (Cambridge, 1972).

Wrigley, E. Anthony, "The Growth of Population in Eighteenth-Century England: A Conundrum Resolved", *Past and Present*, 98 (1983), pp. 121-150.

Wrigley, E. Anthony, *People, Cities and Wealth: The Transformation of Traditional Society* (Oxford, 1987).

Wrigley, E. Anthony and R.S. Schofield, *The Population History of England, 1541-1871: A Reconstruction* (Cambridge, 1981).

Wu, Ching Chao, "Chinese Immigration in the Pacific Area" (Unpublished Dissertation, University of Chicago, 1926).

Wyman, Mark, *D.P. Europe's Displaced Persons, 1945-1951* (Philadelphia etc., 1988).

Wyman, Mark, *Round-Trip to America. The Immigrants Return to Europe 1880-1930* (New York, 1993).

Yang, Anand, *The Limited Raj. Agrarian Relations in Colonial India, Saran District, 1793-1920* (Delhi, 1989).

Yans-McLaughlin, Virginia, *Family and Community: Italian Immigrants in Buffalo, 1880-1930* (Ithaca, 1977).

Yans-McLaughlin, Virginia (ed.), *Immigration Reconsidered. History, Sociology and Politics* (New York, 1990).

Yen, Ching-Hwang, "The Overseas Chinese and Late Ch'ing Economic Modernization", *Modern Asian Studies* 16 (1982), pp. 217-232.

Yen, Ching-Hwang, *Coolies and Mandarins: China's Protection of Overseas Chinese During the Late Ch'ing Period (1851-1911)* (Singapore, 1985).

Young, Arthur, *Bismarck's Policy Toward the Poles, 1870-1890* (Ph.D., University of Chicago, 1970).

Zanden, Jan Luiten van, *The Rise and Decline of Holland's Economy: Merchant Capitalism and the Labour Market* (Manchester, 1993).

Zarama, Jose Rafael, *Reseña histórica*, (Pasto, 1942).

Zaslavsky, Victor and Robert J. Brym, *Soviet-Jewish Emigration and Soviet Nationality Policy* (London and Basingstoke, 1983).

Zelinsky, Wilbur, "The Hypothesis of the Mobility Transition", *The Geographical Review*, LX (1971), pp. 219-249.

Zimmermann, Michael, "Ausgrenzung, Ermordung, Ausgrenzung. Normalität und Exzess in der polizeilichen Zigeunerverfolgung in Deutschland (1870-1980)", in: Lüdtke, *"Sicherheit" und "Wohlfahrt"*, pp. 344-370.

Zo, Kil Young, "Credit Ticket System for the Chinese Emigration into the United States", *Nanyang University Journal*, 8/9 (1974/5).

Zo, Kil Young, *Chinese Emigration into the United States. 1850-1880* (New York, 1978).

Zolberg, Aristide R., "International Migration Policies in a Changing World System", in: McNeill and Adams, *Human Migration*, pp. 241-286.

Zolberg, Aristide R., "The Formation of New States as a Refugee-Generating Process", *Annals of the American Academy of Political and Social Science*, 467 (May 1983), pp. 24-38.

Zolberg, Aristide R., Astri Suhrke and Sergio Aguayo, *Escape from Violence. Conflict and the Refugee Crisis in the Developing World* (New York, 1989).

Zolberg, Aristide R., "Reforming the Back Door: The Immigration Reform and Control Act of 1896 in Historical Perspective", in Yans-McLaughlin, *Immigration Reconsidered*, pp. 315-339.

Zubrzycki, J., *Polish Immigrants in Britain. A Study of Adjustment* (The Hague, 1956).

Zubrzycki, J., "International Migration in Australia and the South Pacific", in: Kritz et al., *Global Trends in Migration*, pp. 158-180.

Zucchi, John E., *The Little Slaves of the Harp. Italian Child Street Musicians in Nineteenth-Century Paris, London, and New York* (Montreal etc., 1992).

Zunz, Olivier, *The Changing Face of Inequality: Urbanization, Industrial Development, and Immigrants in Detroit, 1880-1920* (Chicago, 1982).

Zunz, Olivier, "Genèse du pluralisme américain", *Annales ESC*, 42 (March -April 1987), pp. 429-444.

Zunz, Olivier, John Bodnar "Forum: American History and the Changing Meaning of Assimilation", *Journal of American Ethnic History*, 4 (1985), pp. 53-76.

Zysberg, André, *Les galériens. Vies et destins de 60.000 forçats sur les galères de France 1680-1748* (Paris, 1987).

Subject Index

Name Index

Geographical Index

Notes on Contributors

Ida Altman (1950) is Professor of History at the University of New Orleans. She is author of *Emigrants and Society. Extremadura and Spanish America in the Sixteenth Century* (Berkeley/Los Angeles, 1989; Madrid, 1991) and co-editor, with James Horn, of *"To Make America". European Emigration in the Early Modern Period* (Berkeley/Los Angeles, 1991). Other publications include "Spanish Society in Mexico City After the Conquest", *Hispanic American Historical Review*, 21 (1991), "The Contact of Cultures: Perspectives on the Quincentenary", *American Historical Review*, 99 (1994) (co-authored with Reginald Butler), and *Community and Colonization in the Spanish Empire: Brihuega and Puebla, 1560-1620* (forthcoming).

Robin Cohen (1944) is Professor of Sociology at the University of Warwick and a former director of the Centre for Research in Ethnic Relations. He is author of *The New Helots. Migrants in the International Division of Labour* (Aldershot, 1987), *Frontier of Identity. The British and the Others* (London, 1994) and *Global Diasporas. An Introduction* (London, 1997). He is editor of *The Cambridge Survey of World Migration* (Cambridge, 1995).

David Eltis (1940) is Professor of History at Queen's University, Kingston, Canada, Fellow of the W.E.B. Du Bois Institute, Harvard University and Research Lecturer at the University of Hull, England. He is author of *Economic Growth and the Ending of the Transatlantic Slave Trade* (New York, 1987) and co-editor of *The Abolition of the Atlantic Slave Trade. Origins and Effects in Europe, Africa and the Americas* (Madison, 1981) and *Routes to Slavery. Direction, Mortality and Ethnicity in the Transatlantic Slave Trade, 1595-1867* (London, 1997; co-edited with David Richardson).

Pieter C. Emmer (1944), is Professor at the Department of History, University of Leiden, The Netherlands. His area of specialisation: The history of the expansion of Europe in the Atlantic. Major publications on migration: *The Atlantic Slave Trade. New Approaches/La traite des noirs par l'Atlantique. Nouvelles approches* (Paris, 1976; co-edited with J. Mettas and J.-C. Nardin), *Colonialism and Migration; Indentured Labour Before and After Slavery* (Dordrecht, 1986; editor), *European Expansion and Migration. Essays on the International Migration from Africa, Asia and Europe* (New York and Oxford, 1992; co-edited with Magnus Mörner), and *The Dutch in the Atlantic Economy* (Aldershot, 1998).

Georg Fertig (1962), is lecturer in social and economic history at the Historisches Seminar, Universität Münster. His book *Lokales Leben, atlantische Welt. Die Entscheidung zur Auswanderung vom Reich nach Nordamerika im 18. Jahrhundert* is to be published in 1999. Recent articles have appeared in *Contuinity and Change* (1998) and *Tel Aviver Jahrbuch für deutsche Geschichte* (1998). His current interests include the study of kinship and factor markets in nineteenth-century rural Westphalia.

Donna Gabaccia (1949) is Charles H. Stone Professor of American History, University of North Carolina at Charlotte. Her publications include: *From Sicily to Elizabeth Street* (Albany, 1984), *Militants and Migrants. Rural Sicilians Become American Workers* (New Brunswick and London, 1988), *From the Other Side. Women and Immigrant Life in the US* (Bloomington, 1994), and *We Are What We Eat. Ethnicity and the Business of Food* (Cambridge, MA, 1998).

Nancy L. Green is Directrice d'Études at the École des Hautes Études en Sciences Sociales in Paris. She is author of *The Pletzl of Paris: Jewish Immigrant Workers in the Belle Époque* (New York, 1986), *Et ils peuplèrent l'Amérique: L'odyssée des émigrants* (Paris, 1994) and *Ready-to-Wear and Ready-to-Work. A Century of Industry and Immigrants in Paris and New York* (Durham, 1997).

Arjan de Haan (1963) is a historical sociologist. He has worked as a lecturer at the Erasmus University Rotterdam and as research fellow at the University of Amsterdam and the School of Oriental and African Studies, University of London. His main research interests include poverty, migration and labour markets, and he has also worked on social security, social exclusion and poverty monitoring in developing countries. His contribution to this volume is based on field and archival research in the United Kingdom and India. Results of this research were also published in *Unsettled Settlers, Migrant Workers and Industrial Capitalism in Calcutta* (Hilversum, 1994). At present, he is a Social Development Adviser at the Social Development Division of the Department for International Development, London.

Dirk Hoerder (1943) teaches North American social history at the University of Bremen, Germany. His areas of interest are European labour migration in the Atlantic economies, worldwide migration system, migrants' experiences as reflected in Canadian immigrant autobiographies. He has been director of the Labor Migration Project, dealing with the political consciousness and acculturation of European labour migrants in North America. His publications include *Labor Migration in the Atlantic Economies. The European and Northern American Working Classes during the Period of Industrialization* (Westport, 1985) and, edited with Leslie Page Moch, *European Migrants. Global and Local Perspectives* (Boston, 1996). He has recently taught at York University, Toronto, and is preparing a study on autobiographical writings of immigrant men and women in Canada, 1880s-1930s.

Colin Holmes (1938) is Professor of History at the University of Sheffield. He has published extensively on the history of racism. Among his publications are *Anti-Semitism in British Society, (1876-1939)* (London, 1978), *John Bull's Island. Immigration and British Society, 1871-1971* (Basingstoke, 1988) and *A Tolerant Country?* (London, 1991). He has edited more recently, jointly with Geoffrey Alderman, a *Festschrift* for W.J. Fishman, *Outsiders and Outcasts* (London, 1993). He is also joint-editor of the journal *Immigrants and Minorities*.

Jan Lucassen (1947) is Director of Research of the International Institute of Social History, Amsterdam, and Professor of International and Comparative Social History, Vrije Universiteit, Amsterdam, The Netherlands. His major publications include *Migrant Labour in Europe 1600-1900. The Drift to the North Sea* (London, 1987), *Newcomers. Immigrants and their Descendants in the Netherlands 1550-1995* (Amsterdam, 1997; together with Rinus Penninx), and *Die lippischen Ziegler im 18. und 19. Jahrhundert. Entstehung und Entwicklung eines 'ethnischen Berufs'* (Osnabrück, 1999).

Leo Lucassen (1959) is Associate Professor at the History Department of Amsterdam University and Director of the Research programme "Immigration in the Netherlands 1860-1960", financed by the Dutch Council for Scientific Research (NWO). He got his PhD in 1990 and since published extensively on gypsies and itinerant groups, among others in *Immigrants and Minorities* (1992), the *International Review of Social History* (1993), and *Crime, History and Societies* (1997). In 1996 his book *Zigeuner. Die Geschichte eines polizeilichen Ordnungsbegriffes in Deutschland, 1700-1945* appeared and in 1998 *Gypsies and other itinerant groups*, written together with Annemarie Cottaar and Wim Willems. His current interest is in migration control and state formation.

Kenneth Lunn (1949) is Reader in Social History at the School of Social and Historical Studies at the University of Portsmouth. He edited *Race and Labour in Twentieth-Century Britain* (1985) and, with Tony Kushner, *Traditions of Intolerance* (1989) and *The Politics of Marginality?* (1990). He is an editor of *Labour History Review* and his most recent work, a study of race, ethnicity and the labour movement in Britain since the mid-nineteenth century will be published in 1999.

Leslie Page Moch (1944) is Professor of History at Michigan State University. She is author of *Paths to the City. Regional Migration in Nineteenth-Century France* (Beverly Hills [etc.], 1983), *Moving Europeans. Migration in Western Europe since 1650* (Bloomington and Indianapolis, 1992), and (with Rachel Fuchs) "Pregnant, Single and Far From Home: Migrant Women in Nineteenth-Century Paris", *American Historical Review*, 95 (1990). She is editor (with Dirk Hoerder) of *European Migrants. Global and Local Perspectives* (Boston, 1996) and (with Michael Hanagan and Wayne te Brake) of *Challenging Authority. The Historical Study of Contentious Politics* (Minneapolis and London, 1998).

Eric Richards (1940) is Professor of History at Flinders University, Adelaide, Australia. Among his publications are *A History of the Highland Clearances* (2 vols, London, 1982, 1985), *Visible Immigrants: Neglected Sources for the History of Australian Immigration* (co-editor, Canberra, 1989), *Poor Australian Immigrants in the Nineteenth Century. Visible Immigrants: Two* (editor, Canberra, 1991), *Visible Women. Female Immigrants in Colonial Australia* (editor, Canberra, 1996), and *The Twentieth-Century Australian Immigrant* (co-editor; Canberra, 1998).

Ralph Shlomowitz (1941) is Reader in History at The Flinders University of South Australia, Adelaide. He is author of *Mortality and Migration in the Modern World* (Aldershot, 1996).

Aristide R. Zolberg (1931) is University-in-Exile Professor at the Graduate Faculty of the New School for Social Research in New York City, and Director of the International Center for Migration, Ethnicity, and Citizenship. He is a member of the editorial board of *International Migration Review* and *Journal of Refugee Studies* (Oxford). Recent publications relevant to migration include *Escape from Violence: Conflict and the Refugee Crisis in the Developing World* (Oxford, 1989; co-authored with Astri Suhrke and Sergio Aguayo); "The Future of International Migrations", *Working Papers. Commission for the Study of International Migration and Cooperative Economic Development*, No. 19 (February 1990); and "Bounded States in a Global Market: The Uses of International Labor Migrations", in Pierre Bourdieu and James S. Coleman (eds), *Social Theory for a Changing Society* (Boulder, 1991). He is currently completing a book on the role of immigration policy in American political development, and a work on the contemporary world-wide migration crisis, *Crowding at the Gates: The Past and Future Immigration Crisis.*

INTERNATIONAL AND COMPARATIVE SOCIAL HISTORY

1. *Racism and the Labour Market: Historical Studies.* Edited by Marcel van der Linden and Jan Lucassen in collaboration with Dik van Arkel, Els Deslé, Fred Goedbloed, Robert Kloosterman and Kenneth Lunn. 1995.

2. *Social Security Mutualism: The Comparative History of Mutual Benefit Societies.* Edited by Marcel van der Linden in collaboration with Michel Dreyfus, Bernard Gibaud and Jan Lucassen. 1996.

3. *The International Confederation of Free Trade Unions.* Edited by Marcel van der Linden. 2000.

4. *Migration, Migration History, History: Old Paradigms and New Perspectives.* Edited by Jan Lucassen and Leo Lucassen. 1997, 1999, 2005.

5. *Free and Unfree Labour: The Debate Continues.* Edited by Tom Brass and Marcel van der Linden. 1997.

6. *The Rise and Development of Collective Labour Law.* Edited by Marcel van der Linden and Richard Price. 2000.

7. *Urban Radicals, Rural Allies: Social Democracy and the Agrarian Issue, 1870–1914.* Edited by Aad Blok, Keith Hitchins, Raymond Markey and Birger Simonson. 2002.

8. *Between Cross and Class: Comparative Histories of Christian Labour in Europe 1840–2000.* Edited by Lex Heerma van Voss, Patrick Pasture and Jan De Maeyer. 2005.